THE ROUGH GUIDE TO
ROME

MAR   2018

ROUGH
GUIDES

This eighth edition updated by
Agnes Crawford and Maria Pasquale

Contents

OPPOSITE SANTI LUCA E MARTINA, WITH THE VITTORIANO IN THE BACKGROUND PREVIOUS PAGE ROMAN FORUM

Introduction to
Rome

When most people think of Rome they imagine sights and monuments: the Colosseum, Forum, the Vatican and St Peter's – giant, see-before-you-die sights that are reason enough for a visit. And it's true that there is perhaps no more monumental city in the world than Rome; yet the city is so much more than the sum of these parts. There's an unpretentiousness to it and its inhabitants that belies the historical significance, and marks it out from its rivals further north. It's almost as if Rome doesn't have to try too hard, aware that it is simply the most fascinating city in Italy – and arguably the world.

Packed with the relics of well over two thousand years of inhabitation, you could spend a month in Rome and still only scratch the surface. There are the city's celebrated **ancient** features, but Rome boasts an almost uninterrupted historical sequence of spectacular monuments – from early Christian basilicas, Romanesque churches and Renaissance palaces, right up to the fountains and churches of the Baroque period, which perhaps more than any other era has determined the look of the city today. The modern epoch has left its mark too, with the ponderous **Neoclassical architecture** of the post-Unification period and the self-aggrandizing edifices of the Mussolini years. All these various eras crowd in on one another to an almost overwhelming degree: there are medieval churches atop Imperial palaces, Renaissance *Palazzi* above ancient temples; houses and apartment blocks incorporate fragments of eroded Roman columns, carvings and inscriptions; roads and piazzas follow the lines of ancient theatres and stadiums.

Culturally Rome is relatively provincial, and its **food**, while delicious, is earthy rather than refined. But its atmosphere is like no other city – a busy capital, yet an appealingly relaxed place, with a centre that has been relatively little affected by chains and multinationals. The city does have a **modern edge**, and the opening of prestige new buildings and a general updating of the city centre have given a sense that Rome has at last joined Europe's mainstream. Whether its character will change remains to be seen.

ABOVE TREVI FOUNTAIN

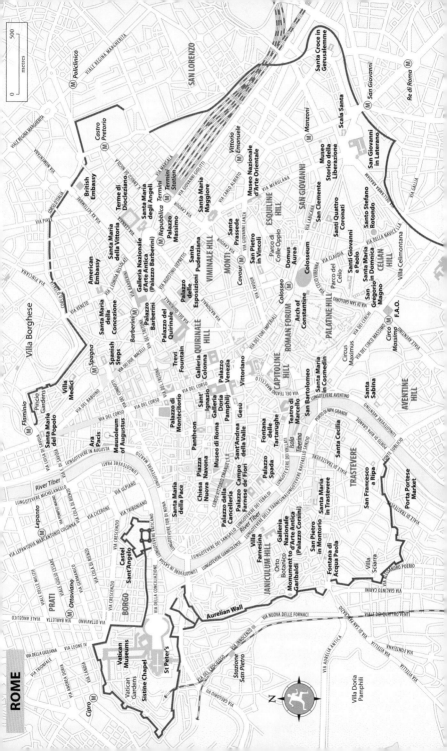

What to see

Rome's city centre is divided neatly into distinct blocks. The warren of streets that makes up the **Centro Storico** occupies the hook of land on the east bank of the River Tiber. From here Rome's central core spreads out: east across Via del Corso to the major shopping streets and alleys around the Spanish Steps – the **Tridente**; south across Corso Vittorio Emanuele II to **Campo de' Fiori** and around; to the major sites of the **ancient city** to the southeast; and to the huge expanse of the **Villa Borghese** park to the north. The west bank of the river, distanced from the main hum of the rest of the city, is home to the **Vatican** and **St Peter's**, and, to the south, **Trastevere** – even in ancient times a distinct entity from the city proper.

But where should you start in any tour of Rome? There are the obvious key sights, and you should try to see these if you can. But if you're here for only a day or two it would be a pity not to spend time just exploring the **Centro Storico**, whose churches, palaces and back alleys are a fascinating glimpse into the city's history. Central Rome is full of reminders of the glories of the **ancient** city: most obviously the **Colosseum**, and **Forum** and **Palatine**, but also the **Domus Aurea**, the **Capitoline Museums** and the museums of the **Museo Nazionale Romano** (at the Baths of Diocletian, Crypta Balbi, Palazzo Massimo and Palazzo Altemps) and of course the **Pantheon**, perhaps the most intact structure of the period. **Baroque Rome** is everywhere you look, in piazzas, church facades, street furniture and fountains, and most notably in **St Peter's Basilica**, one of the grandest Baroque creations in Christendom. Rome is also a city of great **art collections**, some of them the property of illustrious Roman families and still displayed in their palaces, such as the **Galleria Doria Pamphilj**; others are now property of the state and housed in appropriately grand buildings including the **Palazzo Barberini** and **Galleria Borghese**.

To see most of the city centre, the best way to get around is to walk. The same goes for the ancient sites, and the Vatican and Trastevere – although you might want to jump on a bus to cross the river. Keep public transport for the longer hops, down to **Testaccio** or **Via Appia Antica**, and, of course, for trips out of the city – to the excavations at **Ostia** and **Tivoli**, or one of the nearby **beaches**.

When to go

Rome is a year-round city, and you can really visit at any **time of year**. If you can though, avoid coming in July and August, when the weather is hot and sticky, and those Romans who don't make their living exclusively from the tourist industry have left town; many businesses close in August. The weather is more comfortable in April–June, September and October, when days will be warm but not unbearably so. The quietest times of year are November and early December, and late January to early February. Especially midweek in these periods, sights are delightfully deserted, though the weather can be very wet.

20

things not to miss

It's not possible to see everything that Rome has to offer in one visit – and we don't suggest you try. What follows, in no particular order, is a selective taste of the city's highlights, from outstanding art collections and historic architecture to picturesque parks. All highlights are colour-coded by chapter and have a page reference to take you straight into the Guide, where you can find out more.

1

1 THE PANTHEON
Page 35

By far the most intact of Rome's ancient monuments, and still sporting the city's widest dome.

2 PIZZA
Page 245

There's nothing quite like thin, crispy-based Roman pizza, fresh from a wood-burning oven.

3 MUSEO NAZIONALE ROMANO
Pages 39 & 123

Palazzo Altemps and Palazzo Massimo make up the greatest part of the Museo Nazionale Romano, and between them hold some of the city's finest ancient finds.

4 GALLERIA BORGHESE

A fantastic array of Bernini sculptures together with superb collections of Renaissance paintings in a beautifully restored seventeenth-century villa.

5 GELATO

The traditional – and best – way to finish off an evening out.

6 ROMAN FORUM AND PALATINE

The heart of the ancient world is almost unrecognizable today, but no less evocative for that.

7 VATICAN MUSEUMS

One of the world's largest museum complexes, jam-packed with treasures that include iconic parts of the building itself, such as the Sistine Chapel and Raphael Rooms.

8 TREVI FOUNTAIN

Stumbling upon the Trevi Fountain by accident, especially first thing in the morning, is one of the greatest of all Rome experiences.

7

8

13

14

15 CAMPO DE' FIORI
Page 48

The morning market here is one of Rome's oldest, while in the evening the square's bars and restaurants form one of the city centre's main nightlife hubs.

16 CAPITOLINE MUSEUMS
Page 64

The world's oldest public museum, and one of the very finest for ancient sculpture, is set in a jumble of ancient, Renaissance and modern buildings on Rome's Capitol.

17 VILLA BORGHESE
Page 169

The city centre's largest open space has plenty to occupy you – superb galleries, a zoo and boating lake.

18 COLOSSEUM
Page 72

The most photographed of Rome's monuments, and no wonder. In terms of size and ingenuity, it's hard to beat.

19 ST PETER'S BASILICA
Page 190

One of the largest churches in the world in the world's smallest country.

20 PROTESTANT CEMETERY
Page 143

This evocatively overgrown corner of Testaccio is the final resting place of Keats and Shelley.

Itineraries

There's no greater pleasure than wandering around Rome with no particular destination in mind, but if time is tight you might want to follow one of our itineraries to pursue a special interest or to make sure you squeeze everything in. Follow our suggestions to the letter or just dip in and out, the choice is yours.

DAY ONE

Capitoline Hill Rome began here, and the museums that flank the elegant square are among the city's key sights. **See p.63**

Roman Forum Some of the most ruined ruins you'll see, but also the most atmospheric. See p.77

Colosseum The most recognizable and perhaps the greatest ancient Roman monument of them all. **See p.72**

Lunch *Terra e Domus – Enoteca della Provincia di Roma* opposite the Vittoriano, makes a perfect and delicious lunch stop on your way from the Colosseum to the Trevi Fountain. See p.252

Trevi Fountain No trip to the city could be complete without a visit here. **See p.101**

Ara Pacis Enclosed in an impressive purpose-built modern structure, this ancient altar's amazing frieze displays the imperial family during the time of Augustus. **See p.98**

Galleria Borghese The Bernini sculptures here are the pure essence of Rome. See p.169

Dinner A meal in lively Trastevere is a must – and you can't go wrong at *Da Enzo*. See p.261

DAY TWO

St Peter's Basilica It would be a pity to leave Rome without seeing perhaps the city's greatest Baroque attraction. **See p.190**

Vatican Museums So much more than the Sistine Chapel – this staggering complex of museums is not to be missed. **See p.194**

Lunch *Dal Toscano*, a long-established Tuscan restaurant close by the Vatican walls, is a good place to recover from museum fatigue. **See p.264**

Piazza di Spagna The Spanish Steps, Keats-Shelley House and the square itself are among the city's most compelling attractions. See p.94

Piazza Navona One of the Centro Storico's loveliest open spaces, and close to the church of San Luigi dei Francesi and Palazzo Altemps. See p.42

The Pantheon Rome's most intact ancient sight, and near one of the city's great churches, Santa Maria sopra Minerva. **See p.35**

The Ghetto Stroll through the old Jewish Quarter, an ancient part of the city centre. See p.56

Dinner *Piperno* is the best of the Ghetto's restaurants, with fantastic Roman food served in lovely surroundings. **See p.251**

FOODIE ROME

Dagnino We love the coffee and pastries at this Sicilian stalwart, which is among the city's best places to start the day. **See p.256**

Testaccio The food stalls at the morning market here are one of the city's best traditional sources of fresh meat and produce. **See p.142**

Eataly Just in case the Testaccio market didn't have what you were looking for, this Ostiense behemoth may be the answer, a glorious multistorey homage to the best Italian edible goodies. **See p.144**

Città del Gusto Down in the depths of Trastevere, this is home to the country's foremost food organization; it runs cookery and wine-tasting sessions and courses, plus it has a shop. **See p.256**

Roscioli Foodie heaven, arguably where you'll find the best *carbonara* in town, alongside fresh bread from their bakery across the road. **See p.251**

Antica Caciara Trasteverina Fortified by lunch, cross the river to peek in at one of the city's oldest and best cheese shops. **See p.296**

DOT Experience great creative cooking with a Sicilian twist for your evening meal. **See p.262**

Gelateria del Teatro Finish the day in Italian style, at this fabulous *gelateria* serving great combinations of ice cream and sorbets made in the traditional way. **See p.247**

HIDDEN ROME

Museo Storico della Liberazione Just around the corner from the basilica of San Giovanni, this is one of the city's most moving attractions, housed in the former HQ of the Gestapo during the Nazi occupation. **See p.134**

Villa Torlonia This lovely park holds a number of compelling attractions, from the whimsical Casina delle Civette to Mussolini's World War II bunker, recently opened to the public for the first time. **See p.183**

Galleria Colonna One of the city's finest family palace collections of art, yet only open Saturday mornings, so relatively unknown. **See p.101**

Rooms of St Ignatius Just next to the entrance to the much-visited Gesù church, few visitors also take in the intriguing rooms of St Ignatius, with their amazing false perspective by Borromini. **See p.55**

Museo Criminologico For those fascinated by the Mafia and Italian organized crime, this is an intriguing if somewhat gruesome glimpse of that world. **See p.52**

Museo Storico dell'Arte Sanitaria Ancient medical museums assert a strange fascination, and this one, tucked away at the back of the modern hospital of Santo Spirito, is no exception. **See p.210**

Priorato di Malta The gardens and Piranesi church of the secretive home of the Knights of Malta are open to tour groups only, but anyone can peek through the keyhole for its famous view of the dome of St Peter. **See p.138**

PORTA SAN PAOLO STATION

Basics

Getting there

There are regular direct flights to Rome from the UK and the US, while airlines from Australia, New Zealand and South Africa fly via Asian or European cities. Rome has two airports: Leonardo da Vinci, better known as Fiumicino, which serves the majority of scheduled flights; and Ciampino, the Ryanair hub, which also handles charter flights.

Air fares depend more than ever on how far **in advance** you book, the **season**, and the day of the week and time of day you want to travel. Travelling between June and August, when the weather is best, will cost more than in the depths of winter (excluding Christmas and New Year). As always, the cheapest tickets come with restrictions: any changes incur additional fees. The lowest-priced air tickets are generally cheaper than those for the long train or bus journey.

Flights from the UK and Ireland

There are plenty of direct flights from the UK and Ireland to Rome. Of the scheduled airlines flying from the **UK**, British Airways (🌐 britishairways.com) flies several times a day from London Heathrow, with a couple of services from London Gatwick too, while national carrier Alitalia (🌐 alitalia.com) has daily flights from London Heathrow and London City. Of the low-cost airlines, easyJet (🌐 easyjet .com) fly from London Gatwick (daily), London Luton (4–5 weekly) and Bristol (4–7 weekly) to Fiumicino; Ryanair (🌐 ryanair.com) fly from London Stansted (daily), East Midlands (3 weekly), Manchester (daily), Edinburgh (4 weekly) and Glasgow (2 weekly) to Ciampino; Norwegian (🌐 norwegian.com) from London Gatwick (6 weekly), Manchester (up to 1 weekly) and Edinburgh (6 weekly end March to Oct) to Fiumicino; and Jet2 (🌐 jet2.com) from Leeds/Bradford (3 weekly), Manchester, Newcastle (2 weekly) and Glasgow (2 weekly) to Fiumicino. The site 🌐 flycheapo.com is a good source of information on low-cost flights in Europe.

From **Ireland**, Ryanair fly daily from Dublin to Ciampino, Jet2 has a couple of flights weekly from Belfast to Fiumicino, while Aer Lingus (🌐 aerlingus .com) has at least one daily nonstop flight from Dublin to Fiumicino.

Book far enough in advance with one of the low-cost airlines and you can pick up a ticket for around £60 return excluding hold baggage, even in summer; book anything less than three weeks in advance and prices can triple. Scheduled airline fares, booked within a month of travel, will cost £150–250 during winter, spring and autumn, and £250–350 in summer; booking in advance in summer will save you £100 or so.

Flights from the US and Canada

Alitalia (🌐 alitalia.com) fly the widest choice of direct routes between the **US** and Rome, with daily nonstop flights from New York, Boston, Los Angeles and Atlanta. Of the American carriers that operate nonstop services, Delta (🌐 delta.com) fly from New York and Atlanta; American Airlines (🌐 aa.com) fly from Chicago, Philadelphia and New York; and United (🌐 united.com) from Newark, Washington DC, and Chicago (mid-May to mid-Sept). In addition, many European carriers fly (via their hubs) to Italy from major US and Canadian cities: for example British Airways (🌐 britishairways.com) fly via London, Lufthansa (🌐 lufthansa.com) via Frankfurt and KLM (🌐 klm.com) via Amsterdam. Nonstop scheduled fares don't vary as much as you might think, and you'll often be basing your choice on routes, timings and ticket restrictions and even the airline's reputation for comfort and service. It's a long flight, around nine hours from New York and Boston, twelve hours from Chicago and fifteen hours from Los Angeles, so it's as well to be fairly comfortable and arrive at a reasonably sociable hour.

The cheapest **round-trip fares** to Rome, travelling midweek in low season, start at around US$650 for indirect flights from New York, or US$1300 for nonstop flights, rising to US$750 (US$1500 nonstop) in spring and fall, and US$950 (US$1600 nonstop) during the summer. Add

---

A BETTER KIND OF TRAVEL

At Rough Guides we are passionately committed to travel. We believe it helps us understand the world we live in and the people we share it with – and of course tourism is vital to many developing economies. But the scale of modern tourism has also damaged some places irreparably, and climate change is accelerated by most forms of transport, especially flying. All Rough Guides' flights are carbon-offset, and every year we donate money to a variety of environmental charities.

another US$100–200 for flights from other US destinations.

Air Canada (**W** aircanada.com) and Alitalia operate nonstop flights **from Toronto and Montréal** to Rome, a journey of around nine hours from Toronto, or eight hours from Montréal; fares are around Can$600 nonstop in low season, and around Can $800 nonstop in summer.

Flights from Australia, New Zealand and South Africa

There are no nonstop flights to Italy **from Australia** or **New Zealand**. From either country you are likely to get most flexibility by travelling with Emirates (**W** emirates.com), British Airways (**W** britishairways .com) or Qantas (**W** qantas.com.au). Round-trip fares to Rome from the main Australian cities go for Aus$1100–1500 in low season (European winter), and around Aus$1800 in high season (European summer); from New Zealand, round-trip fares cost from around NZ$1800 in low season up to NZ$3000 in high season.

There are no direct flights from **South Africa** to Rome, and most flights make one European stop using one of the big carriers – Emirates, KLM (**W** klm .com) and South African Airways (**W** flysaa.com) all offer decent deals. Reckon on paying around ZAR5000 return from Johannesburg, or around ZAR7000–8000 from Cape Town or Durban.

Trains

Travelling **by train** to Rome won't save you money, but it can be an enjoyable and leisurely (as well as environmentally friendly) way of getting there, and you can stop off in other parts of Europe on the way. The choice of **routes** and fares is complex, but most trains from the UK pass through Paris and head down through France to northern Italy and then on to Rome. Advance booking is essential and can often save you quite a lot of money; there are discounts for under-26s and special offers are common.

The journey takes around 21 hours. The best way to do it is to leave London on an afternoon Eurostar train to Paris, then take the Thello sleeper train overnight to Milan, where you arrive the next morning and change for a high-speed train to Rome. A return **fare** from London to Rome can be found for as little as £247 for the two legs (London–Paris from £72 return, Paris–Rome for £175 return), travelling in a six-berth couchette; if you opt for a two-berth sleeper the cheapest ticket for the Paris–Rome return is £310. The train has a decently priced restaurant car

and, if you opt for a sleeper, is a wonderfully comfortable way to travel – see the rail-planning site **W** seat61.com for all the options, or **W** uk.voyages -sncf.com – though bear in mind that there's usually more availability, and tickets may be cheaper, if you book direct with the national train operators.

Package tours and specialist operators

There's no shortage of operators organizing **packages to Rome**, many of which offer specialist tours. For an ordinary city break, you can reckon on spending £450–750 for two people staying for three nights in a three- to four-star hotel between April and October, including flights, though special offers can sometimes cut prices drastically, especially for late bookings. **Specialist tours** with guest lecturers tend to cost around £2000 for a week. Travelling from the US, you can expect to pay from around US$1500 for a week in a three-star hotel, although tours limited to Rome can be hard to find – most take in Tuscany, or focus on the three cities of Rome, Florence and Venice. We've listed some of the better specialist operators below.

RAIL CONTACTS

Eurostar UK ☎ 03432 186 186, **W** eurostar.com.
Man in Seat Sixty-One **W** seat61.com.
Rail Europe US ☎ 1800 622 8600, **W** raileurope.com; Canada ☎ 1800 361 7245, **W** raileurope.ca.
Traintours4u ☎ 020 7619 1080, **W** traintours4u.co.uk.
Voyages-sncf UK ☎ 0844 848 5848, **W** uk.voyages-sncf.com.

AGENTS AND OPERATORS

TRAVEL AGENTS

North South Travel UK ☎ 01245 608 291, **W** northsouthtravel .co.uk. Friendly, competitive travel agency, offering discounted fares worldwide. Profits are used to support projects in the developing world, especially the promotion of sustainable tourism.
STA Travel UK ☎ 0333 321 0099, US ☎ 1800 781 4040, Australia ☎ 134 782, New Zealand ☎ 0800 474 400, South Africa ☎ 0861 781 781; **W** statravel.co.uk. Worldwide specialists in independent travel; also student IDs, travel insurance, car rental, rail passes and more. Good discounts for students and under-26s.
Travel CUTS Canada ☎ 1800 667 2887, US ☎ 1800 592 2887; **W** travelcuts.com. Canadian youth and student travel firm.
USIT Ireland ☎ 01 602 1906, Northern Ireland ☎ 028 9032 7111; **W** usit.ie. Ireland's main student and youth travel specialists.

PACKAGE TOURS

Central Holidays US ☎ 1800 539 7098, **W** centralholidays.com. Offers tours twinning Rome with the Amalfi Coast, among other popular holiday spots.

CIT Australia ☎ 1300 380 992, Ⓦ cit.com.au. A variety of escorted and self-drive tours that start off in Rome.

Citalia UK ☎ 01293 731 605, Ⓦ citalia.co.uk. Long-established Italy specialists.

Explore Holidays Australia Ⓦ exploreholidays.com.au. Multi-city breaks that include three to five nights in Rome.

SPECIALIST AND CULTURAL TOURS

Abercrombie & Kent UK ☎ 01242 547 760, US ☎ 1800 554 7016, Ⓦ abercrombiekent.com. This high-end operator offers occasional art-focused tours to Rome led by experts from Christie's.

ACE Cultural Tours UK ☎ 01223 841 055, Ⓦ aceculturaltours .co.uk. Specialist, academic-led tours focusing on such subjects as art, architecture and gardens.

Andante Travel UK ☎ 01722 713 800, Ⓦ andantetravels.co.uk. Archeology excursions, including tours of Lazio's countryside, and "Hidden Rome", which gives special access to the secret archives of the Vatican.

Bellini Travel UK ☎ 020 7602 7602, Ⓦ bellinitravel.com. An upmarket company specializing in Italy that puts together bespoke itineraries.

Ciceroni Travel UK ☎ 01869 811167, Ⓦ ciceroni.co.uk. Small-group tours led by experts, often focusing on private visits to villas and gardens.

Fine Art Travel UK ☎ 020 7437 8553, Ⓦ finearttravel.co.uk. High-end art tours.

Kirker Holidays UK ☎ 020 7593 1899, Ⓦ kirkerholidays.com. Luxury themed breaks to Rome, including one that explores the villas and gardens around Rome, as well as an "Art, opera and architecture" tour.

Martin Randall Travel UK ☎ 020 8742 3355, Ⓦ martinrandall .com. Themed cultural tours led by lecturers that take in hard-to-access sites, including an out-of-hours visit to the Sistine Chapel.

Peter Sommer UK ☎ 01600 888 220, Ⓦ petersommer.com. This company specializing in cultural tours has now introduced a small-group Explore Rome tour, led by two archeologists.

RHS Garden Holidays UK ☎ 0800 804 8710, Ⓦ worldwide .rhsgardenholidays.com. A selection of garden-themed tours led by RHS experts includes the six-day "Eternal Gardens of Rome".

Arrival

Reaching the centre of Rome is pretty straightforward for air and rail travellers. You'll most likely end up at Termini station, close to the top attractions and the bulk of accommodation.

By air

Both of Rome's airports are a short hop from the city centre. If you take a taxi or bus to the centre, remember that Rome's traffic can add significantly to your journey time (though not your fare, as rates from the airports are fixed).

Fiumicino airport

Fiumicino, or FCO (Ⓦ www.adr.it; enquiries ☎ 06 65951) is Rome's largest airport, about 30km southwest of the city centre, near the coast. There are four terminals, T1, T2, T3 and T5 (for US airlines and El-Al). All but T5 (for which there is a shuttle bus) are within walking distance of one another.

The airport is connected to the centre of Rome by a direct train, the **Leonardo Express**, which takes 32 minutes to get to Termini station and costs €14; services begin at 6.23am and then leave every 15–30 minutes until 11.23pm. In the other direction, trains leave Termini at 5 and 35 minutes past each hour from 5.35am to 10.35pm, from platforms 23 and 24 on the far right-hand side of the station.

Alternatively, there are **slower trains** every fifteen minutes (every 30min on Sun) to Trastevere (27min), Ostiense (32min) and Tiburtina (48min) stations; tickets cost €8. Ostiense and Tiburtina are stops on Rome's metro (€1.50; see box, p.23), or you can catch city bus #75 or #130 from Ostiense, #492 or #649 from Tiburtina, or tram #8 from Trastevere to the city centre (€1.50).

Several **bus services** link the airport with Termini and other points around the centre, a journey of around 45 minutes to an hour. Some offer cheaper fares if booked in advance online. All fares quoted below are one-way. COTRAL has around eight services a day to Termini's Piazza dei Cinquecento (1.15am–7pm; €5 online, €7 on board; Ⓦ cotralspa .it); SIT Bus Shuttle runs to Via Marsala 5, by Termini, and to Via Crescenzio in the Vatican area (8.30am–11.50pm; every 30–45min; €6; Ⓦ sitbusshuttle.it); Terravision runs to Via Marsala 29, by Termini (5.35am–11pm; every 30min; €5; Ⓦ terravision.eu); and T.A.M buses run to Via Giolitti on the south side of Termini, and to Stazione Ostiense (5.40am–11.30pm; roughly every 30min; €6; Ⓦ tambus.it).

Taxis from Fiumicino to the city centre cost a flat-rate (*tariffa fissa*) €48 for up to four people including one bag each. The journey time to the city centre is about 40–50 minutes.

Ciampino airport

The city's second airport, **Ciampino**, or CIA (☎ 06 65951, Ⓦ www.adr.it), is also pretty close to the city, only 15km southeast, but it's much smaller than Fiumicino and there are no direct rail connections between the airport and city centre. Terravision (Ⓦ terravision.eu), SIT bus (Ⓦ sitbusshuttle.it) and Schiaffini (Ⓦ romeairportbus.com) run **bus services** to Termini, which pull up on Via Marsala, right by the station (4am–midnight; every 30min–1hr; around 40min; around €4 one-way). If you don't want to get off at Termini, and are staying near a metro stop on the A line (near the Spanish Steps or Via Veneto areas, for example), you could take an ATRAL bus from the airport to Anagnina metro station at the end of metro line A (6.40am–10.40pm; every 40min; 20–30min; €1.20 one-way, plus €1.20 per suitcase; ⓦatral-lazio.com); from Anagnina you can take the metro to your destination (€1.50).

Taxis cost a flat €30 and the journey time to the city centre is 30–40 minutes. However, be warned that many drivers don't like taking people into the city centre from Ciampino, especially for this fixed rate, and it can sometimes be hard to persuade someone to take you; stand your ground if no one seems to want to put their hand up, and don't pay more than €30 plus tip.

By train

Travelling **by train** from most places in Italy, or indeed Europe, you arrive at the central **Termini station**. There are **left-luggage** facilities by platform 24 (open daily 6am–11pm; €6 per piece for the first 5hr, €1/hr from 6 to 12hr, then 50c/hr). Other services in the vast complex include a tourist information office (see opposite) and the usual car rental outlets on the Via Giolitti side, a post office and lots of shops. The station is the hub of the city's two principal metro lines, and the only point at which they cross. Piazza dei Cinquecento, on the station's western side, is the terminus for many of the city's buses; there's also a taxi rank here.

Among **other train stations** in Rome, **Tiburtina** is a stop for some north–south intercity trains, and certain parts of Lazio and elsewhere, as are Trastevere, San Pietro, Ostiense and Tuscolana; if you're staying near any of these and travelling out of town it's always worth checking if you can pick up a train there and avoid Termini altogether. Selected routes **around Lazio** are also handled by Termini's Regionali platforms (near the Fiumicino platform, a further 5min walk beyond the end of the regular platforms). The Roma-Nord line (*trenino*) station on

> ### TRAIN ENQUIRIES AND TICKETS
>
> For general enquiries contact **Trenitalia** (ⓣ892 021 or ⓣ06 6847 5475, ⓦtrenitalia. it). For enquiries about schedules and prices, call ⓣ06 3000 (24hr). There's a ticket office at Termini on the first concourse (daily 6.30am–10pm), as well as ticket machines dotted around the station.

Piazzale Flaminio runs to Viterbo and stations in between, and the Roma Lido/Porta San Paolo station next to Piramide metro station serves stations down to Ostia Lido (including Ostia Antica).

By bus

The main station for **buses** arriving in the city from outside the Rome region is **Tiburtina**, also the city's second train station. From here, take metro line B to Termini for buses, trains and line A.

By car

Coming into the city **by car** can be quite confusing and isn't really advisable unless you're used to driving in Italy and know where you are going to park (see p.26). However, renting a car is worth considering for day-trips out of town (see p.26).

If you're on the A1 highway coming from the north take the exit "Roma Nord"; from the south, follow exit "Roma Est". Both lead you to the **Grande Raccordo Anulare** (GRA), which circles the city and is connected with all of the major arteries into the city centre: the Via Cassia from the north; Via Salaria from the northeast; Via Tiburtina or Via Nomentana from the east; Via Appia Nuova and the Pontina from the south; Via Prenestina and Via Casilina or Via Cristoforo Colombo from the southeast; and Via Aurelia or Via Flaminia from the northwest.

From Ciampino, either follow Via Appia Nuova into the centre or join the GRA at junction 23 and follow the signs to the centre. **From Fiumicino**, just follow the A12 motorway into the city centre; it crosses the river just north of EUR, from where it's a short drive north up Via Cristoforo Colombo to the city walls and, beyond, to the Baths of Caracalla. Note that the centre of Rome has traffic restrictions during the day; see p.26.

Getting around

As in most Italian cities, the best way to get around Rome is to walk – you'll see more and will better appreciate the city. Rome wasn't built for motor traffic, and it shows in the congestion, the pollution and the bad tempers of its drivers. However, the city has good public transport on the whole – a largely efficient blend of buses, a few trams and a three-line metro – which you'll almost certainly need to use at some point if you

USEFUL TRANSPORT ROUTES

BUSES

#23 Piazzale Clodio–Piazza Risorgimento–Ponte Vittorio Emanuele–Ponte Garibaldi–Via Marmorata–Piazzale Ostiense–Centrale Montemartini–Basilica di S. Paolo.

#30 Express (Mon–Sat only) Piazzale Clodio–Piazza Mazzini–Piazza Cavour–Corso Rinascimento–Largo Argentina–Piazza Venezia–Lungotovere Aventino–Via Marmorata–Piramide–Via C. Colombo–EUR.

#40 Express Termini–Via Nazionale–Piazza Venezia–Largo Argentina–Piazza Pia/Castel Sant'Angelo.

#60 Express Piazza Venezia– Via Nazionale– Porta Pia–Via Nomentana.

#62 Stazione Tiburtina–Via Nomentana/Villa Torlonia–Porta Pia–Piazza Barberini–Via del Corso–Piazza Venezia–Corso V. Emanuele–Lungotevere Santo Spirito–Piazza Pia.

#64 Termini–Piazza della Repubblica–Via Nazionale–Piazza Venezia–Largo Argentina–Corso V. Emanuele–Stazione S. Pietro.

#75 Via Poerio (Monteverde)–Via Induno–Porta Portese–Testaccio–Circus Maximus–Colosseum–Via Cavour–Termini.

#118 Via Appia Antica–Terme di Caracalla–Circus Maximus–Piazza Venezia–Colosseum–Terme di Caracalla–Via Appia Antica.

#492 Stazione Tiburtina–Termini–Piazza Barberini–Via del Corso–Piazza Venezia–Largo Argentina–Corso del Rinascimento–Piazza Cavour–Piazza Risorgimento–Cipro (Vatican Museums).

#590 Same route as metro line A but with access for disabled; runs every 1hr 30min.

#660 Largo Colli Albani–Via Appia Nuova–Via Appia Antica.

#714 Termini–Santa Maria Maggiore–Via Merulana–San Giovanni in Laterano–Terme di Caracalla–EUR.

#910 Termini–Piazza della Repubblica–Galleria Borghese–Auditorium–Piazza Mancini.

MINIBUSES

These **small buses** negotiate circular routes through the narrow streets of Rome's centre.

#116 Porta Pinciana–Via Veneto–Piazza Barberini–Piazza di Spagna–Corso Rinascimento–Campo de' Fiori–Piazza Farnese–Ponte Vittorio Emanuele–Terminal Gianicolo.

#117 San Giovanni in Laterano– Colosseum–Via Cavour–Via Nazionale–Piazza di Spagna– Piazza Trinità dei Monti–Piazza del Popolo.

TRAMS

#2 Piazzale Flaminio–Viale delle Belle Arti–Palazzetto dello Sport–Piazza Mancini.

#3 Viale delle Belle Arti–Piazza Buenos Aires–Viale Regina Margherita–San Lorenzo–Piazza di Santa Croce in Gerusalemme–Colosseum–Circus Maximus–Piazzale Ostiense.

#8 Stazione Trastevere–Piazza Mastai–Viale Trastevere–Via Arenula/Largo Argentina–Piazza Venezia.

#14 Termini–Piazza Vittorio Emanuele–Porta Maggiore–Via Prenestina (Pigneto).

#19 Porta Maggiore–San Lorenzo–Piazzale Verano–Viale Regina Margherita–Viale Belle Arti–Villa Giulia–Ottaviano–Piazza Risorgimento.

NIGHTBUSES

#N1 Same route as metro line A.

#N2 Same route as metro line B.

#N7 Piazzale Clodio–Via Ripetta–Corso del Rinascimento–Largo Argentina–Piazza Venezia–Via Nazionale–Termini.

#N8 Viale Trastevere–Piazza Venezia–Via Nazionale–Termini.

#N10 Piazzale Ostiense–Lungotevere De' Cenci–Via Crescenzio–Viale Belle Arte–Viale Regina Margherita–Via Labicana–Colosseum–Circus Maximus–Piazzale Ostiense.

want to see anything outside the immediate centre.

ATAC (Azienda Tramvie ed Autobus del Comune di Roma) runs the city's **bus, tram and metro service** and on the whole is pretty efficient; its website – ⓦatac.roma.it – has plenty of **information** in English and an excellent route planner; there's also an enquiries line (Mon–Sat 8am–8pm; ☎06 57003), but it's Italian-only. The Muoversi a Roma website (ⓦmuovi.roma.it) has a journey planner that uses real-time data to find the quickest route and is available as an app.

There's also an **information booth** (daily 8am–8pm) in front of Termini on Piazza dei Cinquecento, as well as basic transport information displayed outside.

By bus and tram

The city's **bus and tram** service is on the whole pretty good – cheap, reliable and as quick as the clogged streets of the city centre allow. Remember to board through the rear doors and punch your ticket as you enter. There is also a small network of **electric minibuses** that negotiate the narrow backstreets of the old centre. Buses generally run from around 5.30am until midnight, when infrequent **nightbuses** take over, accessing most parts of the city through the night; it's worth keeping spare tickets handy as it can be difficult to buy one in the early hours. Nightbuses are easily identified by the letter N before the bus number; on bus stops, look for the owl symbol.

TOURS

A number of companies run **organized trips** around the city centre. For general orientation and a glance at the main sights, the City Sightseeing open-top bus (see below) is good value. For a more in-depth tour you're better off with one of the walking-tour specialists below.

WALKING TOURS

Context Travel Via Baccina 40 ☎ 06 9672 7371, ⓦ contexttravel.com. Excellent small-group walking tours (maximum 6 people) of sights and neighbourhoods, led by engaging experts, on subjects ranging from architecture to gastronomic Rome – and of course they do all the major sights too. One of the best options if you want something both in-depth and personal. Tours from €65 per person for a 2hr tour.

Katie Parla ⓦ katieparla.com. The private food, wine and beer tours led by food critic and writer Katie Parla focus on different areas of the city; various themed tours are available too, including "Food and Archaeology" and "Roman Jewish Cuisine". Private tours (maximum of six participants) cost €300 for the group.

Understanding Rome ☎ 338 1984 375, ⓦ understandingrome.com.
Qualified Rome guide and architectural historian Agnes Crawford leads private tailor-made tours of Rome and environs. As well as the Colosseum and the Vatican, some less well-trodden itineraries include her "Roads and Water" tour, which explores a section of an aqueduct and visits the Appian Way. From €250 per group for a 3hr tour.

BUS TOURS

City Sightseeing ⓦ city-sightseeing.com/tours/italy/rome .htm. There are several hop-on-hop-off buses in Rome, operating on much the same route around the main sights, and on similar double-decker buses with audioguide included in the ticket price. The red City Sightseeing buses depart from Via Marsala 7 outside Termini every 10min from 9am to 7pm. 24hr tickets cost €22, 48hr tickets €28 and 72hr tickets €32.

Roma Cristiana ☎ 06 698 961,
ⓦ operaromanapellegrinaggi.org. The Vatican's tourist bus service, with commentary, links Rome's major basilicas and other Christian sites, starting in front of Termini on Piazza dei Cinquecento, and also at St Peter's. Services run daily every 30min between 9am (9.30am St Peter's) and 6pm, and tickets cost €15, or €20 for 24hr; you can also buy tickets that include public transport (€22/€35 for 24/48hr). Tickets can be bought on board, or at various Roma Cristiana meeting points (detailed on the website).

CAR AND BIKE TOURS

Rome 500 Experience ☎ 06 7049 4983, ⓦ rome500exp. com. Self-drive or chauffeured guided tours of Rome in a convoy of vintage Fiat 500s. Options include a Rome driving tour (from €190), and a route visiting the locations of the film *The Great Beauty* (from €210), both lasting 3hr.

TopBike Rental & Tours ☎ 06 488 2893, ⓦ topbikerental. com. This reliable operator runs a variety of bike tours, from "Panoramic Rome" (4hr 30min; €49) to a tour of the Appian Way and Catacombs (6hr; €79).

For **day-trips out of town**, COTRAL (☎ 06 7205 7205, ⓦ cotralspa.it) run a number of useful bus routes: to Tivoli and Palestrina (from Ponte Mammolo metro station; line B); to Cerveteri (from Cornelia metro station; line A); to Nettuno, near Anzio (from Laurentina metro station; line B); to the Castelli Romani and Nettuno (from Anagnina metro station; line A); and to Bracciano, Viterbo and around (from Saxa Rubra station; on the Roma-Nord line and connected by train with the station at Piazzale Flaminio, on metro line A).

By metro

Rome's **metro** runs from 5.30am to 11.30pm daily, except on Fridays and Saturdays, when it closes at 1.30am. The metro consists of two main lines, **A (red) and B (blue)**, which cross at Termini station; line B1, which branches off line B towards the northern suburbs, is of little use to tourists. The first section of **line C** was finished in 2014, and in 2017 it connected with Line A at San Giovanni. However, its city-centre stations, at the Colosseum and Piazza Venezia, won't be completed until 2020 at the earliest. The metro can be good for quick hops across the centre: useful stops include the Colosseum, Piazza Barberini, Piazza del Popolo (the stop is called Flaminio), Piazza di Spagna, Ottaviano (for St Peter's) and Cipro (for the Vatican Museums).

The metro system also incorporates the major **overground trains** that head out to the suburbs: these include the Roma-Lido line, which connects the city to Ostia; and the Roma-Laziale and Roma-Nord lines, which run respectively east and north of the city centre.

By taxi

The easiest way to get a taxi is to find the nearest **taxi rank** (*fermata dei taxi*). The most centrally located are at Corso Rinascimento (Piazza Navona); Largo Argentina; Piazza Barberini; Santa Maria

TICKETS AND PASSES

Flat-fare tickets (BIT) cost €1.50 each and are good for any number of bus or tram rides and one metro ride within 100 minutes of validating them. You need to punch your ticket when you start the ride, and a second time if you use the metro; otherwise you can be fined. **Tickets** are available from tobacconists (*tabacchi*), newsstands, some coffee bars, and ticket machines located in all metro stations and at major bus stops. You can also get a **day-pass** (BIG), valid for 24 hours from the first use, for €7; a 48-hour pass costs €12.50; a 72-hour pass costs €18; or a seven-day pass (CIS, valid until midnight on the seventh day) costs €24. A **monthly pass** costs €35, and is valid for the calendar month that's printed on the pass. Public transport is free with the **Roma Pass** and **Omnia Vatican & Rome Pass** (see p.32). One-day BIRG tickets (**regional transport passes**) for COTRAL and ATAC services are well worth buying if you are going out of Rome for the day (see box below). Finally, it's worth knowing that there are hefty spot **fines** of up to €100 for **fare-dodging**, and pleading a foreigner's ignorance will get you nowhere.

Maggiore; Piazza Belli (Trastevere); Piazza dei Cinquecento (Termini); Piazza del Popolo; Piazza San Silvestro; Piazza di Spagna; Piazza Venezia and Via Veneto (Porta Pinciana). Alternatively, you can **call** a taxi (☎ 06 0609), although these cost more – €3.50 for the call, plus the meter starts ticking the moment the taxi is dispatched to collect you.

After much legal to-ing and fro-ing, and protests by local taxi drivers, the app-based taxi service **Uber** was allowed to operate legitimately in Rome in 2017. Vehicles are restricted to those licensed for private driver services (NCC), so are not as numerous as in other major cities. However, it does mean vehicles are usually smart and many are eight-seaters.

Meters start at €3 (€4.50 on Sun, €6.50 10pm–6am); your first piece of luggage is free, then it's €1 per item; the meter clicks up at the rate of €1 or so every kilometre. A journey from one side of the city centre to the other should cost around €10, or around €15 on Sunday or at night. Pick-ups from Termini station incur a supplement of €2. Taxis are white, and all carry a **rate card** in English giving the current tariff, and the extra charges for luggage, late-night, Sundays and holidays, and airport journeys.

By bike and scooter

Renting a bike or scooter is an efficient way of nipping around Rome's clogged streets. You'll see bike stands belonging to the Roma-Bike scheme all over the centre; unfortunately, this bike-sharing programme is open to residents only (and has not been a success, thanks to the Roman preference for four wheels over two). However, there are plenty of places offering bike rental (see below); rates are around €4/hr or €13/day for bikes, and €30–80/day for scooters, and you'll need to have a full driving licence. You can also rent bikes on the Via Appia Antica (see p.148). **Tours** of the city and surrounding area by bike are also available (see box opposite). Note that traffic can be treacherous and cycling is not a relaxing experience outside the narrow streets and pedestrianized areas of the Centro Storico, and the Villa Borghese park: cycle lanes are few and far between.

BIKE RENTAL OUTLETS

Barberini Via della Purificazione 84 ☎ 06 488 5485, ⓦ rentscooter.it. Rents bicycles and scooters. Daily 9am–7pm.

TRAVEL AROUND LAZIO

The **Lazio transport system** is divided into zones which spread concentrically out from the city. If you're considering travelling outside Rome, it's possible to buy **season tickets** to travel within them. The **BIRG** (Biglietto Integrato Regionale Giornaliero) is valid all day (until midnight) for unlimited travel on the state railway, COTRAL buses and the Rome metro, but not trains to the airport. Prices range from €3.30 to €14, depending on the number of zones (up to seven including the city centre). A €9.30 ticket, covering four zones, for example, ferries you between Rome and Viterbo. The **BTR** (Biglietto Turistico Regionale) is valid for three days and costs from €8.90 to €39.20, depending on the zone. You can also buy a weekly pass – the **CIRS** (Carta Integrata Regionale Settimanale) – which costs from €13.50 to €61.50. Vendors – train and bus ticket offices, newspaper stands and tobacconists – can advise you on which zones you need to include, or see ⓦ atac.roma.it.

Bici e Baci Via del Viminale 5 ☎ 06 482 8443; Via Cavour 302 ☎ 06 9453 9240; Vicolo del Bottino 8 ☎ 06 678 6788; ⓦ bicibaci.com. Three city-centre locations, or bikes, scooters and mopeds can be dropped off and picked up from your hotel. Check out, too, the basement scooter museum at their Via Cavour location. Daily 8am–7pm.

Collalti Via del Pellegrino 80a–82 ☎ 06 6880 1084, ⓦ collaltibici .com. Bike rental and repairs by the hour or day, just round the corner from Campo de' Fiori. Mon–Sat 9am–1pm & 3.30–7pm.

Treno e Scooter Rent Piazza dei Cinquecento, Termini ☎ 06 4890 5823, ⓦ trenoescooter.com. Bikes and scooters for hire by the day; on the right as you come out of the station. Daily 9am–2pm & 4–7pm.

By car

Driving in central Rome can be a nightmare, and is something to be avoided at all costs. In any case, much of the Centro Storico is within the **ZTL** (*zona a traffico limitato*), in which traffic is restricted during the day; if you are driving to a hotel in the centre, check if they are in the ZTL and if they can get you permission to enter. Fines are hefty for drivers ignoring the restrictions.

Only residents with a permit are allowed to **park** for free in central Rome, so you will always need to pay. You can park on the street for around €1.20 an hour (8am–8pm) – places will usually be designated by blue lines – and there are coin-operated pay-and-display parking meters. There are 24hr **garages** in Villa Borghese, in front of Termini station, at Terminal Gianicolo (which is a short walk to the Vatican) and next to each of the end-of-the-line metro stations, from where it's easy to get into the city centre. All charge around €2.20/hr or €18/day.

In the event of a **breakdown**, call ☎ 803 116 to speak to ACI (the national motoring association), or consult the *Yellow Pages* (*Pagine Gialle*) under "Autoriparazioni" for specialized repair shops.

If you plan to **rent a car**, you'll find all the usual suspects have desks at Fiumicino, Ciampino, Termini and elsewhere in the city, including the area on and around Via Veneto. It's a good idea to take out Collision Damage Waiver (CDW) and Personal Accident Insurance (PAI) on top of the third-party insurance that comes as standard.

Media

The city's free daily (Italian-language) newspaper – *Metro* – is available in bars and cafés all over town, and provides weather reports, what's-on info and useful phone numbers. If you want to get into a bit more depth or to practise your **Italian, you might want to dip into one of the Italian dailies – though be advised that however good your Italian is, most of the country's national newspapers offer a pretty turgid read.**

Of the big **national newspapers**, the posh paper is the right-of-centre *Corriere della Sera*, to which *La Repubblica* is the left-of-centre alternative – both have Rome news supplements daily. The **Rome papers** are the popular *Il Messaggero*, the right-leaning *Il Tempo* and the Vatican daily *L'Osservatore Romano*, which also prints an English edition once a week. You'll notice that the sports coverage in all these papers is relatively thin. If you want in-depth football reporting you need to try one of three national **sports dailies** – either the pink *Gazzetta dello Sport*, the Rome-based *Corriere dello Sport* or *Tuttosport*.

For **what's-on and listings information**, the twice-monthly English expat magazine, *Wanted in Rome* (€2; ⓦ wantedinrome.com), is a useful source of information, especially if you're looking for an apartment or work, and is available at central newsstands. For those with a bit of Italian, the daily arts pages of *Il Messaggero* list movies, plays and major musical events, and Thursday's *La Repubblica* includes the "Trova Roma" supplement, another handy guide to current offerings. Finally, **English-language newspapers**, such as *The International Herald Tribune* and *The Financial Times*, are available the same day of publication, usually after lunch, at newsstands all over town.

Money

Italy's currency is the euro (€), split into 100 cents. There are seven euro notes – in denominations of 500, 200, 100, 50, 20, 10 and 5 euros, each a different colour and size – and eight different coin denominations, with 2 and 1 euros, then 50, 20, 10, 5, 2 and 1 cents. For the latest exchange rates check ⓦ xe.com.

The easiest way to get euros is simply to use your **debit card** in an ATM machine (*bancomat*); there's usually a charge, but it's no more expensive than getting money any other way. The daily limit for withdrawal is €250. It's more expensive to use a **credit card** to withdraw cash; check charges before you travel. Credit and debit cards are widely accepted in hotels and most restaurants, though some of the smaller restaurants, B&Bs and shops are cash-only, so check first. Visa and MasterCard are the most commonly accepted cards.

Banking hours are normally Monday to Friday from 8.30am until 1.30pm, and then for an hour in the afternoon (usually between 2.30 & 4pm). Outside banking hours, the larger hotels will change money, and there are plenty of exchange bureaux – normally open evenings and weekends. Try Western Union, which is available at lots of banks and locations throughout the city. The last resort should be any of the many *Ufficio Cambio* kiosks, almost always offering the worst rates (despite "no commission" signs).

LOST OR STOLEN CREDIT CARDS

CREDIT CARDS
American Express ☎ 800 914 912 or ☎ 06 72282.
MasterCard ☎ 800 870 866.
Visa ☎ 800 819 014.

Travel essentials

Climate

Visiting Rome at any time of year is a pleasure, although some months are of course better than others in terms of **climate**. If you can, avoid visiting in July and August, when the weather is prone to being hot, sticky and humid. Temperatures are usually more comfortable in May, June and September, when most days will be warm but not unbearably so, and it's almost always less humid. April and October are usually good weather-wise, warm enough if prone to the odd shower. The winter months can be pleasant, and temperatures are usually mild, but you will almost certainly have some rain, especially in November and December.

Crime and personal safety

Rome is a pretty safe city by any standards, but particularly when compared to its counterparts in the US and UK. The main thing is to make sure you're not too obvious a target for petty criminals by taking some **common-sense precautions**. Most of the crime you're likely to come across will be **bag-snatching**, where gangs of either street kids or *scippatori* ("snatchers") operate. *Scippatori* work on foot or on scooters, disappearing before you've had time to react; the kids are more likely to crowd you in a group, trying to work their way into your bags or pockets while you're trying to shoo them away. As well as handbags, they whip wallets, slash the side of a purse, tear off visible jewellery and, if they're really adroit, unstrap watches. You can minimize the risk of this happening by being discreet: don't flash anything of value, keep a firm hand on your camera, and carry shoulder bags slung across your body. On crowded buses and metros you're more at risk, so keep an eye on your possessions at all times. It's also worth being vigilant when withdrawing money from ATMs. Be aware of anyone standing too close or trying to distract you – they may be trying to read your PIN or clone your card using a "skimmer" machine. Contact your bank or credit card provider immediately if you suspect you're a victim of **card fraud** (see above).

There are not really any parts of town you should avoid. Some of the areas around **Termini** can be a bit rough, but the neighbourhood is changing and in any case it's more seedy than dangerous. Deserted stretches around **Ostiense or Testaccio** are probably worth avoiding at night, but again this is just to be on the safe side rather than because of any track record of violent crime in these areas.

If the worst happens, you may be forced to have some dealings with the **police**. The Italian police is principally divided between the **Vigili Urbani**, mainly concerned with directing traffic and issuing parking fines; the **Polizia di Stato**, the main crime-fighting force; and the **Carabinieri**, with their military-style uniforms and white shoulder belts, who also deal with general crime, public order and drug control. The Polizia enjoy a fierce rivalry with the Carabinieri and are the ones you'll perhaps have most chance of coming into contact with, since thefts should be reported to them. Rome's main

AVERAGE MONTHLY TEMPERATURES AND RAINFALL												
	Jan	Feb	Mar	Apr	May	Jun	Jul	Aug	Sep	Oct	Nov	Dec
TEMPERATURE												
max/min (°C)	12/3	13/4	15/5	18/8	23/11	27/15	30/17	30/18	27/15	22/11	16/7	13/4
max/min (°F)	53/37	55/38	59/41	65/46	73/52	81/58	87/63	87/64	80/59	71/51	61/44	55/39
RAINFALL												
mm	103	99	68	65	48	34	23	33	68	94	130	111

questura or **police station** is at Piazza del Collegio Romano 3, just behind the Palazzo Doria Pamphilj (☎ 06 4686).

Note that in Italy everyone is required by law to carry **ID** at all times, so it's worth making a photocopy of your passport or other ID just in case.

Culture and etiquette

Rome is very used to tourists, but the rules for visiting **churches** are much as they are all over Italy: **dress modestly**, which usually means covered shoulders and no shorts (not even Bermuda-length ones), and try to avoid wandering around during a service.

In restaurants, you are not expected to leave a **tip**, but of course it's appreciated if you do; one or two euros per person is plenty.

Electricity

The **electricity supply** is 220V, though anything requiring 240V will work. Most plugs have three round pins, though you'll find the older two-pin plug in some places; an adapter is very useful.

Entry requirements

EU citizens can enter Italy and stay as long as they like on production of a **passport** valid for the duration of your stay. Citizens of the United States, Canada, Australia and New Zealand need only a passport, too (valid for at least three months beyond the planned date of departure from Italy), but are limited to stays of three months. South Africans require a Schengen visa, which entitles you to travel through many of the countries in the Eurozone. All other nationals should consult the Italian embassy in their own country about visa requirements.

If planning on staying for **more than ninety days**, EU citizens must visit the local *ufficio anagrafe* (registry office) to inform them of the planned length of stay and obtain a stamped **Dichiarazione di Presenza** ("declaration of presence"), within eight days of arrival. Non-EU citizens need to apply for a **Permesso di Soggiorno** ("permit to stay") specifying the reason for their stay (for work, study and so on). You can pick up a "kit" at the post office (see p.31), which contains the necessary forms and instructions (in Italian only). Once completed, the forms should be submitted at the post office; keep the receipt as proof. *Permessi* can take up to three months to obtain.

FOREIGN EMBASSIES IN ROME

Australia Via A. Bosio 5 ☎ 06 852 721, ⓦ italy.embassy.gov.au /rome/home.html.

Britain Via XX Settembre 80a ☎ 06 4220 0001, ⓦ gov.uk /government/world/organisations/british-embassy-rome.

Canada Via Zara 30 ☎ 06 85444 3937, ⓦ canadainternational. gc.ca/italy-italie.

Ireland Villa Spada, Via Giacomo Medici ☎ 06 585 2381, ⓦ dfa.ie/irish-embassy/italy.

New Zealand Via Clitunno 44 ☎ 06 853 7501, ⓦ nzembassy.com/ italy.

US Via Veneto 121 ☎ 06 46741, ⓦ italy.usembassy.gov.

Health

As a member of the European Union, Italy has **free reciprocal health agreements** with other member states. EU citizens are entitled to treatment within Italy's public healthcare system at reduced cost, or sometimes for free if on a temporary stay, on production of a **European Health Insurance Card** (**EHIC**). The EHIC is free of charge and valid for at least three years, and it basically entitles you to the same treatment as an insured person in Italy. In the UK, you can apply for the card by calling ☎ 0300 330 1350 or applying online at ⓦ www.ehic.org.uk; it was unclear at the time of writing whether this benefit would still be available after Brexit. In Ireland, you can fill in an application form at your local health office or online (ⓦ hse.ie). The card should take 7–10 days to come through, but it's worth allowing a week or so longer. Non-EU citizens should take out health insurance, though the Australian Medicare system also has a reciprocal healthcare arrangement with Italy.

Vaccinations are not required, and Rome doesn't present any more health worries than anywhere else in Europe; the worst that's likely to happen to you is suffering from the extreme heat in summer. The **water** that you'll see flowing from public fountains all over town is perfectly safe to drink,

EMERGENCIES

For help in an emergency, call one of the following national telephone numbers:
Police or any emergency service, including ambulance (*Soccorso Pubblico di Emergenza*) ☎ 113.
Carabinieri ☎ 112.
Ambulance (*Ambulanza*) ☎ 118.
Fire (*Vigili del Fuoco*) ☎ 115.
Road assistance (*Soccorso Stradale*) ☎ 116.

ROUGH GUIDES TRAVEL INSURANCE

Rough Guides has teamed up with WorldNomads.com to offer great travel insurance deals. Policies are available to residents of over 150 countries, with cover for a wide range of adventure sports, 24hr emergency assistance, high levels of medical and evacuation cover and a stream of travel safety information. Roughguides.com users can take advantage of their policies online 24/7, from anywhere in the world – even if you're already travelling. And since plans often change when you're on the road, you can extend your policy and even claim online. Roughguides.com users who buy travel insurance with ⓦ WorldNomads.com can also leave a positive footprint and donate to a community development project. For more information, go to ⓦ roughguides.com/travel-insurance.

except where there are *acqua non potabile* signs. It's worth taking **insect repellent**, as the countryside around Rome is rather prone to mosquitoes.

Staff in **pharmacies** (*farmacia*) are well qualified to give you advice on minor ailments and to dispense prescriptions. Pharmacies are generally open Monday to Friday 8.30am–1pm and 4–7.30pm, and Saturday 8.30am–1pm. Outside these hours, check the notice posted on the pharmacy door for the nearest night pharmacy or head to a 24hr pharmacy (see below). If you need treatment, go to a **doctor** (*medico*), or if you are seriously ill or involved in an accident, go straight to the **Pronto Soccorso** (Accident and Emergency) of the nearest **hospital**, or phone ☎113 and ask for *ospedale* or *ambulanza*. The most central hospitals are Fatebenefratelli, San Giovanni and Santo Spirito (see below).

DOCTORS

AlphaMed Via Zanardelli 36 ☎ 06 6830 9493. Central medical practice with English-speaking doctors. Mon–Fri 9am–8pm.
Tobias Wallbrecher Via Domenico Silveri 30 ☎ 06 638 0569, ⓦ twallsancosma.familydoctors.net. English-speaking family doctor close to the Vatican. Mon–Fri 9am–1pm & 4–7pm.

DENTISTS

Absolute Dentistry Via G. Pisanelli 3 ☎ 06 3600 3837, 24hr emergency line ☎ 339 250 7016, ⓦ absolutedentistry.it. English-speaking dentist.
Arrigo Peri Via Mecenate 77 ☎ 06 488 1614.

HOSPITALS

Fatebenefratelli On the Isola Tiberina ☎ 06 68371.
San Giovanni Via A. Aradam 8 ☎ 06 77051.
Santo Spirito Near the Vatican at Lungotevere in Sassia 1 ☎ 06 68351.
Bambino Gesù Piazza Sant'Onofrio, Trastevere ☎ 06 68591. The city's children's hospital.
Rome American Hospital Via E. Longoni 69 ☎ 06 22551. A private multi-speciality hospital with bilingual staff and a 24hr emergency line.

PHARMACIES

Internazionale Piazza Barberini 49 ☎ 06 487 1195. 24hr.
Piram Via Nazionale 228 ☎ 06 488 0754. 24hr.

Insurance

Even though EU healthcare privileges apply in Italy, you'd do well to take out an **insurance policy** before travelling to cover against theft, loss, illness or injury. A typical policy usually provides cover for the loss of baggage, tickets and – up to a certain limit – cash or cheques, as well as cancellation or curtailment of your journey. Most policies exclude so-called **dangerous sports** unless an extra premium is paid. Many policies can be chopped and changed to exclude coverage you don't need – for example, sickness and accident benefits can often be excluded or included at will.

If you do take **medical cover**, ascertain whether benefits will be paid as treatment proceeds or only after your return home, and whether there is a **24-hour medical emergency number**. When securing **baggage cover**, make sure the per-article limit will cover your most valuable possession. If you need to **make a claim**, you should keep receipts for medicines and medical treatment, and if you have anything stolen, you must obtain an official statement from the police (see p.27).

Internet

Internet cafés are not as ubiquitous as they once were but you should never be stuck for a place to get online, particularly around Termini station. Reckon on paying around €3/hr. Note that by law, internet cafés are required to check your ID, so be sure to carry this with you. Most hotels have wi-fi access, and many have a computer for guests' use; wi-fi is increasingly offered in cafés and bars too.

INTERNET CAFÉS

AntiCafé Via Veio 4b ☎ 06 7049 4442, ⓦ anticafe.eu. Near Piazza di San Giovanni in Laterano, AntiCafé is a bit different to the average internet café: when you come in you're given a card that records the time you arrived. You have free access to food and drink at the counter, free internet and free books and board games. When you're ready to leave, you're probably charged for the time spent in the café, starting at €4 for the first hour. Mon–Fri 9am–11pm, Sat & Sun 10am–11pm.

Yex Piazza Sant'Andrea delle Valle 1 ☎ 06 9727 3136. A bureau de change with attached internet café, near Campo de' Fiori. Daily 10am–8pm.

Laundries

You can usually get your **laundry** done in your hotel, but if you can't, a laundry (*lavanderia*) is probably just a short walk away. Try Wash and Dry (🅦 washedry.it), which has branches around town including at Via Avignonesi 17 and Via della Pelliccia 35 (both daily 8am–10pm). All offer a wash including soap and tumble-drying for €7–10 for a 6kg (15lb) load.

Lost property

For **property lost** on a train try the lost property office at Termini station (daily 7am–10pm; ☎ 06 4730 6682); on metro line A, try the office at Giulio Agricola station (Mon, Wed & Fri 9.30am–12.30pm; ☎ 06 4695 7068); on the B line, try the office at Piramide station (Mon–Fri 8am–1pm; ☎ 06 4695 8164). Items of property lost elsewhere are taken first to the police station nearest to where they were found, then after about a fortnight to Rome's lost property office at Circonvallazione Ostiense 191 (July & Aug Mon–Fri 8.30am–1pm; Sept–June Mon,

Tues, Wed & Fri 8.30am–1pm, Thurs 8.30am–5pm; ☎ 06 6769 3214).

Maps

For **walking around the city** you should find the maps in this book more than adequate for your needs. If you require something more detailed, then the best choice is perhaps the 1:12,500 *TCI* map (€7.90), which includes good coverage of the outskirts and suburban neighbourhoods. For public transport, **metro maps** are posted up in every station, and we've included one at the end of this book. Additionally, Lozzi publishes maps of Rome and of Lazio in various sizes (from €3), available from newsstands and bookshops (see p.292).

Opening hours and public holidays

The city's **opening hours** are becoming more flexible, but much of Rome still follows a traditional Italian routine. Most **shops and businesses** in Italy open Monday to Saturday from around 9am until 1pm, and from about 4pm until 7 or 8pm, although many shops close on Saturday afternoons and Monday mornings; a few of the more international businesses have longer hours, around 9am–7.30pm Monday to Saturday, and often 11am–7pm on Sunday. Traditionally, everything except big city-centre shops, and bars and restaurants, closes on Sunday, though there's

---

RESTORATION ROME

Though traditionally unwilling to accept corporate cash to fund restoration, in recent years cash-strapped Italy has turned to **private sponsors** – most notably big names in Italian fashion – in a bid to save its precious monuments. Keen to put their name to such a prestigious cause, sponsors have vied to pledge ever-larger sums, and the city is seeing a large-scale renovation of its heritage sites as a result. The **Trevi Fountain** has been spruced up courtesy of Fendi; leather brand Tod's have coughed up €25 million to restore the **Colosseum** (the facade was finished in 2015 and work has now moved inside); and Bulgari recently sponsored the restoration of the **Spanish Steps**. Despite the obvious value to the national patrimony, these projects have their detractors, who are concerned that in relying so heavily on corporate sponsorship Rome is selling its soul; Tod's, for example, have negotiated the right to mention the Colosseum's restoration in its brand materials for up to fifteen years (though nothing at the site itself indicates who is paying for it). Those working on the **Domus Aurea**'s ongoing restoration are trying a different tack: crowdfunding – but with €39 million needed to complete the job, this may take some time.

As for the smaller sights, you may well find places **closed for restoration** (*chiuso per restauro*), and it's usually pretty uncertain when they might reopen. If there's something you really want to see and you don't know when you'll be back in Rome, it might be worth trying to persuade a workman or priest/curator to show you around.

usually a *pasticceria* (pastry shop) open in the mornings, and in general Sunday opening is becoming more common.

Most **museums and galleries** are closed on Mondays; hours are given throughout the Guide. Many large museums run **late-night openings** in summer (till 10pm or later Tues–Sat, or 8pm on Sun). Some archeological sites – such as the Colosseum – also hold summer night visits, which are ideal for avoiding both heat and crowds.

Most major **churches** open in the early morning, at around 7 or 8am, and close around noon or 1pm, opening up again at 4pm and closing at 6 or 7pm; hours may be shorter during the winter months. At any time of year, some of the less-visited churches will open only for early-morning and evening services, and some are closed at all times except Sundays and on religious holidays; if you're determined to take a look, you may have to ask around for the key, or make an appointment with the custodian.

The other factors to be aware of are **public holidays** (see below) and the fact that in **August**, particularly during the weeks either side of Ferragosto (Aug 15), most of Rome flees to the coast; at this time many shops, bars and restaurants close and the only people around are other tourists.

PUBLIC HOLIDAYS

New Year's Day Jan 1
Epiphany Jan 6
Pasquetta Easter Monday
Liberation Day April 25
Primo Maggio May 1
Day of the Republic June 2
Festa di Santi Pietro e Paolo June 29
Ferragosto Aug 15
Ognissanti Nov 1
Immacolata Concezione Dec 8
Christmas (Natale) Dec 25
Santo Stefano (St Stephen) Dec 26

Phones

The **country code** for Italy is ☎+39. You can use your **mobile phone** – or *telefonino* – in Italy, and indeed you will hardly see an Italian without his or her mobile clasped to the ear. Data roaming charges, which used to be extortionate, have now been scrapped within the EU, though British travellers may face high charges again when Brexit bites (if indeed it does); check with your provider before you travel.

CALLING HOME FROM ITALY

To make an international call, dial the international access code (in Italy it's 00), then the destination's country code, before the rest of the number. Note that the initial zero is omitted from the area code when dialling the UK, Ireland, Australia and New Zealand from abroad.

Australia international access code + 61
New Zealand international access code + 64
UK international access code + 44
US and Canada international access code + 1
Ireland international access code + 353
South Africa international access code + 27

Post

General information on Italian **postal services** is available on ☎803 160 or at ⊕poste.it. Rome's main **post office** (*ufficio postale*) is on Piazza San Silvestro (Mon–Fri 8.20am–7.05pm, Sat 8.20am–12.35pm); other post offices can be found at Via Firenze 36 off Via Veneto, Via Isonzo 17 near Villa Borghese, and at Termini station. Hours vary, but tend to be Monday to Friday 8.30am to 6pm, Saturday 8.30am to 1pm.

Stamps (*francobolli*) are sold in *tabacchi* too, as well as in some gift shops; they will often also weigh your letter. If your letter is urgent make sure you send it "*posta prioritaria*", which has varying rates according to weight and destination. In Rome you can also use the **Vatican postal system**, which is quicker, and you get the benefit of an exotic postmark. However, not unreasonably, you have to use Vatican stamps and post your items from the Vatican itself. For this there are post offices and boxes in Piazza San Pietro (Mon–Sat 8.30am–6.30pm) and in the Vatican Museums (same hours as the museums).

Smoking

Smoking is banned in all public indoor spaces in Italy, including restaurants, bars and clubs. Some establishments have separate smoking rooms, though this is rare.

Time

Rome is one hour ahead of GMT, six hours ahead of Eastern Standard Time and nine hours ahead of Pacific Standard Time.

ROME ONLINE

Ⓦ **060608.it** Comprehensive information on sights, transport and events.

Ⓦ **inromenow.com** Fairly up-to-date and very wide-ranging guide to the city.

Ⓦ **parlafood.com** Not just a great online guide to the best of Rome's food and drink, but a dynamic and delectable culinary website and blog.

Ⓦ **racheleats.wordpress.com** A mouthwatering food blog by a Brit living in Rome.

Ⓦ **rome.angloinfo.com** Good current information directed

at expats and English speakers living in the city.

Ⓦ **romeguide.it** Site of the "Il Sogno" co-operative, which aims to place young people in tourist industry jobs in Rome. A useful resource on sights and good for up-to-date information on concerts and events too.

Ⓦ **romeing.it** A very useful source of what's-on information, updated regularly, and with engaging features too.

Ⓦ **turismoroma.it** Rome's official tourist website.

Ⓦ **understandingrome.com/blog** Some thoughts for exploring lesser-known sights off the beaten track.

Toilets

There are **public lavatories** on Piazza Zanardelli, just north of Piazza Navona, and on Piazza di Spagna, but these are something of a rarity in Rome. The only others are on Via dei Fori Imperiali, near the entrance to the Forum; in St Peter's Square, just to the left of the entrance to the basilica; in Piazza Vittorio Emanuele; and in Termini station and some city-centre metro stations. The facilities in *McDonalds*, department stores and in the lobbies of five-star hotels are always worth trying if you're desperate.

Tourist information

There are official **tourist information booths** at Fiumicino in Terminal 3 (daily 8am–7.45pm), in the Arrivals hall at Ciampino Airport (daily 9am–6.30pm) and inside Termini at Via Giolitti 34 (daily 8am–8pm). You'll also find **green information kiosks** or **PIT** (daily 9.30am–7pm) in key locations around the city centre (see below) that are useful for free maps, directions (the staff usually speak English) and details about nearby sights – though they can be pretty clueless if you want anything less obvious. The Rome **tourist office website** (Ⓦturismoroma.it) can help take up some of the slack, and has plenty of information in English. The council-run **tourist information line** ☎06 0608 is open daily 9am–9pm (calls charged at local rates). For practical information on **transport** and local services, call ☎06 0606, a 24hr helpline run by the council and staffed by English speakers.

INFORMATION KIOSKS

Castel Sant'Angelo Via della Conciliazione 4.
Colosseum Via dei Fori Imperiali.
Piazza Barberini Via di San Basilio 51.

Piazza Navona Piazza delle Cinque Lune.
Portico d'Ottavia Via di Santa Maria del Pianto 1.
Trevi Fountain Via Minghetti.
Vatican Piazza San Pietro.
Via Nazionale Palazzo delle Esposizioni.

Tourist passes and discounts

There is no museum pass that will get you into all the main attractions in Rome, though the **Roma Pass** (☎06 0608, Ⓦromapass.it) covers most places you'll want to visit (the most notable exception is the Vatican Museums). Available from all museums in the circuit and tourist information kiosks, it costs €38.50 (valid for three days), or €28 (valid for two days). It entitles you to travel free on buses, trams and the metro, gives free admission to two of some 45 museums or sights of your choice (the vast majority of places participate) and reduced entry to others – and, perhaps most importantly, allows you to avoid the queues at big sights (quite a lifesaver at the Colosseum).

The Vatican's **Omnia Vatican & Rome Pass** (Ⓦomniakit.org) gives pre-paid, fast-track access to the Vatican Museums, St Peter's, Mamertine Prison, the Colosseum, Forum and Palatine, as well as discounts to the same museums covered by the Roma Pass (plus free entry into one); you also get free transport around the city, plus a trip on the Roma Cristiana bus tour of the city (see box, p.24). However, it's expensive (€113; valid for 3 days), so you're paying a lot to jump the queues, and for the Vatican Museums you can do this anyway simply by booking online for €20. It's only really just about worth it if you visit all the sites (some of which are free anyway) and would have bought a three-day travel pass.

If you don't want to splash out, it's handy to know that some sights are grouped together to make it easier and cheaper to visit them. The Forum,

Palatine and Colosseum can be visited on a **combined ticket**, and much of Rome's ancient sculpture and other artefacts have been gathered together in the **Museo Nazionale Romano**, which operates on four main sites: Palazzo Massimo, the Terme di Diocleziano, Crypta Balbi and the Palazzo Altemps; you can buy a ticket from each location that permits entry to all the others for just €7 and is valid for three days. The **Archaeologia Card** (€25; valid for 7 days; ☎06 3996 7700, ⓦcoopculture.it) gets you in to all sites of the Museo Nazionale Romano, as well as the Colosseum, Forum, Palatine, Baths of Caracalla, Tomb of Cecilia Metella and Villa dei Quintilii. It can be bought at the ticket offices of the sites involved.

All state-run sights are **free on the first Sunday of the month** – which means potentially big savings on entrance fees, but, inevitably, bigger crowds too. Public museums are free for **under-18s**, with **under-25s** resident in the EU paying a discounted price. Many theatres and cinemas will also offer discounts.

Travellers with disabilities

Rome can be quite a challenge for those with **disabilities**: there are lots of steps, navigating the cobblestones can be tricky with a wheelchair, and Italy as a whole is just not as accessible as a lot of northern Europe and North America. Most stops on **metro** line A are accessible for disabled persons (though not San Giovanni, Repubblica, Barberini, Spagna and Flaminio); bus #590 (every 1hr 30min) does the same route and can also accommodate those with disabilities. On metro line B, Circo Massimo, Colosseo and Cavour do not have accessibility, but all other stations do. Eighteen **bus lines** are now wheelchair-

---

STUDYING IN ROME: ACADEMIES AND LIBRARIES

The **American Academy** is at Via Angelo Masina 5, 00153 Rome (☎06 58461, ⓦaarome.org); the **British School at Rome** is at Via Gramsci 61, 00197 Rome (☎06 326 4939, ⓦbsr.ac.uk). The best **library** is the one at the American church of **Santa Susanna**, Via XX Settembre 15 (☎06 482 7510), which costs €45 a year (plus a refundable deposit of €40), and also has a good noticeboard for finding work, accommodation and so on (Tues 10am–1pm, Wed 3–6pm, Thurs 10am–1pm, Fri 1–4pm, Sun 10am–12.30pm). Reference libraries include those of the **American Studies Center**, Via M. Caetani 32 (Mon–Thurs 9am–5.30pm, Fri 9am–2pm; ☎06 6880 1613, ⓦcentrostudiamericani.org), and the British School at Rome (see above; Mon–Fri 9am–6.45pm; annual membership €30).

---

accessible: H, 44, 46, 60, 80, 81, 85, 87, 90, 170, 360, 490, 558, 590, 650, 660, 664 and 671.

There's useful information on **accessible tourism** in Rome, though in Italian only, on the Roma Per Tutti website (ⓦwww.romapertutti.it); see also ⓦaccessibleitaly.com for information on accessibility and tours.

France San Luigi dei Francesi ⓦsaintlouis-rome.net.
Germany Santa Maria dell'Anima ⓦwww.santa-maria-anima.it.
Scotland St Andrews ⓦpresbyterianchurchrome.org.
Spain Santa Maria di Monserrato.
US (Catholic) Santa Susanna ⓦwww.santasusanna.org.
US (Episcopalian) San Paolo entro le Mura ⓦstpaulsrome.it.

ROME'S SPECIAL CHURCHES

In the course of visiting and reading about Rome you may come across the concept of the city's four **patriarchal basilicas**: St Peter's, San Giovanni in Laterano, San Paolo fuori le Mura and Santa Maria Maggiore. These are the four most important churches in Rome, and therefore of the Catholic Church, and they symbolically represent the various parts of the world where the Catholic faith has reached. Apart from Santa Maria Maggiore, each one is technically part of the Vatican state (ie not Italian territory), and each has a **Holy Door** that is only opened – by the pope – every 25 years. San Giovanni in Laterano used to be the home of the pope and the Vatican, and is still technically the cathedral of Rome. Over the centuries pilgrims have always made a point of visiting these churches, plus the three other so-called **"pilgrimage" churches** – San Lorenzo fuori le Mura (occasionally included as a patriarchal basilica), Santa Croce in Gerusalemme and the Santuario Madonna del Divino Amore outside the city. It's a tradition that continues to this day, though Christian visitor numbers are these days swelled several-fold by tourists and other visitors.

The Centro Storico

The real heart of Rome is the Centro Storico or "historic centre", which makes up the greater part of the roughly triangular chunk of land that bulges into a bend in the Tiber. In the days of Ancient Rome, when it was known as the Campus Martius ("the Field of Mars"), this low-lying area lay outside the city centre and was mostly given over to military training (hence the Mars bit) and sporting arenas. Later, it became the heart of the Renaissance city, and nowadays it's here that most people find the Rome they have been looking for – a city of pretty piazzas, crumbling *palazzi*, Renaissance churches, Baroque fountains and the odd ancient ruin. In whichever direction you wander, there's something to see; indeed, it's part of the appeal of this area that even the most aimless ambling leads you past effortlessly beautiful and historic spots.

The Pantheon

Piazza della Rotonda • Mon–Sat 8.30am–7.30pm, Sun 9am–6pm, public hols 9am–1pm • Free • ☎ 06 6830 0230, Ⓦ pantheonroma.com •
Bus to Largo di Torre Argentina

Piazza della Rotonda is one of the city's most picturesque squares, invariably thronged
with sight-weary tourists, hawkers and street musicians, besieging the café tables that
fringe the edge. The waters of the fountain in the middle, an eighteenth-century
construction topped by one of Rome's eight ancient Egyptian obelisks, are a soothing
influence, but the main focus of interest is the **Pantheon**, which forms the square's
southern edge – easily the most complete ancient Roman structure in the city, and,
along with the Colosseum, visually the most impressive.

Originally a temple that formed part of Marcus Agrippa's redesign of the Campus
Martius in around 27 BC – hence the inscription on the porch facade, which translates
as "Marcus Agrippa, son of Lucius, three-time consul, built this" – the building was
entirely rebuilt by the **Emperor Hadrian** and finished around 125 AD. It remains a
formidable architectural achievement, and is the best preserved of the city's ancient
monuments. Consecrated as a Christian site in 609 AD, it was dedicated to **Santa
Maria ad Martyres** in an allusion to the Christian bones said to have been brought here
from the catacombs. A thousand years later, the bronze ceiling of the portico was
stripped by Pope Urban VIII, to be melted down for the baldacchino in
St Peter's and the cannons of the Castel Sant'Angelo. Some of this "stolen" bronze later
found its way back here when, after Unification, the cannons were in turn melted
down to provide materials for the tombs of two Italian kings, which are housed in the
right and left chapels.

Inside, you get the best impression of the **engineering expertise** of Hadrian: the
diameter is precisely equal to its height (43.3m), the oculus (hole in the centre of the
dome) is 8.7m across. To this day, it's the world's largest unreinforced concrete dome.
In its heyday, the interior would have been even more richly decorated: as well as the
surviving coloured marble lining the interior, the coffered ceiling was once heavily
stuccoed and the niches filled with statues of Roman gods.

The Pantheon also houses the **tomb of Raphael**, between the second and third chapels
on the left, with an inscription by the humanist cardinal Pietro Bembo: "Living, great
Nature feared he might outvie Her works, and dying, fears herself may die."

Elephant Statue

Just behind the Pantheon, outside the church of Santa Maria sopra Minerva, Bernini's
Elephant Statue is one of Rome's delightful small statues – and the celebrated Baroque
artist's most endearing piece of work. It shows a cheery elephant trumpeting under the
weight of the obelisk that he carries on his back – a reference to Pope Alexander VII's
reign and an illustration that strength should support wisdom.

Santa Maria sopra Minerva

Piazza della Minerva 42 • Mon–Fri 6.45am–7pm, Sat 6.45am–12.30pm & 3.30–7pm, Sun 8am–12.30pm & 3.30–7pm •
☎ 06 6992 0384, Ⓦ www.basilicaminerva.it • Bus to Largo di Torre Argentina

The church of **Santa Maria sopra Minerva** is Rome's only **Gothic church**, though its
soaring lines have since been overburdened by marble and frescoes. Built in the late
thirteenth century on the ruins of a temple to Minerva, it is also one of the city's
art-treasure churches, crammed with the tombs and self-indulgences of wealthy Roman
families. The splendid **Carafa Chapel**, in the south transept, is decorated with frescoes
by Filippino Lippi; the central wall shows the Assumption, a bright, effervescent piece
of work. Inset, as it were hanging from ribbons wrapped around the legs of cherubs in
the corners of the room, is a smaller painting of the Annunciation showing Oliviero
Carafa, the cardinal who commissioned the chapel, being presented to the Virgin by

1

1

Thomas Aquinas. On the left-hand wall of the chapel is the later tomb (by Pirro Ligorio) of Pope Paul IV, nephew of Cardinal Oliviero Carafa and the Inquisitor who would build the walls of the Jewish Ghetto and introduce the Index of Forbidden Books. On the right-hand wall, Aquinas confounds a group of heretics in sight of two beautiful young boys. The children, visible in the foreground on the right, are the future Medici popes **Leo X** and **Clement VII**; the equestrian statue of Marcus Aurelius, destined for the Capitoline Hill, is just visible in the background.

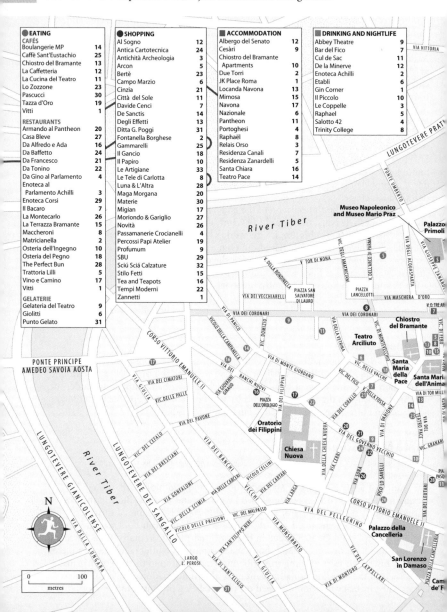

● EATING

CAFÉS
Boulangerie MP	14
Caffè Sant'Eustachio	25
Chiostro del Bramante	13
La Caffetteria	12
La Cucina del Teatro	23
Lo Zozzone	11
Pascucci	30
Tazza d'Oro	19
Vitti	1

RESTAURANTS
Armando al Pantheon	20
Casa Bleve	27
Da Alfredo e Ada	16
Da Baffetto	24
Da Francesco	21
Da Tonino	22
Da Gino al Parlamento	4
Enoteca al Parlamento Achilli	3
Enoteca Corsi	29
Il Bacaro	7
La Montecarlo	26
La Terrazza Bramante	15
Maccheroni	8
Matricianella	2
Osteria dell'Ingegno	10
Osteria del Pegno	18
The Perfect Bun	28
Trattoria Lilli	5
Vino e Camino	17
Vitti	1

GELATERIE
Gelateria del Teatro	9
Giolitti	6
Punto Gelato	31

● SHOPPING
Al Sogno	12
Antica Cartotecnica	24
Antichità Archeologia	3
Arcon	5
Bertè	23
Campo Marzio	6
Cinzia	21
Città del Sole	11
Davide Cenci	7
De Sanctis	14
Degli Effetti	13
Ditta G. Poggi	31
Fontanella Borghese	2
Gammarelli	25
Il Gancio	18
Il Papiro	10
Le Artigiane	33
Le Tele di Carlotta	8
Luna & L'Altra	28
Maga Morgana	20
Materie	30
Migian	17
Moriondo & Gariglio	27
Novità	26
Passamanerie Crocianelli	4
Percossi Papi Atelier	19
Profumum	9
SBU	29
Sciù Scià Calzature	32
Stilo Fetti	15
Tea and Teapots	16
Tempi Moderni	22
Zannetti	1

■ ACCOMMODATION
Albergo del Senato	12
Cesàri	9
Chiostro del Bramante Apartments	10
Due Torri	2
JK Place Roma	1
Locanda Navona	13
Mimosa	15
Navona	6
Nazionale	6
Pantheon	11
Portoghesi	4
Raphaël	8
Relais Orso	3
Residenza Canali	7
Residenza Zanardelli	5
Santa Chiara	16
Teatro Pace	14

■ DRINKING AND NIGHTLIFE
Abbey Theatre	9
Bar del Fico	7
Cul de Sac	11
De la Minerve	12
Enoteca Achilli	2
Etabli	6
Gin Corner	1
Il Piccolo	10
Le Coppelle	3
Raphael	5
Salotto 42	4
Trinity College	8

The lives of Leo and Clement come full circle in the church, where they are both buried, and remembered by two very grand tombs on either side of the high altar – Leo on the left, Clement on the right. To the left of the high altar *Christ Bearing the Cross*, is a serene work that **Michelangelo** completed for the church in 1521. Beneath the altar is the tomb of St Catherine of Siena, who died in a convent here in 1380. The room where she died is viewable through the sacristy, though you may need to ask someone to open it for you. You can leave the church by the passage to the left of the altar,

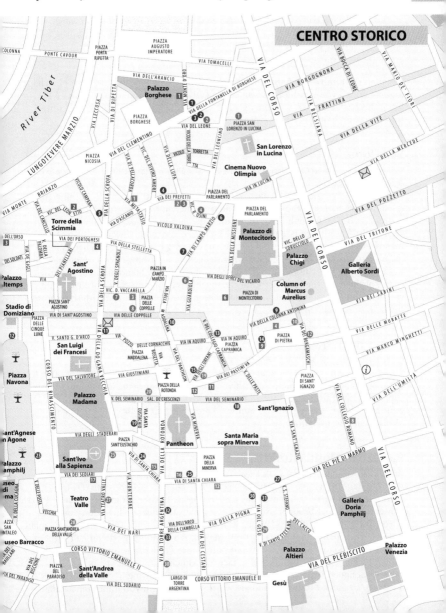

1

> ## CLERICAL FASHIONS
>
> Opposite the church of Santa Maria sopra Minerva, Via dei Cestari and Via di Santa Chiara host Rome's **clerical fashion district**, longtime home to a number of shops selling liturgical garments to priests, monks and nuns. Oddly enough, anyone is welcome to browse and even buy: should you be interested, a full set of cardinal's outfits, including a change of cassocks, a skullcap and something for special occasions, will set you back about €1500. Perhaps the most famous store of all is Gammarelli, Via di Santa Chiara 34 (Mon–Fri 8.30am–7pm; ☎ 06 6880 1314, ⓦ gammarelli.com), in business since 1798. This is the official supplier to the pope, and it's this historic shop that's charged with delivering three sizes of white (or, strictly, ivory) garments to the Vatican during papal elections to ensure that, whoever is elected, there will be something ready in the new pope's size.

taking in the **tomb of Fra Angelico**, who also died here in 1455, just in front of a chapel that contains a very soothing *Madonna and Child* by Benozzo Gozzoli, from 1449. From this back entrance, you emerge onto Via Sant'Ignazio, just around the corner from the church of the same name.

Sant'Ignazio

Piazza di Sant'Ignazio · Mon–Sat 7.30am–7pm, Sun & Aug 9am–7pm · ☎ 06 679 4406, ⓦ chiesasantignazio.it · Bus to Largo di Torre Argentina, Via del Corso or Piazza Venezia

Piazza di Sant'Ignazio, a lovely little square laid out like a theatre set, is dominated by the facade of the Jesuit church of **Sant'Ignazio**. The saint isn't actually buried here; appropriately, for the founder of the Jesuit order, he's in the main Jesuit church, the Gesù, a little way south (see p.54). But it's a spacious structure, worth visiting for a marvellous **Baroque ceiling** by Andrea Pozzo, showing the entry of St Ignatius into paradise – a spectacular work, employing sledgehammer trompe-l'oeil effects, notably in the mock cupola painted into the dome of the crossing. Stand on the disc in the centre of the nave, the focal point for the ingenious rendering of perspective: figures in various states of action and repose, conversation and silence, fix you with stares from their classical pediments.

Piazza di Pietra

Bus to Largo di Torre Argentina, Via del Corso or Piazza Venezia

On the northern side of Piazza di Sant'Ignazio lies **Piazza di Pietra**, a pleasant open space dominated by the giant Corinthian columns of an ancient Roman temple, still supporting their frilled peristyle and incorporated in true Roman style into the building behind. The temple was built by Antoninus Pius in 145 AD in memory of his predecessor, Hadrian.

Palazzo di Montecitorio

Piazza di Montecitorio · First Sun of the month 10am–6pm; closed July, Aug & first week of Sept; hourly guided tours (Italian only); 30min · Free; pick up tickets first at the Punto Camera, Via del Parlamento 9a · ☎ 06 67601, ⓦ camera.it · Bus to Via del Corso

A couple of minutes' walk north of Piazza di Pietra, the obelisk in the centre of **Piazza di Montecitorio** was brought to Rome by Augustus to celebrate his victory over Cleopatra and set up in the Campus Martius, where it formed the gnomon of a giant sundial. The square takes its name from the **Palazzo di Montecitorio** on its northern side, a Bernini creation from 1650 and home since 1871 to the lower house of the Italian parliament. The building is in fact two knocked into one: the original Bernini-designed structure, and another incorporating the main Hall of Deputies. Visits are by guided tour only and are worth considering if you understand Italian.

Next door to Palazzo Montecitorio is **Piazza Colonna**, home to Palazzo Chigi – the prime minister's official residence – and the Column of Marcus Aurelius (see p.92).

Torre della Scimmia

A few minutes' walk west of the Palazzo di Montecitorio, on Via dei Portoghesi, take a look at the **Torre della Scimmia** – literally the "Tower of the Monkey" – which grows almost organically out of a fork in the road above a *palazzo*. The story goes that in the seventeenth century, a pet monkey kidnapped a child and carried it to the top of the tower; the father of the child called upon the Virgin for help, and the monkey promptly clambered down, delivering the child to safety. By way of thanks, the man erected a shrine to the Virgin accompanied by a glowing lamp, which you can still see at the top of the tower.

Sant'Agostino

Piazza di Sant'Agostino 80 · Daily 7.30am–noon & 4–7.30pm · ☎ 06 68801962 · Bus to Corso del Rinascimento

Along Via dei Pianellari, the Renaissance facade of the church of **Sant'Agostino** takes up one side of a drab piazza of the same name. Its towering facade is an example of late fifteenth-century austerity, and belies three masterpieces within: this was the church of Rome's creative community in the sixteenth century, and as such drew wealthy patrons and well-connected artists. Just inside the door, the serene statue of the *Madonna del Parto*, by **Sansovino**, is traditionally invoked during pregnancy, and is accordingly surrounded by offerings in pink and baby blue.

Further into the church, take a look at Raphael's vibrant fresco of Isaiah, on the third pillar on the left, beneath which is another work by Sansovino, a craggy *St Anne, Virgin and Child*. But the biggest crowds gather around the first chapel on the left, where the *Madonna di Loreto*, painted in 1605 by Caravaggio, is a characteristic work of what was at the time almost revolutionary realism, showing two peasants praying at the feet of a sensuous Madonna and Child, their dirty feet and scruffy clothes contrasting with the pale, delicate feet and skin of Mary.

Palazzo Altemps

Piazza Sant'Apollinare 46 · Tues–Sun 9am–7.45pm · €7 combined ticket with Palazzo Massimo (p.123), Terme di Diocleziano (p.123) & Crypta Balbi (p.55); valid for 3 days; free first Sun of the month · ☎ 06 3996 7700, ⓦ archeoroma.beniculturali.it · Bus to Corso del Rinascimento

A five-minute walk west of Sant'Agostino, Piazza Sant'Apollinare is the home of the beautiful **Palazzo Altemps**. Begun in 1477 and completed just under a hundred years later, it now houses a branch of the **Museo Nazionale Romano**, which contains the cream of the museum's collections of Roman statuary. Divided between two storeys of the palace, in rooms which open off an elegant courtyard, most of what is on display derives from the collection of the seventeenth-century Roman cardinal, Ludovico Ludovisi. Some pieces were purchased by Ludovisi to adorn his villa on the Quirinal Hill, while others were found in the grounds of the villa itself, which occupied the site of a former residence of Julius Caesar.

The ground floor

First up, at the far end of the courtyard's loggia, is a statue of Emperor Antoninus Pius, who ruled from 138 to 161 AD, and, around the corner, a couple of marvellous heads of Zeus and Pluto, a large **bronze bust** of Marcus Aurelius, a bust of Julia, the disgraced daughter of Emperor Augustus, and a grave-looking likeness of the philosopher Demosthenes, from the second century AD. Further rooms hold more riches: there are two almost identical statues of Apollo the Lyrist, a magnificent statue of Athena taming

1

a serpent, pieced together from fragments found near the church of Santa Maria sopra Minerva, an Aphrodite from an original by Praxiteles, a frieze from a third-century sarcophagus showing the labours of Hercules and, just off the far corner of the courtyard, a shameless Dionysus with a satyr and panther, found on the Quirinale Hill.

Restoration works on the *palazzo* brought to light the remains of a Roman domus from the fourth to fifth century AD, which you can peer down at from a room off the south side of the courtyard.

The first floor

Upstairs, you get a slightly better sense of the original sumptuousness of the building – some of the frescoes remain, and the north loggia retains its original late-sixteenth-century decoration, simulating a vine-laden pergola, heavy with fruit, leaves and gambolling cherubs and now home to a series of busts of Roman emperors. The objects on display are if anything even finer than those downstairs. The **Painted Views room**, so called for the bucolic scenes on its walls, has a fine statue of Hermes, restored in the seventeenth century in an oratorical pose according to the fashion of the time. The room next door, with its fresco of a display of wedding gifts against a floral background, has a wonderful statue of a warrior at rest called the **Ludovisi Ares**, which may represent Achilles and was restored by Bernini in 1622, as well as a charmingly sensitive portrayal of Orestes and Electra, from the first century AD by a sculptor called Menelaus – his name is carved at the base of one of the figures.

Beyond are even more treasures, and it is hard to know where to look first. One room retains a frieze telling the story of **Moses** as a cartoon strip, with each scene displayed by nude figures as if on an unfurled tapestry. In the room itself is a colossal head of **Hera**, now thought to be a head of **Antonia** (Mark Antony's daughter and mother of Caligula and Claudius), and – what some consider the highlight of the entire collection – the famous **Ludovisi Throne**: an original fifth-century BC Greek work embellished with a delicate relief portraying the birth of Aphrodite. She is shown being hauled from the sea, where she was formed from Uranus's genitals, while on each side reliefs show a flute player and a woman sprinkling incense over a flame – rituals associated with the worship of Aphrodite.

Further on, there is a depiction of Aphrodite after a bath, a first-century AD boy strangling a goose and a relief of Dionysus in the former cardinal's bedroom – a bold, almost modern profile of a face in red marble. Beyond the bedroom is the Great Room of Galata, whose huge hearthside is embellished with caryatids and ibex – the symbol of the Altemps family – and which holds the *Suicide of Galatian*, apparently commissioned by Julius Caesar to adorn his Quirinale estate. Also here, an incredible sarcophagus depicts a battle between the Romans and barbarians in graphic, almost visceral sculptural detail, while in the small room next door there are some quieter, more erotic pieces – a lovely Pan and Daphne, a satyr and nymph, and the muses Calliope and Urania. Once you've made it to here, you'll be ready for a quick peek at the chapel, off the opposite end of the Great Room of Galata, and a skim back through your favourite pieces, before leaving one of Rome's best collections of classical art.

Palazzo Primoli

Bus to Corso del Rinascimento

Around the corner from Palazzo Altemps, at the end of Via Zanardelli, the sixteenth-century **Palazzo Primoli** was the home of a descendant of Napoleon, Joseph Primoli. It houses two minor museums that may command your attention on the way to the Vatican, just across the Tiber from here.

1

Museo Mario Praz

Via Giuseppe Zanardelli 1 • Tues–Sun hourly tours 9am–1pm & 2.30–6.30pm; 50min • Free • ☎ 06 686 1089

The first of Palazzo Primoli's two museums, the **Museo Mario Praz**, on the top floor, was the home of one Mario Praz, a teacher of English literature, art historian and writer who lived here for fifteen or so years until his death in 1982. It is kept pretty much as the elegant and cultured Praz left it, its nine rooms stacked to the gills with books, magazines, paintings and ornate furniture. Praz lived in a larger apartment in the Palazzo Ricci on Via Giulia before moving here and amassed heaps of stuff – a period described in his signature book, *La Casa della Vita*. Tours of the apartment give you a glimpse of the vanished way of life of an aesthete.

Museo Napoleonico

Piazza di Ponte Umberto 1 • Tues–Sun 10am–6pm • Free • ☎ 06 687 4240, ⓦ museonapoleonico.it

On the ground floor of the Palazzo Primoli, facing the river, the **Museo Napoleonico** is reasonably interesting even if you're not an enthusiast for the great Frenchman and his dynasty, which had a considerable influence on nineteenth-century Italy. Rome was home for the Bonapartes in the 1820s, after Pauline married Camillo Borghese; Napoleon's mother, Letizia, also lived nearby (on Via del Corso) – and this museum contains a rather weighty assortment of their personal effects. There's a letter from Napoleon himself from his exile in St Helena, a room devoted to Pauline Borghese, busts and paintings, a Napoleonic bike, and portraits of Napoleon's nieces, Carlotta and Zenaide, hung among a number of Carlotta's own quite adept paintings. You can even find a plaster cast of Pauline Borghese's right breast, done in situ by Canova, for his famous statue in the Galleria Borghese.

Via dei Coronari

Bus to Corso del Rinascimento

Down Via Zanardelli from the Museo Napoleonico, you reach narrow **Via dei Coronari**, the fulcrum of Rome's antiques trade. Although the prices are as high as you might expect in such a location, there's a huge number of shops (the street consists of virtually nothing else), and it's an enjoyable place to browse even if you're not buying.

Piazza Navona

Bus to Corso del Rinascimento or Corso Vittorio Emanuele II

Piazza Navona, Rome's most famous square and as picturesque as any in Italy, is the focus of the surrounding area. The best time to come is at night, when the inevitably tourist-geared flavour of the place is at its most vibrant, with crowds hanging out around the **fountains** or people-watching while nursing a pricey drink at a table outside one of the **bars**, or watching the **buskers** and **street artists** entertain the throng. Piazza Navona takes its name from the Greek word for "struggle", *agone* – due to the games that were traditionally held here – and its shape from the first-century AD Stadium of Domitian (see opposite). Until the mid-fifteenth century, the ruins of the arena were still here, overgrown and disused, but the square was given a facelift in the mid-seventeenth century by the Pamphilj Pope Innocent X, who built most of the grandiose palaces that surround it.

Palazzo Pamphilj

Piazza Navona • Closed to the public

Remodelled by Pamphilj Pope Innocent X, the **Palazzo Pamphilj** – the largest of the grandiose palaces – fills much of the southwestern side of Piazza Navona. It's now home to the Brazilian embassy and is not open to the general public – which is a shame, given the fact that one of its state rooms has a lavish frescoed ceiling by Pietro da Cortona, depicting the adventures of Aeneas, which you can glimpse at night if the lights are on in the embassy.

Sant'Agnese in Agone

Piazza Navona • Tues–Sat 9.30am–12.30pm & 3.30–7pm, Sun 10am–1pm & 4–8pm • ☎ 06 6819 2134, ⓦ santagneseinagone.org

Pope Innocent X commissioned the church of **Sant'Agnese in Agone** next door to the Palazzo Pamphilj, initially from Carlo Rainaldi and later from Borromini, who took over after Rainaldi was sacked for being too slow. The story goes that the 13-year-old St Agnes was stripped naked before the crowds in the stadium as punishment for refusing to marry, whereupon she miraculously grew hair to cover herself. She was later martyred by a sword blow to her throat; nowadays she is the patron saint of young girls. The saint is depicted (fully clothed) being consumed by flames in the right-hand chapel; her skull is encased in a reliquary in a chapel at the back of the church, which, typically squeezed into the tightest of spaces by Borromini, is supposedly built on the spot where it all happened.

The fountains

Opposite the church of Sant'Agnese in Agone, the **Fontana dei Quattro Fiumi** (Fountain of the Four Rivers), one of three that punctuate the square, is a masterpiece of 1651, by Bernini, Borromini's arch-rival. Each male reclining figure represents one of what were considered at the time to be the four great rivers of the world – the Nile, Danube, Ganges and Plate – though only the horse, symbolizing the Danube, was actually carved by Bernini himself. It's said that the figures are shielding their eyes in horror from Borromini's church facade (Bernini had never had time for the work of his less prolific contemporary, Borromini), but the fountain had actually been completed before the facade was begun. The rocky outcrop is topped with a Roman-era faux **Egyptian obelisk,** carved with meaningless hieroglyphs and brought here by Pope Innocent X from the Circus of Maxentius.

Bernini also had a hand in the fountain at the southern end of the square, the so-called Fontana del Moro, designing the central figure of the Moor in what is another fantastically playful piece of work, surrounded by toothsome dolphins and other marine figures. The fountain at the opposite end of the square, the Fontana del Nettuno, is equally fanciful, depicting Neptune struggling with a sea monster, surrounded by briny creatures in a riot of fishing nets, nymphets, beards, breasts, scales and suckers.

Stadio di Domiziano

Via di Tor Sanguigna 3 • Mon–Fri & Sun 10am–7pm, Sat 10am–8pm • €8 • ☎ 06 4568 6100, ⓦ stadiodomiziano.com • Bus to Corso del Rinascimento

Just north of Piazza Navona lie the remains of the **Stadio di Domiziano** (Stadium of Domitian), built in around 86 AD. The stadium is responsible for the piazza's distinctive oval shape: the piazza was built on top of the remains of the stadium's arena, and its buildings incorporate the original lower arcades. The Emperor Domitian commissioned the stadium as a Roman venue for the Greek athletic games, of which he was a fan. It was used mainly for running races (the name comes from the Greek stadion, or race-track), as well as competitions that combined sport with intellectual pursuits – boxing followed by Latin poetry, say – though these were never as popular with the bloodthirsty Romans as the gladiatorial contests taking place at the Colosseum.

The underground site holds the well-preserved remains of a small section of the stadium, the towering archways giving a sense of its former size: it once held around thirty thousand spectators. There's little else to see, though temporary exhibitions add some interest; if you don't want to pay the entrance fee you can get a reasonable view from the balcony at street level on Piazza di Tor Sanguigna.

San Luigi dei Francesi

Piazza San Luigi dei Francesi 5 • Daily 10am–12.30pm & 3–6.45pm; closed Thurs pm • ☎ 06 688 271, ⓦ saintlouis-rome.net • Bus to Corso del Rinascimento or Corso Vittorio Emanuele II

On the eastern side of Piazza Navona, the French national church of **San Luigi dei Francesi** is well worth a visit, mainly for the works by **Caravaggio** that were painted specifically for the Contarelli Chapel (the last chapel on the left) where they still hang today. *The Calling of St Matthew* takes place in a tavern, an example of the characteristically earthy settings favoured by Caravaggio of the biblical scene. Bring some coins to turn the lights on.

Palazzo Madama

Corso del Rinascimento 11 • Guided tours (Italian only) Sept–July first Sat of the month 10am–6pm, every 20min; 40min • Free; arrive at Piazza Madama 11 from 8.30am onwards to book a tour for later that day • ☎ 06 6706 2177, ⓦ senato.it • Bus to Corso del Rinascimento, Corso Vittorio Emanuele II or Largo di Torre Argentina

Just south of San Luigi, there's a constant police presence around the seventeenth-century **Palazzo Madama**, which owes its name to the "madame" Margaret of Parma, the illegitimate daughter of Charles V, who lived here in the sixteenth century, before its fancy Baroque facade was added. Nowadays, it holds the chamber and many of the offices of the Italian upper house or Senate – a rather ageist institution whose 315 representatives have to be at least 40 years old and elected every five years only by Italians over 25. **Tours**, conducted in Italian, take in the main debating chamber and various public spaces and form a good complement to tours of the lower house of the Italian parliament, located in the Palazzo di Montecitorio (see p.38).

Sant'Ivo alla Sapienza

Corso del Rinascimento 40 • Sun 9am–12.15pm; closed July & Aug • ☎ 06 686 4987, ⓦ sivoallasapienza.eu • Bus to Corso del Rinascimento, Corso Vittorio Emanuele II or Largo di Torre Argentina

Between the Pantheon and Piazza Navona, accessible from Corso del Rinascimento, the rather blank facade of the **Palazzo della Sapienza** used to be the site of Rome's university (which retains the palace's name) and cradles an elegant Borromini-designed courtyard and the church of **Sant'Ivo alla Sapienza.** Inside, it's comparatively featureless, but very cleverly designed – impressively light and spacious given the small space the church is squeezed into, rising to a tall parabolic cupola.

Santa Maria dell'Anima

Via Santa Maria dell'Anima 64 • Daily 9am–12.45pm & 3–7pm • ☎ 06 6828 1802, ⓦ santa-maria-anima.it • Bus to Corso Vittorio Emanuele II

A few steps west off Piazza Navona is Via Santa Maria dell'Anima, where the church of **Santa Maria dell'Anima** takes its name from the statue of the Virgin on its facade, between two pleading souls in purgatory. It's another darkly cosy Roman church, wide and squat and crammed into an impossibly small space. Nowadays, it's the Catholic German national church in Rome, and a richly decorated affair, almost square in shape, with a protruding main sanctuary flanked by Renaissance tombs. The tomb on the right, a beautiful, rather sad concoction, is that of the last non-Italian pope until John Paul II, the Netherlandish Hadrian VI, who died in 1523. His brief reign was characterized by a thwarted struggle to address the issues raised by Martin Luther. At the far end of the church, above the altar, you can just about make out a dark and glowing *Virgin with Saints* by Giulio Romano.

Santa Maria della Pace

Piazza Santa Maria della Pace • Mon, Wed & Sat 9am–noon • ☎ 06 686 1156 • Bus to Corso del Rinascimento

Just beyond Santa Maria dell'Anima, the church of **Santa Maria della Pace** dates originally from the late fifteenth century but has a facade and portico that were added a couple of hundred years later by Pietro da Cortona. If you're lucky enough to find it open, you can see Raphael's frescoes of various sibyls above the Chigi chapel (first on the right), executed in the early sixteenth century. If the church is shut, you can see the frescoes from the window of the café of the Chiostro del Bramante (see below).

Chiostro del Bramante

Via Arco della Pace 5 • Mon–Fri 10am–8pm, Sat & Sun 10am–9pm; last entry 1hr before closing • ☎ 06 6880 9035,
ⓦ chiostrodelbramante.it

Perhaps the most impressive part of Santa Maria della Pace – and the one part of the building you can be sure of seeing – is the attached **Chiostro del Bramante**, finished in 1504, a beautifully proportioned, two-tiered cloister that is given over to temporary **art exhibitions**. It also has a good café and bookshop that you don't need an entrance ticket to visit (see p.246) and rents rooms (see p.230).

Museo di Roma

Piazza San Pantaleo 10 • Tues–Sun 10am–7pm; last entry 1hr before closing • €11 • ☎ 06 0608, ⓦ museodiroma.it • Bus to Corso Vittorio Emanuele II

Backing onto Piazza Navona, the eighteenth-century Palazzo Braschi is the home of the large, sporadically interesting **Museo di Roma**, which has a permanent collection relating to the history of the city from the Middle Ages to the present day. The building itself is probably the main event, particularly the magnificent **Sala Nobile** where you go in, the main staircase and one or two of the renovated rooms, not least the exotically painted Sala Cinese and Sala Egiziana. But there's interest in some of the **paintings**, too, which show the city during different eras – St Peter's Square before Bernini's colonnade was built; jousting in Piazza Navona and the Cortile Belvedere in the Vatican; big gatherings and processions in the Campidoglio and Piazza del Popolo – and frescoes from demolished palaces provide decent enough highlights. There are also portraits and busts of the most eminent Roman families, most of whom produced a pope at one time or another – not only the Braschi, but also the Corsini, Chigi and Odescalchi. These names resonate around historic parts of the city today, and their faces gaze out of the rooms here with deadly and penetrating self-importance.

Piazza Pasquino

Just south of Piazza Navona, immediately behind Palazzo Braschi, the battered torso of **Pasquino** is easy to miss, even in the small triangular space of **Piazza Pasquino**, in the corner of which it still stands. Pasquino is perhaps the best known of Rome's "talking statues" (see box, p.63) of the Middle Ages and Renaissance times, to which anonymous comments on the affairs of the day would be attached – comments that had serious as well as humorous intent. Pasquino gave us the word "pasquinade", meaning a satire or lampoon of a public figure, though whether the comments and photocopied poems that grace the statue these days live up to it or not is debatable.

Via del Governo Vecchio and around

Bus to Corso Vittorio Emanuele II

In the heart of the old city, **Via del Governo Vecchio** leads west from Piazza Pasquino through one of Rome's liveliest quarters. The street was named for the Palazzo Nardini at no. 39, which was once the seat of the governors of Rome (currently under restoration). However, this part of Rome is best known for its cool independent shops and boutiques and its vigorous restaurants and bars that fill the narrow streets with a buzzing nightlife.

Oratorio dei Filippini

At the western end of Via del Governo Vecchio, the small square of **Piazza dell'Orologio** is so called because of the quaint clocktower that is its main feature. The clock is part of the **Oratorio dei Filippini**, designed by Borromini, which backs onto the Chiesa Nuova (see below) and is part of the same complex: the followers of San Filippo Neri (founder of the Chiesa Nuova) attended musical gatherings here as part of their worship, hence the musical term "oratorio". Nowadays it's given over to the **Casa delle Letterature**, a research centre dedicated to nineteenth-century literature, which hosts temporary exhibitions – sneak in for a look at its elegant orange-tree-shaded courtyard.

Chiesa Nuova

Piazza della Chiesa Nuova • Daily 7.30am–noon & 4.30–7.30pm; winter closes 7pm • ☎ 06 687 5289, ⓦ vallicella.org

The church of Santa Maria in Vallicella – or the **Chiesa Nuova**, as it's more often known – backs onto Via del Governo Vecchio and is another highly ornate Baroque church, which is strange, because its founder, **San Filippo Neri**, didn't want it decorated at all. Neri was an ascetic man, who tended the poor and sick in the streets around here for most of his life and commissioned this place of worship on the site of an earlier structure, Santa Maria in Vallicella, which had been donated to him and his followers by Pope Gregory XIII in 1577. Neri died in 1595, and this large church, as well as being his last resting place (he lies in the chapel to the left of the apse), is his principal memorial. Inside, three paintings by Rubens hang at the high altar, centring on the *Virgin with Angels*. Pietro da Cortona's ceiling paintings, meanwhile, show the Ascension of the Virgin in the apse, and, above the nave, the construction of the church and Neri's famous "**vision of fire**" of 1544, when a globe of fire entered his mouth and dilated his heart – a physical event which apparently affected his health thereafter. You can usually book a guided tour of San Filippo Neri's **rooms** in the church, which include his bedroom and private chapel, though these were closed for restoration at the time of writing.

MARKET AT CAMPO DE' FIORI

Campo de' Fiori and the Ghetto

The area surrounding the vibrant market square of Campo de' Fiori, between Corso Vittorio Emanuele II and the Tiber, can be seen as Rome's old centre part two. As in the Centro Storico proper, cramped streets open out onto small squares flanked by churches, although it's more of a working quarter – less monumental, with more functional buildings and shops – and the main square of Campo de' Fiori, with its fruit-and-veg stalls and lively bars, forms a marked contrast to the pavement artists and sleek cafés of Piazza Navona. To the east, the Campo de' Fiori area merges into the atmospheric streets and scrabbly Roman ruins of the old Jewish Ghetto, a small but thriving neighbourhood which nuzzles close to the city's giant central synagogue, and leads to the Isola Tiberina, while just north of here lies the major traffic intersection and ancient Roman site of Largo di Torre Argentina.

Campo de' Fiori

Market Mon–Sat 8am–1pm; clean-up is about 2–5pm, when the square is least appealing • Bus to Largo di Torre Argentina

The long oblong of **Campo de' Fiori** is home to a lively fruit and vegetable market. Surrounded by restaurants and cafés, the square is busy pretty much all day. Its role as heart of the area's nightlife, and the consequent glut of bars and outdoor drinkers (largely foreign students), has taken away some of its charm, in the evenings at least, but for all that, it still remains one of the city's most appealing squares.

No one really knows how the square came by its name, which means "field of flowers". One theory holds that it was derived from the Roman Campus Martius, which used to cover most of this part of town. Another claims it is named after Flora, the mistress of Pompey, whose theatre used to stand on what is now the northeast corner of the square – part of a huge complex which stretched as far as Largo Argentina. This was the site of Julius Caesar's assassination on the Ides of March, 44 BC. You can still see parts of the theatre in a number of buildings in the area, including the basement of the *Da Pancrazio* restaurant, on tiny Piazza del Biscione. The semicircular Via de' Grotta Pinta retains the curve of the theatre's seating.

Subsequently, Campo de' Fiori was an important point on papal processions between the Vatican and the major basilicas of Rome (notably San Giovanni in Laterano), and was also a site of public executions. The most notorious killing here is commemorated by the **statue of Giordano Bruno**, in the middle of the square. Bruno was a late sixteenth-century freethinker who followed the teachings of Copernicus and was denounced to the Inquisition; his trial lasted for years under a succession of different popes, and finally, when he refused to renounce his philosophical beliefs, he was burnt at the stake.

Palazzo Farnese

Piazza Farnese • Tours in English Wed 5pm, in French or Italian Mon, Wed & Fri 3pm, 4pm & 5pm • 45min • €9; book at least 1 week in advance (at least 1 month in advance for a tour in English in high season) and bring your passport; no admission to under-10s • Ⓦ inventerrome.com • Bus to Corso Vittorio Emanuele II

Just south of Campo de' Fiori, Piazza Farnese is a quite different square, with great fountains spurting out of carved lilies – the Farnese emblem – into marble tubs brought from the Baths of Caracalla, all overlooked by the sober bulk of the **Palazzo Farnese** itself, now the French embassy. Commissioned in 1514 by Alessandro Farnese – later Pope Paul III – from Antonio di Sangallo the Younger, the building was worked on after the architect's death by Michelangelo, who added the top tier of windows and cornice. It's certainly worth visiting if you can (book well in advance) – the Farnese were great enthusiasts and collectors, and classical statues litter the hallways and salons of the palace. Even from the outside, however, it's a tremendously elegant and powerful building – indeed, of all the fabulous locations that Rome's embassies enjoy, this has to be the best.

First floor

On the first floor or *piano nobile*, the **Salone d'Ercole** has a copy of the so-called Farnese Hercules (the original of which used to stand here but is now in Naples), surrounded by busts of Roman emperors in a room decorated with the feats of Hercules by Federico Zuccari. Zuccari also had a hand in the room next door, the **Sala dei Fausti Farnesiani** or "Room of the Farnese Deeds", which is decorated with frescoes by Francesco Salinati illustrating the great acts of the family – though this is sadly not always open for tours, as it's used for official functions.

Carracci Gallery

The real treasure of the Palazzo Farnese is at the back of the building – the Bolognese painter Annibale Carracci's *Loves of the Gods*, a ceiling fresco cycle finished in 1603 and sitting in the **Carracci Gallery**. It's a work of such magnificent vitality, with complex and dramatically arranged figures, great swathes of naked flesh and vivid colours, that it is often seen as the first great work of the Baroque era. Commissioned by Odoardo Farnese, the main painting, centring on the marriage of Bacchus and Ariadne, which is supposed to represent the binding of the Aldobrandini and Farnese families, leaps out of its frame in an erotic hotchpotch of cavorting, a fantastic, fleshy spectacle of virtuoso technique and perfect anatomy, surrounded by similarly fervent works illustrating various classical themes. Between and below them, nude figures peer out – amazing exercises in perspective that seem almost to be alongside you in the room. Carracci did the main plan and the central painting himself, but left the rest to his brother and cousin, **Agostino** and **Ludovico**, and assistants such as **Guido Reni** and **Guercino**, who went on to become some of the most sought-after artists of the seventeenth century. It's a great piece of work, perhaps only eclipsed in Rome by the Sistine Chapel itself, and it's sad to note that Carracci, disillusioned by the work and bitter about the relative pittance he was paid for it, didn't paint much afterwards and died penniless a few years later.

Make sure you also see the **Camerino**, a small room displaying Carracci's work after his arrival in Rome in 1595; it was these frescoes that enabled him to receive the commission for the larger gallery.

Galleria Spada

Piazza di Capo di Ferro 3 • Daily except Tues 8.30am–7.30pm • €5; free first Sun of the month • ☎ 06 683 2409, ⓦ galleriaborghese.it • Bus to Corso Vittorio Emanuele II

If you can't get in to the Palazzo Farnese, you'll have to make do with the Palazzo Spada, a couple of blocks east down Via Capo di Ferro. Walk right through the courtyard to the back of the building to reach the **Galleria Spada**. Although its four rooms, decorated in the manner of a Roman noble family, aren't spectacularly interesting unless you're a connoisseur of seventeenth- and eighteenth-century Italian painting, it does show what a collector's eye Cardinal Bernardino Spada, in particular, had. Highlights include two portraits of Spada by **Reni** and **Guercino**, alongside a *St Jerome*, also by Reni; *Cleopatra*, by **Lavinia Fontana**, who outranked both her father and husband as a sixteenth-century artist; the father and daughter Caravaggisti **Orazio and Artemesia Gentilleschi** are represented, as are works by Italian-influenced Dutch artists like **Jan van Scorel**. The building itself is great: its facade is frilled with stucco adornments and, left off the small courtyard, there's a crafty trompe l'oeil by **Borromini** – a tunnel whose actual length is multiplied about four times through the architect's tricks with perspective.

Ponte Sisto

Immediately behind the Palazzo Spada lies the river and a pedestrian bridge across to Trastevere, the **Ponte Sisto**. Built by Pope Sixtus IV in 1479 on the site of a ruined structure, it was the first bridge to be built across the Tiber since Roman times. It is a relatively narrow structure, and the inscriptions on each side of the entrance recall Sixtus IV's achievements, although they do not record the fact that the money to build it came from Cardinal Juan de Torquemada – uncle of the notoriously grisly tyrant of the Inquisition. One thing you can't see from the bridge itself is a large round hole in the middle, which functioned as an overflow in times of flood.

Via Giulia and around

Bus to Chiesa Nuova or Corso Vittorio Emanuele II

Via Giulia runs parallel to the Tiber from the Ponte Sisto, and was laid out by Julius II to connect the bridge with the Vatican. The street was conceived as the centre of papal Rome, and Julius commissioned Bramante to line it with imposing palaces. Bramante didn't get very far with the plan, as Julius was shortly after succeeded by Leo X, but the street soon became a popular residence for wealthier Roman families. It is still packed

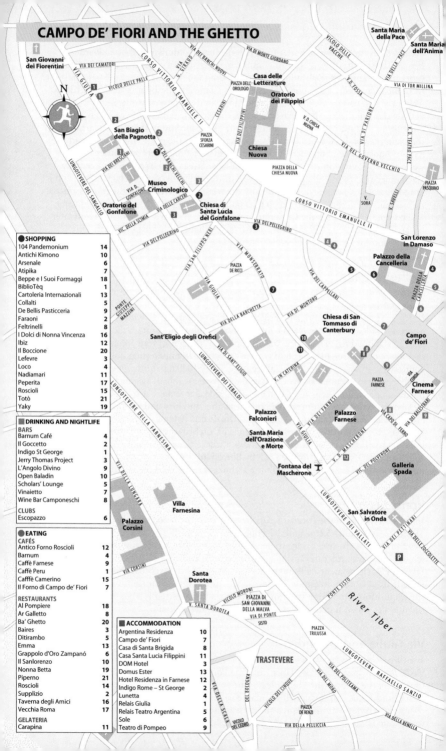

CAMPO DE' FIORI AND THE GHETTO

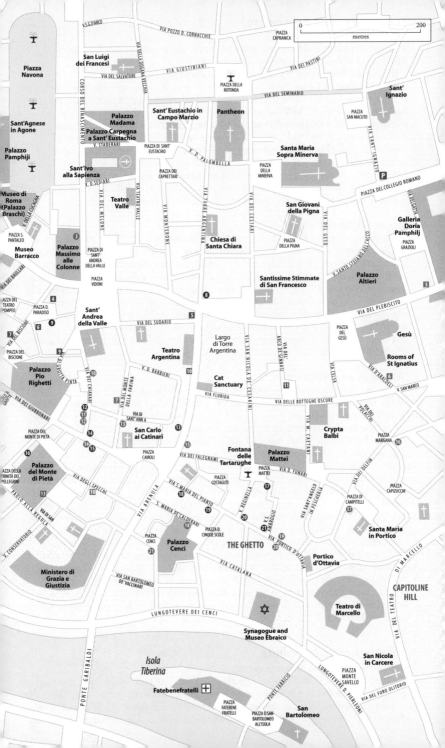

2

with stylish **palazzi** and has some **antiques shops**, and as such makes for a nice wander, with plenty to tickle your interest along the way.

The playful **Fontana del Mascherone**, right behind the Farnese palace and topped with the Farnese emblem, is the first point of interest. Beyond, the **arch** across the street, designed by Michelangelo, is the remnant of a Renaissance plan to link the Farnese palace with the **Villa Farnesina** across the river. After the arch you come to the church of **Santa Maria dell'Orazione e Morte**, decorated with skulls; a medieval fraternity brought the unidentified dead found on the streets of Rome here to give them a Christian burial. Further along, the **Palazzo Falconieri**, recognizable by the quizzical falcons crowning each end of the building, and now the home of the Hungarian Academy, was largely the work of Borromini, who enlarged it in 1646–49. At the time of writing, public access to the *palazzo* was suspended until further notice; for more information contact ✉ accademiadungheria2@gmail.com.

Museo Criminologico

Via del Gonfalone 29 • Tues & Thurs 9am–1pm & 2.30–6.30pm, Wed, Fri & Sat 9am–1pm • €2 • ☎ 06 688 9941, 🌐 museocriminologico.it

On the corner of Via Gonfalone, the **Museo Criminologico** offers a small but intriguing look at crime in general and Italy's underworld in particular. There are some gruesome early **instruments of torture** – manacles, lashes, head braces – a display on the unfortunate Beatrice Cenci (see p.57) and a selection of guillotines, nooses and various articles worn by the condemned, although inevitably the most interesting stuff – if you can read Italian – is that most pertinent to the world of Italian crime: the Mafia, the Brigate Rosse and Italian prison life. All in all, it is a perfect antidote to the more effete Renaissance splendours of Via Giulia, although it's worth knowing that Italy's Anti-Mafia Bureau has its headquarters at nearby Via Giulia 52, which explains the robust police presence outside.

San Giovanni dei Fiorentini

Piazza dell'Oro 1 • Daily 7.25am–noon & 5–7pm • ☎ 06 6889 2059, 🌐 sangiovannideifiorentini.net

At the far end of Via Giulia, right by the river, the church of **San Giovanni dei Fiorentini** is set on its own small square, Piazza dell'Oro, and is the burial place of the seventeenth-century architect **Borromini**. Its eighteenth-century facade is as monumental as any of Rome's churches, but inside it is a relatively plain affair, originally built by Sansovino on the orders of the Medici pope, Leo X, who wanted to see an expression of Florentine pride in what was then the heart of Rome. The church was finished in the early 1600s by **Carlo Maderno**, who added the dome, and is buried here, along with Borromini, who helped him after finishing work on the nearby Palazzo Falconieri. Beneath here, Raggi's flamboyant seventeenth-century altarpiece depicts the Baptism of Christ, and in the nearby south transept, Salvatore Rosa's *Martyrdom of Saints Cosmas and Damian* – the patrons of the Medici – has a fleeing male nude figure in the foreground that Rosa challenged Michelangelo to beat: "Let Michelangelo come and see if he can paint a better nude than this!" The chapel to the right of the high altar has a faded fresco by **Filippino Lippi** that is said to have miraculous powers. Look out, too, for the naive statue of a young John the Baptist in the south aisle, above the sacristy door, next to which there's a bust of another Florentine pope, Clement XII, carved by Bernini. San Giovanni extends a special welcome to pets, and you'll often see churchgoers wandering in with dogs, cat baskets and the like.

Palazzo della Cancelleria

Piazza della Cancelleria 1 • Bus to Corso Vittorio Emanuele II

Walking east along Corso Vittorio Emanuele II from the Chiesa Nuova, you come to the grand **Palazzo della Cancelleria**, the seat of the papal government that once ran the city (it is still extraterritorial Vatican property); Bramante is thought to have had a hand in its design, and this gorgeous edifice exudes a cool poise quite at odds with the rather grimy nature of its location. You can't usually get in to see the interior, but you can stroll into the marvellously proportioned, multitiered courtyard, which is a treat enough in itself.

San Lorenzo in Damaso

Piazza della Cancelleria 1 • Daily 7.30am–noon & 4.30–8pm

Just off Corso Vittorio Emanuele II, the church of **San Lorenzo in Damaso** forms part of the Palazzo della Cancelleria complex and is one of the oldest churches in Rome; tradition says a church was first built here within the house of Pope Damasus I in the late fourth century. It was rebuilt at the same time as the palace in the late fifteenth century and has since been often restored, most recently in the late nineteenth century. A painting by Federico Zuccaro, *The Coronation of the Virgin*, hangs over the altar (though it's hard to see behind the massive canopy), and there's a twelfth-century icon of the Virgin Mary in the chapel to the left of it.

Museo di Scultura Antica Giovanni Barracco

Corso Vittorio Emanuele II 166a • Tues–Sun: June–Sept 1–7pm; Oct–May 10am–4pm • Free • ☏ 06 0608, ⊛ museobarracco.it • Bus to Corso Vittorio Emanuele II

Set back slightly from busy Corso Vittorio Emanuele II, the so-called Piccola Farnesina palace was built by Antonio Sangallo the Younger. The palace itself actually never had anything to do with the Farnese family, and took the name "little Farnese" because of the lilies on the outside of the building, which were confused with the Farnese heraldic lilies. It's home to the **Museo di Scultura Antica Giovanni Barracco** on the first and second floors, a small but extremely fine-quality collection of ancient sculpture that was donated to the city in 1902 by one Baron Barracco. There are ancient Egyptian pieces, including two sphinxes from the reigns of Hatshepsut and Rameses II, an austere head of an Egyptian priest, a bust of a young Rameses II and statues and reliefs of the god Bes from various eras.

Look out for ceramics and statuary from the Greek classical period – essentially the fourth and fifth centuries BC and Roman copies of the same period – which include a lovely, almost complete figurine of Hercules, a larger figure of an athlete copied from an original by Polyclitus, a highly realistic dog washing herself, and a complete and very beautiful votive relief dedicated to Apollo. A small room at the front of the building contains later Roman pieces, most notably a small figure of Neptune from the first century BC and an odd, almost Giacometti-like column-sculpture of a hermaphrodite, along with beautifully realistic portrait busts of both anonymous and public figures such as Sophocles and Euripides. The charming busts of two young Roman boys opposite date from the first century AD.

Sant'Andrea della Valle

Piazza Vidoni 6 • Daily 7.30am–12.30pm & 4.30–7.30pm • ☏ 06 686 1339 • Bus to Largo di Torre Argentina

East of Campo de' Fiori, and dominating a busy stretch of Corso Vittorio Emanuele II, the church of **Sant'Andrea della Valle** has the distinction of sporting the city's second-tallest dome (after St Peter's), built by Carlo Maderno, and also of being the location for the first scene of the opera *Tosca* by Puccini. Inside, it's one of the most Baroque of Rome's churches, a high, barn-like building whose dome is decorated with paintings of the Glory of Paradise by Giovanni Lanfranco. The marvellous set of frescoes in the apse illustrating the life of St Andrew are by Lanfranco's contemporary, Domenichino, and centre on the monumental scene of the saint's crucifixion on the characteristic transverse cross. In a side chapel on the right, you may recognize some good-looking copies of not only Michelangelo's *Pietà* (the original is in St Peter's), but also of his figures of Leah and Rachel from the tomb of his patron, Julius II, in the church of San Pietro in Vincoli (see p.113).

Largo di Torre Argentina

Many bus routes pass through Largo di Torre Argentina; tram #8 runs from Via Arenula, just off the square, to Trastevere

Largo di Torre Argentina is a good-sized square, frantic with traffic that circles around the excavated ruins of four (Republican-era) temples and the channel of an ancient public lavatory. It's more a place to catch a bus than to linger deliberately, though you may want to spend a moment amid the traffic to contemplate the most famous event to take place here: the assassination of Julius Caesar.

Cat Sanctuary

Largo di Torre Argentina · Daily noon–6pm · Free · ☎ 06 4542 5240, ⓦ romancats.com

You can visit the **Cat Sanctuary** down the steps on the southwestern corner of Largo di Torre Argentina, and, if you wish, donate money or buy a feline gift from their small shop, or even "adopt" a cat for a monthly fee. Around 250 cats live in the excavations here, most of them domestic creatures dumped by their owners, and the people who look after them are all volunteers and receive no support from the city. In fact, the helpers here care for all of the city centre's four thousand or so stray cats, whose colonies spread from the Forum to the ruins at Piazza Vittorio Emanuele.

Teatro Argentina

Largo di Torre Argentina 52 · ☎ 06 6840 00311, ☎ 06 0608 (museum bookings), ⓦ teatrodiroma.net

On the western side of Largo di Torre Argentina, the **Teatro Argentina** was the venue for the first performance of Rossini's *Barber of Seville*, in 1816. It was not a success: Rossini was apparently booed into taking refuge in a nearby pastry shop. Now hidden behind a nineteenth-century facade, the theatre dates back to 1731; it was built above the Curia of Pompey (part of the Theatre of Pompey complex which extended as far as Campo de' Fiori), which was being used as the temporary home of the Senate when Julius Caesar was assassinated here in 44 BC. Today, it is one of the city's most important theatres. Its small **museum** (open to group tours only, by appointment) houses displays on historic productions and the history of the district, as well as objects from the original building.

Palazzo Altieri

Piazza del Gesù 49

Via del Plebiscito, a dark, rather gloomy thoroughfare, links Largo Argentina with Piazza Venezia, 500m or so away. Halfway down on the left, flanking the north side of Piazza del Gesù, the grey decaying bulk of the **Palazzo Altieri** was a monster of a project in its time that – a contemporary satire posted on the Pasquino statue (see p.45) quipped – looked set to consume Rome by its very size. The Altieri pope, Clement X, had the palace built around the house of an old woman who refused to make way for it: the two spyhole windows that were left can still be seen above the ground-floor windows, three windows to the right of the main entrance. Unfortunately, you can't visit the palace, which is now used as offices.

The Gesù

Via degli Astalli 16 · Daily 7am–12.30pm & 4–7.45pm · ☎ 06 697 001, ⓦ chiesadelgesu.org · Bus to Piazza Venezia or Largo di Torre Argentina

Lording it over Piazza del Gesù is the church of the **Gesù**, an appropriately dramatic symbol of the Counter Reformation. It was the first **Jesuit church** to be built in Rome, soon after the Order's foundation in the mid-sixteenth century. High and wide, with a single-aisled nave and short transepts edging out under a huge dome, it was ideal for the large, fervent congregations that the movement wanted to draw; indeed, it has since served as the model for Jesuit churches everywhere and is still well patronized. The facade is by **Giacomo della Porta**, the interior the work of **Vignola**, and the glitzy tomb of the order's founder who also commissioned this church, St Ignatius, in the north transept, is topped by a huge globe of lapis lazuli representing the Earth. Opposite, the tomb of sixteenth-century Jesuit missionary **St Francis Xavier**, decorated with a painting by **Carlo Maratta** showing his death on a Chinese island, holds a reliquary containing the saint's severed arm; the rest of his (incorruptible) body remains a focus of pilgrimage in Goa, India. Otherwise, it's the staggering richness of the church's gold interior that will impress, especially the paintings by the Genoese painter **Il Baciccia** in the dome and the nave, extravagant Baroque decorations added a century after the building's construction. The ceiling of the nave is decorated with Il Baciccia's bombastic *Triumph of the Name of Jesus*, an ingenious trompe l'oeil that oozes out of its frame in a tangle of writhing bodies, flowing drapery and stucco angels stuck like limpets.

2

Rooms of St Ignatius

Via degli Astalli 16 • Mon–Sat 4–6pm, Sun 10am–noon • Free

To the right of the Gesù church, the **Rooms of St Ignatius** occupy part of the first floor of the Jesuit headquarters. St Ignatius lived here from 1544 until his death in 1556, and there are just three simple chambers, where the saint and founder of the Jesuit order studied, worshipped and received visitors. One was his private chapel, and the other two hold artefacts from his life – his shoes, vest and cloak, the robe he was buried in, his writing desks and original documents, and a bronze bust of the great man based on his death mask. But the true draw here is the **decorative corridor** just outside. Designed by **Andrea Pozzo** in 1680, it's a superb exercise in perspective, an illusion of a grand hall in what is a relatively small space. Stand on the rose in the centre and the room's architectural fancies, putti, garlands and scallop shells are precise and true; walk up and down and the ceiling beams bend, the figures stretch and the scrollwork buckles – giving the bizarre feeling of a room shifting before your eyes. It's a feast of technical trickery and grandiose brushwork – all in weird contrast to the basketball courts that occupy the quadrangle down below.

Crypta Balbi

Via delle Botteghe Oscure 31 • Tues–Sun 9am–7.45pm; hourly tours of the excavations (10.45am–4.45pm); 15min • €7 combined ticket with Palazzo Altemps (p.39), Palazzo Massimo (p.123) & Terme di Diocleziano (p.123); valid for 3 days; free first Sun of the month • ⊕ 06 3996 7700, ⓦ archeoroma.beniculturali.it • Bus to Largo di Torre Argentina

Crypta Balbi, on the corner of Via Michelangelo Caetani and Via delle Botteghe Oscure, is the site of a Roman theatre, the remains of which later became incorporated

---

ALDO MORO

Via Michelangelo Caetani is the site of a memorial to the former Italian prime minister **Aldo Moro**, whose body was left here in the boot of a car on the morning of May 9, 1978, 54 days after his kidnap by the **Brigate Rosse**, or "Red Brigades". It was a carefully chosen spot, not only for the impudence it showed on the part of the terrorists in that it was right in the centre of Rome, but also for its position midway between the headquarters of the Communist and Christian Democrat parties. A plaque (and sometimes a wreath) marks the spot, and tells part of the story of how Moro, a reform-minded Christian Democrat, was the first right-wing politician to attempt to build an alliance with the then popular Italian Communists. Whether it was really left-wing terrorists who kidnapped him, or darker, right-wing forces allied to the establishment, or perhaps a combination of the two, there's no doubt that Moro's attempt to alleviate the Right's postwar monopoly of power found very little favour with others in power at the time – though that didn't make his death any less of a shock.

During the "**Mani pulite**" years that followed, corruption in both politics and business was supposed to have been exposed and eliminated, but arguably little changed: the prime minister who took over after Moro's death was none other than the elder statesman of Italian politics **Giulio Andreotti**, whose alleged involvement with the Mafia saw him twice tried – and acquitted – for collusion, in 2004 for the last time. Political cynicism resurfaced in the 1990s and is still much in evidence today; as such, the tragedy of Moro's death still carries a lot of resonance for Romans.

into a number of medieval houses. An above-ground exhibition, with lots of explanation in English, takes you through the evolution of the site in great detail – especially interesting if you want to know more about the often under-represented medieval history of the city. Every hour from 10.45am until 4.45pm (except on the first Sunday of the month and when rain makes the site slippery) a staff member accompanies visitors down to the theatre proper, where excavations are ongoing; try to glean what you can from the various arches, theatre segments, latrines, column bases and supporting walls that make up the cellar of the current building. The real interest is in the close dissection of one city block over two thousand years – an exercise that could presumably be equally well applied to almost any city corner in Rome.

The Ghetto

Bus to Largo di Torre Argentina

Across Via Arenula from the Campo de' Fiori area, the contrast with stately Via Giulia can be felt immediately in the crumbling area of the **Ghetto**. Its narrow, confusing switchback streets and alleys makes for one of Rome's most atmospheric neighbourhoods, and one of its most resurgent, with lots of kosher cafés and restaurants serving some of the city's best traditional Roman cuisine, and a host of other Jewish-related shops (see box below).

Portico d'Ottavia

Largo 16 Ottobre 1943 • Daily 9am–7pm, winter till 5pm • Free

The main artery of the Jewish area is **Via Portico d'Ottavia**, a short pedestrian street which leads southeast from Via Arenula to the **Portico d'Ottavia**, restored by Augustus and dedicated to his sister around 23 BC, and then rebuilt by Septimius Severus in 203 AD. The site is currently being excavated. Information panels trace the changing functions of this patch of land, from a colonnaded square holding temples and libraries in the first century BC to a fish market in the Middle Ages – hence the name of the neighbouring church, Sant'Angelo in Pescheria (St Angelo in the Fish Market). The site walkway continues to the Teatro di Marcello.

Teatro di Marcello

Between Via Portico d'Ottavia and Via del Teatro di Marcello • Daily 9am–7pm, winter till 6pm • Free

The **Teatro di Marcello** has served many purposes over the years: planned by Julius Caesar and built by Augustus, it was pillaged in the fourth century. In the Middle Ages it became

---

THE JEWS OF ROME

Rome's **Jewish population** traces its origins to the second century BC, when the Roman Republic forged an alliance with Judea. With sporadic exceptions, they were not a generally persecuted group until 1555, when Pope Paul IV issued a series of punitive laws that forced them into what was then one of the city's most squalid districts, right by the river and prone to flooding from the Tiber. A wall was built around the area, and all Jews, in a chilling omen of things to come, were made to wear yellow caps and shawls when they left the district; they were also only allowed to practise two professions: buying and selling clothes and money-lending. Later, after Unification, the **ghetto** was opened up, but during the 1930s, under Mussolini's racial legislation, which was part of his alliance with Hitler, they were once again barred from certain professions and prohibited from marrying non-Jews. The **Nazi occupation** in 1943 brought inevitable deportations and over two thousand people died in the camps of northern Europe. However the majority of Rome's Jewish population survived and currently numbers roughly sixteen thousand (around half Italy's total). Although only a fraction of that number actually live in the Ghetto, largely because of the historical significance, and the presence of the **Tempio Maggiore**, the most important of the city's synagogues, it remains the hub of the city's Jewish community, with new kosher restaurants and shops opening all the time.

a formidable fortified palace for a succession of Rome's ruling families, including the Orsini family. It provides a grand backdrop for classical concerts in the summer.

Piazza Mattei

On the north side of Via Portico d'Ottavia, narrow Via della Reginella leads to **Piazza Mattei**, whose **Fontana delle Tartarughe**, or "Turtle Fountain", is a delightful late-sixteenth-century creation, restored by Bernini, who added the turtles. The **Palazzo Mattei**, designed by Carlo Maderno, flanks one side of the square, and stretches down Via dei Funari ("Ropemakers' Street") to the corner of Via Michelangelo Caetani. The palace is now partly occupied by the Centro degli Studi Americani, and during opening hours it's possible to wander into the courtyard, where the antique friezes and statues still give some sense of the power and grandeur of this once-great Roman family, former patrons of a young Caravaggio, who lived here for a short time.

Santa Maria in Portico

Piazza di Campitelli 9 • Daily 7am–noon & 4–7pm • ☎ 06 6880 3978, ⓦ santamariainportico.it

Santa Maria in Portico (or Santa Maria in Campitelli) is a heavy, ornate church built by **Carlo Rainaldi** in 1667 to house an ancient enamel image of the **Virgin Mary**, deemed to have miraculous powers following respite from a plague. The image was originally housed in another church on Via Portico d'Ottavia, but was moved here by Pope Alexander VII so as to be in more appropriately splendid surroundings. Everything in the church focuses on this small framed picture, encased in an incredibly ornate golden altarpiece, which fills the entire space between the clustered columns of the apse. It's actually quite hard to see, but **votive images** all around the church give you a close-up look. There's not much else in the church, although the paintings, including a dramatic *Virgin with Saints* by Luca Giordano, in the second chapel on the right, represent Baroque at its most rampant; while opposite, a chapel contains the body of **St John Leonardi**, who was made the patron saint of pharmacists by Benedict XVI in 2006, and who wrote a history of the church's revered icon in the early seventeenth century.

Palazzo Cenci

Piazza delle Cinque Scole

Just south of Via Portico d'Ottavia, **Piazza delle Cinque Scole**, named for the building which housed synagogues of each of the five Jewish groups present in Rome during the time of the Ghetto that once stood here (regulations stipulated that each of the papal cities should have only one synagogue; here five were squeezed into one). It is overlooked by one side of the **Palazzo Cenci**, which huddles into the dark streets here. It's a reminder of the untimely death of **Beatrice Cenci**, who was executed, with her stepmother, on the Ponte Sant'Angelo in 1599 for the murder of her wicked (and allegedly incestuous) father – a story immortalized in verse by Shelley and in paint by an unknown artist whose portrait of the unfortunate Beatrice still hangs in the Palazzo Barberini (see p.105).

Synagogue and Museo Ebraico

Lungotevere dei Cenci • **Museum** April to mid-Sept Mon–Thurs & Sun 10am–5.15pm, Fri 10am–3.15pm; mid-Sept to March Mon–Thurs & Sun 10am–5pm, Fri 9am–2pm; closed Sat & Jewish hols • €11 • **Synagogue tours** Hourly, included in cost of museum ticket; same days and hours as museum; 30min • ☎ 06 6840 0661, ⓦ lnx.museoebraico.roma.it

At the far end of Via Portico d'Ottavia is the area's principal Jewish sight: the huge **synagogue**, built in 1904 and dominating the streets around and indeed the river beyond with its bulk. Carabinieri stand guard 24 hours a day outside, ever since a PLO attack on the building in 1982 killed a two-year-old boy (Stefano Gaj Taché, for whom the piazza at the Synagogue's entrance is named) and injured many others.

The **Museo Ebraico**, in the bowels of the building, spreads through several rooms and covers several major themes including **Jewish ritual** in Rome; the Roman or Italian rite pre-dates the diaspora, and is neither Ashkenazi nor Sephardic. Detailed panels (in English, Italian, and Hebrew) give information on the **history** of the Jews in Rome and the Ghetto in particular, and of course the **war years**, when over two thousand citizens were deported from the area, and only fifteen returned. Also on display are decorative and liturgical pieces from the previous synagogues (*le Cinque Scole*, the five "schools" – see p.57), a variety of ritual clothes and textiles and wartime posters and propaganda. The **tour** takes in both the smaller Sephardic synagogue in the basement, as well as the extremely grand **Tempio Maggiore** (the main synagogue) upstairs, and gives good background on the building and the Roman Jewish community in general.

Isola Tiberina

On the river side of the synagogue, **Ponte Fabricio** crosses the Tiber to the **Isola Tiberina**. Built in 62 BC, it's the only classical bridge to remain intact without help from the restorers (the Ponte Cestio, on the other side of the island, was partially rebuilt in the last century). The **island** itself offers a calm respite from the city centre proper, and is mostly given over to Rome's oldest **hospital**, the **Fatebenefratelli**, founded in 1548 – appropriately, it would seem, as the island was originally home to a third-century BC temple of Asclepius, the Roman god of healing. Beyond the Isola Tiberina, you can see the remains of the **Ponte Rotto** (Broken Bridge) on the river, all that remains of the first stone bridge to span the Tiber. Built between 179 and 142 BC, it collapsed at the end of the sixteenth century.

San Bartolomeo all'Isola

Piazza di San Bartolomeo all'Isola • Mon–Sat 9.30am–1.30pm & 3.30–5.30pm, Sun 9.30am–1pm • ⓦ sanbartolomeo.org

Opposite the Fatebenefratelli's entrance, the church of **San Bartolomeo all'Isola** stands on the original site of the temple of Asclepius, and is worth a peep inside for its ancient columns, probably rescued from the temple, and an ancient wellhead on the altar steps, carved with figures relating to the founding of the church, including St Bartholomew himself. The saint also features in the painting above the altar, hands tied above his head, on the point of being skinned alive – his famous and gruesome mode of martyrdom.

Piazza Venezia and the Capitoline Hill

For many people, the modern centre of Rome is Piazza Venezia – not so much a square as a road junction, and a busy one at that, but a good place to start your wanderings, midway between the Renaissance centre and most of the city's ancient ruins. Flanked on all sides by imposing buildings, the piazza is a definite focal point, and a spot you'll find yourself returning to time and again. The great white bulk of the Vittorio Emanuele monument also makes it Rome's best landmarked open space by some way. The Vittoriano, as it's known, is one of the key sights in the city, not least for its splendid views. Behind it lie the Piazza del Campidoglio and the unmissable museums on the Capitoline Hill, the first-settled and most central of Rome's seven hills.

Piazza Venezia and around

Many bus routes converge on Piazza Venezia; tram #8 connects the piazza with Trastevere

There's not much need to hang about on **Piazza Venezia** itself: it's more a place to catch a bus or pick up a taxi than soak up the atmosphere. A legacy of nineteenth-century Rome, it looked quite different a couple of hundred years ago, when it was the domain of the Venetian Pope Paul II, whose Palazzo Venezia dominated this part of the city, its gardens reaching around its south side, where the Vittoriano now stands.

The Vittoriano

Piazza Venezia 3 • Daily 9.30am–5.30pm, winter till 4.30pm; lifts Mon–Thurs 9.30am–6.30pm, Fri–Sun 9.30am–7.30pm; last entry 45min before closing • Free; lifts €7 • ☎ 06 678 0664

The other buildings on Piazza Venezia pale into insignificance beside the marble monstrosity rearing up across the street from San Marco – the Vittorio Emanuele Monument or **Vittoriano**, erected at the end of the nineteenth century as the "Altar of the Nation" to commemorate Italian Unification. It has been variously likened to a typewriter (because of its shape), and, by American GIs, to a wedding cake (the white marble used will never mellow with age). King Vittorio Emanuele II, by all accounts a modest man, probably wouldn't have thought much of it. Indeed, the only person who seems to have benefited from the building is the prime minister at the time who was a deputy for Brescia, from where (perhaps not entirely coincidentally) the marble was supplied.

There are things to see inside the monument (see below), but it's the **outside** of the structure that should command most of your attention, and it's great to clamber up and down the sweeping terraces and flights of steps which once upon a time you could only gaze at from the street. The structure is full of the weighty **symbolism** that was typical of the period. The figures either side of the entrance represent the two seas that surround Italy – the Tyrrhenian (on the right) and the Adriatic (on the left). At the top of the first lot of stairs is the Tomb of the Unknown Soldier, flanked by eternal flames and a permanent guard of honour, behind which a huge 1920s bas-relief represents the nation, focused on a figure of Minerva – for Rome – in the centre.

Up another flight of stairs sits the figure of Vittorio Emanuele II on horseback, at 10m by 12m one of the **world's largest statues** (his moustache alone is 3m long, and apparently twenty people once had lunch in the horse's belly); the figures on the frieze on the plinth represent the major cities of the Italian Republic. Above here, the huge, sweeping **gallery** stretches the width of the monument, with figures symbolizing the regions of Italy, while behind, glass **lifts** whisk you to the top of the monument for amazing views from between the massive *quadriglie*, or chariots, on each side. The whole thing is undeniably impressive, if only for the sheer audaciousness of its conception. Wherever you stand, though, the **views** of the city are wonderful – perhaps because it's the one place in Rome from which you can't see the Vittoriano.

The museums

Via di San Pietro in Carcere • **Museo del Risorgimento** Daily 9.30am–6.30pm; closed first Tues of the month • €5; free first Sun of the month • **Museo Nazionale dell'Emigrazione Italiana** Mon–Thurs 9.30am–6.30pm, Fri–Sun 9.30am–7.30pm • Free • **Ala Brasini** Temporary art exhibitions; check website for details • ⊕ ilvittoriano.com

In the southeastern wing of the monument, the echoing chambers of the so-called **Complesso del Vittoriano** host temporary art and other exhibitions. Also inside the Vittoriano, the engaging **Museo del Risorgimento** follows the long corridor that runs around the back of the building, full of busts, weaponry and mementoes of the Unification struggle and beyond. The small **Museo Nazionale dell'Emigrazione Italiana**, in the western wing, explores the role Italian emigration has played in the country's history. There's also a gallery of flags from various Italian regiments, which gives onto the **Tomb of the Unknown Soldier** itself, along with the story of the transportation and ceremonial interment of the body in 1921. The **Brasini Wing** (Ala Brasini) houses temporary art exhibitions.

Palazzo Venezia

Via del Plebiscito 118

Taking up the western side of Piazza Venezia is the first large Renaissance palace in the city, **Palazzo Venezia**, built in the mid-fifteenth century and for several centuries the embassy of the Venetian Republic. Famously, **Mussolini** moved in here while in power, occupying the vast Sala del Mappamondo (unfortunately only visitable

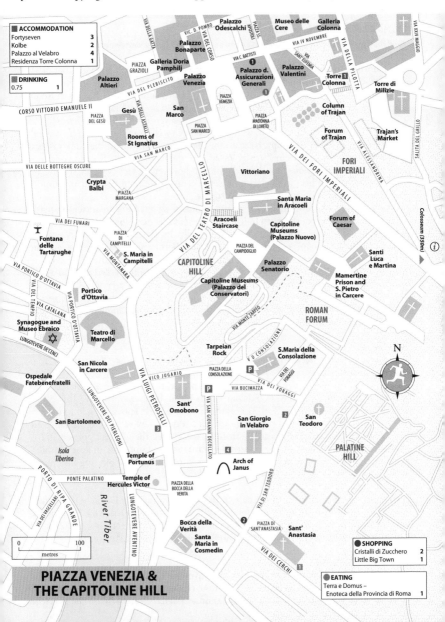

PIAZZA VENEZIA &
THE CAPITOLINE HILL

during occasional temporary exhibitions). In those days, the palace lights would be left on to give the impression of constant activity in what was the centre of the Fascist government and war effort. The room opens onto the balcony overlooking the piazza from which Il Duce declared Italy's entrance into the Second World War.

These days, Palazzo Venezia is a venue for occasional temporary exhibitions and home, on the first floor, to the **Museo Nazionale di Palazzo Venezia**, an under-visited museum mostly dedicated to Early Renaissance works.

Museo Nazionale di Palazzo Venezia

Via del Plebiscito 118 • Tues–Sun 8.30am–7.30pm; last entry 1hr before closing • €5; free first Sun of the month • ☎ 06 6999 4388, ⓦ museopalazzovenezia.beniculturali.it

The paintings in the **Museo Nazionale di Palazzo Venezia** include a large number of fifteenth-century devotional works from central and northern Italy. Among numerous Crucifixions and Madonnas, look out for the polychromatic wooden **statues** in Room 4, notably two figures from a Magi group from Le Marche and a lovely *Madonna and Child* from Lazio, both thirteenth-century; an early seventeenth-century *Deposition of Christ* by **Borgianni** in Room 6, in which Christ is viewed from the feet up by way of clever use of perspective (a copy, basically, of Mantegna's painting of the same subject). The ceiling paintings in room 7 are by **Vasari**, and depict Ceres, the Roman goddess of agriculture and the various months and seasons; they were in fact designed for another building and moved here in the late nineteenth century. Room 8 holds an arresting double portrait of two young men by **Giorgione**.

Beyond here, a corridor lined with ceramics, including jars from an ancient monastic pharmacy, skirts the courtyard to link with the *palazzetto* next door (sometimes closed), where you can find a couple of rooms of beautifully displayed **bronzes** – a wide array of figures, animals and copies of ancient sculptures by **Bernini** and **Giambologna**, among others. Around the corner are more sculptural pieces, including a tortured head of Seneca, by **Guido Reni**, and **Algardi**'s representation of San Filippo Neri with an angel, a study of St Theresa for Bernini's statue in the church of Santa Maria della Vittoria, and some designs for the Trevi Fountain by **Pietro Bracci**. Walk out to the palace's upper loggia for a view over the palm-filled courtyard – the **loggia** is crammed full of ancient sculptural fragments, and the **gardens** are some of the prettiest in Rome.

San Marco

Piazza di San Marco 52 • Mon 4–7pm, Tues–Sat 7.30am–12.30pm & 4–7pm, Sun 7.30am–12.30pm & 4–7.30pm • ☎ 06 679 5205, ⓦ sanmarcoevangelista.it

Adjacent to the Palazzo Venezia, on its southern side, the church of **San Marco**, accessible from Piazza San Marco, is one of the oldest basilicas in Rome. This dark, cosy church was founded in 336 AD on the spot where the apostle is said to have lived while in the city. It was rebuilt in 833 and added to by various Renaissance and eighteenth-century popes – Paul II restored it and added the graceful portico and gilded ceiling. The church has a beautiful Cosmati-work floor, and an apse **mosaic** which dates from the ninth century and shows Pope Gregory IV offering his church to Christ, above a gracious semicircle of sheep that bear more than a passing resemblance to llamas.

Back outside, tucked away in the corner, the statue of the busty harridan is "**Madam Lucretia**", actually an ancient depiction of the Egyptian goddess Isis. Like Pasquino, a few hundred metres away, she is one of Rome's so-called talking statues (see box opposite), commenting in a satirical fashion on the affairs of the day.

Palazzo Bonaparte

On the northern side of Piazza Venezia, the canyon of Via del Corso, Rome's main street, begins its journey to the other side of the city centre at the Piazza del Popolo, its opening stretch flanked by the nineteenth-century **Palazzo Bonaparte** on the left, with

ROME'S TALKING STATUES

As the home of the papacy, Rome has long been a political city, and its people have always enjoyed commenting on and arguing about the important issues of the day. In Renaissance times, the antics of the Church, in particular the pope and the powerful Roman families who vied to fill the post, were the subject of intense curiosity and scrutiny. A number of "**talking statues**" – usually ancient, unidentified pieces, among them Madam Lucretia (see opposite) outside the basilica of San Marco; Pasquino (see p.45) just off Piazza Navona; the "baboon" on Via del Babuino; the "facchino", or porter, on Via Lata, just off Via del Corso; and Marforio (see p.66), now in the courtyard of the Palazzo Nuovo – were a focus for this. They were hung with witty rhymes and notes commenting on the hubris and foolishness of the movers and shakers of the papal city, a kind of gossip-column-cum-parliamentary-sketch where people would gather to talk and laugh at their political masters.

its green-shuttered balcony. It was from this vantage point that Napoleon's mother Letizia Bonaparte, who lived here after her son was deposed until her death in 1836, used to keep an eye on the comings and goings outside, though nowadays it's privately owned and the shutters are usually closed.

3

Palazzo Valentini

Piazza Foro Traiano 85 • Tours Mon & Wed–Sun 9.30am–6.30pm; 1hr 30min • €12, booking essential • ☎ 06 32810, ⊛ palazzovalentini.it

Just off Piazza Venezia, the solid, late sixteenth-century **Palazzo Valentini** is the home of the government of the metropolitan area and as such is a busy place, full of scurrying office workers and folk trying to find their way to appointments. It's also the location of archeological **excavations** including ancient Roman baths and a residential complex, which are open to the public. Visits are by **guided tour** only; these are high-tech affairs, breathlessly narrated and deliberately dramatic, but they succeed pretty well in bringing the excavations to life, with glass floors and catwalks taking you through the site, and technology that re-creates the structures as they might have looked in ancient times. The tour is in two parts, first taking you through the **baths complex**, where there are patches of marble and opus sectile floor, fragments of statuary, columns and other artefacts that were found down here, along with part of a neighbouring house – equally fine, and with stretches of mosaic flooring in between medieval foundations. The second part of the tour focuses on the nearby **Trajan's Column** (see p.88), with a virtual reconstruction that allows a close-up look at the column's bas-reliefs.

Capitoline Hill

Bus to Piazza Venezia

The real pity about the Vittoriano is that it obscures views of the **Capitoline Hill** behind – once, in the days of imperial Rome, the spiritual and political centre of the Roman Empire. The upside of this is that it gives a perfect route to the Capitoline, via the café right behind the Vittoriano and a passageway that delivers you right by the back entrance of Santa Maria in Aracoeli (see p.64), and just above the Piazza del Campidoglio.

The Capitoline's name derives from its position as the *caput mundi*, or "**head of the world**", and its influence and importance resonate to this day, not least in language – "capitol" and "capital" originated here, as did "money", which comes from the temple to Juno Moneta that once stood on the hill and housed the Roman mint. The Capitoline also played a significant role in medieval and Renaissance times: the flamboyant fourteenth-century dictator, **Cola di Rienzo**, stood here in triumph in 1347 and was murdered on the same spot by an angry mob seven years later – a humble nineteenth-century statue marks the place where he is said to have died. **Michelangelo** gave the hill's Piazza del Campidoglio its present form, redesigning it as a symbol of Rome's regeneration after the city was sacked by the troops of Holy Roman Emperor Charles V in 1527. These days, the Capitoline forms a tight, self-contained group of essential attractions, with the focus on its pair of **museums** and the **church** of Santa Maria in Aracoeli.

Santa Maria in Aracoeli

Piazza del Campidoglio 4; access via Aracoeli staircase, or avoid the steps by going via Piazza del Campidoglio • Daily: May–Sept 9am–7pm; Oct–April 9.30am–5.30pm • ☎ 06 6976 3839

The church of **Santa Maria in Aracoeli** crowns the highest point on the Capitoline Hill and is built on the site of a temple to Jupiter where, according to legend, the Tiburtine Sibyl foretold the birth of Christ. The flight of steps that leads up here, the **Aracoeli Staircase**, was erected by Cola di Rienzo in 1348 and is one of the city's steepest climbs. The church, one of Rome's most ancient basilicas, is worth the effort. Inside, in the first chapel on the right, there are some fine **frescoes** by Pinturicchio recording the life of San Bernardino, with realistic tableaux of landscapes and bustling town scenes. There are also some older, more recently uncovered fragments of fresco by Pietro Cavallini further down the same aisle, most notably a beautiful *Madonna and Child* – which is in keeping with the church's best-known feature, the so-called **Santo Bambino**, a small statue of the child Jesus carved from the wood of a Gethsemane olive tree. Said to have healing powers, the statue was traditionally called out to the sickbeds of the ill and dying all over the city, its coach commanding instant right of way through the heavy Rome traffic. The Santo Bambino was stolen in 1994, however, and a copy now stands in its place, in a small chapel to the left of the high altar.

Piazza del Campidoglio and the Capitoline Museums

Both museums are on Piazza del Campidoglio • Tues–Sun 9am–8pm; last entry 1hr before closing • €15, €16 combined ticket with Centrale Montemartini (p.145) • ☎ 06 0608, ⊕ museicapitolini.org

Next door to the Aracoeli Staircase, the **Cordonata** is an elegant, smoothly rising ramp, and as such a much gentler climb. Topped with Roman statues of Castor and Pollux, it leads to **Piazza del Campidoglio**, one of Rome's most perfectly proportioned squares, designed by Michelangelo in the last years of his life for Pope Paul III, who was determined to hammer Rome back into shape for a visit by the Holy Roman Emperor, Charles V. In fact, Michelangelo died before his plan was completed (the square wasn't finished until the late seventeenth century), but his designs were faithfully executed, balancing the piazza, redesigning the facade of what is now Palazzo dei Conservatori and projecting an identical building across the way, known as Palazzo Nuovo. These buildings, which have been completely renovated in recent years, are home to the **Capitoline Museums** and feature some of the city's most important ancient sculpture.

Both are angled slightly to focus on **Palazzo Senatorio**, Rome's town hall, with its double staircase and fountain, flanked by statues representing the Tiber and the Nile. In the centre of the square, Michelangelo placed an equestrian **statue of Emperor Marcus Aurelius**, which had previously stood unharmed for years outside San Giovanni in Laterano; early Christians had refrained from melting it down because they believed it to be of the Emperor Constantine (the first Roman ruler to acknowledge and follow Christianity). The original is now beautifully displayed in the new wing of the Palazzo dei Conservatori, and a copy has taken its place at the centre of the piazza.

If you see no other museums of ancient sculpture in Rome, try at least to see the Capitoline Museums, the most venerable of the city's collections, and the oldest public museum in the world (the first room of ancient sculpture was donated to the city by Pope Sixtus IV in 1471). They're divided into two parts, one devoted only to **sculpture**, the other more extensive and wide-ranging with a gallery of **paintings** as well. You should, if possible, see at least part of both rather than choosing one; tickets remain valid all day, so you can easily take a break for a stroll around the other Capitoline sights in between.

Palazzo dei Conservatori

The **Palazzo dei Conservatori**, which occupies the right-hand side of the Piazza del Campidoglio, is perhaps the natural place to start a tour of the Capitoline Museums, home as it is to the ticket office and the larger, more varied collection, with ancient sculpture on the first floor and in the new wing at the back, and paintings on the second floor. It has undergone quite a transformation in recent years with the incorporation of the Palazzo Caffarelli-Clementino into the museum, with its new wing housing some large ancient statuary, most notably the equestrian statue of Marcus Aurelius and the foundations of the Capitoline's ancient temple of Jupiter, revealed during construction in 2000.

Ground and first floors

Some of the museum's ancient sculpture is littered around the ground-floor **courtyard** by the entrance – most impressively the feet, hand and other fragments of a gigantic statue, believed to be of the Emperor Constantine, and one of the most popular images of Rome. Upstairs, the first room you enter is the massive **Sala degli Orazi e Curiazi**, where the curators of the collections used to meet and which is appropriately decorated with giant late-sixteenth-century frescoes showing legendary tales from the early days of the city – the *Discovery of the She-wolf*, at the western end, faces the *Rape of the Sabine Women* at the opposite end, while presiding over all are colossal statues of Pope Urban VIII and his successor Innocent X, by Bernini and Algardi respectively. Fittingly, it was the venue for the signing of the Treaty of Rome in 1957, and for the presentation of the EU's ill-fated draft constitution nearly fifty years later.

The rooms that follow have more friezes and murals showing events from Roman history, notably the **Sala dei Capitani**, which celebrates various generals with statues in Roman military dress, among them Marco Antonio Colonna, who famously defeated the Turks at Lepanto in 1571, and Carlo Barberini (brother of Pope Urban VIII), by Bernini and Algardi. The corner room beyond contains the so-called *Spinario*, a Roman statue of a boy picking a thorn out of his foot, and a striking bronze head, known as *Brutus*, from the fourth century BC. The sacred symbol of Rome, the Etruscan bronze she-wolf nursing **Romulus and Remus**, the mythic founders of the city, gets a room to itself next door; the twins themselves are not Etruscan but were added by Pollaiuolo in the late fifteenth century. On the walls, the Fasti are an amazing record of magistrates and other political figures from the height of the Augustan age, rescued from the Forum.

The next-door room is given over to two bronze Roman geese and a bust of Michelangelo, which Daniele da Volterra based on the artist's death mask, while further on there are more **Roman sculptures** – eagles this time – in a room with the breast-laden Diana of Ephesus. Retrace your steps slightly for the **Sala di Annibale**, covered in wonderfully vivid fifteenth-century paintings recording Rome's wars with Carthage, and so named for a rendering of Hannibal seated impressively on an elephant, and the **Sala degli Arazzi**, which holds eighteenth-century tapestries depicting works belonging to the Capitoline Museums; look out also for the Vatican Museums' *Laocoön* and *Belvedere Apollo* in the frescoed frieze.

Further on, in the airy **new wing**, the original **statue of Marcus Aurelius**, formerly in the square outside, takes centre stage. Alongside it stand a giant bronze statue of Constantine (or at least its head, hand and orb) and a rippling gilded bronze Hercules, found nearby at the Forum Boarium. Behind are part of the foundations and a retaining wall from the Capitoline's original temple of Jupiter, discovered when the work for the new wing was undertaken.

There are some great exhibits around the main hall here: some remnants from the **Iron Age** on the Capitoline, statuary rescued from ancient gardens on the Esquiline Hill, including a statue of the Emperor Commodus – the son of the decidedly more heroic Marcus Aurelius – as Hercules, the milk-white Esquiline Venus and plenty more besides. When museum fatigue sets in, you can climb up to the second-floor **café**, whose terrace commands one of the best views in Rome. The **café** (and the view) is also accessible without buying a ticket for the museum by using the Palazzo Caffarelli entrance on Piazzale Caffarelli.

Second floor

The second-floor picture gallery (*pinacoteca*) holds **Renaissance painting** from the fourteenth to the late seventeenth century, with labels in Italian and English. The collection fills nine rooms, and **highlights** include a couple of portraits by Van Dyck and a penetrating *Portrait of a Crossbowman* by Lorenzo Lotto; a pair of paintings from 1590 by Tintoretto – a *Baptism of Christ* and a *Flagellation*; some nice small-scale work by Annibale Carracci; and a very fine early work by Ludovico Carracci, *Head of a Boy*. There are also several sugary pieces by Guido Reni, executed at the end of his life, including *St Sebastian*. In one of two large galleries, there's a vast picture by Guercino depicting the *Burial of Santa Petronilla* (an early Roman martyr who was the supposed daughter of St Peter), which used to hang in St Peter's and arrived here via the Quirinale palace and the Louvre. It is displayed alongside several other works by the same artist, notably a lovely, contemplative Persian Sibyl and a wonderful picture of Cleopatra cowed before a young and victorious Octavius (later Augustus), as well as two paintings by Caravaggio, one a version of the young John the Baptist which hangs in the Galleria Doria Pamphilj, the other a famous canvas known as *The Fortune-Teller* – an early work that's an adept study in deception. The large room at the back holds paintings from the Sacchetti collection, which includes a number of works by Pietro da Cortona, among them portraits of his patron Marchese Matteo Sacchetti and the steely Pope Urban VIII, as well as his lively depiction of the *Rape of the Sabine Women* – credited with kick-starting the Baroque age in 1630.

Palazzo Nuovo

The **Palazzo Nuovo**, the smaller of the wings, is across the square from the Palazzo dei Conservatori, also accessible by way of an underground **walkway** that holds the **Galleria Lapidaria**, a collection of Roman marble inscriptions. Don't miss the breathtaking **view** over the Forum from the Tabularium (up a flight of stairs on your right, two-thirds of the way along the gallery). The walkway emerges in the **palace courtyard**, which is guarded by a vast statue of Mars in battle armour, and dominated by the large **Fountain of Marforio**, a bearded figure known as one of Rome's "talking statues" (see box, p.63), renowned in Renaissance times for speaking out in satirical verse against the authorities.

The **first floor** collections concentrate some of the best of the city's Roman sculpture into half a dozen or so rooms and a long gallery crammed with elegant statuary. There's the remarkable, controlled statue of the *Dying Gaul*, a Roman copy of a Greek original; a naturalistic *Boy with Goose* – another copy; an original, grappling *Eros and Psyche*; a *Satyr Resting*, after a piece by Praxiteles, that was the inspiration for Nathaniel Hawthorne's book *The Marble Faun*; and the red marble *Laughing Silenus*, another Roman copy of a Hellenistic original. In the main **Salone**, statues of an old and a young centaur face each other, and a naturalistic hunter holds up a rabbit he has just killed. Walk through from here to the **Sala degli Imperatori**, with its busts of Roman emperors and other famous names, including a young Augustus and a cruel Caracalla, and the **Sala dei Filosofi**, with portrait busts of lots of well-known ancient thinkers including Socrates and Pythagoras, as well as political wheeler-dealers such as Cicero. Also, don't miss the *Capitoline Venus* – a coy, delicate piece, again based on a work by Praxiteles, housed in a room on its own.

Tarpeian Rock

After seeing the Capitoline Museums, take a walk around behind the **Palazzo Senatorio** for another great view down over the Forum, with the Colosseum in the background.

There's a copy of the statue of Romulus and Remus suckling the she-wolf here, while on the right, Via di Monte Tarpeo follows the brink of the old **Tarpeian Rock** – named after Tarpeia, who betrayed the city to the Sabines – from which traitors were thrown in ancient times.

Mamertine Prison

Clivo Argentario 1 · Tues, Thurs, Sat & Sun 8.30am–12.30pm & 2–4.30pm; last entry 30min before closing · €10 · ☎ 06 6992 4652, ⓦ operaromanapellegrinaggi.org · Bus to Via dei Fori Imperiali

Steps lead down from the Piazza del Campidoglio to a series of viewing terraces at the edge of the Forum and, at the bottom, **San Pietro in Carcere**, a low-vaulted church that lies above the ancient **Mamertine Prison**. Spies, vanquished soldiers and other enemies of the state, including St Peter and St Paul, were incarcerated here during Roman times. You can descend to the murky depths of the jail by yourself, or take the audio tour. Either way, you can see the column to which St Peter was chained, along with the spring the saint is said to have used to baptize his guards and other prisoners. There's a make-do altar and a cross – upside-down, because this was how Peter was (at his own request) crucified. At the top of the staircase, hollowed out of the honeycomb of stone, is an imprint claimed to be of St Peter's head as he tumbled down the stairs (though when the prison was in use, the only access was through a hole in the ceiling, which is still there). The audio tour focuses on the spiritual importance of the site, taking in a film on the life and times of the saint and finishing with a bit of evangelizing in the church above.

Santi Luca e Martina

Via della Curia 2 · Sat 8am–8pm · ☎ 06 679 8848 · Bus to Via dei Fori Imperiali

Opposite San Pietro in Carcere, the church of **Santi Luca e Martina** is two churches in one, an elegant building that has been here since the eighth century, when it was dedicated to the little-known Christian martyr Martina, who preached on this site back in the third century AD. Later, it was given by Sixtus V to the artists' group, Accademia San Luca, who additionally dedicated it to St Luke, the patron saint of painters, and had it rebuilt in the mid-seventeenth century by Pietro da Cortona, who in turn is buried in the church in a tomb of his own design. These days, the upper church is dedicated to Santa Martina, with a statue of the saint on the altar, and the lower to St Luke, with an altar by Pietro da Cortona and two works by Alessandro Algardi: a bas-relief of the *Deposition of Christ* and a terracotta *Pietà*.

San Nicola in Carcere

Via del Teatro di Marcello 46 · Church Mon–Sat 7am–7pm, Sun 7am–5pm; excavations Mon–Fri 10am–6pm, Sat & Sun 10am–5pm · Excavations €3 · ☎ 06 6830 7198, ☎ 347 381 1874 (excavations) · Bus to Via del Teatro di Marcello

Immediately south of the Capitoline Hill, a little way down Via del Teatro di Marcello, is the church of **San Nicola in Carcere**, built in the eighth century on the site of three Republican temples. It was later dedicated to St Nicholas, the patron saint of seafarers – this used to be the riverfront, and was the site of a lively fish market. The church is nice enough, but the real interest is in the **ancient remnants** it incorporates. The nave is formed by a wonderful mixture of ancient columns, both Ionic and Corinthian, while down below, informal guided tours of the excavations show how the church is supported by the central Temple of Juno and the columns of two temples either side. You can walk down the narrow Roman street that ran between the temples, squeezing between the massive blocks of the central temple and the column bases of the Temple of Janus that hold up one side of the church – columns that are clearly visible on the outside, too.

Santa Maria della Consolazione

Piazza della Consolazione 94 • Mon–Sat 6.30am–6.30pm, Sun 10am–6.30pm • ☎ 06 678 4654 • Bus to Via del Teatro di Marcello

The church of **Santa Maria della Consolazione**, just off Via del Teatro di Marcello, on the eastern side of the Capitoline Hill, was originally the chapel of a hospital that used to exist just behind. Inside, the Mattei chapel, immediately to the right of the entrance, has a wonderful series of **frescoes** by Zuccari depicting scenes from the life of Christ, including a naturalistic and dynamic flagellation scene on the left.

San Teodoro

Via di San Teodoro 7 • Mon–Fri & Sun 9.30am–12.30pm • ☎ 06 678 6624 • Bus to Via del Teatro di Marcello

A few steps from the church of Santa Maria della Consolazione, between the Capitoline and Palatine hills, the round church of **San Teodoro** is Rome's Greek national church; it's an ancient structure, though one that has been somewhat smoothed over inside by the paint and plaster of later years. St Theodore was martyred on this spot in the fourth century AD, and the church originally dates from the sixth century. The apse **mosaics** are contemporary with the original church, and show Christ with saints, including a bearded Theodore, next to St Peter on the right.

Piazza della Bocca della Verità and around

Metro Circo Massimo or bus to Lungotevere Aventino or Via del Teatro di Marcello

Down towards the Tiber, Via di Teatro di Marcello becomes Via Luigi Petroselli and meets the riverside highway at **Piazza della Bocca della Verità**, also known as the **Forum Boarium** owing to its function as a cattle market in ancient times. The square takes its name from the Bocca della Verità, one of the city's biggest tour-bus attractions, housed in the portico of the church of Santa Maria in Cosmedin. This aside, the main reason for visiting the square is to take a look at its two well-preserved Roman temples.

Temples of Portunus and Hercules Victor

Piazza della Bocca della Verità • The Temple of Hercules Victor can be visited on twice-monthly pre-booked guided tours (Italian only) on the first and third Sun of the month at 10.30am; 1hr • €5.50 • ☎ 06 3996 7700, Ⓦ coopculture.it

The **Temple of Portunus** and the **Temple of Hercules Victor**, just off the western side of the Piazza della Bocca della Verità, are two of the city's better-preserved Roman temples; the latter has long been known as the **Tempio Rotondo** because of its circular shape. Both date from the end of the second century BC and are fine examples of Republican-era places of worship; the Temple of Hercules Victor is, for what it's worth, the oldest surviving marble structure in Rome.

Santa Maria in Cosmedin

Piazza della Bocca della Verità 18 • Daily 10am–5pm • ☎ 06 678 7759

Most people don't bother to enter the church of **Santa Maria in Cosmedin**, which is a shame, because it's one of Rome's most beautiful and typical medieval basilicas, with a thirteenth-century baldacchino over a pink, ancient Roman bathtub that serves as the altar and a colourful and ingenious Cosmati mosaic floor. The sacristy acts as a gift shop and displays one of the church's greatest treasures – an eighth-century mosaic of the *Adoration of the Magi*. However, the church's fame rests on the so-called **Bocca della Verità** ("Mouth of Truth") in the portico outside. In medieval times, this ancient Roman drain cover in the shape of an enormous face would apparently swallow the hand of anyone who hadn't told the truth; it was particularly popular with husbands anxious to test the faithfulness of their wives. Today, there are queues throughout the day of people waiting to have their photograph taken with their hand inside, following in the footsteps of Gregory Peck in *Roman Holiday* (1953).

San Giorgio in Velabro and around

Via del Velabro 19 • Tues, Fri & Sat 10am–12.30pm & 4–6.30pm • ☎ 06 6979 7536, ⓦ sangiorgioinvelabro.org

On its northern side, Piazza della Bocca della Verità peters out peacefully at the squat, weathered **Arch of Janus**, possibly built in honour of the deified Constantine around 356 AD; its two rows of scalloped niches would have held statues, but none survives. Beyond it is the campanile of the church of **San Giorgio in Velabro**, a stunted echo of that of Santa Maria across the way. Inside is one of the city's barest and most beautiful old basilicas, an ancient-columned nave lit by bare stone windows carved with an intricate design. Only the late twelfth-century fresco in the apse, the work of Pietro Cavallini, lightens the melancholy mood, showing Christ and the Virgin, and various saints, including St George on the left, to whom the church is dedicated – and whose cranial bones lie in the reliquary under the high altar canopy, placed here in 749 AD shortly after the original basilica was built.

Immediately to the left of the church, the building incorporates a small, fenced-off arch, erected by the Forum Boarium market traders in honour of Septimius Severus and his family – whose portraits you can see on the inside, apart from that of his son Geta which, like the version on Septimius Severus's arch in the main forum, was erased after his assassination by his brother Caracalla. Opposite the church, behind an iron gate, you can see the arches of the **Cloaca Maxima**, the ancient city's main sewer, which emerges on the Tiber just to the left of the nearby Ponte Palatino.

Sant'Anastasia

Via di San Teodoro 1 • 24hr • ☎ 06 678 2980 • Bus to Via del Teatro di Marcello

Tucked right up against the Palatine Hill, just off the Circo Massimo, the basilica of **Sant'Anastasia** is a very ancient church, founded by a Roman noblewoman (called Anastasia) in the fourth century and later dedicated to the saint of the same name. It's a great example of how Roman churches can be very old but have been so refurbished over the years that they feel anything but. The church has extensive remains of a Roman house below its floor, but these are normally closed to the public. It is a designated centre of "**Perpetual Adoration**", which means it's open all the time, with someone always present at prayer.

Ponte Palatino

The busy **Ponte Palatino**, which connects the Capitoline side of the river to Trastevere on the opposite bank, is sometimes known as the "English Bridge" because traffic on the bridge drives on the left (facilitating U-turns from the right to left bank of the river). Look closely at the right bank of the river from the bridge itself and you should be able to spot the giant arch placed there to take the outflow of the ancient Cloaca Maxima sewer, now overgrown with trees and bushes.

THE COLOSSEUM

Ancient Rome

There are remnants of Rome's ancient glories all over the city and environs, but the greatest concentration is in the area southeast from the Capitoline Hill, which we've called "ancient Rome". Mussolini ploughed the Via dei Fori Imperiali through here in the 1930s with the intention of exploiting the city's imperial heritage as a backdrop to the military parades that he used to advertise his own imperial ambitions. You can easily spend a day or more lazily picking your way through the rubble of what was once the heart of the ancient world. An obvious place to start exploring is the Colosseum, Rome's most iconic sight, before moving on to the Forum – immediately below the Capitoline Hill – and the greener heights of the Palatine Hill. Try also to see the excellent museum at Trajan's Markets, and the Domus Aurea, part of Nero's opulent palace.

Colosseum

Daily: mid-Feb to mid-March 8.30am–5pm; mid- to end March 8.30am–5.30pm; April–Aug 8.30am–7.15pm; Sept 8.30am–7pm; Oct 8.30am–6.30pm; Nov to mid-Feb 8.30am–4.30pm; last entry 1hr before closing • €12 combined ticket with Forum (p.77) & Palatine Hill (p.84); valid for 2 days; last Sun of the month free • ☎ 06 3996 7700, ⓦ coopculture.it • Metro Colosseo or bus to Colosseo, Via Cavour or Via dei Fori Imperiali

The **Colosseum** is Rome's most awe-inspiring ancient monument, and one which, unlike the Forum, needs little historical knowledge or imagination to deduce its function. This enormous structure was so solidly built, that despite the depredations of nearly two thousand years – earthquakes, fires, riots, wars and, not least, plundering for its seemingly inexhaustible supply of ready-cut travertine blocks – it still stands relatively intact, a readily recognizable symbol not just of the city of Rome, but of the entire ancient world. Inevitably, it's not nearly as grand as it once was – sections are missing, it's badly cracked and there are gaping holes where internal metal brackets once linked the great blocks together – but a huge, 25-million-euro renovation, funded by Italian shoe giant Tod's, has very successfully cleaned and restored the exterior and was working its way round the interior at the time of writing.

The Colosseum is the prototype of all sports stadia, and until 2000 it appeared on all winners' medals in the Olympics. Today, it graces the Italian 5c coin. To avoid the worst of the crowds it's best to pre-book tickets (see box below) and come first thing in the morning before the tour buses have arrived or last thing in the evening before it closes.

Once inside the arena, you're free to wander round most of the **ground level**, circling the remains of the arena and observing its maze of brick walls, but you'll get a better view from the **lower tier**, reached by steep **stairways** leading up from the entrance. Here also, in the connecting corridor, is a space for temporary exhibitions on all things Roman, a display of fragments of masonry and a decent bookshop. More stairs lead to the **upper tier** – even here you are still only about halfway up the original structure – though this and the arena and underground areas are visitable only on guided **tours** (see box below).

Beginnings

A **lake** once lay where the Colosseum stands today, drained by a small stream that wove between the Palatine and Celian hills before emptying into the Tiber. Things changed after the great **fire** of 64 AD, when Nero set about building his outrageous palace, the Domus Aurea (see p.76). The lake became part of the palace gardens, an imperial

---

TICKETS AND TOURS

A single **ticket** covers the **Colosseum, Forum and Palatine Hill** and is valid for two days; you're allowed to visit each attraction once during this time, and the Forum and Palatine Hill count as one site, so have to be visited at the same time. **Queues** can be a problem, particularly at the Colosseum, and while they do move quickly, during summer they're rarely less than 100m long and are often besieged by touts. Your best bet is to buy your ticket **online in advance** (booking fee of €2 in addition to the ticket price; ⓦcoopculture.it), which reduces queueing times, or buy it at either entrance to the Forum early in the morning when things are usually quieter. Holders of the Archaeologia Card, RomaPass or Omnia Vatican & Rome Pass (see p.32) are allowed to use a different queue. Even with pre-booked tickets there is a security check which can cause further queues. The best advice to minimize these is to arrive before 9.30am or as late as opening hours allow in the afternoon.

There are guided tours for groups of up to twenty of the Colosseum daily (10.15am–3pm; roughly every 30min–1hr; 45min; €5), and of the Forum on Fridays, Saturdays and Sundays at 11am and 12.30pm (1hr; €5). The Colosseum also offers daily tours of the upper tier, arena floor and underground spaces – areas usually closed to the public (sometimes not available in winter or in adverse weather conditions; €9; advance booking essential). In addition, **night tours** of the Colosseum are available (usually end April to mid-Oct Mon, Thurs, Fri & Sat 8.10pm–midnight; last entry 10.40pm; €20), which include a visit to the underground areas. All tours can be booked through ⓦcoopculture.it.

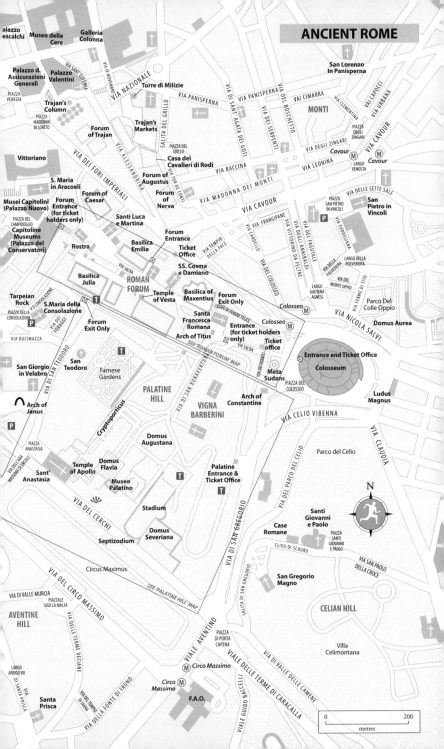

ANCIENT ROME

alazzo
escalchi
Museo delle Cere
Galleria Colonna

San Lorenzo In Panisperna

Palazzo d. Assicurazioni Generali
Palazzo Valentini

VIA SANT'EUFEMIA
VIA IV NOVEMBRE

PIAZZA VENEZIA

Trajan's Column

PIAZZA MADONNA DI LORETO

Forum of Trajan

Vittoriano

S. Maria in Aracoeli

Musei Capitolini (Palazzo Nuovo)

PIAZZA DEL CAMPIDOGLIO

Capitoline Museums (Palazzo dei Conservatori)

Rostra

Tarpeian Rock

PIAZZA DELLA CONSOLAZIONE

S.Maria della Consolazione

VIA DELLA CONSOLAZIONE

VIA DEL FORAGGI

VIA BUCIMAZZA

San Giorgio in Velabro

Arch of Janus

PIAZZA ANASTASIA

VIA DELL'ARA MASSIMA ERCOLE

Sant' Anastasia

VIA DI SAN TEODORO

San Teodoro

Farnese Gardens

VIA NAZIONALE

Torre di Milizie

VIA PANISPERNA

Trajan's Markets

SALITA DEL GRILLO

VIA SANT'AGATA DEI GOTI

PIAZZA DEL GRILLO

Casa dei Cavalieri di Rodi

Forum of Augustus

VIA TOR DE' CONTI

Forum of Nerva

VIA DEI FORI IMPERIALI

VIA ALESSANDRINA

Forum of Caesar

Santi Luca e Martina

Basilica Emilia

ROMAN FORUM

VIA SACRA

Basilica Julia

Temple of Vesta

Forum Entrance (for ticket holders only)

Forum Entrance

Ticket Office

SS. Cosma e Damiano

Basilica of Maxentius

Santa Francesca Romana

Arch of Titus

SEE 'ROMAN FORUM' MAP

Forum Exit Only

Forum Exit Only

VIA DI SAN BONAVENTURA

PALATINE HILL

VIGNA BARBERINI

Cryptoporticus

Domus Augustana

Temple of Apollo

Domus Flavia

Museo Palatino

Stadium

Domus Severiana

Septizodium

VIA DEL CERCHI

Circus Maximus

SEE 'PALATINE HILL' MAP

Palatine Entrance & Ticket Office

VIA DI SAN GREGORIO

VIA PANISPERNA

VIA DI SANT'AGATA DEI GOTI

VIA DEI SERPENTI

VIA DEL BOSCHETTO

VIA CIMARRA

MONTI

VIA CLEMENTINA

VIA URBANA

VIA CAPOCCI

PIAZZA DEGLI ZINGARI

VIA DEGLI ZINGARI

VIA BACCINA

VIA MADONNA DEI MONTI

VIA CAVOUR

VIA LEONINA

Cavour

LARGO VENOSTA

Cavour

VIA FRANGIPANE

VIA CARDELLO

VIA DEL TEMPIO DELLA PACE

VIA DEGLI ANNIBALDI

VIA DEL COLOSSEO

VIA DELLE SETTE SALE

PIAZZA SAN PIETRO IN VINCOLI

San Pietro in Vincoli

VIA EUDOSSIANA

VIA DEL FAGUTALE

VIA VITTORINO DA FELTRE

VIA DELLA POLVERIERA

LARGO DELLA POLVERIERA

VIA DEL MONTE OPPIO

LARGO GAETANA AGNESI

Parco Del Colle Oppio

VIA TERME DI TITO

Colosseo

Colosseo

CLIVO DI VENERE FELICE

Forum Exit Only

Entrance (for ticket holders only)

Ticket office

VIA SACRA

VIA NICOLA SALVI

Domus Aurea

Meta Sudans

Entrance and Ticket Office

Colosseum

PIAZZA DEL COLOSSEO

VIA CELIO VIBENNA

Ludus Magnus

VIA CLAUDIA

Arch of Constantine

Parco del Celio

VIA DEL PARCO DEL CELIO

Case Romane

Santi Giovanni e Paolo

PIAZZA SANTI GIOVANNI E PAOLO

CLIVO DI SCAURO

VIA SAN PAOLO DELLA CROCE

San Gregorio Magno

CELIAN HILL

Villa Celimontana

SALITA DI SAN GREGORIO

AVENTINE HILL

VIA DI VALLE MURCIA

PIAZZALE UGO LA MALFA

VIA DELLE TERME DECIANE

LARGO ARRIGO VII

VIA DI SANTA PRISCA

Santa Prisca

VIA DEL TEMPIO DI DIANA

VIA DELLA FONTE DI FAUNO

Circo Massimo

Circo Massimo

F.A.O.

VIALE AVENTINO

PIAZZA DI PORTA CAPENA

VIALE DELLE TERME DI CARACALLA

VIALE GUIDO BACCELLI

VIA DI VALLE DELLE CAMENE

N

0   200

metres

BEASTLY HAPPENINGS AT THE COLOSSEUM

The Romans flocked to the Colosseum for many things, but **gladiatorial contests** were the big attraction. Gladiatorial **combat** as a Roman tradition was a direct import from the Etruscans, who thought it seemly to sacrifice a few prisoners of war or slaves at the funeral games of an important person. By the second century BC, such contests had become so institutionalized in Rome that a **gladiatorial school**, or Ludus Magnus (see p.76), was installed in the city – a rather grim affair, consisting of a barracks for gladiators and a ring in which they could practise with blunt weapons, under supervision.

Gladiatorial combat was probably the greatest and cruellest of all **bloodsports**. At the start of the games, the gladiators would enter through the monumental door at the eastern end of the arena. They would make a procession around the ring and halt in front of the emperor's box, where they would make their **famous greeting**, "Hail Caesar, we who are about to die salute you." Gladiators were divided into several **classes**, each performing different types of combat. There was the heavily armed "Samnite", named after the type of arms the Romans had captured on the defeat of that tribe in 310 BC, equipped with heavy armour, an oblong bronze shield, a visored helmet with crest and plumes, and a sword (*gladius*). Usually a Samnite would be pitted against a combatant without armour, equipped only with a cast net and a trident, whose main protection was that he was unencumbered and therefore could be fleet of foot. He had, however, only one cast of his net in which to entangle the Samnite and kill him with his trident. Neither man was allowed to flee from the arena, and, once captured or disarmed, the roaring mob would be asked whether the loser should be killed or allowed to live. If he had put up a good fight he would usually be spared; if he had not fought as valiantly as he should, he would be **slaughtered** on the spot. The early Christian Church waged a long and often unpopular campaign against gladiatorial combat, and in the end they carried the day: in 404 AD, a monk named **Telemachus** tried to separate two fighting gladiators, and the crowd stoned him to death, prompting the Emperor Honorius to abolish gladiatorial fighting altogether.

The other activities conducted in the Colosseum involved **animals**. In the hundred-day games that inaugurated the Colosseum, something like nine thousand beasts were massacred – roughly twelve killings a minute – and during the 450 years of activity here several breeds of African elephant and lion were rendered extinct. There were also gladiatorial games which involved "**hunting**" wild animals, and sometimes creatures would be pitted against each other – bears would be tied to bulls and have to fight to the finish, lions would take on tigers, dogs would be set against wolves and so on. The last games involving animals were conducted in the year 523 AD, after which the Colosseum gradually fell into disuse and disrepair.

4

plaything where mock nautical battles could be enacted. Four years later, Nero was dead, and, after a trio of quick-fire emperors, **Vespasian** seized power and soon set a new course. To prove that the wayward days of Nero were over and the city was being given back to the people, Vespasian drained the lake and began the construction of the Flavian Amphitheatre, as it was originally known, in 70 AD. Incredibly, given the size of the project, the Colosseum was inaugurated by Vespasian's son Titus just eight years later, an event celebrated by a hundred days of continuous **games**; it was finally completed by **Domitian**, Titus's brother and the third of the Flavian emperors.

Construction and organization

Prior to Vespasian, gladiatorial and other bloody games had been conducted in a makeshift stadium in the Roman Forum, near the Curia. The stands were temporary and constructed of wood, and had to be erected and taken down every time there were games. It is said that seventy thousand Hebrew slaves did the heavy work at the Colosseum. Fifty thousand cartloads of pre-cut travertine stone were hauled from the quarries at Tivoli, a distance of 27km. In the depths of what must have been the muddy bottom of the lake, a **labyrinth** was laid out, walling in passages for the contestants and creating areas for assembling and storing sets, scenery and other requirements for gladiatorial contests. The overall structure was tastefully designed, with close attention paid to decoration. On the outside, the arena's three **arcades** rose in strict classical fashion to a flat surface at the top punctuated only by windows, where there was a series of supports for **masts** that protruded at the upper limit. These masts, 240 in total, were used to extend a canvas awning over the spectators inside the arena.

Inside, beyond the corridors that led up to the **seats**, lavishly decorated with painted stucco, there was room for a total of around sixty thousand people seated and ten thousand or so standing; the design was such that all seventy thousand could enter and be seated in a matter of minutes. **Seating** was allocated according to social status, with the emperor and his attendants naturally occupying the best seats in the house, and the social class of the spectators diminishing further up the stands. There were no ticket sales as we conceive of them; rather, tickets were distributed through – and according to the social status of – Roman heads of households. These "**tickets**" were in fact wooden tags, with the entrance, row, aisle and seat number carved on them. Inside the amphitheatre, the **labyrinth** below was covered over with a wooden floor, punctuated at various places for trapdoors and lifts to raise and lower the animals that were to take part in the games. The **floor** was covered with canvas to make it waterproof, and the canvas was covered with several centimetres of sand to absorb blood; in fact, our word "arena" is derived from the Latin word for sand. There was also a busy sideline in sponges soaked in the blood of the newly departed – the blood was said to cure epilepsy.

Around the Colosseum

Once you've seen the Colosseum, it's worth having a wander around outside. If you feel you must be photographed with one of the (entirely unauthorized) costumed centurions, arrange a price first (€5 is a general rule), or be prepared for distinct unpleasantness. Alternatively, focus your attentions on the impressive **Arch of Constantine**; make the short walk, too, to the somewhat hidden church of **Santa Francesca Romana** for an alternative view of the Forum and to see the saint's body, among other miraculous relics. Also worthwhile is a visit to what survives of Nero's pleasure palace, the **Domus Aurea**.

Arch of Constantine

On the opposite side of the Colosseum stands the huge **Arch of Constantine**, placed here in 315 AD, after Constantine had consolidated his power as sole emperor with a triumph over his co-ruler Maxentius. The deterioration of the arts during the later stages of the Roman Empire, and perhaps a desire to evoke the "glory years" of the second century, meant that most of the sculptural decoration on the arch was looted from earlier monuments. The round medallions are taken from a temple dedicated to the Emperor Hadrian's lover, Antinous, who was deified after his premature death, and show Antinous and Hadrian engaged in the hunt. Sculptures on top of the columns, removed from the Forum of Trajan, show Dacian prisoners captured in Trajan's war there. Perhaps finest of all are the reliefs between these warriors which were carved for the Emperor Marcus Aurelius. The large **inscription** in the centre was made for the arch and dedicates it to Constantine for his triumph over the "tyrant" Maxentius.

Meta Sudans

Between the Arch of Constantine and the Colosseum, at a pivotal point in the Via Sacra, stood a monumental fountain or **Meta Sudans**, the outline of which can still be seen today in the form of a circular brick foundation. A "meta" was the marker in the centre of a racecourse, and was usually an obelisk or some other large, easily visible object. In this case, it was a conical fountain that was probably dedicated to Apollo, and produced a slow supply of water that resembled sweat, hence its name – the "**Sweating Meta**". The low brick walls nearby are believed to be the foundations for the moorings of Nero's lake.

Ludus Magnus

Piazza del Colosseo • Tunnels open to groups only; call ☎ 06 0608

To the east of the Colosseum, the sunken brick ruins at the foot of Via di San Giovanni in Laterano are what's left of the **Ludus Magnus**, the main training school for gladiators. The complex included a small arena built by Domitian that was surrounded by gladiators' barracks, connected to the Colosseum by tunnels – some of which still exist.

Santa Francesca Romana

Piazza di Santa Francesca Romana 4 • Daily 10am–noon & 3–5pm • ☎ 06 679 5528

Standing on the edge of the Forum, but reached by way of a narrow side road from the Colosseum (across the road from the metro station), the church of **Santa Francesca Romana** is sometimes known as **Santa Maria Nova** after the church of Santa Maria Antiqua, which it replaced as a place of worship in the tenth century. The church was subsequently dedicated to a fifteenth-century Trastevere noblewoman and later nun who did good works for the poor and experienced a vision of her guardian angel that lasted several years – quite long enough to get her beatified. The church is a fascinating building on many levels. Highlights include a series of beautiful twelfth-century mosaics in the apse, above a venerated depiction of the Madonna and Child from the same era and the elaborate tomb of Pope Gregory XI, who brought the papacy back to Rome from Avignon in the late fourteenth century. Close by – to the right of the high altar in the transept – protective grilles have been bolted over two **flagstones** brought here from the Via Sacra. Legend asserts that the dips on the flagstones bear the imprint of the knees of St Peter, who knelt in prayer to ask God to punish Simon the Sorcerer, who was busy flying through the air; God obliged, and Simon crash-landed. Not far from here, steps lead down into the crypt, where the skeletal body of St Francesca lies prone, clothed, holding a prayer book and surrounded by votive photos.

Domus Aurea

Viale della Domus Aurea 1 • Sat & Sun 9am–5pm; last entry 3.45pm; admission by guided tour only, limited to groups of 25 people; visits last 1hr 15min; check the website for the latest information • €12 • Book in advance on ☎ 06 3996 7700 or ⓦ coopculture.it; you can follow the progress of the restoration on the blog ⓦ archeoroma.beniculturali.it/cantieredomusaurea/en

Almost opposite the Colosseum is the park of **Colle Oppio**, built on the Oppian Hill, one of the peaks of the ancient Roman Esquiline. A fairly undistinguished open space (and a slightly unsavoury spot after dark), it does, however, hold the remnants of two important Roman structures: the imposing fenced-off remains of Trajan's Baths – a public baths built in 109 AD that's still being excavated – and Nero's magnificent **Domus Aurea**, which lies underneath the baths complex.

Currently undergoing a decade-long, €39-million restoration, the Domus Aurea, or "Golden House", partially reopened to the public in late 2014. The "house" was a vast undertaking built on the summit and into the sides of the Oppian Hill, after a fire of 64 AD (allegedly started by Nero) devastated over half of ancient Rome, conveniently clearing the way for Nero to start building his villa complex: a series of banqueting rooms, nymphaea, small baths, terraces and gardens, looking over what was at the time a lake fed by the underground springs and streams that drained from the surrounding hills (now the valley of the Colosseum). Much of the site remains unexcavated, but scholars estimate that its vast bulk and surrounding parkland extended for a square kilometre or more, reaching the slopes of the Palatine, Esquiline and Celian hills. The excavated area alone – a fraction of the whole – is equivalent to three football pitches.

Rome was used to Nero's excesses, but it had never seen anything like the Golden House before. The facade was said to have been coated in solid gold; there was an elaborate bath complex; one of the dining rooms, the Coenatio Rotunda on the Palatine (see p.86), rotated slowly and was rigged up to shower flower petals and natural scent on guests; and the grounds held vineyards, woods full of game, and the great lake where mock nautical battles were staged. Behind the lake, by the entrance vestibule of the palace, Nero erected a gilded bronze statue of himself as a sun god which is described by Suetonius as being 120 feet tall. When the palace was finished, Nero is reputed to have remarked "Good, now I can at last begin to live like a human being!", but he didn't get to enjoy it for long – he died four years later, victim of a Senate-sponsored revolution, and Vespasian tore much of the exposed facade down in disgust, draining the lake and building the Colosseum in its place. The public baths of Titus, and then Trajan, were built over the Colle Oppio section of the palace, and it was pretty much forgotten until its **wall paintings** were discovered by Renaissance artists, including Raphael and Pinturicchio. When these artists first visited these rooms, they had to descend ladders into what they first believed was some kind of mystical cave, or **grotto**; their attempts to imitate what they found here gave us the word "grotesque".

The rooms

Visitors are given hard hats before entering the excavation site. The temperature inside always hovers at around 10°C and this, combined with the ninety percent humidity, makes it necessary to wear a sweater or jacket even in the middle of the Roman summer. The house can at first be confusing – Trajan's attempts to obliterate the palace with his baths complex mean that the baths' foundations merge into parts of the palace, and vice versa. The lively and engaging **tours** take you past various covered fountains, service corridors and terraces to the **Room of the Gilded Vault**, with its original ceiling dotted with holes made by the Renaissance painter-explorers. Most spectacular is the **Octagonal Room**, with a hole in the middle of its domed ceiling and a stepped artificial waterfall. Most of the rooms are decorated in the so-called Third Pompeiian style, with garlands of flowers, fruit, vines and foliage, interspersed with mythical animals and fanciful depictions of people looking back through windows at the viewer.

The tours also deal with the problems faced by the restorers: the roots of the mature trees in the park above have embedded themselves in the roof, and the weight of the soil is considerable, especially when it rains and water filters through, damaging the frescoes. The long-term plan is to remove the existing park and create a landscaped garden on a thinner layer of soil, to ease the pressure on the palace below.

Roman Forum

Entrances Largo della Salaria Vecchia, halfway down Via dei Fori Imperiali; at the Arch of Titus near the Colosseum; on Via di San Gregorio (via the Palatine) **Exits** Largo della Salaria Vecchia; Via di San Gregorio (via the Palatine); behind the Arch of Septimius Severus, near the Capitoline Hill; by the Basilica of Maxentius and the church of Santa Francesca Romana; behind the Basilica Giulia on to Via di Teodoro • Daily: Mid-Feb to mid-March 8.30am–5pm; mid- to end March 8.30am–5.30pm; April–Aug 8.30am–7.15pm; Sept 8.30am–7pm; Oct 8.30am–6.30pm; Nov to mid-Feb 8.30am–4.30pm; last entry 1hr before closing • €12 combined ticket with Colosseo (p.72) & Palatine Hill (p.84); valid for 2 days; free first Sun of the month • W coopculture.it • Metro Colosseo or Circo Massimo

The original **Roman Forum** was the centre of Republican-era Rome. During the reign of Augustus, Rome reached an estimated population of a million and in many places stretched out as far as the Late Imperial Aurelian Wall (see box, p.147) in a sprawl of

---

THE DECLINE AND FALL OF THE FORUM

In 667 AD, **Constans II**, ruler of the Eastern empire, paid a state visit to Rome. He came to the Forum, and, seeing all the temples and basilicas held together with bronze and iron cramps, decided that they would serve better in his war against Islam and ordered all the metal to be transported back home and forged into spear-points, arrowheads and armour. It took just twelve days to dismantle the metal props, but the result was a disaster: everything was captured en route to Constantinople by Saracen raiders, and the columns and arches supporting all the buildings in the Forum fell down with the next earth tremor. By the early ninth century, hardly anything remained standing, leaving it ripe for the looters of later years – one reason why so little is left today

apartment blocks (*insulae*). The Forum was home to its political and religious institutions, its shops and market stalls, and was a meeting place for all. Under Julius Caesar's dictatorship, and then during the imperial era, Rome's increased importance as a world power led to the building of the extensions now known as the "Imperial Fora" nearby (see p.86).

A **fire** in the third century AD caused a great deal of damage, and although repairs were made, Rome was by this time in an inexorable state of decline, and the unstoppable rise of Christianity only served to accelerate the process, particularly for its pagan temples and institutions. After the fall of the city to barbarian invaders, the whole area was left in ruin, its buildings looted for the construction of other parts of Rome during both medieval and Renaissance times; the heart of the Empire became a quarry for spare parts. The odd church or fortification was built incorporating the more viable piles, accounting for those buildings which survive amid the rubble. **Excavation** of the site didn't start until the beginning of the nineteenth century, and has continued pretty much without stopping ever since: constant restorations and continued excavations mean areas can be closed off, but the general trend is a very positive one: more of the sites are accessible than ever before.

These days, the Forum is one of the city's **top attractions**, but it can be a bit muddling, since you need a good imagination and some grasp of history to really appreciate the place. But these ten or so acres were once the heart of an empire which dominated the Mediterranean and beyond, and are a very real testament to a power that held a large chunk of the world in its thrall for close on five centuries, and whose influence reverberates right up to the present day – in language, in architecture, in political terms and systems, even in the romance that time has lent to its ruins. Our **suggested route** around the Forum begins at the Largo Salaria Vecchia entrance with the **western section**, and continues east from the **Temple of Vesta**.

Via Sacra

Get oriented and start your explorations at the **Via Sacra**, which dog-legs its way through the core of the Forum, from below the Capitoline Hill in the west to the far eastern extent of the site. This was the best-known street of ancient Rome, along which

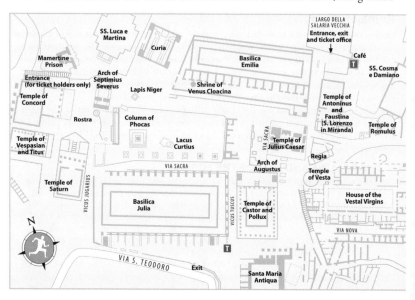

victorious emperors and generals would process to give thanks at the Capitoline's Temple of Jupiter. It's possible, however, that the modern street isn't the original Via Sacra, and was in fact only given the name in the 1550s, when the Holy Roman Emperor, Charles V, visited Pope Paul III and the only triumphal arch they could find to march under was the Arch of Septimius Severus (see p.81).

Regia

As you come down the ramp from the entrance you'll see shallow steps flanking the Via Sacra ahead of you and to the left; these are part of the **Regia**, or House of the Kings, an extremely ancient – and ruined – group of foundations that probably date from the reign of the second king of Rome, Numa, who ruled from 715 to 673 BC. There was a shrine of Mars here, housing the shields and spears of the god of war, which generals embarking on a campaign rattled before setting off. If the shields and spears rattled of their own accord, it was a bad omen, requiring purification and repentance rites. The Regia later became the residence of Julius Caesar, who moved here in 45 BC – an imperious act which contributed to his downfall.

Temple of Antoninus and Faustina

Opposite the Regia are the vast looming columns of the **Temple of Antoninus and Faustina,** the best-preserved temple in the Forum. It survives because it was converted into the church of **San Lorenzo in Miranda** during the seventh century (it is said that St Lawrence was martyred here, barbecued alive in the Forum). The six huge Corinthian columns of Euboean marble across its front are still connected by an inscribed lintel, dedicating the temple by order of the Senate to the god Antoninus (usually known as Antoninus Pius for his religiosity) and his wife, the deified empress Faustina – Roman emperors who weren't too dreadful were deified upon their deaths, a privilege often extended to their immediate family. On the sides of the building part of the original frieze of griffins, candelabra and acanthus scrolls can be seen. Otherwise, the brick stairs leading up to the floor of the temple are a modern reconstruction, while the Baroque facade of the church dates from 1602. Note the curious position of the main door, marooned halfway up the facade; when the church was built in the seventeenth

4

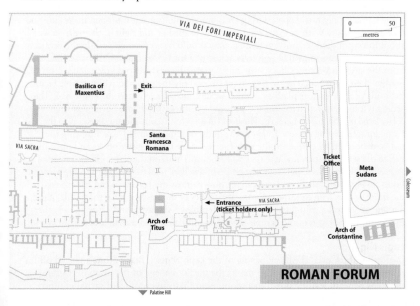

VIA DEI FORI IMPERIALI

0 50
metres

Basilica of Maxentius

Exit

Santa Francesca Romana

VIA SACRA

Ticket Office

Meta Sudans

Colosseum

← Entrance (ticket holders only) VIA SACRA

Arch of Titus

Arch of Constantine

ROMAN FORUM

Palatine Hill

century the door would have been at ground level. It's a very visible reminder of the change in ground level of this low-lying valley after the millennium of deposits of waste, rubble, and river silt that followed the definitive collapse of the western Empire in the late fifth century.

Temple of Julius Caesar

Next to the Regia, the assorted piles of rubble that have been immersed in preservative cement are the remains of the **Temple of Julius Caesar**, a grand edifice erected two years after Julius Caesar's assassination, as part of his posthumous deification (the first mortal to be deified). The small semi-circular green roof on the edge of the rubble covers the spot where Caesar was cremated and upon which the temple was built.

Basilica Emilia

The football pitch of broken columns on the other side of the entrance ramp to the site from the Temple of Antoninus and Faustina, and opposite the Temple of Julius Caesar, marks the site of the **Basilica Emilia**, built in the second century BC to house law courts, and, in the little booths and boutiques flanking its south side, moneychangers. Also on the basilica's south side, a modern plaque signs the circular stone foundation of the **shrine of Venus Cloacina**, the waters of which were used for ritual purification. The shrine was built where the Cloaca Maxima canal entered the Forum before slicing down to the River Tiber, thereby draining the Forum, which was originally marshland.

Curia

The large cube-shaped building at the west end of the Basilica Emilia is the **Curia**, built on the orders of Julius Caesar as part of his programme for expanding the Forum – it connects with the Forum of Caesar outside – although what you see today is a third-century AD reconstruction built during the era of the Emperor Diocletian. The Senate met here during the Republican period, and augurs would come to announce the wishes of the gods. For centuries, the Curia served as a church until it was (fairly aggressively) restored in the 1930s, and its bronze doors – which had been removed in the seventeenth century to San Giovanni in Laterano, where they remain – were replaced with reproductions.

The Curia is only rarely open during temporary exhibitions; if it is open make sure you take a look inside. Within, three wide stairs rise to the left and right of the hall, on which about three hundred senators on folding chairs could be accommodated. In the centre is the **speaker's platform**, with a porphyry statue of a toga-clad figure. Otherwise, apart from the late third-century floor, elegantly patterned in red, yellow, green and white marble, there's not much left of its ancient decor, only the grey and white marble facing each side of the speaker's platform, which would once have covered the entire hall. The ceiling is a modern replacement, and in Imperial times would have been gilded.

The large marble reliefs here, the **Plutei of Trajan** – found outside and brought to the Curia for safekeeping – show Trajan in the midst of public-spirited acts, forgiving the public debt owed by citizens to the state (porters carry large register books and place them before the seated emperor, where they will be burnt) and, on the right, giving a woman a sack of money, a representation of the emperor's welfare plan for widows and orphans. Look closely at the reliefs, and you can see how parts of the Forum would have looked at the time: in one, a fig tree, the columns and arches of the Basilica Julia, the facade of the Temple of Saturn, a triumphal arch and the Temple of Vespasian and Titus; in the other, the columns and eaves of the Temple of Castor and Pollux and the Arch of Augustus.

Lapis Niger

In front of the Curia, the black paving of the **Lapis Niger** ("Black Stone"; fenced off for restoration at the time of writing) marks the traditional site of the tomb of Romulus, the steps beneath leading down to a monument that was considered sacred ground during classical times. The excavation work at the Lapis Niger means that the Via Sacra is currently a dead end; for the best view of the monuments described below, you are advised to double back and take the parallel path, past the Basilica Julia, in the direction of the Capitoline Hill, at the foot of which you can admire at close quarters the Arch of Septimius Severus.

Arch of Septimius Severus

At the end of the Via Sacra stands the conspicuous **Arch of Septimius Severus**, constructed in the early third century AD by his sons Caracalla and Geta to mark their father's victories in what is now Iran. The friezes on it recall Severus and in particular Caracalla, who ruled Rome with undisciplined terror for seven years. The space where Geta was once commemorated is blank – Caracalla, who had inherited the empire jointly, had him executed in 213 AD, and his name expediently removed from the arch altogether.

Rostra

To the left of the arch of Septimius Severus (as you look across the Forum, the Capitoline Hill behind you), the low brown wall of the **Rostra** faces the wide-open scatter of paving, dumped stones and beached columns that makes up the central portion of the Forum, which in its heyday would have been crowded with politicians, tribunes and traders. The Rostra was the place where important speeches were made, and it was probably from here that Mark Antony spoke about Caesar after his death.

Temples of Saturn, Vespasian and Titus, and Concord

As you look at the Rostra, behind your right shoulder is the **Temple of Saturn**. The oldest temple in the Forum, it dates originally from 497 BC, although the base and eight columns you see today are the result of a series of restorations carried out between 42 BC and 380 AD. The temple was also the Roman treasury and mint. Next to the temple, three columns still stand from the **Temple of Vespasian and Titus** of the 80s AD. Still further to the right, behind the Arch of Septimius Severus, the large pile of brick and cement rubble is all that remains of the **Temple of Concord**, dedicated by Tiberius in 10 AD.

4

Vicus Jugarius

A short slope at the end of the Via Sacra brings you to the **Vicus Jugarius** ("Street of the Yoke-makers"). The street once formed part of the ancient trade route to the Tiber.

Basilica Julia

On the opposite side of the Forum from the Curia are the long, shallow steps of the **Basilica Julia**, built by Julius Caesar in the 50s BC after his return from the Gallic Wars. All that remain are a few column bases and one nearly complete column, and you can't climb the stairs – although you can still see the odd game board carved into the marble steps (one is visible on the far left end of the steps as you look at them), where idlers in the Forum played their pebble-toss games.

Column of Phocas and Lacus Curtius

Opposite the Basilica Julia, on the other side of the Via Sacra, the so-called **Column of Phocas** is a commemorative column that has managed to retain its dedicatory inscription. Further along, guardrails lead into a kind of alcove in the pavement, which overlooks the site of the **Lacus Curtius** – the spot where, according to legend, a chasm opened in the city's earliest days and the soothsayers determined that it would be closed only when Rome had sacrificed its most valuable possession into it. Marcus Curtius, a Roman soldier who declared that Rome's most valuable possession was a loyal citizen, hurled himself and his horse into the void, and it duly shut.

Temple of Castor and Pollux

As you pass the Basilica Julia, you'll see the **Temple of Castor and Pollux** ahead of you on the right, a vast concrete rubble base denuded of its marble cladding from which three graceful Corinthian columns rise, heroic survivors. The temple was dedicated in 484 BC to the divine twins, or Dioscuri, the offspring of Jupiter by Leda, who appeared miraculously to ensure victory for the Romans in a key battle. The story goes that a group of Roman citizens were gathered around a water fountain on this spot fretting about the war, when Castor and Pollux appeared and reassured them that the battle was won – hence the temple, and their adoption as the special protectors of Rome.

Temple of Vesta and the House of the Vestal Virgins

Further ahead, opposite the **Temple of Antoninus and Faustina**, is the site of the **Temple of Vesta**. It burnt down on several occasions (a hazard of housing the eternal flame), but three columns stand (heavily restored), perched on top of a curving brick wall. Vesta was the Roman goddess of the hearth and home, and her cult was an important one in ancient Rome. Her temple was in the charge of the **Vestal Virgins** (see box below), who resided in the neighbouring **House of the Vestal Virgins**, behind the temple and immediately to the east. The building, a second-century AD reconstruction of a structure originally built by Nero, was a very comfortable palace: four storeys of rooms set around a central courtyard. The rooms are mainly ruins now, though they're fairly recognizable, and you can get a good sense of the shape of the place from the picturesque remains of the courtyard, still with its pool in the centre and fringed by a few statues of the women themselves.

Temple of Romulus

Opposite the House of the Vestal Virgins, next to the **Temple of Antoninus and Faustina**, is the curved facade of the building usually identified as the **Temple of Romulus** (the son of the Emperor Maxentius, named for the founder of Rome a thousand years or so after the other Romulus). Dating from 309 AD, it has been sanctified and for centuries served as the vestibule for the church of Santi Cosma e Damiano (see p.88). It retains its original bronze doors and is occasionally open when temporary exhibitions are housed inside.

Basilica of Maxentius

Past the Temple of Romulus, the short path on the left rises up to the towering **Basilica of Maxentius**, sometimes called the Basilica of Constantine, which is, in terms of size and ingenuity, probably the Forum's most impressive structure. Begun by Maxentius, the structure was continued by his co-emperor and rival, Constantine, after he had defeated him at the Battle of Ponte Milvio in 312 AD. By the time the basilica was built, Roman architects and engineers were expert at building with poured cement. It's said that Michelangelo studied the hexagonal coffered arches here when working on the

---

THE VESTAL VIRGINS

The **Vestal Virgins** had the responsibility of keeping the sacred flame of Vesta alight in the Temple of Vesta, and were obliged to remain chaste for the thirty years that they served (they usually started at around age 10). If the flame should go out, the woman responsible was scourged; if she should lose her chastity, she was buried alive (her male partner-in-crime was flogged to death in front of the Curia). Vestal virgins could resign their post if they wished, but the importance of their office did accord them special privileges: a choice section in the Colosseum was reserved for them; only they and the empress could ride in a wheeled vehicle within the confines of the city; and they had the right to pardon any criminal who managed to get close enough to one of them to beseech their mercy.

design of St Peter's, and Renaissance architects frequently used its apse and arches as a model. Incidentally, the church you can see through the metal fence is that of Santa Francesca Romana – very much worth a look, but only accessible from outside the Forum (see p.77).

Arch of Titus

The Via Sacra climbs east up to the **Arch of Titus**, which stands commandingly on a low arm of the Palatine Hill, looking one way down the remainder of the Via Sacra to the Colosseum, and back over the Forum proper. The arch was built by Titus's brother and successor, Domitian, after the emperor's death and subsequent deification in 81 AD. It commemorates his victories in Judaea in 70 AD and his triumphal return from that campaign. It sets in stone the inauguration of the Flavian dynasty and Rome's return to peace and stability following the disruption that had followed Nero's death. The Forum side of the arch is **much-restored**, though the original interior reliefs survive. They show, on one side: Titus riding in a chariot with Nike, goddess of Victory, and, on the opposite side: spoils removed from the Temple in Jerusalem, with a menorah most notably visible.

Palatine Hill

Access is from the Roman Forum or from Via di San Gregorio, near the Colosseum • Daily: Mid-Feb to mid-March 8.30am–5pm; mid- to end March 8.30am–5.30pm; April–Aug 8.30am–7.15pm; Sept 8.30am–7pm; Oct 8.30am–6.30pm; Nov to mid-Feb 8.30am–4.30pm; last entry 1hr before closing • €12 combined ticket with Colosseum (p.72) & Forum (p.77); valid for 2 days; free last Sun of the month • ⓦ coopculture.it • Metro Colosseo

From the Arch of Titus the uphill path takes you to the **Palatine Hill**, where the city of Rome was legendarily founded by Romulus. It would become the most desirable address during the Roman Republic, and the spot where the emperors' palaces would eventually be built (indeed the hill's name gives us the word "palace"). In a way, it's a more pleasant site to tour than the Forum – larger, greener and less busy. The brick ruins that litter the hill today of course would once have been clad in coloured marble.

The path, paved with ancient stones, leads past olive trees. Bear right at the massive fallen column of Euboean marble, then make a left at the tall brick pier before turning immediately right to follow the box hedges towards the **Farnese Gardens**, one of the first private botanical gardens in Europe. Planted with roses and orange trees, and replanted in the early twentieth century to drawings of the Renaissance gardens laid out here by Cardinal Alessandro Farnese in the mid-sixteenth century, the Farnese gardens occupy what was once the Domus Tiberiana (the extension of the palace built by Tiberius). Beyond the orange trees, a terrace offers a spectacular and unmissable view over the Forum.

Skirting the hill through more beautifully recreated Renaissance gardens, with active excavations of the Domus Tiberiana on your right, you arrive at another terrace with views towards the Tiber (and a convenient vending machine in case you find yourself requiring sustenance). Continue down the staircase to where the Houses of Augustus and Livia (closed indefinitely at time of writing) are believed to have been sited and you come to the central area of the palace structures.

Domus Flavia

The **Domus Flavia**, the work of the Emperor Domitian, was built on top of large sections of the palace of Nero and occupies most of the central part of the Palatine site. It's now almost completely ruined, and you have to imagine the interplay of interior spaces, open courtyards and fountains (in the central area the hexagonal brick structure was the foundation of an elaborate fountain). Such was Domitian's terror of assassination that he had the walls of his palace clad in Cappadocian marble, whose mirror-like surface allowed him to see when anyone was approaching.

Domus Augustana

Next to the Domus Flavia are the remains of the area now called the **Domus Augustana**, a nineteenth-century label which refers to the "Augustuses" (emperors in general, not "the" Augustus in particular). In fact it is also part of the complex built by Domitian with some later additions. Some traces of surviving marble decorations can still be found, for example in the space leading to the railing which overlooks the "**Stadium**". This is also a nineteenth-century label, given to a long, sunken garden for its shape; there is no evidence it was ever used for races of any sort.

Museo Palatino

The large grey building behind the Domus Flavia houses the small but interesting **Museo Palatino**, which contains an assortment of statues, pottery and architectural fragments excavated on the Palatine during the last 150 years. The **ground floor** has finds from the early years of Rome and the original Iron Age village that predated it, with the last rooms jumping forward to the imperial age. Especially interesting in the last room is a collection of specimens of the sorts of coloured stones that once decorated the palace, with a map showing their provenance: a geological map of empire. The **first floor** displays decorations from the House of Augustus and its Temple to Apollo, as well as some exquisite marble inlay that once decorated the palace of Nero. The last room houses busts of various emperors, including Nero, Antoninus Pius, and a very young Marcus Aurelius.

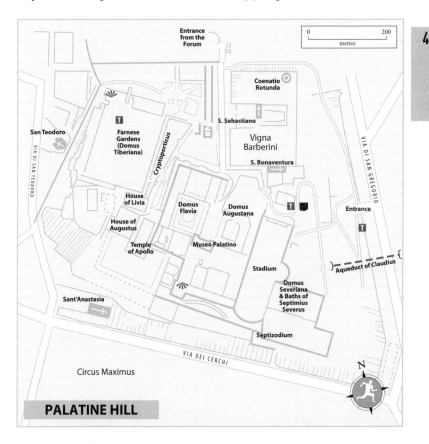

PALATINE HILL

Domus Severiana and the Septizodium

The far side of the "Stadium" garden is overlooked by the substantial remains of the **Domus Severiana**, which was built at the behest of the Emperor Septimius Severus towards the end of the second century AD – as were the adjoining **Baths of Septimius Severus** and, further to the south, the **Septizodium**. Little remains of the last two structures, but, from the site of the Septizodium (a large decorative facade built to impress visitors as they arrived in Rome), there are grand views over the Circus Maximus towards the Aventine Hill.

Vigna Barberini and Coenatio Rotunda

From the Domus Severiana head past the vending machines towards an olive grove (with the church and monastery of St Buonaventura above on your left). This path leads to the quiet space of the **Vigna Barberini** which has benches and a great view of the Colosseum. Here are the remains of a temple built by Emperor Heliogabalus in 218–222 AD and dedicated to the Syrian sun god with whom he identified. Further on, right on the corner of the Palatine and overlooking the Colosseum, you can see the base of the four-metre-thick pillar at the heart of the so-called **Coenatio Rotunda**, or Nero's rotating dining hall, which was part of the Domus Aurea (see p.76) and was said by Suetonius to "perpetually revolve, both day and night, in the manner of the celestial bodies". He went on, "the ceilings, inlaid with ivory, scattered flowers while a device of pipes sprinkled sweet oil upon the guests".

4 Circus Maximus

Free access • Metro Circo Massimo or bus to Circo Massimo

The southern side of the Palatine Hill drops down to the **Circus Maximus**, a green strip bordered by heavily trafficked roads. Once the city's main venue for chariot races, it was used for over a thousand years (with multiple rebuildings) from the period of the ancient and semi-legendary kings of Rome. At the pinnacle of Rome's power it had a capacity of up to 300,000 spectators, and if it were still intact would no doubt match the Colosseum for grandeur. As it is, a litter of stones at the Viale Aventino end is all that remains, together with a little medieval tower built by the Frangipani family at the southern end, behind a chain-link fence. The huge **obelisk** that now stands in front of the church of San Giovanni in Laterano (see p.132) – at 385 tonnes and over 30m high the largest in the world – was once the central marker of the arena, and it's known that the obelisk now in Piazza del Popolo once stood here too. The last race was held at the Circus Maximus in 549 AD, but it still retains something of its original purpose as an occasional venue for festivals, concerts and large gatherings (estimates said a million people crowded in here to celebrate Roma winning the Italian league in 2001).

Imperial Forums

Via dei Fori Imperiali • No access • Metro Colosseo or bus to Via dei Fori Imperiali

By the time the imperial era arrived, the original Forum (see p.77) was no longer large enough to serve the demands of the empire, and the city's public institutions began to spread with the construction of a series of **Imperial Forums**. Julius Caesar had begun the expansion upon his declaration as dictator in 49 BC with a new Senate building, a basilica, and a temple to Venus (his purported ancestor), which together formed the **Forum of Caesar**. After his assassination, his nephew and successor Augustus added his own forum and so did later emperors – Vespasian, Nerva and Trajan. Trajan's forum necessitated the building of the semicircular structure known as Trajan's Markets (see p.88), a sort of retaining wall for the Quirinal Hill which was partially cut away to make more room for forum building.

VIA DEI FORI IMPERIALI

Up until the 1930s, the ruins of the ancient city centre were surrounded by a warren of medieval streets. A vast **archeological park** had been created in the area in the late nineteenth century by the so-called Passeggiata Archeologica; travellers on Grand Tours could ride in their carriages past the Forum, Colosseum, Circus Maximus and Baths of Caracalla. Mussolini's enthusiasm for road-building put paid to all this, however, when in 1932 he ordered the construction of the **Via dei Fori Imperiali**, a soulless boulevard that cuts southeast from Piazza Venezia through the heart of Rome's ancient sites.

The possibility of the restoration of the archeological park is sporadically mooted, but at least strolling between the major sights is a more tranquil experience now that the Via dei Fori Imperiali has been closed to private vehicles – though for the time being the views are partially obscured by the ongoing works on Metro Line C.

Forum of Caesar

The **Forum of Caesar**, the first of the "Imperial" Forums to be built, occupies a sunken plot of ground on the south side of Via dei Fori Imperiali. The main survivors are the three columns and mini-pediment of the temple of Venus Genetrix, the Roman goddess of motherhood and mother of Aeneas, from whom Caesar claimed descent – a claim which enraged Roman republicans.

Forum of Nerva

The **Forum of Nerva** is also known as the "transitional forum" for its role in connecting the Forum of Augustus with the original Forum: Nerva's construction ran north–south under what is now Via dei Fori Imperiali. It was built by the crazed and cruel Emperor Domitian, but only finished after his murder by his successor, the elderly Emperor Nerva, who completed the Temple of Minerva and naturally dedicated the complex to himself; two columns supporting a gateway set in a stretch of wall close to the foot of Via Cavour are pretty much all that is left.

Forum of Augustus

The shattered remains of the **Forum of Augustus** date from 42 BC; the walkway linking the main boulevard with Via Alessandrina marks the boundary with the adjacent Forum of Trajan. Among a sea of broken columns, the most conspicuous remains are the monumental staircase, elevated platform and four marble columns of what was once the Temple of Mars the Avenger, put up by **Augustus** in memory of his uncle and adoptive father, Julius Caesar, after the last of his assassins had been defeated. The temple is backed by a large wall of grey stone erected to prevent fire spreading into the forums from the densely inhabited neighbourhood of Suburra which occupied the area between the fora and the slopes of the Esquiline Hill. The distinctive brick loggia round the corner to the left of the wall is the **Casa dei Cavalieri di Rodi**, a fifteenth-century structure that houses the Order of the Knights of St John – hence the red flag with a cross that's usually flown from its arcaded gallery.

Forum of Trajan and Basilica Ulpia

The **Forum of Trajan**, once an elaborate complex of monuments, apartments and shops, is today recalled by a flotilla of battered stone columns marooned in a sunken area beside the road and in front of the semicircular Trajan's Markets. These are the remains of the **Basilica Ulpia**, an immense structure, 176m long by 59m wide, which was devoted to the administration of justice. The basilica had five aisles and a huge apse at either end, but although the central nave is discernible from the large paved area behind the Column, the remains are really very scant.

Trajan's Column

Built at the very pinnacle of Roman power and prestige, **Trajan's Column** was erected to celebrate the emperor's victories in Dacia (modern Romania) in 113 AD. About 30m high, the column is covered from top to bottom with **reliefs** commemorating the highlights of the campaign with some 2500 figures carved on a series of marble drums. The **carving** on the base shows the trophies brought back and bears an inscription saying that the column was dedicated to Trajan by the Senate and People of Rome and that its height is that of the original height of the land removed to accommodate the building of the new Forum. The **statue** on the top is of St Peter, placed here by Pope Sixtus V in the late sixteenth century, and made from the bronze doors of Sant'Agnese fuori le Mura on Via Nomentana (see p.184).

Trajan's Markets

Via IV Novembre 94 · Daily 9.30am–7.30pm; last entry 1hr before closing · €14 · ☎ 06 0608, ⓦ mercatiditraiano.it · Bus to Via Nazionale

Built into the side of the Quirinal Hill – and reached via a flight of steps beside Trajan's Column – **Trajan's Markets** encompass a perfectly preserved crescent of shops, administrative offices, and arcades that don't leave as much to the imagination as many parts of the ancient city. The **great hall** by which you enter is an impressive two-storeyed space, flanked by rooms that house displays on each of the Imperial Fora. Exhibits include a large marble head of Constantine, a torso of a warrior and a cupid frieze from the Temple of Venus Genetrix in the Forum of Caesar (see p.87). Interestingly, the marble head was discovered in an old sewer and may have been thrown there during a pagan revolt against Constantine that swept Rome in 326 AD. You can descend from the hall to the cobbled, shop-lined **Via Biberatica**, which winds around the bottom of the arcade and the side of the hall, before clambering up the stairs to look at the fragments of masonry and statuary in the museum. From the belvedere at this level, there is also a great view of the Forum of Trajan down below. The uppermost section leads to a garden by the **Torre delle Milizie.**

Torre delle Milizie

Via IV Novembre

The **Torre delle Milizie**, behind Trajan's Markets, is a twelfth-century fortification, a remnant of the centuries of muddled violence which characterised the struggle for control over the city after the collapse of the Empire and throughout the Middle Ages. The top was destroyed by a blast of lightning in the fifteenth century and acquired its lean from an earthquake in 1348.

Santi Cosma e Damiano

Via dei Fori Imperiali 1 · Daily 9am–1pm & 3–7pm · Free, but €1 donation for presepio · ☎ 06 692 0441

The **Temple of Romulus** in the Roman Forum (see p.82) was converted into the entrance vestibule of the church of **Santi Cosma e Damiano** in the early sixth century. A thousand years later it underwent major modifications and is today entered from Via dei Fori Imperiali (the discreet entrance is to the left of the Forum entrance), by way of a quiet Renaissance cloister. The exquisite mosaics in the apse are among the oldest works of Christian art in the city, dating from the early sixth century. They show the two saints (and brothers) being presented to Christ by St Peter and St Paul, flanked by St Felix on the left and St Theodore on the right. You can also visit the Neapolitan **presepio** or "**Christmas crib**", displayed in a room in a corner of the cloister, a detailed piece of work with dozens of figures spread among the ruins of ancient Rome.

The Tridente and Trevi

The northern part of Rome's city centre is sometimes known as the Tridente, owing to the trident shape of the roads leading down from the apex of Piazza del Popolo – Via del Corso in the centre, Via di Ripetta to the west and Via del Babuino to the east. It comprises some of the busiest streets in the city, with a host of shopping and sights along Via del Corso and up towards Piazza di Spagna, where the Spanish Steps are a magnet for tourists and locals alike. To the south, the area around the Trevi Fountain is similarly thronged, though the fountain itself is of course well worth seeing. Most of the Tridente has heavy traffic restrictions, a welcome change for those keen to indulge in the district's main pursuits: shopping and people-watching.

5

Via del Corso

Metro Spagna or bus to Via del Corso

The central prong of the Tridente, **Via del Corso** is central Rome's main thoroughfare, linking Piazza Venezia at its southern end with Piazza del Popolo to the north. You can follow it all the way up, zigzagging in and out of the sights of the Centro Storico. The streets on the western side focus on the ancient Roman dome of the **Pantheon** (see p.35) and further north on the offices of the **Italian parliament** and Prime Minister (see p.39), while on the opposite side it gives onto the swish shopping thoroughfares that lead up to Piazza di Spagna.

Named after the races that used to take place along here throughout the Middle Ages and the Renaissance, the street has had its fair share of **famous residents** during the years: Goethe lived at no. 18 for two years, close to the Piazza del Popolo end (see p.96); the Shelleys – Percy and Mary – lived for several years in the Palazzo Vesporio, at Via del Corso 375 (now a bank), during which time they lost their son William to a fever (see p.143). Since the middle of the last century, Via del Corso has become Rome's principal **shopping** street, home to mid-range boutiques and chain stores that make it a busy stretch during the day, full of hurrying pedestrians, but a relatively dead one come the evening.

Galleria Doria Pamphilj

Via del Corso 305 • **Gallery** Daily 9am–7pm; last entry 1hr before closing; Sat 11am guided tour with Baroque music • €12, including audioguide in English; guided tours with music €30, including entrance fee • **Private apartments** Guided tours on the hour 10am–1pm & 3–6pm • €5 • ☎ 06 679 7323, ☎ 388 1975 179 (guided tours with music), ⊛ dopart.it/roma • Bus to Piazza Venezia

North from Piazza Venezia, the first building on the left of Via del Corso, the **Palazzo Doria Pamphilj**, is among the city's finest Rococo palaces, with a facade added in 1734 to a building that was the product of years of construction and remodelling dating back to Roman times, when a storehouse stood on this site. The beautiful courtyard with its citrus trees and central fountain (accessible without a ticket) is a delightful oasis away from the chaotic Via del Corso. The Doria Pamphilj family were (and are) one of Rome's most illustrious – they still own the building and live in part of it. They were also prodigious collectors of art, in particular **Prince Camillo Pamphilj**, who was the first member of the family to live here in the mid-seventeenth century. As a result, the **Galleria Doria Pamphilj** is one of Rome's best late-Renaissance art collections.

The picture gallery

The **picture gallery**, through which you're taken on the audio tour by the urbane Jonathan Pamphilj, starts in the elegant **reception hall** of the original palace, crammed with landscape paintings by the seventeenth-century French artist, Dughet. The Pamphilj pope is much in evidence (all major Roman families produced a pope), with splendid portraits of Innocent X. There's also a **ballroom** with a corner stage, from which the band played, and a small private chapel, which contains the apparently incorruptible body of the Roman martyr St Theodora, swathed in robes, and the relics of St Justin under the altar. The picture gallery proper extends around a lush courtyard, the paintings mounted in the style of the time, crammed in frame-to-frame, floor-to-ceiling. On the first corner, there's a badly cracked bust of Innocent X by **Bernini**, which the sculptor apparently replaced in a week with the more famous version at the other end of the hall, in a small room off to the left. In the same room, Velázquez's famous painting of the same man is quite different, depicting a rather irritable character regarding the viewer with impatience. "It's too real!", its subject is supposed to have exclaimed when he saw it.

The rest of the collection is just as rich in interest, and there are many works worth lingering over. These include perhaps Rome's best concentration of **Dutch and Flemish paintings**, among them a rare Italian work by Brueghel the Elder, showing a naval battle being fought outside Naples, complete with Vesuvius, Castel Nuovo and other familiar landmarks; a highly realistic portrait of two old men by Quentin **Metsys**; and a Hans

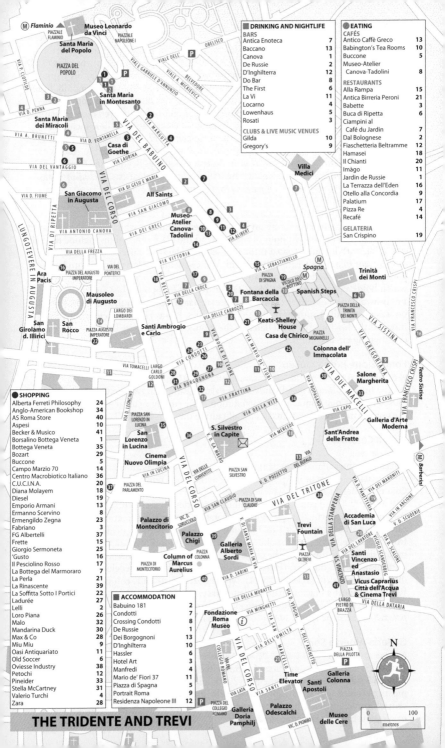

DRINKING AND NIGHTLIFE

BARS

Antica Enoteca	7
Baccano	13
Canova	1
De Russie	2
D'Inghilterra	12
Do Bar	8
The First	6
La Vi	11
Locarno	4
Lowenhaus	5
Rosati	3

CLUBS & LIVE MUSIC VENUES

Gilda	10
Gregory's	9

EATING

CAFÉS

Antico Caffè Greco	13
Babington's Tea Rooms	10
Buccone	5
Museo-Atelier Canova-Tadolini	8

RESTAURANTS

Alla Rampa	15
Antica Birreria Peroni	21
Babette	3
Buca di Ripetta	6
Ciampini al Café du Jardin	7
Dal Bolognese	2
Fiaschetteria Beltramme	12
Hamasei	18
Il Chianti	20
Imàgo	11
Jardin de Russie	1
La Terrazza dell'Eden	16
Otello alla Concordia	9
Palatium	17
Pizza Re	4
Recafé	14

GELATERIA

San Crispino	19

SHOPPING

Alberta Ferreti Philosophy	24
Anglo-American Bookshop	34
AS Roma Store	40
Aspesi	10
Becker & Musico	41
Borsalino Bottega Veneta	1
Bottega Veneta	35
Bozart	29
Buccone	5
Campo Marzio 70	14
Centro Macrobiotico Italiano	36
C.U.C.I.N.A.	20
Diana Molayem	18
Diesel	19
Emporio Armani	13
Ermanno Scervino	8
Ermenegildo Zegna	23
Fabriano	3
FG Albertelli	37
Frette	15
Giorgio Sermoneta	25
'Gusto	16
Il Pesciolino Rosso	17
La Bottega del Marmoraro	7
La Perla	21
La Rinascente	39
La Soffitta Sotto I Portici	22
Ladurée	27
Lelli	26
Loro Piana	26
Malo	32
Mandarina Duck	30
Max & Co	28
Miu Miu	9
Oasi Antiquariato	11
Old Soccer	6
Oviesse Industry	38
Petochi	12
Pineider	33
Stella McCartney	31
Valerio Turchi	4
Zara	28

ACCOMMODATION

Babuino 181	2
Condotti	7
Crossing Condotti	8
De Russie	1
Dei Borgognoni	13
D'Inghilterra	10
Hassler	4
Hotel Art	3
Manfredi	6
Mario de' Fiori 37	11
Piazza di Spagna	5
Portrait Roma	9
Residenza Napoleone III	12

THE TRIDENTE AND TREVI

5

Memling *Deposition*. There's another Metsys painting – the fabulously grotesque *Moneylenders and Their Clients* – close by Annibale **Carracci**'s wonderfully bucolic *Flight into Egypt*, one of a set of lunettes displayed here which was completed by his pupil Albani. Nearby, there's a bust of Camillo's wife, Olimpia Aldobrandini Pamphilj, from whose uncle, Cardinal Pietro Aldobrandini, much of the collection of paintings came. In the so-called Aldobrandini room, among some beautifully displayed classical statuary, busts, sarcophagi and figurines, are three paintings by **Caravaggio**. These include a tender *Repentant Magdalene* and a marvellous *Rest on the Flight into Egypt* – a truly lyrical work that shows an angel playing violin to Joseph and Mary, and so real it's actually possible to play the piece of score Joseph is holding. Beyond, the **Primitives Room** holds paintings on wood panels by Italian and Flemish artists, including Hans Memling's touching *Compassion for the Dead Christ with a Donor*.

The private apartments

Hourly guided tours take in the **private apartments**, some of which were lived in until recently, hence the family photos dotted around the place. The rooms include the **Sala del Trono**, with its stately papal throne, raised on a dais and turned to the wall, except in the event of a papal visit; the beautiful, Venice-themed **Saletta Verde**, with lagoon-green furnishings and an extravagant Murano glass chandelier; and the **Sala Azzurra**, which holds a portrait of Lady Mary Talbot, wife of Filippo Andrea and the first Englishwoman to enter the family; the spectacular gilded cot in the bedroom further on was used at the baptisms of the couple's babies. It was Filippo, incidentally, who installed the luscious Bath of Diana on the ground floor, with its Pompeii-style frescoes and inviting circular steps.

Fondazione Roma Museo

Via del Corso 320 • ☎ 06 2276 1260, ⓦ fondazioneromamuseo.it • Bus to Via del Corso

A little further along Via del Corso from Palazzo Pamphilj, **Palazzo Cipolla** holds the **Museo Fondazione Roma**, a major exhibition space run by a cultural foundation, which puts on temporary exhibitions: a dose of culture on shop-heavy Via del Corso.

Piazza Colonna

Bus to Via del Tritone

Piazza Colonna is flanked on its north side by the late sixteenth-century **Palazzo Chigi**, the official residence of the prime minister and as such not open to the public. The **Column of Marcus Aurelius**, which gives Piazza Colonna its name, was erected between 180 and 190 AD to commemorate military victories in northern Europe, and, like the column of Trajan which inspired it, is decorated with reliefs depicting scenes from the campaigns. The statue of St Paul on top was added by Sixtus V, made from bronze from the ancient doors of the church of Sant'Agnese fuori le Mura (see p.184). The square used to be the site of the city's principal coffee-roasters' market, so was always a busy spot, and it still has an elegant backdrop in the Palazzo Wedekind, home to the offices of Rome's *Il Tempo* newspaper, whose dozen or so Ionic columns, originally Roman, support a gracious balustraded terrace.

On its western side, Piazza Colonna leads through to Piazza Montecitorio and the *palazzo* of the same name, home to Italy's Chamber of Deputies (see p.38).

Galleria Alberto Sordi

Piazza Colonna • Daily 10am–10pm • ☎ 06 6919 0769, ⓦ galleriaalbertosordi.it • Metro Barberini or bus to Largo Chigi or Piazza Venezia

Across Via del Corso from Piazza Colonna, the Beaux Arts shopping arcade of **Galleria Alberto Sordi** was restored in the mid-2000s and named in memory of one of Rome's most celebrated film stars. It provides a welcome escape from this ultra-busy part of central Rome; it's also a handy short-cut to the Trevi Fountain, and there are a couple of pleasant cafés on the concourse.

San Lorenzo in Lucina

Piazza di San Lorenzo in Lucina • Daily 8am–8pm; underground tours first Sat of the month at 5pm; €2 • ☎ 06 687 1494 • Bus to Via del Tritone

The church of **San Lorenzo in Lucina**, with its manifestly ancient campanile and columned portico, stands out among the largely undistinguished buildings surrounding the **Piazza di San Lorenzo in Lucina**. It originally dates from the fifth century but was rebuilt in the twelfth. Much of the interior dates from a seventeenth-century remodelling, and there are several features of interest, not least a section of the griddle on which St Lawrence was roasted (see p.126), in the first chapel on the right – though this is almost impossible to see. A little further down, on the same side, the tomb of the French painter Nicolas Poussin is a delicate nineteenth-century marble affair by his compatriot Chateaubriand; Poussin spent much of his life in Rome and died here in 1665. Beyond, take a look at Bernini's bust of the moustachioed doctor of Innocent X, Fonseca, in the next chapel but one, and the *Crucifixion* by Guido Reni, in the apse. There are also **excavations** under the church which you can visit on the first Saturday of the month; these include parts of the original basilica, along with Roman frescoes and insulae from the second and third centuries AD.

Outside the church, the pedestrianized, triangular square of **Piazza di San Lorenzo in Lucina** is a pleasant space, less known to tourists than other more famous squares in the area; spread with café tables, it makes a nice place to stop for a coffee or a bite to eat.

Santi Ambrogio e Carlo

Via del Corso 437 • Daily 7am–7pm • ☎ 06 682 8101, ⓦ arciconfraternitasantiambrogioecarlo.it • Bus to Via del Tritone

The church of **Santi Ambrogio e Carlo** – or "San Carlo al Corso", as it's more often known – is the Milanese church in Rome, dedicated to its most famous bishop (Ambrose, who died in 397 AD) and Charles Borromeo, who was a humble and reforming archbishop of Milan around 1200 years later. The dome is one of the largest in the city and crowns a vast and highly decorative seventeenth-century church; the chapel at the back is home to a reliquary containing the heart of Charles Borromeo.

Casa di Goethe

Via del Corso 18 • Tues–Sun 10am–6pm; guided tours (in Italian) Sun at 11am • €5; tours included in price • ☎ 06 3265 0412, ⓦ casadigoethe.it • Metro Flaminio or bus to Piazzale Flaminio

A short way down Via del Corso from Piazza del Popolo, the **Casa di Goethe** is a genuinely engaging small German-run museum. There seem to be houses all over Italy that Goethe stayed in, but he did spend over two years in this one, and wrote much of his classic travelogue *Italian Journey* here – indeed, each room is decorated with a quotation from the book. Goethe had long dreamed of travelling to Italy, inspired by a journey his father made years earlier, and he came here – incognito, as Filippo Miller – in 1786, after touring the north of the country. His routine here was a **bohemian** one, associating with expat artists and writers, far removed from his life in Germany, where he was a celebrated writer. The house has been restored as a modern exhibition space and holds books, letters, prints and drawings, plus a reconstruction of his study in Vienna. Among the objects on display are Piranesi prints of public spaces in Rome, watercolours by Goethe himself and drawings by the German artist **Tischbein**, with whom he shared the house, including a lovely one of Goethe leaning out of the window over Via del Corso and a more formal painting of him reclining in the foreground of an idealized Roman *campagna* landscape. The latter inspired Andy Warhol to paint his own portrait of Goethe in 1982, which now hangs in the same room.

5

Piazza di Spagna

Metro Spagna

The area around **Piazza di Spagna** is travellers' Rome. Historically, it was the artistic quarter of the capital, and wealthy young men and women on eighteenth- and nineteenth-century Grand Tours would come here in search of the colourful and exotic. **Keats** and **Giorgio de Chirico** are just two of the many artists and writers who have lived on Piazza di Spagna; **Goethe** had lodgings on Via del Corso (see p.93); and places such as *Antico Caffè Greco* (see p.252) and *Babington's Tea Rooms* (see p.252) were the meeting-places of a local artistic and expat community for almost two centuries. Today, these institutions have been supplemented by latter-day traps for the tourist dollar, local residents are more likely to be investment bankers than artists or poets, and Via Condotti and the surrounding streets are strictly international designer territory, with some of Rome's fanciest stores. But the air of a Rome being discovered – even colonized – by foreigners persists, even if most of those hanging out on the Spanish Steps are flying-visit teenagers.

Piazza di Spagna itself underlines the area's international credentials, taking its name from the Spanish embassy, which has stood here since the seventeenth century – though, oddly enough, part of the square was once known as Piazza di Francia for the French church of **Trinità dei Monti** at the top of the Spanish Steps (see opposite). It's a long, thin straggle of a square, almost entirely enclosed by buildings, fringed by high-end clothes and jewellery shops, and normally thronged with tourists, but, for all that, it's one of the city's most appealing open spaces, especially first thing in the morning when the crowds are yet to descend.

The square centres on the distinctive, boat-shaped **Fontana della Barcaccia**, a collaboration between Pietro Bernini and his more famous son, Gianlorenzo. It is said to commemorate the great flood of Christmas Day 1598, when a barge from the Tiber was washed up on the slopes of Pincio Hill, close by.

The large **Colonna dell'Immacolata** at the southern end commemorates Pius IX's official announcement, in 1854, of the dogma of the Immaculate Conception. On 8 December (the Feast of the "Immacolata", a public holiday in Italy), the pope holds an outdoor mass by the monument.

Keats-Shelley House

Piazza di Spagna 26 • Mon–Sat 10am–1pm & 2–6pm • €5 • ☎ 06 678 4235, ⓦ keats-shelley-house.org

Facing directly onto Piazza di Spagna, opposite the Barcaccia fountain, the house where the poet John Keats died in 1821 now serves as the **Keats-Shelley House**, an archive of English-language literary and historical works and a museum of manuscripts and literary mementoes relating to the Keats circle of the early nineteenth century – namely Keats himself, Percy and Mary Shelley, and Byron (who at one time lived across the square). Its four rooms contain manuscripts, letters and the like, and various personal effects of Keats, Shelley, Byron and associates, including an ancient silver scallop-shell reliquary containing locks of Keats's, Shelley's, Milton's and Elizabeth Barrett Browning's hair and an alabaster urn with Shelley's jawbone. Keats's death mask, stored in the room in which he died from tuberculosis, captures a resigned grimace.

Keats didn't really enjoy his time in Rome, referring to it as his "**posthumous life**": he came here only under pressure from doctors and friends when, it transpired, it was already too late. He was also tormented by his love for **Fanny Brawne**, whom he had left behind in London, and he spent months in pain before he finally died, at the age of just 25, confined to the house with his artist friend Joseph Severn, to whom he remarked that he could already feel "the flowers growing over him". Keats's grave, next to Severn's, is in the Protestant Cemetery (see p.143). If you really want to get into the Romantic poet experience, there's an apartment on the third floor available to rent through the UK-based Landmark Trust (see box, 240).

Casa de Chirico

5

Piazza di Spagna 31 · Tues–Sat & the first Sun of every month 10am–1pm; closed Aug; entry by guided tour (in English) at 10am, 11am or noon; advance booking essential · €7 · ☏ 06 679 6546, ⓦ fondazionedechirico.org

Almost next door to the Keats-Shelley House, the fourth-floor **Casa de Chirico** was the home of the Greek-Italian metaphysical artist Giorgio de Chirico for thirty years, until his death in 1978, and is now a small, evocative museum. His wife, **Isa**, lived on here until 1990, when she too died, after which the apartment was donated to the city. It's kept pretty much as she left it, and it gives a fantastic glimpse into how De Chirico lived, as well as having a great many of his paintings on display.

There are works from his **classic period** in the entrance hall and first living area, including portraits of himself, often dressed up, and others of his wife, who modelled for him until he died. The chair in which he used to watch TV sits by the door, while the next-door living room is filled with paintings from his last few years, all harking back to his **proto-surrealist heyday**. Upstairs, in keeping with the untouched nature of the house, De Chirico's cell-like bedroom is left with his books and rather uncomfortable-looking single bed, while, across the hall, the video player in Isa's bedroom is marked with stickers placed there to remind her how it worked. At the end of the corridor, De Chirico's **studio**, lit by a skylight in the terrace above, holds his brushes and canvases, more books and records, a portrait of his mother and a photo of his brother, Andrea, also a writer and artist.

If you're keen to see more of De Chirico's work, it's worth visiting the Museo Carlo Bilotti in Villa Borghese (see p.175), which has some of his paintings on display.

The Spanish Steps

If you don't think you can make it to the top of the steps on foot, use the lift in the entrance of Spagna metro station, down Vicolo del Bottino

The **Spanish Steps** (Scalinata di Spagna) sweep down in a cascade of balustrades and balconies a few steps from Giorgio de Chirico's house, the hangout, during the nineteenth century, of young hopefuls waiting to be chosen as artists' models. The scene has not changed much; it is still a venue for international posing and fast pick-ups late into the summer nights. It was, in fact, a largely **French initiative** to build the steps – before their construction, the French church of Trinità dei Monti was accessible only by way of a rough path up the steep slope. After a few decades of haggling over the plans, the steps were finally laid in 1725, and now form one of the city's most distinctive attractions, built to a design, by one **Francesco de Sanctis**, that is deliberately showy, perfect for strollers to glide up and down while chatting and looking each other up and down. The steps also contain a religious message – the three flights and three landings are an allusion to the Holy Trinity.

Trinità dei Monti

Piazza della Trinità dei Monti · Tues, Wed & Fri–Sun 6.30am–8pm, Thurs 6.30am–midnight · ☏ 06 679 4179 · Metro Spagna or bus to Trinità dei Monti

At the top of the Spanish Steps is the **Trinità dei Monti**, a largely sixteenth-century church designed by **Carlo Maderno** and paid for by the French king. Its rose-coloured Baroque facade overlooks the rest of Rome from its hilltop site, and it's worth clambering up here just for the views. The church also has a couple of impressive works by Daniele da Volterra, notably a soft, beautifully composed fresco of the Assumption in the third chapel on the right, whose array of finely realized figures includes a portrait of his teacher Michelangelo (he's the greybeard on the far right); while a Deposition, across the nave in the second chapel on the left, has another ingenious arrangement, with Christ hauled down from the cross as his mother and other figures grieve below. The French seventeenth-century artist

5

Poussin considered this work, which was probably painted from a series of cartoons by Michelangelo, as the world's third-greatest painting (Raphael's *Transfiguration* was, he thought, the best).

Villa Medici

Viale della Trinità dei Monti 1 • Guided tours of the villa and gardens (in Italian, French & English) Tues–Sun, 10am, 11am, noon, 2pm, 3pm, 4.30pm, 6pm; those in English are at 11am & 3pm. Tours last 1hr 30min • €12 • ☎ 06 67611, ⓦ villamedici.it • Metro Spagna or bus to Trinità dei Monti

Walking north from the top of the Spanish Steps, you reach the sixteenth-century **Villa Medici**. This was where **Galileo** was imprisoned in the 1630s by the Vatican's Holy Office for heretically claiming that the Earth was not the centre of the universe but instead revolved around the Sun. He was forced to recant his theory and say seven penitential psalms a week. Nowadays, the **villa** is home to the French Academy, visitable on guided **tours**, and occasionally for temporary exhibition. You visit a couple of the villa's frescoed rooms, but the formal gardens are the real draw; tours take in the little **Studiolo** on the far side of the gardens, decorated by Jacopo Zucchi in the mid-sixteenth century with frescoes of lush vegetation, birds and depictions of the villa itself, and the **Gipsoteca** just beyond, full of casts of classical sculpture, while the views of the city from the villa's terrace are among the best in Rome. There's also a very comfy **café**, with lots of sofas from which to enjoy the views. The academy puts on exhibitions and concerts throughout the year; check the website for upcoming events.

Via del Babuino

Metro Spagna

Leading north from Piazza di Spagna to Piazza del Popolo, **Via del Babuino** and the narrow **Via Margutta**, where the film-maker Federico Fellini once lived, set the tone for the area, which in the 1960s was the core of a thriving arts community and home to the city's best galleries and a fair number of its artists. High rents forced out all but the most successful, and the neighbourhood now supports a prosperous trade in antiques and designer fashions. Via del Babuino – literally "Street of the Baboon" – gets its name from the statue of **Silenus** (Fontana del Babuino), which reclines about halfway down on the left. In ancient times, the wall behind was a focus for satirical graffiti, although it is now coated with graffiti-proof paint. A little further down on the left is the church of **All Saints**, the official Anglican church of Rome; its solid steeple and brick construction, erected in the late nineteenth century, serves as a further reminder of the English connections in this part of town.

Museo-Atelier Canova-Tadolini

Via del Babuino 150a • Daily 8am–midnight • ☎ 06 3211 0702, ⓦ canovatadolini.com

Right by the statue of Silenus, the **Museo-Atelier Canova-Tadolini** is really a café-restaurant (see p.252), but a highly original one, littered as it is with the sculptural work of four generations of the Tadolini family. The nineteenth-century sculptor Canova donated the building to Adam Tadolini, his most promising student, in 1818, and the family occupied the building for the next 150 years. It's one of the more intriguing spots in the area for a coffee.

Piazza del Popolo

Metro Flaminio or bus to Piazza del Popolo or Piazzale Flaminio

At the far end of Via del Babuino, the oval-shaped expanse of **Piazza del Popolo** is a dignified meeting of roads laid out in 1538 by Pope Paul III (Alessandro Farnese) to make an impressive entrance to the city; it owes its present symmetry to Valadier, who added the central fountain in 1814. The monumental **Porta del Popolo** went up in 1655, the work of Bernini, whose patron Alexander VII's Chigi family symbol – a pile of hills surmounted by a star – can clearly be seen above the main gateway. During summer, the steps around the obelisk and fountain, and the cafés on either side of the square, are popular hangouts. But the piazza's real attraction is the unbroken view it gives all the way back down Via del Corso, between the twin churches of **Santa Maria dei Miracoli** and **Santa Maria in Montesanto**, to the central columns of the Vittoriano.

Santa Maria del Popolo

Piazza del Popolo 12 • Mon–Thurs 7.15am–12.30pm & 4–7pm, Fri & Sat 7.30am–7pm, Sun 7.30am–1.30pm & 4.30–7.30pm • €1 to illuminate paintings • ☎ 06 361 0836, ⓦ santamariadelpopolo.it

On the far side of Piazza del Popolo, hard against the city walls, **Santa Maria del Popolo** holds some of the best range of Renaissance and Baroque art of any Roman church, with works by Raphael, Bramante, Pinturicchio, Sansovino and Caravaggio. It was originally erected here in 1099, over the burial place of Nero, in order to sanctify what was believed to be an evil place (the emperor's ghost had "appeared" here several times), but took its present form in the fifteenth century. Inside, there are frescoes by Pinturicchio in the first chapel of the south aisle, including a lovely *Adoration of Christ*, full of tiny details receding into the distance. Pinturicchio also did some work in the next chapel but one – the altarpiece *Madonna and Child and Saints* – and in the Bramante-designed apse, which in turn boasts two fine tombs by Andrea Sansovino.

The **Chigi chapel**, the second from the entrance in the northern aisle, was designed by **Raphael** for Agostino Chigi in 1516 (he lies in the tomb on the right, his brother Sigismondo on the left), although most of the work was actually undertaken by other artists and not finished until the seventeenth century. The odd pyramid-shaped memorials on either side have come in for lots of speculation in recent years, due to Dan Brown's fictional conspiracy theories – in *Angels & Demons*, its statues helped lead to the secretive Illuminati. Michelangelo's protégé, Sebastiano del Piombo, was responsible for the altarpiece; and two of the sculptures in the corner niches, of Daniel with the lions, on the left as you enter, and Habakkuk, diagonally opposite, are by Bernini.

However, it's two pictures by **Caravaggio**, in the left-hand Cerasi chapel of the north transept, that attract the most attention. These are typically dramatic works: one, the *Conversion of St Paul*, shows Paul and horse bathed in a beatific radiance; while the other, the *Crucifixion of St Peter*, has Peter as an aged but strong figure, dominated by the musclebound figures hoisting him up. Like his paintings in the churches of San Luigi dei Francesi and Sant'Agostino (see p.44 & p.39), both works were considered extremely risqué in their time, their heavy chiaroscuro and deliberate realism too much for the Church authorities; one contemporary critic referred to the *Conversion of St Paul*, a painting dominated by the exquisitely lit horse's hindquarters, as "an accident in a blacksmith's shop". In the middle, Carracci's boldly coloured altarpiece, with its golds and pinks, offers a massive contrast.

Museo Leonardo da Vinci

Piazza del Popolo 12 • Daily 10am–7pm • €10 • ☎ 06 361 0836, ⓦ davincithegenius.com

Next to Santa Maria del Popolo, the small **Museo Leonardo da Vinci**, focusing on Leonardo's designs and machines, is perhaps worth a look, especially if you have curious kids in tow, though the entrance fee is a bit steep and there are no Leonardo originals here at all. Full-size wooden reproductions – some interactive – have been created from sketches taken from Leonardo's codices and include the scary-looking "multi-directional gun machine" and floats designed to strap onto soldiers' feet to enable them to walk on shallow water.

5

Via di Ripetta
Bus to San Claudio or Via del Corso

Leading from Piazza del Popolo to the Centro Storico, **Via di Ripetta** was laid out by Pope Leo X to provide a straight route out of the city centre from the old river port area here. Midway along, **Piazza del Augusto Imperatore** is made up of largely Mussolini-era buildings surrounding a peaceful ring of cypresses and the giant, circular Mausoleo di Augusto.

Mausoleo di Augusto
Piazza del Augusto Imperatore • Closed for restoration at the time of writing

The massive **Mausoleo di Augusto** is the burial place of the emperor and his family. Augustus died in 14 AD, giving way to his son Tiberius, who ruled until 37 AD (the last ten years from the island of Capri), when his nephew's son Caligula took over and effectively signalled the end of the Augustan age, and the order, prosperity and expansion that defined it. As Augustus himself had it, according to Suetonius: "I found Rome built simply out of bricks: I left her clad in marble." The mausoleum was transformed into many buildings over the years, including a medieval fortress, and in 2017 its floundering long-term **restoration** was revived by sponsorship from the TIM phone company.

Ara Pacis
Lungotevere in Augusta, at Via Tomacelli • Daily 9.30am–7.30pm; last entry 1hr before closing • €11 • ☏ 06 0608, ⊕ arapacis.it • Metro Flaminio

On the west side of Piazza del Augusto Imperatore, the **Ara Pacis** or "Altar of Augustan Peace" is now enclosed in a purpose-built structure designed by the New York-based architect **Richard Meier** to replace the barely watertight structure built during the Fascist era. Its angular lines and sheer white surfaces of local travertine limestone dominate the river side of the square. A marble block enclosed by sculpted walls, the altar was built in 13 BC, probably to celebrate Augustus's victory over Spain and Gaul and the peace it heralded. Much of it had been dug up piecemeal over the years, but the bulk was uncovered in the middle of the last century, in the heart of the Campus Martius, a few hundred yards south, where it had originally stood. Putting it back together was no easy task: Fascist-era excavation involved digging down to a depth of 10m and freezing the water table, after which many other parts had to be retrieved from museums the world over, or plaster copies made.

The result, on the surrounding walls especially, is a superb example of **imperial Roman sculpture**, particularly in the victory procession itself, on the mausoleum side of the altar. This is a picture of a family at the height of its power, with little inkling of the scandal and tragedy that would afflict it in years to come. The first part of the frieze is almost completely gone, but the head of Augustus is complete, as are the figures that follow: the priests with their skullcap headgear, then, behind the figure carrying an axe, Augustus's great general, Marcus Agrippa, hooded, clutching a rolled piece of parchment, with his son Gaius pulling on his toga. Then, respectively, come Augustus's wife Livia, followed by her son (and Augustus's eventual successor) Tiberius and niece Antonia, the latter caught simply and realistically turning to her husband, Drusus, while holding the hand of her son Germanicus. Of the various other children clutching the togas of the elders, the last is thought to be the young Claudius, while the old man towards the end may be Maecenas, once Augustus's most trusted adviser. On the front of the altar is a frieze of Aeneas, whom Augustus claimed as his ancestor, making a sacrifice, while on the back is a well-preserved representation of Mother Earth bestowing peace and prosperity on Rome, holding two babies in her arms – perhaps Lucius and Gaius, Augustus's grandchildren and his intended successors. On the river side of the altar, the veiled figure is believed to be their mother, Julia, Augustus's daughter, with Lucius in front of her. Julia later married her stepbrother Tiberius and was constantly disgraced for

CLOCKWISE FROM TOP PIAZZA DEL POPOLO (P.96); TREVI FOUNTAIN (P.101); LIBRARY IN KEATS-SHELLEY HOUSE (P.94) >

5

her promiscuity about Rome; both her children died young, before they could take on the responsibility that Augustus had planned for them.

Via Sistina

Metro Spagna

Leading south from the top of the Spanish Steps to Piazza Barberini, **Via Sistina** was the first of Pope Sixtus V's planning improvements to sixteenth-century Rome, a dead-straight street designed to connect Santa Maria Maggiore to Trinità dei Monti – which it almost still does, under a variety of names – and in the other direction to Piazza del Popolo, which it never quite managed. Nowadays, it's the quickest way of getting to the Via Veneto and Quirinale areas from the Spanish Steps.

Galleria d'Arte Moderna di Roma

Via Francesco Crispi 24 • Tues–Sun 10am–6.30pm (last entry 6pm) • €7.50 • ☎ 06 060 608, ⓦ galleriaartemodernaroma.it • Metro Barberini

Not to be confused with Rome's main modern art museum (see p.176), the **Galleria d'Arte Moderna di Roma**, just off Via Sistina, is a much smaller affair – only about 150 works are on display at any one time – housed in a former Carmelite convent. Rotating pieces from the museum's 3000-strong collection of nineteenth- and twentieth-century paintings, drawings and sculptures include works by prominent Italian artists such as Giacomo Manzù, Giacomo Balla and Scipione, and there are interesting temporary exhibitions too.

Sant'Andrea delle Fratte

Via di Sant'Andrea delle Fratte 1 • Daily: summer 6.30am–noon & 4.30–7.30pm; winter 6.30am–12.30pm & 4–7pm • ☎ 06 679 3191 • Metro Spagna or bus to Via del Tritone

A hundred metres or so southwest of Via Sistina, **Sant'Andrea delle Fratte** is tucked into a tight spot – like so many churches by **Borromini**, who designed the characteristic campanile. This is another church in which the great men of the Baroque era came together: inside, the apse is flanked by two histrionic angels designed by Bernini, originally intended for the Ponte Sant'Angelo, the bridge which connects the Centro Storico and Prati. To the left of the north door, a plaque remembers **Angelica Kauffmann**, an accomplished late-eighteenth-century Swiss painter and great friend of the English artist Joshua Reynolds, who lived in Rome and was a good friend of Goethe (see p.93), while the door in the opposite aisle gives way to a very pleasant tree-filled cloister.

San Silvestro in Capite

Piazza di San Silvestro 17a • Mon–Sat 7am–7pm, Sun 9am–12.45pm & 3.30–6.30pm • ☎ 06 697 7121 • Bus to Via del Tritone

On the eastern side of Via del Corso, Piazza San Silvestro was once a busy bus terminus but is now a quieter pedestrian square, complete with benches (though distinctly lacking in shade). Nonetheless, nowhere illustrates better how history sits cheek-by-jowl with the modern world in Rome than the church of **San Silvestro in Capite**. The peaceful, plant-filled terracotta courtyard that you walk through to get in feels a million miles away from the traffic of the Corso nearby. Inside, the blackened skull of John the Baptist that gives the church the second half of its name is displayed in a small chapel that doubles as a side entrance. The church itself was at one point the centre of the Franciscan movement in Rome, home to Margherita Colonna who espoused the then left-field beliefs of St Francis and whipped up a storm in the Catholic hierarchy. These days, its interior is classic overstuffed Roman Baroque, although the dark, ancient feel suits its long and illustrious history well.

Trevi Fountain and around

5

Piazza di Trevi • Metro Barberini or bus to Via del Tritone or Via del Corso

South of San Silvestro, across Via del Tritone, a tight web of narrow, apparently aimless streets opens out onto one of Rome's more surprising sights – the **Trevi Fountain**, or Fontana di Trevi, a huge, very Baroque gush of water over statues and rocks built onto the backside of a Renaissance palace; it's fed by one of Rome's most celebrated water sources, the **Acqua Vergine**, which also surfaces at the Barcaccia Fountain in Piazza di Spagna.

There were many designs for the Trevi Fountain dating from the late fifteenth century, but work only eventually began in 1732, when **Niccolò Salvi** won a competition held by Clement XII to design the fountain. Even then it took thirty years to finish the project. Salvi died in the process: his lungs fell victim to the time he spent in the dank waterworks of the fountain. The Trevi Fountain is now, of course, the place you come to chuck in a coin if you want to guarantee your return to Rome, though you might remember Anita Ekberg throwing herself into it in *La Dolce Vita* (there are police to discourage you from doing the same thing).

In 2015–16, the fountain underwent a €2.2 million **restoration** – the most comprehensive in its history – funded by the Italian fashion house Fendi.

Santi Vincenzo ed Anastasio

Vicolo dei Modelli 73 • Daily 9am–8pm • ☎ 06 678 3098

Diagonally opposite the Trevi Fountain, the church of **Santi Vincenzo ed Anastasio** is the parish church of the Quirinale Palace, and, bizarrely, holds in marble urns the hearts and viscera of the 22 popes who used the palace as a papal residence. Two tablets – one either side of the high altar – record each of the popes whose bits and pieces lie downstairs, from Sixtus V, who died in 1590, to Leo XIII, who passed away in 1903.

Accademia di San Luca

Piazza dell'Accademia di San Luca 77 • Mon–Sat 10am–7pm • Free • ☎ 06 679 8850, ⓦ accademiasanluca.eu

A short walk from the Trevi Fountain, following Via della Stamperia towards Via del Tritone, the **Accademia di San Luca** is first and foremost Rome's school of art; it has a small collection of art and hosts regular exhibitions. The building itself is worth visiting, in any case, for its **Borromini ramp**, which spirals up from the main lobby instead of a staircase, but it's also worth a peep at the collection in the third-floor gallery, which includes a handful of sculptures by Canova, including a bust of Clement XIII and a rare self-portrait, some pieces by the nineteenth-century Danish sculptor Bertel Thorvaldsen, architectural drawings and a host of portraits of prominent academicians over the years, from Algardi and Bernini to Vanvitelli.

Vicus Caprarius - Città dell'Acqua

Vicolo del Puttarello 25 • Tues–Fri 11am–5.30pm, Sat & Sun 11am–7pm • €3; tours €6 (in English; advance booking essential) •
☎ 339 778 6192, ⓦ vicuscaprarius.com

Just around the corner from the Trevi Fountain, the so-called **Vicus Caprarius - Città dell'Acqua** holds two ancient Roman structures: one an imperial-era domus, the other a building that was at some point converted into a series of cisterns. Walkways weave among the ruins and take in a few finds from the site. The site is small and difficult to work out, but the visit doesn't take long, and it is an intriguingly different angle on this part of town, well worth the entry fee.

Galleria Colonna

Via della Pilotta 17 • Sat 9am–1.15pm; guided tours in English at noon; terrace café March–Oct Sat same hours; gardens not open to the public • €12; guided tours included in price • ☎ 06 678 4350, ⓦ galleriacolonna.it • Bus to Piazza Venezia

A short stroll south from the Trevi Fountain brings you to the **Galleria Colonna**, part of the Palazzo Colonna complex, whose gardens stretch up the hill from here, linked to

5

the palace by bridges over the narrow street. The gallery is outranked by many of Rome's other palatial collections, but it's worth visiting, not only for its small yet high-quality collection of art, but also for the glimpse it gives you of the home of one of Rome's most powerful papal families.

The so-called **Battle Column** room has two lascivious paintings of Venus and Cupid facing each other across the room – one by Bronzino on the far side, the other by Ghirlandaio – that were once considered so risqué that clothes were painted on in 1840 (they were removed during a restoration a few years ago). There are more fleshy creations by Ghirlandaio in the same room, while the ceiling paintings in the adjacent chandelier-decked **Great Hall** glorify the deeds of Marcantonio Colonna, notably his great victory against the Turks at the Battle of Lepanto. Of the paintings, the highlight is perhaps the gallery's collection of landscapes by Dughet (Poussin's brother-in-law), housed in the next room, frescoed with more scenes of the Battle of Lepanto; while other rooms remember the Colonna pope, Martin V, not least the frescoes in the **Room of the Apotheosis** which show him being received into heaven, and Pisanello's pious portrait of him in the next room. Other paintings which stand out here include Annibale Carracci's early and unusually spontaneous *Bean Eater* (though its attribution to him has since been questioned); a *Portrait of a Venetian Gentleman*, caught in a supremely confident pose by Veronese; *Narcissus* and a portrait of an old man by Tintoretto; and Bronzino's lovely *Madonna with Saints Elizabeth and John*.

Santi Apostoli

Piazza dei Santi Apostoli 51 · Daily 7am–noon & 4–7pm · ☎ 06 699 571 · Bus to Piazza Venezia

The back of Palazzo Colonna is taken up by the large church of **Santi Apostoli**, a sixth-century basilica dedicated to the apostles Philip and James. The church's ancient origins are hard to detect now, encased as it is in an eighteenth-century shell and Napoleonic facade, and completely done up with Baroque finery inside. It was once part of the Colonna estate and is a Franciscan church, thanks to the family's early embracing of the movement. Its vast interior is still looked after by the friars, who pad silently around while you take in its clash of Byzantine, Renaissance and Baroque architectural styles. The ceiling paintings are by the Genoese painter Baciccia, more famous for his work in the Gesù (see p.54), and the north aisle contains the nineteenth-century Italian sculptor Canova's first work in Rome, the very grand tomb of Clement XIV above the door to the sacristy. But the church's statue-encrusted portico is perhaps its most impressive feature, commissioned by Pope Julius II, who lived in the palace next door. Santi Apostoli overlooks the equally grandiose **Palazzo Odescalchi** opposite, which was renovated by Bernini in the 1660s. Now home to governmental offices, it is not open to the public.

Museo delle Cere

Piazza dei Santi Apostoli 68 · Daily 9am–9pm; Oct–April closes 8.30pm · €9 · ☎ 06 679 6482, ⓦ museodellecere.com · Bus to Piazza Venezia

A short walk from Piazza Venezia, the **Museo delle Cere** is either quirky or dispiriting, depending on your point of view. The museum of dusty waxworks hosts an array of characters from history and Italian culture and is unlikely to appeal to any but the greatest aficionados of the genre. It starts with the ancients – Cleopatra and Julius Caesar among them – before moving on to various titans of the war and postwar era: Hitler and Himmler; the Yalta conference threesome of Churchill, Stalin and Roosevelt (particularly unconvincing); and Mao and Khrushchev. Things lighten up a bit in other rooms, with singers Pavarotti, Andrea Bocelli and gravel-voiced rock balladeer Zucchero. Somewhat inevitably, the display concludes with a roomful of popes.

SAN CARLO ALLE QUATTRO FONTANE

The Quirinale and Via Veneto

Up above the historic centre, and across Via Nazionale from the Esquiline Hill and Monti, the Quirinale is perhaps the most appealing of the hills that rise up on the eastern side of the centre of Rome, and the first to be properly developed, when, in the seventeenth century, those who could afford it moved up here from the city centre. Nowadays, the district holds some compelling sights, namely the Palazzo del Quirinale (only open on Sundays); the Palazzo Barberini, home to some of Rome's best art; and a couple of the finest Baroque churches in the city. Via Veneto, too, is worth the stroll up from Piazza Barberini: once the capital's most celebrated urban thoroughfare, it still sports the odd hint of Sixties glamour, as well as some distinguished architecture.

Piazza Barberini

At the bottom of the Quirinal Hill, the junction of Via Sistina and the shopping street of Via del Tritone centres on the busy intersection of **Piazza Barberini**, which itself focuses on Bernini's **Fontana del Tritone** – a sea-god gushing a high jet of water from a conch shell in the centre of the square. The fountain lends a unity to the square in more ways than one: traditionally, this quarter of the city was associated with the Barberini, a family who were great patrons of Bernini, and the sculptor's works in their honour are thick on the ground around here. He finished the Tritone fountain in 1643, shortly before designing the smaller **Fontana delle Api**, otherwise known as the "Fountain of the Bees" (the bee is the Barberini family symbol), which you can see nearby at the bottom end of Via Veneto. Unlike the Tritone fountain, you could walk right past this without noticing it; it's a much smaller, quirkier work – a broad scallop shell studded with the eponymous bees.

6

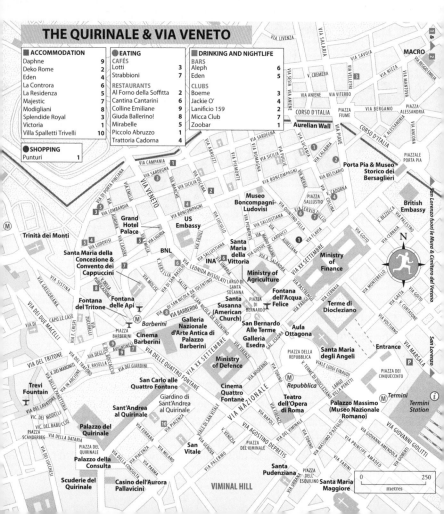

Palazzo Barberini: Galleria Nazionale d'Arte Antica

Via delle Quattro Fontane 13 • **Gallery** Tues–Sun 8.30am–7pm; last entry 1hr before closing • €7, or €9 including Palazzo Corsini (p.162); valid 3 days; free first Sun of the month • ☎ 06 32810, ⊕ barberinicorsini.org • **Apartments** Tours Tues–Fri 11.30am & 4pm, Sat 4pm; advance booking essential • €10 (also allows you entrance to Palazzo Corsini within 10 days of purchase) • ☎ 06 4201 0066 • **Mithraeum** • Tours second and fourth Sat of the month at 10am; advance booking essential • €5.50 • ☎ 06 3996 7700, ⊕ coopculture.it • Metro Barberini or bus to Via del Tritone

On the southeast side of Piazza Barberini, **Palazzo Barberini** is home to a series of apartments which were once occupied by the Barberini family and, more importantly, nowadays house the **Galleria Nazionale d'Arte Antica**, a rich patchwork of art, mainly Italian and focused on the early Renaissance to late Baroque. Perhaps the most impressive feature of the gallery is the building itself, worked on at different times by the most favoured architects of the day – Bernini, Borromini, Maderno – and the epitome of Baroque grandeur. In an impressive show of balanced commissioning, there are **two main staircases**, one by Bernini and a second by his rival Borromini, and the two couldn't be more different – the former an ordered rectangle of ascending grandeur, the latter a more playful and more organic spiral staircase. But the palace's first-floor **Salone di Cortona** is its artistic highlight, with a ceiling frescoed by Pietro da Cortona that is one of the best examples of exuberant Baroque trompe l'oeil you'll ever see: a manic rendering of the *Triumph of Divine Providence* that almost crawls down the walls to meet you. Note that on Sundays and public holidays the top-floor rooms may be closed owing to under-staffing.

Ground floor

The collection is divided into three sections, the first of which, on the **ground floor**, has the oldest works, from the medieval to the early Renaissance. Among the numerous Madonnas, highlights include the *Madonna Advocata* in Room 1, the gallery's oldest work, a panel painting dating from c.1075, and Fra' Filippo Lippi's warmly domestic *Annunciation with donors* in Room 3. In Room 7, look out for Lorenzo Lotto's *Portrait of a Youth*, a slightly off-balance painting that captures the young man's diffidence, in contrast to the self-assured subject of Bellini's *Portrait of a Man* that hangs directly above it.

First floor

The second section, on the first floor, is the core of the collection, with works taking you through the **Renaissance and Baroque eras**, and finishing up with the Salone di Cortona, magnificently empty but for a couple of seats from which to admire the ceiling. In the first rooms, look out for Piero di Cosimo's *St Mary Magdalene* (Room 10), with lovely colour and detail, and Room 11's Pietàs by Giacomo Francia. Room 12 holds Raphael's beguiling *La Fornarina*, a painting of a Trastevere baker's daughter thought to have been the artist's mistress (Raphael signs his name on the bracelet around her bicep, and relatively recent restoration revealed what is thought to be an engagement ring).

In Room 15 are Tintoretto's *Christ and the Woman taken in Adultery* and his son Domenico's *St Jerome*, as well as Titian's lively *Venus and Adonis* and Lotto's *Mystical Marriage of St Catherine*; while Room 16 brings together the collection's impressive array of **portraiture**: Bronzino's rendering of the marvellously erect Stefano Colonna, and a portrait of Henry VIII by Hans Holbein painted immediately before his marriage to his fourth wife, Anne of Cleves; Henry is depicted as a rather irritable but beautifully dressed middle-aged man – a stark contrast to the rather ascetic figure of Erasmus of Rotterdam by Quentin Matsys, which hangs nearby. Just off Room 16 is the palace's chapel, frescoed by Pietro da Cortona. In Room 17, amid the Mannerists there are two unusually small paintings by El Greco, the *Baptism of Christ* and *Adoration of the Shepherds*, thought to be sketches for larger pieces. A recently restored work by Michelangelo's student Daniele da Volterra shows David slaying Goliath. In Room 20 are three works by Caravaggio – *Narcissus, St Francis in Meditation*, and the dramatic *Judith and Holofernes*. By way of Guido Reni's portrait of tragic Beatrice Cenci in Room 24 you proceed into the Grand Salon with its extraordinary Pietro da Cortona ceiling, worth the visit in itself.

6

Top floor

Rooms 25–34 on the top floor pick up the collection by taking you from the **late Baroque era** into the eighteenth century. You begin in Room 25 with works by Neapolitan Baroque painters and their acolytes, most significantly Luca Giordano, whose marvellously realistic *Portrait of a Master Builder* has a wonderfully rough immediacy, and the Calabrian Mattia Preti, whose dark, dramatic canvases again owe a huge debt to Caravaggio. Next door in Room 26, Bernini's portrait of Urban VIII, the Barberini pope, has been rightfully reinstated in the pontiff's own palace. Room 29 displays the work of Rome's late eighteenth-century society painters: Batoni, von Maron and Mengs. Room 30 is rich in landscapes and splendid Venetian scenes by Canaletto and Guardi, while Van Wittel's Rome scenes are an interesting comparison for the sites you've been visiting: many remain entirely unchanged.

The apartments

Access to the apartments is possible by following a guided tour (see above for booking details); it takes in the eighteenth-century **apartments** on the top floor of the *palazzo*, whose sumptuous rooms were home to princess Cornelia Costanza Barberini. The apartments reflect the tastes of the time, not only in their Rococo decor, but also in their emphasis on privacy: a series of passageways for servants run behind the walls, accessed by secret doors concealed in furniture.

Barberini mithraeum

Twice a month, you can visit the **Barberini mithraeum**, a barrel-vaulted room discovered in the garden of the *palazzo* in 1936 but dating back to the second century AD. Dedicated to the cult of Mithras, it contains a vivid fresco showing the Persian god ritually slaying a bull, flanked by smaller comic-strip-style paintings telling his story.

Santa Maria della Concezione

Via Veneto 27 • **Church** Daily 7am–1pm & 3–6pm • ☎ 06 487 1185 • **Convento dei Cappuccini** Daily 9am–7pm • €8.50 (including museum) • ☎ 06 8880 3695, ⓦ cappucciniviaveneto.it

A little way up Via Veneto from Piazza Barberini, on the right, the Capuchin church of **Santa Maria della Concezione** was one of many sponsored creations of the Barberini family in the area (founded in 1626), although it's not a particularly significant building in itself, and its only real treasure is Guido Reni's androgynous *St Michael Trampling on the Devil*, in the first chapel on the right. The Devil in the picture is said to be a portrait of Innocent X, whom the artist despised, and who was apparently a sworn enemy of the Barberini family. Take a look at the tomb slab of the founder of the church, Antonio Barberini, in front of the altar, which has an inscription – "Here lies dust, ashes, nothing" – that is quite at odds with the worldly, wealthy impression you get of the Barberini elsewhere in the city.

Convento dei Cappuccini

The main reason people come to Santa Maria della Concezione is to see the **Convento dei Cappuccini**, to the right of the church, which is famously home to the **bones** of four thousand monks who died between 1528 and 1870, set into the walls of a series of six

---

VIA RASELLA

More or less opposite Palazzo Barberini, **Via Rasella** was the scene of an ambush of a Nazi military patrol in 1944 that led to one of the worst Italian wartime atrocities – the reprisal massacre of 335 innocent Romans at the Ardeatine Caves outside the city walls. A **memorial** now stands on the site of the executions, near the Via Appia Antica (see p.147), and the event is commemorated there every March 24 with a solemn ceremony; it's also documented in the Richard Burton movie *Massacre in Rome* (see p.332).

chapels – a monument to "Our Sister of Bodily Death", in the words of St Francis, that was erected in 1793. Some bones and skulls are simply piled up, but others appear in abstract or Christian patterns or as fully clothed skeletons, their faces peering out of their cowls in twisted expressions of agony. The effect lies somewhere between chilling and ludicrous, and makes for one of the more macabre and bizarre sights of Rome.

As for the **Capuchin order**, they are the most **ascetic** and extreme interpretation of the Franciscan order, dressed in roped habits and traditionally dedicated to a life of poverty. There's an attached **museum** with lots of good background on them (much of it in English), including a couple of short films, devotional items and paintings (including a *St Francis* not entirely convincingly attributed to Caravaggio) and a display on the charismatic Father Mariano of Turin, perhaps the most famous Capuchin friar of modern times, who had his own TV show until his death in 1972 and who now rests here.

Via Veneto and around

Via Vittorio Veneto, usually referred to as **Via Veneto**, bends north from Piazza Barberini up to the southern edge of the Villa Borghese, and is a cool, materialistic antidote to the murky atmosphere of the nearby Capuchin grotto. The pricey bars and restaurants lining the street were once the haunt of Rome's beautiful people, made famous by Fellini's *La Dolce Vita*, but those days are long gone, and Via Veneto is now living off **past glories**, if the *Dolce Vita*-era photos adorning the outside of *Harry's Bar*, *Café de Paris* and its other iconic establishments are anything to go by. The street has a full complement of all the posh hotel names you could possibly think of: the *Excelsior*, *Majestic*, *Imperiale* – they're all here, some more upmarket than others, though nearly all are chains. Via Veneto is also home to some interesting architecture (see box below), and is worth a wander just for that.

Museo Boncompagni-Ludovisi

Via Boncompagni 18 • Tues–Sun 9.30am – 7pm; last entry 1hr before closing • Free • ☎ 06 4282 4074, ⊕ polomusealelazio.beniculturali .it • Metro Barberini or bus to Via Veneto

A five-minute walk east from Via Veneto, the **Museo Boncompagni-Ludovisi** is a small cultural highlight of the neighbourhood, an adjunct to the Modern Art Museum in

---

VIA VENETO ARCHITECTURE

Largely home to nineteenth-century buildings, Via Veneto and Via Bissolati – which branches east about halfway up it – also sport some of the city's best and most imposing **Fascist**-era buildings, many of them the work of the Fascists' favourite architect, Marcello Piacentini. The following buildings are well worth a look.

Ministry for Economic Development Via Veneto 33, on the corner of Via Molise. A brutal Fascist-era edifice built of giant tufa blocks that set off well the bronze door panels of the main entrance, depicting musclebound scenes of industry, agriculture, commerce, transport and the like. If the doors are open, try to get a peek in the lobby, whose staircase and stained glass might well be the model for the all-powerful Ministry in Terry Gilliam's film *Brazil*.

BNL Building Via Bissolati, on the corner of Via Veneto. This brick and travertine building, designed by Piacentini, anchors the corner of Via Veneto, opposite the US embassy.

INA Building Via Bissolati 23. A giant building designed by Piacentini in the 1920s, with friezes of ships on either side of its main door. Its roof terrace served as the setting for Jep Gambardella's birthday party in one of the opening scenes of the 2014 Oscar-winner *The Great Beauty*.

Grand Hotel Palace Via Veneto 70 (⊕ millenniumhotels.com). Designed by Piacentini in 1927, this hotel's solid travertine elegance, punctuated by Art Deco lamps supported by sleek nymphets, is reminiscent of a bygone age – a feel that is emphasized in the bar inside, frescoed with scenes of the wealthy and beautiful people of 1920s Rome.

Villa Borghese (see p.176), with displays of decorative arts and fashion through the ages. Housed in a mid-nineteenth-century *palazzo*, it has a small collection of furniture, porcelain and paintings, but its main focus is **Italian fashion** on the ground floor, with an array of nineteenth- and twentieth-century cocktail and evening dresses, among other items. The frescoed walls, featuring trompe-l'oeil views of the Villa Ludovisi framed by pillars, make a charming backdrop.

6 San Carlo alle Quattro Fontane

Via del Quirinale 23 • Mon–Fri 10am–1pm & 3–6pm, Sat & Sun 10am–1pm; closed afternoons in July & Aug • ☎ 06 488 3261 • Bus to Via Nazionale and a short walk

Via delle Quattro Fontane takes a route right over the Quirinal Hill from Piazza Barberini, and at its crossroads with Via XX Settembre is the seventeenth-century landmark church of **San Carlo alle Quattro Fontane**. This was Borromini's first major solo architectural commission, and in it he displays all the ingenuity he later became known for, elegantly cramming the church into a tiny and awkwardly shaped site that occupies the same floor space as one of the piers supporting the dome inside St Peter's. Tucked in beside the church, the cloister is squeezed into a tight but elegant oblong, topped with a charming balustrade.

Outside the church are the **four fountains** that give the street and church their name, each cut into a niche in a corner of the crossroads that marks the highest point on the Quirinal Hill. Put here in 1593, they represent the Tiber and Aniene rivers and Strength and Fidelity, and make a fine (if busy) spot to look back down towards the Trinità dei Monti obelisk in one direction and the Santa Maria Maggiore obelisk in the other – all part of Sixtus V's grand city plan.

Giardino di Sant'Andrea al Quirinale

Via del Quirinale 27 • Daily 7am–sunset • Free • Bus to Via Nazionale and a short walk

The small, shaded public gardens between the churches of San Carlo alle Quattro Fontane and Sant'Andrea al Quirinale, the **Giardino di Sant'Andrea al Quirinale**, make a good place for a sit-down and a picnic lunch; they also provide a direct route down to Via Nazionale and the Esquiline area beyond. The huge black monument in the middle of the gardens, depicting two rather sinister-looking figures, was placed here in 2014 to commemorate the bicentenary of the founding of the *carabinieri*.

Sant'Andrea al Quirinale

Via del Quirinale 29 • Tues–Sat 8.30am–noon & 2.30–6pm, Sun 9am–noon & 3–6pm • Sacristy and Rooms of St Stanislaus €2 • ☎ 06 487 4565, Ⓦ santandrea.jesuiti.it • Bus to Via Nazionale and a short walk

A few steps southwest of the church of San Carlo alle Quattro Fontane, flanked on the left by gardens (see above), the domed church of **Sant'Andrea al Quirinale** is a flamboyant building that Bernini planned in a flat oval shape to fit into its wide but shallow site. Like San Carlo, it's unusual and ingenious inside, and was the project that Bernini himself was most pleased with. Its wide, elliptical nave is cleverly made into a grand space despite its relatively small size. Once you've taken this in, you can visit the **sacristy** – whose frescoes are similarly artful, with cherubs pulling aside painted drapery to let in light from mock windows – and the upstairs rooms of one **St Stanislaus Kostka**, where the Polish saint lived (and died) in 1568. The rooms have changed quite a lot since then, with paintings by the Jesuit artist Andrea Pozzo illustrating the life of the saint and a chapel focused on a disturbingly lifelike painted statue of Stanislaus lying on his deathbed.

Piazza del Quirinale and around

Bus to Via Nazionale and a short walk

Piazza del Quirinale enjoys an exceptional setting, with views stretching right across the centre of Rome. The main feature of the piazza is the huge statue of the Dioscuri, the name given to Castor and Pollux. These are massive five-metre-high Roman copies of classical **Greek statues**, showing the divine twins, sons of Zeus, who, according to legend, supported the Romans in an important battle (see p.82). The statues originally stood at the entrance to the Baths of Constantine, the ruins of which lay nearby, and were brought here by Pope Sixtus V in the early sixteenth century to embellish the square – part of the pope's attempts to dignify and beautify the city with many large, vista-laden squares and long, straight avenues. Nowadays, it forms an odd concoction with the obelisk, originally from the Mausoleum of Augustus, which tops the arrangement, and the vast shallow bowl in front, which was apparently once resident at the Roman Forum – all in all, a classic example of how Rome has recycled most of its classical debris.

6

Palazzo del Quirinale

Piazza del Quirinale • Sun 8.30am–noon; closed end June to early Sept • €10 • ☎ 06 46991, ⓦ quirinale.it • Metro Barberini or bus to Via Nazionale

Fronting onto the Piazza del Quirinale is the **Palazzo del Quirinale**, a sixteenth-century structure that was the official summer residence of the popes until Unification, when it became the **royal palace**; it's now the home of Italy's president (a largely ceremonial role). It's worth braving the security for a glimpse of the style in which popes, despots, kings and now presidents like to live, with a fine set of state rooms and some very accomplished works of art – though note the limited opening hours. On Sundays from October to June **concerts** (usually free) take place in the Pauline Chapel, broadcast live on national radio at noon; get to the chapel when it opens at 11.30am to bag a seat.

Salone dei Corazzieri and Cappella Paolina

The first and perhaps most impressive of the works in the palace is Melozzo da Forli's fifteenth-century fresco of Christ, on the staircase off the courtyard, a fragment of a work that was painted for the apse of Santi Apostoli – other pieces are in the Pinacoteca of the Vatican Museums (see p.195). Inside, the spectacular first room, the **Salone dei Corazzieri**, was partly decorated by Carlo Maderno and essentially intended to glorify the life of Paul V, with frescoes interspersing the life of Moses with scenes showing the pope greeting various foreign emissaries and ambassadors. In case you were in any doubt of Paul V's achievements, Maderno throws in monochrome representations of some of his big building projects, including the Acqua Paola at one end of the room and St Peter's and the Quirinale itself at the other end. You can't always enter Maderno's **Cappella Paolina**, through the next door, though it's no great loss: its dimensions are precisely the same as the Sistine Chapel but it couldn't be more different, studded with a tasteless decorative ceiling, its walls covered in colourless nineteenth-century representations of the Apostles.

Salone del Balcone and beyond

More grand rooms follow: the **Salone del Balcone** was where Pius IX gave his blessing on his election as pope; and the next room contains a copy of Raphael's *John the Baptist* by Giulio Romano. The three rooms beyond used to be one enormously long space but were remodelled during Napoleon's occupation of the place; even now, they cut quite a dash, frescoed under the direction of Pietro da Cortona in 1656 to a commission by Pope Alexander VII, with big biblical events depicted in accomplished and naturalistic style by a variety of artists, culminating in a dazzling *Adoration of the Shepherds* by Carlo Maratta. The final rooms are largely decorated in the style of the Savoy kings, who took over the palace in the nineteenth century, but the last room you see, the **Salone delle Feste** – originally the Sala Regia, where Paul V received foreign dignitaries – still packs quite a punch, its ceiling massively higher than the others at 16m, and decorated with Agostino Tassi's pseudo-oriental perspectives.

Scuderie del Quirinale

Via XXIV Maggio 16 • Opening times vary but usually Mon–Thurs & Sun 10am–8pm, Fri & Sat 10am–10.30pm • Exhibitions usually around €10 • ☎ 06 3996 7500, Ⓦ scuderiequirinale.it

The eighteenth-century **Scuderie del Quirinale** faces the Palazzo del Quirinale from across the square, completing the triangle of buildings that make up the piazza. Originally the papal stables, it has been imaginatively restored as display space for temporary exhibitions which are almost unfailingly excellent. The equestrian spiral staircase that winds up to the main exhibition rooms is impressive, and the modern glass staircase added to the side of the building offers by far the best view over Rome from the Quirinale. There's also a decent restaurant and café, and an excellent art bookshop on the ground floor.

6

Casino dell'Aurora Pallavicini

Via XXIV Maggio 43 • Casino open first day of the month 10am–noon & 3–5pm; closed Jan • Free • ☎ 06 8346 7000, Ⓦ casinoaurorapallavicini.it • Bus to Via Nazionale

Opposite the Scuderie del Quirinale, the **Palazzo Pallavicini-Rospigliosi** was originally commissioned by Cardinal Scipione Borghese in 1603, on the site of the Baths of Constantine, specifically to be near the papal action at the Palazzo del Quirinale. There's a decent collection of Baroque painting in the gallery inside, but this can only be visited in large groups and by appointment; the only part of the palace you can turn up unannounced to see is the **Casino dell'Aurora Pallavicini**, and this only once a month. The Casino is attached to the gardens on the left, where you can admire the Roman sarcophagi that frieze the facade, which is wonderfully well preserved and full of tangled figures and exotic animals. It's a theme that is continued inside, with depictions of Roman triumphs at each end. However, the main focus is Guido Reni's ceiling fresco, *Aurora Scattering Flowers before the Sun* – a typically accomplished and smooth work, but somehow lacking in drama. In each corner, the poised and bucolic scenes of each season provide a nice counterpoint.

Via XX Settembre

Bus to Via XX Settembre

Via XX Settembre spears out towards the **Aurelian Wall** – the city walls (see box, p.147) – from Via del Quirinale. It's not Rome's most appealing thoroughfare by any means, flanked as it is by the deliberately faceless bureaucracies of the national government, erected after Unification in anticipation of Rome's ascension as a new world capital. It was, however, the route by which Italian troops entered the city on September 20, 1870, after the French troops defending the city had withdrawn; the place where they breached the wall is marked with a column.

Santa Susanna

Via XX Settembre 15 • ☎ 06 4201 4554, Ⓦ santasusanna.org

Halfway up Via XX Settembre and just north of Piazza della Repubblica is the church of **Santa Susanna**, the headquarters of **American Catholics in Rome**. One of an elegant cluster of facades, the church is a prominent landmark, although behind its well-proportioned Carlo Maderno frontage it's not an especially notable building in itself, except for some bright and soothing frescoes.

Fontana dell'Acqua Felice

Via XX Settembre

Santa Susanna looks across the busy junction to the **Fontana dell'Acqua Felice**, which is playfully fronted by four basking lions, and focuses on a massive, bearded figure of Moses in the central one of three arches. Marking the end of the Acqua Felice aqueduct, the fountain forms part of Pope Sixtus V's late sixteenth-century attempts to spruce up the city centre with large-scale public works.

San Bernardo alle Terme

Via Torino 94 • Daily 6.30am–noon & 4–7pm • ☎ 06 488 2122

Opposite Santa Susanna and the Fontana dell'Acqua Felice, the church of **San Bernardo alle Terme** is so named (from *terme* – baths or springs) for the fact that it was once part of the vast, late third-century complex of Diocletian's baths (which extended as far as the platforms of Termini station), and with its coffered ceiling and roof light, it's like a mini-Pantheon inside, although it is highly restored.

Santa Maria della Vittoria

Via XX Settembre 17 • Mon–Sat 8.30am–noon & 3.30–6pm, Sun 3.30–6pm • ☎ 06 4274 0571

Immediately opposite the Fontana dell'Acqua Felice, the church of **Santa Maria della Vittoria** was, like Santa Susanna, built by Carlo Maderno. Its interior is one of the most elaborate examples of Baroque decoration in Rome: the ceiling and walls are pitted with carvings, and statues are crammed into remote corners as in an overstuffed attic. The church's best-known feature, Bernini's carving of the *Ecstasy of St Teresa*, the centrepiece of the sepulchral **chapel of Cardinal Cornaro**, set the tone for the church's later decorations with its dramatic representation of **St Teresa of Avila** in the throes of a divine visitation. She is shown in a niche bathed in gilded light as members of the Cornaro family look on from theatre-boxes on either side of the chapel. St Teresa is one of the Catholic Church's most enduring mystics, and Bernini records the moment when, in 1537, she had a vision of an angel piercing her heart with a dart. St Teresa's ecstasy verges on the worldly as she lies back in groaning submission beneath a mass of dishevelled garments and drapery.

British Embassy

Via XX Settembre 80a • ☎ 06 4220 0001

At the northeast end of Via XX Settembre, the **British Embassy** building cuts quite a dash behind its high security-controlled gates and fences, a striking modern statement amid the neighbourhood's heavy nineteenth-century *palazzi*. The previous building was destroyed by a terrorist bomb in 1946, and the diplomats were forced to camp out for a couple of decades at the Villa Wolkonsky (the official residence of the Ambassador), near San Giovanni. The new building right next to Michelangelo's **Porta Pia** (see below) was designed with characteristic panache by Sir Basil Spence and opened in 1971. It is set on **stilts** above a courtyard and pool complete with a Henry Moore sculpture, though sadly, you'll be lucky to get more than a passing glimpse given the heavy military presence outside.

Porta Pia

Marking the northern end of Via XX Settembre, the **Porta Pia** was one of the last works of Michelangelo, erected under Pope Pius IV in 1561, and one of the major remaining gates in the third-century AD **Aurelian Wall** (see box, p.147) – constructed by the emperor of the same name in 275 AD to protect the city from attack. Only the interior facade follows Michelangelo's design; the exterior facade is nineteenth-century. The gate is where the walls of the city were breached on September 20, 1870. This marked the definitive end of the Papal States, and Rome became the capital of the new Italian state.

Museo Storico dei Bersaglieri

Piazzale di Porta Pia 2 • Closed indefinitely for restoration at time of writing; access is currently by appointment only (✉ museo _bersaglieri@esercito.difesa.it) • Free • ☎ 06 486 723

The Porta Pia houses the small **Museo Storico dei Bersaglieri**, dedicated to a crack squad of troops founded in 1836 (they're the ones with the large floppy feathers in their hats) and with displays on the founder, Alessandro La Marmora, along with sections on the Unification struggle, World War II and other conflicts.

Monti, Termini and the Esquiline

Immediately north of the Colosseum, the Esquiline is the highest and largest of the city's seven hills, an area of vineyards and olive groves that was one of the most fashionable residential quarters of ancient Rome. These days it's somewhat scruffier, home to Termini station and the bulk of Rome's budget hotels. The busy artery of Via Cavour heads downhill from here to Monti, one of the city centre's most appealing corners, with grocery stores and restorers' workshops, as well as buzzy bars and cool boutiques. It's an atmospheric neighbourhood that rewards aimless strolling, but there are plenty of engaging sights in the area too, not least the the fabulous Basilicas of Santa Maria Maggiore and Santa Prassede, and the splendid museum at Palazzo Massimo. East of Termini, San Lorenzo is the city's student district, low-key by day, buzzing at night.

Monti

Metro Cavour or bus to Via Cavour or Via Nazionale

Between the busy thoroughfares of Via Cavour and Via Nazionale, and up as far as the church of Santa Maria Maggiore, lies the small district of **Monti**. Once the ancient city's slum area, it's now an atmospheric, lively quarter centred on Piazza Madonna dei Monti and the narrow streets radiating out from it.

Piazza Madonna dei Monti

Monti's social centre is **Piazza Madonna dei Monti**, a small, vibrant open space at the end of Via dei Serpenti and Via del Boschetto. The architect **Giacomo della Porta** designed the fountain in the centre, where, legend has it, heathen girls and boys were once brought to be baptized into the Catholic Church. It makes a nice spot for a drink or something to eat, whether you're exploring the neighbourhood or not; indeed, it has the advantage of being just five minutes' walk from the Colosseum and is an atmospheric place at night when it's crammed with people hanging out and drinking.

7

Madonna dei Monti

Via della Madonna dei Monti 41 • Daily 7.30am–10pm • ☎ 06 485 531

The large building next to the Piazza Madonna dei Monti, at the bottom of Via dei Serpenti, is the church of the **Madonna dei Monti**, built in 1580 on the site of a convent, where a miraculous image of the Virgin was found. Its high dome and generous proportions make it well worth a peep; the church is the work of Giacomo della Porta, designer of the fountain in the piazza.

San Pietro in Vincoli

Piazza di San Pietro in Vincoli 4a • Daily 8am–12.30pm & 3–7pm; closes 6pm Oct–March • ☎ 06 9784 4952 • Metro Cavour or bus to Via Cavour

At the bottom end of Via Cavour, steps lead from the street's southern side up to the tranquil piazza in front of the church of **San Pietro in Vincoli**, one of Rome's most delightfully plain places of worship, built to house an important relic – the two sets of chains (*vincoli*) that held St Peter when he was in jail in Jerusalem and in Rome, which later miraculously joined together. The chains of St Peter can still be seen in the *confessio* beneath the high altar, in a beautiful gold and rock crystal reliquary. During the papacy of Sixtus IV, the church was the cardinal seat of the pope's nephew, Giuliano della Rovere; he in turn became Pope Julius II, the patron who commissioned Michelangelo to paint the ceiling of the Sistine Chapel.

Tomb of Pope Julius

Most people come to the church of San Pietro in Vincoli for the **tomb of Pope Julius II** at the far end of the southern aisle, which occupied **Michelangelo** on and off for much of his career. Michelangelo reluctantly gave it up to paint the Sistine Chapel, and was never able to return to it for very long, being always at the beck and call of successive popes, who understandably had little interest in promoting the glory of one of their predecessors. Michelangelo's intended design was to be much larger; the final, abbreviated version was finished after his death. The only statue certain to have been completed by him is the splendid *Moses*. Unfinished statues of male nudes, usually referred to as the "Slaves", are today to be found at the Accademia Gallery in Florence and the Louvre in Paris.

Moses, shown after he descended from Sinai to find the Israelites worshipping the golden calf, is one of the artist's most captivating works, and the rest of the composition – completed by later artists – seems dull and static by comparison. Following medieval tradition, Michelangelo shows Moses with **horns** (a medieval mistranslation of the "radiance of the Lord" that Exodus tells us shone around his head). Nonetheless, this powerful statue is so lifelike that Michelangelo is alleged to have struck its knee with his hammer and shouted, "Speak, damn you!" The rest of the group was finished by Michelangelo's **pupils**, while the statue of Julius II at the top, by Maso del Bosco,

MONTI, TERMINI AND THE ESQUILINE

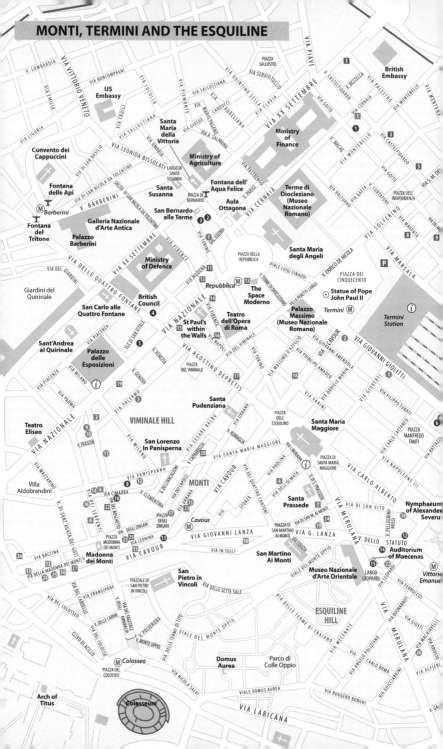

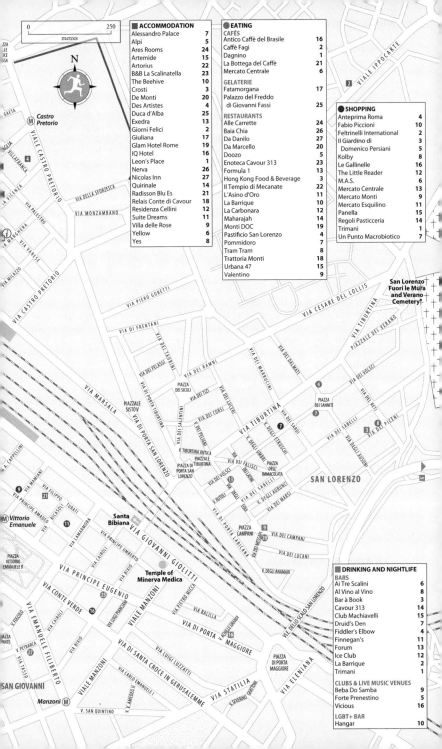

0	250
metres	

N

Castro Pretorio Ⓜ

■ ACCOMMODATION
Alessandro Palace	7
Alpi	5
Ares Rooms	24
Artemide	15
Artorius	22
B&B La Scalinatella	23
The Beehive	10
Crosti	3
De Monti	20
Des Artistes	4
Duca d'Alba	25
Exedra	13
Giorni Felici	2
Giuliana	17
Glam Hotel Rome	19
IQ Hotel	16
Leon's Place	1
Nerva	26
Nicolas Inn	27
Quirinale	14
Radisson Blu Es	21
Relais Conte di Cavour	18
Residenza Cellini	12
Suite Dreams	11
Villa delle Rose	9
Yellow	6
Yes	8

■ EATING
CAFÉS
Antico Caffè del Brasile	16
Caffè Fagi	2
Dagnino	1
La Bottega del Caffè	21
Mercato Centrale	6

GELATERIE
Fatamorgana	17
Palazzo del Freddo di Giovanni Fassi	25

RESTAURANTS
Alle Carrette	24
Baia Chia	26
Da Danilo	27
Da Marcello	20
Doozo	5
Enoteca Cavour 313	23
Formula 1	13
Hong Kong Food & Beverage	3
Il Tempio di Mecenate	22
L'Asino d'Oro	11
La Barrique	10
La Carbonara	12
Maharajah	14
Monti DOC	19
Pastificio San Lorenzo	4
Pommidoro	7
Tram Tram	8
Trattoria Monti	18
Urbana 47	15
Valentino	9

● SHOPPING
Anteprima Roma	4
Fabio Piccioni	10
Feltrinelli International	2
Il Giardino di Domenico Persiani	3
Kolby	8
Le Gallinelle	16
The Little Reader	12
M.A.S.	6
Mercato Centrale	13
Mercato Monti	9
Mercato Esquilino	11
Panella	15
Regoli Pasticceria	14
Trimani	1
Un Punto Macrobiotico	7

San Lorenzo Fuori le Mura and Verano Cemetery

SAN LORENZO

Vittorio Emanuele Ⓜ

Santa Bibiana

Temple of Minerva Medica

SAN GIOVANNI

Manzoni Ⓜ

■ DRINKING AND NIGHTLIFE
BARS
Ai Tre Scalini	6
Al Vino al Vino	8
Bar à Book	3
Cavour 313	14
Club Machiavelli	15
Druid's Den	7
Fiddler's Elbow	4
Finnegan's	11
Forum	13
Ice Club	12
La Barrique	2
Trimani	1

CLUBS & LIVE MUSIC VENUES
Beba Do Samba	9
Forte Prenestino	5
Vicious	16

LGBT+ BAR
Hangar	10

modelled on an Etruscan coffin lid, sadly fails to evoke the character of this apparently active, courageous and violent man – who was in fact laid to rest at St Peter's.

North aisle and apse

During the summer months it can be a bit of a scrum to see the tomb, but it is also worth wandering around the building's less congested areas. In the north aisle, there's a seventh-century **mosaic** of St Sebastian, and to the right of the door is the tomb of the Pollaiuolo brothers, Antonio and Piero, the fifteenth-century Tuscan sculptors responsible for Sixtus IV's elaborate tomb in St Peter's (see p.193). The **frescoes** in the apse are pretty fabulous, too: three late sixteenth-century works by Giacomo Coppi that tell the story of Peter's chains.

San Lorenzo in Panisperna

Via Panisperna 90 • Usually open immediately before Mass only (Mon–Fri 7.45am, Sat 6pm, Sun 11am & 6pm) • ☎ 06 483 667

If you happen to be passing immediately before a service (note the very limited opening hours), it's worth making a brief stop at the church of **San Lorenzo in Panisperna**, north of San Pietro in Vincoli. It was traditionally where monks distributed bread and ham ("*pane e perna*") to the poor – hence the name of the street. Outside, the modern statue is of St Bridget of Sweden, who, in the fourteenth century, founded an order of nuns back in her home country, and begged here on behalf of the poor after she came to Rome. The church houses the **chapel** where St Bridget was buried before being shipped back to Sweden, and has a nice **courtyard**, along with a large fresco of the martyrdom of St Lawrence in the apse, painted by Pasquale Cati, one of Michelangelo's lesser-known pupils. Another chapel holds the grill on which it's said the saint was martyred.

Santa Pudenziana

Via Urbana 160 • Daily 8.30am–noon & 3–6pm • ☎ 06 481 4622

Just off Via Cavour, the church of **Santa Pudenziana**, down below street level, has extremely ancient origins. It was dedicated to Pudenziana, said to have been St Praxedes's sister. Tradition has it that their father Pudens harboured St Peter in his house on this site. The two relics once housed in the church – the chair that St Peter used as his throne and the table at which he said Mass – have both long gone, to the Vatican and the Lateran, respectively. But the church still has one feature of ancient origin, the superb fifth-century **apse mosaics** – the oldest Christian figurative mosaics in Rome. Despite interference during various remodellings of the church's interior, they are fluid and beautiful works, centring on a golden enthroned Christ surrounded by the Apostles – not quite all of them, you'll notice, owing to the fact that the mosaic was reduced in size when the church was restored in the sixteenth century, and they cut off one from either side. Nonetheless, the mosaic is marvellous, not least for the graphic

---

AN AUGUST SNOWFALL

Unlike the other great places of pilgrimage in Rome, Santa Maria Maggiore was not built on any special Constantinian site, but instead went up during the fifth century after the Council of Ephesus decreed the Virgin to be the Mother of God. Subsequent diffusion of the **cult of the Virgin** saw churches venerating Our Lady springing up all over the Christian world. According to legend, the Virgin Mary appeared to Pope Liberius in a dream on the night of August 4, 352 AD, telling him to build a church on the Esquiline Hill, on a spot where he would find a patch of newly fallen **snow** the next morning. The snow would outline exactly the plan of the church that should be built there in her honour – which, of course, is exactly what happened, and the first church here was called Santa Maria della Neve ("of the snow").

On August 5 each year, a special **ceremony** celebrates the miraculous snowfall: at midday Mass, white rose petals are showered on the congregation from the ceiling, and at night, the fire department operates an artificial snow machine in the piazza in front.

SIXTUS V

Although he reigned for only five years, from 1585 to 1590, **Sixtus V**'s papacy was one of Rome's most memorable. He laid out several **new streets**, notably the long, straight thoroughfare that runs from the top of Trinità dei Monti to Santa Maria Maggiore (at various points Via Sistina, Via delle Quattro Fontane and Via Depretis); he erected many of the present **obelisks** that dot the city, including those in Piazza San Pietro and Piazza San Giovanni; and he launched an attack on **bandits** in the surrounding countryside and **criminal gangs** in the city. As a priest at the time remarked: "I am in Rome after an absence of ten years, and do not recognize it, so new does all appear to me to be: monuments, streets, piazzas, fountains, aqueducts, obelisks and other wonders, all the works of Sixtus V."

Sixtus was, like Julius II, a man of action and a Franciscan friar. He was perhaps most famously responsible for the execution of Beatrice Cenci (see p.57), although his reign was also notorious for stripping the Roman Forum of its marbles and the Colosseum of its stone for St Peter's. He also demolished the Septizodium, at the southeast end of the Palatine Hill, marble from which decorated his tomb.

7

arrangement of the Apostles that remain, the expressiveness of their features, each one of which is purposefully different from the next, and the cityscape in the background.

Santa Maria Maggiore

Piazza di Santa Maria Maggiore · **Basilica** Daily 7am–6.45pm · Free · ☎ 06 6988 6800, ⓦ www.vatican.va/various/basiliche /sm_maggiore/index_en.html · **Museum** Daily 9.30am–6.30pm · €3 · ⓦ museoliberiano.net · **Loggia and apostolic palace** Daily tours 9am–6.30pm · €5 · **Domus Romana** Tours Sat 10am & Sun 4pm; book in advance · €5 · Metro Termini or bus to Via Cavour

Backing onto Via Cavour at Piazza dell'Esquilino, **Santa Maria Maggiore** is one of Rome's four papal **basilicas**, and as such is extra-territorial Vatican property. Built in the fifth century by Pope Sixtus III on the site of an earlier church, it has undergone multiple modifications and restorations but has never been completely rebuilt, and retains some of its fifth-century mosaic decoration. The facade was encased in an eighteenth-century shell during the papacy of Benedict XIV, while the campanile, the highest in Rome, was built in 1377 under Pope Gregory XI.

Santa Maria Maggiore is noted for two special **ceremonies**. The first, on August 5, remembers an unseasonal snowfall (see box opposite). The other takes place on Christmas morning, when the reliquary containing the basilica's most prized possession, part of the crib of Christ, is processed around the church and then displayed on the high altar.

The nave

The present structure dates from about 420 AD and was completed during the reign of Sixtus III, pope between 432 and 440 AD. The original building survives intact, its broad **nave** fringed on both sides with strikingly well-kept **mosaics** (binoculars help), most of which date from the time of Pope Sixtus III and recount, in comic-strip form, incidents from the Old Testament. The ceiling, which shows the arms of the Spanish Borgia popes, Calixtus III and Alexander VI, was gilded in 1493 with gold sent by Queen Isabella as part payment of a loan from Innocent VIII to finance the voyage of Columbus to the New World.

Sistine Chapel

In the right transept is the **Sistine Chapel** (the one in the Vatican is named for Pope Sixtus IV, this one for Sixtus V, who ruled a century later). Decorated with marble taken from the Roman Septizodium (see p.86), it features frescoes and reliefs portraying events from Sixtus V's reign. In the middle, a bronze baldacchino carried by four angels covers another small chapel. The chapel also contains the tomb of another zealous and reforming pope, Pius V, whose statue faces that of Sixtus; he's probably best known for excommunicating Queen Elizabeth I of England, in 1570.

Pauline Chapel

Outside the Sistine Chapel is the modest tomb slab of the Bernini family, including Gian Lorenzo himself, to the right of the sanctuary steps. Across the nave in the left transept, the sumptuous **Pauline Chapel** is home to the tombs of the Borghese pope, Paul V, on the left, and his immediate predecessor Clement VIII, opposite. The floor is decorated with the Borghese arms, an eagle and dragon, and the magnificently gilded ceiling shows glimpses of heaven. The altar, of lapis lazuli and agate, holds a Madonna and Child dating from the twelfth or thirteenth century.

The confessio and altar

Between the two chapels, the **confessio** contains a kneeling statue of Pope Pius IX, the longest-serving pope in history, and the last one to hold real power – he lost control of Rome following the invasion of the troops of Vittorio Emanuele on September 20, 1870, and retreated into the walls of the Vatican for the remaining eight years of his life. The reliquary here is said to have fragments of the crib of Christ inside, in rock crystal and silver, while the high altar, above it, houses the relics of St Matthew, among other Christian martyrs. But it's the **mosaics** of the arch that really dazzle – a vivid representation of scenes from the life of Christ – the Annunciation, the Adoration of the Magi (in which Christ is depicted not as a child, unusually, but as a king himself) plus the Massacre of the Innocents on the left and the Presentation in the Temple and Herod Receiving the Magi on the right. The central apse mosaics are later, but are no less impressive, commissioned by the late-thirteenth-century pope, Nicholas IV, and showing the Coronation of the Virgin, with angels, saints and the pope himself.

Museum

The **museum** underneath the basilica (access through the small souvenir shop on the right just inside the main entrance to the church) boasts a wide variety of relics, even by Roman standards – including a hair of the Virgin, and the arms of saints Luke and Matthew. There are also architectural drawings of the basilica, as well as the usual liturgical garments. The standout exhibit, though, is the collection of carved figures from a nativity scene, or **presepio**, by Arnolfo di Cambio – originally created in 1291 to decorate a chapel that was intended to hold the basilica's holy crib relics.

The loggia and apostolic palace

The loggia with its splendid mosaics is well worth a visit (ask when the next tour is at the museum ticket desk). The **loggia**, above the main entrance, has some magnificent mosaics showing Christ among various saints, sitting above four scenes that tell the story of the miracle of the snow: the one on the far left shows Mary appearing to Pope Liberius; the one on the far right shows the miraculous snowfall. Tours also take in the **apostolic palace** above the basilica, including the "**Room of the Popes**", which was the work of Paul V, and as a result has his insignia on every door to prove it, as well as a fabulous wooden ceiling decorated with his Borghese coat of arms. The room is so-called for its portraits of popes associated with Santa Maria Maggiore, but more interesting are the various devotional items on display, including a copy of a letter by the hand of St Peter that John Paul II had made for the basilica. Bernini's splendid **spiral staircase** next door tops it all off.

Domus Romana

As if Santa Maria Maggiore's Christian relics weren't enough, excavations under the basilica have also uncovered a large first-century AD Roman villa, the **Domus Romana**. **Tours** take in the most accessible parts, which have fragments of Roman mosaics and frescoes, including some stunning geometric work and the remains of an ancient pictorial calendar, as well as the walls and roof tiles from the original fourth-century basilica.

CLOCKWISE FROM TOP LEFT SANTA MARIA MAGGIORE (P.117); AI TRE SCALINI BAR (P.269); MOSAIC, PALAZZO MASSIMO (P.123);
FONTANA DELLE NAIADI, PIAZZA DELLA REPUBBLICA (P.122) >

Santa Prassede

Via di Santa Prassede 9a • Daily 7am–noon & 4–6.30pm; Sat & Sun opens at 8am • €1 to light the mosaics • ☎ 06 488 2456

Across the road from Santa Maria Maggiore, the ninth-century church of **Santa Prassede** occupies an ancient site where it's claimed St Praxedes harboured Christians on the run from persecution. She is said to have collected the blood and remains of the martyrs and placed them in a well where she herself was later buried; a red marble disc in the floor of the nave marks the spot. In the southern aisle, the chapel of St Zeno was built by Pope Paschal I as a **mausoleum** for his mother, Theodora, and is decorated with marvellous ninth-century mosaics that make it glitter like a jewel-encrusted box. Theodora is depicted on the left-hand arch. The chapel also contains a fragment of a column that Christ was supposedly tied to when he was scourged. In the apse are more ninth-century mosaics, showing Christ between saints Peter, Pudenziana and Zeno (on the right) and saints Paul, Praxedes and Paschal I (on the left). Note that Paschal's halo (like Theodora's) is in a rectangular form, indicating that he was alive when the mosaics were created.

San Martino ai Monti

Viale del Monte Oppio 28 • Daily 8am–noon & 4–7pm • ☎ 06 478 4701

Two minutes from Santa Prassede, the church of **San Martino ai Monti** backs onto the piazza of the same name and is another place of worship that dates back to the earliest days of Christianity. It was dedicated to St Sylvester in the sixth century, with St Martin of Tours a later addition, and incorporates an ancient Roman structure. Almost entirely rebuilt in the 1650s, the grand ceiling shows the arms of the Medici, specifically the family's last pope, Leo XI, who ruled very briefly in 1605. A series of frescoes lining the aisles depict scenes of the Roman countryside and the interiors of the old Roman basilicas of St Peter and San Giovanni before they were gussied up in their present Baroque splendour – St Peter's is at the far end of the north aisle, San Giovanni in the same aisle by the door.

Piazza Vittorio Emanuele II and around

Metro Vittorio Emanuele or bus to Via Cavour or Termini

Two minutes' walk southeast from Santa Maria Maggiore, **Piazza Vittorio Emanuele II** was the centre of a district which became known as the "*quartiere piemontese*" when this was a residential area for high-ranking civil servants in the machines of the new Italian state after Unification. The arcades of the square, certainly, recall central Turin, as do the solid palatial buildings that surround it. These days, the area is best known for its daily **market**, in two covered halls between Via Ricasoli and Via Lamarmora, one selling clothes, the other food (Mon–Sat 7am–2pm). The area is central Rome's **immigrant quarter**, with a heavy concentration of African, Middle Eastern, Indian and Chinese shops and restaurants.

Long divested of its original glamour, Piazza Vittorio retains a not unappealing shabby, down-at-heel grandeur: in summer, the grubby central park holds outdoor **film showings**, which means during the day it's full of people taking the weight off their feet and staring at giant empty screens. There's also a children's playground, and in the northeastern corner of the piazza, an eighteen-metre-high pile of Roman bricks is all that is left of a monumental public fountain known as the **Nymphaeum of Alexander Severus** (emperor from 222 to 235 AD) – a distribution point for water arriving in the city by a branch of the Acqua Claudia aqueduct and now home to a prosperous colony of cats. Have a look, too, at the **Porta Magica**, the only remnant of the seventeenth-century Villa Palombara; the doorway is flanked by two mysterious, bearded, almost Buddha-like figures and inscriptions which some claim refer to the ancient art of alchemy.

Museo Nazionale d'Arte Orientale
Via Merulana 248 • Tues–Sun 8am–7pm (last entry 6.30pm) • €6; free first Sun of the month • ☎ 06 469 7481, ⓦ museorientale
.beniculturali.it

A short walk from Piazza Vittorio, on the busy Via Merulana, the imposing Palazzo Brancaccio houses the **Museo Nazionale d'Arte Orientale** – a first-rate collection of oriental art, the best in Italy. Beginning with Marco Polo in the thirteenth century, the Italians have always had connections with the East, and the quality of this collection of Islamic, Chinese, Indian and Southeast Asian art reflects this fact – not to mention making a refreshing break from the multiple ages of Western art you are exposed to in Rome. There are finds dating back to 1500 BC from a necropolis in Pakistan; architectural fragments, artworks and jewellery from Tibet, Nepal and Pakistan; a solid collection from China, with predictable Buddhas and vases alongside curiosities such as Han dynasty figures and a large Wei dynasty Buddha with two bodhisattvas; and coins from twelfth-century Iran and northwest India.

Auditorium of Maecenas
Largo Leopardi 2 • Open to organized groups only • ☎ 06 0608

Outside the Museo Nazionale d'Arte Orientale, Largo Leopardi is home to the remains of the so-called **Auditorium of Maecenas**, the sole remnant of a villa that was home to the trusted friend and adviser of Augustus; the rest was swept up and incorporated into Nero's Domus Aurea (see p.76) long after Maecenas's death. A ramp leads down into a large room with a hemicycle of marble steps, once thought to have been seating (hence the name), but now thought to have been part of an elaborate fountain. Some fresco decorations depicting garden scenes survive, although they are inevitably damaged.

Santa Bibiana
Via Giolitti 154 • Daily 7.30–11am & 5–7.30pm • ☎ 06 466 5235

A couple of blocks northeast of Piazza Vittorio Emanuele II, right up against the train tracks, the church of **Santa Bibiana** is an inauspicious location for Bernini's first church in Rome. A rebuilding of a much older church, it incorporates a number of ancient columns, including the one at which the fifth-century martyr is supposed to have been tortured. The **statue** of the saint, however, in a niche on the high altar, is pure, theatrical Bernini, completed in 1626, and gives a hint of what was to come in his later work, most notably in the church of Santa Maria della Vittoria, on the other side of Termini station (see p.125).

Temple of Minerva Medica
Viale Manzoni 64 • No public access

Just down the train tracks from the church of Santa Bibiana, the structure usually referred to as the **Temple of Minerva Medica** (an erroneous eighteenth-century identification) is in fact the substantial ruin of a late-imperial dining hall, part of a large villa-garden complex. Visible from the railway line, it signals your arrival in Rome by train. It's not open to the public, but you can appreciate its size and structure well enough from the outside where it nestles, patiently, between the railway and tram tracks.

Via Nazionale
Metro Repubblica or bus to Via Nazionale

Following the dip between the Viminal and Quirinal hills, **Via Nazionale** connects Piazza Venezia and the centre of town with Termini station and the surrounding area. The road was laid out after Unification, and some of its buildings, such as the Palazzo delle Eposizioni and the Banca d'Italia, are characteristic examples of the Beaux Arts bombast favoured by the new Italian state. At the bottom end of the road, at the junction of Via XXIV Maggio, the palm-filled gardens of the **Villa Aldobrandini** are a pleasant respite from the traffic, high above the street and reached from the entrance on Via Mazzarino.

Palazzo delle Esposizioni

Via Nazionale 194 • Tues–Thurs & Sun 10am–8pm, Fri & Sat 10am–10.30pm; limited opening hours in Aug • Admission varies, but usually €10–12.50 • ☎ 06 3996 7500, ⓦ palazzoesposizioni.it

About halfway along Via Nazionale, the imposing **Palazzo delle Esposizioni** was designed in 1883 by Pio Piacentini (father of the more famous Marcello, the favoured architect of Mussolini) and now hosts regular large-scale exhibitions and cultural events. It also houses a cinema, an excellent art and design bookshop and a café in its basement.

St Paul's within the Walls

Via Napoli 58, at Via Nazionale • Mon–Fri 9.30am–4.30pm • ☎ 06 488 3339, ⓦ stpaulsrome.it

The American Episcopal church of **St Paul's within the Walls** was the first non-Catholic church to be built inside the walls of the city after the Unification of Italy in 1870 and is a peaceful and spiritual haven after the humdrum bustle of Via Nazionale. Dating from 1879, it was built in a neo-Gothic style by the British architect George Edmund Street (architect of the Royal Courts of Justice in London) and is worth a quick peek inside for its works by **English artists**. The leaf-pattern ceramic tiles that line the walls of each side of the nave were designed by William Morris, while the apse mosaics, by the Pre-Raphaelite artist Edward Burne-Jones, depict one of the church's founders, the American financier J.P. Morgan, as St Paul, alongside his family, Garibaldi, General Ulysses Grant and Abraham Lincoln. The 1913 mosaics on the western wall are by George Breck, director of the American Academy at the time.

Piazza della Repubblica and around

Metro Repubblica or bus to Via Nazionale

At the top of Via Nazionale, **Piazza della Repubblica** (formerly Piazza Esedra) is typical of Rome's nineteenth-century regeneration, a stern and dignified semicircle of buildings tracing the footprint of the caldarium of the Baths of Diocletian, the remains of which lie beneath. Once rather dilapidated, it is now – with the help of the stylish *Hotel Exedra* and Rome's second branch of Eataly (see box, p.144) – once again resurgent. The arcades make a fine place to stroll, despite the traffic, which roars ceaselessly around the Fontana delle Naiadi's languishing nymphs and sea monsters.

Santa Maria degli Angeli

Piazza della Repubblica • Mon–Sat 7am–6.30pm, Sun 7am–7.30pm • ☎ 06 488 0812

If Piazza della Repubblica follows the semicircular outline of part of the Baths of Diocletian, completed in 306 AD, more tangible remains lie across the piazza, converted into the church of **Santa Maria degli Angeli**. The space gives the best impression of the size and grandeur of Diocletian's bath complex. It's a huge, open building, with an interior standardized by Vanvitelli into a rich eighteenth-century confection after a couple of centuries of piecemeal adaptation (started by an aged Michelangelo). The pink **granite pillars** – at 3m in diameter the largest in Rome – are original, imported from Egypt, and the main transept formed the main hall of the baths; only the crescent shape of the facade remains from the original caldarium (it had previously been hidden by a newer facing). The **meridian** that strikes diagonally across the floor in the south transept, flanked by representations of the twelve signs of the zodiac, was until 1846 the regulator of time for Romans (now a cannon is fired daily at noon from the Janiculum Hill).

Aula Ottagona

Via Giuseppe Romita 8 • Open during temporary exhibitions only

To the left of Santa Maria degli Angeli as you look at it is another remnant of Diocletian's bath complex, the **Aula Ottagona** (Octagonal Hall), formerly a planetarium and now part of the Museo delle Terme di Diocleziano (see below). The large domed room contains marble statues taken from the baths of Caracalla and Diocletian, and two remarkable statues of a boxer and athlete from the Quirinal Hill. Excavations underground – accessible by stairs – show the furnaces for heating water for the baths and the foundations of another building from the time of Diocletian.

Terme di Diocleziano

Via Enrico di Nicola 79 • Tues–Sun 9am–7.30pm; last entry 1hr before closing • €8 combined ticket with Palazzo Altemps (p.39), Crypta Balbi (p.55) & Palazzo Massimo (below); valid for 3 days; free first Sun of the month • ☎ 06 3996 7700, ⓦ archeoroma.beniculturali.it

The buildings that surround Santa Maria degli Angeli are, like the church itself, also recycled parts of Diocletian's Baths – the complex was enormous, originally measuring 376m by 361m – and include the round church of San Bernardo alle Terme, off Via XX Settembre, and the round building in the other direction, at the corner of Via Viminale and Via delle Terme di Diocleziano. The rest of the baths – the huge halls and courtyards on the side towards Termini – have been renovated and, together with the Carthusian monastery attached to the church, now hold the **Museo delle Terme di Diocleziano**. Especially focused on a beautifully displayed epigraphic collection, and in an extraordinary setting, the museum is part of the Museo Nazionale Romano, along with Palazzo Massimo across the street (see below), Palazzo Altemps (see p.39), and the Crypta Balbi (see p.55). The ticket is valid for all four locations over a three-day period, making it extremely good value.

The museum is fronted by a fragrant **garden**, which is open to all and centres on a large krater fountain with little cupids holding up its rim. The most evocative part of the museum is the large **cloister** of the former monastery, crammed with statuary, funerary monuments and sarcophagi and fragments from all over Rome. There's a lot to pick through, but standouts include the animal heads found in the Forum of Trajan, a fine, headless, seated statue of Hercules from the second century AD and a nice, if again damaged, statue of a husband and wife. The upstairs gallery wraps around the cloister and includes finds dating back to the seventh century BC. The downstairs section is devoted to inscriptions, beautifully displayed, with informative information panels in Italian and English. The natatio (open-air bathing pool) and the "Grande Aule" (the large halls) give the best idea of all of the scale of the original bath complex. Room X is especially interesting and houses reconstructed tomb structures; in the centre, an exquisite funerary sculpture of a boy on a horse once held the ashes of the child.

Palazzo Massimo

Largo di Villa Peretti 1 • Tues–Sun 9am–7.45pm; last entry 45min before closing • €8 combined ticket with Palazzo Altemps (p.39), Crypta Balbi (p.55) & Museo delle Terme di Diocleziano (above); valid for 3 days; free first Sun of the month • ☎ 06 3996 7700, ⓦ archeoroma .beniculturali.it

Across from Santa Maria degli Angeli, **Palazzo Massimo** is home to one of the two principal parts of the **Museo Nazionale Romano** – the other is in the Palazzo Altemps (see p.39). It's a superb collection of Greek and Roman **antiquities**.

Basement

The basement has displays of exquisite gold **jewellery** from the second century AD – necklaces, rings, brooches, all in immaculate condition – and some fine gold imperial hairnets. There's also – startlingly – the mummified remains of an eight-year-old girl, along with a fantastic **coin collection**, from the first bronze coinage of the fourth century BC to the surprisingly sophisticated coins of the Republic and imperial times, right up to the lira and concluding with a display devoted to the euro.

Ground floor

The ground floor of the museum is devoted to statues from the **early Empire**, including a gallery on the right with an unparalleled selection of unidentified busts found all over Rome. Their lack of clear identity is no barrier to appreciating them; they are amazing pieces of portraiture, and as vivid a representation of patrician Roman life as you'll find. Look out for the so-called *Statue of the Tivoli General*, the face of an old man mounted on the body of a youthful athlete – sometimes believed to be a portrait of L. Munatius Plancus, the military officer who named Octavian "Augustus" (literally "Reverend") and so officially started the cult of the emperor. At the far end of the courtyard are more busts, this time identifiable as members of the i**mperial family**: a bronze of Germanicus, a marvellous small bust of Caligula, several representations of Livia, Tiberius, Antonia and Drusus and a life-size statue of Augustus, piously dressed as the high priest of Rome with his toga covering his head. The highlights of the ground floor are the Greek bronzes of a Hellenistic prince holding a spear, from the second century BC, and a wounded boxer at rest, from a century earlier.

7

First floor

The first-floor gallery is a useful catalogue of Roman **imperial dynasties** in chronological order. The craggy determination of Vespasian and the pinched nobility of Nerva, among the busts lining the corridor, are in complete contrast to Room 2, where Trajan appears as Hercules next to his wife Plotina, opposite a bust of his cousin Hadrian, who is in turn next to his lover Antinous. These were some of the most successful years of the Empire, which continued with the reign of Antoninus Pius, shown in a heroic nude pose and in several busts, flanked by likenesses of his daughter Faustina Minor. Faustina was the wife of Antonius's successor, Marcus Aurelius, whose bust is in the corridor outside. He was succeeded by his son Commodus, whose reign would mark the end of the glory years and the beginning of a slow and inexorable decline. Further on we see the North African Severan dynasty, with the fierce-looking Caracalla gazing across, past his father Septimius Severus, to his brother Geta, whom he later murdered.

Next door we find a sleeping hermaphrodite, an almost complete Dionysus that was fished out of the Tiber, and bronzework from two imperial galleys found in southern Lazio, at Lake Nemi, dating from the time of Caligula. A balustrade from one of the galleys is studded with figures, each one different with a face on each side, handles are decorated with the faces of panthers, wolves and lions, and rudders come in the shape of forearms. On the other side of the courtyard are more astonishing pieces, this time from various imperial villas outside Rome, many of them copies of **Greek originals**, including figures of Apollo and Dionysus, an Amazon and a barbarian, full of movement and vigour, as well as more dynastic busts discovered at Hadrian's villa in Tivoli and a beautiful statue of a young girl holding a tray from Augustus's villa at Anzio.

Second floor

The second floor takes in some of the finest Roman frescoes and mosaics you'll see in Rome, and is divided into three sections. There is an exquisite room of **frescoes** from the **Villa di Livia**, depicting an orchard dense with fruit and flowers and patrolled by partridges, doves and other birds. On the same side of the courtyard are floor **mosaics** showing naturalistic scenes – sea creatures, people boating – from the so-called **Villa di Baccano** on Via Cassia, a sumptuous mansion probably owned by the imperial Severan family. Four mosaic panels taken from a bedroom, featuring four chariot drivers and their horses, are so finely crafted that from a distance they look as if they've been painted, while further on is a very rare example of *opus sectile*, an inlay technique imported from the eastern provinces in the first century AD. Pieces of coloured stones, mother-of-pearl, and glass of various sizes and shapes are used instead of tesserae, to create pictures and geometric patterns.

More mosaics decorate the corridor outside, with floors showing Nile scenes, complete with crocodiles and hippos, while others come from Anzio, including one showing a reclining Hercules holding a cup and club while a wild boar emerges from a nearby cave. The final section displays **wall paintings** rescued during the building of the Tiber embankments in the late nineteenth century from what was believed to be the riverside villa of Augustus's daughter Julia and his trusted general Agrippa, built at Trastevere for their wedding. The decoration is sumptuous in the extreme, including a room painted with garlands and an Egyptian-style frieze, and two small bedrooms (*cubiculae*) painted deep red and covered with different figures.

Termini

Behind the Palazzo Massimo is the low white facade of **Termini station** (so named for its proximity to the "Terme", the Baths of Diocletian, nothing to do with being the terminus of Rome's rail lines) and the vast, bus-crammed hubbub that is **Piazza dei Cinquecento** in front. The station is a striking building from any angle, an ambitious piece of modern architectural design, completed in 1950. There is a complex of shops and cafés both on the main concourse and in the basement, where you can also find a small section of Rome's original city wall, the **Servian Wall** (see box, p.139), next to *McDonalds*. A larger section is also visible above ground, to the left of the station's main entrance as you look at it. In front of the bus station is a five-metre-high cloaked **statue of Saint John Paul II** by Oliviero Rainaldi, unveiled in 2011 to general dismay on account of the pontiff's severe-looking face. Though reworked the following year to reveal a newly smiling pope, it remains fairly unpopular, and the sweeping cloak has been compared to a giant pissoir.

7

San Lorenzo

Tram or bus to Piazzale Tiburtino

East of Termini, and accessible on foot under the train tracks from Via Giovanni Giolitti, the district of **San Lorenzo** spreads from the tracks to the main campus of Rome's university, at the far end of Via Tiburtina. Sheltering behind a short stretch of the **Aurelian Wall** (see box, p.147), it's an originally working-class area, latterly popular with students, that retains something of the air of a local neighbourhood, quite different from the rest of the city centre. Via Tiburtina provides its main spine; it is flanked by a couple of small parks and playgrounds, off which are streets that are home to some good and often inexpensive local **restaurants** (see p.256).

Cimitero del Verano

Piazzale del Verano 1 · Daily 7.30am–7pm; Oct–March closes 6pm; last entry 1hr before closing · ☎ 06 4923 6349 · Tram or bus to Piazzale del Verano

Just past the junction of Via Tiburtina and Via Cesare de Lollis, facing a square flanked by monumental masons and flower-sellers, the **Cimitero del Verano** cemetery has been the largest **Catholic burial-place** in Rome since 1830. It's worth a visit for the grandiose tombs, such as the she-wolf-topped stone of the poet, journalist and activist **Goffredo Mameli**, just inside, on the left. A contemporary of Garibaldi, Mameli wrote the lyrics to the Italian national anthem, *Il Canto degli Italiani*, in 1847, and fought on the side of Unification forces, receiving the bayonet wound that killed him in 1849, at the age of just 22.

San Lorenzo fuori le Mura

Piazzale del Verano 3 · Daily: summer 7.30am–12.30pm & 4–8pm; winter 7.30am–12.30pm & 3.30–7pm · ☎ 06 446 6184 · Tram or bus to Piazzale del Verano

The San Lorenzo area takes its name from the church of **San Lorenzo fuori le Mura** (literally "outside the walls") on Via Tiburtina, right by the Verano cemetery. One of the seven great **pilgrimage churches** of Rome, it's a beautifully austere example of an Early Christian basilica, though it underwent a major (and successfully sympathetic) restoration after Allied bombing, aimed at the railway lines, hit the area in 1943, killing over two thousand people. Given its location, the church is often used for funerals. It is fronted by a columned portico, decorated with twelfth-century frescoes, and has a lovely twelfth-century cloister to its side. The original church was built by Constantine on the site of **St Lawrence**'s burial place. The saint was reputedly burned to death on a gridiron, halfway through his ordeal uttering the immortal words, "Turn me, I am done on this side."

Inside the church

San Lorenzo is actually a combination of three churches: one is a sixth-century reconstruction of Constantine's church by **Pope Pelagius II**, which now forms the chancel; another is a fifth-century church from the time of **Sixtus III**; and the third, joining the two, is a basilica from the thirteenth century by **Honorius II**. Inside, there are features from all periods: there's a fantastic ancient **Roman sarcophagus** by the main door; the **tomb** of one Cardinal Fieschi; a **Cosmati floor**, perhaps the city's most impressive; a thirteenth-century **pulpit**; and a **paschal candlestick** with a twisted stem.

The **baldacchino** in the choir is dated from 1147 and sits on its own colourful Cosmati floor, beyond which a thirteenth-century bishop's throne is perfectly placed to see the sixth-century mosaic on the inside of the triumphal arch – a depiction of Pope Pelagius II, St Stephen and St Lawrence offering his church to Christ (the underneath of the arch is decorated with fruit and flowers). Beneath here, in the *confessio* under the raised choir, lie the bodies of the two saints and more **mosaics**, nineteenth-century this time, adorning the tomb of Pope Pius IX. The body of the last pope to rule Rome was carried here under cover of darkness in 1881, in a procession that was disrupted by a gang of Italian nationalists who attempted to throw his corpse into the river. Turn your back on the tomb, and you'll see the stone on which St Lawrence's body is said to have been laid after his death, preserved behind glass. Finally, upstairs again, through the sacristy, is the church's small Romanesque **cloister**, one of Rome's simplest and most peaceful, with a well-tended garden and fishpond in the middle, and a fragment of a bomb remembering the bombardment of the church in World War II.

SAN CLEMENTE

The Celian Hill and San Giovanni

Immediately behind the Colosseum, the Celian Hill is the most southerly of Rome's seven hills and one of its most peaceful, with few major roads and the park of Villa Celimontana at its heart. The area just east of here is known as San Giovanni, after the basilica complex which lies at the end of the long, narrow thoroughfare of Via San Giovanni in Laterano and which was, before the creation of the separate Vatican city-state, the headquarters of the Catholic Church. It's a mixed area, mainly residential, but it has some compelling sights in the basilica of San Giovanni itself, the church of Santa Croce in Gerusalemme beyond and the amazing triple-layered church of San Clemente – all in all a worthy add-on to a morning spent at the Colosseum.

Santo Stefano Rotondo

Via di San Nicola da Tolentino 13 • **Church** July–Oct Tues–Sat 9.30am–12.30pm & 3–6pm, Sun 9.30am–12.30pm; Nov–June Tues–Sat 9.30am–12.30pm & 2–5pm, Sun 9.30am–12.30pm • ☏ 06 4211 9130, ⓦ www.santo-stefano-rotondo.it • **Mithraeum** Closed for restoration at the time of writing • Metro San Giovanni or bus to Piazza di San Giovanni in Laterano

Ten minutes' walk from the Colosseum down Via Claudia, and not on the Celian Hill proper, the round church of **Santo Stefano Rotondo** is a truly ancient structure, built in the 460s AD and consecrated by Pope Simplicius to commemorate Christianity's first martyr, St Stephen. Its four chapels form the shape of a cross in a circle, atmospherically lit by the 22 windows of the clerestory. The interior is a magnificent and moody circular space, made up of two concentric rings, but the feature that will really stick in your mind is the series of stomach-turning frescoes on the walls of the outer ring, showing various saints being martyred in different ways: impaling, drawing and quartering, disembowelment, boiling in oil, hanging, beheading – according to Charles Dickens, who visited in 1845, "such a panorama of horror and butchery no man could imagine in his sleep, though he were to eat a whole pig raw, for supper".

Underneath the church is a second-century **mithraeum** (closed for restoration at the time of writing), whose walls are covered in frescoes relating to the cult of the Persian god Mithras. The site is thought to have been chosen because of its proximity to military barracks in the neighbourhood; the cult was popular among soldiers.

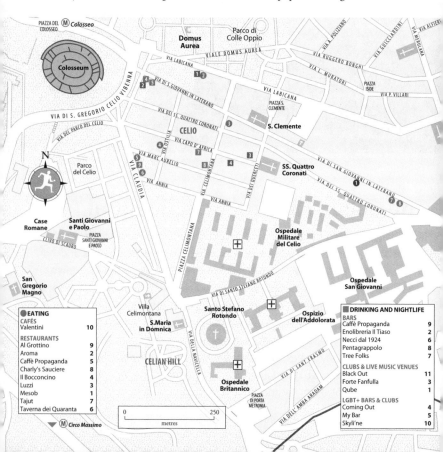

⬤EATING	
CAFÉS	
Valentini	10
RESTAURANTS	
Al Grottino	9
Aroma	2
Caffè Propaganda	5
Charly's Sauciere	8
Il Bocconcino	4
Luzzi	3
Mesob	1
Tajut	7
Taverna dei Quaranta	6

⬛ DRINKING AND NIGHTLIFE	
BARS	
Caffè Propaganda	9
Enolibreria Il Tiaso	2
Necci dal 1924	6
Pentagrappolo	8
Tree Folks	7
CLUBS & LIVE MUSIC VENUES	
Black Out	11
Forte Fanfulla	3
Qube	1
LGBT+ BARS & CLUBS	
Coming Out	4
My Bar	5
Skyli'ne	10

Santa Maria in Domnica

Piazza della Navicella 10 • Daily 9am–noon & 3.30–6pm • ☎ 06 7720 2685 • Metro San Giovanni or Circo Massimo, or bus to Piazza San Giovanni in Laterano

Across Via della Navicella from the church of Santo Stefano Rotondo, Piazza della Navicella was named after the "navicella" or Roman stone boat that sits outside the church of **Santa Maria in Domnica**. This is a bare and beautiful sixth-century church, with a sixteenth-century ceiling showing more boats – in particular Noah's Ark – and the arms of the Medici, though its most significant features by far are its apse mosaics. Above the apse, a ninth-century mosaic of Christ has some wonderfully individualized apostles and angels, while in the apse itself another mosaic shows Paschal I, who restored the church, kneeling at the feet of the Virgin.

Villa Celimontana

Access from Piazza della Navicella, next door to Santa Maria in Domnica, or from Piazza Giovanni e Paolo • Dawn–dusk • Metro San Giovanni or Circo Massimo, or bus to Circo Massimo

The shady **Villa Celimontana** park was built on the site of an ancient zoo that was home to some of the animals that were to die in the nearby arena. Nowadays, the park makes a nice spot for a picnic, with lots of leafy walkways and grassy slopes, and you could do worse than take a stroll through before moving on to the other sights of the Celian Hill.

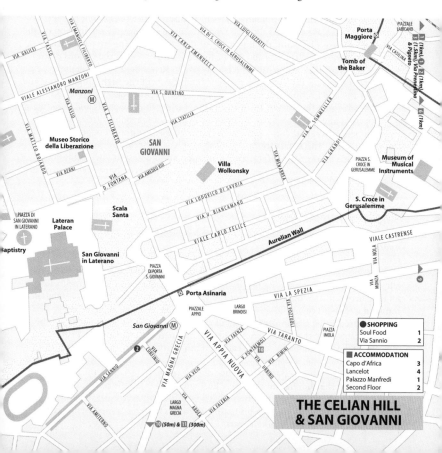

Santi Giovanni e Paolo

Piazza dei Santi Giovanni e Paolo 13 · Mon–Sat 8.30am–noon & 3.30–6pm, Sun 8.30am–12.45pm & 3.30–6pm · ☎ 06 700 5745 · Metro Circo Massimo or bus to Circo Massimo

Right outside one entrance to the Villa Celimontana park, at the Celian Hill's summit, the church of **Santi Giovanni e Paolo**, marked by its campanile studded with colourful tiles, is set in a peaceful **piazza** and is a popular location for weddings – despite the adolescent autograph hunters who occasionally throng outside the TV studios behind the gate opposite. Originally founded by a Roman senator called Pammachius, the church acts as an unofficial memorial to conscientious objection, dedicated to two dignitaries who were beheaded here in 361 AD after refusing military service. The remnants of what is believed to be their house are now open to the public in the **Case Romane** (see below). Inside the church's dark interior, thronged with chandeliers, a railed-off tablet in mid-nave marks the shrine where the saints were martyred and buried; while outside in the far corner of the square, beneath the campanile, you can see the arches of part of a **Temple of Claudius**, the remains of which extend far down the hill towards the Colosseum.

Case Romane

Clivo di Scauro · Mon & Thurs–Sun 10am–1pm & 3–6pm · €8 · ☎ 06 7045 4544, ⓦ caseromane.it · Metro Circo Massimo or bus to Circo Massimo

The excavations of the **Case Romane** (Roman Houses) under the church of Santi Giovanni e Paolo are accessed through what was once an ancient Roman shop on the picturesque Clivo di Scauro, the buttresses of the church arching over the narrow, ancient Roman street. The rise and fall of Rome is catalogued in the various phases of the residences on the site: from grand houses of the Republic, through densely populated apartment buildings for the petit bourgeoisie of the high Empire, to grand houses of the late Empire when the city's population decline was unstoppable. Highlights include the **Stanza dei Genii**, frescoed with winged youths and cupids, and the courtyard and the **Ninfeo di Proserpina**, which has a marvellous fresco of Persephone (Proserpina) and Venus sandwiched between cupids in boats, fishing and loading supplies. The **antiquarium** beautifully pulls together finds from the site, among them a *Christ with Saints* fresco, ceramics, amphorae and fascinating small domestic artefacts: an intact imperial-age spoon, a bronze reel, bone sewing needles and oil lamps.

San Gregorio Magno

Piazza di San Gregorio 1 · Daily 9am–1pm & 3.30–7pm; ring the bell marked "portineria" to gain admission · ☎ 06 700 8227 · Metro Circo Massimo or bus to Circo Massimo

Continuing down Clivo di Scauro from Santi Giovanni e Paolo and the Case Romane under a succession of brick arches leads to the church of **San Gregorio Magno** on the left. It occupies a commanding position above the roar of traffic on the road below, looking across to the umbrella pines of the Palatine Hill opposite. **St Gregory the Great** founded a monastery on the site, and was a monk before becoming pope in 590 AD. Stabilizing Rome after the fall of the empire, he effectively established the powerful papal role that would endure for the best part of the following 1500 years; he also despatched St Augustine in the early seventh century to convert England to Christianity.

Today's rather ordinary Baroque **interior** doesn't really do justice to the historical importance of the church, but the lovely **Cosmati floor** remains intact, and the chapel of the saint at the end of the south aisle has a beautifully carved bath showing scenes from St Gregory's life along with his marble throne, a beaten-up specimen that actually predates the saint by five hundred years.

Sant'Andrea, Santa Barbara and Santa Silvia

Piazza di San Gregorio 2 • Guided tours available Tues, Thurs, Sat & Sun 9.30am–12.30pm; advance booking essential • Free • ☎ 06 7049 4966

Just to the left of the church entrance, on the site of the original monastery, stand a church and two chapels surrounded by cypress trees. The church of **Sant'Andrea**, in the middle, contains two large frescoes narrating the martyrdom of the saint – one, by Domenichino, a busy, vibrant piece showing a grey-bearded Andrew at the mercy of brutal soldiers, and a second by Guido Reni depicting *St Andrew with Sts Peter and Paul*. Either side of Sant'Andrea are the chapels of **Santa Barbara** and **Santa Silvia**, both filled with more frescoes, the former in particular covered with scenes of Gregory the Great, and containing the table at which St Gregory is said to have fed twelve paupers daily with his own hands for years.

Missionario della Carità

Piazza di San Gregorio 2 • Tues-Fri 9–11.30am & 4.30–6.30pm • Free

Across the garden from the church of Sant'Andrea is the Rome headquarters of the organization founded by St Theresa of Calcutta (her bust stands in front of San Gregorio Magno, a gift from the Indian government). A whitewashed and peaceful haven located in the former chicken-houses of the San Gregorio monastery since the 1970s, the **Missionario della Carità** houses around thirty women. They're a busy group, among other things looking after the hostel for the needy next door to the main church. But there are usually novices to show you the simple chapel in which they gather every morning at 5am, and of course the small room that Mother Theresa occupied on her frequent visits to Rome, with its tiny bed and other effects – her plate and cutlery, prayerbooks and items of clothing, along with a reliquary containing a piece of tissue stained with her blood.

8

Santi Quattro Coronati

Piazza dei Santi Quattro Coronati 20 • Mon–Sat 10–11.45am & 4–5.45pm; Aula Gotica open for twice-monthly tours (check website for dates) • Church free; cloister and San Silvestro chapel donation expected; Aula Gotica tours €10 • ☎ 06 7047 5427, ⓦ aulagoticasantiquattrocoronati.it • Metro Colosseo or Manzoni, or bus to Via Labicana

Between San Giovanni in Laterano and the Colosseum, the church of **Santi Quattro Coronati**, up the steps off Via dei Santi Quattro Coronati, is dedicated to four soldier martyrs who died because they refused to worship a statue of Asclepius during the persecutions of Diocletian. Originally built in 1110 by Pope Paschal II, it's a fortified, somewhat dishevelled building whose interior feels quiet and ancient, a world away from the crowds around the Colosseum below. The atmosphere is intensified by the pretty **cloister**, accessed through a door in the north aisle, which is elegantly proportioned and contains a small, neat garden.

The church itself has an extra-wide apse and some very old frescoes on the south and west walls, as well as a giant series of apse paintings showing the martyrdom of the soldiers, and a *matroneum*, or women's gallery – something rarely seen nowadays. A convent of Augustinian nuns lives here now, and it's they who administer entrance to the **San Silvestro chapel**, accessible from the second courtyard, which contains frescoes painted in 1248. They comprise a beautifully preserved comic strip that tells the story of how the fourth-century pope Sylvester cured the Emperor Constantine of leprosy (he's the one covered in spots) and then baptized him. A pox-free Constantine is also shown giving his crown to the pope in a symbolic transfer of power, and all of it takes place beneath an enthroned Christ surrounded by saints.

In the convent, the **Aula Gotica** (Gothic Hall) holds some beautiful frescoes depicting the zodiac, the seasons and the months of the year, among other subjects. Dating back to the thirteenth century, the frescoes were discovered in 2002 under a thick layer of plaster, thought to have been applied after the 1348 plague for hygiene reasons. The Aula Gotica is only accessible with a guided tour that runs twice a month.

San Clemente

Via Labicana 95 · Mon–Sat 9am–12.30pm & 3–6pm, Sun 12.15–6pm; last entry to excavations 30min before closing · Church free; lower church excavations €10 · ☎ 06 774 0021, ⊕ basilicasanclemente.com · Metro Colosseo or Manzoni, or bus to Via Labicana

Halfway down Via San Giovanni in Laterano, the church of **San Clemente** is a cream-coloured twelfth-century basilica that brilliantly encapsulates continuity of history in the city – it is in fact a conglomeration of three places of worship from three very different eras in the history of Rome. Pope St Clement I, to whom the church is dedicated, was the third pope after St Peter (and is said to have been ordained by him), reigning from 90 AD until 99 AD, when he was exiled and martyred in the Crimea. His relics are kept in this church, and they have been venerated here from the very earliest times.

The basilica

The street-level church is a superb example of a medieval **basilica**: its facade and courtyard face east in the archaic fashion, and there are some splendid twelfth-century mosaics in the apse. The choir is partitioned off with beautiful white marble slabs repurposed from the older lower basilica; they are decorated with the earliest known papal insignia in the city, the monogram of Pope John II, who reigned from 533 to 535 AD. The gilded ceiling bears the arms of Pope Clement XI, from the early years of the eighteenth century, during whose papacy the church was remodelled. Perhaps the highlights of the main church, though, are the fifteenth-century **frescoes** by Masolino in the chapel, whose soft, yet vivid, colours show scenes from the life of St Catherine on the left: at the top, the saint – in the blue dress – attempts (in vain) to convert the Emperor Maxentius to Christianity, and in fact succeeds in converting his wife (in green), for which the wife is beheaded. In the centre, St Catherine is shown being pulled apart by two wheels – hence the name of the famous firework – until an angel intervenes and she too is beheaded (in the far-right panel). The central fresco shows the Crucifixion, with Mary Magdalene clinging to the cross, while Christ's mother Mary is distraught in the foreground.

The lower church and temple of Mithras

Downstairs, you can visit the excavated nave of an **earlier church**, dating back to the late fourth century. The frescoes of what was the entrance portico show the *Miracle of San Clemente* and the transferral of his body from St Peter's to San Clemente. At the western end of this church, steps lead down to the labyrinthine third level, which contains a **Mithraic temple** of the late second century. The temple was converted from the central courtyard of a Roman house built after the fire of 64 AD. In the temple is a statue of Mithras slaying the bull, as well as the sloping podium upon which the worshippers lounged during their ceremonies. The underground river that formerly fed the lake in front of the Domus Aurea can be heard rushing to its destination in the Tiber, behind the Circo Massimo, a reminder that Rome is built on very shaky foundations indeed. Next door to the Roman house, across a narrow alleyway, are the ground-floor rooms of a **first-century imperial building**, all of which can be explored by the spooky light of fluorescent tubes set in the ceiling and along the mossy brick walls.

San Giovanni in Laterano

Piazza di San Giovanni in Laterano 4 · **Basilica** Daily 7am–6.30pm · Free · **Cloisters** Daily 9am–6pm · €2 · **Baptistery** Daily 9am–12.30pm & 4–6.30pm · Free · ☎ 06 6988 6433 · Metro San Giovanni or bus to Piazza di San Giovanni in Laterano

The basilica of **San Giovanni in Laterano** is the cathedral of Rome, and the mother church of the Catholic world. The Lateran Treaty of 1929 accorded this and the other patriarchal basilicas extraterritorial status.

There has been a church on this site since the fourth century, the first established by Constantine. The present building, reworked by Borromini in the mid-seventeenth century, evokes – like San Clemente and Santo Stefano – Rome's staggering wealth of history, with a host of features from different periods: the statue of Constantine in the porch was found on the Quirinal Hill, while the doors of the church itself were taken from the Curia, or Senate House, of the Roman Forum. The obelisk that stands on the north side of the church is the oldest (and largest) in Rome, dating from the fifteenth century BC and brought here from Thebes by Constantine, originally for the Circus Maximus, but raised here by Sixtus V.

The large orange building next door is the **Lateran Palace** (no public access). This was the medieval home of the popes (before they decamped to the more easily fortified Vatican) and was originally much bigger. In the sixteenth century, extensive remodelling saw much of the medieval building demolished; a large road was driven through what was once the papal dining hall, and the Scala Santa (see p.134), once part of the complex, is now stranded on a traffic island.

The basilica

The interior of San Giovanni has been extensively reworked over the centuries. Much of what you see today dates from the seventeenth century, when the Aldobrandini pope, Clement VIII, had the church remodelled for Holy Year. The **gilded ceiling** of the nave has as its centrepiece the papal arms of Pope Pius VI, from the late 1700s, while the ceiling in the crossing bears the Aldobrandini family insignia. In the right transept is the tomb of Pope Innocent III, who died in 1216 and was buried here in the late 1800s at the behest of Pope Leo XIII, when he had this wing of the crossing remodelled. Leo XIII himself, who died in 1903, is buried opposite.

The first pillar on the left of the right-hand aisle shows a fragment of **Giotto**'s fresco of Boniface VIII, proclaiming the first Holy Year in 1300, a gentle work with gorgeous colours that is at odds with the immensity and grandeur of the rest of the building. On the next pillar along, a more recent monument commemorates Sylvester I – "the magician pope", bishop of Rome during much of Constantine's reign – and incorporates part of his original tomb, said to sweat and rattle his bones when a pope is about to die.

As for the **nave** itself, it's lined with eighteenth-century statues of the apostles in flashy and dramatic Rococo style, each one of which gives a clue as to their identity or manner of death: St Matthew, the tax collector, is shown with coins falling out of a sack; St Bartholomew holds a knife and his own skin (he was flayed alive); St Thomas holds a set square (he's the patron saint of architects) and St Simon a saw (he was, apparently, sawn to death). At the head of the nave, the heads of St Peter and St Paul, the church's prize relics, are kept secure behind the papal altar. The mosaics in the apse are undeniably impressive, but fake – they were added in the later nineteenth century to replace the lost originals – but the **baldacchino** just in front is most definitely genuine. A splash of Gothic grandeur made by the Tuscan sculptor Giovanni di Stefano in the fourteenth century, it shelters the glassed-over bronze tomb of Martin V, the Colonna pope who was responsible for returning the papacy to Rome from Avignon in 1419.

The cloisters

Outside the church, the **cloisters**, accessed via a door by the north transept, are one of the most pleasing parts of the complex, decorated with early thirteenth-century Cosmati work and with fragments of the original basilica. Rooms off to the side form a small **museum**, displaying various papal artefacts (including the vestments of Boniface VIII).

The baptistery

Next door to the basilica, the **baptistery** has been carefully restored, along with the side of the church itself, after a car bombing in 1993. It is the oldest surviving baptistery in the Christian world, an octagonal structure built during the fifth century that has been the model for many such buildings since. Oddly, it doesn't really feel its age, although the mosaics in the chapel on the far side and the bronze doors to the chapel on the right, brought here from the **Baths of Caracalla**, quickly remind you where you are.

Scala Santa and Sancta Sanctorum

Piazza di San Giovanni in Laterano 14 • **Scala Santa** April–Sept Mon–Sat 6am–2pm & 3–7pm, Sun 7am–2pm & 3–7pm; Oct–March Mon–Sat 6am–2pm & 3–6.30pm, Sun 7am–noon & 3–6.30pm • Free • **Sancta Sanctorum** Mon–Sat 9.30am–12.40pm & 3–5.10pm; last entry 30min before closing • €3.50 • ☎ 06 772 6641 , Ⓦ scala-santa.it • Metro San Giovanni or bus to Piazza di San Giovanni in Laterano

Across Piazza di Porta San Giovanni from the San Giovanni basilica is a building housing the **Scala Santa**, said to be the staircase from Pontius Pilate's house down which Jesus walked after his trial. It was said to have been brought to Rome by St Helena, mother of Constantine, and was within the complex of the Lateran Palace during the Middle Ages. Its current form was determined by Pope Sixtus V, for whom the new building was constructed after his demolition of much of the former papal palace to make way for the road we see today. At the top of the staircase is the splendid **Sancta Sanctorum**, or chapel of St Lorenzo – formerly the pope's private place of worship. The 28 steps are protected by boards, and the only way you're allowed to climb them is on your knees, which pilgrims do regularly – although there are staircases either side for the less penitent. The Sancta Sanctorum holds an ancient (sixth- or seventh-century) painting of Christ that is attributed to an angel, hence its name – *acheiropoeton*, or "not done by human hands".

Museo Storico della Liberazione

Via Tasso 145 • Wed, Sat & Sun 9.30am–12.30pm, Tues, Thurs & Fri 9.30am–12.30pm & 3.30–7.30pm; closed Aug • Free (donations welcome) • ☎ 06 700 3866, Ⓦ viatasso.eu • Metro Manzoni or bus to Via Merulana or Via Labicana

Five minutes' walk from the San Giovanni basilica, the **Museo Storico della Liberazione** occupies three floors of the building in which Nazi prisoners were held and interrogated during the wartime Occupation. It's a moving place and deliberately low-key – the original cells have been left as they were, with their windows bricked up by the SS, while the two isolation cells are marked with the desperate notes and messages from the people held here. The other cells focus on different themes of the Occupation: one is dedicated to the 335 victims of the Fosse Ardeatine massacre (see p.150), another to prisoners who died at Forte Bravetta on the outskirts of the city. You can also see the former kitchen that was the cell of Colonel Giuseppe Montezemolo, who led the Resistance and was executed at the Fosse Ardeatine, complete with scraps of his clothing and other personal effects. The top floor has German propaganda notices, pages from clandestine newspapers and anti-German media, as well as photos, lists of names and notices given to families during the

---

VILLA WOLKONSKY'S TREASURES

An overgrown garden can conceal all sorts of treasures, particularly in Rome. In the 1930s a Russian princess, Zenaide Wolkonsky, built an imposing villa – now known as the **Villa Wolkonsky** – near Piazza di San Giovanni in Laterano. The gardens were the princess's pride and joy, and she filled them with statuary and artefacts from a nearby Roman necropolis, and hosted literary gatherings here for the likes of Sir Walter Scott, Stendhal and Nikolai Gogol. Subsequently, the villa had several owners until it was sold to the German government in 1920. Used as a headquarters of the Gestapo in World War II, the villa was sequestered in 1945 and has served as the residence of British ambassadors ever since.

Until recently, the garden of the villa was a rambling affair, but recent landscaping brought to light a wealth of artefacts concealed beneath the tangled foliage. As gardeners hacked through the undergrowth they uncovered some 350 precious pieces, including some extremely rare stone reliefs from ancient Roman tombs depicting freed slaves, their wives and children. A derelict greenhouse has been restored to house the collection, though at present – due to the high security at the ambassador's residence – the "greenhouse museum" is only open to tours from gardening or archeological organizations (last Thurs of the month, except Aug & Dec; book in advance through ✉ inforome@fco.gov.uk).

deportation of the Jews from the Ghetto. Twenty minutes after receiving these they had to be ready to leave; most of them never returned.

Via Sannio

Metro San Giovanni or bus to Piazzale Appio

Across the far side of the square in front of San Giovanni in Laterano, the **Porta Asinaria**, one of the city's grander gateways, marks the Aurelian Wall (see box, p.147). If you're here in the morning, you could visit the somewhat grubby market (Mon–Sat until about 2pm) on **Via Sannio** just beyond, with numerous stalls shadowing the wall touting cheap bags, jewellery, clothes and underwear, and then continue on for five minutes to **Piazzale Metronio**, from where you can follow the line of the **Aurelian Wall** as far as **Porta San Sebastiano** and the Aurelian Wall museum, Museo delle Mura (see p.146) – a twenty-minute walk in total.

Santa Croce in Gerusalemme

Piazza di Santa Croce in Gerusalemme · **Church** Daily 7am–12.45pm & 3.30–7.30pm, Ⓦ santacroceroma.it · Free · **Archeological area** Guided tours (Italian only) first and third Sat of the month at 10.15am; 1hr · €5.50 · **Vegetable garden** Occasional pre-booked visits · €15 · ☏ 06 7061 3053, Ⓦ coopculture.it · Metro San Giovanni or bus or tram to Viale Carlo Felice or Piazza di Santa Croce in Gerusalemme

Five minutes' walk from the San Giovanni basilica, by way of Viale Carlo Felice, the ancient church of **Santa Croce in Gerusalemme** is one of the seven pilgrimage churches of Rome, believed to stand on the site of the palace of Constantine's mother St Helena, and home to the relics of the True Cross that she brought back from Jerusalem. Parts of it date from the fourth century AD, although the beautiful Renaissance apse frescoes by Antoniazzo Romano are late fifteenth-century, and show the discovery of the fragments of the Cross, under a seated Christ – a marvellously Technicolor, naturalistic scene showing trees and mountains and the saint at the centre, with the True Cross and a kneeling cardinal. Steps behind lead down to the original level of Helena's house – now a chapel dedicated to the saint and decorated with marvellous Renaissance mosaics and with a statue of St Helena in a niche, beneath which messages are left. The tiles on the stairs are an inscription relating to the discovery of the True Cross and were produced at the same time as the apse frescoes.

The relics chapel

The **relics** that St Helena kept so carefully are stored in a Mussolini-era **chapel** up some steps at the end of the left aisle, incorporating three pieces of the Cross itself, a nail and a couple of thorns, though most spectacular perhaps is a piece of the supposed wooden tablet with Pilate's imputation against Jesus, showing his name in Hebrew, Greek and Latin, found in the vestibule outside. Off to the right there's a copy of another, equally famous, relic, the **Shroud of Turin**. Take time to ponder the chapel at the bottom of the staircase too – a rather sad shrine to local girl Antonietta Meo, who died in 1937 at the age of 6 having written 162 letters to God. Some of these are on display, along with some toys, clothes and other effects. She is the youngest person ever to have been canonized by the Catholic Church.

The vegetable garden and archeological area

There's a lovely **vegetable garden** adjoining the church, which is looked after by monks, with a gate designed by the Greek-Italian artist Jannis Kounellis in 2007. The **archeological area** holds the scattered remains of the **Castrense amphitheatre** – apart from the Colosseum, Rome's only example. Able to accommodate 3500 spectators, it is thought to have been constructed by the Emperor Elagabalus around 220 AD.

National Museum of Musical Instruments

Piazza di Santa Croce in Gerusalemme 9a • Tues–Sun 9am–7pm; last entry 6.30pm • €5; free first Sun of the month • ☎ 06 701 4796, ⓦ museostrumentimusicali.beniculturali.it• Metro San Giovanni or bus or tram to Viale Carlo Felice or Piazza di Santa Croce in Gerusalemme

The first floor of the palace next door to Santa Croce is the home of the **National Museum of Musical Instruments**, an interesting display of Italian and European instruments that has surprisingly good background information and labelling in English. There are early Roman and Etruscan pieces, lots of stringed instruments, mechanical and church instruments, instruments used by travelling musicians and early pianofortes. The star of the show is the seventeenth-century Barberini harp.

Porta Maggiore

Metro Manzoni or bus or tram to Piazza di Porta Maggiore

Just to the north of the church of Santa Croce in Gerusalemme, towards the train tracks, the **Porta Maggiore** (the "Main Gate") sits amid a grubby tangle of tram lines and buses. The highest point to the east of the city, it was the entrance point to the city for five aqueducts. Originally built before Rome needed to defend herself with walls, it served as a monumental arch of the double-decker **aqueduct: Acqua Claudia** and **Anio Novo**, completed in 52AD. When viewed side on, the channels through which the water once ran are visible. The more attractive travertine arch stands out from the tuff arcades (complete with dedicatory inscription) and was built to span the important vie Labicana and Praenestina: roads which left the city towards the east. It was subsequently incorporated into the Aurelian Wall (see box, p.147).

The grand **Tomb of the Baker**, in white travertine, just outside the gate, is a monument from about the reign of Augustus. The baker in question was a public contractor who made a fortune selling bread to the army. The round holes and the cylinders on the outside of the tomb represent the tools used for the measurement of grain, and the frieze shows scenes from the bread-making process.

Pigneto

Tram to Piazzale Prenestino, bus to Ponte Casilino or local train from Termini to Ponte Casilino

A ten-minute walk from the Porta Maggiore, **Pigneto** was originally a working-class district of apartment blocks, low-rise villas and cottages, which grew up around the rail lines in the nineteenth century. It has always been slightly different – it was a favourite haunt of **Pasolini**, who shot some of his movies here – and these days it's one of Rome's most up-and-coming neighbourhoods. Far from being entirely gentrified, it retains a slight edge – although the completion of the metro line C station that recently opened on Via del Pigneto will surely hasten its regeneration.

The pedestrianized strip of **Via del Pigneto** hosts a colourful morning fruit and vegetable **market** (Mon–Sat). Via del Pigneto and the surrounding streets are home to a number of good restaurants, cafés and bars (see p.270).

PYRAMID OF CAIUS CESTIUS

The Aventine Hill and south

The leafy Aventine Hill – once the heart of plebeian Rome – is now a smart residential area and one of the city's most pleasant corners. South and west of the hill are two distinct neighbourhoods: Testaccio, a working-class enclave that's become increasingly hip and gentrified and is home to much of the city's nightlife, as well as lots of good restaurants and one of the best produce markets; and the more up-and-coming Ostiense, beyond the ancient city wall, worth a visit for the Centrale Montemartini branch of the Capitoline Museums. Between these districts is Rome's Non-Catholic (also known as the "Protestant") Cemetery, where the poets Keats and Shelley are buried. Further south lie the magnificent basilica of San Paolo fuori le Mura and the Via Appia Antica with its atmospheric catacombs, and beyond, EUR – Rome's futuristic 1930s experiment in town planning.

9

Santa Sabina and around

Piazza Pietro d'Illiria 1 • Daily 8.15am–12.30pm & 3.30–6pm • ☎ 06 579 401 • Bus to Lungotevere Aventino

On the opposite side of the Circus Maximus to the Palatine Hill, the Aventine is the most southerly of Rome's seven hills, a leafy, residential neighbourhood that's home to **Santa Sabina**, the principal church of the Dominicans in Rome. It's a strong contender for the city's most beautiful basilica, a high and wide structure, with a nave and portico that were restored back to their fifth-century appearance in the 1930s. In the **portico**, look at the main doors at the far end, which are contemporary with the church and boast eighteen panels carved with Christian scenes, forming an illustrated Bible that includes (top left) the oldest representation of the Crucifixion in Rome. **Inside**, the windows above the arches of the nave are among the most beautiful features of the church, each one different, letting in light by way of lacy patterns carved into the stone. The mosaic inscription on the wall above the doors heralds the achievements of Celestino I, flanked by two female figures representing converted Jews and pagans. Immediately below, in the corner, a smooth piece of black marble, pitted with holes, was apparently thrown by the Devil at St Dominic himself while at prayer, shattering the marble pavement but miraculously not harming the saint.

It's claimed that the orange trees in the **garden** behind the church (which you have to ask to see) are descendants of those planted by St Dominic himself. Whatever the truth of this, the views from the gardens are splendid – right across the Tiber to the centre of Rome and St Peter's. Beyond here you can be taken up to see the room where the saint stayed: it's now a small, heavily decorated chapel, but the timbered far end hints at a more spartan authenticity. The **cloister**, accessible by way of a door off the portico, has been under restoration for some time.

Giardino degli Aranci

Daily 7am–dusk

Take the time to wander into the **Giardino degli Aranci** public gardens next to Santa Sabina, planted with orange trees and immortalized in the 2013 Paolo Sorrentino film *The Great Beauty*. The gardens are a favourite with strolling couples, drawn by the wonderful panorama from here across the river towards the Vatican.

Sant'Alessio

Piazza di Sant'Alessio 23 • Open for weddings and concerts only • ☎ 06 574 3446

A short walk beyond Santa Sabina, the church of **Sant'Alessio** was originally a Romanesque structure but now mostly dates from the eighteenth century, apart from a nice mosaic floor and two tiny mosaic-covered columns in the apse. Alessio, a popular medieval saint, is said to have left his betrothed on their wedding night and travelled for years as a beggar, eventually returning to his father's house incognito and living there as a servant until he died – hence the wooden staircase in the left aisle, which denotes his secret "below stairs" existence. There are nice gardens by the church with good views of St Peter's.

Priorato di Malta

Piazza dei Cavalieri di Malta 4 • Closed to the public; visits possible on Sat morning by group tour only; email ✉ a.amato@orderofmalta.int

The road across the Aventine widens out at the Piazza dei Cavalieri di Malta, where you'll find the **Priorato dei Cavalieri di Malta** on the right, a priory that is one of several buildings in the city belonging to the Knights of Malta; it has a celebrated **view of the dome of St Peter's** through the keyhole of its main gate. The little piazza has marble triumphal insignia designed by Piranesi to celebrate the Knights' dramatic history.

Piranesi also designed the church of **Santa Maria del Priorato** inside, which you can see, along with the lovely gardens, on group tours organized in advance. The church was rebuilt by Piranesi in 1765, the only structure that the famous engraver built. Its elaborate decor is typical of Roman churches, but it differentiates itself with its monochromatic sculptural simplicity. Virtually all the decoration is in grey stone or marble, or covered in stucco, and the effect is impressively uniform – a fact that Piranesi, caught in thoughtful pose in a statue on the right, is no doubt contemplating. The **gardens** are quite formally planted, with roses and topiary, but lush, too, with palms and subtropical plants that in combination with the high walls and entry restrictions give the feel of a secret, cloistered domain – in short, exactly what a city garden should be. They're beautifully tended, focusing on a small fountain and cage of doves in the centre, though to be honest, the views are no better than the ones from the Giardino degli Aranci (see opposite).

Sant'Anselmo

Piazza dei Cavalieri di Malta 5 • Church daily 9am–6pm; shop Tues–Sun 10am–1pm & 3–6pm • ☎ 06 57911, ⓦ www.anselmianum.com

Opposite the Priorato di Malta, spare five minutes or so for the church of **Sant'Anselmo**, a Benedictine complex containing a church and college, with pleasant gardens and a shop selling all manner of produce, Benedictine and otherwise: limoncello, *grappa*, *amaro*, as well as chocolate, beer, books, CDs and toiletries. The church is a plain basilica built in the last decade of the nineteenth century – not of much interest in itself, but known for its Gregorian chant and reasonably regular concerts, usually held on Sunday evenings.

San Saba

Piazza Bernini 20 • Mon–Sat 8am–noon & 4–7.10pm, Sun 9.30am–1pm & 4–7.30pm • ☎ 06 6458 0140

Across busy Piazza Albania from the Aventine Hill, the church of **San Saba** was built in the tenth century over a seventh-century structure constructed by monks who had fled here from the Middle East to escape the Arab advance. Topped with a fifteenth-century loggia and fronted by a pleasant, if scruffy, walled garden, it's worth visiting for its wonderful Cosmati-work door and floor, and an interior that feels very ancient, with a wonderful mixture of Roman pillars and thirteenth-century frescoes in a short additional left aisle and the beautifully proportioned apse.

The Baths of Caracalla

Viale delle Terme di Caracalla 52 • Mon 9am–2pm, Tues–Sun 9am–1hr before sunset; last entry 1hr before closing • €6 combined ticket with Tomb of Cecilia Metella (p.152) and the Villa dei Quintili (p.153); free first Sun of the month • ☎ 06 3996 7700, ⓦ coopculture.it • Metro Circo Massimo or bus to Viale delle Terme di Caracalla

Southeast of the Aventine, the **Baths of Caracalla** give a far better sense of the monumental scale of Roman architecture than most of the extant ruins in the city – so much so that Shelley was moved to write his Romantic play *Prometheus Unbound* here in 1819. The baths are no more than a giant shell now, but the walls still rise to very nearly their original height. There are many fragments of mosaics – none spectacular, but quite a few bright and well preserved – and it's easy to discern a floor plan. Set in extensive walled gardens, the baths were built around the long spine of the central hall,

---

SERVIAN WALL

On Piazza Albania, at the end of traffic-choked Viale Aventino and a world away from the leafy heights of the Aventine Hill, there's a rare stretch of the so-called **Servian Wall** – the first wall to properly enclose Rome. Although it was built in the fourth century BC, it has been (erroneously) named after the sixth-century Roman king Servius Tullius since time immemorial. Other stretches of the Servian Wall can be seen outside and in the basement at Termini.

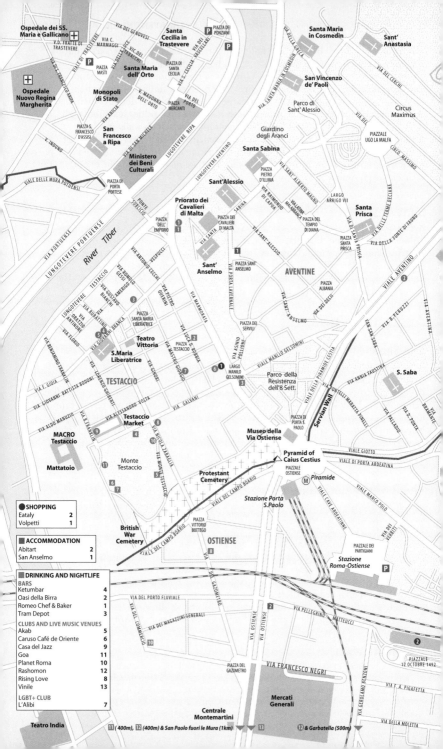

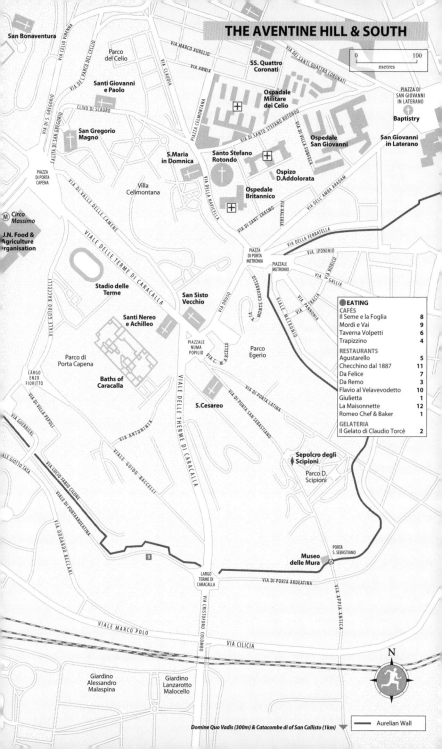

9

or frigidarium, at each end of which are vast courtyards – *palestrae* – which were used for sports before bathing. Off to the left of the frigidarium was the tepidarium, and beyond this the domed chamber of the circular caldarium, which is easier to see outside the baths themselves. On the other side of the frigidarium was the *natatio* or swimming pool, a huge open space which would have been accessed by way of the *apodyteria*, or changing rooms, on either side – you can get the best sense of this by following the signed route from the entrance.

As for Caracalla, he was one of Rome's most brutal emperors, responsible for the murder of his brother, Geta. The baths are the summer venue of the **Teatro dell'Opera** (one of Mussolini's better ideas), and attending an opera performance here is a thrilling way to see the baths at their most atmospheric (see p.280).

The underground areas
Occasionally open for temporary exhibitions

A network of **tunnels** 6m high and wide extends for 4km under the baths; these once accommodated storage rooms for wood, furnaces to heat water, and an army of scurrying slaves to keep it all going. Also underground (though not usually accessible) is a large **Mithraic temple**, the city's biggest, where followers of the cult of Mithras would butcher bulls and bathe in their blood.

Santi Nereo ed Achilleo

Via delle Terme di Caracalla 28 · Usually open for Mass only: Mon–Sat 8am, 10am & 7pm, Sun & church holidays 10am, 11am, noon, 6.30pm & 7pm · ⓦ vallicella.org · Metro Circo Massimo or bus to Viale delle Terme di Caracalla

Just outside the Baths of Caracalla, the church of **Santi Nereo ed Achilleo** makes for a peaceful spot after the crowds at the baths, and is of interest for the ninth-century mosaic on the arch above its apse, which depicts Christ and three prostrate apostles, between a scene of the Annunciation on the left and a Virgin and Child on the right. The beautiful Cosmati work on the marble choir screen and the altar itself also merits a look, as does the ornate throne sitting on two lions in the apse, said to have been preached from by Gregory the Great (see p.319). St Gregory is shown preaching to various cardinals in an apse fresco that's full of charming detail: you'll notice one of the cardinals – second from the right – has trouble hearing, while others confer as to what the great pope might be saying.

Back outside the church, on the far side of the Piazzale Numa Pompilio roundabout, Via di Porta San Sebastiano leads onto the Via Appia Antica which heads towards the catacombs and other archeological delights, a few kilometres south (see p.147).

Testaccio

Metro Piramide or bus to Piazzale Ostiense

On the far side of the Aventine Hill, across Via Marmorata, the working-class neighbourhood of **Testaccio** was in ancient times a rubbish dump for the nearby river port (see Monte Testaccio below). In modern times it was long synonymous with the slaughterhouse (Mattatoio) that sprawls down to the Tiber just beyond. The slaughterhouse closed long ago, and these days the neighbourhood is a curious mixture of the old and the new: traditional trattorias celebrate their use of offal alongside veggie restaurants and cool cafés, and there's a busy gay and alternative club scene that exists cheek-by-jowl with the car-repair shops gouged into Monte Testaccio. The tight-knit community groups around a couple of main squares – Piazza di Santa Maria Liberatrice and Piazza Testaccio. The latter, with its restored 1920s amphora fountain, is a charming spot on summer evenings, with children playing football and people chatting on the benches. It was for decades the home of a (rather ramshackle) daily **food market** (the gouges in the trees still show where the roof was), but this moved to a purpose-built new complex opposite the Mattatoio on Via Galvani several years ago, and is well worth a visit (Mon–Sat 7am–1pm).

MACRO Testaccio and La Pelanda

Piazza Orazio Giustiniani 4 • Tues–Sun 4–10pm • €8.50, or €14.50 including the other branch of MACRO (p.182); valid for 7 days • ☎ 06 8535 6892, ⓦ museomacro.org

The slaughterhouse, or **Mattatoio**, was once the area's main employer and is now a huge, partly derelict complex, housing the *centro sociale* "Villaggio Globale", a space used for concerts and offbeat events in summer, stabling for the city's horse-and-carriage drivers and a branch of the Museum of Contemporary Art of Rome (see p.182), **MACRO Testaccio**, just inside the main gate, where a couple of large pavilions stage adventurous temporary exhibitions. Further into the site is **La Pelanda**, a cultural space that also hosts temporary exhibitions.

Monte Testaccio

Entrance at Via Nicola Zabaglia 24; visits occasionally possible on request • ☎ 06 0608

Bang in the middle of Testaccio, a fifty-metre-high mound of historic landfill known as **Monte Testaccio** gives the area its name. Over several centuries, the ancient Romans broke terracotta amphorae up into small shards and laid them down in an orderly manner, sprinkling quicklime on them to dissolve the residual wine or oil. It's estimated that there are around 53 million amphorae here and it makes for an odd sight, the ceramic curls clearly visible through the tufts of grass that crown its higher reaches, the bottom layers hollowed out over the decades first by tavernae, then by the workshops of car and bike mechanics, and, now, clubs and bars.

Protestant Cemetery

Via Caio Cestio 6 • Mon–Sat 9am–5pm, Sun 9am–1pm • Donation of at least €3 expected • ☎ 06 574 1900, ⓦ cemeteryrome.it

On the far side of Monte Testaccio, off Via Marmorata, although originally for British Protestants who died in Rome, the "**Protestant" Cemetery** has long been the burial place of non-Catholics of all nationalities, so you'll also find atheists, members of the Eastern Orthodox Church, and the odd Jew or Muslim buried here. It is nonetheless one of the shrines to the English in Rome, and a fitting addition to a visit to the Keats-Shelley House on Piazza di Spagna (see p.94).

Most visitors come to see the grave of **Keats**, who lies next to his friend, the painter **Joseph Severn**, in the furthest corner of the less crowded, older part of the cemetery (turn left from the entrance), his stone inscribed as he wished with the words "Here lies one whose name was writ in water". Severn died much later than Keats but asked to be laid here nonetheless, together with his brushes and palette. Just behind Severn and Keats lies the little grave of Severn's infant son; behind, a plaque on the wall remembers the Swedish doctor and writer Axel Munthe, his wife Hilda and their two sons. As for **Shelley**, his ashes were brought here at Mary Shelley's request and interred, after much obstruction by the papal authorities, in the newer part of the cemetery, on the left as you enter, at the top, against the ancient Aurelian wall. The Shelleys had visited several years earlier, the poet praising it as "the most beautiful and solemn cemetery I ever beheld". It had been intended that Shelley should rest with his young son, William, who died while they were in Rome and was also buried here, but his remains couldn't be found (although his small grave is nearby). Mary Shelley was so broken-hearted by the deaths of her son and husband that it was twenty years before she could bring herself to visit their graves.

Shelley's great friend, the writer and adventurer **Edward Trelawny**, lies next to him, while in front of Shelley's grave is a slab marking the final resting-spot of the American Beat poet **Gregory Corso**, who died in 2001 and was buried next to his hero Shelley, at his request. To the right, an ancient headless torso, marked simply "Belinda", signals the grave of Belinda Lee, a little-known Hollywood starlet, who died in her mid-twenties in

9

a car crash in Hollywood in 1961, after a scandalous affair with one of the Orsini princes. Among other famous residents, the cemetery boasts the founder of the Italian Communist Party, **Antonio Gramsci** (on the far right-hand side of the cemetery and about halfway back). His *Scritti Politici* were written while he was imprisoned by the Fascist regime. The Italian novelist **Carlo Emilio Gadda** is nearby. If you're at all interested in star-spotting you should either borrow or buy the comprehensive **booklet** available at the entrance.

British War Cemetery
Via Nicola Zabaglia • Mon–Fri 7am–noon & 1–3.30pm; opens 8am in winter • ☎ 06 509 9911

Between Monte Testaccio and the Aurelian Wall, the **British War Cemetery** is the less famous counterpart to the Protestant Cemetery across the road, but it's no less contemplative a spot. It's the final resting-place of the four hundred or so young men from Britain and parts of the Commonwealth who were killed in action during 1943 and 1944 in the battle to liberate Italy and ultimately Rome. Planted with lawns and framed by the arches of the old Roman wall behind (in which a stone from Hadrian's Wall is embedded), it's a beautifully kept and peaceful place, with birdsong easily drowning out the hum of traffic on nearby Via Ostiense.

Ostiense

The Porta San Paolo overlooks a major traffic junction from which Via Ostiense spears off south. The **Ostiense** neighbourhood, close to already gentrified Testaccio, is also an up-and-coming area, dotted with hip bars and restaurants, as well as a number of interesting sights.

Pyramid of Caius Cestius
Piazzale Ostiense • **Pyramid** Open to the public on second & fourth Sat of the month at 11am; entry by guided tour only (in Italian); book in advance; 1hr • €5.50 • ☎ 06 3996 7700 • **Cat shelter** Daily 2–4pm • ⓦ igattidellapiramide.it • Metro Piramide or bus to Piazzale Ostiense

Overlooking the Protestant Cemetery, the most distinctive landmark in this part of town is the **Pyramid of Caius Cestius**. Cestius, who died in 12 BC, had spent time in Nubia, and his pyramid-shaped tomb evokes his exotic travels, albeit in ever-so-Italian gleaming white marble. Part of Cestius's will decreed that all his slaves should be freed; the tomb was thrown up by them in only 330 days of what must have been joyful building. You can visit the **cats** that live here, and the volunteers who care for them, in the afternoon.

Museo della Via Ostiense
Piazza di Porta San Paolo 3 • Tues–Sun 9am–1.30pm; closed Sun in Aug • Free • ☎ 06 574 3193 • Metro Piramide or bus to Piazzale Ostiense

Housed in the old Porta San Paolo, the **Museo della Via Ostiense** is devoted to the Via Ostiense, the ancient link between Rome and its port of Ostia. There's not a huge

---

EATALY

High-end supermarket chain **Eataly** opened its first Rome branch in 2012, in a hangar-like building on Piazzale XII Ottobre, Ostiense (daily 10am–midnight; ☎ 06 9027 9201, ⓦ eataly .net/it), a ten-minute walk from Piramide metro station. While some feel this multistorey temple to food is uncomfortably far from the traditional Italian shopping experience, many Romans have embraced it, and a second branch opened in Piazza della Repubblica in 2015 – ousting *McDonald's*, no less. You can make up your own mind as you wander the three floors, stuffed with restaurants, bars and shops, where you can buy everything from beers bottled in the on-site microbrewery to gourmet biscuits. Even if you leave empty-handed – prices are higher here than elsewhere – you'll find Eataly's air-conditioned spaces a welcome relief on a hot day.

amount of interest here, but if you have half an hour to kill on your way to catch a train to Ostia Antica from the Porta San Paolo station opposite, the model of Ostia is worth studying, as is that of the old port of Trajan. There are sepulchral monuments and other items that used to line the old road, and you can stand on top of the gate to contemplate the traffic chaos outside.

Centrale Montemartini

Via Ostiense 106 • Tues–Sun 9am–7pm • €7.50, or €12.50 combined ticket with Capitoline Museums, €16 when temporary exhibitions are running • ☎ 06 0608 • ⓦ centralemontemartini.org • Ten minutes' walk from Metro Piramide, or bus to Via Ostiense

The former electricity generating plant of **Centrale Montemartini** was perhaps the first thing to put Ostiense on the map and is well worth the journey. It was originally requisitioned to display the cream of the Capitoline Museums' sculpture while the main buildings were being renovated, but was so popular that it became the Capitoline's permanent outpost. The huge rooms of the power station are ideally suited to showing off ancient sculpture, although checking out the massive turbines and furnaces has a fascination of its own.

The **Machine Hall** houses the head, feet and an arm from a colossal statue, once 8m high, found in Largo di Torre Argentina, as well as various heads, some of emperors (Claudius, Tiberius, Domitian), a large Roman *Athena* and a fine statue of a Roman soldier from the Esquiline Hill, tucked away in a corner. In the adjacent **Furnace Hall**, the most obvious features are the furnace itself at the far end and a fragmented mosaic of hunting scenes that occupies half the floor – deer and boar, and figures on horseback or crouching to trap their prey in nets. Among the sculptures on display is an amazing third-century BC statue of a girl seated on a stool with legs crossed, a statue of the Muse Polymnia, leaning on a rock and staring thoughtfully into the distance, and a wonderful pair of magistrates, one old, one young, but both holding the handkerchief that they would use to herald the start of competitions and circuses.

Garbatella

Metro Garbatella

East of Via Ostiense is the vast derelict expanse of the Mercati Generali, beyond which lies **Garbatella**, one of the city's more interesting nineteenth-century residential developments, planned as new housing for the growing city in the 1920s. Originally known as the Borgata Giardino, it was – and to some extent still is – a solid, left-leaning, working-class district. An odd mixture of undistinguished postwar apartment blocks and low-rise cottages set in leafy gardens that evoke a peaceful, suburban feel, it makes quite a change from the industrial grittiness that pervades so much of this part of the city. If Garbatella has a centre, it's **Piazza Damiano Sauli**, whose shabby civic buildings centre on a trio of brick arches, through which you can walk to wander the area's shady lanes. It's becoming rather gentrified, as you might expect, but the district as a whole remains fairly close to its old roots, with a solid base of support for AS Roma.

San Paolo fuori le Mura

Via Ostiense 186 • **Basilica** Daily 7am–6.30pm • Free • **Cloister, chapel and archeological area** Daily 9am–1pm & 3–6pm • €4 • ☎ 06 4543 4185, ⓦ abbaziasanpaolo.net • Metro San Paolo or bus to Via Ostiense

Some 2km south of the Porta San Paolo, the basilica of **San Paolo fuori le Mura**, or "St Paul's outside the Walls", is one of the four patriarchal basilicas of Rome (and thus not technically Italian territory). It occupies the supposed site of St Paul's tomb, where St Paul – joint patron saint of Rome, with St Peter – was laid to rest after being beheaded at Tre Fontane (see p.156). Of the four basilicas, this has probably fared the least well over the years. It was apparently once the grandest, connected to the Aurelian Wall by a colonnade over a kilometre in length, made up of eight hundred

9

marble columns, but a ninth-century sacking by the Saracens and a devastating fire in 1823 (a couple of cack-handed roofers spilt burning tar, almost entirely destroying the church) means that the building you see now is largely a nineteenth-century reconstruction.

The interior

The church is a very successful – if somewhat clinical – rehash of the former building. Perhaps even more than St Peter's, it impresses with sheer size and grandeur, and whether you enter by way of the cloisters or the west door, it's impossible not to be awed by the space of the building inside, its crowds of columns topped by round-arched arcading, and the **medallions** of all the popes fringing the nave and transepts above, starting with St Peter to the right of the apse and ending with Benedict XVI at the top of the south aisle. Of all the basilicas of Rome, this gives you the feel of what an ancient Roman basilica must have been like: the huge, barn-like structure, with its clerestory windows and roof beams supported by enormous columns, has a powerful and authentic sense of occasion.

Some parts of the building did survive the fire. In the south transept, the paschal candlestick at the head of the nave, behind two large statues of St Peter (on the left) and St Paul (on the right), is a remarkable piece of **Romanesque carving**, supported by half-human beasts and rising through entwined tendrils and strangely human limbs and bodies to scenes from Christ's life, the figures crowding in together as if for a photocall; it's inscribed by its makers, Nicola d'Angelo and Pietro Vassalletto. The bronze, eleventh-century doors at the end of the south aisle were also rescued from the old basilica, as was the thirteenth-century tabernacle by Arnolfo di Cambio, under which a slab from the time of Constantine, inscribed "Paolo Apostolo Mart", is supposed to lie – although it's hard to get a look at this. The arch across the apse is original, too, embellished with **mosaics** (donated by the Byzantine empress Galla Placidia in the fifth century) that show angels, saints Peter and Paul, the symbols of the Gospels and Christ giving a blessing. The mosaics in the apse date from 1220 and show Luke, Paul, Peter and Andrew and the kneeling figure of Honorius III kissing the feet of Christ.

The cloister, chapel and pinacoteca

The **cloister**, through the shop, is probably Rome's finest piece of Cosmati work, its spiralling, mosaic-encrusted columns enclosing a peaceful rose garden. Around the cloister are arranged archeological fragments, and just off here, the **relics chapel** houses a set of artefacts, including the remains of Pope Gregory VII. Beyond is the **pinacoteca**, a gallery of ecclesiastical art, vestments, silverware and the like.

The archeological area

Off the cloister, an **exhibition gallery**, opened to the public in 2015, holds vessels from the treasury, alongside inscriptions and fragments of statuary recently excavated in the early medieval monastic complex south of the basilica. You can get up close to the **excavations** by taking the glass staircase near the shop, where raised walkways take you through the site. Helpful information panels help make sense of the rubble, though it was a work in progress at the time of writing.

Museo delle Mura

Via di Porta San Sebastiano 18 • Tues–Sun 9am–2pm • Free • ☎ 06 0608, ⓦ museodellemuraroma.it • Bus to Porta San Sebastiano

From Porta San Paolo, it's about 2km around the Aurelian Wall (see box opposite) to the fifth-century Porta San Sebastiano, where the **Museo delle Mura** occupies a couple of floors of the gate. It's the best place to get a sense of the wall's history, with displays of Aurelian's original plans and lots of photos of the past and present walls that are

AURELIAN WALL

The **Aurelian Wall** was built by the Emperor Aurelian (and his successor Probus) between 271 and 275 AD to protect the city from invasion. It is the largest ancient Roman monument in the city, running for 18 km. If you are a real enthusiast, you can walk the circumference in an eight-hour day with a pause for lunch. However, for a taster, one of the best-preserved stretches runs between Porta San Paolo and Porta San Sebastiano – where you'll find a museum about the Wall, the Museo delle Mura (see opposite) – following Via di Porta Ardeatina: cross the road from Piramide metro station, turn right and follow the walls, keeping them always on your left. Other stretches can be seen at Porta Pia (see p.111), San Lorenzo (see p.125), Porta Asinaria (see p.135) and Porta San Pancrazio (see p.167).

helpful in showing what is original and what are medieval additions, and how different structures have been incorporated into the walls over the years. The museum tells you more about the walls and the various gates than you really need to know, but you can climb up to the top of the gate for great views over the Roman countryside beyond, and walk a few hundred metres along the walls themselves – towards the east – before having to return to the museum.

Sepolcro degli Scipioni

Via di Porta San Sebastiano 9 · Open to organized groups by reservation only · €4 · ☎ 06 0608 · Bus to Porta San Sebastiano

Leading from the Baths of Caracalla to the Porta San Sebastiano, the Via Porta San Sebastiano, like the Via Appia further south, would once have been lined with the tombs of rich families. One of these, the **Sepolcro degli Scipioni**, lies a short walk from the Museo delle Mura. The Scipios were one of the great Republican dynasties, generals in the Punic Wars against Carthage; the family tomb complex was in use between the third century BC and the first century AD. It was discovered in 1780 and the earliest of the sarcophagi, that of Scipio the Bearded (c.297 BC), was transported to the Vatican where it is passed by thousands every day (a replica is in the original find position). The site is atmospheric and a neighbouring frescoed columbarium, a sort of condominium for funerary urns, is part of the same archeological visit, giving some idea of the sort of accommodation that the majority of Romans would have occupied in death.

Via Appia Antica

Starting at the Porta San Sebastiano on the edge of the city centre, the **Via Appia Antica** (or "Appian Way") is the first and the most famous of the consular roads that once radiated out in all directions from the ancient city. It was built by the censor Appius Claudius in 312 BC, hence its name, and during classical times it was the most important of all the Roman trade routes, the so-called "Queen of Roads". It ran through Campania as far as the port of Brindisi, some 500km southeast, from where sea links connected with the eastern provinces of the Empire.

The best-known Christian sites along the Appia Antica are the underground burial cemeteries or **catacombs** of the early Christians. Ancient Roman legislation forbade burial within the city walls, for logical reasons, and most Romans were cremated. As Christianity became more popular, more and more people required burial and these state-sanctioned complexes developed (they were never secret), tunnelling through the friable tuff on multiple levels. There are catacombs in other parts of the city – those under the church of Sant'Agnese on Via Nomentana (see p.184) are some of the best – but of the five visitable complexes in Rome, three are on the Appian Way. They were in use between the first and the fourth centuries; today they are almost entirely emptied of bodies, but the symbols of the early Church and the names of its faithful remain.

9

The three principal complexes are within walking distance of each other, though it's not really worth trying to see them all – the layers of shelves lose their fascination for all but the most enthusiastic after a while. If you only go for one, you'd do best to focus on **San Sebastiano** (which boasts both pagan and Christian tombs) and explore the other attractions nearby.

VIA APPIA ANTICA ESSENTIALS

GETTING THERE

By bus The best bet if you're concentrating on Via Appia Antica proper – that is, just the catacombs and the attractions close by – is to take one of the buses that run south along Via Appia Antica and conveniently stop at or near most of the main attractions. Bus #118 stops at Via del Teatro di Marcello (to the right of the staircase up to the Campidoglio), the Colosseum, the Circus Maximus and Terme di Caracalla and makes several stops on Via Appia Antica, including Domine Quo Vadis, San Sebastiano, San Callisto and the Villa dei Quintili. You can also take bus #218 from San Giovanni in Laterano (Metro San Giovanni), which goes down Via Ardeatina, or bus #660, which runs from Colli Albani metro station to just beyond the Tomb of Cecilia Metella. If you get off the bus at the Appia Antica information office (see below) you can pick up a map first.

On foot From Porta San Sebastiano you can take in everything on foot; it takes about 15min to reach Domine Quo Vadis, 10min from there to San Callisto, and from there another 10min to San Sebastiano, and 5min to the Fosse Ardeatine or Domitilla.

By bike Perhaps the best way of all to get around is to rent a bike (€3/hr for the first 3hr, or €15/day) from the Parco Appia Antica information office (see below). The office can also arrange bike and walking tours. You can cycle (or walk)

from Quo Vadis to San Sebastiano, via San Callisto, without touching the road, which can be busy, and beyond San Sebastiano it's quiet and relatively traffic-free.

By guided tour Enjoy Rome's Catacombs and Roman Countryside tour (Mon, Tues, Thurs, Fri & Sat at 10am; 3hr; €59; ☎ 06 445 0734, ⊛ enjoyrome.com) takes in a set of catacombs, as well as other Appian Way sights (groups of up to 25). Expert guide Agnes Crawford runs private tours at ⊛ understandingrome.com. Her Roads and Water tour looks at the infrastructure of the ancient city by focusing on the Appian Way and the Claudian aqueduct. Pre-booking is essential; 3hr; €340 for up to 3 people; private driver service and entrance fees included.

TOURIST INFORMATION

Parco Regionale dell'Appia Antica The information office for the area – which is a regional park – is at Via Appia Antica 58, right at the start of the park, on the right before you get to Domine Quo Vadis (end March to end Oct Mon–Sat 9.30am–1pm & 2–5.30pm, Sun 9.30am–6pm; end Oct to end March 9.30am–1pm & 2–5pm, Sun 9.30am–5pm; ☎ 06 513 5316, ⊛ parcoappiaantica.it); you can pick up a good map and other information on the various Appia Antica sights and rent bikes here (see opposite). Their website has lots of good information in

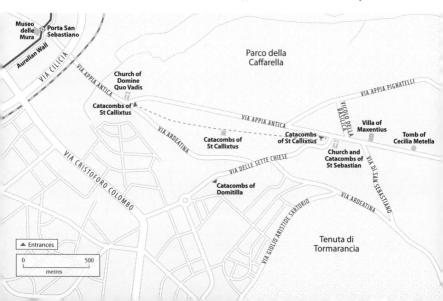

English, including recommended walking tours and places to go horseriding in the area.

EATING

It's nice to take a picnic if you're making a day of it, but there are also good restaurants: *L'Archeologia*, just past the church at Via Appia Antica 125 (☎ 06 788 0494; closed Tues), and *Cecilia Metella*, right opposite at Via Appia Antica 139 (☎ 06 512 6769; closed Mon); neither is especially cheap but both are pleasant and have nice gardens.

Domine Quo Vadis

Via Appia Antica 51 • Daily 8am–6pm; closes 7pm in summer • ☎ 06 512 0441

About 500m from Porta San Sebastiano (an unappealing stretch of pavement-less road best avoided on foot), where the road forks, the church of **Domine Quo Vadis** is the first obvious sight, and signals the start of the catacomb stretch of road. Legend has this as the place where St Peter saw Christ while fleeing certain death in Rome and asked, "Where goest thou, Lord?", to which Christ replied that he was going to be crucified once more, leading Peter to turn around and accept his fate. The small church houses a replica of a piece of marble that is said to be marked with the footprints of Christ from the meeting on this spot; the original is in the church of San Sebastiano (see p.150).

Catacombe di San Callisto

Via Appia Antica 110–126 • Daily except Wed 9am–noon & 2–5pm; closed end Jan to end Feb; tours 45min • €8 • ☎ 06 513 0151, ⓦ catacombe.roma.it

Opposite the church of Domine Quo Vadis, a tree-lined road leads across the fields a kilometre or so to the **Catacombe di San Callisto** – also accessible from Via Appia Antica itself close to the church of San Sebastiano, and from Via Ardeatina. They're the largest of Rome's catacombs, and the regular tours in English are usually run by priests, taking in a bit of preliminary explanation before heading into the high-vaulted passages, which stretch for some 30km and once held around half a million bodies. This complex was founded in the second century AD, and many of the early popes are buried here in the papal crypt, including Callixtus himself. St Callixtus was in fact the guardian of the cemetery before he became pope; he was later killed in a riot and buried here in 222 AD, along with Sixtus II and seven other early popes. The

9

numerous passages and burial vaults are as atmospheric as you would expect and also feature some well-preserved seventh- and eighth-century **frescoes**, as well as the **crypt of Santa Cecilia**, who was buried here after her martyrdom, before being shifted to the church dedicated to her in Trastevere (see p.164) – a copy of Carlo Maderno's famous statue marks the spot.

Catacombe di Santa Domitilla

Via delle Sette Chiese 282 • Daily except Tues 9am–noon & 2–5pm; tours (in English) 45min • €8 • ☎ 06 511 0342, ⓦ domitilla.info

In the opposite direction from the San Callisto exit, up Via delle Sette Chiese on the left, the **Catacombe di Santa Domitilla** are quieter than those of San Callisto. The catacombs stretch from underneath a renovated fourth-century basilica that was erected to the martyrs Achilleus and Nereus, Roman citizens who were killed for their Christian beliefs and eventually buried here during the reign of Diocletian. Domitilla was a Roman noblewoman who donated the land that the catacombs occupy. The network stretches for around 17km in all and is thought to contain around 150,000 tombs. Tours wind about a small section beneath the church, taking in several late-fourth-century BC frescoes and the usual wall etchings and niches.

Mausoleo delle Fosse Ardeatine

Via Ardeatina 174 • Mon–Fri 8.15am–3.15pm, Sat & Sun 8.15am–4.45pm; museum closes 15min earlier • Free

Near the alternative entrance to the San Callisto catacombs, the **Mausoleo delle Fosse Ardeatine** commemorates the massacre of over three hundred civilians during the Nazi occupation of Rome, after the resistance had ambushed and killed 32 soldiers on Via Rasella in the centre of the city (an event remembered in the 1973 film *Massacre in Rome*). The Nazis killed ten arbitrarily chosen civilians for every dead German, burying the bodies here and then exploding mines to cover up their crime. The bodies were dug up after the war and reinterred in the mausoleum. Chapels have been installed in the so-called **Grotta dell'Eccidio**, where the bodies were found; they now rest in an extremely moving nearby area under serried rows of stone slabs, each with a name, age, profession, and photo apart from the odd "*ignoto*" (unknown). Just above here a path leads to a small **museum** with newspaper cuttings telling the story of the event, and various other artefacts relating to the Nazi occupation, resistance and eventual liberation.

Catacombe di San Sebastiano

Via Appia Antica 136 • Mon–Sat 10am–5pm • €8 • ☎ 06 785 0350, ⓦ catacombe.org

The **Catacombe di San Sebastiano**, the first complex to be developed in the first century, are situated beneath a much-renovated church that was originally built by Constantine above the catacombs where Saint Sebastian was buried, and where the bodies of Sts Peter and Paul are said to have been kept for protection during the Barbarian invasions. In the church, the first chapel on the left holds a statue of Sebastian as he lay dying, built above his original tomb, while opposite, among various relics is the original slab of marble supposedly imprinted with the feet of Christ that you may have seen in the church of Domine Quo Vadis.

Downstairs, half-hour tours wind around the catacombs, dark corridors showing signs of early Christian worship – paintings of doves and fish, a contemporary carved oil lamp and inscriptions dating the tombs themselves. The most striking features, however, are not Christian at all, but three **pagan tombs** (one painted, two stuccoed), discovered when archeologists were burrowing beneath the floor of the basilica upstairs. These were buried when Constantine is said to have raised his chapel to Peter and Paul, and although the remains of St Peter were later removed to the Vatican, and St Paul to San Paolo fuori le Mura, the graffiti up the staircase from

CLOCKWISE FROM TOP LEFT SHELLEY'S GRAVESTONE (P.143); BATHS OF CARACALLA (P.139); CENTRALE MONTEMARTINI (P.145) >

PERCY BYSSHE SH

COR DIUM

ATUS IV AUG. MDCCX

II JUL. MDCCCXXI

him that doth fade,
a sea=change
h and strange

FRANCO TOSI
LEGNANO
ITALIA

9

the pagan tombs record the fact that this was indeed, albeit temporarily, where the two apostles rested.

Villa and Circus of Maxentius

Via Appia Antica 153 • Tues–Sun 10am–4pm • Free • ☎ 06 06068, ⓦ villadimassenzio.it

A couple of hundred metres further on from the San Sebastiano catacombs, the group of brick ruins trailing off into the fields to the left are the remains of the **Villa and Circus of Maxentius**, a large complex built by the Emperor in the early fourth century AD before his defeat by Constantine. It's a clear, long oval of grass, similar to the Circus Maximus (see p.86) back in town, but slightly better preserved and in a rather more bucolic location. You can make out the twelve starting gates to the circus, or racetrack, the enormous towers that contained the mechanism for lifting the gates at the beginning of the races and the remains of a basilica. The remains of the imperial villa stand above the circus, built on top of – and incorporating the vestiges of – a second-century structure, which in turn was built over one dating to the late Republic. To the left of the racetrack are the circular ruins of what was once a magnificent mausoleum. The **Tomb of Romulus** was built to commemorate the son of Maxentius who was deified after his death aged 5 or 6. The small circular temple in the Forum (see p.77) is believed to have been dedicated to him. A farmhouse built against the mausoleum has been restored and is destined to become a museum area.

Tomb of Cecilia Metella

Via Appia Antica 161 • Tues–Sun 9am–1hr before sunset; last entry 1hr before closing • €6 combined ticket with Baths of Caracalla (p.139) and Villa dei Quintili (see opposite); free first Sun of the month • ☎ 06 3996 7700

Further along the Via Appia is the circular **Tomb of Cecilia Metella** from the Augustan period, converted into a castle in the fourteenth century. It's believed to be the tomb of the daughter of one Quintus Metellus Creticus, who was a consul around 70 BC. Metella married the son of Marcus Crassus, who – with Julius Caesar and Pompey – was one of a short-lived "first triumvirate" of rulers of the late Roman Republic. The vast tomb on a conveniently raised spot of land (the end of the lava flow of the Alban Hills) was the perfect place for a look-out point, and was integrated into the medieval fortress of the Caetani family (the family of Pope Boniface VIII). The small museum area incorporates the courtyards of the medieval fortress.

Capo di Bove

Via Appia Antica 222 • Mon–Sat 10am–4pm, Sun 10am–6pm • Free • ☎ 06 3996 7700

About 500m beyond Cecilia Metella, the **Capo di Bove** consists of the remains of an ancient Roman bath complex, possibly part of the vast estate of Herodius Atticus, a Greek aristocrat and senator, and one-time tutor of Marcus Aurelius. You can make out most of the rooms of the baths, as well as a few fragments of mosaic floors. The building beyond the site holds the photography archive of journalist and politician **Antonio Cederna**, the driving force behind Italy's first environmental movement, who was passionate about the Via Appia Antica and did much to protect it from development during the postwar building boom which laid waste to so much of the Campagna Romana.

South to the Villa dei Quintili

Beyond Cecilia Metella, the Via Appia Antica hits proper countryside, and the road heads straight south: some stretches are still made up of the original Roman slabs, with the road's verges littered with ancient rubble, including tombs, shrines, gateposts and watchtowers, most of them excavated during the nineteenth century. There's no bus out here, but it's by far the most atmospheric stretch of the ancient Via Appia, and a lovely walk or cycle through open countryside and past multiple gated villas. Where else can

ROME'S AQUEDUCTS

Eleven major **aqueducts** supplied ancient Rome with water, built between the fourth century BC and third century AD. At its height the population of the city was around a million, and between them the aqueducts ensured that an estimated cubic metre of water entered the city per capita every day – far more than the per capita water supply of any city before or since. The aqueducts were designed to allow water to flow freely towards the city under the force of gravity. The majority of aqueducts were tunnelled through the hills; it was only when they got closer to the city and the elevation required to maintain the gradient dropped away too rapidly that the water would run along a conduit raised on arches, providing the gradual gradient necessary to allow the water to reach the city with the required pressure.

you enjoy a picnic on the ancient stones of a Roman funerary memorial? Follow the road as far as the Villa dei Quintili (see below), which can be accessed by a (poorly signposted) entrance off Via Appia Antica 251.

Villa dei Quintili

Via Appia Nuova 1092; access also possible at Via Appia Antica 251 (see above) • Tues–Sun 9am–1hr before sunset; last entry 1hr before closing • €6 combined ticket with Tomb of Cecilia Metella (see opposite) and Baths of Caracalla (p.139); free first Sun of the month • ☏ 06 3996 7700 • Colli Albani Metro, then bus #664

The **Villa dei Quintili** crowns the crest of a hill not far from the main road out to Ciampino. It's one of the largest and most complete suburban villas close to Rome, and dates from the mid-second century AD. As you might expect from the position of the place, the Quintili were an influential Roman family; two brothers were consuls under Commodus, and subsequently executed by him in 182 AD on spurious charges of treason.

The main building contains a one-room **museum** with finds from the villa and surrounding area: a large statue of Zeus and three heads of Hermes, a lovely head of a woman and another of a man from the residential section of the villa, a fragment of a relief of Mithras slaying the Bull from the villa's baths, and three almost perfect wall designs of male nude figures in *opus sectile*. The villa itself is up a track on the mound of the hill, enjoying panoramic views of the Roman countryside on all sides. On the northern side, the massive **bath complex** has steps leading down to its well-preserved caldarium, in which a rectangular pool is overlooked by massive windows designed to keep the temperature inside comfortably warm. A few rooms over, the frigidarium is perhaps the best-preserved room in the complex, with considerable traces of its mosaic floor and two columns at the far end. Retracing your steps, you can also walk the corridors of the residential part of the villa; while on the far side of the complex you can wander into what must have been a hugely impressive main reception hall, whose large windows would have made the most of the countryside views. A number of spaces have beautifully restored mosaics in situ.

Parco degli Acquedotti

Via Lemonica 256 • A few minutes' walk from Subaugusta Metro

The **Parco degli Acquedotti** is a lovely spot, where two aqueducts (see box above) snake between the pines of suburban Rome. Of the pair, the **Acqua Claudia** (towards the Via Appia Nuova side, by Via Appio Claudio) is unusually intact, its arches leading off south into the far distance. Looking north, along its more ruinous stretches, you can see central Rome, marked by the dome of St Peter's. The other, lower aqueduct is the **Acqua Felice**, which is supplemented by a modern pipe. They are an impressive sight, and make a nice place for a picnic.

9 ## Cinecittà

Via Tuscolana 1055 · Daily except Tues 9.30am–6.30pm; tours in English at 11:30am & 4pm · €20 · ☎ 06 722 931, Ⓦ cinecittastudios.it · Metro Cinecittà

Still the largest film-making complex in Europe and one of the biggest in the world, **Cinecittà**, set in its own oasis of umbrella pines on the southeastern edge of the city, is steeped in history and legend. Built in the 1930s and opened by Mussolini in 1937, its first few years were given over to propaganda movies glorifying the Fascist regime. But after World War II, its reputation for quality and low costs plus its accessible location brought some of the big Hollywood producers here to make historical epics such as *Ben-Hur* and *Cleopatra* (the latter one of the most expensive films ever made at the time), as well as more low-key classics such as *The Pink Panther*.

Of course, all the great Italian directors used Cinecittà, too: **Fellini** made nearly all of his movies here, and Vittorio De Sica, **Franco Zeffirelli**, **Luchino Visconti**, Pasolini and many others were regular visitors during their 1960s and 1970s heyday; it was also the creative home of **Sergio Leone**'s spaghetti westerns. And the studio still thrives, after a major corporate takeover and a serious upgrade of its facilities in the 1990s. **Bernardo Bertolucci** made much of his *Last Emperor* here in 1987, and more recently **Martin Scorsese** used its giant sound stages to recreate the streets of New York for *Gangs of New York*; HBO also came here – where else? – to film their epic, *Rome*, in 2005, and the *Ben-Hur* remake and *Zoolander 2* were both filmed here in 2015. Although part of the complex was damaged by a serious fire in 2007, it finally caught up with its counterparts in the US and opened to the public for tours in 2012. The studios' latest venture, a €250-million movie-themed amusement park, called **Cinecittà World** (see p.311), opened 25km west of the studios in 2014.

Studio tours

Don't expect anything approaching the structure or scale of big Hollywood studio tours, but if you have an interest in Italian cinema **"Cinecittà Shows Off"** is worth the metro ride. The small museum traces the studios' history, with technology, props and costumes, and you don't have to be that much of a movie buff to enjoy the Liz and Dick *Cleopatra* garb. Other costume highlights include La Gradisca's red coat worn in Fellini's *Amarcord* and Cameron Diaz's dress from *Gangs of New York*. A new permanent exhibition, **"Shooting in Cinecittà"**, covers seventy years of filming at the studios, touching on various genres, from Italian comedy to spaghetti westerns, ending with a screening room dedicated to Sergio Leone's *Once Upon a Time in America*.

There are also **guided tours** of some of the sets; at the time of writing, the recreations of late Republican Rome for HBO's *Rome* series were undoubtedly the main highlight. When you're done, you can relax at the studio café.

EUR

Metro EUR Fermi, Palasport or Magliana, or bus to Via Cristoforo Colombo or Piazza Marconi

From Piazza di Porta San Paolo and the Piramide metro station, Via Ostiense leads south to join up with Via Cristoforo Colombo, which in turn runs down to **EUR** (pronounced "eh-oor") – the acronym for the district originally intended for the "Esposizione Universale Roma" in 1942, designed by Marcello Piacentini, Mussolini's favourite architect. In the end, the exhibition didn't take place for obvious reasons, but the planned "city within a city" went ahead anyway, though much of the building work wasn't finished until 1960, when the site was repurposed as a hub for the Olympics.

The core of EUR is not so much a neighbourhood as a statement in stone, a slightly soulless grid of square buildings, long vistas and wide processional boulevards linked tenuously to the rest of Rome by metro but light years away from the city in feel. Especially on a Sunday, it has the intriguing but unsettling atmosphere of a De Chirico painting writ large. The district's great flaw is that it's not really built for people: the streets are designed for easy traffic flow and the shops and cafés are easily outnumbered by offices, although the columned buildings provide shade in numerous arcades. Tree-lined Viale America is one of the pleasanter boulevards to stroll down. Of the main structures, it's the prewar, Fascist-era constructions that are of most interest; the postwar development of the area threw up bland office blocks for the most part. Come here for EUR's museums, or if you have a yen for modern city architecture and planning. **Piazza Marconi** is the nominal centre of EUR, where the wide, classically inspired boulevards intersect to swerve around a friezed obelisk dedicated to the inventor of radio in the centre; EUR's museums are within easy reach of here.

Palazzo della Civiltà del Lavoro

A few minutes' walk from Piazza Marconi, in the northwest corner of EUR, the **Palazzo della Civiltà del Lavoro** is a visual highlight – Mussolini-inspired architecture at its most assured, and chauvinistic: the inscription around the top reads "One Nation, of Poets, Artists, Heroes, Saints, Thinkers, Scientists, Navigators and Travellers". With a heroic statue on each corner, it's a successful and imposing structure, and far and away the best piece of architecture in EUR. Some have called it the "square Colosseum",

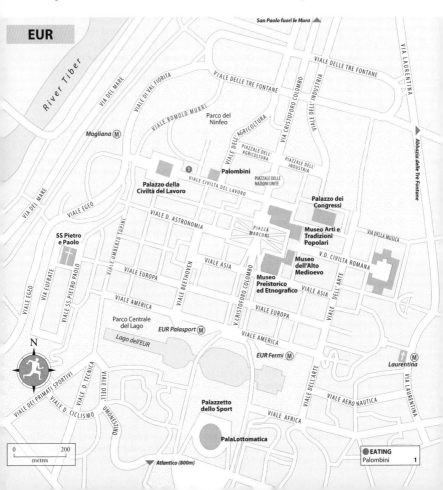

EUR

San Paolo fuori le Mura

River Tiber

VIA LAURENTINA

VIALE DELLE TRE FONTANE

VIA DEL MARE

VIALE DI VAL FIORITA

VIALE DELLE TRE FONTANE

VIALE ROMOLO MURRI

VIA CRISTOFORO COLOMBO

VIALE DELL'INDUSTRIA

Parco del Ninfeo

Magliana Ⓜ

Abbazia delle Tre Fontane

VIALE DELL'AGRICOLTURA

PIAZZALE DELL'AGRICOLTURA

PIAZZALE DELL'INDUSTRIA

ⓘ **Palombini**

Palazzo della Civiltà del Lavoro

VIALE CIVILTÀ DEL LAVORO

PIAZZALE DELLE NAZIONI UNITE

Palazzo dei Congressi

VIA DEL MARE

VIALE EGEO

VIALE D. ASTRONOMIA

PIAZZA MARCONI

Museo Arti e Tradizioni Popolari

VIA DELLA MUSICA

SS Pietro e Paolo ✝

VIALE UMBERTO TUPINI

V.D. CIVILTÀ ROMANA

VIALE ASIA

Museo dell'Alto Medioevo

VIALE SS PIETRO PAOLO

VIA EUFRATE

VIALE EUROPA

VIALE BEETHOVEN

VIALE ASIA

VIALE DELL'ARTE

VIALE EGEO

Museo Preistorico ed Etnografico

V. CRISTOFORO COLOMBO

VIALE AMERICA

VIALE EUROPA

Parco Centrale del Lago

EUR Palasport Ⓜ

VIALE AMERICA

Lago dell'EUR

EUR Fermi Ⓜ

ⓘ Ⓜ
Laurentina

N

VIA LAURENTINA

VIALE DEI PRIMATI SPORTIVI

VIALE D. TECNICA

VIALE DELL'UMONESIND

VIALE D. CICLISMO

VIALE DELL'ARTE

Palazzetto dello Sport

VIALE AERO NAUTICA

VIALE AFRICA

0 ___ 200
metres

PalaLottomatica

▼ Atlantico (800m)

● **EATING**
Palombini   1

9

which sums up its mixture of modern and classical styles perfectly. It recently underwent a massive restoration sponsored by Fendi who have taken the lease for their HQ. Occasional exhibitions celebrating Italian design of various sorts allow free access to the ground floor, so it's worth asking at the gate.

Museo Nazionale delle Arti e delle Tradizioni Popolari

Piazza Marconi 8 • Tues–Sun 8.30am–7.30pm; last entry 45min before closing • €4, €10 combined ticket with other EUR museums, valid 3 days; free first Sun of the month • ☎ 06 592 6148, ⓦ idea.mat.beniculturali.it

The **Museo Nazionale delle Arti e delle Tradizioni Popolari** is a run-through of applied arts, costumes, and religious artefacts from the Italian regions. It's hardly essential viewing unless you have a specific interest, but it's exhaustive and gives a great insight into the diverse and intensely regional nature of Italy, not to mention how close the country is to its roots and traditions – an odd juxtaposition in the heart of EUR. Everything is labelled in Italian, so you might want to bring a dictionary.

Museo Nazionale Preistorico ed Etnografico Luigi Pigorini

Piazza Marconi 14 • Mon–Sat 9am–6pm, Sun 9am–1.30pm • €6, €10 combined ticket with other EUR museums, valid for 3 days; free first Sun of the month • ☎ 06 549 521, ⓦ pigorini.beniculturali.it

The **Museo Nazionale Preistorico ed Etnografico Luigi Pigorini** is Rome's natural history and ethnographic museum rolled into one, and it does a pretty good job, arranged in manageable and easily comprehensible order. Enthusiasts will find its prehistoric section exhaustive. The ethnographic collection, much of which originated in the collection of the seventeenth-century Jesuit Athanasius Kircher, has artefacts from South America, the Pacific and Africa.

Museo dell'Alto Medioevo

Viale Lincoln 3 • Tues, Fri & Sat 9am–2pm, Wed, Thurs & Sun 9am–7.30pm • €4, €10 combined ticket with other EUR museums, valid for 3 days; free first Sun of the month • ☎ 06 5422 8199, ⓦ archeoroma.beniculturali.it/en/museums/national-museum-early-middle-ages

Housed in the same building as the Pigorini museum, further down the colonnade, the **Museo dell'Alto Medioevo** concentrates on artefacts from the fifth to the tenth centuries – local finds mainly, including some beautiful jewellery from the seventh century and a delicate fifth-century gold fibula found on the Palatine Hill.

Museo della Civiltà Romana

Piazza Agnelli 10 • Closed indefinitely at the time of writing • ☎ 06 0608, ⓦ museociviltaromana.it

Of all the museums, the most interesting is the **Museo della Civiltà Romana**, though it's currently closed for restoration. Amid the reconstructed statuary, tablets and inscriptions, the ordinary stuff impresses most – small bronze lamps, medical instruments, carved zodiac charts, musical instruments and the like. Among many reconstructions, the long corridor housing large casts of the reliefs from Trajan's Column is instructive, to say the least. The *pièce de résistance* is a room-filling model of Rome during the time of Constantine to a 1:250 scale that you can look down on from above – perfect for setting the rest of the city in context.

Abbazia delle Tre Fontane

Viale Acqua Salvie 1 • Daily: grounds 6am–8.30pm; Santi Vincenzo e Anastasio 6.30am–12.30pm & 3–8.45pm; Santa Maria alla Scala Coeli 8am–1pm & 3–6pm; Chiesa della Martirio di San Paolo 8am–1pm & 4–6pm; shop 9.30am–1.30pm & 3.30–7.30pm • ☎ 06 540 1655, ⓦ abbaziatrefontane.it • 10min walk from Laurentina Metro or bus #761 from the Basilica di San Paolo

The perfect antidote to the brutalist experiment of EUR is just a ten-minute walk away: the **Abbazia delle Tre Fontane**, a complex of churches founded on the spot where St Paul was martyred – it's said that when the saint was beheaded his head bounced and three springs erupted where it touched the ground. In those days this was a malarial area, and it was all but abandoned during the Middle Ages, but in the second half of the nineteenth century Trappist monks drained the swamp and planted eucalyptus trees in the vicinity; monks still distil a eucalyptus-based chest remedy here, as well as an exquisite liqueur, chocolate bars, wine, toiletries and all manner of other monastic products – all sold at the small **shop** and bar by the entrance. The three churches were rebuilt in the sixteenth century and restored by the Trappists. They're not particularly outstanding buildings, appealing more for their peaceful location, which is relatively undisturbed by visitors, than any architectural distinction. The **gatehouse**, on the way out, contains ceiling frescoes from the thirteenth century that show the possessions of the abbey at the time. They're in a pretty bad state, but you can make out a few heads of Christ and a kind of picture map of Italy in the thirteenth century.

The churches

The first and largest of the Tre Fontane **churches**, originally built in 625 and rebuilt and finally restored by the Trappists, is **Santi Vincenzo e Anastasio**, its gloomy atmosphere exacerbated by the fact that most of the windows are of a thick marble that admits little light – although the stained-glass ones, dating from the Renaissance with papal heraldry from that period, are beautiful. The three fountains in the floor, supposedly formed by the saint's bouncing head, have long since run dry.

To the right, the church of **Santa Maria alla Scala Coeli** owes its name to a vision that St Bernard had here in which he saw the soul he was praying for ascend to heaven; the Cosmatesque altar where this is supposed to have happened is down the cramped stairs, in the crypt, where St Paul was allegedly kept prior to his beheading. Beyond, the **Chiesa della Martirio di San Paolo** lies at the end of a tree-lined path and holds the pillar to which St Paul was tied in the right transept and a couple of very well-preserved mosaic pavements from Ostia Antica. Try to be here, if you can, in the early morning or evening, when the monks come in to sing Mass in Gregorian chant – a moving experience.

GALATEA BY RAPHAEL, VILLA FARNESINA

Trastevere and the Janiculum Hill

Sheltered under the Janiculum Hill, Trastevere was the artisan area of the city
in classical times, neatly placed for the trade that came upriver from Ostia
and was unloaded nearby. Located across the river and outside the city walls
(the name means literally "across the Tiber"), its separation lent the
neighbourhood a strong identity that lasted well into the twentieth century.
Although these influences are long gone, it's still one of the city's most
appealing neighbourhoods for a stroll, with some very worthwhile sights,
notably the Villa Farnesina and the churches of Santa Maria and Santa Cecilia.
Its narrow streets and closeted squares are peaceful in the morning, but
lively come the evening, as dozens of trattorias set out tables along the
cobbled streets – and they're still buzzing late at night, when its lively bars
take over.

ARRIVAL AND DEPARTURE   **TRASTEVERE**

By tram or bus The easiest way to reach Trastevere from the Centro Storico and other parts of the city centre is on tram #8 from Piazza Venezia or Via Arenula, just off Largo di Torre Argentina; from Termini take bus H.

On foot Trastevere is easily reachable on foot from the Centro Storico: it's a 15min walk from Largo di Torre Argentina or Piazza Navona, cross the river by the pedestrian Ponte Sisto.

Piazza Belli and Viale di Trastevere

10

Right by the river, the traffic junction of **Piazza Belli** marks the beginning of **Viale di Trastevere**, which cuts the district in two, separating the more discovered and touristy, but still lovely, part to the west (covered below) from the quieter and more undisturbed streets to the east (see p.164). The brick building with the crenellations and tower on Piazza Belli is known as the **Casa di Dante**, although it's doubtful that the poet ever stayed here; while the top-hatted **statue** opposite is of the Roman poet Giuseppe Gioacchino Belli – "the poet of the people of Rome", according to the inscription – who in the nineteenth century produced thousands of sonnets in dialect recording life in the city and waged a long campaign against the reactionary Pope Gregory XVI. After the pope's demise, Belli quipped "I really liked Pope Gregory, because it gave me so much pleasure to speak ill of him."

San Crisogono

Piazza Sonnino 44 • Mon–Sat 7.30–11.30am & 4–7pm, Sun 8am–1pm & 4–7.30pm • Crypt €3 • ☎ 06 581 0076

Next door to Piazza Belli is Piazza Sonnino, where the church of **San Crisogono** is a large, typically Roman basilica, with a nave lined with ancient columns and one of the city's finest Cosmati floors. The church itself is relatively featureless, apart from a beautiful thirteenth-century apse mosaic showing the church's name saint and St James; it's the remains of the earlier buildings below that mark the church out – two buildings really, an early Christian structure from the third century AD and a later fifth-century basilica whose substantial remnants cover almost the entire footprint of the main church. There are some very worn frescoes – St Chrysogonus himself in the centre of the apse, and a saint healing a sick man (covered in spots) in the north aisle – as well as various bits of Roman stonework, including a couple of impressively carved sarcophagi.

Santa Maria in Trastevere

Piazza di Santa Maria in Trastevere • Daily 7.30am–9pm • ☎ 06 581 4802

The heart of Trastevere is **Piazza di Santa Maria in Trastevere**, which is named after the church of **Santa Maria in Trastevere** in its northwest corner, built on a site where a fountain of oil is said to have sprung on the day of Christ's birth, and held to be the first Christian place of worship in Rome. The greater part of the structure now dates from 1140, after a rebuilding by Innocent II, a pope from Trastevere. These days many people come here for the church's **mosaics**, which are among the city's most impressive: those on the cornice were completed a century or so after the rebuilding and show the Madonna surrounded by ten female figures with lamps – once thought to represent the Wise and Foolish Virgins. Inside, there's a nineteenth-century copy of a Cosmatesque pavement of spirals and circles, and more twelfth-century mosaics in the apse, Byzantine-inspired works which depict a solemn yet sensitive parade of saints thronged around Christ and Mary, while underneath a series of panels shows scenes from the life of the Virgin by the painter Pietro Cavallini. Beneath the high altar on the right, an inscription – "FONS OLEI" – marks the spot where the oil is supposed to have sprung up, to the right of which there is a chapel crowned with the crest of the British monarchy – placed here by Henry, Cardinal of York, when he and his family, the Stuarts, lived in exile in Rome.

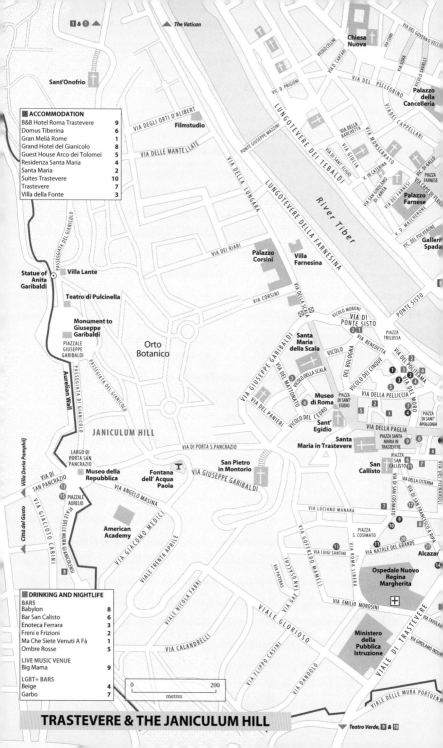

TRASTEVERE & THE JANICULUM HILL

The Vatican

Sant'Onofrio

ACCOMMODATION
B&B Hotel Roma Trastevere	9
Domus Tiberina	6
Gran Meliá Rome	1
Grand Hotel del Gianicolo	8
Guest House Arco dei Tolomei	5
Residenza Santa Maria	4
Santa Maria	2
Suites Trastevere	10
Trastevere	7
Villa della Fonte	3

Filmstudio

Chiesa Nuova

Palazzo della Cancelleria

Palazzo Farnese

Galleria Spada

River Tiber

Palazzo Corsini

Villa Farnesina

Statue of Anita Garibaldi

Villa Lante

Teatro di Pulcinella

Monument to Giuseppe Garibaldi

PIAZZALE GIUSEPPE GARIBALDI

Orto Botanico

Santa Maria della Scala

Museo di Roma

Sant' Egidio

Santa Maria in Trastevere

PONTE SISTO

PIAZZA TRILUSSA

Aurelian Wall

JANICULUM HILL

Largo di Porta San Pancrazio

Museo della Repubblica

Fontana dell' Acqua Paola

San Pietro in Montorio

San Callisto

PIAZZA SAN CALLISTO

PIAZZALE AURELIO

American Academy

Villa Doria Pamphilj

Città del Gusto

PIAZZA S. COSIMATO

Alcazar

Ospedale Nuovo Regina Margherita

DRINKING AND NIGHTLIFE
BARS
Babylon	8
Bar San Calisto	6
Enoteca Ferrara	3
Freni e Frizioni	2
Ma Che Siete Venuti A Fà	1
Ombre Rosse	5

LIVE MUSIC VENUE
Big Mama	9

LGBT+ BARS
Beige	4
Garbo	7

Ministero della Pubblica Istruzione

0 — 200 metres

Teatro Verde, 9 & 10

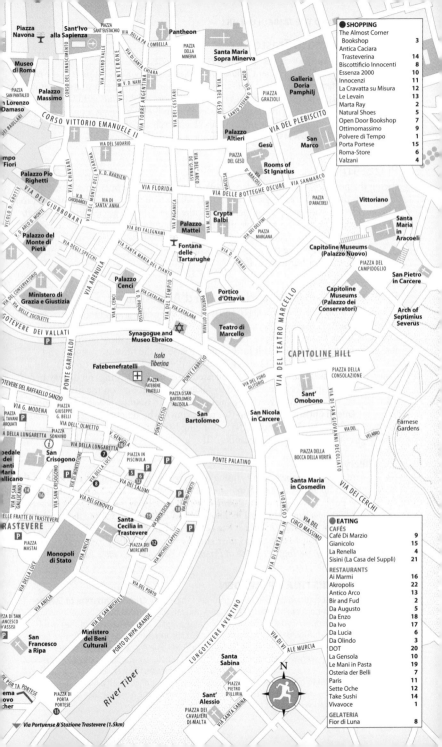

Museo di Roma in Trastevere

Piazza di Sant'Egidio 1b • Tues–Sun 10am–8pm; last entry 7pm • €9.50 • ☎ 06 589 7123, ⓦ museodiromaintrastevere.it

The long triangle of **Piazza di Sant'Egidio**, in the heart of Trastevere, is home to the **Museo di Roma in Trastevere**, a small but well-chosen collection of artefacts illustrating Roman folklore. The displays include paintings of an older, more rural Rome and life-sized tableaux showing scenes of nineteenth-century Roman life – an *osteria*, a pharmacy, a *saltarello* dance and the like. The museum also has a lively programme of temporary exhibitions, with photos and paintings of Rome and its inhabitants to the fore.

10

Piazza Trilussa

Facing the pedestrian Ponte Sisto (see p.49), **Piazza Trilussa** is a busy open space that focuses on the steps up to its grand 1613 fountain, where the waters of the Acqua Paola emerge. On the other side, the upper torso of the poet Trilussa, after whom the square is named, casually leans on a marble plinth as if declaiming his poems – one of which is printed beneath him. Trilussa is actually the pen-name (and an anagram) of Carlo Alberto Salustri, who, like the nineteenth-century Roman poet Belli (see p.159), wrote in dialect – often for humorous effect.

Palazzo Corsini: Galleria Nazionale d'Arte Antica

Via della Lungara 10 • Daily except Tues 8.30am–7.30pm • €5, or €9 including Palazzo Barberini (p.105); valid for 10 days; free first Sun of the month • ☎ 06 6880 2323, ⓦ galleriacorsini.beniculturali.it

On the edge of Trastevere proper, the **Palazzo Corsini** – sister gallery to the Palazzo Barberini (see p.105) – was built for Cardinal Riario in the fifteenth century, and totally renovated between 1732 and 1736 by Ferdinando Fuga for the cardinal and art collector Neri Maria Corsini. Corsini collected most of the paintings on display here now, a relatively small collection that only takes up a few rooms on the first floor of the giant palace, which dwarfs everything in the immediate vicinity. It was a fitting final home for **Queen Christina of Sweden** (see box below), who renounced Protestantism and with it the Swedish throne in 1655, bringing her library and fortune to Rome, to the delight of the Chigi pope, Alexander VII.

The gallery

It's not hard to imagine the queen roaming the lofty rooms and draughty corridors of the palace – such is its haunting grandeur – and her bedchamber features among the rooms open to the public. Among the **art**, Room 1 (which doubles as the ticket office) boasts some fairly harmless landscapes by Dughet, followed in Room 2 by more heavyweight works such as the Neapolitan Salvator Rosa's large and graphic vision of Prometheus having his entrails ripped out. Off to the right, the Cardinal Gallery has a real mixture: Lanfranco's *St Peter Healing St Agatha in Prison*, Fra Bartolomeo's *Holy Family and St John*

QUEEN CHRISTINA OF SWEDEN

One of the most cultured women of the seventeenth century, **Queen Christina of Sweden** was passionate about philosophy, mathematics and religion, and a knowledgeable patron of the arts. Having renounced the Swedish throne at the age of 28, the "Minerva of the north" moved to Rome, living first in Palazzo Farnese (see p.48) and then at the Palazzo Corsini (see above) for a number of years, dying in the palace in 1689. She is one of only five women to be buried in St Peter's, notwithstanding her rejection of Catholic convention: she often turned out in men's clothes, removed the strategically placed fig leaves on the statues in her palace and made no attempt to hide her bisexuality, at one stage having affairs with a nun and a cardinal at the same time, and giving the English ambassador at the time a real surprise by introducing her latest female companion as her "bedfellow".

the Baptist, Van Dyck's sensitive *Madonna of the Straw*, a copy of Raphael's famous portrait of Julius II, and – on a more low-key note – a tavern scene by David Teniers.

In the next room the focus is on the curious **Corsini Throne**, thought to be a Roman copy of an Etruscan throne from the second or first century BC. Hewn out of marble, its back is carved with warriors in armour and helmets, below which wild boar the size of horses are pursued by hunters. The base is decorated with scenes of a sacrifice, notably the minotaur devouring a human being – only discernible by the kicking legs that protrude from the feasting beast. The throne is overlooked by two penetrating paintings by Rubens – *Testa d'Uomo* and *Testa di Vecchio* – alongside a famous portrayal of *Salome with the Head of John the Baptist* by Guido Reni. Next door, **Queen Christina's bedchamber**, where she died in 1689, is decorated with frescoes by an unknown artist – cupids and grotesques with scenes of the miracles of Moses – and on the wall is a portrait of the queen as Diana by Justus van Egmont and a depiction of the Pantheon by Charles-Louis Clérisseau, though it's a rather fanciful interpretation, squeezing the Pyramid of Cestius and Arch of Janus into the background. Two rooms further on is Caravaggio's youthful, highly stylized *St John the Baptist*, as well as paintings by more Neapolitans – in this case Luca Giordano and Giuseppe de Ribera.

10

Orto Botanico

Largo Cristina di Svezia 24 • Entry at the top of Via Corsini; no entry from the Palazzo Corsini • Mon–Sat: April to end Oct 9am–6.30pm; end Oct to March 9am–5pm, closed public holidays • €8 • ☎ 06 4991 7107 ⊛ ortobotanicoitalia.it/lazio/romalasapienza

The grounds of the Palazzo Corsini are the site of the **Orto Botanico**, which, after Padua's botanical garden, is the most important in Italy – and a good example of eighteenth-century garden design. It's a pleasantly unkempt expanse these days, a low-key bucolic retreat clasping the side of the Janiculum Hill. You can clamber up to high stands of bamboo and ferns cut by rivulets of water and stroll through a wood of century-old oaks, cedars and conifers. A grove of acclimatized palm trees stands in front of the so-called Fountain of the Tritons, a rather grand name for the relatively small-scale fountain that forms the centrepiece of the lower part of the gardens. There's a herbal garden with medicinal plants, greenhouses holding succulents and cacti, and a collection of orchids that bloom in springtime and early summer. A garden of aromatic herbs has been put together for the blind; the plants can be identified by their smell or touch, and are accompanied by signs in Braille. The garden also has the distinction of being home to one of the oldest plane trees in Rome, between 350 and 400 years old, situated by the monumental staircase.

Villa Farnesina

Via della Lungara 230 • Mon–Sat 9am–2pm, second Sun of the month 9am–5pm • €6; second Sun of the month (with obligatory guided tour) €12 • ☎ 06 6802 7268, ⊛ villafarnesina.it

Across the road from the Palazzo Corsini, the small **Villa Farnesina** is a fabulous example of a Renaissance pleasure villa. Built during the early sixteenth century by Baldassare Peruzzi for the banker Agostino Chigi, it is a unique building, known for its frescoes and contributed to by some of the masters of the Renaissance. Chigi situated his villa here to be close to the papal court and away from his business cronies.

Beyond the entrance, in the first room, is Raphael's **Galatea** fresco, which depicts the eponymous sea nymph on her scallop-shell chariot, drawn by dolphins – described by Kenneth Clark as "the greatest evocation of paganism of the Renaissance". It seems that Raphael fitted it in between his Vatican commissions for Julius II, but the painter and (not always reliable) art historian Vasari claims that Michelangelo, passing by one day while Raphael was canoodling with his mistress, "La Fornarina", finished the painting for him. The rest of the room is a mixed bag thematically with bucolic country scenes and, in one of the lunettes, a giant, monochrome head, which was once said to have been painted by Michelangelo, but is now attributed to the architect of the building, Peruzzi. The other lunettes feature scenes from Ovid's *Metamorphoses* by Sebastiano del Piombo and the ceiling shows Chigi's horoscope constellations, again frescoed by Peruzzi.

In the next room, the Raphael-designed painting of **Cupid and Psyche** in a glassed-in loggia was completed in 1517 by the artist's assistants, Giulio Romano, Francesco Penni and Giovanni da Udine. Here again, Vasari claims Raphael didn't complete the work because of his infatuation with his mistress, whose father's bakery was situated nearby, but more likely he was simply so overloaded with commissions that he couldn't possibly finish them all. Whoever was responsible, it's mightily impressive, a flowing, animated work bursting with muscular men and bare-bosomed women. Actually, it would have made even more of an impact if completed as planned, because the blue would have been much brighter – what you see is just the preparatory colour.

Upstairs, the **Sala delle Prospettive** features trompe-l'oeil balconies giving views onto contemporary Rome – one of the earliest examples of the technique. This room leads through to Chigi's **bedroom**, decorated with Sodoma's extremely bold and colourful scenes from the life of Alexander the Great and his wife Roxane.

Santa Cecilia in Trastevere

Piazza di Santa Cecilia, off Piazza dei Mercanti • Basilica & crypt Mon–Sat 9.30am–1pm & 4–7.15pm, Sun 11.30am–12.30pm & 4.30–6.30pm; singing gallery Mon–Sat 10am–12.30pm, Sun 11.30am–12.30pm • Basilica free; crypt €2.50; singing gallery €2.50 • ☎ 06 589 9289

In the quieter, eastern half of Trastevere, the basilica of **Santa Cecilia in Trastevere** is set in a pretty courtyard. Its slightly antiseptic eighteenth-century appearance belies the more ancient church beneath (look for the ninth-century bell tower; the facelift was superficial). The church stands on the site of the third-century home of **St Cecilia**, whose husband Valerian was executed for refusing to worship Roman gods and who herself was subsequently persecuted for her Christian beliefs. The story has it that Cecilia was locked in the caldarium (hot room) of her own baths for several days, but refused to die, singing her way through the ordeal (Cecilia is the patron saint of music). Her head was finally half hacked off with an axe, though it took several blows before she finally expired.

Below the high altar, under a Gothic baldacchino, Stefano Maderno's limp **statue** of the saint shows her incorruptible body as it was found when exhumed in 1599, with three deep cuts in her neck – a fragile, intensely human piece of work that has helped make Cecilia one of the most revered Roman saints. Behind all this presides an apse **mosaic** from the ninth century showing Paschal I, who founded the current church, being presented to Christ by St Cecilia flanked by various saints. The excavations of the baths and the rest of the Roman house are on view in the **crypt** below – a series of dank rooms with some fragments of mosaic and a gaudily decorated chapel at the far end – but more alluring by far is the **singing gallery** above the nave of the church, where Pietro Cavallini's partially visible late thirteenth-century **fresco of the Last Judgement** is all that remains of the decoration that once covered the entire church. For access (hours above) ring the buzzer at the door up a couple of steps to the right of the church's entrance. It's a powerful painting, an amazingly fluid, naturalistic piece of work for the time, with each of the Apostles, ranked six each side of Christ, captured as an individual portrait, while Christ sits in quiet, meditative majesty in the centre, flanked by angels.

San Francesco a Ripa

Piazza di San Francesco d'Assisi 88 • Daily 7am–1pm & 2.30–7pm • ☎ 06 581 9020, ⓦ sanfrancescoaripa.com

Not far from Santa Cecilia, the church of **San Francesco a Ripa** is best known for its association with St Francis, who once stayed here. You can see the actual room that he slept in, which is now a shrine displaying the rock he used as a pillow, on a free guided tour – ask

CLOCKWISE FROM TOP LEFT PORTA PORTESE MARKET (P.166); VILLA FARNESINA (P.163); PIAZZA DI SANTA MARIA IN TRASTEVERE (P.159) >

the attendant; the shrine is beyond the sacristy and up some steep stairs. The church is also the burial place of the twentieth-century Italian artist Giorgio de Chirico (see p.95), who lived in Rome until his death in the 1970s and is buried behind the first chapel on the left, in a simple white room named after the painter (ask the sacristan if you'd like to see it). But perhaps the most visually memorable item in the church is the writhing, orgasmic statue of a minor saint, the *Blessed Ludovica Albertoni*, that Bernini sculpted towards the end of his career; it's located in the last chapel on the left. As a work of Baroque sauciness, it bears comparison with his more famous *Ecstasy of St Teresa* in the church of Santa Maria della Vittoria (see p.111); both show a very earthily realized divine ecstasy.

10

Porta Portese

Via Portuense · Sun 7am–2pm

Trastevere at its traditional if somewhat disreputable best can be witnessed on Sunday mornings, when the **Porta Portese flea market** stretches from the Piazza di Porta Portese down Via Portuense to Trastevere train station in a congested medley of antiques, old motor spares, cheap clothing, household goods, bric-a-brac and assorted junk. Haggling is the rule, and come early if you want to buy – most of the bargains, not to mention the "back of the lorry" goods, have gone by 10am, by which time the crush of people can be intense; keep a good hold of your wallet or purse. It's pretty much all over by lunchtime.

Janiculum Hill

Bus #115 crosses the hill from Viale di Trastevere to the Gianicolo terminal on the Vatican side

The **Janiculum Hill** may not be one of the original seven hills of Rome, but it is the one with the best and most accessible views of the city centre. It also has several **monuments** honouring those Italians who fought with Garibaldi here in 1849: the enemy were the French, who were attempting to put Pius IX back in control of the Papal States after he had been ignominiously driven out by his rebellious subjects. It takes about fifteen minutes to walk to the top of the hill from Trastevere, and there are several possible routes, but perhaps the most enjoyable is to follow Vicolo del Cedro and then take the steps up to Via Garibaldi at a point near San Pietro in Montorio. Alternatively, you can avoid the steps by sticking to Via Garibaldi.

San Pietro in Montorio

Piazza di San Pietro in Montorio 2 · Church Mon–Fri 8.30am–noon & 3–4pm, Sat & Sun 8.30am–noon; Tempietto Tues–Fri 9.30am–12.30pm & 2–4.30pm, Sat 9am–3pm · Free · ☎ 06 581 3940, ⊕ sanpietroinmontorio.it

Now part of a complex that includes the Spanish Academy and Spanish ambassador's residence, the church of **San Pietro in Montorio** was built on a site once believed to have been the place of the saint's crucifixion. The compact interior is particularly intimate – it's a favourite for weddings – and features some first-rate paintings, among them, on the right-hand side at the start of the nave, Sebastiano del Piombo's vivid and muscular *Flagellation*. Also, don't miss Bramante's little **Tempietto**, a small circular building in the courtyard to the right of the church's front door, built on what was supposed to have been the precise spot of St Peter's martyrdom; perfectly proportioned and neatly executed, like a classical temple in miniature, it's one of the seminal works of the Renaissance. Access to the Tempietto is through the Spanish Academy.

Fontana dell'Acqua Paola

Just above the church of San Pietro di Montorio, the **Fontana dell'Acqua Paola**, constructed for Paul V in 1612 with marble from the Roman Forum, gushes water at a bend in the road. It's a very grandiose affair whose ancient water supply is provided by Lake Bracciano, way to the north of Rome, and in turn goes on to feed the fountain down below on Piazza Trilussa.

Passeggiata del Gianicolo

Just beyond the Fontana dell'Acqua Paola, turn right down leafy **Passeggiata del Gianicolo**, which threads its way along the ridge at the top of the Janiculum Hill to **Piazzale Giuseppe Garibaldi**, where there's an equestrian monument to Garibaldi – an ostentatious work from 1895. There are panoramic views of the city from the terrace in front of the statue and just below is the spot from which a cannon is fired at noon each day for Romans to check their watches, leaving a whiff of powder in the air and setting all the car alarms off. Just beyond the *piazzale* is a **statue of Anita Garibaldi**, a fiery, melodramatic work (she cradles a baby in one arm, brandishes a pistol with the other and is galloping full speed on a horse) that recalls the important part she played in the 1849 battle and also marks her grave – she died later in the campaign. Immediately opposite this statue, the Renaissance **Villa Lante** (rarely open) is a jewel of a place that is now the home of the Finnish Academy in Rome and gives a panoramic view of the city.

10

Sant'Onofrio

Piazza di Sant'Onofrio 2 • Daily 7.30am–1.30pm; closed Aug • ☏ 06 686 4498, museum ☏ 06 687 7341 (Tues 4–6pm)

At the bottom of the Janiculum Hill, next to the Bambino Gesù children's hospital, the church of **Sant'Onofrio** sits on the road's bend, with an L-shaped portico and one of the city's most delightful small cloisters to the right. The sixteenth-century Italian poet Torquato Tasso, friend of Mannerist sculptor Benvenuto Cellini and author of *La Gerusalemme Liberata* (Jerusalem Delivered), moved into the cloister in the last weeks of his life and died here the day before being garlanded as poet laureate at the Capitoline Hill. If you call in advance you may be able to arrange to visit the poet's cell, which holds some manuscripts, his chair, his death mask and personal effects. Just beyond the church by a small amphitheatre you'll find **Tasso's Oak**, the gnarled old oak tree where he is said to have whiled away his last days.

Around Largo di Porta San Pancrazio

An arm of the Passeggiata del Gianicolo leads back from the Piazzale Garibaldi to the **Porta San Pancrazio**, a city gate built during the reign of Urban VIII, destroyed by the French in 1849, and rebuilt by Pope Pius IX five years later. It has recently been restored yet again and now houses the modest **Museo della Repubblica Romana e della Memoria Garibaldina** (Tues–Fri 10am–2pm, Sat & Sun 10am–6pm; last entry 1hr before closing; free; ☏ 06 0608, ⊕ museodellarepubblicaromana.it), which has a series of exhibitions on Garibaldi's efforts to hold the French army at bay here on the Janiculum in 1849.

To either side of the Porta are the heavily restored, brown-brick remains of the **Aurelian Wall** (see box, p.147), begun in the third century AD. On the west side of the Porta is **Piazzale Aurelio**, the start of the old Roman Via Aurelia, and close by are the numerous buildings of the **American Academy** in Rome. By the time you get up here you might also be ready for a drink, in which case the American Academy's local, *Bar Gianicolo* (see p.261), right on the square, is the perfect spot for a drink and a bite to eat.

Villa Doria Pamphilj

Via Aurelia Antica • Daily 7am–dusk • ☏ 06 0608

Just beyond the Porta San Pancrazio, down Via di San Pancrazio, is the entrance to the grounds of the **Villa Doria Pamphilj**, the largest of Rome's parks, laid out in the mid-seventeenth century for Prince Camillo Pamphilj. The stately Baroque villa is not open to the public, but the sprawling greenery that surrounds it is an enchanting mix of formal parterres and shady glades, dotted with fountains and statues, and wilder tracts.

From the main gate, a path leads downhill and round to the right for around 250m, emerging at the villa. From here, follow the path southwest past the house for around 500m to reach the tree-fringed **lake**, fed at its northern end by a once-grand cascade of tiny waterfalls and grottoes, and inhabited by scores of turtles that bask photogenically on its banks.

VILLA BORGHESE

Villa Borghese and north

Some of the area immediately north of Rome's city centre is taken up by its most central park, the Villa Borghese, which serves as valuable outdoor space for both Romans and tourists, as well as hosting some of the city's best museums. The neighbourhoods beyond, Flaminio and the other residential districts of north-central Rome, were until recently not of much interest in themselves, except perhaps for the Foro Italico across the river – worth visiting to watch football and see the Fascist-era monumental sports centre. But the Auditorium Parco della Musica complex and the cutting-edge MAXXI have inspired fresh interest in the area. To the east, beyond the upscale Parioli neighbourhood and vast Villa Ada park, Via Nomentana and the neighbourhoods either side are worth the journey for the Villa Torlonia park and two of Rome's most ancient and atmospheric churches.

Villa Borghese and around

The area outside the Aurelian walls, to the north and northeast of the city, was once a district of market gardens, olive groves and patrician villas, trailing off into open country. During the Renaissance, these vast tracts of land were appropriated as summer estates by the city's wealthy, most of which were affiliated at some point to the papal court. One of the most notable estates, the **Villa Borghese**, was the summer playground of the Borghese family and is now a public **park**, home to the city's most significant concentration of **museums**, including the **Galleria Borghese**, which houses the resplendent art collection of the aristocratic family – a Roman must-see in anyone's book – and the **Villa Giulia**, built by Pope Julius III for his summer repose and now the National Etruscan Museum. The park was bought by the city at the beginning of the twentieth century and is a huge area, its woods, lake and grass, crisscrossed by roads, as near as you can get to peace in the city centre. Besides the museums, you'll also find a boating lake, a zoo – the "Bioparco" (see p.310) – and a cinema for children (see p.311).

ARRIVAL AND DEPARTURE — VILLA BORGHESE

By bus Bus #360 runs from Termini to the top end of Via Pinciana, close to the Galleria Borghese; bus #63 runs from Piazza Venezia to Via Salaria, a short walk away; and bus #116 goes through the Centro Storico (with stops on Via Giulia, Piazza della Cancelleria near Campo de' Fiori, and Via del Tritone), terminating at Porta Pinciana on the park's south side.

By metro The park is a short walk from Spagna and Flaminio metro stations, both on Line A.

By tram Tram #3 runs right around the city centre (with stops at the Colosseum and Porta Maggiore) to La Galleria Nazionale (the modern art museum) on the northern side of the park, passing the Bioparco and zoological museum on the way. Tram #19 runs from the Vatican to Villa Borghese, stopping at Villa Giulia, the modern art museum and the Bioparco, before heading southeast towards Villa Torlonia.

On foot Alternatively, you can just stroll up from the Spanish Steps or Piazza del Popolo to the Pincio Gardens, where you can pick up your own transport for getting around the park (see below).

GETTING AROUND AND ACTIVITIES

Vehicle rental You can rent bikes (from €4/hr, €10/4hr), go-karts (€5/hr), rollerblades (€5/hr), golf buggies (€10/30min; €15/hr), Segways (€10/30min, €15/hr) or a *risciò* (a sort of pedal-driven chariot with a small electric motor; €12/hr for 2 people, €20/hr for 4 people) from various places in the park, and all make getting around much easier. Most options are available from two places in the Pincio Gardens (one on the corner of Viale dell'Obelisco and Viale dell'Orologio, and a second by the water clock); outside the Casa del Cinema; and outside the zoo. Segways

are available from a booth on the Piazza del Popolo side of the Pincio Gardens; golf buggies can be found a short walk away at Piazzale delle Canestre.

Boat rental You can rent rowing boats for (€3/20min) on Villa Borghese's "Laghetto" (little lake) in the middle of the park, near Museo Carlo Bilotti.

Tourist train Villa Borghese's "*trenino*" (daily 10.30am–7pm) makes a 25min circuit of the park and costs €3 per person. There are stops outside the *Cinecaffè* on the park's southern side, outside Galleria Borghese and at the Pincio Gardens.

Pincio Gardens

On the edge of the Villa Borghese, overlooking Piazza del Popolo, the **Pincio Gardens** were laid out by Valadier in the early nineteenth century. Fringed with dilapidated busts of classical and Italian heroes, they give fine views over the roofs, domes and TV antennae of central Rome, right across to St Peter's and the Janiculum Hill. The benches are pleasantly shaded and a good place to take some weight off your feet. The nineteenth-century **water clock** at the back is a quirky attraction, and there's a carousel, a decent café-restaurant (see p.263), and a couple of places to rent bikes (see above).

Galleria Borghese

Piazzale del Museo Borghese 5 • Tues–Sun 9am–7pm; admission on timed tickets every 2hr (last entry 5pm); pick up tickets 30min before admission time • €15 including reservation fee; €2 first Sun of the month • Pre-booked visits obligatory (at least a week in advance; at least a month May–Oct) at ☎ 06 32810 or ⊛ galleriaborghese.it or ⊛ tosc.it

The **Galleria Borghese**, housed in a lavish villa (the "Casino" or "little house") on the far eastern side of the park, was built in the early seventeenth century as a "museum of the universe" and, together with the gardens, was turned over to the state in lieu of unpaid taxes in 1902. The gallery has since taken its place as one of Rome's great treasure-houses and should not be missed; be sure to book in advance.

Some history

When Camillo Borghese was elected pope and took the papal name Paul V in 1605, he elevated his favourite nephew, **Scipione Caffarelli Borghese**, to the cardinalate and put

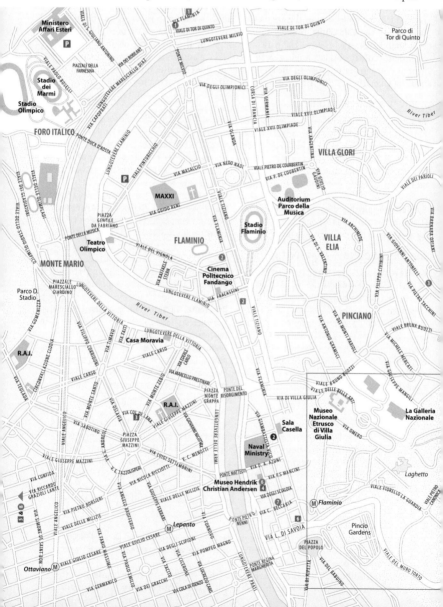

him in charge of diplomatic, ceremonial and cultural matters at the papal court. Scipione possessed an infallible instinct for recognizing artistic quality, and, driven by ruthless passion, he used fair means or foul to acquire prized works of art. He was also shrewd enough to patronize outstanding talents such as Gian Lorenzo Bernini, Caravaggio, Domenichino, Guido Reni and Rubens. To house the works of these artists, as well as his collection of antique sculpture and other pieces, he built the Casino, predictably sparing no expense. The gallery is a celebration of the ancient

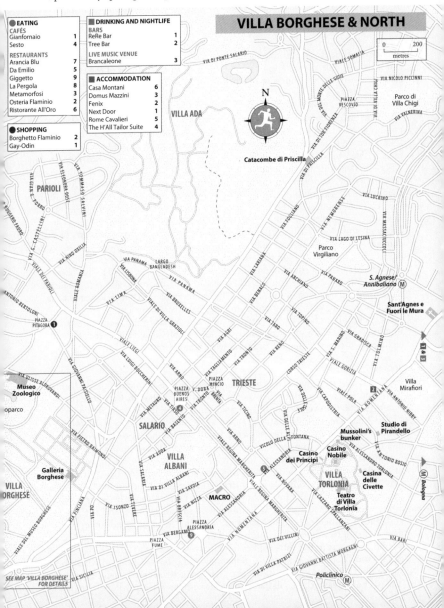

PAULINE BORGHESE

Pauline Borghese, the sister of Napoleon and married to the reigning Prince Borghese, was a shocking woman in her day, with grand habits. There are tales of jewels and clothes, of the Negro who used to carry her from her bath, of the servants she used as footstools and, of course, of her long line of lovers. The statue of her in the Villa Borghese was considered outrageous by everyone but herself: when asked how she could have posed almost naked, she simply replied, "Oh, there was a stove in the studio." The couch on which she reposes originally had a kind of clockwork mechanism inside, which allowed the statue to rotate while the viewer remained stationary.

splendour of the Roman Empire: over the years its art collection has been added to, and its rooms redecorated – most notably during the last quarter of the eighteenth century, when several ceilings were repainted to match the artworks in each room.

11

The portico and entrance hall

The main gallery entrance is through a portico, which displays classical sculpture, notably several large statues of Dacian prisoners from the time of the Emperor Trajan. (Note that on Sundays and when weather is bad, entrance is from inside the basement ticket office.) Inside, the main hall has a splendid **ceiling** by Marino Rossi, painted in 1775–78, depicting the foundation and early history of Rome – Jupiter is in the centre, surrounded by various moral and spiritual attributes and historical and mythological characters such as Romulus, Remus and the she-wolf. On the floor, a series of Roman mosaics from about 320 AD depict gladiators fighting and killing various animals and each other – a circle with a line drawn through it next to the name indicates the deceased, and blood gushes gruesomely from the pierced throats and hearts of the animals. Among a number of notable statues, there's a *Bacchus* from the second century AD, a *Fighting Satyr* and, on the wall facing the entrance door, a melodramatic piece in marble of Marcus Curtius flinging himself into the chasm (see p.81) – his horse is a Roman sculpture and the figure is by Bernini's father. There are also colossal heads of the emperors Hadrian and Antoninus Pius on the right, and a female head of the Antonine period, with a lotus flower to represent Isis, on the left.

The ground floor beyond the entrance hall contains sculpture, a mixture of ancient Roman items and seventeenth-century works, roughly linked together with late eighteenth-century ceiling paintings showing scenes from the Trojan War.

Rooms, 1, 2 and 3

Room 1, on your right as you enter, contains paintings depicting the Judgement of Paris, and as its centrepiece Canova's famous **statue of Pauline Borghese** posed as Venus (see box above), with flimsy drapery that leaves little to the imagination. Room 2 has a marvellous **statue of David** by Bernini, finished in 1624, when the sculptor was just 25. The face is a self-portrait, said to have been carved with the help of a mirror held for him by Scipione Borghese himself, and its expression of grim determination is perfect. There's more work by Bernini in Room 3, where his statue of **Apollo and Daphne** is a dramatic, poised work that captures the split second when Daphne is transformed into a laurel tree, with her fingers becoming leaves and her legs tree trunks. Mocked by Apollo, Cupid had taken revenge by firing a golden arrow which infected the god with immediate and ardent love, and shooting Daphne with a leaden one designed to hasten the rejection of amorous advances. Daphne, the daughter of a river god, called on her father to help her avoid being trapped by Apollo, who was in hot pursuit; her father changed her into a laurel tree just as Apollo took her into his arms – a desperately sad piece of drama to which Bernini's statue does full justice. This statue also caused a great scandal when it was unveiled. The poet and playwright, Maffeo Barberini, who later became Pope Urban VIII, wrote a couplet in Latin, which is inscribed on the base, claiming that all who pursue fleshly lusts are doomed to end up holding only ashes and dust.

Rooms 4 and 5

The walls of Room 4, the so-called **Emperors' Hall**, are flanked by red porphyry seventeenth- and eighteenth-century busts of Roman emperors, facing another Bernini sculpture, the **Rape of Proserpine**, dating from 1622, a coolly virtuosic work that shows the story of the carrying off to the underworld of the beautiful goddess Proserpine, daughter of Ceres, goddess of the fertility of the earth. The brutal Pluto grasps the girl in his arms, his fingers digging into the flesh of her thigh as she fights off his advances, while the three-headed form of Cerberus snaps at their feet.

In the small Room 5 next door, there's a marvellous **statue of a sleeping hermaphrodite**, from the first century AD, and a large porphyry Roman bathtub with feline feet that are almost modern in style.

Room 6

The earliest of the large sculptures by Gianlorenzo Bernini (possibly with the help of his father) is in Room 6, the **Room of Aeneas and Anchises.** In the centre is a larger-than-life statue of Aeneas carrying his father out of the burning city of Troy, his infant son Ascanius by his side. The statue portrays a crucial event in Roman myth when, after the defeat of the Trojans, Aeneas escaped with his family and embarked on the long voyage that ended up on the shores of what became Latium, his descendants

11

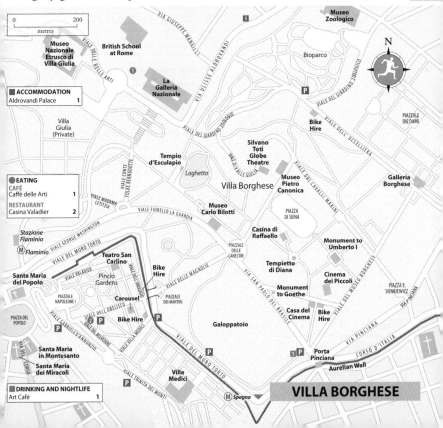

eventually founding the city of Rome. The old man carries the statues representing their family household gods, while Ascanius bears a flaming pot containing what became the Vestal Fire. Also here, in the far corner, is a late, and unfinished, work by Bernini, *Truth Revealed by Time*, created near the end of his career when he had been accused of faulty architectural work in part of St Peter's. Truth, with a sappy look on her face, clutches the sun, representing Time, to her breast.

Rooms 7 and 8

Room 7, the **Egyptian Room**, holds artefacts, friezes and paintings with an Egyptian theme, Roman floor mosaics and a statue of a satyr on a dolphin dating from the first century AD. Room 8 contains six paintings by Cardinal Scipione Borghese's protégé **Caravaggio**, including the large *Madonna of the Palafrenieri* from 1605, a painting that at the time was considered to have depicted the Christ child far too realistically to hang at St Peter's; when it was rejected, Scipione snapped it up at cut price for his collection. Take note also of Caravaggio's self-portrait as the Sick Bacchus as you enter, gazing lasciviously at the coy boy with the basket of fruit opposite. Diagonally opposite, St Jerome is captured writing at a table illuminated only by a source of light that streams in from the upper left of the picture. Painted near the end of Caravaggio's turbulent life, *David Holding the Head of Goliath*, on the right wall, was sent to Scipione Borghese from exile, where he had fled in 1606 to escape capital punishment for killing a man in a duel. The head of Goliath, portrayed in the last agonies of death, is believed to be a self-portrait, and the painting was designed to curry favour with the all-powerful cardinal and gain Caravaggio a pardon. The cardinal managed to get him off, but the artist died of malaria after landing in Italy at Porto Ercole, north of Rome, in 1610.

The picture gallery

Upstairs – accessed by a spiral staircase (there's also a small lift) off the Hall of the Emperors – the picture gallery houses one of the richest small collections of **paintings** in the world. The first room, **Room 9**, has several important works by Raphael, his teacher Perugino and other masters of the Umbrian School from the late fifteenth and early sixteenth centuries, not least Raphael's *Deposition* over the fireplace, produced in 1507 for a noble of Perugia in memory of her son, and pillaged from Perugia cathedral by associates of Cardinal Scipione. Look also for Raphael's *Lady with a Unicorn* and *Portrait of a Man*; the three works together demonstrate the evolution in the artist's style as he moved from Perugino's workshop to the Florentine artistic scene. The room also contains a beautiful, sensitive *Virgin with Child* by Giuliano Romano, while, nearby, Andrea del Sarto tackles the same subject with slightly more gusto.

Room 10 contains more early-sixteenth-century paintings, prominent among which are Cranach's *Venus and Cupid with a Honeycomb*, from 1531, and Brescianino's *Venus and Two Cupids*, from about 1520 – both remarkable at the time for their departure from classical models in their treatment of their subjects. The Cranach Venus, dressed in a diaphanous robe, shows Cupid and his honeycomb, demonstrating the dangers of carnal love. Opposite, they are complemented perfectly by Correggio's saucy *Danae*.

Retracing your steps to **Room 12**, look out for two early-sixteenth-century copies of Leonardo's *Leda and the Swan* (the original has been lost); Lorenzo Lotto's touching *Portrait of a Man*, a soulful study that hints at grief over a wife lost in childbirth, symbolized by the tiny skull and rose petals under the subject's right hand; and, in the large **Gallery of Lanfranco** at the back of the building, a series of self-portraits done by Bernini at various stages of his long life. Next to these are a lifelike bust of Cardinal Scipione executed by Bernini in 1632, accurately portraying him as a worldly connoisseur of fine art and fine living, and a smaller bust of Pope Paul V, also by Bernini. Next door's *Young Man and Faun* is the sculptor's earliest-known work, from 1615.

Beyond here, **Room 15** has Dosso Dossi's *SS Cosma e Damiano* and Jacopo Bassano's lively and naturalistic *Last Supper*, while in **Room 19** there are two paintings by Domenichino: the *Cumaean Sibyl* and a large *Diana*, the latter showing the goddess and her attendants celebrating and doing a bit of target practice – one of them has just shot a pheasant through the head and everybody else is jumping with enthusiasm; in the foreground a young nymph, lasciviously bathing, looks out with a lustful expression. Scipione was so keen on the work that he apparently imprisoned the artist until he agreed to sell it.

Room 20, the **Room of Psyche**, holds, along with works by Bellini and the other Venetians of the early 1500s, Titian's *Sacred and Profane Love*, painted in 1514 when he was about 25 years old, to celebrate the marriage of the Venetian noble Niccolò Aurelio (whose coat of arms is on the sarcophagus). It shows his bride, Laura Bagarotto, dressed in white representing Sacred Love, and Venus, representing Profane Love, carrying a lamp symbolizing the eternal Love of God. The bride cradles a bowl of jewels that refer to the fleeting happiness of life on earth.

Museo Carlo Bilotti

Viale Fiorello la Guardia • June–Sept Tues–Fri 1–7pm, Sat & Sun 10am–7pm; Oct–May Tues–Fri 10am–4pm, Sat & Sun 10am–7pm • Free • ☏ 06 0608, ⓦ www.museocarlobilotti.it

Housed in the orangery of the Villa Borghese, the **Museo Carlo Bilotti** is, like the Galleria Borghese, made up of a family bequest, this time of Carlo Bilotti – a perfume and cosmetics baron who, until his death in 2006, collected art and hobnobbed with the brightest and best in the international art world. Portraits of him by Larry Rivers, and of his wife and daughter by Andy Warhol, add to the slightly self-congratulatory air of the place. However, the paintings are beautifully displayed, and act as a nice adjunct to the modern art museum ten minutes' walk away.

Most of the 22 works exhibited here are by the great modern Italian painter **Giorgio de Chirico**. It's a small but varied collection, and you get a good sense of De Chirico's versatility, from the Impressionistic *Nude Woman from Behind* to his almost perversely traditional *Self-Portrait with the Head of Minerva* and the pastiche Canaletto scene that hangs next to it. The weird stuff with which De Chirico made his name is here too, including *Metaphysics with Biscuits* and *Melancholy of a Street*, and plays on the *Archeologists* theme you might have seen at La Galleria Nazionale (see p.176), although these are 1960s copies of canvases he produced during his earlier "metaphysical" period. Free temporary exhibitions are also often housed in the space. The restored Casina del Lago, opposite, holds a little café, with tables outside on a shady terrace.

If you are a fan of De Chirico's work, head to the Casa de Chirico (see p.95, pre-booking required), a kilometre or so southwest of here near the Spanish Steps.

Museo Pietro Canonica

Viale Pietro Canonica 2 • Tues–Sun: June–Sept 1–7pm; Oct–May 10am–4pm • Free • ☏ 06 0608, ⓦ museocanonica.it

Across the road from the large oval of the Piazza di Siena, the **Museo Pietro Canonica** occupies the house and studio of the nineteenth-century Italian sculptor. Canonica was an establishment artist and as such not only did the city bequeath him this impressive, castellated bolt-hole to live in, but the museum devoted to him is virtually a roll-call of European historical names. Canonica seemingly knew everyone and sculpted everybody, and one room alone contains busts of a king of England (Edward VII), the man who took Turkey to independence (Mustafa Kemal Atatürk), numerous Italian royals and nineteenth-century dignitaries, and Pope Benedict XV (a supplement to the artist's memorial to him in St Peter's). Other rooms document nineteenth-century world history – Simón Bolívar astride a stallion (1954), Atatürk again, this time leading the Turkish charge, and an equestrian statue of King Faisal of Iraq (1933) – to name only the most prominent examples of an epic collection.

The museum also includes **Canonica's studio** on the ground floor, still with his tools and the piece he was working on when he died in 1959, along with a couple of portraits of the great man and some of his own botched attempts at landscapes – which show that he was probably right to stick to sculpture. Upstairs are the **apartments** Canonica occupied with his wife, who continued to live here until she died in 1987. The rooms are left much as they were then (and are rather musty) with original furniture, the living room with a piano and a musical score on it (Canonica was also an accomplished musician and composer) and family photographs. Oddly, there is only one that shows Canonica himself, a holiday snap taken in the mountains, on the right side of the dining room.

Silvano Toti Globe Theatre

Largo Aqua Felix • ☎ 06 0608, ⓦ globetheatreroma.com

Next door to the Pietro Canonica museum, Rome's very own **Globe Theatre** is a strange sight, a typically flamboyant cultural initiative of former Rome mayor Walter Veltroni, built in 2003. Like its more famous counterpart in London, it's a copy of the sixteenth-century London original and is built entirely of wood (though the roof is not thatched) with a capacity of around 1250, a third of which is standing, facing a rectangular, canopied stage. It stages performances of Shakespeare's plays – in Italian – throughout the summer most evenings at about 9pm.

La Galleria Nazionale

Viale delle Belli Arti 131 • Tues–Sun 8.30am–7.30pm; last entry 45min before closing • €10 • ☎ 06 3229 8221, ⓦ lagallerianazionale.com

Two of the Villa Borghese's most important museums are situated on the northwestern side of the park, on the Viale delle Belle Arti, in the so-called "Academy Ghetto" – the Romanian, British, Dutch, Danish, Egyptian and other cultural academies are all situated here. The **Galleria Nazionale** is a huge Neoclassical construction housing a wide selection of nineteenth- and twentieth-century Italian (and a few foreign) names. However, the museum's compact and surprisingly engaging collection is beautifully displayed – and can make a refreshing change after several days of having the senses bombarded with Etruscan, Roman and Renaissance art. There is also a smart **café** with a sunny terrace, the *Caffè delle Arti*, out the back door at Via Gramsci 73, which is part of the gallery complex (though doesn't require a ticket) and is the best place to grab something to eat and drink if you're wilting.

A massive rehang entitled "Time is Out of Joint" in 2017 saw the dramatic juxtaposition of pieces from different periods, breaking with the traditional chronological arrangement. Another rehang in a similar vein is scheduled for 2018. Star pieces in the collection include a giant statue of Hercules by Antonio Canova in the central room. Other nineteenth-century Italian artists represented include the sculptor Pietro Tenerani and Nino Costa. There are several pieces by major **Impressionists and post-Impressionists** – Cézanne, Degas, Monet, Van Gogh, along with impressive early figurative works by Italian artists such as Umberto Boccioni and Giacomo Balla. The rhetoric of national glory and sacrifice of the Italian Unification is represented by pieces such as Fattori's *Battle of Custoza*, and impressionistic and "Belle Époque" portraits by – among others – Giuseppe de Nittis and Morelli's pupil Antonio Mancini.

Works such as Boccioni's *Portrait of Maestro Busoni* and Balla's series, *The Sick People*, *The Madman* and *The Beggar*, catalogue the birth of Futurism. A lovely self-portrait of a doubtful Giorgio de Chirico accompanies the artist's unsettling metaphysical paintings, as well as those of his contemporaries Gino Severini and Giorgio Morandi. Look out, too, for Gerardo Dottori's series of fascist panels from 1935, paeans to the brutal modern world of weapons and machinery revered by the Futurists. Other big names include Modigliani, Mondrian, Miró and Klimt.

Post-World War I pieces include drawings and paintings by Pirandello, Giacometti figures, and work by non-Italian pioneers such as Jackson Pollock, Henry Moore, Cy Twombly – who lived in Rome more than half his life – and Karel Appel.

THE ETRUSCANS

The **Etruscans** remain something of a historical mystery. We know that they lived in central Italy – in Etruria – from around 900 BC. The official line was that they were conquered by the Romans; however, the last three kings of Rome (sixth century BC) were Etruscans, rendering the matter slightly less cut-and-dried than the Roman Empire might have wanted us to believe. Whether they were native to the region, or whether they had originally migrated here from overseas, specifically from **Asia Minor**, remains a matter of debate. The Romans borrowed heavily from their civilization (it was by way of the Etruscans that wine, olive oil and gladiatorial combat first arrived in Italy). The Etruscans were also masters at working in terracotta, gold and bronze, and accomplished carvers in stone, and it is these skills – together with their obvious sensuality and the ease with which they appeared to enjoy life – that make a visit to the Villa Giulia so beguiling.

Museo Nazionale Etrusco di Villa Giulia

Villa Giulia Piazzale di Villa Giulia 9 • Tues–Sun 8.30am–7.30pm; last entry 6.30pm • €8; free first Sun of the month • ☎ 06 322 6571, ⓦ villagiulia.beniculturali.it • **Villa Poniatowski** Via di Villa Giulia 34 • Thurs 10am–1pm, Sat 3–6pm; advance booking (at least 2 days) obligatory • Free entry with Villa Giulia ticket • ☎ 06 321 9698 (Mon–Fri 2–5pm), ✉ arteingioco@libero.it

11

Right on the western edge of the Villa Borghese, Villa Giulia, five minutes' walk away from Via Flaminia, is a harmonious collection of courtyards, loggias, gardens and temples put together in a playful Mannerist style for Pope Julius III in the mid-sixteenth century. It's home to the **Museo Nazionale Etrusco di Villa Giulia**, which, along with the Etruscan collection in the Vatican, is the world's primary collection of Etruscan treasures, and a good introduction – or conclusion – to the Etruscan sites in Lazio, which between them contributed most of the artefacts on display here. Part of the collection is now housed in **Villa Poniatowski**, a two-minute walk from the main museum, though at the time of writing you had to pre-book to visit these rooms.

Rooms 1–13: Vulci and Cerveteri

Rooms 1–6 hold finds from the Etruscan city of **Vulci**, including two pieces of sculpture in Room 1, one showing a man astride a sea horse, a recurring theme in ancient Mediterranean art, and an oddly amateurish centaur – basically a man pasted to the hindquarters of a horse – both dating from the sixth century BC. The next rooms contain bronze objects from the seventh and sixth centuries BC – urns used to contain the ashes of cremated persons, among which a beautiful example in the shape of a finely detailed dwelling hut stands out – and a number of terracotta votive offerings of anatomical parts of the human body, their detail alluding to the Etruscans' accomplishments in medicine. A gold dental bridge shows their skill at dentistry too.

Rooms 9–13 focus on finds from the Etruscan tombs at **Cerveteri**: hundreds of vases, pots, drinking vessels and other items, and, among a number of busts and images, clearly portraits of real people, including a depiction of a man with a cauliflower right ear and a finely stitched cut to the right of his mouth – clearly a tough customer. The octagonal Room 12 holds the remarkable **Sarcophagus of the Married Couple**, one of the most famous pieces in the museum. Dating from the sixth century BC, and actually containing the ashes of the deceased rather than the bodies, it's a touchingly lifelike portrayal of a husband and wife lying on a couch. He has his right arm around her; she is offering him something from her right hand, probably an egg – a recurring theme in Etruscan art. Their clothes are modelled down to the finest detail, including the laces and soles of their shoes, and the pleats of the linen and lacy pillowcases. In case you're wondering, the holes in the backs of their heads, and at other spots, are ventilation holes created to prevent the terracotta from exploding when the hollow piece was fired.

Room 13b has items and reconstructions from the enormous temple excavated at **Pyrgi**, Cerveteri's seaport, in the 1960s, including replicas of gold foil plates thought at one time to offer a Rosetta Stone-like key to the Etruscan language; the plates are Etruscan, Punic and Greek, and represent some of the oldest pre-Roman inscriptions ever found.

Rooms 14–21

Upstairs, in the balcony over the *Sarcophagus of the Married Couple*, there are displays on the **Etruscan language**, and on the *cistae* – drum-like objects, engraved and adorned with figures, that were supposed to hold everything the body needed after death – recovered from tombs around Praeneste. A special area is devoted to the beautiful and justifiably famous **Ficorini Cista**, made by an Etruscan craftsman named Novios Plautios for a lady named Dindia Malconia and probably a wedding present. Further on you'll find mostly bronzes, mirrors, candelabra, religious statues and tools used in everyday life. Notice, particularly, the elongated statues of priests and priestesses, some of whom hold eels in their hands and are engaged in some kind of rite. There is also a realistic bronze statuette of a ploughman at work, plodding along behind his oxen.

Rooms 25 and 27: jewellery

Visits to the collection of Castellani gold in Room 27 (Tues–Sun 10am, noon, 3pm & 5pm) are bookable at least 1 week in advance; contact **✉** sba-em.soprintendente@beniculturali.it

The Castellani, three generations of famous Italian goldsmiths, amassed an astonishing collection of ancient **jewellery** – one of the finest in existence – between the eighteenth and nineteenth centuries, now displayed in rooms 25 and 27. Marvellously intricate Etruscan pieces, worked into tiny horses, birds, camels and other animals, are displayed alongside the work of the **Castellani** themselves. The nineteenth-century pieces are equally fascinating, notable for their delicate micromosaics and fine filigree work.

Rooms 31–34: the Faliscan area

A gallery containing several hundred examples of Etruscan **pottery**, terracotta and bronze items, including charcoal braziers and pieces of armour, and, remarkably, a trumpet that has not sounded for two thousand years, leads you to the upper floor of the west wing, which is devoted to the **Falisci**, a people from northeast Lazio who spoke a dialect of Latin but were culturally Etruscans. There's also information on the excavations at Narce, Capena, Civita Castellana and other sites in the Faliscan area. Highlights include a drinking horn in the shape of a dog's head that is so lifelike you almost expect it to bark; a *holmos*, or small table, to which the maker attached 24 little pendants; and a bronze disc breastplate from the seventh century BC decorated with a weird, almost modern abstract pattern of galloping creatures.

Rooms 35–36: Falerii

Downstairs, rooms 35–36 hold finds from the **Falerii sanctuaries** at Sassi Caduti and Lo Scasato, dedicated to Apollo – Etruscan artistry at its best, with gaudily coloured terracotta figures that leer, run, jump and climb; a beautiful, lifelike torso of Apollo, dating from around the start of the fourth century BC; and a bust of Juno which has the air of a dignified matron, the flower pattern on her dress still visible, as are her earrings, necklace and crown.

Rooms 37–40: Veii

Rooms 37–40 display items found in **Veii**. Look out for the precious **Chigi vase** in Room 38, a polychromatic wine pitcher dating back to around 650 BC, with intricately decorated friezes, including a tableau of the Judgement of Paris – the earliest existing depiction of the myth. In the following rooms there are items from the Sanctuary of Apollo at Portonaccio, among them the terracotta statues of Hercules and Apollo disputing over the sacred hind which Apollo had shot and Hercules claimed.

Villa Poniatowski

You have to book ahead to enter the sixteenth-century **Villa Poniatowski**'s richly frescoed rooms, which hold more artefacts with obvious connections to the Etruscans, with items from Umbria and from southern Lazio, including Tivoli, the Sanctuary of Diana at Lake Nemi and the ancient town of Satricum, south of the Alban hills. Among the highlights are a sarcophagus carved out of an oak log; cases of terracotta votive offerings – anatomical parts, babies in swaddling clothes and models of temples and houses; bronze pots with griffins' heads looking in to see what's cooking; and a wonderful bronze throne from Palestrina with elaborately worked scenes of hunting, military parades and horse racing.

Museo Hendrik Christian Andersen

Via P.S. Mancini 20 • Tues–Sun 9am–7.30pm • Free • ☎ 06 321 9089 • Metro Flaminio or tram to Via Mancini

West of the Villa Borghese, around ten minutes' walk north from Piazzale Flaminio, the **Museo Hendrik Christian Andersen** is a delightful, small collection – and one of the best of Rome's lesser-known free attractions. Affiliated to the modern art museum, it's devoted to the work of the eponymous Norwegian–American sculptor and painter, who was a friend and contemporary of Henry James and lived in Rome for almost half his long life. His old studio contains some of his giant Neoclassical sculptures in grand and heroic poses; it's hard to imagine a room more crammed full of elegantly shaped buttocks and penises. Don't miss the cast for his tomb in the Protestant Cemetery (see p.143), where he is buried with other members of his family.

Andersen wasn't just a sculptor: in the gallery next door are his 1912 plans for a utopian world city, a planned centre of civilization on so epic a scale that, not surprisingly, it was never built, although Mussolini later got behind it and it's conceivable that his EUR (see p.154) was based at least in part on Andersen's ideas. Upstairs, where the artist lived, is more restrained, now given over to his modest paintings of landscapes around Lazio and Campania, as well as a handful of family holiday snaps and scribbled postcards – personal insights into Andersen's full and creative life in Italy.

MAXXI

Via Guido Reni 4a • Tues, Wed & Fri–Sun 11am–7pm, Thurs 11am–10pm; last entry 1hr before closing • €12 • ☎ 06 320 1954, ⓦ fondazionemaxxi.it • Metro Flaminio, then tram #2

A ten-minute tram ride north of Piazza del Popolo, **MAXXI** is a museum of twenty-first-century art and architecture. Opened to much fanfare in 2010, in a landmark building by the late Zaha Hadid, it makes a great modern accompaniment to Renzo Piano's nearby Auditorium complex. Built around a former military barracks, it's mainly a venue for temporary exhibitions, but there are a few small permanent collections, too, which showcase late twentieth-century Italian works of art and the archives of influential Italian architects such as Pier Luigi Nervi. The building, a simultaneously jagged and curvy concrete spaceship that looks like it's just landed in this otherwise rather ordinary part of the city, is worth a visit in its own right, with a towering lobby encompassing the inevitable café and bookshop, and bright, curvaceous galleries leading one into the other, connected by walkways that flow through the complex like passages in some giant termite mound. There's also a larger bookshop and café-restaurant in the converted buildings across the pleasant courtyard.

Auditorium Parco della Musica

Viale Pietro de Coubertin 30 • April–Oct Mon–Sat 11am–8pm, Sun 10am–8pm; Nov–March Mon–Sat 11am–6pm, Sun 10am–6pm; Museo Archeologico same hours as Auditorium but April–Oct Mon–Sat closes 6pm; free; Museo Aristaios same hours as Auditorium but April–Oct Mon–Sat opens 10am; free; Museo degli Strumenti Mon–Wed & Fri–Sun 11am–5pm; €9 • ☎ 06 8024 1281, ⓦ auditorium .com • Metro Flaminio, then tram #2, or bus to Viale de Coubertin

In the heart of the Flaminio district, Rome's **Auditorium Parco della Musica**, a multifunctional music complex, is in fact three auditoriums in one, their large bulbous shapes making them look like three giant, lead-skinned armadillos crouched together. Designed by everyone's favourite Italian architect, **Renzo Piano**, and opened in spring 2006, it's a clever building: the foyers all join up and, above, the three buildings make a large amphitheatre, used for outdoor performances in the piazza below. It's clever, too, in the way that it has incorporated the remains of a Republican-era villa between two of the concert halls; the villa was discovered when building began, and actually halted the project for two years while it was excavated.

Each concert hall is conceived and designed for a different kind of musical performance: the smallest, the **Sala Petrassi** on the right side, accommodates seven hundred people and is used for concerts of contemporary music; the middle **Sala Sinopoli** holds 1200; while the largest of the three, the eastern **Sala Santa Cecilia**, can seat 2700 listening to big symphonic works, and is now home to Rome's flagship orchestra, the Accademia Nazionale di Santa Cecilia. The amphitheatre, known as the **Cavea**, is an atmospheric venue for summer music concerts.

11

You can walk right around the building outside, exploring the park in which it is set. The main entrance is on Viale Pietro de Coubertin, home to a great book and music shop, or you can cut through to the park from Viale Maresciallo Pilsudski.

The Auditorium also holds a few **museum** spaces, which are worth a browse while you're waiting for a concert to start. The **Museo Archeologico** has a model of the ancient villa and displays artefacts found at the site during construction works; the **Museo Aristaios** holds ancient pottery from the private collection of composer and conductor Giuseppe Sinopoli, who died in 2001; and the **Museo degli Strumenti** has more than five hundred musical instruments, with a focus on Italian strings from the seventeenth to the twentieth centuries. There's also a contemporary-art exhibition space, **Auditorium Arte**.

Ponte Milvio

Metro Flaminio, then tram #2

Immediately north of the Flaminio district, the Tiber sweeps around in a wide hook-shaped bend that is crossed by the **Ponte Milvio**, the old, originally Roman, footbridge where the Emperor Constantine defeated Maxentius in 312 AD. It provides wonderful views of the meandering Tiber, with the city springing up green on the hills to both sides and the silty river running fast below. Until recently, the bridge was famously festooned with **padlocks**, placed here by lovers who then threw the keys into the river – an enactment of a ritual popularized by Federico Moccia's best-selling novel, *Ho Voglia di Te* (I Want You), published in 2006. The lampposts that the padlocks were attached to eventually started to collapse beneath the weight, and the council removed the padlocks; there's now a website – ⓦlucchettipontemilvio.com – where you can attach a virtual padlock as a symbol of your undying love.

Like the bridge, the area on the northern side of the river, around Piazzale di Ponte Milvio, attracts a youthful crowd these days, who increasingly flock here for the cool bars and restaurants that have sprung up in the neighbourhood. There's a cheap and cheerful **market**, too.

Foro Italico

Piazza Lauro de Bosis · Metro Ottaviano, then bus #32 to Piazza Lauro de Bosis

It's just ten minutes' walk from Ponte Milvio – past the huge Italian Foreign Ministry building – to the **Foro Italico** sports centre, one of the few parts of Rome to survive intact pretty much the way Mussolini planned it. Repurposed as one of the hubs of the 1960 Olympic Games, the Foro Italico is still used as a sports centre but is worth visiting as a relic of the architecture of the Fascist era as much anything else. Opposite the **Ponte Duca d'Aosta**, which connects the Foro Italico to the town side of the river, is a vast white marble **obelisk** capped with a gold pyramid engraved MUSSOLINI DUX. The marble finials at the side of each end of the bridge show soldiers in various heroic acts, loading machine guns and cannons, charging onto the face of enemy fire, carrying the wounded and so forth, each bearing the face of Mussolini himself – a very eerie sight indeed.

Beyond the bridge, an avenue patched with more mosaics revering "Il Duce" leads up to a fountain surrounded by images of muscle-bound figures revelling in sporting activities. Either side of the fountain are the two main **stadiums**: the larger of the two, the **Stadio Olimpico** on the left, was used for the Olympic Games in 1960 and remodelled for the World Cup final in 1990. It is still the venue for Rome's two football teams on alternate Sundays (see p.304), although AS Roma are perennially planning to move to a new (and as yet unbuilt) stadium in the city's southern outskirts. The smaller **Stadio dei Marmi** (Stadium of Marbles) is ringed by sixty great male statues, groins modestly hidden by fig leaves, in a variety of elegantly macho poses – each representing both a sport and a province of Italy: an unwitting exercise in homoerotic bombast.

11

Monte Mario

Dawn–dusk · Metro Ottaviano, then bus #32 to Piazzale Maresciallo Giardino

Rome's highest hill at 139m, **Monte Mario** lies a mile or so north of the Vatican, easily visible by the telegraph masts that top its summit, as well as the dome of the city's former observatory. Unsurprisingly, the views from the top are among the city's best, though the park itself is sadly looking rather neglected these days. You can follow a path up from Via Gomenizza, on the far side of Piazzale Maresciallo Giardino.

Parioli

The area immediately to the east of the Auditorium, and north of Villa Borghese, is the **Parioli** district, which extends roughly over as far as the massive Villa Ada park (see below), and whose quiet, winding streets, large villas and lush, leafy gardens make up one of Rome's wealthier neighbourhoods. Its main street, Viale dei Parioli, is home to some decent restaurants, and the Villa Glori park provides a splash of green on its northern edge, but the main reason you might find yourself here is before or after attending a concert at the Auditorium, or maybe after a trip to Villa Ada.

Villa Ada

Entrances at Via Salaria, Via di Ponte Salario and Via Panama · Daily 7am–dusk · Bus to Piazza Verbano or Via Panama

Immediately east of Parioli, the enormous expanse of **Villa Ada** is one of Rome's largest public parks, flanked on the far side by Via Salaria – the old trading route between the

---

CASA MORAVIA

It's rarely open, and you have to book in advance, but if you can time it right try to get to the **Casa Museo Alberto Moravia**, on the west bank of the River Tiber at Lungotevere Vittoria 1 (☎06 0608, ⓦfondoalbertomoravia.it, ⓦmuseiincomuneroma.it; Metro Lepanto, then bus #280). Moravia moved to this apartment in 1963, after he had split from his wife, the writer Elsa Morante. He was a very Roman writer, living all his life in the city, and the apartment is left just as it was when he died in 1990, with a retro kitchen, large Tiber-facing terrace and book-lined study, all decorated with paintings by various twentieth-century Italian artists. The apartment is open on the first Saturday of each month (except Aug) for guided tours at 10am and 11am (tours €5); booking is obligatory, on ☎06 3972 8186 or ☎348 320 6721 or by email: ⓔbellitalia88@bellitalia88.it.

Romans and Sabines, so called because the main product transported along here was salt. The Villa Ada was once the estate of King Vittorio Emanuele III (the original royal villa is now the site of the Egyptian embassy) and is a nice enough place in which to while away an afternoon, with a bucolic atmosphere that is a world away from the busy streets of the city centre. The lake on the Via Salaria side is full of turtles, and you can rent bicycles, canoes or ponies from the southerly reaches of the park, where there is also a children's playground.

Catacombe di Priscilla

Via Salaria 430 · Tues–Sun 9am–noon & 2–5pm · €8 · ☎ 06 8620 6272, ⓦ catacombepriscilla.com · Bus to Via di Priscilla or Viale Libia

Just outside Villa Ada, the **Catacombe di Priscilla** are among Rome's most extensive early Christian burial complexes, a frescoed labyrinth of tunnels on three levels that can be visited on regular (obligatory) guided tours. This complex is far less busy than the Appian Way catacombs. Several important martyrs ended up here, including Praxedes and Pudenziana. Tours last half an hour and take in a number of locations. Highlights include the so-called Greek Chapel, whose frescoes – painted between the second and fourth centuries AD and showing the Adoration of the Magi, Daniel in the lions' den, the resurrection of Lazarus, Noah, and the sacrifice of Isaac – are more impressive than those you'll see in any of Rome's other catacombs. There is also the earliest known depiction of the Virgin and Child, though this could simply be a picture of a mother and child, both of whom were probably buried here.

Quartiere Coppedè

Bus to Piazza Buenos Aires

South of Villa Ada is the **Trieste** district, home to the whimsical architecture of the so-called **Quartiere Coppedè**. Via Dora signals the start of the neighbourhood, a series of Art Nouveau buildings designed by the Florentine architect Gino Coppedè at the end of the nineteenth century. Its centre, **Piazza Mincio** (accessible through the arch on Via Dora), is less a collection of buildings and more the backdrop for a Ruritanian opera, with turrets, grotesque faces, creatures and columns all jumbled together in a riot of eclectic design. The centrepiece is the fountain, topped by frogs, and with more frogs underneath spewing water into scallop shells held by straining men.

MACRO

Via Nizza 138 · Tues–Sun 10.30am–7.30pm · €10, or €12.50 including MACRO Testaccio (p.143), valid for 7 days · ☎ 06 8535 6892, ⓦ museomacro.org · Bus to Piazza Fiume

The Museum of Contemporary Art of Rome, or **MACRO**, is housed in the old Peroni brewery stables, just beyond Piazza Alessandria. The complex of buildings opened in 1999 as an arts and culture centre, and a new wing designed by French architect Odile Decq was opened in 2010, enlarging the space for exhibitions and adding a roof terrace and sleek suspended walkways. There is a permanent collection of contemporary works, mainly focusing on Italian artists since the 1960s, but the large exhibition halls are mostly used to host temporary exhibitions, plus there's a library, bookshop, restaurant and café.

Via Nomentana and around

From the Porta Pia and busy Corso d'Italia – in effect part of the central ring road that girdles the city centre – the wide boulevard of **Via Nomentana** is an ancient Roman route that leads northeast through a plush neighbourhood of large nineteenth-century villas and apartment blocks. It's a useful rather than a picturesque route, but the neighbourhood home to a number of attractions.

Villa Torlonia

Via Nomentana 70; access also possible from Via Siracusa and Via Spallanzani • **Gardens** Daily dawn–dusk • Free • **Museums** Tues–Sun 9am–7pm; last entry 45min before closing • Casino Nobile €7.50; Casina delle Civette €6; joint ticket for Casino Nobile and Casina delle Civette €9.50; buy tickets at the Via Nomentana entrance • ☎ 06 0608, Ⓦ museivillatorlonia.it • **Theatre** Guided tours (in Italian) Tues, Sat & Sun, usually at 10am • €5 • Ⓦ casadeiteatri.roma.it/teatro-di-villa-torlonia • Bus to Via Nomentana or Corso Trieste

A few hundred metres down Via Nomentana from the Porta Pia is one of Rome's most under-appreciated sites: the large nineteenth-century estate of **Villa Torlonia**, which in the 1930s was given by the banker **Prince Giovanni Torlonia** to **Mussolini** to use for as long as he needed it. The palm-tree-filled park – a lovely retreat on a hot day – holds an array of attractions, which have been restored to their former glory over the last few years. Villa Torlonia is also the site of some third-century AD Jewish catacombs, which extend under the gardens for 4–5km, though these are not at present open to the public.

Casino Nobile

Mussolini lived in the Villa Torlonia from 1925 to 1943, occupying the central **Casino Nobile**, all for the nominal rent of one lira a year. Designed by Valadier in the early nineteenth century, the house was a sumptuous place to live. Various rooms are decorated with cycles of frescoes whose unifying theme is frolicking and nakedness, alongside a general deference to bygone ages, with ancient Roman tableaux, including Antony and Cleopatra, hieroglyphics and portraits of great artists and thinkers. The Mussolinis didn't alter the house much, just installing a couple of en-suite bathrooms between their bedrooms on the first floor (since removed) and strengthening the basement to withstand an air raid ("Mussolini's bunker", as it is known, has reopened after a period of closure; check website for latest information); the gardens became a bit of a playground, with tennis courts and a riding track for Il Duce to show off in.

11

Casino dei Principi

Close to the Casino Nobile, the smaller **Casino dei Principi** is now used for temporary exhibitions, but was originally a farm building that was remodelled and used as an annexe to the main villa, to which it's connected by a tunnel. Its most impressive permanent feature is the room at the end, decorated in the mid-nineteenth century with views of the Bay of Naples.

Casina delle Civette

Don't miss the **Casina delle Civette**, the "small house of the owls", in the southeastern corner of the estate. This is something unusual in Rome – a Liberty-style dwelling full of Art Nouveau features, such as stained glass, wood panelling and inlays, which contribute to the kind of complete design vision that was common at the end of the nineteenth century. Though originally designed in 1840, the building was transformed in 1917 by one Vincenzo Fasoli into a comfortable residence for a Roman aristocrat – in this case Prince Torlonia – in the fashionable style of the time. The house's name derives from the prince's love of owls and their dominance in the decoration of the building (although much of this hasn't survived). Indeed, the prince was keen on all things of the night, as his upstairs bedroom shows, decorated as it is with a night sky and a bat-encrusted chandelier. The bird scheme continues in the **Room of the Swallows** (with its stucco birds in each corner, and swallow-themed stained glass), and there are owls in the stained-glass windows at the front of the house and the relief above the back door.

Villino Medievale

The so-called **Villino Medievale** has been turned into the comfortable *La Limonaia* café-restaurant, where you can sit outside in a leafy garden, and an interactive science and technology kids' attraction known as **Technotown** (in Italian only; Tues–Sun 9.30am–7pm; €10; Ⓦ technotown.it).

Teatro di Villa Torlonia

Villa Torlonia's **Teatro di Villa Torlonia** was commissioned by Prince Alessandro Torlonia to celebrate his marriage to Teresa Colonna in 1841, but it wasn't finished until 1874. It was decorated by one Costantino Brumidi, who had found fame in the US after painting the frescoes of the Capitol building in Washington DC. After years of neglect, the theatre was sumptuously restored in 2013 and now hosts regular concerts and other performances (see p.280).

Studio di Pirandello

Via Antonio Bosio 13b • Mon–Thurs 9am–3.30pm, Fri 11am–7pm • Free • ☎ 06 4429 1853, ⓦ studiodiluigipirandello.it • Metro Bologna

Five minutes' walk from Via Nomentana, and about the same from Piazza Bologna's metro station, the building known as the **Studio di Pirandello** was the home of the Italian writer for twenty years, and he spent the last three years of his life, until his death in 1936, in the second-floor apartment here. This was more or less outside the city centre at that time, and he would have had a clear view of Villa Torlonia from his bedroom balcony. The apartment has been left untouched from that time, with Pirandello's desk in the corner of the main sitting room left as if he had just got up to make a cup of coffee; the engraved cigar box was given to him by the Italian writer and politician Gabriele d'Annunzio, and the landscapes that hang behind were painted by Pirandello himself, and complement the portraits done by his son Fausto, who lived downstairs with his family.

Sant'Agnese fuori le Mura

Via Nomentana 349 • **Sant'Agnese** Daily 7.30am–noon & 4–7.30pm • **Catacombs** End March to Oct Mon–Sat 9am–noon & 4–6pm, Sun 4–6pm; end Oct & Dec to end March Mon–Sat 9am–noon & 3–5pm, Sun 3–5pm; closed Nov; tours (in English) take 30min • €5 • **Santa Costanza** Mon–Sat 9am–noon & 3–6pm, Sun 3–6pm • ⓦ santagnese.org • Bus to Via Nomentana

About a mile up Via Nomentana from the Porta Pia, the church of **Sant'Agnese fuori le Mura** is dedicated to the 13-year-old saint who was martyred in Domitian's Stadium in 303 AD (see p.43). It's part of a small complex of early Christian monuments that also includes the catacombs underneath and the neighbouring church of Santa Costanza, and in fact is the modern-day survivor of an enormous basilica complex that was built here by Constantine at the same time as the other ancient basilicas (dedicated to St Peter, St Paul, and St Lawrence) – the remains of the Constantinian basilica can be seen in the grounds.

Sant'Agnese

Apart from some later modifications, the church of **Sant'Agnese** is much as it was when it was built by Pope Honorius I in the seventh century, close to Constantine's original but by then ruined (and much larger) structure – which had in turn been built over St Agnes's grave. Entrance is either through the outside courtyard or down a long staircase plastered with fragments of Roman reliefs and inscriptions. The interior has been updated in Baroque style, but the apse mosaic is contemporary with Honorius's building, showing Agnes next to the pope, who holds a model of his church, in typical Byzantine fashion. If you don't want to take the tour of the catacombs, you can still see St Agnes's tomb in the crypt (see below); take the stairs to the right of the apse.

The catacombs

The **catacombs** that sprawl below the church are among the best preserved and most crowd-free in Rome – indeed if you have time for only one set of catacombs during your stay in Rome (and they really are all very much alike), you could make it these. Originally dating back to the late second century, they became much expanded over subsequent years as the cult of St Agnes grew, and at their peak there were around 55,000 bodies buried here. Tours take you through the choicest passages, picking out often touching inscriptions to beloved wives, husbands and children, into a vaulted family chapel, and conclude with the tomb of Agnes herself beneath the altar, moved here by Paul V from its original burial place nearby. Agnes lies inside a sarcophagus alongside her sister but minus her head, which remains in the church dedicated to her on Piazza Navona (see p.43).

Santa Costanza

The church of **Santa Costanza** is a gem not to be missed; a splendid illustration of the transition from paganism to Christianity in Rome. Built in 350 AD as a mausoleum for Constantia, the daughter of the Emperor Constantine, the church is the only intact part of Constantine's original basilica, a round structure which follows the traditional shape of the great pagan tombs (consider those of Hadrian and Augustus elsewhere in the city); indeed the mosaics on the vaulting of its circular ambulatory – fourth-century depictions of vines, leaves and birds – would have been as at home on the floor of a Roman domus as they were in a Christian church. The porphyry sarcophagus of St Constantia herself was moved to the Vatican Museums in the eighteenth century (see p.194), and what you see in the church is a plaster copy.

11

BERNINI'S BALDACCHINO

The Vatican

On the west bank of the Tiber, directly across from Rome's historic centre, the Vatican City has been an independent sovereign state since 1929. St Peter, considered by Roman Catholics to be the first of the popes, is believed to have been martyred and buried in the area that the Romans called the Vatican Field. Subsequently, a church dedicated to Peter was built by the Emperor Constantine over his tomb, and the Vatican palaces developed nearby. Stretching north from St Peter's, these papal palaces are now home to the Vatican Museums – one of the largest, most compelling, and perhaps most exhausting museum complexes in the world. The Castel Sant'Angelo, a huge fortress that was once a refuge for the popes in times of danger, is also well worth visiting, while east of the Vatican the well-heeled Prati district has some of the city's best restaurants.

ARRIVAL AND DEPARTURE

THE VATICAN

By bus The useful #64 bus runs from Termini to St Peter's via Via Nazionale, Piazza Venezia and Largo di Torre Argentina. Bus #40 travels a similar route but is an express service, terminating by Castel Sant'Angelo. Watch out for your bags on both buses, as they are notoriously popular with pickpockets.

By metro St Peter's is a 5min walk from Ottaviano station, while the Vatican Museums are a 10min walk.

On foot The Vatican is easily reachable from the Centro Storico – it takes about 20min to walk from Piazza Navona to St Peter's. The best route is across Ponte Sant'Angelo.

Piazza San Pietro

Perhaps the most famous of Rome's many piazzas, Bernini's vast **Piazza San Pietro** doesn't disappoint, though its size is not really apparent until you're right on top of it. In fact, in tune with the spirit of the Baroque, the church was supposed to be even better hidden than it is now: Bernini planned to complete its colonnade with a triumphal arch linking the two arms, so obscuring the view until you were well inside the square, but this was never carried out and the arms of the piazza remain open, symbolically welcoming the world into the lap of the Catholic Church.

The **obelisk** in the centre of the piazza was brought to Rome from Egypt by Caligula in 36 AD, and it stood for many years in the centre of Nero's Circus on the Vatican Hill (to the left of the church); according to tradition, it marked the site of St Peter's martyrdom. It was moved here in 1586, when Sixtus V ordered that it be erected in front of the basilica, a task that took four months and was apparently carried out in silence, on pain of death. The matching **fountains** on either side are the work of Carlo Maderno (on the right) and Bernini (on the left). In between the obelisk and the two fountains, a circular stone set into the pavement marks the focal points of an ellipse, from which the four rows of columns on the perimeter of the piazza line up perfectly, so that the colonnade appears to be supported by a single line of columns.

12

SPECIAL VATICAN VISITS AND TOURS

VATICAN GARDENS AND NECROPOLIS

Most of the Vatican's sights of interest are easily accessible; others require a little forward planning. The **Vatican Gardens**, which are dotted with sculptures and fountains and offer great views of St Peter's, can only be visited on a guided tour, either on foot (daily except Wed & Sun; 2hr; €32) or by open-top bus with a pre-recorded audioguide (tours Mon–Sat 9am, 10am, 1pm; 45min; €36); book in advance through ⓦ museivaticani.va. Tickets include entry to the Vatican Museums, so you'll probably want to make a day of it.

You can also take a **tour** of the **Vatican Necropolis**, including the believed burial place of St Peter. This is run by the excavation office of St Peter's Basilica (ⓦ scavi.va). Pre-booking is essential well in advance by email. Send available dates, number and names of participants, and the language which you require to ⓔ scavi@fsp.va. The tour costs €12 and is not open to under 15s.

PAPAL AUDIENCES

It is possible to attend a **papal audience**; these take place on Wednesdays at 10.30am (there are no audiences in July and August) when the pope is in Rome, either in the piazza or in the Audience Hall of Paul VI on the south side of St Peter's. These are by no means one-to-one affairs – you'll be with thousands of others. Seats are allocated on a first-come-first-served basis, entrance is free and tickets can be requested here: ⓦ www.vatican.va/various/prefettura/en/biglietti_en .html, and post or fax to the office of the Prefettura della Casa Pontificia, 00120 Città del Vaticano (ⓕ 06 6988 5863); tickets need to be collected from just inside the bronze door on the right-hand side of St Peter's Square, between 3 and 7pm on the day before the audience, or between 7 and 9am on the day itself. The pope also appears each Sunday at noon to bless the crowds on St Peter's Square; this requires no ticket.

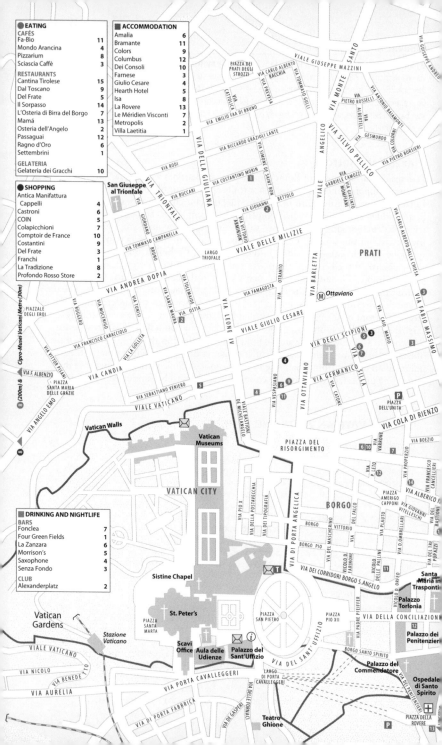

EATING

CAFÉS
Fa-Bio	11
Mondo Arancina	4
Pizzarium	8
Sciascia Caffè	3

RESTAURANTS
Cantina Tirolese	15
Dal Toscano	9
Del Frate	5
Il Sorpasso	14
L'Osteria di Birra del Borgo	7
Mamá	13
Osteria dell'Angelo	2
Passaguai	12
Ragno d'Oro	6
Settembrini	1

GELATERIA
Gelateria dei Gracchi	10

SHOPPING
Antica Manifattura Cappelli	4
Castroni	6
COIN	5
Colapicchioni	7
Comptoir de France	10
Costantini	9
Del Frate	3
Franchi	1
La Tradizione	8
Profondo Rosso Store	2

ACCOMMODATION
Amalia	6
Bramante	11
Colors	9
Columbus	12
Dei Consoli	10
Farnese	3
Giulio Cesare	4
Hearth Hotel	5
Isa	8
La Rovere	13
Le Méridien Visconti	7
Metropolis	2
Villa Laetitia	1

DRINKING AND NIGHTLIFE

BARS
Fonclea	7
Four Green Fields	1
La Zanzara	6
Morrison's	5
Saxophone	4
Senza Fondo	3

CLUB
Alexanderplatz	2

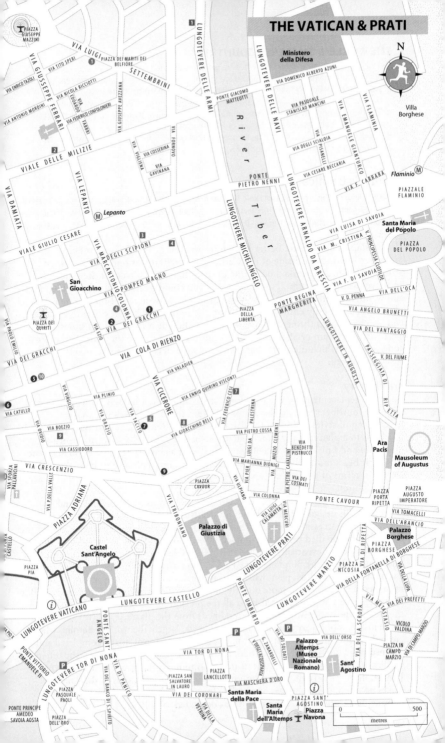

THE VATICAN & PRATI

PIAZZA GIUSEPPE MAZZINI

VIA LUIGI LUCIANI

VIA TITO SPERI

PIAZZA DEI MARITI DEI BELFIORE

VIA ENRICO TAZZOLI

VIA NICOLA RICCIOTTI

SETTEMBRINI

VIA GIUSEPPE FERRARI

VIA ANTONIO MORDINI

VIA FEDERICO CONFALONIERI

VIA RODRIGO FABBRI

VIA GIUSEPPE AVEZZANA

LUNGOTEVERE DELLE ARMI

LUNGOTEVERE DELLE NAVI

Ministero della Difesa

VIA DOMENICO ALBERTO AZUNI

PONTE GIACOMO MATTEOTTI

VIA PASQUALE STANISLAO MANCINI

VIA EMANUELE GIANTURCO

VIA FLAMINIA

Villa Borghese

VIALE DELLE MILIZIE

VIA COSSERINA

VIA VIGLIENA

VIA FORNOVO

VIA GAVINANA

River

Tiber

VIA DEGLI SCIALOIA

VIA SCHIANELLI

VIA CESARE BECCARIA

Flaminio

VIA DAMIATA

VIA LEPANTO

Lepanto

PONTE PIETRO NENNI

LUNGOTEVERE MICHELANGELO

VIA F. CARRARA

PIAZZALE FLAMINIO

VIALE GIULIO CESARE

VIA MARCANTONIO COLONNA

VIA MARC DEGLI SCIPIONI

San Gioacchino

VIA POMPEO MAGNO

PIAZZA DEI QUIRITI

VIA EZIO

VIA DEI GRACCHI

VIA PAOLO EMILIO

VIA DEI GRACCHI

VIA COLA DI RIENZO

PIAZZA DELLA LIBERTA

LUNGOTEVERE ARNALDO DA BRESCIA

PONTE REGINA MARGHERITA

VIA LUISA DI SAVOIA

VIA M. CRISTINA

VIA PRINCIPESSA CLOTILDE

Santa Maria del Popolo

PIAZZA DEL POPOLO

VIA F. DI SAVOIA

V.D. PENNA

VIA DELL'OCA

VIA ANGELO BRUNETTI

VIA DEL VANTAGGIO

V. DEL FIUME

PASSEGGIATA DI RIPETTA

LUNGOTEVERE IN AUGUSTA

VIA VALADIER

VIA CICERONE

VIA ENNIO QUIRINO VISCONTI

VIA FEDERICO CESI

VIA VIRGILIO

VIA PLINIO

VIA ORAZIO

VIA TACITO

VIA CATULLO

VIA OVIDIO

VIA BOEZIO

VIA GIOACCHINO BELLI

VIA PIETRO COSSA

PALESTRINA

VIA CASSIODORO

VIA MARIANNA DIONIGI

VIA PIER

VIA LUIGI DA

VIA MUZIO CLEMENTI

VIA PIETRO CAVALLINI

VIA BENEDETTI PISTRUCCI

VIA DEI COSMATI

Ara Pacis

Mausoleum of Augustus

VIA CRESCENZIO

VIA SFORZA PALLAVICINI

VIA P. DELLA VALLE

PIAZZA CAVOUR

VIA ULPIANO

VIA COLONNA

PONTE CAVOUR

PIAZZA PORTA RIPETTA

PIAZZA AUGUSTO IMPERATORE

VIA TOMACELLI

VIA DELL'ARANCIO

Palazzo Borghese

PIAZZA ADRIANA

Castel Sant'Angelo

PIAZZA PIA

VIA TRIBONIANO

Palazzo di Giustizia

LUNGOTEVERE PRATI

PONTE UMBERTO

VIA LUIGI CALAMATTA

VIA MERCONI

Palazzo Borghese

PIAZZA BORGHESE

PIAZZA NICOSIA

VIA DELLA FONTANELLA DI BORGHESE

VIA DELLA LUPA

VIA DI RIPETTA

VIA DELLA SCROFA

VIA METASTASIO

VIA DEI PREFETTI

VICOLO VALDINA

LUNGOTEVERE VATICANO

PONTE SANT'ANGELO

LUNGOTEVERE CASTELLO

PONTE VITTORIO EMANUELE II

LUNGOTEVERE TOR DI NONA

VIA TOR DI NONA

VIA DEL BANCO DI S. SPIRITO

G. ZANARDELLI

VIA DEI SOLDATI

VIA AGOSTINELLI

Palazzo Altemps (Museo Nazionale Romano)

VIA DELL'ORSO

PIAZZA IN CAMPO MARZIO

VIA DI CAMPO MARZIO

PONTE PRINCIPE AMEDEO SAVOIA AOSTA

PIAZZA PASQUALE PAOLI

PIAZZA DELL'ORO

VIA DEI CORONARI

PIAZZA SAN SALVATORE IN LAURO

PIAZZA LANCELLOTTI

VIA MASCHERA D'ORO

Santa Maria della Pace

VIA DELLA VETRINA

Santa Maria dell'Altemps

PIAZZA SANT'AGOSTINO

Sant' Agostino

Piazza Navona

0	500
	metres

> ### THE WORLD'S SMALLEST COUNTRY
>
> The Vatican ruled Rome until 1870, when Italian Unification led to an impasse, and a period of over fifty years in which a series of popes are said not to have left the Vatican. After reaching an uneasy agreement with Mussolini, the Vatican became a **sovereign state** in 1929, and nowadays has its own radio station, daily newspaper (*L'Osservatore Romano*), postal service (see box, p.193) and security service in the colourfully dressed Swiss Guards (a corps which dates back to 1506); it also has its own version of the euro complete with the pope's head (collectors' items, incidentally, should you be given one). Its relationship with the Italian state nowadays is, not surprisingly, anything but straightforward.

St Peter's Basilica

Basilica Daily: April–Sept 7am–7pm; Oct–March 7am–6.30pm; free guided tours in English Tues & Thurs at 8.15am from the Vatican info office on the left-hand side of the square • Free • **Grottoes** Daily: April–Sept 8am–6pm; Oct–March 7am–5.30pm • Free • **Treasury** Daily: April–Sept 8am–7pm; Oct–March 8am–6.15pm • €6 • **Dome** Daily: April–Sept 8am–6pm; Oct–March 8am–5pm • €8 via lift, €6 using the stairs • **☎** 06 6988 1662

The Basilica di San Pietro, better known to many as St Peter's, cannot fail to impress: the principal shrine of the Catholic Church, it was built on the site of St Peter's tomb, and worked on by the greatest Italian architects of the sixteenth and seventeenth centuries. Not so long ago you could freely stroll around the piazza and wander into the basilica when you felt like it. Now much of the square is fenced off, and you can only enter St Peter's from the right-hand side (exiting to the left); you also have to go through security first, and the queues can be long unless you get here before 9am or after 5pm. Bear in mind that you need to observe the **dress code** to enter, which means no bare knees or shoulders – a rule that is very strictly enforced.

12

Brief history

Built as a replacement for the run-down structure erected here by Constantine in the early fourth century on the site of St Peter's tomb, St Peter's is a strange hotchpotch of styles, bridging the gap between the Renaissance and Baroque eras. It was built to a plan initially conceived at the beginning of the sixteenth century by **Bramante** and finished off, heavily modified, over a century later by **Carlo Maderno**. In size, it beats most other churches hands down (although it's not officially the largest in terms of area – that honour belongs to the Basilica of Our Lady of Peace, Côte d'Ivoire).

Bramante had originally conceived a Greek-cross plan rising to a high central dome, but this design was altered after his death and revived only with the elderly **Michelangelo**'s accession as chief architect. Michelangelo was largely responsible for the dome, but he too died before its completion (in 1564). He was succeeded by Vignola, and the dome was eventually finished in 1590 by Giacomo della Porta. Carlo Maderno, under orders from the Borghese pope Paul V, took over in 1605, and stretched the church into a Latin-cross plan, which had the practical advantage of accommodating more people and followed more directly the plan of Constantine's original basilica. But in so doing he completely unbalanced all the previous designs, not least by obscuring the view of the dome (which he also modified) from the piazza.

The inside, too, is very much of the Baroque era, largely the work of **Bernini**, who created many of the most important fixtures. The church was finally completed and reconsecrated on November 18, 1626, exactly 1300 years to the day after the original basilica was first consecrated. At least the inscription on the facade – "Paul V, Roman, Pontiff, in the year 1612, the seventh in his pontificate, in honour of the Apostles" – leaves no doubt as to who was responsible for getting the job finished: as Pasquino commented at the time, "I thought it was dedicated to St Peter!"

Michelangelo's Pietà

The entrance to the basilica is through the door to the left of the Holy Door, which is only opened every Jubilee year. These are usually every 25 years, with the next one due in 2025. Inside, the first chapel on the right houses **Michelangelo's Pietà**, completed when he was just 24. Ever since an attack by a vandal in 1972, it has sat behind glass, strangely remote from the life of the rest of the building. When you look at the piece, its fame comes as no surprise: it's a sensitive and individual work, draping the limp body of a grown man across the legs of a woman with grace and ease. Etched into the strap across Mary's chest are words proclaiming the work as Michelangelo's – the only piece ever signed by the sculptor and apparently done after he heard that his work, which had been placed in Constantine's basilica, had been misattributed by onlookers.

The nave

In the north aisle of the **nave**, diagonally opposite the *Pietà*, are monuments to two of the few women buried at St Peter's: the colourful Queen Christina of Sweden (see box, p.162), in the shape of a huge medallion (she's buried in the grottoes downstairs), and

12

ST PETER'S

0   20
metres

Tomb of Paul III
Tomb of Urban VIII
Cattedra of St Peter
N
Bernini's Baldacchino
Monument to Alexander VII
St Veronica
St Helena
Entry to the Grottoes
Confessio
Entrance to the Treasury
St Longinus
St Andrew
John XXIII
St Peter
Tomb of Innocent VIII
Monument to Countess Mathilda of Tuscany
Chapel of the Blessed Sacrament
Monument to Clementina Sobieska
Monument to Queen Christina of Sweden
Tomb of St John Paul II
Benedict XV
Exit from the Dome
Statue of Charlemagne
Monument to the Stuarts
Michelangelo's Pietà
Statue of Constantine
Holy Door

Bernini's statue of Countess Mathilda of Tuscany, on the next pier along. The chapel after that of the *Pietà* houses the tomb of Saint John Paul II, canonized in 2013. The next major chapel on the right, halfway up the north aisle, is the wonderful gilded Baroque **Chapel of the Blessed Sacrament**, designed by Borromini, with work by Pietro da Cortona, Domenichino and Bernini; it is reserved for prayer (no photography) and is usually curtained off.

At the end of the aisle, the remains of John XXIII lie under a wax effigy, and get a lot of attention from pilgrims, a suitably humble memorial to a humble pope. John is remembered with more pomp by a modern relief in a chapel on the other side of the basilica in the penultimate chapel on the south aisle, opposite a kneeling rendering of an equally pious pope, Benedict XV, the work of Pietro Canonica (see p.175). On a pillar almost opposite is Antonio Pollaiuolo's tomb of the late-fifteenth-century pope, Innocent VIII – banker to Queen Isabella of Spain and the financier of Columbus's voyage to the New World – the only tomb to survive from the Constantinian basilica. In the upper statue of the monument the pope holds what looks like a mason's trowel – in fact the spearpoint of Longinus, given to him by the Ottoman sultan Bajazet II to persuade him to keep the sultan's brother and rival in exile in Rome. On the last pillar of the south aisle is an austere monument by Canova depicting the last of the Stuart pretenders to the British throne, while opposite, over the exit from the dome, is a monument to Clementina Sobieska, the wife of James Edward Stuart, here referred to as King James III – the third of the three women buried in St Peter's.

12

The crossing

Under the **crossing** of the transepts and the nave, the dome is breathtakingly imposing, rising high above the supposed site of St Peter's tomb. With a diameter of 44m, it is only 1.5m smaller than the Pantheon, and the letters of the inscription inside its lower level are nearly 2m high. It's supported by four enormous piers, decorated with reliefs depicting the basilica's "major relics": St Veronica's handkerchief, which was used to wipe the face of Christ and is adorned with his miraculous image; the lance of St Longinus, which pierced Christ's side; and a piece of the True Cross, in the pier of St Helen (the head of St Andrew, which was returned to the Eastern Church by Pope Paul VI in 1966, was also formerly kept here). On the right side of the nave, near the pier of St Longinus, the bronze statue of St Peter is another of the basilica's most venerated monuments, carved in the thirteenth century by Arnolfo di Cambio; its right foot has been polished smooth by the attentions of pilgrims. On holy days the statue is dressed in papal tiara and vestments.

The baldacchino

Bernini's **baldacchino** is the centrepiece of the sculptor's Baroque embellishment of the interior, a massive 26m high, cast from 927 tonnes of bronze removed from the ceiling at the entrance portico of the Pantheon in 1633. Its wild spiralling columns are modelled on columns in the Constantine basilica, in turn said to have been brought to Rome by Helena, mother of Constantine, from the Temple of Solomon. You'll also notice the bees that adorn just about anything to do with the Barberini family – in this case Bernini's patron was Pope Urban VIII of the Barberini family.

The apse

Bernini's feverish sculpture decorates the **apse**, too, his vast bronze *Cathedra Petri* enclosing what tradition says to be the chair of St Peter. Gilded stucco rays of light, angels and clouds burst out from around the central alabaster window, at its centre the image of a dove with a wingspan of 2m. Below, four doctors of the Church support the throne (the two with bishops' mitres are St Augustine of Hippo and

St Ambrose, representing the Western Church; the two to the rear are portraits of St John Chrysostom and St Athanasius of the Eastern Church). On the right, the **tomb of Urban VIII**, also by Bernini, is less grand but more dignified, while on the left, the tomb of **Paul III**, by Giacomo della Porta, was moved up and down the nave of the church before it was finally placed here to balance that of Pope Urban.

Monument to Alexander VII
In the south transept, the last of Bernini's works in the church is his splendidly Baroque monument to **Alexander VII**. Perhaps the most dramatic papal monument of them all, it shows a winged skeleton clutching an hourglass, a vivid *memento mori* (reminder of death), struggling to escape from beneath the heavy marble drapery; above, the Chigi pope kneels victorious in prayer, triumphant over death. On the left sits Charity, on the right, Truth Revealed by Time; behind are Hope and Faith.

The treasury
An entrance off the south aisle, under a giant monument to Pius VIII, leads to the **treasury museum**. At the entrance a wall tablet records the names of all the popes buried in St Peter's. Along with more recent additions, it holds artefacts from the earlier church: a spiral marble column (the other survivors form part of the colonnade around the interior of the dome), once thought to be from the old temple of Jerusalem; a wall-mounted tabernacle by Donatello showing the dead Christ being revealed by angels (the latter carved by Michelozzo); a rich blue-and-gold dalmatic that is said to have belonged to Charlemagne (though this has since been called into question); the vestments and tiara for the bronze statue of St Peter in the nave of the basilica; and the massive late-fifteenth-century bronze tomb of Sixtus IV by Pollaiuolo, an enormously influential piece of the Early Renaissance. Don't miss the beautifully carved fourth-century early Christian tomb of Junius Bassus, once prefect of Rome.

12

The grottoes
Steps lead down behind Bernini's statue of St Andrew to the **Vatican grottoes** (not accessible when the area in front of the high altar is fenced off during Masses, usually 4.30–6pm), which extend right under the main footprint of the main church. The area is only partially accessible. Some column bases from Constantine's original basilica are visible, as well as a number of papal tombs (the majority of the popes are buried here) and a glimpse into the chapel of the *confessio*, the area below the high altar which is the closest point to the believed place of the tomb of Peter and the most sacred place in the church.

Canova's statue of Pius VI dominates the central aisle, while the tombs in the south aisle include a plain slab commemorating the Blessed Paul VI; and the sarcophagus of John Paul I, who reigned for just 33 days in 1978. Leaving, you emerge outside the basilica, so it's best to visit the grottoes last.

VATICAN POST
The Vatican's own **postal service** is widely thought to be quicker and more reliable than the standard Italian post; many Romans make a special trip to the Vatican to ensure the speedy delivery of important letters. Perhaps unsurprisingly, more letters are sent each year per inhabitant from the Vatican postcode (00120) than from anywhere else in the world.

To send a postcard with a Vatican postmark (and a Vatican stamp), head to one of the post offices to the left of St Peter's (as you approach), or behind the right-hand colonnade (Mon–Sat 8.30am–6.30pm), or inside the Vatican Museums (same hours as museums).

The roof and dome

You can get up to the **roof** and **dome** by taking the far right-hand gate of the portico of the basilica (after the security checks in the right-hand colonnade) following the signs for the "Cupola". An early start is advised to minimize queuing and, even with the lift (which takes care of two hundred steps), there's a long climb via a narrow stairway that spirals up the dome – another three hundred or so steps that grow increasingly cramped as you get higher. The views from the gallery around the interior of the base of the dome give you a fantastic sense of the vast size of the church, and the roof has views all around, though sadly you can't get right up behind the statues of the Apostles any longer. There's a small café serving coffee and soft drinks, along with a souvenir shop, and from here you make the final ascent to the lantern at the top of the dome, from which the views over the Vatican and Rome are as glorious as you'd expect. Bear in mind, though, that it is a fairly claustrophobic climb through the double shell of the dome to reach the lantern; you should give it a miss if you're uneasy with heights or confined spaces. The exit leads you back into the south aisle of the church itself.

Vatican necropolis

The baldacchino and *confessio* are supposed to mark the exact spot of the **tomb of St Peter**, and excavations in the 1940s under Pius XII did indeed turn up – directly beneath the baldacchino and the remains of Constantine's basilica – a row of Roman family tombs with inscriptions confirming that the Vatican Hill was a well-known burial ground in classical times. It is possible to take a **tour** of the **Vatican necropolis** in English, but you need to book well in advance (see box, p.187). The tombs are decorated with frescoes, mosaic floors and stucco figures, and surround an ancient tomb that is believed to be that of the apostle. You can see what's left of the canopy that used to cover it, a graffitied wall and behind it a transparent plastic box – one of nineteen such boxes – that may contain his remains, or at least those of an elderly man who died in the first century AD.

12

Vatican Museums

Viale Vaticano 13 • Mon–Sat 9am–6pm, last entry at 4pm; last Sun of each month 9am–2pm, last entry at 12.30pm; closed public and religious holidays; May–Sept also open Fri 7–11pm, last entry 9.30pm • €16; all tickets pre-booked online €4 extra; last Sun of the month free • ☎ 06 6988 4676, Ⓦ museivaticani.va

A fifteen-minute walk out of the northern side of the piazza takes you up to the only part of the Vatican Palace that you can visit independently, the **Vatican Museums**. If you have found any of Rome's other museums disappointing, the Vatican is probably the reason why: so much booty from the city's history has ended up here, and so many of the Renaissance's finest artists were in the employ of the pope, that the result is a set of museums so stuffed with antiquities as to put most other European collections to shame.

As its name suggests, the complex actually holds a collection of museums on very diverse subjects, with displays of classical statuary, Renaissance painting, Etruscan relics and Egyptian artefacts, not to mention the furnishings and decoration of the palace itself. There's no point in trying to see everything in one visit. Once inside, you have a choice of routes, but the only features you really shouldn't miss are the **Raphael Rooms** and the **Sistine Chapel** – and there are plenty of signs to make sure you don't. Above all, decide how long you want to spend here, and what you want to see, before you start; you could spend anything from an hour to the better part of a day inside, and it's easy to collapse from museum fatigue before you've even got to your most important target of interest. Be conservative – the distances between different sections alone can be vast and very tiring.

Finally, bear in mind that in high season, at least, there may be a queue to get into the museums; online reservations are always a good idea. From May to September the Vatican Museums are open on Friday evenings, which are a less busy option.

Pinacoteca

If the **Pinacoteca** is on your list, it's best to visit it first – turn right at the top of the stairs. A relatively new museum, opened in 1932, and housed in a separate building, it ranks possibly as Rome's best picture gallery, with works from the early primitives right up to the nineteenth century.

The Gothic period to the Umbrian School

The display is chronological, and starts with a beautiful collection of works from the **Gothic period**, among them an amazing, almost mosaic-like *Last Judgement* by Niccolò and Giovanni from the second half of the twelfth century in the first room, and the stunning Stefaneschi triptych by Giotto in the next room painted after 1300 for the old church of St Peter's, where it remained until 1506 when it was removed for the building of the new church. In the rooms that follow are lovely pieces by Fra Angelico, Filippo Lippi and Benozzo Gozzoli, while the next room has the **naturalistic works** of Marco Palmezzano and Melozzo da Forlí's musical angels – fragments of a fresco commissioned for the church of Santi Apostoli by Giuliano della Rovere, the future Pope Julius II. The central figure of the Risen Christ from the same fresco has been at the Palazzo del Quirinale since the eighteenth century (see p.109). Giuliano della Rovere also makes an appearance in Melozzo's *Sixtus IV Opening the Vatican Library* in the same room – he's the tonsured figure in the red robes of a cardinal, before his uncle Pope Sixtus (the man for whom the Sistine Chapel was named). On the far left is Giuliano's brother Giovanni, then the prefect of Rome. The next room holds Carlo Crivelli's magnificently angst-ridden *Pietà*, while beyond here lie the rich backdrops and elegantly clad figures of the **Umbrian School** painters, Perugino and Pinturicchio.

12

THE VATICAN PALACE AND THE MUSEUMS' LAYOUT

Rather like Rome, the **Vatican Palace** complex wasn't built in a day. It is a patchwork of palace buildings constructed over many decades, interwoven with purpose-built museum spaces, dating from the eighteenth to the twentieth centuries. The three-hundred-metre-long corridor that makes up much of the "museum" space was built to join the original palace next to St Peter's, constructed around 1450, with a newer building, the Belvedere, built on the higher ground to the north by Innocent VIII in 1490 as a summer residence. Bramante oversaw the connection of the two buildings in the 1500s, creating a vast, three-tier courtyard used for festivals and banquets, until it was divided into separate quadrangles in the late sixteenth century. The construction of the nineteenth-century Braccio Nuovo divided the area even further, resulting in its current form.

The museums occupy four principal structures: the **original Palace** at the end nearest St Peter's; the **Belvedere Palace** to the north (above the museum entrance), and the long **galleries**. In the middle of it all are the three **courtyards**: the **Cortile del Belvedere** at the southern end; the small **Cortile della Biblioteca** in the middle, created by the construction of the Vatican Library and the Braccio Nuovo; and, the northernmost of the three, the **Cortile della Pigna** – named after the huge bronze pine cone mounted in the niche at the end, an ancient Roman artefact that was found close to the Pantheon. In classical times this was a fountain with water pouring out of each of its points. Also in this courtyard is a large modern bronze sculpture of a sphere within a sphere by Arnaldo Pomodoro, and a pleasant outdoor café.

The old main entrance to the museums was created by Pope Pius XI, in 1932, and its huge bronze spiral staircase, the work of Giuseppe Momo, provides a dignified **exit** to the museums. On it are displayed the heraldic arms of all the popes from 1447 (Nicholas II) to Pius XI's predecessor (Benedict XV), while the staircase is in the form of a double helix, one half ascending, the other descending. The new museum **entrance** was built next door in 1999.

Finally, bear in mind that the collections of the Vatican Museums are in a constant state of restoration, and are often closed and shifted around with little or no notice, though the most important departments are usually open; check ⓦ museivaticani.va for up-to-date details.

12

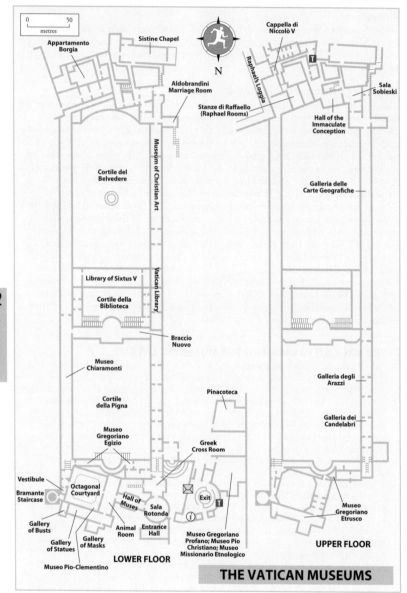

Sistine Chapel

Cappella di Niccolò V

Appartamento Borgia

Aldobrandini Marriage Room

Stanze di Raffaello (Raphael Rooms)

Raphael's Loggia

T

Sala Sobieski

Hall of the Immaculate Conception

N

Museum of Christian Art

Cortile del Belvedere

Galleria delle Carte Geografiche

Library of Sixtus V

Vatican Library

Cortile della Biblioteca

Braccio Nuovo

Museo Chiaramonti

Cortile della Pigna

Pinacoteca

Galleria degli Arazzi

Galleria dei Candelabri

Museo Gregoriano Egizio

Greek Cross Room

Vestibule

Octagonal Courtyard

Bramante Staircase

Hall of Muses

Sala Rotonda

Exit

T

i

Museo Gregoriano Etrusco

Gallery of Busts

Animal Room

Entrance Hall

Gallery of Statues

Gallery of Masks

Museo Gregoriano Profano; Museo Pio Christiano; Museo Missionario Etnologico

UPPER FLOOR

Museo Pio-Clementino

LOWER FLOOR

THE VATICAN MUSEUMS

0   50
metres

Raphael and Leonardo

Room VIII is dedicated to **Raphael**; it contains three vast paintings, and, in climate-controlled glass cases, the tapestries that were made to his designs to be hung in the Sistine Chapel during conclave. The cartoons from which these tapestries were made are now in the Victoria and Albert Museum in London. Of the three paintings, the *Coronation of the Virgin*, on the right, was done when Raphael was only 19 years old; the *Transfiguration*, in the middle, was his last major painting; and the *Madonna of*

Foligno, on the left, shows saints John the Baptist, Francis of Assisi and Jerome, and was painted as an offering after a cannonball (in the centre of the painting) struck the house of the donor, Sigismondo de' Conti (kneeling on the far right). In the next room, Leonardo's **St Jerome** is unfinished, too, but it's a remarkable piece of work, with Jerome a rake-like ascetic torn between suffering and a good meal. Look closely at this painting and you can see that a 25-centimetre square, the saint's head, was reattached to the canvas after the painting was used as upholstery for a stool in a cobbler's shop in Rome for centuries.

Caravaggio and beyond

Caravaggio's *Descent from the Cross*, a few rooms on, gets more attention, a warts-and-all canvas that unusually shows the Virgin Mary as a middle-aged mother grieving over her dead son, while the men placing Christ's body on the bier are models that the artist recruited from the city streets – a realism that is imitated successfully in Reni's *Crucifixion of St Peter* in the same room: the Baroque at full throttle. Take a look, too, at the most gruesome painting in the collection, Poussin's *Martyrdom of St Erasmus*, which shows the saint stretched out on a table with his hands bound above his head in the process of having his small intestine wound onto a drum – basically being "drawn" prior to "quartering". The views over the Vatican Gardens nearby, with the dome of St Peter's in the background, provide a suitable antidote if you need it.

Museo Gregoriano Egizio

12

The **Museo Gregoriano Egizio**, founded in the nineteenth century by Gregory XVI, has a distinguished collection of ancient **Egyptian artefacts**. It holds some vividly painted mummy cases (and two mummies), along with the alabaster vessels in which the entrails of the deceased were placed. There is also a partial reconstruction of the Temple of Serapis from Hadrian's Villa near Tivoli, along with another statue of his lover Antinous, who drowned close to the original temple in Egypt and so inspired Hadrian to build his replica – dressed here as Osiris. The Egyptian-style statues in shiny black basalt next door are also Roman imitations, as is the reclining figure of the Nile river god, complete with crocodile. Hadrian collected some original Egyptian bits and pieces, too, some of which are housed in the room which curves around the niche containing the pine cone, including various Egyptian deities – look out for the laughing dwarf god Bes.

The next rooms contain Egyptian bronzes from the late pharaonic period and early days of the Roman Empire, including a group of items from the cult of Isis, which became popular in Rome itself. Beyond are a couple of rooms with clay tablets inscribed in cuneiform writing from Mesopotamia; Assyrian, Sumerian and Persian bas-reliefs on stone tablets; and, in the last room, a lovely relief of a kneeling winged god from 850 BC.

THE LAOCOÖN STATUE

The **Laocoön** is perhaps the most famous classical statue ever, referred to by Pliny who thought it carved from a single piece of marble, and written about by Byron – who described its contorted realism as "dignifying pain". The statue depicts the prophetic Trojan priest with his sons being crushed by serpents, sent by the gods to punish him for warning his fellow citizens of the danger of the Trojan horse. Dating from the first-century BC, it was discovered near Nero's Domus Aurea in 1506 by a ploughman who had inadvertently dug through the roof of a buried part of Trajan's Baths. Some scholars theorize that the statue is in fact a sixteenth-century fake by Michelangelo, which isn't as mad is it sounds – Michelangelo did design a substitute arm for the statue, and this was found to be an almost exact match for the "original".

Museo Pio-Clementino

The **Museo Pio-Clementino** is home to some of the Vatican's best classical statuary, and is perhaps the only must-see apart from the Sistine Chapel and Raphael Rooms. Its vestibule contains a copy of Lysippos's fourth-century BC statue *Apoxyomenos*, showing an athlete scraping dirt from his body. The adjoining **Octagonal Courtyard** holds two statues that proved a huge influence on Renaissance artists: the serene *Apollo Belvedere*, in the left corner as you go in, a Roman copy of a fourth-century BC original; and the first-century BC **Laocoön** in the far left corner (see box, p.197).

Diagonally opposite the *Apollo Belvedere* is a statue of Hermes that Poussin thought the greatest male nude he'd ever seen, while diagonally opposite the *Laocoön* is a group of nineteenth-century Classical figures by Canova. In between the two stands a statue of Venus from the second century AD, said to be a portrait of Marcus Aurelius's wife Faustina.

Animal Room and Gallery of Masks

Leave the courtyard between the two howling dogs and you're in the **Animal Room**, named for its animal sculptures, although only a few are of ancient provenance and perhaps the most impressive features are the floor and wall mosaics, all from Hadrian's Villa at Tivoli.

Hall of the Muses

After the Animal Room, the frescoed **Hall of the Muses**, so called for the statues that line its central section, has as its centrepiece the so-called **Belvedere Torso**, which was found in Campo de' Fiori during the reign of Julius II. It's signed by Apollonius, a Greek sculptor of the first century BC, and is generally thought to be a near-perfect example of male anatomy. Its portrayal, either of Hercules sitting on his lion skin or Ajax resting, was studied by most key Renaissance artists, including Michelangelo, who incorporated its turning pose into his portrait of *Christ in the Last Judgement* in the Sistine Chapel.

Sala Rotonda

A short corridor leads to the **Sala Rotonda**, centring on a vast bowl from the Domus Aurea and with a floor paved with a third-century AD Roman mosaic from the town of Otricoli, north of Rome, depicting battles between men and sea monsters. There is more classical statuary around the room, notably a huge gilded bronze statue of a rather dim-witted-looking Hercules, also from the second century AD and the only surviving gilded bronze statue on display in the Vatican Museums. On either side of the statue are busts of the Emperor Hadrian and his lover Antinous, who is also depicted in the same room, to the right of the entrance, as a huge statue dressed as Bacchus. Opposite this is a beautiful white marble statue of Claudius, in the guise of Jupiter, with his oak-leaf crown and an eagle at his feet.

Greek Cross Room

Beyond, the **Greek Cross Room** is decorated in Egyptian style, although the pharaonic statues flanking the entry door are second-century imitations: Roman fakes made for Hadrian's Villa at Tivoli. In the middle of the floor is another Roman mosaic, its central figure a second-century AD representation of Minerva, while the two huge porphyry boxes are the sarcophagi of Helena and Constantina. On Helena's, soldiers vanquish their enemies, while that of Constantina, the daughter of the emperor, shows putti carrying grapes, loaves of bread and lambs – perhaps a reference to the Eucharist, as she was a devout Christian.

Museo Gregoriano Etrusco

A grand staircase, the Simonetti Staircase, leads up to the **Museo Gregoriano Etrusco** (usually only open in the morning) which holds sculpture, funerary art and applied art from the sites of southern Etruria – a good complement to the Etruscan collection at the Villa Giulia (see p.177).

The Regolini-Galassi tomb
The second room houses finds from the seventh-century BC **Regolini-Galassi tomb**, which was discovered near Cerveteri (and named for the archeologists who discovered it). It contained the remains of three Etruscan nobles, two men and a woman; the breastplate of the woman and her huge fibula (clasp) are of gold. Take a look at the small ducks and lions with which they are decorated, fashioned in microscopic beadwork. There's also armour, a bronze bedstead, a funeral chariot and a wagon, as well as several enormous storage jars, in which food, oil and wine were contained for use in the afterlife.

The Mars of Todi and finds from Northern Lazio
Beyond here are **Etruscan bronzes**, including weapons, candelabra, barbecue sets (skewers and braziers); beautiful make-up cases known as *cistae*; and, most notably, the *Mars of Todi*, a three-quarter-size votive statue found in the Umbrian town of Todi. On a flap of the figure's armour an inscription gives the name of the donor. Further on, there is a large collection of Etruscan sarcophagi and stone statuary from Vulci, Tarquinia and Tuscania in northern Lazio. Particularly interesting here are the finely carved horses' heads from Vulci and the sarcophagus of a magistrate from Tarquinia, which still bears traces of the paint that its reliefs were coloured with. There is also Etruscan jewellery, with exquisite goldsmith work, crowns of golden oak and laurel leaves, necklaces, earrings and rings set with semiprecious stones and a fibula complete with the owner's name etched on it in such small writing that a magnifying glass is provided for you to read it.

The Statue of Adonis and Greek krater
Heading up some stairs from this room, you come to a series of large rooms which look out from the north side of the Belvedere Palace and offer stunning views of the hill of Monte Mario. Inside, you'll find lots of vases, assorted weapons and items of everyday household use, as well as a magnificent terracotta **statue of Adonis** lying on a lacy couch, found near the town of Tuscania in the 1950s. Finally, don't miss the **Greek krater**, among a lot of Greek pottery found in Etruscan tombs, which shows Menelaus and Ulysses asking the Trojans for the return of Helen.

Galleria dei Candelabri
Outside the Etruscan Museum, the staircase leads back down to the main – and consequently crowded – route to the Sistine Chapel, taking you first through the **Galleria dei Candelabri**, the niches of which are adorned with huge candelabra taken from imperial Roman villas. This gallery is also stuffed with ancient sculpture, its most memorable piece a copy of the famous statue of Diana of Ephesus, her appendages usually interpreted as breasts.

Galleria degli Arazzi
Beyond the Galleria dei Candelabri, the **Galleria degli Arazzi** has, on the left, Flemish tapestries (*arazzi*) to designs by the school of Raphael, which show scenes from the life of Christ and, on the right, tapestries made in Rome at the Barberini workshops during the late 1600s, showing scenes from the life of Maffeo Barberini, who became Pope Urban VIII in 1623.

Galleria delle Carte Geografiche
The Galleria degli Arazzi leads on to the **Galleria delle Carte Geografiche** (Gallery of the Maps), which is as long (120m) as the previous two galleries put together. It was

decorated in the late sixteenth century as part of the Papal palace at the behest of Pope Gregory XIII, the reformer of the calendar, to show all of Italy, the major islands in the Mediterranean and the papal possessions in France, as well as large-scale maps of the maritime republics of Venice and Genoa. The maps are fantastic, illustrative yet precise, and this gallery, with its ceiling frescoes showing scenes that took place in the area depicted in each adjacent map, is considered by many to be the most beautiful in the entire museum complex. The elaborate ceiling stuccoes frame frescoes showing stories from the lives of the saints connected to the territories below.

Hall of the Immaculate Conception and the Sala Sobieski

After the Gallery of the Maps, there is a hall with more tapestries and, to the left, the **Sala Sobieski**, with its nineteenth-century painting of the Polish king driving Turks out of Europe. Beyond is the **Hall of the Immaculate Conception**, which sports nineteenth-century frescoes of Pope Pius IX declaring the Doctrine of the Immaculate Conception of the Blessed Virgin Mary on December 8, 1854. From here all visitors are directed to a covered walkway suspended over the lower palace courtyard, which leads through to the Raphael Rooms.

Raphael Rooms

The **Raphael Rooms**, or Stanze di Raffaello, are, apart perhaps from the Sistine Chapel, the Vatican's greatest work of art. This set of rooms formed the private apartments of Pope Julius II, and when he moved in here he commissioned Raphael to redecorate them in a style more in tune with the times. Raphael died before the scheme was complete, but the two rooms that were completed by him, as well as others completed by pupils, are among the highlights of the Renaissance.

Stanza di Costantino

The first of the Raphael Rooms you come to, the **Stanza di Costantino**, was not in fact the work of Raphael at all, but painted partly to his designs about five years after he died by his pupils Giulio Romano, Francesco Penni and Raffaello del Colle, between 1525 and 1531. It shows scenes from the life of the Emperor Constantine, who made Christianity the official religion of the Roman Empire. The enormous painting on the wall opposite the entrance is the *Battle of the Milvian Bridge* by Giulio Romano and Francesco Penni – a depiction of the decisive battle in 312 AD between the warring co-emperors of the West, Constantine and Maxentius. With due regard to the laws of propaganda, the victorious emperor is in the centre of the painting mounted on his white horse, while the vanquished Maxentius drowns in the river to the right, clinging to his black horse. The painting to your left as you enter, the *Vision of Constantine* by Giulio Romano, shows Constantine telling his troops of his dream-vision of the Holy Cross inscribed with the legend "In this sign you will conquer". Opposite, the *Baptism of Constantine*, by Francesco Penni, is a flight of fancy; Constantine was baptized on his deathbed about thirty years after the battle of the Milvian Bridge.

Stanza di Eliodoro

The **Stanza di Eliodoro** is the first of the Raphael Rooms proper, with a fresco on the right of the entrance, the *Expulsion of Heliodorus from the Temple*, that tells the story of Heliodorus, the agent of the Hellenistic King Seleucus IV, who was slain by a mysterious rider on a white horse while trying to steal the treasure of Jerusalem's Temple. It's an exciting piece of work, painted in the years 1512–14 for Pope Julius II, and the figures of Heliodorus, the horseman and the fleeing men are adeptly done, the figures almost jumping out of the painting into the room. The group of

CLOCKWISE FROM TOP LEFT SCHOOL OF ATHENS, RAPHAEL ROOMS (P.202); THE SWISS GUARD; PIAZZA SAN PIETRO FROM THE TOP OF THE BASILICA (P.187); STATUE OF ST PETER, PIAZZA SAN PIETRO (P.187) >

figures on the left, however, is more interesting – Pope Julius II in his papal robes, Giulio Romano, the pupil of Raphael, and, to his left, Raphael himself in a self-portrait.

On the left wall as you enter, the *Mass of Bolsena* is a bit of anti-Lutheran propaganda, and relates a miracle that occurred in the town in northern Lazio in the 1260s, when a German priest who doubted the transubstantiation of Christ found the wafer bleeding when he broke it during a service – the napkin onto which it bled can be seen in the cathedral at Orvieto, 90km north of Rome. The pope facing the priest is another portrait of Julius II. The composition is a neat affair, the colouring rich, the onlookers kneeling, turning and gasping as the miracle is realized. On the window wall opposite, the *Deliverance of St Peter* shows the saint being assisted in a jail-break by the Angel of the Lord – a night scene, whose clever chiaroscuro predates Caravaggio by nearly one hundred years. It was painted by order of Pope Leo X, as an allegory of his imprisonment after a battle that took place in Ravenna a few years earlier. Finally, on the large wall opposite, the *Expulsion of Heliodorus from the Temple, Leo I Repulsing Attila the Hun* is an allegory of the difficulties that the papacy was going through in the early 1500s and shows the chubby cardinal Giovanni de' Medici, who succeeded Julius II and became Leo X in 1513. Leo later had Raphael's pupils paint a portrait of himself as Leo I, so, confusingly, he appears twice in this fresco, as pope and as the equally portly Medici cardinal just behind.

Stanza della Segnatura

12

The next room, the **Stanza della Segnatura**, or Pope's Study, is probably the best known – and with good reason. Painted in the years 1508–11, when Raphael first came to Rome, the subjects were again the choice of Julius II, and, composed with careful balance and harmony, it comes close to the peak of the painter's art.

The **School of Athens**, on the near wall as you come in, steals the show, a representation of the triumph of scientific truth, in which all the great minds of antiquity are represented. Plato and Aristotle discuss philosophy at the centre of the painting: Aristotle, the father of scientific method, motions downwards; Plato, pointing upwards, indicating his philosophy of otherworldly spirituality, is believed to be a portrait of Leonardo da Vinci. On the far right, the crowned figure holding a globe was meant to represent the Egyptian geographer, Ptolemy; to his right the young man in the black beret is Raphael, while in front, demonstrating a theorem to his pupils on a slate, the figure of Euclid is a portrait of Bramante. Spread across the steps is Diogenes, lazily ignorant of all that is happening around him, while to the left, Raphael added a solitary, sullen portrait of Michelangelo as Heraclitus writing – a homage to the artist, apparently painted after Raphael saw the first stage of the Sistine Chapel almost next door. Other identifiable figures include the beautiful youth with blonde hair on the left looking out of the painting, Francesco Maria della Rovere, placed here by order of Julius II.

Della Rovere, the Duke of Urbino, also appears as the good-looking young man to the left of the seated dignitaries in the painting opposite, the *Disputation over the Sacrament*, an allegory of the Christian religion and the main element of the Mass, the Blessed Sacrament – which stands at the centre of the painting being discussed by all manner of popes, cardinals, bishops, doctors, even the poet Dante.

Stanza dell'Incendio di Borgo

The final room, the **Stanza dell'Incendio di Borgo**, was the last to be decorated, to the orders (and the general glorification) of Pope Leo X, and in a sense it brings together three generations of work. The ceiling was painted by Perugino, Raphael's teacher, and the frescoes completed to Raphael's designs by his pupils (notably Giulio Romano). The most striking of them is the *Fire in the Borgo*, facing the main window – an oblique reference to Leo X restoring peace to Italy after Julius II's reign but in fact describing an event that took place during the reign of Leo IV, when the pope stood in the loggia of the old St Peter's and made the sign of the cross to extinguish a fire. As with so many of these paintings, the chronology is deliberately crazy: Leo IV is in fact a portrait of Leo X, while on the left, Aeneas carries his aged father Anchises out of the burning city of Troy, two thousand years earlier.

Appartamento Borgia

Outside the Raphael Rooms, head down to the **Appartamento Borgia**, which was inhabited by Julius II's hated predecessor, Alexander VI – a fact which persuaded Julius to move into the new set of rooms he called upon Raphael to decorate. Since 1972, host to the galleries of modern religious art, the Borgia rooms were almost exclusively decorated by Pinturicchio in the years 1492–95, on the orders of Alexander VI, though sadly the lighting is poor – more focused on the modern art than it is on the ceilings.

The first room is named after its ceiling decorations of the twelve sibyls, and a further room shows Euclid kneeling at Geometry's throne above the fireplace, but it's the frescoes in the third room, the **Sala dei Santi**, that are especially worth seeing, typically rich in colour and detail and depicting the legend of Osiris and the Apis bull – a reference to the Borgia family symbol. Among other images is a scene showing St Catherine of Alexandria disputing with the Emperor Maximilian, in which Pinturicchio has placed his self-portrait behind the emperor. The Arch of Constantine is clearly visible in the background. The figure of St Catherine is said to be a portrait of Lucrezia Borgia, and the room was reputedly the scene of a decidedly un-papal party to celebrate the first of Lucrezia's three marriages, which ended up with men tossing sweets down the fronts of the women's dresses.

The religious collection is spread throughout the main apartments and the forty or so rooms include works by some of the most famous names in the **modern art** world: a typically tortured Van Gogh *Pietà*; an exquisite pastel drawing of *Joan of Arc* by Redon;

12

JULIUS II AND THE ORIGINS OF THE SISTINE CHAPEL FRESCOES

When construction was completed in 1483 during the reign of Pope Sixtus IV, the Sistine Chapel ceiling was painted as a blue background with gold stars to resemble the night sky. Over the altar there were two additional paintings by Perugino and a large picture of the Virgin Mary. Sixtus IV was succeeded by Innocent VIII, who was followed by Alexander VI, the Borgia pope who, after the brief reign of Pius III, was succeeded in 1503 by Giuliano della Rovere, who took the name **Julius II**. Though a Franciscan friar, he was a violent man with a short temper; his immediate objective as pope was to try to regain the lands that had been taken away from the papacy during the reigns of Innocent VIII and Alexander VI by the French, Germans and Spanish. For this purpose he started a series of wars and secret alliances.

Julius II was also an avid collector and patron of the arts, and he summoned to Rome the best artists and architects of the day. Among these was **Michelangelo**, who, perhaps through a series of political intrigues orchestrated by Bramante and Raphael, was assigned the task of decorating the Sistine Chapel. Work commenced in 1508. Oddly enough, Michelangelo hadn't wanted to do the work at all: he considered himself a sculptor, not a painter, and was more eager to get on with carving Julius II's tomb – now in San Pietro in Vincoli (see p.113) – than the ceiling, which he regarded as a chore. Pope Julius II, however, had other plans, drawing up a design of the twelve Apostles for the vault and hiring Bramante to design a scaffold for the artist to work from. Michelangelo was apparently an awkward, solitary character: he had barely begun painting when he rejected Bramante's scaffold as unusable, fired all his staff and dumped the pope's scheme for the ceiling in favour of his own. But the pope was easily his match, and there are tales of the two men clashing while the work was going on – Michelangelo would lock the doors at crucial points, ignoring the pope's demands to see how it was progressing, and legend has the two men at loggerheads at the top of the scaffold one day, resulting in the pope striking the artist in frustration.

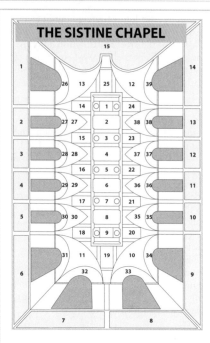

THE SISTINE CHAPEL

12

liturgical vestments designed by Matisse; a fascinating *Landscape with Angels* by Salvador Dalí, donated by King Juan Carlos of Spain; and one of Francis Bacon's studies of *Innocent X after Velázquez*.

Sistine Chapel

Steps lead up from the Appartamento Borgia to the **Sistine Chapel** (Cappella Sistina), a huge, barn-like structure built for Pope Sixtus IV between 1473 and 1483. It serves as the pope's official private chapel and is also the scene of the conclaves of cardinals for the election of each new pontiff. The ceiling paintings here, and the *Last Judgement* on the wall behind the altar, together make up arguably the greatest masterpiece in Western art, and the largest body of painting ever planned and executed by one man – **Michelangelo**. They are also probably the most viewed paintings in the world: it's estimated that on an average day about twenty-five thousand people trudge through here to take a look, and during the summer and on special occasions the number of visitors can exceed thirty thousand. It's useful to carry a pair of binoculars with you in order to see the paintings better, but bear in mind that it is strictly forbidden to take pictures of any kind in the chapel, including video, and it is also officially forbidden to speak – although this is something that is often ignored despite the best efforts of the museum staff.

The wall paintings

Upon completion of the structure, Sixtus brought in several prominent painters of the Renaissance to decorate the walls. The overall project was under the management of Pinturicchio and comprised a series of paintings showing (on the left as you face the altar) scenes from the life of Moses and, on the right, scenes from the life of Christ. There are paintings by, among others, **Perugino**, who painted the marvellously composed cityscape of *Jesus Giving St Peter the Keys to Heaven*; **Botticelli**, with the *Trials of Moses* and *Cleansing of the Leper*; and **Ghirlandaio**, whose *Calling of St Peter and St Andrew* shows Jesus calling the two fishermen to be disciples, surrounded by onlookers, against a fictitious medieval landscape of boats, birds, turrets and mountains. Some of the paintings were in fact collaborative efforts, and it's known that Ghirlandaio and Botticelli in particular contributed to each other's work. Anywhere else they would be pored over very closely indeed. As it is, they are often overlooked in favour of Michelangelo's more famous work.

The ceiling frescoes

Michelangelo's frescoes depict scenes from the Old Testament, from the *Creation of Light* at the altar end to the *Drunkenness of Noah* over the door. The sides are decorated with prophets and sibyls and the ancestors of Jesus. Julius II (see box, p.203) lived only a few months after the Sistine Chapel ceiling was finished, but the fame of the work he had commissioned soon spread far and wide. Certainly, it's staggeringly impressive, all

---

THE SISTINE CHAPEL: MICHELANGELO'S PROGRESS

Restorers have been able to chart the **progress of Michelangelo** as he moved across the vault. Images on fresco were completed before the plaster dried, and each day a fresh layer of plaster would have been laid, on which Michelangelo would have had around eight hours or so before having to finish for the day. Comparing the different areas of plaster, it seems the figure of Adam, in the key *Creation of Adam* scene, took four days; God, in the same fresco, took three. You can also see the development of Michelangelo as a painter when you look at the paintings in reverse order. The first painting, over the door, the *Drunkenness of Noah*, is done in a stiff and formal style, and is vastly different from the last painting, the *Creation of Light*, over the altar, which shows the artist at his best, the perfect master of the technique of fresco painting.

the more so for the addition in 2015 of seven thousand LED lights, which throw the frescoes into three-dimensional detail.

The ceiling frescoes: side panels

Entering from behind the altar, you are supposed, as you look up, to imagine that you are peering into heaven through the arches of the imaginary architecture that springs from the sides of the chapel, supported by little putti caryatids and *ignudi* or nudes, bearing shields and the oak-leaf garlands of the Della Rovere family of Julius II. Look at the pagan **sibyls** and biblical **prophets** which Michelangelo also incorporated in his scheme – some of the most dramatic figures in the entire work, and all clearly labelled by the painter, from the sensitive figure of the Delphic Sibyl to the hag-like Cumaean Sibyl, whose biceps would put a Bulgarian shot-putter to shame. Look out, too, for the figure of the prophet Jeremiah – a brooding self-portrait of an exhausted-looking Michelangelo.

The ceiling frescoes: central panels

We've detailed the paintings of the **central panels** in the chart (see p.204), but, specifically, they start with the *Creation of Light* – God's arms bowed, beard flowing, as he separates light from darkness – and move on, consecutively, to the *Creation of the Sun and the Moon*, in which Michelangelo has painted God twice, once with his back to us hurling the moon into existence and simultaneously displaying another moon to the audience; the *Separation of Land and Water*; and, in the fourth panel, probably the most famous of all these paintings, the *Creation of Adam*, in which God sparks Adam into life with the touch of his finger. God's cape billows behind him, where a number of figures stand – representatives of all the unborn generations to come after Adam. The startled young woman looking at Adam is either Eve or the Virgin Mary, here as a witness to the first events in human history.

The fifth panel from the altar shows the *Creation of Eve*, in which Adam is knocked out under the stump of a Della Rovere oak tree and God summons Eve from his side as he sleeps. She comes out in a half-crouch position with her hands clasped in a prayer of thanksgiving and awe. The sixth panel is the powerful *Temptation and Expulsion from the Garden of Eden*, with an evil spirit, depicted as a serpent, leaning out from the Tree of Knowledge and handing the fruit to Adam. On the right of this painting the Angel of the Lord, in swirling red robes, is brandishing his sword of original sin at the nape of Adam's neck as he tries to fend the angel off, motioning with both hands. The eighth panel continues the story, with the *Story of the Flood*, the unrighteous bulk of mankind taking shelter under tents from the rain while Noah and his kin make off for the Ark in the distance. Panel seven shows the *Sacrifice of Noah* as he and his family make a sacrifice of thanksgiving to the Lord for their safe arrival after the flood; one of Noah's sons kneels to blow on the fire to make it hotter, while his wife brings armloads of wood. Lastly, there's the *Drunkenness of Noah*, in which Noah is shown getting drunk after harvesting the vines and exposing his genitals to his sons – it is strictly prohibited in the Hebrew canon for a father to show his reproductive organs to his children. Oddly enough, Noah's sons are naked too.

The Last Judgement

The Last Judgement, on the altar wall of the chapel, was painted by Michelangelo more than twenty years later, between 1535 and 1541. Michelangelo wasn't especially keen to work on this – he was still engaged on Julius II's tomb, under threat of legal action from the late pope's family – but Pope Paul III, an old acquaintance of the artist, was keen to complete the decoration of the chapel. Michelangelo tried to delay by making demands that were likely to cause the pope to give up entirely, insisting on the removal of two paintings by Perugino and the closing of a window that pierced the end of the chapel. Furthermore, he insisted that the wall be replastered, with the top 15cm out of the perpendicular to prevent the accumulation of soot and dust. Surprisingly, the pope agreed.

The painting took **five years**, again single-handed, and is probably the most inspired and most homogeneous large-scale painting you'll ever see, Michelangelo's technical virtuosity taking a back seat to the sheer exuberance of the work. The human body is fashioned into a finely captured set of exquisite poses, in which even the damned can be seen as a celebration of the human form. Perhaps unsurprisingly, the painting offended some, and even before it was complete **Rome was divided** as to its merits, especially regarding the etiquette of introducing a display of nudity into the pope's private chapel. But Michelangelo's response to this was unequivocal, lampooning one of his fiercer critics, the pope's master of ceremonies at the time, Biagio di Cesena, as Minos, the doorkeeper of hell, with ass's ears and an entwined serpent in the bottom right-hand corner of the picture. Later the pope's zealous successor, **Pius IV**, objected to the painting and would have had it removed entirely had not Michelangelo's pupil, **Daniele da Volterra**, appeased him by carefully – and selectively – adding coverings to some of the more obviously naked figures, forever earning himself the nickname of the "breeches-maker". During the major restoration between 1982 and 1997, most of the overpainted breeches were discreetly removed.

Briefly, the painting shows the Day of Judgement, when the bodily resurrection of the dead takes place and the human race is brought before **Christ** to be either sent to eternity in Paradise or condemned to suffer in Hell. The centre is occupied by Christ, turning angrily as he gestures the condemned to the underworld. **St Peter**, carrying his gold and silver keys, looks on in astonishment at his Lord filled with rage, while **Mary** averts her eyes from the scene. Below Christ a group of angels blasts their trumpets to summon the dead from their sleep. Somewhat amusingly, one angel holds a large book, the book of the damned, while another carries a much smaller one, the book of the saved. On the left, the dead awaken from their graves, tombs and sarcophagi (one apparently has the likeness of Martin Luther) and levitate into the heavens or are pulled by ropes and the napes of their necks by angels who take them before Christ. At the bottom right, **Charon**, keeper of the underworld, swings his oar at the damned souls as they fall off the boat into the waiting gates of Hell. Among other characters portrayed are many martyred saints, **the Apostles**, Adam and, peeking out between the legs of the saint on the left of Christ, **Julius II**, with a look of fear and astonishment.

12

Museum of Christian Art

After the Sistine Chapel, you're channelled all the way to the exit by way of the **Museum of Christian Art**, including many pieces of early Christian funerary art from the catacombs. A small room off to the left contains a number of ancient Roman frescoes and mosaics, among them the celebrated **Aldobrandini Wedding**, a first-century BC Roman fresco that shows the preparations for a wedding in touching detail. Other items in a room that is extremely rich in interest include frescoes showing scenes from the *Odyssey*, and another, later piece from Ostia depicting a ship being loaded with grain, as well as some fantastic mosaics of wild beasts.

Vatican Library

The Museum of Christian Art corridor turns into the **Vatican Library**, home to around a million books and manuscripts (only open to researchers) and decorated with scenes of Rome and the Vatican as it used to look. Beyond, the corridor opens out into the dramatic **Library of Sixtus V** on the right, a vast hall built across the courtyard in the late sixteenth century to glorify literature – and of course Sixtus V himself.

Braccio Nuovo

Off the Cortile della Pigna, the **Braccio Nuovo** and Museo Chiaramonti (see p.208) both hold classical sculpture, although be warned that they are the Vatican at its most overwhelming – close on a thousand statues crammed into two long galleries – and you need a keen eye and much perseverance to make any sense of it all. The Braccio Nuovo was built in the early 1800s to display **classical statuary** that was particularly prized, and it contains, among other things, probably the most famous extant image of Augustus addressing the army, hand outstretched, found on the Via Flaminia, near the Villa di Livia (the cupid riding the dolphin is a reference to the imperial family's descent from Venus and her son Aeneas). There's also a nice statue of Silenus clutching an infant Dionysus nearby, and a bizarre-looking statue depicting the Nile, whose yearly flooding was essential to the fertility of the Egyptian soil. It is this aspect of the river that is represented here: crawling over the hefty river god are sixteen babies, thought to allude to the number of cubits the river needed to rise to fertilize the land.

Museo Chiaramonti

The three-hundred-metre-long **Chiaramonti gallery** is especially unnerving, lined with the chill marble busts of hundreds of nameless, blank-eyed ancient Romans, along with the odd deity (such as a colossal head of Neptune from Hadrian's villa). It pays to have a leisurely wander, for there are some real characters here: sour, thin-lipped matrons with their hair tortured into pleats, curls and spirals; kids, caught in a sulk or mid-chortle; and ancient men with flesh sagging and wrinkling to reveal the skull beneath. Many of these heads are ancestral portraits, kept by the Romans in special shrines in their houses to venerate their familial predecessors, and in some cases family resemblances can be picked out. The fine head of Athena, on the right, has kept her glass eyes, a reminder that most of these statues were originally painted to resemble life, with eyeballs where now a blank space stares out.

Museo Gregoriano Profano

There's a further grouping of **museums** in the modern building next door – and their lack of popularity can be something of a relief from the crowds in the rest of the museum. The first, the **Museo Gregoriano Profano,** however, is usually closed, but should you find it open you'll find some splendid classical sculpture, mounted on scaffolds for all-round viewing, including mosaics of athletes from the Baths of Caracalla and Roman funerary work, notably the Haterii tomb friezes, which show backdrops of ancient Rome and realistic portrayals of contemporary life. It's thought the Haterii were a family of construction workers and that they grabbed the opportunity to advertise their services by incorporating reliefs of the buildings they had worked on (including the Colosseum), along with a natty little crane, on the funeral monument of one of their female members.

Museo Pio Cristiano

The **Museo Pio Cristiano**, adjacent to the Museo Gregoriano Profano, has intricate early Christian sarcophagi and, most famously, an expressive late-third-century AD statue of the Good Shepherd – a subject you'll see on many of the other fourth-century sarcophagi nearby. One of the best is the "Two Brothers" sarcophagus from 325 AD, swathed in biblical scenes and meditations on the deceased.

Borgo and Prati

The area surrounding the Vatican City is known as the **Borgo**, traditionally the service area for the papal palaces. It is full of hotels, restaurants and scurrying tourists and pilgrims – as it has been since the King of Wessex founded the first hostel for pilgrims here in the eighth century. The neighbouring nineteenth-century neighbourhood of **Prati** (named after the meadows that used to lie here), just to the north, is one of Rome's wealthiest quarters, with some excellent restaurants, and a lively shopping district around Via Cola di Rienzo.

Castel Sant'Angelo

Lungotevere Castello 50 • Tues–Sun 9am–7.30pm; last entry 1hr before closing • €10, free first Sun of the month • ☎ 06 681 9111, ⓦ castelsantangelo.com • Metro Lepanto, or bus to Piazza Pia or Via Crescenzio

The great circular hulk of **Castel Sant'Angelo** was designed and built by the Emperor Hadrian as his own mausoleum. The original building was a grand monument, faced with white marble, surrounded by statues and topped with cypresses, similar in style to Augustus's mausoleum across the river. It was renamed in the sixth century, when Pope Gregory the Great witnessed a vision of St Michael here that ended a terrible plague. The mausoleum's position near the Vatican was not lost on the papal authorities, who converted the building for use as a fortress and built a raised walkway (the **Passetto di Borgo**) to link it with the Vatican as a refuge in times of siege or invasion – a route utilized on a number of occasions, most notably when the Medici pope, Clement VII, sheltered here for several months during the Sack of Rome in 1527. Incidentally, the **café** on the top floor of the Castel Sant'Angelo offers one of the best views of Rome.

Inside the mausoleum, a spiral ramp leads from the monumental **entrance hall** up into the centre of the mausoleum itself, passing through the chamber where the emperor was entombed and over a drawbridge, one of the defensive modifications made by the Borgia pope, Alexander VI, in the late fifteenth century. It continues to the main level at the top, where a small palace was built to house the papal residents in appropriate splendour.

After the Sack of Rome, Pope Paul III had some especially fine renovations made, including the beautiful **Sala Paolina**, which features frescoes by Pierno del Vaga, among others. The gilded ceiling here displays the Farnese family arms, and on the wall is a trompe-l'oeil fresco of one of the family's old retainers coming through a door from a darkened room. You'll also notice Paul III's personal motto, *Festina lente* ("make haste slowly"), scattered throughout the ceilings and in various corners of all his rooms. Elsewhere, some rooms hold swords, armour, guns and the like, while others are lavishly decorated with grotesques and paintings (don't miss the bathroom of Clement VII on the second floor, with its prototype hot and cold water taps and mildly erotic frescoes). Below are **dungeons** and storerooms (generally open for tours during the Notti d'Estate a Castel Sant'Angelo festival in summer), which can be glimpsed from the spiralling ramp, testament to the castle's grisly past as the city's most notorious Renaissance prison – Benvenuto Cellini and Cesare Borgia are just two of its more famous detainees.

Outside the Castel Sant'Angelo, the **Ponte di Sant'Angelo** is flanked by angels carved to designs by Bernini and known as his "breezy maniacs".

Ospedale di Santo Spirito

Lungotevere in Sassia 1/Borgo Santo Spirito 2 • Closed for restoration at the time of writing • ☎ 06 6821 0854, ⓦ en.santospiritoinsassia.it

One of the cornerstones of the Borgo neighbourhood is the **Ospedale di Santo Spirito**, the oldest hospital in Rome, founded in the eighth century by Pope Innocent III, who, as legend has it, was moved after dreaming of dead and unwanted babies being tossed into the Tiber. It was later developed by Sixtus IV as a hospital for pilgrims; the oldest buildings date from this time. These two giant halls, each 60m long and joined by an octagonal hall that used to serve as the main entrance, served as wards until 2000, and now form part of an events and conference centre, hosting gala dinners and fashion shows. **Frescoes** illustrating the lives and deeds of Innocent III and Sixtus IV, twelve of whose building projects around Rome are illustrated, line the main walls, while outside the main door a window contains a barrel in which *proietti*, or abandoned babies, were left anonymously – alongside a slot for donations. Behind the two halls the hospital still functions, and once the current restoration works are complete, tours will take in two cloisters, one originally designated for nuns, the other for monks, and the elegant main courtyard of the later Palazzo del Commendatore.

12

Museo Storico dell'Arte Sanitaria

Lungotevere in Sassia 3 · Mon, Wed & Fri 10am–noon, Sat & Sun by appointment · €7; book in advance · ☎ 06 678 7864, ⓦ museiscientificiroma.eu/artesanitaria

Around the corner to the river side of the Santo Spirito complex, just before the modern entrance to the hospital, is the **Museo Storico dell'Arte Sanitaria**, housed behind an old medical lecture theatre, and hosting a rather macabre jumble of ancient medical artefacts. There's a model of the original hospital, anatomical models of body parts and casts, horrible pickled babies in jars, vile-looking scalpels, forceps and syringes as well as the inevitable old-style pharmacy – not for the squeamish.

Day-trips from Rome

You may find there's quite enough of interest in Rome to keep you occupied during your stay. But it can be a hot, oppressive city, and if you're around long enough you really shouldn't feel any guilt about seeing something of the countryside. Two of the most popular day-trip attractions are admittedly ancient Roman sites (Ostia Antica and Hadrian's Villa at Tivoli), but just the process of getting to them can be energizing. North of the city, the Etruscan sites of Cerveteri and Tarquinia, and historic Viterbo, are atmospheric alternatives, and Bracciano has an airy lakeside location. To the south, the Castelli Romani provide the most appealing stretch of countryside close to Rome, and the coastal town of Anzio one of its most accessible beaches, although there are many choices if all you want to do is flop (see box, p.225).

13

Tivoli and around

Perched high on a hill and looking back over the plain, **TIVOLI** has always been something of a retreat from the city, owing to its fresh mountain air and pleasant position on the Aniene River. In classical days it was a retirement town for wealthy Romans; later, during the Renaissance, it again became the playground of the moneyed classes, attracting some of the city's most well-to-do families out here to build villas. Nowadays, the leisured classes have mostly gone, but Tivoli does very nicely on the fruits of its still-thriving travertine business, exporting the precious stone worldwide (the quarries line the main road into town from Rome), and supports a small airy centre that preserves a number of relics from its ritzier days. To do justice to its celebrated villas, Villa d'Este, Villa Gregoriana and Villa Adriana – especially if the latter is on your list – you'll need most of the day; set out early, and try to be in Tivoli by mid-morning at the latest.

Villa d'Este

Piazza Trento 5 • Tues–Sun: Jan 8.30am–4pm; Feb 8.30am–4.30pm; April 8.30am–6.30pm; May–Aug 8.30am–6.45pm; Sept 8.30am–6.15pm; Oct 8.30am–5.30pm; Nov & Dec 8.30am–4pm • €8; free first Sun of the month • ☏ 199 766 166, ⊕ www.villadestetivoli.info • The Villa d'Este is a 2min walk from Tivoli's Piazza Garibaldi

Tivoli's major sight is the **Villa d'Este**, across the main square of Piazza Garibaldi. Once a convent, it was transformed into a country villa by Pirro Ligorio in 1550 for Cardinal Ippolito d'Este, and is now often thronged with visitors even outside peak season. The villa itself is worth a visit: it has been recently restored to its original state, with beautiful Mannerist frescoes in its seven ground-floor rooms showing scenes from the history of the d'Este family in Tivoli.

But most people come here to see the **gardens**, which peel away down the hill in a succession of terraces. It's probably the most contrived garden in Italy, but also the most ingenious, almost completely symmetrical, its carefully tended lawns, shrubs and hedges interrupted at decent intervals by one playful fountain after another. The **fountains** are collectively unique and a must-see if you're in Tivoli; just make sure that you don't touch or drink the water – it comes directly from the operating sewers of Tivoli.

Among the highlights, the central, almost Gaudí-like **Fontana del Bicchierone**, by Bernini, is one of the simplest and most elegant. On the right lies the **Fontana dell'Ovato**, topped with statues on a curved terrace around artificial mountains, behind which is a rather dank arcade; beyond are the dark, gushing Grottoes of the Sibyls. Behind this the **Fontana dell'Organo** is a giant and very elaborate water organ, whose air pipes are forced by water valves, and play every couple of hours. Right in front, the similarly large **Fontana del Nettuno** ejects a massive torrent down into a set of central fish ponds, while at the far end the many pendulous breasts of the somewhat denuded **Fontana di Diana Efesina** gush yet more water. Finish up on the far side of the garden, where the **Rometta** or "Little Rome" has reproductions of the city's major buildings and a boat holding an obelisk.

Villa Gregoriana

Piazza Tempio di Vesta • Tues–Sun: March, Nov & Dec 10am–4pm; April–Oct 10am–6.30pm; last entry 1hr before closing • €6 • ☏ 0774 332 650, ⊕ villagregoriana.it • Turn right off Piazza Garibaldi to Piazza Santa Croce and follow Via del Trevio through the pedestrianized old town to Piazza del Plebiscito, where Via Palatina continues down to the bridge over the gorge; cross over, and the back entrance is just around the corner on the left – a 10min walk in all

Tivoli's other main attraction, the **Villa Gregoriana**, isn't actually a villa at all, but an impressively wild set of landscaped gardens, created when Pope Gregory XVI diverted the flow of the river here to ease the periodic flooding of the town in 1831. At least as interesting and beautiful as the d'Este estate, it remains less well known and less visited, and has none of the latter's conceits – its vegetation is lush and overgrown, descending into a gorge over 60m deep. It's harder work than the Villa d'Este – if you blithely saunter down to the bottom of the gorge, you'll find that it's a long way back up the other side – but it is in many ways more rewarding.

There are two main **waterfalls** – the larger Grande Cascata on the far side, and a small Bernini-designed one at the neck of the gorge. The best thing to do is walk the main path in reverse, starting at the back entrance, over the river, and winding down to the bottom of the canyon. The ruins of a Republican-era villa cling to the far side of the gorge, and you can peek into them and then catch your breath down by the so-called Grotto of the Mermaid, before scaling the other side to the Grotto

ACCOMMODATION

Camping Fabulous	4
Camping Tiber	1
La Posta Vecchia	2
Plus Camping Roma	3

DAY-TRIPS

13

of Neptune, reached by a tunnelled-out passage through the rock, where you can sit right by the roaring falls, the dark, torn shapes of the rock glowering overhead. The path leads up from here to an exit and the substantial remains of an ancient **Temple of Vesta**, which you'll have seen perched on the side of the hill, and which marks the main entrance to the villa. You can take a breather at the small **café** here, and the view is probably Tivoli's best – down into the chasm and across to the high green hills that ring the town.

Villa Adriana

Largo Marguerite Yourcenar 1 • Daily 9am–1hr before sunset; ticket office closes 1hr before • €8, or €11 if there's an exhibition on; free first Sun of the month • ☏ 06 3996 7900, ⓦ villaadriana.beniculturali.it • The CAT #4 or #4X bus from Tivoli's Piazza Garibaldi stops right outside the villa (roughly every 45min, 6 daily on Sun); buses also run direct from Rome (see below)

Once you've seen the two villas in town you've really seen Tivoli – the rest of the town is nice enough but there's not much to it. But just outside, at the bottom of the hill, the **Villa Adriana** puts the achievements of the Tivoli popes and cardinals very much into the shade. This was probably the largest and most sumptuous villa in the Roman Empire, the retirement home of the Emperor Hadrian between 135 AD and his death three years later, and it occupies an enormous site. You need time to see it all; there's no point in doing it at a gallop and, taken with the rest of Tivoli, it makes for a long day's sightseeing.

The site

The site is one of the most soothing spots around Rome, its stones almost the epitome of romantic, civilized ruins. The imperial palace buildings proper are in fact one of the least well-preserved parts of the complex, but much else is clearly recognizable. Hadrian was a great traveller and a keen architect, and parts of the villa were inspired by buildings he had seen around the world. The massive **Pecile**, for instance, through which you enter, is a reproduction of a building in Athens. The **Canopus**, on the opposite side of the site, is a liberal copy of the sanctuary of Serapis near Alexandria, its long, elegant channel of water fringed by sporadic columns and statues leading up to a temple of Serapis at the far end. Near the Canopus a **museum** displays the latest finds from the ongoing excavations, though most of the extensive original discoveries have found their way back to Rome and many museums in Europe. Walking back towards the entrance, make your way across the upper storey of the so-called Pretorio, a former warehouse, and down to the remains of two **bath complexes**. Beyond is a fish pond with a **cryptoporticus** (underground passageway) winding around underneath. It's enjoyable to walk through the cryptoporticus and look up at its ceiling, picking out the names of the seventeenth- and eighteenth-century artists (Bernini, for one) who visited and wrote their signatures here using a smoking candle. Behind this are the relics of the emperor's imperial apartments. The **Teatro Marittimo**, adjacent, with its island in the middle of a circular pond, is the place to which it's believed Hadrian would retire at siesta time to be sure of being alone.

ARRIVAL AND DEPARTURE TIVOLI

By bus COTRAL buses for Tivoli leave every 10min from outside Ponte Mammolo metro station in Rome (line B), dropping off on Tivoli's main square, Piazza Garibaldi (journey time 45min). There are 7 buses a day (Mon–Sat) from Ponte Mammolo to Villa Adriana (ⓦ www.cotralspa.it), dropping off 300m from the site; the more frequent Rome–Tivoli buses stop 1km from the site – ask the driver to drop you off.

By train Trains run hourly from Tiburtina station (on metro line B) to Tivoli (journey time 30–50min).

EATING AND DRINKING

Reginella Via Sante Viola 4/6 ☏ 0774 333 729. A couple of minutes' walk from the Villa d'Este, this friendly, casual sandwich shop with outdoor tables also serves a range of craft beers and salads, as well as fried snacks and

home-made burgers. Daily 11am–midnight/1am.
Sibilla Via Sibilla 50 ☎0774 335 281, ⓦristorante
sibilla.com. Overlooking the Villa Gregoriana, and right by
the back entrance, this is the most scenically situated

restaurant in Tivoli. It also serves some of its best food, with
great pasta in particular (ravioli *alla gricia* €12), and has a
fantastic setting; try and bag an outside table. Tues–Sun
12.30–3.30pm & 7.30–10pm.

Ostia Antica

Map 23 Ostia Antica

Viale dei Romagnoli 717 • Tues–Sun: Nov to mid-Feb 8.30am–4.30pm; mid-Feb to late-March 8.30am–5pm; end March to Aug
8.30am–7.15pm; Sept 8.30am–7pm; Oct 8.30am–6.30pm; last entry 1hr before closing; Museo Ostiense 9.30am–1hr before the site
closing time; the Case Decorate can be visited on Sun at 10.30am, booking obligatory; Castle of Julius II closed for restoration • €8, free first
Sun of the month • ☎06 5635 0215, ☎06 5635 8044 (Case Decorate bookings), ⓦostiaantica.beniculturali.it

There are two Ostias. One is the busy seaside resort of Lido di Ostia (see box, p.225),
while the other is one of the finest ancient Roman sites you'll find, comprising the
excavated remains of the port of **OSTIA ANTICA**. These ruins are on a par with anything
you'll see in Rome itself and easily merit a half-day out.

The site of Ostia Antica marked the coastline in classical times, and the town which
grew up here was the port of ancient Rome, a thriving place whose commercial activities
were vital to the city further upstream – until the Emperor Constantine developed a
new port nearby (of which nothing survives). Until the 1970s, the site was only open
one day a week and few people realized how well the port had been preserved by the
Tiber's mud, but in recent decades more and more of the port has been unearthed and
nowadays it's much easier to conjure the look and feel of a Roman town from this than
from any amount of pottering around the Forum – or even Pompeii. It's an evocative
site too, in part at least because it's relatively unvisited, but it is also very spread out, so
be prepared for a fair amount of walking. Carry some **water** and maybe even bring a
picnic – there's a **café-restaurant** on the site, but it's nothing special. Also, be aware that
signage on the site is poor.

A number of **decorated houses** (*case decorate*) dotted around the site can be viewed on
Sunday mornings only (advance booking essential).

The site

From the entrance, the **Via Ostiense** leads west, passing an ancient burial ground on the
left (the Romans always buried their dead outside the city walls), before reaching the
scant remains of the **Porta Romana**, once a main gate. Beyond, the **Decumanus
Maximus**, main street of Ostia, passes the tumbledown **Baths of the Cisiarii** on the right
and the **Baths of Neptune**, where a viewing platform overlooks a well-preserved floor
mosaic of mythological creatures. Further on, also on the right, a pavement **mosaic** is
inscribed with a cup that marks what would have been a bar, the **Caupona of
Fortunatus**. **Via della Fontana** which leads off here is a wonderfully preserved street, and
gives a good idea of a typical Roman urban layout, with its ground-floor shops and
upper-floor apartments. The fountain that gives the street its name is on the right, a
long coffin-shaped thing that would have been a source of fresh water for the homes
and businesses nearby. About halfway along, turn right down Via della Palestra and on
the left is the **Barracks of the Vigiles**, or nightwatch, where the courtyard includes a
shrine devoted to the cult of the emperor.

Piazzale delle Corporazioni

Back on Decumanus Maximus, it's just a few metres to the town's commercial centre,
Piazzale delle Corporazioni, where the remains of shops and trading offices still fringe
the central square. These represented commercial enterprises from all over the ancient
world and each was once fronted by a mosaic of boats, fish and suchlike to denote their
trade as well as their origin (Carthage, for example). Flanking the southern side of the
square, the **theatre** has been much restored but is nonetheless impressive, enlarged by

13

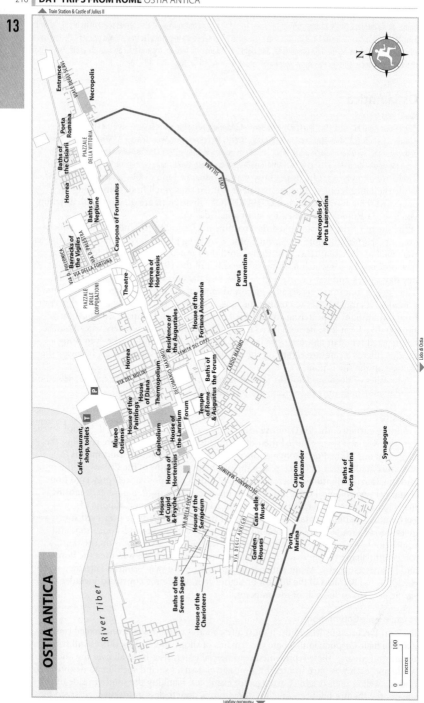

OSTIA ANTICA

Septimius Severus in the second century AD to hold up to four thousand people; it hosts theatre performances during the summer.

House of Diana and Thermopolium

Further along, the Decumanus Maximus runs past the substantial remains of one of Ostia's largest **horrea** (warehouses), buildings that once stood all over the city. Turn right up **Via dei Molini**, then left, to reach the **House of Diana**, probably the best-preserved private house in Ostia, with a dark series of rooms set around a central courtyard and a mithraeum (a shrine devoted to the cult of Mithras) at the back. Just along the street is the delightful **Thermopolium**, an ancient Roman café, complete with seats outside, a high counter, display shelves and even wall paintings of parts of the menu. At the back is a marble wall slab which once held hooks for hanging coats, beyond which is what would have been a small courtyard with a fountain. Opposite the Thermopolium, steps lead to the top of the **House of the Paintings**, giving a fine view over the site. The house itself is sometimes locked but if you can get in you'll be rewarded with a wonderful mosaic fragment showing birds and people.

The Capitolium, Forum and House of the Lararium

Just beyond the Thermopolium, you'll spy the high brick walls of the **Capitolium**, Ostia's most important temple dating from the second century AD, fronted by a wide flight of steps and overlooking the shattered columns of both the **Forum** and the **Temple of Rome and Augustus**. Continuing on down the Decumanus Maximus, next up is the **House of the Lararium**, on the right, a well-preserved courtyard complex that served as a combined market and religious centre with several shrines. Further on, the Porta Occidentale or western gate, at the junction of the Decumanus Maximus and Via delle Foce, is marked by what may have been a **fish shop**, judging by its floor mosaics, still with its shelves and marble table. There are more *horrea* off to the right of the crossroads, superbly preserved and complete with pediment over the entrance and names inscribed on the marble; although you can't enter, you can peer into the courtyard.

Via delle Foce

At the Porta Occidentale, veer right along Via delle Foce to visit one of the most sacred parts of Roman Ostia, where three Republican temples cluster together, possibly dating back to the time of Sulla. The ruins are a little hard to decipher, but immediately behind them is the third-century **House of Cupid and Psyche**, which has a courtyard you can walk into and holds a copy of the statue of Cupid and Psyche that you can see in the museum (see p.218); its rooms are clearly discernible on one side, a colourful marbled floor at the top and a columned nymphaeum, with marble niches, on the right.

Baths of the Seven Sages, House of the Charioteers and the Porta Marina

Keep on down Via delle Foce and you soon reach the **Baths of the Seven Sages** on the left, with its round arcaded courtyard and wonderfully intact floor mosaic. Steps lead up to the roof for good views over this part of the site and the fragments of wall paintings below. The atmospheric arcaded passageways of the complex lead to the **House of the Charioteers**, which you can ascend for more excellent views, beyond which Via degli Aurighi takes you back to the main Decumanus Maximus. A right turn takes you down to the **Porta Marina**, or sea gate, marked by the **Caupona of Alexander** on the left, a wine shop with flower mosaics identifying the owner and showing various forms of combat. Beyond here the road continues on for a little way to what was once the sea – but is now just the main road.

13

Museo Ostiense

Next door to the site's café-restaurant, the half-dozen rooms of the **Museo Ostiense** are full of sculptural finds from the site which are well worth seeing. In a room to the left as you enter is a statue of *Mithras Slaying the Bull* from one of Ostia's mithraeums. The central room has a fine headless male figure in repose, his foot resting on a column base, and a figure of Trajan in full battledress, between two busts of him and another of Hadrian, along with a likeness of Commodus as a young boy. The room beyond contains a statue of Septimius Severus next to his wife, Julia Domna, as the goddess Ceres, while, opposite, a beautifully preserved figure of Maxentius and his sister Fausta look on. In a room off here are various carved sarcophagi found on Via Ostiense, all amazingly well preserved, including one of a young boy, decorated with cupids.

Castle of Julius II

Near the entrance to the ruins, the **Castle of Julius II** was commissioned by the future pope and is an impressive example of fifteenth-century military architecture. Used as a papal residence over the centuries, it was abandoned after a flood in 1587 turned the surrounding area into marshland. It was closed for restoration at the time of writing, but the pretty entrance courtyard is worth a look and *L'Alimentari* next door is a good spot for a snack or lunch.

ARRIVAL AND DEPARTURE   OSTIA ANTICA

By train Take the metro to Piramide station (line B), then go up the escalator, turn left and go down the steps to Roma-Lido station, where you can take a train to Ostia Antica; you can do the whole journey with a single €1.50 metro ticket. The site is a 5min walk from the station.

By car There's a car park at the site (parking €2.50).

Cerveteri

CERVETERI provides the most accessible Etruscan taster from Rome. The settlement here dates back to the tenth century BC and was once a trading heavyweight, one of the Mediterranean's largest centres. Cerveteri, also known as Caere, ranked among the top three cities in the twelve-strong Etruscan federation, its wealth derived largely from the mineral-rich Tolfa hills to the northeast – a gentle range that gives the plain a much-needed touch of scenic colour. In its heyday, the town spread over 8km (something like thirty times its present size), controlling territory 50km up the coast. Rot set in from 351 BC, when the Romans assumed control without granting full citizenship rights. The present town is a thirteenth-century creation, dismissed by D.H. Lawrence – and you really can't blame him – as "forlorn beyond words".

Necropoli di Banditaccia

Piazzale Mario Moretti • Tues–Sun 8.30am–1hr before sunset • €8, or €10 combined ticket with the Museo Nazionale Cerite; free first Sun of the month • ☏ 06 994 0001, ⬜ tarquinia-cerveteri.it • The necropolis site is just over 1km away from the bus stop at Piazza Aldo Moro (see opposite) and is well signposted from the town; you can take bus D from the piazza but it's a fairly simple walk

The **Necropoli di Banditaccia**, or Etruscan Necropolis, is the largest extant Etruscan burial site: from the seventh to first century BC, the Etruscans constructed a literal city of the dead here, weird and fantastically well preserved, with complete streets and homes. Some tombs are strange round pillboxes carved from cliffs; others are covered in earth to create the barrows that ripple the surrounding plateau. Archeologists speculate that women were buried in separate small chambers within each "house" – easy to distinguish – while the men were laid on deathbeds (occasionally in sarcophagi) hewn directly from the stone. Indeed archeological evidence suggests that the position of women in Etruscan society was roughly on a par with that of men. Cremated slaves lie in urns alongside their masters – civilized by comparison with the Romans, who simply threw them into mass burial pits. Of the nineteen show-tombs, try to see the **Tomba Bella** (Tomb of the Bas-Reliefs), **Tomba dei Letti Funebri** (Tomb of the Funeral Beds) and the **Tomb of the Capitals**.

Museo Nazionale Cerite

Piazza Santa Maria 1 • Tues–Sun 8.30am–6.30pm • €8, or €10 combined ticket with the Necropoli di Banditaccia • ☎ 06 994 1354, ⓦ tarquinia-cerveteri.it

Housed in the sixteenth-century Castello Ruspoli, at the top of Cerveteri's old quarter, the **Museo Nazionale Cerite** is well worth a visit. Most of the best Etruscan stuff from here was whisked away long ago to the Villa Giulia in Rome (see p.177), but the museum has two large rooms containing a decent fraction of the huge wealth that was buried with the Etruscan dead – vases, terracottas and a run of miscellaneous day-to-day objects, with 3D displays highlighting decorative details.

ARRIVAL AND DEPARTURE   CERVETERI

By bus The best way to get to Cerveteri is from Rome's Cornelia station on metro line A by COTRAL bus (every 20–50min; 1hr); buses drop off in Piazza Aldo Moro. The same Rome–Cerveteri bus also links to the train station, 7km away (see below).

By train Trains from Termini, Ostiense, Trastevere and San Pietro stations run to Ladispoli-Cerveteri station (every 30min–1hr; 45min). From here there's a COTRAL bus (a 5min walk from the station, at the crossroads of Via Cagliari and Via Taranto; €1.10), which runs to the necropolis site hourly.

ACCOMMODATION AND EATING

La Posta Vecchia Palo Laziale, Ladispoli ☎ 06 994 9501, ⓦ lapostavecchia.com. Situated by the sea about 40km northwest of Rome, just outside Ladispoli, oil baron John Paul Getty's former villa is a luxurious and romantic hotel choice, with a beautiful garden, tennis court, a spa and small pool overlooking the water. Trains run regularly from Termini to Ladispoli station, from where it's a short taxi ride. **€250**

Tuchulcha Via della Necropoli Etrusche 28 ☎ 338 203 5860. There's a café in the necropolis area. Alternatively, this little trattoria on the necropolis road, named after an Etruscan demon, serves hearty country-style food and crisp Cerveteri white wines. Expect to pay around €25 per head for lunch with wine. No credit cards. Tues–Sun 1–3pm & 8–10pm.

Tarquinia

The necropolis at **TARQUINIA** is second only to Cerveteri among northern Lazio's Etruscan sites. The town itself is pleasant, its partial walls and crop of medieval towers making it a good place to pass an afternoon after seeing the ruins. Its museum is also the region's finest outside Rome.

Necropoli di Tarquinia

Via Monterozzi Marina • Tues–Sun: summer 8.30am–7.30pm; winter 8.30am–1hr before sunset • €6, or €8 including museum; free first Sun of the month • Buses (every 30min–1hr, less frequent on Sun) run from the central Barriera San Giusto, or it's a 20min walk: follow Via Umberto I from Piazza Cavour, pass through the Porta Romana, cross Piazza Europa, follow Via IV Novembre/Via delle Croci up the hill, and the site is on the left; a free shuttle runs between the necropolis and the museum every 20–30min 9.15am–12.10pm & 4–7.20pm • ☎ 06 8852 2517, ⓦ tarquinia-cerveteri.it

Once the artistic, cultural and probably political capital of Etruria, the ancient wooden city of Tarquinia has now all but vanished and all that is left is the **Necropoli di Tarquinia**, also known as the Necropolis of Monterozzi. The city was founded in the tenth century BC, with its population peaking at around 100,000, but the Roman juggernaut triggered its decline six hundred years later and only a warren of graves remains. Since the eighteenth century, six thousand tombs have been uncovered (nine hundred in 1958 alone), with many more to go. Grave-robbing is common (thieves are known as *tombaroli*) and it's rare for a tomb to be found intact; the most recent tomb to be excavated with its contents intact, belonging to an Etruscan aristocrat, was unearthed in 2013. Before that, the last non-looted tomb was found thirty years earlier.

Some **frescoes** depict the inhabitants' expectations of the afterlife: scenes of banqueting, hunting and even a *ménage à trois*. The famed **Tomba dei Caronti** makes a

13

darker prediction with demons greeting the deceased. The earliest paintings emphasize mythical and ritualistic scenes, but the sixth- to fourth-century works – in the dell'Orco, degli Auguri and della Caccia e Pesca tombs – show greater social realism. This style is a mixture of Greek, indigenous Etruscan and eastern influences: the ease and fluidity point to a civilization at its peak. Later efforts grow increasingly morbid with purely necromantic drawings – enough to discourage picnic lunches on the pleasant, grassy site.

Museo Nazionale Tarquiniense

Piazza Cavour 2 • Tues–Sun 8.30am–7.30pm • €6, or €8 including necropolis; free first Sun of the month • ☎ 06 8852 2517, ⓦ tarquinia-cerveteri.it

In the centre of Tarquinia, the **Museo Nazionale Tarquiniense** has a choice collection of Etruscan finds, sensitively housed in the attractive Gothic-Renaissance Palazzo Vitelleschi. The ground floor exhibits superb sculpted sarcophagi, many decorated with warm and human portraits of the deceased. Upstairs are displays of exquisite Etruscan gold jewellery, painted ceramics, bronzes, candlesticks, heads and figures. The impressive top floor houses the collection's finest piece – the renowned **winged horses** (fourth century BC), probably from a temple frieze. The **Sala delle Armi** boasts panoramic views of the countryside and sea.

Tarquinia Lido

Reachable by bus from the train station or the Barriera San Giusto

Tarquinia Lido is a fairly developed stretch of coast, with lots of bars, restaurants and hotels lining its sandy **beaches**, some of which are free. It might just hit the spot after a dose of the Etruscans – as might the adjacent **nature reserve** and bird sanctuary, adapted from the nearby salt marshes.

ARRIVAL AND DEPARTURE   TARQUINIA

By train Trains run roughly hourly to Tarquinia from Rome's Termini and Ostiense stations, on the same train line as Cerveteri (Tarquinia is about 40min further on); journey time is around 1hr 30min from Termini, about 1hr from Ostiense. The train station is 2km below the town centre, connected with the central Barriera San Giusto by regular bus BC.

EATING AND DRINKING

La Capanna del Buttero Via della Tuscia 21 ☎ 347 545 8184. There's a café in the necropolis, or try this cosy restaurant about a 10min walk away, which serves up rustic local fare, with a big open grill and an emphasis on meaty mains (though there are vegetarian dishes too, as well as gluten-free options). Two courses with wine cost around €30 per person. Oct–May daily except Tues 12.30–2.30pm & 7.30–10.30pm.

Bracciano and around

Around 30km northwest of Rome, and easily accessible by train, **BRACCIANO** is a small town that enjoyed fifteen minutes of fame when Tom Cruise and Katie Holmes got married here in 2006. It's an unassuming place, dominated by the castle where Cruise and his wife celebrated their nuptials, and enjoying a great position on the western shore of the lake that it gives its name to; the lake is a wonderful place to swim, enjoy watersports or just eat in one of the shoreline restaurants.

Castello Odescalchi

Via del Lago 2 • Mid-March to mid-Oct Mon–Fri 10am–6pm, Sat & Sun 10am–7pm; mid-Oct to mid-March Tues–Fri 10am–5pm, Sat & Sun 10am–6pm • €8.50 • ☎ 06 9980 4348, ⓦ odescalchi.it

The imposing **Castello Odescalchi**, which dominates Bracciano, is a late fifteenth-century structure privately owned by the Odescalchi family. The outer walls, now mostly disappeared, contained the rectangular piazza of the medieval town; nowadays, the castle is a little run-down, its interior home to rusting suits of armour and faded

13

frescoes, but the view from the ramparts, over the broad blue oval of the lake, is worth the admission price alone.

Lago di Bracciano

COTRAL buses run from Bracciano to Anguillara and Trevignano (10–12 daily, fewer on Sun); the Rome–Bracciano train also continues to Anguillara (every 30min; 20min)

The closest of northern Lazio's lakes to Rome, the smooth, roughly circular expanse of **Lago di Bracciano** fills an enormous volcanic crater. It's nothing spectacular, with few real sights and a landscape of rather plain, rolling countryside, but is popular with Romans escaping the heat of the city. The lake's shores are fairly peaceful even on summer Sundays, and you can eat excellent lake fish in its restaurants. The best place to swim in the lake is from the beach at **Lungolago Argenti**, below Bracciano town, where you can rent a boat and enjoy a picnic. The shore between **Trevignano** and **Anguillara Sabazia** also boasts fine swimming spots, as well as some good restaurants.

ARRIVAL AND DEPARTURE

By train Bracciano's train station is reasonably central, just a 10min walk from the castle and centre of town. Trains run to Bracciano from Roma Ostiense every 30min (direction Viterbo), and take just over 1hr (less from Trastevere and

BRACCIANO AND AROUND

San Pietro, where they also stop).
By bus There are COTRAL buses to Bracciano from Saxa Rubra station on the Roma Nord line (trains from Flaminio station) every 20–40min, which take around 1hr.

EATING AND DRINKING

Gens Trebonia Via Garibaldi 53, Trevignano ☎ 06 998 5096. This bar-restaurant is a stylish spot for fresh fish on a terrace overlooking the lake, followed by home-made fruit tart; expect to pay around €25 per head. With a great selection of beers, it's a popular place for an *aperitivo*. Tues 5pm–midnight, Wed–Sun noon–midnight.

Ristorantino del Castello Piazza Mazzini 14,

Bracciano ☎ 06 9980 4333, ⓦ ristorantinodelcastello .it. Perhaps the town's best restaurant, this place is right next to the castle, with a cosy, wood-beamed dining room and a roaring fire in winter. Dishes such as sea bass in a potato crust and steak in a balsamic sauce will set you up for a tour of the castle. *Secondi* range from €12 to €20. Tues–Sun 12.30–2.30pm & 7–10pm.

Viterbo

The capital of its province, and indeed of northern Lazio as a whole, **VITERBO** is easily the region's most historic centre, a medieval town which, during the thirteenth century, was something of a rival to Rome. It was, for a time, the residence of popes, a succession of whom relocated here after friction in the capital, and today it retains some vestiges of its vanquished prestige – a handful of grand palaces and medieval churches, enclosed by an intact set of walls. The town is well-kept and refreshingly untouched by much tourist traffic; buses and trains run frequently to Rome and you can comfortably see the sights in a day.

Piazza del Plebiscito

If there is a centre to Viterbo it's **Piazza del Plebiscito**, girdled almost entirely by fifteenth- and sixteenth-century buildings. The lions and palm trees that reflect each other across the square are the city's symbols, repeated, with grandiose echoes of Venice, all over town. You can peek into the fine Renaissance courtyard of the main, arcaded building of the **Palazzo dei Priori**. The council chamber is decorated with a series of murals depicting Viterbo's history right back to Etruscan times in a weird mixture of pagan and Christian motifs – a melange continued across the square in the church of **Sant'Angelo**.

Via San Lorenzo and the Quartiere San Pellegrino

Roads fork in many directions from Piazza del Plebiscito. Most interesting is **Via di San Lorenzo**, which sweeps past the pretty Piazza di Gesù to the macabrely named **Piazza della Morte** – the "Square of Death", so named after the paupers and abandoned

13

corpses that were buried here by the monks. A left from here leads to Viterbo's oldest district, the **Quartiere San Pellegrino**, a tight mess of hilly streets.

Palazzo dei Papi

Via del Ginnasio 8 • Daily: summer 10am–1pm & 3–7pm (Aug closes 8pm); winter 10am–1pm & 3–6pm; last entry 45min before closing • €9 combined ticket with the Museo del Colle del Duomo

At the western end of Via di San Lorenzo, **Piazza San Lorenzo** is flanked by the town's most historic buildings, chief among which is the **Palazzo dei Papi**, a thirteenth-century structure with impressive views from its loggia looking over the green gorge that cuts into central Viterbo. Most of the palace is closed to the public but you can visit the Aula del Conclave, venue of the election of half a dozen or so popes, and the frescoed Sala Gualterio.

The Duomo and Museo del Colle del Duomo

Opposite the Palazzo dei Papi, the Duomo is a plain Romanesque church that has an elegant striped floor and an understated beauty unusual among Italian churches. Some of its treasure is held in the **Museo del Colle del Duomo** next door (summer daily 10am–1pm & 3–7pm, Aug closes 8pm; winter Tues–Sun 10am–1pm & 3–6pm; €9 combined ticket with the Palazzo dei Papi).

Corso Italia and Santa Rosa

Via Roma leads off Piazza del Plebiscito to become Viterbo's main commercial street, **Corso Italia**, scene of a busy *passeggiata* early evening. At its far end, steps lead up from the right side of Piazza Verdi to the church of **Santa Rosa**, where the desiccated corpse of the town's patron saint can be seen in the second chapel on the right – a slightly grotesque, doll-like figure dressed up in a nun's habit. On September 3 each year an icon of the saint, the **Macchina di Santa Rosa**, is paraded through town to the accompaniment of much revelry and fireworks (⊛macchinasantarosa.it).

Museo Nazionale Etrusco

Piazza della Rocca 21b • Tues–Sun 8.30am–7.30pm • €6 • ☎ 0761 325 929

From Piazza Verdi, Via Matteotti leads up to Piazza della Rocca, a large square dominated by the fierce-looking **Rocca Albornoz**, once a papal residence and now home to the **Museo Nazionale Etrusco**, whose archeological collection includes displays of locally unearthed Roman and Etruscan artefacts. The highlight is a well-preserved two-wheeled chariot found, together with the skeletons of two small horses, in an Etruscan tomb dating to 530–520 BC. Restoration of part of the museum was under way at the time of writing.

San Francesco

Piazza di San Francesco • Daily 8am–6.30pm

Just off the opposite side of the square from the Museo Nazionale Etrusco, the church of **San Francesco** is worth a quick look. The high, unusually plain, Gothic church is the burial place of two of Viterbo's popes – Clement IV and Adrian V – both laid in now heavily restored, but impressive, Cosmatesque tombs on either side of the main altar.

ARRIVAL AND INFORMATION   **VITERBO**

By train Unusually for a small town, Viterbo has three train stations; the most useful, the Porta Romana station south of the centre, is on the Roma–Viterbo line from Ostiense, Trastevere and San Pietro (hourly; 1hr 50min from Ostiense).
By bus The main bus depot is a 10min walk from the centre on the Tangenziale Ovest. Take a local train from Flaminio station to Saxa Rubra, from where there are

COTRAL buses every 30min to Viterbo. There are also buses from Viterbo's bus station to Tarquinia (9 daily, fewer on Sun; 1hr).

Tourist information The tourist office is a 2min walk from Piazza Plebiscito at Via Ascenzi 4 (Tues–Sun 10am–1pm & 3–6pm; closes 5pm in Jan & Feb, 7pm May–Aug; ☎0761 325 992).

ACCOMMODATION AND EATING

13

★ **Antica Taverna** Via S. Agostino 12 ☎ 0761 305 502. This cosy, grotto-like trattoria with stone walls and wooden tables serves up excellent pasta dishes and melt-in-the-mouth Fiorentina steaks. A full meal with wine will cost less than €25. Mon 7.30–10.30pm, Tues–Sat 12.30–2.30pm & 7.30–10.30pm, Sun 12.30–2.30pm.

B&B dei Papi Via del Ginnasio ☎ 0761 309 039, ⓦ bbdeipapi.it. Modern design in a fairytale setting. This lovely old vine-clad mansion is right in the town centre and has beautiful rooms furnished with flair and filled with antiques. There's also a suite with a canopy bed. €110

Buongusto Piadineria Corso Italia 107 ☎ 393 661 9127. In the heart of Viterbo's historic centre,

hole-in-the-wall *Buongusto* is the perfect spot for lunch on the run. *Piadine* (flatbreads) are the order of the day here, with numerous different fillings, all fresh and delicious; try the sausage, *cicoria* (bitter greens) and mozzarella. Tues–Thurs 11am–9pm, Fri 11am–10pm, Sat 11am–3pm & 4.30–11pm, Sun 11am–3pm & 4.30–10pm.

Il Grottino Via della Cava 7 ☎ 0761 290 088. The "Little Cave" offers a bountiful *antipasto della casa* (one portion feeds two), tasty pasta dishes and hearty, rib-sticking mains such as rabbit in wine or pork fillet with rosemary and sage, elegantly prepared and served. The service is impeccable, too. Expect to pay around €30 per head for a full meal. Tues–Sat 12.45–2.30pm & 7.45–10pm, Sun 12.45–2.30pm.

The Castelli Romani

Just free of the sprawling southern suburbs of Rome, the sixteen towns that make up the **Castelli Romani** date back to pre-Roman times. These hills – the **Colli Albani** – have long charmed rich and powerful urbanites, who also treasure the spectacular views of Lago Albano and the area's white **wines**, which benefit from the rich volcanic soil and cooling breezes from the nearby Tyrrhenian Sea. The region is now pretty heavily built up, with most of the historic centres ringed by unprepossessing suburbs, and summer weekends see traffic jams of Romans trooping out to local trattorias. But off-peak, it's worth the journey, either as an excursion from Rome or a stop on the way south.

Frascati

At just 20km from Rome, **FRASCATI** is the nearest of the Castelli towns and also the most striking, with a nice old centre and some great places to eat and drink. Its main square, **Piazza Marconi**, is dominated by the majestic **Villa Aldobrandini**, designed by Giacomo della Porta at the start of the seventeenth century. The Baroque *palazzo* is off-limits, but the **gardens** are open (Mon–Fri: summer 9am–1pm & 3–6pm; winter 9am–1pm & 3–5pm; free). Sadly the elaborate water theatre, where statues once played flutes, is not in top form, but the view from the front terrace is superb, with Rome visible on a clear day. You can also visit the impressively remodelled **Scuderie Aldobrandini**, or stables, of the Villa, at Piazza Marconi 6 (Tues–Fri 10am–6pm, Sat & Sun 10am–7pm; €5; ☎ 06 941 7195), where a collection of Roman finds has been assembled from the nearby site of Tusculum and an extra storey added for local art exhibitions.

Just beyond here is the pedestrianized old centre, which revolves around the two squares of **Piazza San Pietro** and **Piazza del Mercato**. Frascati is also the most famous of the Colli Albani **wine** towns: ask at the tourist office for details of winery tours and tastings, and local *fraschette* – rustic, rough-and-ready bars serving up local wine, often produced in the owner's vineyard; these days, food is often served as well.

Abbazia San Nilo, Grottaferrata

Corso del Popolo 128 • Church Mon–Sat 9am–noon & 4–7pm; monastery Sat & Sun: May–Sept tours at 5pm; Oct–April tours at 4pm • Free • ☎ 069 459 309

Some 3km south of Frascati, **GROTTAFERRATA** is also known for its wine and for its eleventh-century **Abbazia San Nilo**, at the bottom of the main Corso del Popolo – a Greek Orthodox monastery surrounded by high defensive walls and a now-empty moat. The monastery itself is only open briefly at weekends, but you can visit the little **church of Santa Maria** any time, which has a very ancient and atmospheric Byzantine-style interior decorated with thirteenth-century mosaics above the high altar, and, in

13

the chapel of St Nilo off to the right, some big, busy frescoes by Domenichino. Look in also on the so-called **Crypta Ferrata**, a first-century AD edifice where Mary appeared to saints Bartholomew and Nilo, whereupon they resolved to build a church here.

Castel Gandolfo

To the southwest of Grottaferrata, the road joins up with the ancient Roman Via Appia, which travels straight as an arrow down the west side of Lago Albano. **CASTEL GANDOLFO** is the first significant stop, best known as the **pope's summer retreat**: between July and September the pope usually gives sporadic midday addresses on Sundays, though it depends on the individual – Pope Francis is an infrequent visitor. Set 400m above Lago Albano, the town is a pleasantly airy place, and enjoys great views over the lake from its terraces. The **Barberini Garden**, attached to the papal palace, has recently been opened to the public for the first time (tours on Sat at 10.30am; 1hr 30min; €26; book in advance through ⓦ www.museivaticani.va). Nearby, the main **Piazza della Libertà** is a pleasant oblong of cafés and papal souvenir shops, at the end of which is the imposing bulk of the Papal Palace itself. Below the town, there's a pleasant lido along the lakeshore with lots of restaurants and pizzerias and a small stretch of grey **beach**. The road leads down from the main highway, just north of Castel Gandolfo's old centre.

Ariccia

ARICCIA enjoys a dramatic location on the ancient Via Appia, poised between two gorges, and with spectacular views on all sides. The main road crosses the town's central piazza, a well-proportioned square that owes its appearance to Baroque master Bernini. His Pantheon-inspired church of Santa Maria dell'Assunzione sits across the Piazza della Repubblica from the massive Palazzo Chigi he built for Pope Alexander VII, the town's main sight.

Palazzo Chigi

Piazza di Corte 14 • Piano nobile guided tours April–Sept Tues–Fri at 11am, 4pm & 5.30pm, Sat & Sun hourly 10.30am–12.30pm & 4–7pm; Oct–March Tues–Fri at 11am, 4pm & 5.30pm, Sat & Sun hourly 10.30am–12.30pm & 3–6pm; Baroque Museum Sat & Sun 10am–1.30pm & 3.30–7pm; Cardinal's Rooms Sat & Sun: April–Sept 10am–12.30pm & 4–7pm; Oct–March 10am–12.30pm & 3–6pm • Piano nobile €8, Baroque Museum €6, Cardinal's Rooms €6, combined ticket for all three sections €14 • ☎ 06 933 0053, ⓦ palazzochigiariccia.it

The **Palazzo Chigi** is a mightily impressive example of a Baroque provincial palace of the seventeenth century, and its *piano nobile* (visitable by guided tour only) is home to the Chigi collections of paintings, sculpture and objects of applied art. On the ground floor, you can visit the private apartment of Cardinal Flavio Chigi, which includes works by Salvator Rosa and Il Baciccio – the artist who painted the ceiling of the Gesù church in Rome. His work here also includes a striking self-portrait in the palace's so-called Baroque Museum, which features pieces by more Rome ceiling painters – Pietro da Cortona and Andrea Pozzo, among others.

Museo delle Navi, Nemi

Via Tempio di Diana 13 • Mon–Sat 9am–6pm, Sun 9am–2pm • €3 • ☎ 06 939 8040

The town of **NEMI**, built high above a tiny crater lake, isn't much to write home about, but it has a wonderful view and is famous for its strawberries and the local **Museo delle Navi** below the town on the lake's northern shore. This vast hangar-like building was purpose-built by Mussolini in the 1930s and contains two ancient Roman pleasure boats, floating villas built by Caligula. In the last days of the German occupation in 1944 they were set on fire, so apart from a few plans and wooden shutters that survived the fire, what you see today are modern reconstructions of the imperial ships. Nevertheless, the museum is worth a visit for naval enthusiasts, and also displays finds from the ships (though the best are in the Palazzo Massimo in Rome), as well as stretches of a Roman road that passes right through the site.

ARRIVAL AND DEPARTURE

By bus COTRAL buses serve most of the major towns in the area from Rome's Anagnina metro station (line A), with services every 15–30min to Frascati (30min), every 15min to Ariccia (40min), 12 daily to Grottaferrata (fewer on Sun; 40min), and 9 daily to Castel Gandolfo (35min).

By train Trains depart hourly from Termini station for Frascati (30min), as well as other towns in the region, Marino (35min), Albano (55min) and Velletri (1hr), from where buses connect to Nemi (Mon–Sat).

INFORMATION

FRASCATI

Tourist office Frascati's tourist office, Frascati Point, is the best for the region and very conveniently located at Piazza Marconi 5 (daily 10am–8pm; ☎06 9401 5378, ⓦ stsmultiservizi.it).

CASTEL GANDOLFO

Tourist office There's a tourist kiosk at Via M. d'Azeglio, near Piazza della Libertà (Sat & Sun 10am–1pm & 3–5pm; ☎331 965 9691).

WHERE TO FLOP: THE BEST BEACHES NEAR ROME

There are plenty of places to head to near Rome if you fancy a day at the **beach** – and on a hot summer's day in the city there's sometimes nothing else for it but to get out of town. Most beaches have pay sections (*stabilimenti*), charging around €10–20 per day, as well as free sections. Some of the best seaside spots are listed below.

LIDO DI OSTIA

Lido di Ostia has for years been the number one, or at any rate the closest and most accessible, seaside resort for Romans. The beaches are fine, and cleaner than they used to be. Most of them are taken up with *stabilimenti* (beach clubs with a restaurant) where you can rent a sunbed and an umbrella, though there are free spots too. Ostia is easy to get to, just half an hour by train from Porta San Paolo station, next door to Piramide metro on line B; get off at Lido Centro or the last stop, Cristoforo Colombo, where the crowds might be thinner. A €1.50 BIT ticket is sufficient.

TORVAIANICA

South of Ostia, towards **Torvaianica**, the water is cleaner and the crowds not so thick, plus there are gay and nudist sections of the beach, and not a lot of development. Buses run from Cristoforo Colombo station in Ostia in summer; take #07 (every 10–15min). The beaches along this stretch are known as the **cancelli**, after the numbered gates to the beach; the higher the number, the better the beach, so it's worth staying on the bus for a bit.

ANZIO

About 40km south of Rome, and fairly free of the pull of the capital, **Anzio** is worth visiting both for its beaches and its history – much of the town was damaged during a difficult Allied landing here on January 22, 1944, to which two military cemeteries (one British; another, at nearby Nettuno, American), as well as a small museum, bear testimony. It was also a favoured spot of the Roman Emperor Nero, the ruins of whose villa spread along the cliffs above and even down onto the beach. Anzio is a good place to eat lunch: it hosts a thriving fishing fleet and some great **restaurants** down on the harbour: *La Cicala*, right by the water at Riviera Zanardelli 11 (☎06 984 6747; closed Wed in winter), is as good as any, with outside seating and decent food and service. The town is easy to get to, with trains every hour from Termini; the journey takes about an hour and it's just a ten-minute walk from the station down to the main square and harbour, with the beaches stretching out north of the centre.

SANTA MARINELLA

Santa Marinella is one of the most popular spots north of the capital, and rightly so. It has a lovely crescent of beach a five-minute walk from the train station, and although most of it is pay-only, the sand is fine and clean and the water shallow – perfect for kids. Trains run every half an hour from Termini, and they take about an hour. There are also one or two good **restaurants**: try *L'Acqua Marina* (☎0766 511 715; closed Tues), ten minutes' walk from the beach at Piazza Trieste 8, which does great fish.

13

EATING AND DRINKING

FRASCATI

Cantina da Santino Via Pietro Campana 27 ☎ 06 9429 8110, ⓦ cantinadasantino.it. Up some steep steps off the main Piazza Marconi, this cave-like place, in business for over sixty years, is one of the few genuine *fraschette* left in town. Take a seat at one of the communal wooden tables and the friendly owner will pour you a tumbler of wine produced in his own vineyard. No food is served but you can bring your own from the nearby market. Daily 10.30am–1.30pm & 4.30–9pm.

★**Grappolo d'Oro** Piazza Filzi ☎ 06 942 2014. One of many *enoteche* in town, with a nice, easy-going vibe, and tables outside or long tables inside under stone arches. There's really good pasta for €7 – *alla gricia, cacio e pepe, carbonara* – along with *porchetta* and lovely plates of prosciutto and buffalo mozzarella. Daily 11.30am–midnight; closed Tues in winter.

Pinocchio Piazza del Mercato 21 ☎ 06 941 6694, ⓦ www.hotelpinocchio.it. With a much more extensive menu than most of the other more basic Frascati offerings, this hotel restaurant serves up lots of *bruschette*, good, ultra-thin Roman pizza from €6.50, a large array of traditional and more inventive pasta dishes from €8, and meat and fish mains for around €16. Mon–Fri 7am–10.45pm, Sat & Sun noon–3pm & 7–10.45pm.

CASTEL GANDOLFO

Trattoria Lo Spuntino Via Oratorio 1 ☎ 06 936 0226, ⓦ ristorantelospuntino.com. Just off Piazza della Libertà, this pint-sized trattoria has a few cosy tables indoors and two tables on the street outside, which enjoy a side-on view of the lake. The cooking is hearty, tasty and well-priced: try *fettuccine* with black truffle (€13) or smoked *scamorza* cheese with ham (€9), or plump for one of the fixed-price menus (€21 for two courses). Mon, Tues & Thurs–Sun 12.30–3pm & 7.30–10pm.

ARICCIA

L'Aricciarola Via Borgo S. Rocco 9 ☎ 06 933 4103. One of a number of restaurants on this street, just outside Ariccia's old centre, with tables outside and a traditional and affordable menu featuring *primi* for €6–8 and main courses for €10–14. They do great *amatriciana* and *cacio e pepe*, or you could try the excellent *pappardelle allo sugo cinghiale* (with wild boar sauce), following it with grilled steak or local pork, all washed down with a litre of local wine for €4. Or just order cheese and cold cuts from the amazing spread at the counter. Tues–Sun 11am–4.30pm & 7pm–midnight.

Palestrina

About 30km south of Rome, **PALESTRINA** was built on the site of the ancient Praeneste, originally an Etruscan settlement and later a favoured resort for patrician Romans. "Cool Praeneste", as Horace called it, was the site of an enormous Temple of Fortune whose foundations more or less determine the modern centre, which steps up the hillside in a series of terraces.

Palazzo Barberini and the Museo Nazionale Archeologico Prenestino

Piazza della Cortina • Daily 9am–8pm; last entry 1hr before closing; guided tours (in Italian) Sun at 11.30am • €5, includes access to sanctuary of Fortuna Primigenia; guided tours €5 • ☎ 06 953 8100, ⓦ coopculture.it

The stepped streets of Palestrina encourage casual strolling, but you need to save your energy for Palestrina's real attraction, the **Palazzo Barberini**, right on top of the hill, which houses the **Museo Nazionale Archeologico Prenestino**, originally built in the eleventh century and greatly modified in 1640. The palace and the terraces below were carved out of a Republican temple which previously stood on this site, and the views are magnificent from the top, surveying the countryside around as far as the eye can see. Among the collection's highlights are a number of ancient Roman pieces found locally: a torso of *Fortune* in slate-grey marble; Etruscan funerary *cistae*; and, the museum's prize possession, a marvellous first-century BC *Mosaic of the Nile* housed at the very top of the building, which traces the flooding river from source to delta, chronicling everyday Egyptian life in amazing detail.

Outside the museum and down the steps are the remains of the **sanctuary of Fortuna Primigenia**, brought to light following the bombing of Palestrina in 1944. The sanctuary dates to the end of the second century BC, though this is thought to have been a place of worship in even earlier times.

ARRIVAL AND DEPARTURE

By bus The COTRAL bus from Rome runs from Ponte Mammolo on metro B (roughly hourly; 1hr), terminating at Via degli Arcioni, from where the trudge up to the town is a steep one.

By car The museum is right at the top of the town; there are parking spaces nearby.

EATING AND DRINKING

Zi' Rico Via E. Toti 2–4 ☎ 06 8308 2532, ⓦ zirico.it. Signed off the main Corso, *Zi' Rico* isn't the sort of restaurant you'd expect to find on a Palestrina backstreet. The decor is elegant – linen tablecloths, bare brick walls, atmospheric lighting – and the food seriously good. The creative *primi* include potato and salt cod ravioli in a chickpea and rosemary cream, while braised veal cheek with Barolo wine sauce is a standout *secondo*; expect to pay upwards of €30 a head. There's a vast wine list too. Tues–Sat 12.30–2.30pm & 8–11pm, Sun 12.30–2.30pm.

RESIDENZA NAPOLEONE III

Accommodation

As you might expect, there's no shortage of accommodation in Rome, and, for much of the year, you can usually find something without too much trouble. In recent years, the amount of lodging has increased significantly at all levels, especially among boutique options, with sumptuous *palazzi* all over the city centre being given designer makeovers in the hope of attracting a better-heeled clientele. There's also a decent range of budget hotels, as well as a sprinkling of hostels. It's always worth booking in advance if you want to snag a bargain, especially in high season: from Easter to July and September to the end of October, and during Christmas and New Year. With the global rise of experiential travel, apartment stays, arranged through Airbnb for example, are becoming ever more popular, especially in sought-after neighbourhoods such as Monti and Trastevere.

You'll enjoy Rome most if you stay right in the heart of things – in the **Centro Storico**, such as around Piazza Navona or near **Campo de' Fiori**. There are plenty of hotels in these areas, and several that aren't all that expensive, but they fill quickly, so you need to book well in advance, if you can. The **Tridente** and the area east of Via del Corso, towards **Via Veneto** and around the **Spanish Steps**, is prime hunting ground for more upscale accommodation, but there are more affordable options here too, and it is a good and central place to base yourself. Consider also staying across the river: in **Prati**, the pleasant nineteenth-century neighbourhood close to the **Vatican** and nicely distanced from the hubbub of the city centre, or in lively **Trastevere** which boasts a number of budget options and is within easy walking distance of the city centre and the major sights. Otherwise, many of the city's hostels and cheaper hotels are located close to **Termini** – convenient if you have to catch an early train or flight, but not the city's most atmospheric quarter, and a bus ride away from the Centro Storico. For those on a tight budget, however, this is where you'll find the widest choice of accommodation: the streets both sides of the station are stacked full of bargain hotels and hostels. South of the station, the recently gentrified area of **Monti** is a vibrant and convenient part of the city to stay in, with its good transport connections and easy access to all the major monuments.

14

ESSENTIALS

RATES

Apart from taxes (see box below), hotel prices are fairly transparent. The rates given in our listings are for the cheapest double room in high season excluding this tax. Rates can change from day to day (or even hour to hour), but as a very rough guide, you'll pay around €130 for a basic en-suite room, without much in the way of decor; €134–195 will get you a few homely touches and perhaps a more central location; for more comfort and a bit of elegance, plan for €220–320, with the price rising the closer you are to the centre; €300–700 (and beyond) is the price of grand, five-star luxury or the most exclusive of the boutique hotels. Hostel beds tend to go for around €30 a night, and private rooms in hostels for €75–95. There are often deals to be had, as hotels try to fill their rooms. Out of season, particularly during the heat of August, there are often excellent last-minute offers that can make some of the city's better hotels accessible to those on more modest budgets. Year-round, most hotels now offer a cheaper, non-refundable price alongside the standard rate (which usually allows you to cancel without charge up to 48 hours before arrival) – often saving you up 10–20 percent on the standard rate.

BOOKING

Hotels are increasingly trying to compete with online **booking sites** and you can often get a good rate by booking direct. The usual international hotel booking sites

(such as ⓦ booking.com, ⓦ laterooms.com, ⓦ lastminute. com and ⓦ expedia.com), are quick and easy options.

FACILITIES

Breakfast A simple continental breakfast is usually included (although it's always a good idea to confirm this), except in high-end places, where you can expect to pay upwards of €30 per person for a sumptuous buffet breakfast.
Internet and TV Almost all hotels now have wi-fi, although the more upmarket and old-fashioned places sometimes charge for this; the majority also offer satellite TV with English-language news stations.
Kitchen facilities A relatively new trend is a hybrid of apartment and hotel, which often has rooms larger than the standard hotel room and occasionally rudimentary kitchen facilities.
Parking Very few hotels in the Centro Storico have their own parking, but they may have a contract with local garages, which charge €25–35 a day.
Swimming pools Unsurprisingly, swimming pools and spas are confined mostly to the five-star hotels, but they are normally open to all – at a price (see box, p.305).
Bars and restaurants Some of the top hotels have great on-site bars and renowned restaurants that are venues in their own right, with fantastic food, great patios or terraces or stupendous views – and sometimes all three (see box, box, p.262 & box, p.272).

ACCOMMODATION TAX

The Rome city authorities levy a **hotel tax** that ranges from €2 per night in campsites and €3.50 in B&Bs and apartments up to €3–7 per night in hotels; it is applied to each occupant for each night, in all overnight accommodation inside Rome's boundaries, and is usually charged separately in cash (although some hotels will accept payment by credit card). Children under the age of 10 are exempt, and you pay nothing after ten days (five for camping).

HOTELS

CENTRO STORICO

Albergo del Senato Piazza della Rotonda 73 ❶ 06 678 4343, ⓦ albergodelsenato.it; map p.36. A classy choice with friendly service and magnificent views of the Pantheon (which is next door) from some rooms. The rooftop bar, with wonderful views of the city, is an atmospheric spot for a nightcap. Big discounts in low season. **€255**

14

Cesàri Via di Pietra 89a ❶ 06 674 9701, ⓦ albergocesari .it; map p.36. In a perfect position close to the Pantheon, this has been a hotel since 1787, as they will be sure to tell you – the Stendhal room was named for their most famous former guest. The quiet, comfortable rooms are elegant and modern, and you can enjoy the hotel's roof terrace at breakfast and for drinks on summer evenings. **€285**

Chiostro del Bramante apartments Arco della Pace 5 ❶ 06 6880 9035, ⓦ chiostrodelbramante.it; map p.36. Just off the lovely Chiostro del Bramante right in the heart of the Centro Storico, close to Piazza Navona, this place has three beautifully furnished apartments: a two-bedroom, a one-bedroom and a large studio. The two-bedroom flat, *La Torretta*, has a rooftop terrace, and all have cooking facilities. Minimum stay three nights. **€200**

Due Torri Vicolo del Leonetto 23 ❶ 06 6880 6956, ⓦ hotelduetorriroma.com; map p.36. Tucked away down a quiet side street just north of Piazza Navona, this little hotel was once a residence for cardinals, after which it served as a brothel. It's been completely remodelled since then but remains cosy, and some rooms have small terraces with rooftop views. They also have a second hotel, the *Fontanella Borghese*, a few streets away at Largo Fontanella Borghese 84 (❶ 06 688 0954, ⓦ fontanellaborghese.com), with similar rates. **€180**

JK Place Roma Via di Monte d'Oro 30 ❶ 06 982 634, ⓦ jkroma.com; map p.36. The ultra-exclusive JK chain, with other locations in Florence and Capri, opened this chic bolthole in the centre of Rome in 2013. It oozes sophisticated style, from the luxurious Art Deco-inspired rooms – with marble-clad bathrooms bigger than some hotel bedrooms – to the airy lounge, dotted with art and sculpture, and the mirror-lined dining room, which sparkles like a jewellery box. Expensive, but a Roman one-off. **€650**

Locanda Navona Via di Tor Millina 35 ❶ 06 6830 8281, ⓦ locandanavona.com; map p.36. This *residenza*, under the same affable management as the *Navona* (see above), has six bright, cosily decorated rooms overlooking this busy intersection just off Piazza Navona. A simple DIY breakfast is provided in the rooms, or there's a great bar under the hotel for breakfast with the locals. **€110**

Mimosa Pantheon Via di Santa Chiara 61 ❶ 06 6880 1753, ⓦ hotelmimosa.net; map p.36. You get what you pay for at this cheap one-star place in the city centre, but its simple rooms have their own bathrooms and a/c, and the hotel enjoys a great position on a quiet street close to Santa Maria sopra Minerva and the Pantheon. Nice family rooms too. **€115**

Navona Via dei Sediari 8 ❶ 06 6830 1252, ⓦ hotelnavona.com; map p.36. Friendly hotel in a building that dates back to the first century AD, built on the ancient Roman baths of Agrippa. Some of the rooms have wonderful coffered ceilings, though the general aesthetic leans towards modern simplicity, with wood floors, designer Perspex chairs and modish padded headboards. It's in a great location, very close to Piazza Navona, though street noise can be a problem at night. Breakfast costs €10 extra. It also has sister hotels, the *Residenza Zanardelli* (see opposite) and *Argentina Residenza* (see opposite). **€120**

Nazionale Piazza Montecitorio 131 ❶ 06 695 001, ⓦ hotelnazionale.it; map p.36. This sixteenth-century *palazzo* in peaceful Piazza Montecitorio, perfectly located halfway between Piazza Navona and Piazza di Spagna, is next door to the Italian parliament and popular with visiting politicians and dignitaries. Rooms range from simple, comfortable "Classic" via the spacious, luxurious "Executive" to the blow-the-budget, two-bedroom Bougainvillea Suite on the roof. The decor is on the old-fashioned side, but none the worse for that. **€290**

Pantheon Via Pastini 131 ❶ 06 678 7746, ⓦ hotel pantheon.com; map p.36. This comfortable four-star hotel is, as you might expect, a stone's throw from the Pantheon, and has plenty of old-school charm. The well-equipped rooms range from the functional, with beamed wooden ceilings, to deluxe junior suites with sky-lit sitting rooms. **€190**

Portoghesi Via dei Portoghesi 1 ❶ 06 686 4231, ⓦ hotelportoghesiroma.it; map p.36. Decent, classically furnished rooms and a very handy location, just off Via della Scrofa and 5min from the heart of the Centro Storico. The rooms at the front are nicer and brighter, though there is some street noise. There's also a good-value apartment (sleeping five), with its own independent entrance. Breakfast on the roof terrace, with a view of St Peter's dome, is a high point. **€200**

Raphaël Largo Febo 2 ❶ 06 682 831, ⓦ raphaelhotel. com; map p.36. Set on a quiet, picturesque piazza just off Piazza Navona, the *Raphaël* is a mix of plush traditional style – antiques, rich colours and an impressive art collection (Picasso ceramics and paintings by Miró, Morandi and De Chirico) – and sleek contemporary furnishings by American architect Richard Meier of Ara Pacis fame (see p.98) on the second and third floors. You can dine in the lovely rooftop restaurant, which offers an extensive vegetarian and vegan menu (book ahead), so close to the church dome that you can see its rivets. **€400**

Relais Orso Via del Orso 88 ❶ 06 9357 9573, ⓦ relaisorso.com; map p.36. With just sixteen rooms and a contrived yet effective contemporary-meets-distressed antique style, this boutique hotel enjoys one of the best locations in the Centro Storico. Rooms aren't large, but the bathrooms are a good size, with walk-in showers; other pluses are Nespresso machines and free minibar, and a late check-out. There's a rooftop bar, too, a pleasant spot for early evening drinks. **€200**

Residenza Canali ai Coronari Via dei Tre Archi 13 ☎ 06 6830 9541, ⓦ residenzacanali.com; map p.36. On a side street close to Piazza Navona, this family-run hotel enjoys a great location and has the rooms and service to go with it. The bright rooms with wood-beamed ceilings all have modern bathrooms and are great value, especially the junior suites, each of which has a private terrace. There are five floors and no lift. **€140**

★ **Residenza Zanardelli** Via G. Zanardelli 7 ☎ 06 6821 1392, ⓦ hotelnavona.com; map p.36. Just north of Piazza Navona, this is the sister hotel of the *Navona* (see opposite), and ever so slightly more lavish, housed in a former papal residence that retains many original fixtures. Rooms are elegant, with antique iron beds, silk-lined walls and modern amenities. **€190**

Santa Chiara Via di Santa Chiara 21 ☎ 06 687 2979, ⓦ albergosantachiara.com; map p.36. A friendly, family-run hotel in a great location, on a quiet street behind the Pantheon. Tastefully furnished rooms, too, some of which overlook the church of Santa Maria sopra Minerva. **€235**

★ **Teatro Pace** Via del Teatro Pace 33 ☎ 06 687 9075, ⓦ hotelteatropace.com; map p.36. This beautifully restored *palazzo*, a few paces from Piazza Navona, was once home to one of the Vatican's most prominent cardinals. Leading off an impressive Baroque spiral staircase (no lift) are four floors of elegant, mostly spacious rooms with original wood beams, floor-sweeping drapes and luxurious bathrooms. **€190**

CAMPO DE' FIORI AND THE GHETTO

Argentina Residenza Via di Torre Argentina 47 ☎ 06 6880 9533, ⓦ argentinaresidenza.com; map p.50. This former noble carriage-house has been converted to a six-room hotel by the *Navona* folk (see opposite), and it's an elegant affair, antique ceilings offsetting the well-chosen modern furnishings and amenities. It's in a perfect location too, in the core of the historic centre but also close to the major transport hub of Largo di Torre Argentina. **€165**

Campo de' Fiori Via del Biscione 6 ☎ 06 6880 6865, ⓦ hotelcampodefiori.com; map p.50. A friendly hotel with rooms that have been renovated in a plush, boutique style, and a large roof terrace affording great views. The hotel also owns two simple small apartments in the piazza (€212 a night for two people) **€225**

DOM Hotel Via Giulia 131 ☎ 06 683 2144, ⓦ domhotelroma.com; map p.50. A relative newcomer to Rome's luxury boutique hotel scene, *DOM Hotel* goes all-out for opulence in its 24 rooms and suites, all moody greys

---

TOP 5 HOTELS WITH VIEWS

Eden See p.233
Fortyseven See p.232
Hassler See p.232
Palazzo Manfredi See p.237
Splendide Royal See p.234

---

and browns, dramatic lighting and splashy statement art. On the ground floor, boudoir-esque restaurant and cocktail bar *The Deer Club*, black-panelled, chandelier-lit and hung with Andy Warhol silkscreens, is thronged with hip young things after dark: great if you want to be in the thick of the action, not so much if you just want a quiet beer before bed. **€360**

Domus Ester Via di San Salvatore in Campo 38 ☎ 06 6813 9414, ⓦ new.estercampodefiori.com; map p.50. Tucked away on a tranquil alley in the heart of the Ghetto, *Domus Ester* offers excellent value given its location, a 5min walk from Campo de' Fiori. The rooms are small but spotless and crisply painted, with wood-beamed ceilings and gleaming bathrooms. A simple breakfast is delivered to your room in the morning by the smiley staff. There are several flights of stairs and no lift. **€110**

Hotel Residenza in Farnese Via del Mascherone 59 ☎ 06 6821 0980, ⓦ residenzafarneseroma.it; map p.50. On a quiet side street right by Palazzo Farnese, rooms here are large and mostly tastefully appointed, while some overlook the French embassy gardens. The staff are very helpful, and the location is handy for both the Centro Storico and Trastevere, just across the bridge. Considerable discounts are often available. **€190**

Indigo Rome – St George Via Giulia 62 ☎ 06 686 611, ⓦ hotelindigorome.com; map p.50. Situated on one of Rome's most beautiful streets, this five-star has been given a snazzy revamp. Its luxurious rooms have playful touches such as outsize photos of the Fiat 500 emblazoned across the walls, and brightly patterned linens. There's a spa with Turkish bath (free access to guests), plus a chic restaurant, *I Sofa*, and a rooftop bar and restaurant (see p.272) in the summer months. **€325**

Lunetta Piazza del Paradiso 68 ☎ 06 6839 5056, ⓦ hotellunetta.com; map p.50. This elegant hotel has thirty boutique-style rooms of various shapes and sizes, as well as a small spa – unheard-of in all but the swishest five-stars – and a bijou bar on the roof. **€270**

Relais Giulia Via Giulia 93 ☎ 06 9558 1300, ⓦ relaisgiulia.com; map p.50. This hotel has minimalist-style rooms in neutral colours that face an interior courtyard, though one of the suites has a balcony overlooking Via Giulia itself. Some of the rooms are a bit small, but the breakfasts are great, and it's brilliantly situated for visiting the Centro Storico, the Ghetto, Trastevere and the Vatican. **€190**

14

14

Relais Teatro Argentina Via del Sudario 35 ☎ 06 9893 1617, ⊛ relaisteatroargentina.com; map p.50. Situated on a side street right by the Teatro Argentina, this B&B doesn't only have a good location but also exhibits great flair in the colours and textiles chosen for the guest rooms. They don't, however, always have staff present, so be sure to coordinate your arrival time. Free breakfast, served in your room, plus a decent DVD collection. €195

Sole Via del Biscione 76 ☎ 06 6880 6873, ⊛ solealbiscione.it; map p.50. This long-standing cheapie enjoys one of the best locations in the centre and has reasonable rooms, plus several roof terraces with spectacular views of the nearby domes. Unusually, there's a garage attached, so this is a good option if you have a car (€20/day). No breakfast. €135

Teatro di Pompeo Largo del Pallaro 8 ☎ 06 687 2812, ⊛ hotelteatrodipompeo.it; map p.50. Built above the remains of Pompey's ancient Roman theatre, the rooms here are comfortable, with high-beamed wooden ceilings, marble-topped furniture and (in some) sweeping views. €140

PIAZZA VENEZIA AND THE CAPITOLINE HILL

Fortyseven 47 Via Petroselli 47 ☎ 06 678 7816, ⊛ fortysevenhotel.com; map p.61. A contemporary boutique hotel with Art Deco-inspired decor and crisply furnished rooms, some of which have great views of the ancient temples opposite and the Circus Maximus beyond, as does the hotel's rooftop *Circus* restaurant. €270

Kolbe Via di San Teodoro 48 ☎ 06 679 8866, ⊛ kolbehotelrome.com; map p.61. This former convent, near the Circus Maximus on the south side of the Palatine, is a tranquil oasis, with a lovely secluded garden. Rooms are on the bland side of contemporary, and the overall feel is one of affordable rather than boutique luxury, but the location is good, especially if you can snag a room overlooking the Forum. €175

Palazzo al Velabro Via del Velabro 16 ☎ 06 679 2758, ⊛ velabro.it; map p.61. A discreet apartment hotel near the Bocca della Verità; some rooms have views of the Arch of Janus and Temple of Hercules, while others look towards the Palatine Hill (some with a small terrace). There's a breakfast café, fitness facilities and 24hr concierge service, too. €205

★ Residenza Torre Colonna Via delle Tre Cannelle 18 ☎ 06 8360 0192, ⊛ torrecolonna.com; map p.61. A 1247 defensive tower built by the noble Colonna family is now a five-room guesthouse decorated in antique-meets-contemporary style, with the original ceilings and frescoes enlivened with splashy modern art on the walls. There's also a rooftop terrace with panoramic views over the Forum and neighbouring Piazza Venezia. €215

THE TRIDENTE AND TREVI

Babuino 181 Via del Babuino 181 ☎ 06 3229 5295, ⊛ romeluxurysuites.com; map p.91. Rome Luxury Suites operates this and two other locations at Margutta 54 and Mario de' Fiori 37 (see opposite). Decorated with contemporary Italian flair, rooms are stylishly comfortable – fluffy pillows, Frette sheets – and large for Rome standards. There's a roof terrace, where breakfast is served, and a concierge service. €350

Condotti Via Mario de' Fiori 37 ☎ 06 679 4661, ⊛ hotelcondotti.com; map p.91. The *Condotti* is cosy and inviting, with rooms that are comfortable, if a little dated; those in the nearby annexe are more modern. The staff are cheerful and welcoming, and the rates aren't bad for the location – right in the heart of Rome's chichi shopping district – and there are often big discounts on the official rates. Rooms in the annexe do not have breakfast included but this is available in the main hotel for €10 per person. €215

Crossing Condotti Via Mario de' Fiori 28 ☎ 06 6992 0633, ⊛ crossingcondotti.com; map p.91. Classy modern suites and apartments furnished with antiques and painted in elegant, neutral tones, all with rudimentary kitchen facilities, free snacks and drinks in a great location close to Piazza di Spagna. Hotel services, too, including daytime staff and a daily linen change, and guests are given an iPad to use around the city. €340

★ De Russie Via del Babuino 9 ☎ 06 328 881, ⊛ roccofortehotels.com; map p.91. The abode of choice for visiting movie stars and well-heeled trendsetters, with stylishly understated doubles, quirkily furnished with plentiful references to the city's ancient heritage. If you're not staying here, you can still experience the buzz downstairs in the courtyard *Stravinskij Bar* (see box, p.272) or splash out on dinner at the fine-dining restaurant *Le Jardin de Russie* (see p.254). €850

Dei Borgognoni Via del Bufalo 126 ☎ 06 6994 1505, ⊛ hotelborgognoni.it; map p.91. A surprisingly big hotel considering its location down a quietish street not far from Piazza di Spagna, this four-star has pleasant, nicely renovated large rooms with a plush, luxurious feel. The bar serves light meals, and there's a cosy library with fireplace. €285

D'Inghilterra Via Bocca di Leone 14 ☎ 06 8997 0284, ⊛ niquesahotels.com/hotel-dinghilterra; map p.91. This old favourite, formerly the apartments of the princes of Torlonia, is pretty good value compared to the cost of hotels of similar quality in this location. Intimacy, opulence, exquisite antiques, frescoed rooms, marble bathrooms and all the delights of the ancient city centre. A nice, old-fashioned bar, too, and the *Café Romano* restaurant is lovely inside or out. €385

Hassler Piazza Trinità dei Monti 6 ☎ 06 699 340, ⊛ hotelhasslerroma.com; map p.91. Location, location, location – at the top of the Spanish Steps, you can't get a much more commanding position above Rome. A luxury hotel with elegant rooms – each one different – and every convenience a guest could possibly require, including a spa and a Michelin-star restaurant, *Imàgo* (see p.253), but what you're paying for is the reputation and – of course – the view. Breakfast costs €29 extra per person. **€695**

Hotel Art Via Margutta 56 ☏ 06 328 711, ⓦ hotelart.it; map p.91. Ingeniously converted from a convent and with an impressive bar and lobby fashioned out of a vaulted chapel, the *Hotel Art* ticks most of the right boxes: it's in a great location, tucked away on Via Margutta, and its design theme is for the most part well realized and luxurious. The rooms are good, too, though some are disappointingly small. **€235**

Manfredi Suite Via Margutta 61 ☏ 06 320 7676, ⓦ hotelmanfredi.it; map p.91. On picturesque Via Margutta, this hotel is moments from the Spanish Steps. The sixteenth-century building once housed a theatre, renamed Teatro delle Dame because it was the first place in the city where women were allowed to perform. The comfortable, traditionally furnished rooms are fairly fancy for the price, and the wine bar, with its triple-domed ceiling, makes a pleasant spot for a drink. **€265**

Mario de' Fiori 37 Via Mario de' Fiori 37b ☏ 06 6992 1907, ⓦ romeluxurysuites.com; map p.91. This small hotel is one of three properties of Rome Luxury Suites, and its elegantly stylish rooms are situated in a great location close to the Spanish Steps. Bathrooms are a good size and rooms well equipped and decently furnished. The only downside is for breakfast: you have to walk to one of their other properties at Via del Babuino 181 (see opposite), but that's no great hardship. **€350**

Piazza di Spagna Via Mario de' Fiori 61 ☏ 06 679 3061, ⓦ hotelpiazzadispagna.it; map p.91. This small hotel, just a few minutes' walk from the Spanish Steps, is a good alternative to the sumptuous palaces that characterize this area. Friendly, and family-owned and -run, it has comfortable rooms, all with a/c and TV, and some with jacuzzis. There's a little roof garden, too. **€165**

★ **Portrait Roma** Via di Bocca di Leone 23 ☏ 06 6938 0742, ⓦ lungarnohotels.com; map p.91. This converted townhouse with fourteen suites, owned by the Salvatore Ferragamo fashion house and dotted with the late designer's shoe lasts and other fashiony details, is a bastion of luxury and comfort. Prices are eye-watering, but the suites are superbly appointed, and there's a lovely rooftop bar. Attention to detail is second to none: music and temperature in the rooms are adjusted according to guests' requirements, and an iPad loaded with the hotel's Rome suggestions is given to each guest for the duration of their stay. Service is unstuffy and ultra-friendly. **€630**

★ **Residenza Napoleone III** Largo Goldoni 56 ☏ 06 6880 8083, ⓦ residenzanapoleone.com; map p.91. In the opulent setting of the sixteenth-century Palazzo Ruspoli, these two suites are perhaps Rome's most tempting blow-the-budget option. The Napoleone Suite is sumptuously furnished with priceless antiques and vast oil paintings – a level of luxury of which the famous one-time resident obviously approved – while the Roof Garden Suite is less grand but still wonderfully homely, decorated with books and antiques, and with a vast roof terrace overlooking the city's rooftops. **€900**

THE QUIRINALE AND VIA VENETO

Daphne Via degli Avignonesi 20 ☏ 06 8934 5781, ⓦ daphne-rome.com; map p.104. Run by an American woman and her Roman husband, this is a welcoming place, just off Piazza Barberini and only 500m from the Trevi Fountain. The rooms are modern, furnished in a minimalist yet warm style, with plenty of creature comforts. There are three family suites, accommodating up to four people. Most double rooms are en suite (two have shared bathroom). The new fifth-floor reception, veranda and breakfast room are spacious, sunny and inviting. **€240**

★ **Deko Rome** Via Toscana 1 ☏ 06 4202 0032, ⓦ dekorome.com; map p.104. This six-room hotel, run by friendly and efficient Marco and Serena, gets everything right, from the glass of prosecco on arrival to the complimentary iPad and free minibar. The rooms are modern and spotless, and it's in a great location, too. It's understandably popular, so book ahead. **€170**

★ **Eden** Via Ludovisi 49 ☏ 06 478 121, ⓦ dorchester collection.com; map p.104. Just off Via Veneto, this former private residence is one of Rome's most enchanting hotels, with an inviting lobby and a fireplace that blazes in winter. At the time of writing, the property had just reopened after an extensive refurbishment. Many of the new opulently styled rooms and suites have spectacular views over Rome, some even with balconies. Unwind at the small spa or take in the views in the fine-dining rooftop restaurant, *La Terrazza dell'Eden* (see p.254), where Fellini had a regular table and conducted most of his interviews. **€920**

La Residenza Via Emilia 22 ☏ 06 488 0789, ⓦ hotel-la -residenza.com; map p.104. Combining the luxury and atmosphere of a grand hotel with the easy-going comforts and intimacy of a private home, this is a great option in the pricey Via Veneto area. Very tranquil too, set well away from the main drag. **€185**

Majestic Via Veneto 50 ☏ 06 421 441, ⓦ hotelmajestic .com; map p.104. A member of the Leading Hotels of the World, Via Veneto's oldest hotel (1889) has ceiling frescoes,

14

TOP 5 LUXURY CHOICES

De Russie See opposite
JK Place Roma See p.230
Palazzo Manfredi See p.237
Portrait Roma See above
Residenza Napoleone III See above

14

TOP 5 BUDGET CHOICES
The Beehive See below
Giorni Felici See p.238
Mimosa See p.230
Next Door See p.240
Sole See p.232

silk hangings and elaborate antiques that are reminders of its nineteenth-century origins, but its elegant, spacious rooms have been brightened for a more contemporary feel, and come with huge marble bathrooms. The upstairs terrace has a good restaurant, bright with antique mirrors and natural light, and run by celebrated chef Massimo Riccioli. **€455**

Modigliani Via della Purificazione 42 ☎ 06 4281 5226, ⓦ hotelmodigliani.com; map p.104. On a quiet street just off Piazza Barberini, this family-run hotel is tastefully decorated and has a delightful garden courtyard. Splash out on one of the superior rooms, whose balconies have a view of St Peter's. There's also a bar where you can order light meals. **€195**

Splendide Royal Via di Porta Pinciana 14 ☎ 06 421 689, ⓦ splendideroyal.com; map p.104. This old Veneto-area favourite exudes neo-Baroque charm with spacious, light bedrooms decorated in rich gold, cream and red; those that face the Aurelian Wall have magical views of the umbrella pines below. Film buffs should check out the lobby chandelier, which once glittered above Burt Lancaster and Claudia Cardinale in *The Leopard*. The rooftop restaurant, *Mirabelle* (see p.256), is highly rated, and views from the bar are second to none. **€385**

Victoria Via Campania 41 ☎ 06 423 701, ⓦ hotelvictoriaroma.com; map p.104. Decorated in imperial Roman style, this Swiss-managed hotel is situated between the super-deluxe grandeur of Via Veneto and the verdant freedom of Villa Borghese. Many rooms enjoy views of the ancient walls and beyond, and there's a fragrant roof garden too. **€180**

★**Villa Spalletti Trivelli** Via Piacenza 4 ☎ 06 4890 7934, ⓦ villaspalletti.it; map p.104. Count Giangiacomo Spalletti Trivelli's family home makes for an elegant yet pleasantly intimate stay, nestled between Via Nazionale and the Quirinale. Its twelve rooms are spacious (the Grand Deluxe Suites can accommodate a family of four) and feature family antiques and a free minibar, and there's a lovely garden and spa, and a cosy library with a roaring fire in winter, making for a special stay. **€560**

THE ESQUILINE, MONTI AND TERMINI

Alpi Via Castelfidardo 84, Termini ☎ 06 444 1235, ⓦ hotelalpi.com; map p.114. One of the more peaceful yet convenient options close to Termini, with spruce and contemporary (if sometimes somewhat small) en-suite doubles – better than you would expect in a hotel of this category – and a flower-filled terrace. **€190**

★**Artemide** Via Nazionale 22, Esquiline Hill ☎ 06 489 911, ⓦ hotelartemide.it; map p.114. The handsome *Artemide* combines an imposing, old-world feel with a warm welcome and service that's second to none. The comfortable rooms come with a free minibar, breakfast is five star, and the rooftop bar is a lovely spot on a sunny day. There's a swish spa too (€30 entry per person, treatments extra) – an unlikely bonus in a four-star. Rates are significantly lower out of season. **€440**

Artorius Via del Boschetto 13, Monti ☎ 06 482 1196, ⓦ hotelartoriusrome.com; map p.114. On a cobbled Monti street and with just ten rooms, decorated in classic style, this family-run hotel is an appealing mid-range option. The attractive courtyard makes a pleasant spot for breakfast in fine weather and for drinks after dark. **€150**

★**B&B La Scalinatella** Via Urbana 48, Monti ☎ 06 488 0547 or 339 5256537, ⓦ lascalinatellaroma.com; map p.114. This fabulous three-room B&B, run by friendly sisters Annamaria and Elisabetta, is in a seventeenth-century *palazzo* in bustling Monti, a 10min walk from the Colosseum. The rooms are beautifully furnished with whitewashed wood beams, antique furniture and spacious modern bathrooms; book the larger "comfort" room if you can. In the sunny brick-vaulted breakfast room, tea served in antique silver teapots and plentiful pastries make a good start to the day. The B&B is three floors up with no lift. **€120**

★**The Beehive** Via Marghera 8, Termini ☎ 06 4470 4553, ⓦ the-beehive.com; map p.114. This cheery and friendly ecological – and economical – hostel/hotel is run by an American couple and has simple, but well-decorated doubles (some with shared bathroom, some en-suite). They also have two dorms, one for women only and one mixed. There's a cosy lounge, an on-site vegetarian café serving breakfast daily, dinner on some evenings, and a peaceful courtyard garden that feels like a real haven so close to Termini. Doubles **€80/100**, dorms **€35**

De Monti Via Panisperna 95, Monti ☎ 06 481 4763, ⓦ hoteldemonti.com; map p.114. Situated on the third floor (no lift) of a sixteenth-century *palazzo* in the heart of trendy Monti, this small hotel has seven spacious, simply but stylishly furnished rooms with nice bathrooms. Very friendly and hospitable, with good breakfasts served in the rooms. **€125**

Des Artistes Via Villafranca 20, Termini ☎ 06 445 4365, ⓦ hoteldesartistes.com; map p.114. One of the better hotels in the Termini area – good value, spotlessly clean and with a wide range of rooms, including dorms. En-suite rooms are comfortable and decorated in tasteful neutrals, and you can eat breakfast or recover from a long day of sightseeing on the breezy roof terrace. Doubles **€140**, dorms **€26**

14

Duca d'Alba Via Leonina 14, Monti ☎ 06 484 471, ⓦ hotelducadalba.com; map p.114. A reliable four-star set in a former nineteenth-century townhouse in the heart of Monti, just steps from the district's best restaurants and nightlife. The stylish, moodily lit rooms are all different; some come with balconies. **€165**

Exedra Piazza della Repubblica 47, Termini ☎ 06 489 381, ⓦ boscolohotels.com; map p.114. Opened in 2003 in a Neoclassical *palazzo* that curves around part of the piazza, the *Exedra* breathed new life into the Termini area, with large, elegantly furnished rooms, a champagne bar and a lovely spa, which includes a small outdoor roof pool (see box, p.305). **€520**

Giuliana Via A. Depretis 70, Termini ☎ 06 488 0795, ⓦ hotelgiuliana.com; map p.114. This Termini area hotel has a loyal following and a friendly and helpful owner. The rooms are very basic and rather dated, but spotless and well maintained. Wi-fi costs extra. **€100**

Glam Hotel Rome Via Nazionale 82, Monti ☎ 06 9934 5430, ⓦ romeglamhotel.com; map p.114. This four-star boutique hotel, a short walk from the Teatro del Opera and all the nightlife and restaurants of Monti, offers modern designer interiors, a seasonal rooftop terrace for drinks or light snacks and free minibars in all rooms. **€210**

IQ Hotel Via Firenze 8, Termini ☎ 06 488 0465, ⓦ iqhotelroma.it; map p.114. Not the most characterful hotel in the city, but very convenient for Termini and the opera house, and it has a large roof terrace for relaxing and a play area for children. The rooms are small, but well-designed and very clean. There's a free gym and sauna, and a coin-operated laundry for do-it-yourselfers. **€230**

Leon's Place Via XX Settembre 90/94, Termini ☎ 06 890 871, ⓦ leonsplacehotel.it; map p.114. This Termini-area boutique hotel is on the edge of an upscale residential area with good shops and dining, and has a small courtyard garden and a spacious lobby with a bar at the far end that serves light meals. Though on the small side, the rooms are sleekly modern – all black and white with splashes of colour and deft design touches – and come with a smartphone charged with 4G internet connection. **€200**

★**Nerva** Via Tor de' Conti 3, Monti ☎ 06 679 3764, ⓦ hotelnerva.com; map p.114. Right by the Roman Forum, the *Nerva* is a modern boutique hotel. Rooms are decorated in cool monochrome with pops of colour in the cushions and art, while the hound's-tooth fabric used in the outsize headboards lends a touch of vintage style, and the

marble bathrooms add more retro glamour. Free afternoon tea and cake are served every day in the lounge, and staff are always on hand to help with local recommendations. **€260**

★**Nicolas Inn** Via Cavour 295, Monti ☎ 06 9761 8483, ⓦ nicolasinn.com; map p.114. A brief stroll from the Colosseum, this B&B is run by a friendly American–Italian couple who are keen to make guests feel at home and offer a concierge service – impressive at this price. The rooms are a good size, spotless and elegant. Breakfast is included but is served in a nearby bar. **€180**

★**Quirinale** Via Nazionale 7, Esquiline Hill ☎ 06 4707, ⓦ hotelquirinale.it; map p.114. Giuseppe Verdi greeted the Teatro dell'Opera crowds here after the 1893 Rome premiere of *Falstaff*, and it's still a pleasantly old-fashioned place, with a fireplace in its lobby. A secret passageway leads directly to the opera house without going onto the street (open to hotel or dinner guests with a performance ticket). The rooms – large and antique-filled with spacious marble bathrooms – are excellent value. **€155**

Radisson Blu Es Via F. Turati 171, Termini ☎ 06 444 841, ⓦ radissonblu.com/eshotel-rome; map p.114. One of the first hotels to spark the renaissance of the Termini area, this place has sleek, minimalist rooms, two restaurants and a state-of-the-art rooftop bar and pool. The location is very convenient for Termini but not in the most upmarket part of town, despite the rates. **€190**

Residenza Cellini Via Modena 5, Esquiline Hill ☎ 06 4782 5204, ⓦ residenzacellini.it; map p.114. The rooms here are pleasant and large with a slightly old-fashioned feel; apartments are also available, complete with spa bath, accommodating from two to eleven people. Staff are extremely friendly. Rooms **€160**, apartments **€195**

Villa delle Rose Via Vicenza 5, Termini ☎ 06 445 1788, ⓦ villadellerose.it; map p.114. This nineteenth-century villa sits amid its own tranquil rose gardens, belying the fact that it's only a block from the train station. The decor is a little tired, but the hotel has bags of old-world charm, and staff are very friendly. Ask for one of the rooms with a terrace. **€100**

Yes Via Magenta 15, Termini ☎ 06 4436 3836, ⓦ yeshotelrome.com; map p.114. About 5min from Termini (and even closer to the airport bus stop), this hotel is not only extremely convenient for the station but also a step up from some of the grotty options in the area – and you'll pay far less here than for a similar room in the centre. Tailored to the needs of Termini's business travellers rather than its backpackers, the rooms are comfortable if a little bland. **€140**

THE CELIAN HILL AND SAN GIOVANNI

Capo d'Africa Via Capo d'Africa 54, Celian Hill ☎ 06 772 801, ⓦ hotelcapodafrica.com; map p.128. A former nineteenth-century convent, this sleek hotel has a brightly modern interior with contemporary art and furniture, and

---

TOP 5 HOTELS FOR FAMILIES

Daphne See p.233
Grand Hotel del Gianicolo See opposite
IQ Hotel See above
Residenza Santa Maria See opposite
Villa Spalletti Trivelli See p.234

the rooms are spacious and very comfortable. Pièce de *résistance* is the roof-terrace breakfast room, which has a good view of Colle Oppio and the Colosseum. **€235**

★ **Lancelot** Via Capo d'Africa 47, Celian Hill ☎ 06 7045 0615, ⓦ lancelothotel.com; map p.128. Just 2min from the Colosseum, this friendly, family-run hotel has rooms with oriental carpets on wood or terrazzo floors, and an attractive bar. Dinner is good, too, served at intimate round tables with other guests. The terrace and some rooms have a view of the Colosseum and the staff are well informed and helpful. Limited parking for €10. **€195**

★ **Palazzo Manfredi** Via Labicana 125, Celian Hill ☎ 06 7759 1380, ⓦ palazzomanfredi.com; map p.128. This hotel couldn't help but be a haven, given the traffic and tourist mayhem outside, but its lobby, rooms and fabulous top-floor restaurant (see p.259) are truly an oasis of peace and tranquillity in one of Rome's busiest tourist hotspots. Its fourteen rooms and suites are thoughtfully and very stylishly furnished and equipped, with big beds, beautiful bathrooms, Nespresso machines, iPads and more, and the views of the Colosseum from some of them are arguably Rome's best. Its restaurant, *Aroma* (see p.259), has a Michelin star and is on the top floor with a breathtaking panoramic terrace. It's a genuinely luxurious boutique hotel experience, and one that's all too rare in Rome – hence the high prices. **€650**

THE AVENTINE HILL AND SOUTH

Abitart Via P. Matteucci 10–20, Ostiense ☎ 06 454 3191, ⓦ abitarthotel.com; map p.140. Just off Via Ostiense, a 5min walk from Piramide metro station (line B), and very handy for going out in Testaccio, *Abitart* has eight quirky art-themed suites – Metaphysical, Pop Art, Deconstructionist and so on – plus standard and superior rooms, some with terrace, decorated in zingy colours. Despite the out-there design, it's mainly aimed at business travellers, so rates are often lower at weekends. A generous breakfast is included, served on the plant-filled terrace in summer. **€140**

★ **San Anselmo** Piazza Sant'Anselmo 2, Aventine Hill ☎ 06 570 057, ⓦ aventinohotels.com; map p.140. One of the most peaceful places you could stay in central Rome's most upscale residential neighbourhood, the *Sant'Anselmo* has beautifully furnished rooms, each with a different theme, from the "Camera della Scrittrice", with Keats quotes emblazoned across the wall, to "Mille e Una Notte" ("Thousand and One Nights"), with its opulent canopied bed. Breakfast is good, there's a nice lounge and garden, and parking is free. Deals available outside high season. **€180**

TRASTEVERE AND THE JANICULUM HILL

B&B Hotel Roma Trastevere Viale di Trastevere 249d ☎ 06 5833 2683, ⓦ hotel-bb.com/en/hotels/roma-trastevere.htm; map p.160. If you're just looking for

somewhere to lay your head, and aren't too fussed about style or services, this is the place. Although decidedly no-frills, with Ikea-style furnishings, it gets all the basics right: rooms are spacious and clean with comfy beds, the a/c and wi-fi work, and it's well-connected to the centre (the tram to Piazza Venezia stops right outside). Just don't expect much in the way of atmosphere or romance. **€80**

Domus Tiberina Via in Piscinula 37 ☎ 06 581 3648, ⓦ hoteldomustiberina.it; map p.160. Located on the quieter side of Trastevere, this small hotel nevertheless lies within a few minutes' walk of the neighbourhood's buzz. Rooms are small but cosily furnished; those in the newer section are bigger. A simple breakfast is served in a nearby café. **€110**

Gran Meliá Rome Via del Gianicolo 3 ☎ 06 925 901, ⓦ granmeliarome.com; map p.160. Once the site of the villa of Nero's mother, Agrippina, this urban resort hotel comes with pools and gardens, a spa (complete with sensory showers and Turkish bath), a library, stylish bars and a gourmet restaurant – *Vivavoce* (see p.263) – under the guidance of award-winning chef, Alfonso Iaccarino. Just above the Tiber, it's an easy walk to Trastevere, the centre and the Vatican. Some of the posher rooms have private terraces with panoramic views. **€450**

Grand Hotel del Gianicolo Viale delle Mura Gianicolensi 107 ☎ 06 5833 3405, ⓦ grandhotelgianicolo.it; map p.160. Commanding the heights of the Janiculum Hill, close to the Doria Pamphilj Park and with views over the entire city, this former convent has a large, mosaic-tiled swimming pool set in subtropical gardens – a major plus in hot weather, though the rooms themselves are looking a little worn. Easy bus connection to the centre of town (20min), and on-site parking. **€200**

Guest House Arco dei Tolomei Via dell'Arco de' Tolomei 27 ☎ 06 5832 0819, ⓦ bbarcodeitolomei.com; map p.160. In an attractively crumbling *palazzo* on Trastevere's quieter, eastern side, this old-world B&B is full of family antiques, but remains decidedly unstuffy. Decor in the rooms is on the chintzy side, but there's a warm, welcoming feel throughout. A generous breakfast is served in the conservatory. **€210**

Residenza Santa Maria Via dell'Arco di San Calisto 20 ☎ 06 5833 5103, ⓦ residenzasantamaria.com; map p.160. In the centre of lively Trastevere but remarkably peaceful, this small *residenza* is run by the owners of the *Santa Maria* (see below), but is a bit better for families or groups, in that four of the six rooms are triples or quads. There are bikes for guests' use and parking is reasonable. **€205**

★ **Santa Maria** Vicolo del Piede 2 ☎ 06 589 4626, ⓦ hotelsantamariatrastevere.it; map p.160. Near Piazza Santa Maria, in the heart of Trastevere, the rooms of this friendly three-star surround an orange-tree-filled garden, making it feel far removed from the city. The hotel has free bikes for guests to use, and serves a free snack buffet in the

14

14

TOP 5 CHOICES UNDER €250

Farnese See opposite
La Scalinatella See p.234
The Beehive See p.234
Residenza Torre Colonna See p.232
Santa Maria See p.237

afternoon. The sun-trap terrace on the roof is a tranquil spot to chill out after a hard day's sightseeing. **€230**

★ **Suites Trastevere** Viale Trastevere 248 ☏ 347 074 4086, ⊛ trastevere.bbsuites.com; map p.160. A tram ride from Trastevere's bustle, at the Porta Portese end of Viale Trastevere, this boutique B&B offers something a bit different. The rooms are themed around Roman sights – one has a trompe l'oeil of the Pantheon's oculus on the ceiling, another is emblazoned with Villa Borghese views. It's pretty over the top and not to everyone's taste, but what sets this B&B apart is its attention to detail: guests are given local mobile phones to use in case of emergencies, and the fridge is stocked with juices, water and fruit for guests to help themselves to during the day. Breakfast – including owner Marco's grandmother's coffee cake – is served at a communal table in the kitchen. **€110**

Trastevere Via Luciano Manara 24–25 ☏ 06 581 4713, ⊛ hoteltrastevere.net; map p.160. A good place to stay if you want to be in the heart of the district, with simply furnished, cosy doubles, triples and quads. Ground-floor windows are double-glazed – a plus in busy Trastevere. The staff are genuinely friendly and very helpful. **€95**

Villa della Fonte Via della Fonte d'Olio 8 ☏ 06 580 3797, ⊛ villafonte.com; map p.160. This attractive, hidden-away place feels almost secret, yet is just a few steps from Piazza Santa Maria in Trastevere. Rooms are larger than average, with terracotta floors, wood beams and high ceilings. Breakfast is taken on the peaceful roof terrace in summer, full of plants and citrus trees. **€180**

VILLA BORGHESE AND NORTH

Aldrovandi Palace Via Ulisse Aldrovandi 15, Villa Borghese ☏ 06 322 3993, ⊛ aldrovandi.com; map p.173. Just north of Villa Borghese, this luxurious hotel has a bright interior looking out over a lovely landscaped garden with swimming pool, and crisp, contemporary and spacious rooms. It's also home to the luxurious La Mer spa. It's a bit of a way from the city centre, but their free car service will whisk you to the Spanish Steps in no time – or you can cycle to town on one of the hotel's bikes. Parking is free. **€360**

★ **Casa Montani** Piazzale Flaminio 9, Villa Borghese ☏ 06 3260 0421, ⊛ casamontani.com; map p.170. Just outside the Porta del Popolo, this self-styled "luxury town house" has only five rooms, all designed by the friendly French–Italian owners and decked out in a chic palette of

neutral colours with touches of luxury, including designer bathrooms and breakfast served in your room on fine porcelain. Book well ahead. **€220**

Fenix Viale Gorizia 5, Nomentano ☏ 06 854 0741, ⊛ fenixhotel.it; map p.170. Just off Via Nomentana, the rather drab exterior of this hotel belies the bright silks, carpets and antique furniture within. It's very comfortable, with magazines everywhere and an eclectic library. Its cheery little restaurant, *Nini*, is reasonably priced, and much favoured by business travellers. Relax in the small garden with an *aperitivo*, on comfy divans under a gauzy gazebo. **€160**

★ **Giorni Felici** Viale Ippocrate 116, Nomentano ☏ 335 838 4927, ⊛ bbgiornifelici.it; map p.114. Feel like a proper Roman at *Giorni Felici* ("Happy Days"), a beautifully furnished apartment with two excellent-value double rooms, each with its own bathroom. The kitsch decor is not to everyone's taste (the psychedelic wallpaper in the breakfast room will certainly wake you up), but it's fun and friendly. You're not far from Termini, and in any case the Bologna neighbourhood is great. **€75**

The H'All Tailor Suite Via Giuseppe Pisanelli 23/25, Piazza del Popolo ☏ 06 3211 0128, ⊛ thehallroma. com; map p.170. Rome's newest five-star boutique hotel is the brainchild of famous Roman restaurateur Riccardo di Giacinto and his partner. In a completely restored palazzo, the fourteen designer-appointed rooms feature bathtubs and exclusive linen, as well as artworks from Rome's contemporary arts gallery, La Mucciaccia. It's home to Riccardo's fine-dining *All'Oro* restaurant (see p.264), where breakfast is also served. **€220**

Rome Cavalieri Via A. Cadlolo 101, Balduina ☏ 06 35091, ⊛ romecavalieri.com; map p.170. Rome's grandest hotel is quite a way out of the city centre, but if you can afford it it's worth staying here once, not only to check out Heinz Beck's legendary three-Michelin-star rooftop restaurant (see p.264) but also to enjoy its curious mix of 1960s glamour and old-fashioned style. The rooms are large and comfortable, with balconies that enjoy perhaps the best and most all-encompassing view of Rome, and there are four lovely pools (three of which are outdoor). Watch out for extra charges, though – for wi-fi and the fitness centre, for example – which can add up over a few days' stay. There are regular free shuttle buses to Piazza Barberini. **€375**

THE VATICAN AND PRATI

Amalia Via Germanico 66 ☏ 06 3972 3356, ⊛ hotelamalia.com; map p.188. Located on an attractive corner of a busy shopping area near the Vatican, this place provides four-star amenities at three-star prices, including quiet (double-glazing on all windows) and nicely renovated double rooms, some with views of St Peter's dome. **€120**

★**Bramante** Vicolo delle Palline 24 ✆ 06 6880 6426, ⓦ hotelbramante.com; map p.188. This welcoming, family-run hotel has a great location on a peaceful Borgo street and elegantly furnished en-suite rooms with spotless bathrooms. Breakfast is a feast, with hot options alongside the usual cereals and pastries. There are steep steps to the rooms, and no lift, but staff are happy to help with luggage. **€150**

Colors Via Boezio 31 ✆ 06 687 4030, ⓦ colorshotel .com; map p.188. This budget hotel in a quiet neighbourhood near the Vatican has well-kept rooms decorated in cheerful colours, plus there's a pleasant rooftop terrace. En-suite rooms go for around €20 more than those with shared bath. **€90**

Columbus Via della Conciliazione 33 ✆ 06 686 5435, ⓦ hotelcolumbus.net; map p.188. On the main route to St Peter's, *Hotel Columbus* is set in the Palazzo dei Penitenzieri, once home to the cardinal who became Pope Julius II. Standard rooms are simply furnished and a little tired; for a touch more luxury it's worth splashing out on a suite, wood-beamed, with terracotta floors and antique furniture. The public areas are comfortable, with elegant sitting areas, and the atmospheric *La Veranda* restaurant with its fifteenth-century frescoed ceiling is lovely by candlelight, or you can dine on the patio in warm weather, where on Sundays, a delicious brunch is served. Free parking. **€185**

Dei Consoli Via Varrone 2d ✆ 06 6889 2972, ⓦ hoteldeiconsoli.com; map p.188. Right in the heart of Prati, this is a reliable choice in the Vatican area, with compact but comfortable rooms, a lovely roof terrace for breakfast and friendly service. Ask for a room overlooking the courtyard for a quieter night's sleep. The Ottaviano metro station is a 5min walk away. Parking is available for €20 a night. **€145**

Domus Mazzini Via Monte Zebio 9, Prati ✆ 06 4542 1592, ⓦ domushotel.it; map p.170. This B&B, run by charming manager Ciro, has just four double rooms, all attractively decorated and very clean. It's a twenty-minute walk from the Vatican but the neighbourhood is pleasant, and, with breakfast taken around a communal table in the kitchen, the place has the feel of staying in someone's home. **€110**

★**Farnese** Via Alessandro Farnese 30 ✆ 06 321 1953, ⓦ farnese.hotelinroma.com; map p.188. Another grand aristocratic residence that has been turned into an upscale hotel. The rooms have handmade walnut furniture, marble bathrooms and soundproof windows and doors. Some feature private balconies, and the rooftop terrace breakfast room offers a great view of the Vatican. Limited free parking. **€190**

Giulio Cesare Via degli Scipioni 287 ✆ 06 321 0751, ⓦ hotelgiuliocesare.com; map p.188. No longer the Villa Patricia, home of an Italian countess, but you may feel charmed like royalty once you step into the elegant foyer. Attentive staff lead you down mirror-lined hallways to rooms with high ceilings and floor-skimming curtains. There are plenty of places to hang out around the hotel too, including a bar and lounge, and a pretty garden with a fountain where you can sit and relax with an *aperitivo*. Limited free parking. **€140**

Hearth Hotel Via Santamaura 2 ✆ 06 3903 8383, ⓦ hearthhotel.com; map p.188. About as close as you can get to the Vatican – the entrance to the museums is just across the street – this converted monastery has large, stylishly furnished rooms with faux-leather headboards and sleek dove-grey furniture. If you're a light sleeper request a room on the quieter side of the building to avoid being woken by the early-morning chatter from the museums' inevitable queue. Breakfast is an elaborate buffet spread, with gluten-free food also available. **€120**

★**Isa** Via Cicerone 39 ✆ 06 321 2610, ⓦ hotelisa.net; map p.188. A 10min walk from the Vatican, this Prati "design hotel" has rooms decorated in chic monochrome or tasteful neutrals, with playful Art Deco touches and shiny marble fittings in the bathrooms. On the roof terrace, where breakfast is taken in the summer months, there's a view of St Peter's prettily framed by the garden trellis, plus a great bar, which lays on free snacks to go with your Campari. **€195**

La Rovere Vicolo Sant'Onofrio 4 ✆ 06 6880 6739, ⓦ hotellarovere.biz; map p.188. Just round the corner from St Peter's and across the bridge from Piazza Navona, this attractive small hotel is tucked away from all the bustle, with a terrace garden that's perfect for relaxing. The rooms are a mixed bag: some are simple and traditional with carpeted floors and Seventies-style headboards, while the "premium design rooms" on the ground floor have been given an arty makeover, with light installations on the walls, exposed brickwork and giant beanbags to lounge on. **€200**

Metropolis Via delle Milizie 26 ✆ 06 3751 2539, ⓦ hotelmetropolisrome.com; map p.188. The Deco origins of the *Metropolis* are played up with modern furnishings inspired by the Twenties and Thirties. Some rooms have a spa bath. It's popular with business travellers (rates are cheaper at weekends) and has a busy bar that lays on periodic wine tastings. **€140**

Le Méridien Visconti Via Federico Cesi 37 ✆ 06 3684, ⓦ lemeridienviscontirome.com; map p.188. Near Piazza Cavour and the Palace of Justice, the former *Visconti Palace Hotel* became a Starwood Marriott property in 2017 and has undergone a complete revamp. The interiors and 240 spacious rooms look colourful and sleek, designed to appeal to business, leisure and younger travellers. There's an excellent buffet breakfast, and the rooftop terrace is opened in the warmer months, offering views onto the streets and domes of Prati. **€245**

14

Villa Laetitia Lungotevere delle Armi 22 ☎ 06 322 6776, ⓦ villalaetitia.com; map p.188. The Fendi fashion family restored this Art Nouveau villa along the Tiber, filling it with antiques from all over the world to complement the marble pillars and ornate ceilings perfectly – just the thing if you're after a gracious, old-world feel. The twenty rooms are split between the upper floors of the villa itself, with views of city, and the "Garden House", overlooking the pretty grounds. There's also an elegant Michelin-starred restaurant, *Enoteca La Torre*, on site. **€170**

HOSTELS

Rome has plenty of **hostels**, although they can get pretty crowded during peak season. Some places separate guests by gender, and most have private rooms as well as dorms. In addition to the options below, *Des Artistes* (see p.234) and *The Beehive* (see p.234) have dorm accommodation. These and the hostels below offer breakfast (usually extra), and none of them has a curfew. However, some places impose age restrictions for dorms.

Alessandro Palace Via Vicenza 42, Termini ☎ 06 446 1958, ⓦ hostelalessandro.com; map p.114. This has been voted one of the top hostels in Europe, and it sparkles with creative style. Pluses include no lock-out or curfew, a roof terrace for cocktail parties, and a funky restaurant that serves up pizza, burgers and the like to hungry backpackers. Wi-fi and satellite TV are free, but breakfast costs extra. You can stay in dorm beds or en-suite private rooms. Dorms **€26**, doubles **€110**

La Controra Via Umbria 7, around Via Veneto ☎ 06 9893 7366, ⓦ lacontrora.com; map p.104. In an excellent location near Piazza Barberini, this hostel has very helpful staff and a relaxed, arty feel, with quirky geometric wallpaper in the dorms and en-suite doubles. The spacious lounge has a big-screen TV and wi-fi, and there's a large communal kitchen. Dorms **€35**, doubles **€90**

★ **Next Door** Via Nomentana 316, Nomentano ☎ 349 522 7371, ⓦ nextdoorguesthouse.com; map p.170. If you're after a party hostel, look elsewhere: this impeccably decorated guesthouse is more about beautiful design than pizza parties. The eight-bed dorm and private rooms are decked out in a mix of moody greys and zingy brights, with ingeniously upcycled furniture throughout: brightly painted wooden chairs hung from the walls make quirky bedside tables, and the table in the common area is made

APARTMENT STAYS

Renting an **apartment** in Rome has many advantages: for families with children or small groups, it can be a cheaper option than a hotel and much more flexible. Short-term rentals are becoming very popular, however, so book well in advance. All of the agencies listed below have accommodation ranging from small city-centre apartments to grand villas outside the city. Several **hotels** also rent apartments, among them *Portoghesi* (see p.230), the *Campo de' Fiori* (see p.231), *Residenza Cellini* (see p.236) and the apartment-hotel *Palazzo al Velabro* (see p.232). Finally, sites like ⓦ airbnb.com and ⓦ housetrip.com have excellent choices in Rome.

APARTMENT AGENCIES

At Home Via Margutta 13 ☎ 06 3212 0102, ⓦ at-home-italy.com. Your best bet for long-stay apartments and relocation services.

Cross-Pollinate ☎ 06 9936 9799, ⓦ cross-pollinate.com. The owners of *The Beehive* (see p.234) also run this fab apartment-booking service with properties in the major cities of Italy and around Europe. Not surprisingly, they're big on Rome, and have a wide variety of different-sized places all over the city, at a range of prices. Above all, they're nice people, with a strong focus on customer service and satisfaction.

Go2Rome Viale Opita Oppio 78 ☎ 06 9784 5999, ⓦ go2rome.com. A great selection of apartments all over the city, from around €90 a night, and very flexible on length of stay, especially out of season. The website's easy to navigate too, with good last-minute offers.

GowithOh ☎ +44 203 499 5148, ⓦ gowithoh .co.uk. Great UK holiday apartment site that focuses on European cities and has a good range of properties in the centre of Rome – mostly at excellent rates.

Homes in Rome Via Ottaviano 73 ☎ 366 139 9908, ⓦ homesinrome.com. Fairly upscale apartments in the city centre, with prices starting at around €130 a night for a one-bedroom to several times that for three to four bedrooms. Has a good selection of larger options.

Landmark Trust ☎ +44 1628 825925, ⓦ landmark trust.org.uk. This charitable organization restores historic properties and rents them out as holiday lets. They have a number of Italian options, including the elegant third-floor apartment of the Keats-Shelley House (see p.94), right by the Spanish Steps, and Sant'Antonio, a six-room former monastery just outside Tivoli, built over a Roman villa believed to have belonged to the poet Horace.

from pinball machines. Breakfast isn't provided but there's a kitchen and large terrace for guests' use. About 20min by bus from the centre. Dorms €30, doubles €70
★**Yellow** Via Palestro 44, Termini ☎06 4938 2682, ⊛the-yellow.com; map p.114. *The Yellow* is hands-down central Rome's best hostel if you're looking to make new friends. There are various types of dorm on offer, from the

dirt-cheap "Backpacker" to the comfier "Flashpacker", plus en-suite private rooms, some with their own kitchen. Self-consciously cool, the hostel encourages a lively scene in the downstairs bar, open day and night, with cheap drinks and regular pub crawls organized, so if you're after somewhere quiet you might want to look elsewhere. Dorms €23, doubles €95

CONVENTS

14

Rome has lots of accommodation run by **religious organizations**. Many are no longer as cheap as they used to be, and hotel websites often have the better bargains, but they can often be found in central locations (see ⊛monasterystays.com for more). Bear in mind that most have strict rules about curfews and often a single-gender policy.

Casa di Santa Brigida Piazza Farnese 96, around Campo de' Fiori ☎06 6889 2596, ⊛brigidine.org; map p.50. In a hard-to-beat location, and with clean and comfortable rooms with private bathroom and no curfew, this is perhaps the best convent in town. It's not cheap, although breakfast is included. They also have a sister residence that costs less, north of the centre at Via delle Isole 34 (☎06 841 4393), near Via Nomentana and Santa Costanza. €150

Casa Santa Lucia Filippini Largo Santa Lucia Filippini 20, Centro Storico ☎06 679 1612, ⊛gliarchi piazzavenezia.it; map p.50. In an excellent location, a stone's throw from the Pantheon, this is a city-centre bargain, though the midnight curfew might not appeal to night owls. The rooms are clean and spacious, if a little spartan, and fresh fruit, tea and coffee are available all day. €140

CAMPING

For those determined to sleep outdoors, there are a few **campsites** – unsurprisingly, some way out of the city. However, they are easy enough to get to and also offer bungalows. Bear in mind they are only open from spring to early autumn.

Camping Fabulous Via Cristoforo Colombo km18, Acilia ☎06 525 9354, ⊛camping.it/lazio/fabulous; map p.213. Set just off Via Cristoforo Colombo, the main road down to the sea, this campsite can be a bit noisy, but the setting is great – shaded by majestic umbrella pines and with a pool, tennis courts, mini-golf and other facilities. If you arrive by bus, come during the day, as the bus stop is a bit isolated and might be tricky in the dark. Take metro line B to EUR Fermi and then bus #709. Tent pitch €10 plus €11.50 per adult, bungalows €95
Camping Tiber Via Tiberina Km1400 ☎06 3361 0733, ⊛campingtiber.com; map p.213. This campsite, right beside the Tiber, is quiet, spacious and friendly, with a supermarket, bar/pizzeria, swimming pool and really hot showers. It has some 100 bungalows, with bath and without, as well as three camping areas. Take the

Roma-Nord train from Piazzale Flaminio (about 20min), then a free shuttle bus (8am–noon & 4–11pm; 10min) from the nearby Prima Porta station. Tent pitch €10 plus €10.50 per person, double bungalow with bath €80
Plus Camping Roma Via Aurelia 831 ☎06 662 3018, ⊛plushostels.com; map p.213. Aimed squarely at young backpackers, this site has tents that can be booked for private groups of up to three, or as a dorm, with beds booked individually. All linen is included, so there's no need for a sleeping bag. Private rooms and bungalows are also available, and there's a pool, jacuzzi, bar, restaurant, cinema, and regular trips and parties. It's a 30–45min trip from town: take metro A to Cipro, then bus #247, or there's a shuttle bus from the metro, as well as a shuttle from the airports (both April–Oct). Tent per person €1, bungalows €55, chalets €60

CAFFÈ DI MARZIO, TRASTEVERE

Eating

Rome is undeniably a major-league city, though it doesn't compare to London or Paris for cutting-edge trendiness, which can be bad news for nightlife, but it's great news for food. The city is changing, to be sure – that wonderful, cheap, traditional trattoria serving high-quality authentic Roman cuisine has become a bit harder to find in the last decade or so, and eating out as a whole has become pricier. But food remains one of the highlights of any trip to the city, and, as long as you choose carefully, you're unlikely to be disappointed with either the quality on offer or the choice.

Most city-centre restaurants offer standard Italian dishes, and many specialize purely in **Roman cuisine** (see box, p.244), but a few more adventurous places have been cropping up of late. Being at the geographical centre of the country, the capital has numerous establishments dedicated to a variety of **regional cuisines** (see box, p.251) and a reasonable number of **ethnic restaurants** (see box, p.253). The city is also blessed with an abundance of decent **pizzerias** (see box, p.263), churning out thin, crispy-baked pizza from wood-fired ovens, as well as loads of good **bars and cafés**, where you can get a sandwich and sometimes a full meal, and there's a **gelateria** on every corner selling good ice cream (see box, p.247). For something a bit different, consider eating at an **enoteca** (wine bar; see box, p.267), where you can sample wines accompanied by platters of cold meats, cheeses and often hot food. If you want to cut costs and hang out with the cool people, you could try one of the many places offering a "free" *aperitivo* buffet with a drink on weekday evenings – we've detailed a few on p.268, but they're also listed throughout the text.

Most Italians start their day in a bar, their **breakfast** consisting of a cappuccino and a *cornetto* – a glazed or jam-, custard- or chocolate-filled croissant, sweeter than the French variety. **Sandwiches** (panini) can be pretty substantial and are served throughout the day for €3–5; bars also offer *tramezzini*, ready-made sliced white bread with mixed fillings – generally less appetizing than panini but still popular and slightly cheaper at around €2–3 a time. Don't forget that **bakeries** and **delis** are also great places to pick up a spot of lunch (see p.296). We also have information on **food markets** (see box, p.302) and city-centre **supermarkets** (see box, p.296).

15

For hot **takeaway food**, **pizza** is the obvious choice; it's sold by the slice (*pizza al taglio*) pretty much everywhere. Expect to pay about €3 for a decent-sized portion, a bit more for higher-quality ingredients at smarter places like *Pizzarium* (see p.264). A **rosticceria** (literally a "roaster", specializing in roasted meat, particularly chicken), or **tavolacalda** (literally "hot table", an informal, usually self-service restaurant or café that serves affordable hot food at lunchtime) is a reliable bet for Roman specialities – *supplì* or *arancini* (deep-fried rice balls), *filetti di baccalà* (pieces of battered cod) and other deep-fried delights, as well as roast potatoes and rotisserie chickens. A complete meal for two at one of these places can cost less than €20, and although they're usually standing-only, some have a counter and a few chairs. Otherwise, **prices** in all but the really swanky places remain pretty uniform throughout the city, as do set menus, especially in traditional Roman restaurants. In an average trattoria, a substantial meal – an antipasto or a pasta dish, plus main course, dessert and house wine – will set you back €30–45 a head, and you can spend much less.

Good websites and blogs for additional restaurant recommendations include ⓦparlafood.com, ⓦracheleats.wordpress.com and ⓦheartrome.com.

CAFÉS AND BARS

There isn't a big difference between **cafés** and **bars** in Rome. Italian bars are typically open from 7am for breakfast and remain open for coffee, tea and snacks throughout the day, closing between 8pm and midnight. Bars do serve alcohol (see p.267) but are rarely places to linger over a drink. We've listed those places where you might like to spend an evening in the following chapter. An establishment calling itself a café is more likely to have seating and be a little less functional than the standard Roman bar, the sort of place you might want to have lunch but probably not dinner. Note that many cafés and bars are closed during part or all of **August**.

RIP-OFF FOOD

In the past decade or so, truly bad food and rip-off prices have become more commonplace in Rome. With this in mind, it may be wise to avoid places that are adjacent to some major monuments such as the Pantheon, Piazza Navona or the Vatican, especially those that usher people in from the street or hand out fliers. The food in these places can be poor, and the prices outlandish, sometimes as much as three times the going rate when invented service charges are added on.

15

BAR ETIQUETTE

It's important to be aware of the procedure when you enter an Italian bar. It's cheapest to drink standing at the counter (there's often nowhere to sit anyway), in which case you pay first at the cash desk (*cassa*), present your receipt (*scontrino*) to the bar person and give your order. It's customary to leave an extra 10c coin on the counter as a tip for each beverage, although no one will object if you don't. If there's waiter service, just sit where you like, though bear in mind that this will cost perhaps twice as much – and often quite a bit more – especially if you sit outside (*fuori*); the difference is usually shown on the price list as a *tavola* (table). You can, however, sit for as long as you like.

DRINKS

Coffee and tea Coffee is generally very good, drunk small and black (espresso, or just *caffè*; €0.80–1 when taken at the counter) or as a cappuccino (€1.20–1.50). If you want your espresso watered down, ask for a *caffè americano*; a *caffè lungo* is an espresso left to run a little longer. Coffee with a shot of alcohol is *caffè corretto*; with a drop of milk,

it's *caffè macchiato*; a full small cup of the same is *caffè macchiato lungo*. Many places also now sell decaffeinated coffee (ask for the brand "Café Hag", even when it isn't), while in summer you might want to have your coffee cold (*caffè freddo*). For a real treat, ask for *granita di caffè* – cold coffee with crushed ice, usually topped with cream. In summer, you can drink iced tea (*tè freddo*) – excellent for taking the heat off; hot tea (*tè caldo*) comes with lemon (*con limone*), unless you ask for milk (*con latte*). Milk itself is rarely drunk on its own; you can get warm milk with a dash of coffee (*latte macchiato* or *caffè latte*) and sometimes as milk shakes – *frappe* or *frullati*.

Soft drinks A *spremuta* is a fresh fruit juice, squeezed at the bar, usually orange, but sometimes lemon or grapefruit. There are also crushed-ice *granitas*, offered in several flavours, and available with or without whipped cream (*panna*) on top. Otherwise, there's the usual range of fizzy drinks and concentrated juices; the home-grown Italian version of Coca-Cola, Chinotto, is less sweet and works well with a slice of lemon.

Water Tap water (*acqua del rubinetto*) is quite drinkable,

CUCINA ROMANA

Rome is rightly proud of its own cuisine (*cucina Romana*), and has numerous restaurants serving **local specialities** to a clientele that would be satisfied with nothing less. Roman cooking is dominated by the earthy preferences of the working classes, with a little influence from the city's millennia-old Jewish population thrown in. Pasta is a staple, and sauces are hearty and satisfying, while meat dishes famously lean towards various unspeakable parts of cows and lambs. You can eat Roman cuisine all over the city centre, but there are some restaurants that do the classics better than anywhere else: Roman-Jewish specialities like *carciofi alla giudia* ("Jewish-style artichokes"), or the meat and offal dishes typical of Testaccio such as *coda alla vaccinara* (oxtail stew) and *pajata* (calf's intestine). And some places excel at all three. A glossary of **food and drink terms** is given later in the Guide (see p.336).

PASTA

The most popular varieties of pasta are **tonnarelli** or **bucatini** – thick, hollow spaghetti, basically – which stand up well to the coarse, gutsy **sauces** the Romans prefer: *cacio e pepe* (pecorino and ground black pepper); *alla carbonara* (with beaten eggs, cubes of pan-fried *guanciale* – cured pork jowl – or pancetta, and pecorino cheese); *alla gricia* (with pecorino and *guanciale*); and *all'amatriciana* (with tomato and *guanciale*). Spaghetti *alle vongole* (with baby clams) is also common, best when a little *peperoncino* is added to give it an extra kick, and *maccheroni alla ciociara*, with slices of sausage, prosciutto and tomato is another favourite. Pasta *al la pajata* (with calf's intestines) is an old Roman standard, as are **gnocchi**, in Rome usually served with a meat sauce and traditionally eaten on Thursdays.

MAIN COURSES

The classic Roman meat dish is *abbacchio*, milk-fed **lamb** roasted to melting tenderness with rosemary, sage and garlic; you'll also find it *allo scottadito* – grilled and eaten with the fingers. *Saltimbocca alla romana*, thin slices of **veal** cooked with a slice of prosciutto and sage on top, is ever popular. Otherwise, Roman meat dishes are defined by the so-called *quinto quarto* (fifth quarter) of the animal: basically **offal**, which you'll still find on the menus of traditional places, especially those in the old slaughterhouse district of Testaccio. One of the most palatable dishes is *coda alla vaccinara*, oxtail stewed in a rich sauce of tomato and celery. You'll also come across *pajata* (the intestines of an unweaned calf – a very Roman speciality), as well as

and you won't pay for it in a bar. Mineral water (*acqua minerale*) is a more common choice, either still (*liscia* or *naturale*) or sparkling (*con gas* or *frizzante*) – about €1.50 for a small bottle.

RESTAURANTS AND PIZZERIAS

There are good restaurants in the **Centro Storico**, though one needs to know where to look; that said, with a little research it's still surprisingly easy to find places that are not tourist traps. The **Tridente** and around **Campo de' Fiori** are similarly well served, and the neighbouring **Ghetto** is full of appealing restaurants (kosher and non) serving traditional Roman-Jewish cuisine. Until recently, the area around **Termini** had a reputation for being packed with cheap yet dubious places to eat, but the new Mercato Centrale is doing much to challenge this. This multi-level food hall caters for all tastes and budgets. North of Termini, the nearby student area of **San Lorenzo** is also a great option for cheap and simple but quality eats. South of the centre, **Testaccio** is well endowed with decent, moderately priced trattorias, a few serving the best of Rome's offal specialities, while across the river, **Trastevere** is Rome's traditional restaurant enclave and is accordingly thronged with eating options – and people. The result is that the number of authentic trattorias in the area has declined over recent years, but you can still find good – and often great – meals here, at all price levels.

THE MENU

Antipasto and starters/pasta An Italian meal traditionally starts with the antipasto (literally "before the meal"), consisting of various cold cuts of meat, cheeses or vegetable dishes. A plateful of antipasti from a self-service buffet will cost from about €10 a head depending on the

restaurant; an item chosen from the menu will be around the same. Bear in mind that, if you're moving on to pasta, let alone a main course, you may need quite an appetite to tackle this. The next course, *il primo*, consists of a soup or pasta dish, and it's fine to eat just this and nothing else; pasta dishes go for around €8–12 (though pricey places

15

lingua (tongue), *rognone* (kidney), *milza* (spleen – delicious as a pâté on toasted bread) and *trippa* (tripe). Look out too for *testerelle d'abbacchio* (lamb's head baked in an oven with herbs and oil) and *coratella* (lamb's heart, liver, lungs and spleen cooked in olive oil with lots of black pepper and onions). More conventionally, **fish** also features, usually as cod (*baccalà*), and best eaten Jewish-style, deep-fried in batter – like British fish and chips, but without the chips, and sometimes eaten as a starter or snack.

PIZZA, SNACKS AND FRITTI

Rome is surpassed only by Naples in the quality of its **pizzas**, and even this is arguable if you prefer the thin and crispy Roman variety, best when baked in a wood-burning oven (*forno a legna*). Other Roman street food includes various deep-fried specialities, or **fritti**, like *supplì* (fried rice balls with mozzarella), *arancini* (*supplì* with added tomato), as well as **spit-roast** chicken and *porchetta* – pork stuffed with herbs and roasted on a spit; you'll find the latter most commonly in the Castelli Romani, where it's munched between thick hunks of rustic bread.

VEGETABLES

Artichokes (*carciofi*) are the quintessential Roman vegetable, best in late winter and early spring, either served *alla romana* (stuffed with garlic and Roman mint and stewed) or *alla giudia*, flattened and deep-fried in olive oil. Another not-to-be-missed side dish is **fiori di zucca** (batter-fried courgette blossoms stuffed with mozzarella and a sliver of anchovy). Among **other vegetables**, you can find heavenly roast potatoes cooked with rosemary and served with lamb or chicken; great fresh asparagus in spring; *puntarelle* (chicory salad) and various broccoli-like greens in winter; and haricot and borlotti bean dishes year-round.

CHEESE AND DESSERTS

The king of Roman cheeses is **pecorino romano**, sharp, salty and crumbly and used in cooking instead of parmesan. The very best **buffalo mozzarella** from Campania has also become more common in Rome, which is close enough to Naples for it to be rushed up here and eaten fresh.

As for desserts, you may want to try a **tartufo** – chocolate ice cream covered in chocolate, basically – or just have an ice cream on its own: the city centre's **gelaterie** are among the country's best, and there's nothing like enjoying your dessert Italian-style, strolling through the streets after the sun has gone down; we've listed our pick of the best (see box, p.247).

15

will charge more).

Main courses *Il secondo* – the meat or fish course – is usually served alone, except for perhaps a wedge of lemon, a garnish of salad or a potato or two. Watch out when ordering fish, which will either be served whole or by weight: 250g is usually plenty for one person, or ask to have a look at the fish before it's cooked. Main fish or meat courses will normally be €12–20 (more only in the smartest restaurants). Vegetarians will find plenty of options: many pasta dishes and pizzas, of course, are made entirely without meat; lentils and other beans and pulses are a part of traditional cookery; and wonderful fresh vegetables and cheeses are always available. Side dishes – *contorni* – are ordered and served separately, and sometimes there won't be much choice: potatoes will often come roasted (*patate arroste*) or as chips (*patatine fritte*); salads are either green (*verde*) or mixed (*mista*).

Desserts After *il secondo*, you nearly always get a choice of *frutta* (fresh fruit) and a selection of *dolci* (desserts) – sometimes just ice cream, but often more elaborate items such as *zuppa inglese* (sponge cake or trifle). Many Italians wouldn't dream of going out to eat and not ordering a full five-course meal, plus wine, mineral water, coffee and a *digestivo* such as an *amaro* (home-made herb liqueur) – but don't feel you have to follow suit; you can order as little

or as much as you want, and no one will raise an eyebrow. Sharing courses between two is also perfectly acceptable. There are tips on what to drink later in the Guide (see p.267).

OPENING HOURS AND THE BILL

Opening hours Roman restaurants keep pretty rigid opening hours, generally from 12.30pm to 2.30 or 3pm and from 7.30pm to 11pm, although some stay open later, especially in summer, and bear in mind that last orders are likely to be a little bit earlier. Many places are closed for two or more weeks in August, sometimes the entire month (though less than in the past). We have specified after each listing where this is the case, but it is often worth double checking – restaurants' holiday plans are rarely written in stone. It's always an idea to book a table, particularly in more popular spots and towards the weekend.

The bill Getting the bill (*il conto*) can sometimes be a struggle – nothing moves fast in Rome when it comes to mealtimes. Almost everywhere adds a cover charge of around €2 a head; on your bill it will either be labelled as "*coperto*" or "*pane*". Service should not be an additional charge but included in prices; tipping is not required, but rounding up the bill by a few euros is common practice.

CENTRO STORICO

CAFÉS AND BARS

Boulangerie MP Via di Panico 6 ☎ 06 9357 7230; map p.36. When Roman baker Matteo Piras opened his first shop close to the French embassy his flair for French baking quickly had diplomats beating a path to his door for fantastic baguettes and croissants, while savvy politicians wandered over from Parliament to seek his creative panini or grab a slice of pizza. In 2015, he moved towards the river (just across from Castel Sant'Angelo) to a new location with more seating. Most of the food and ingredients are organic, and there are always tasty vegan options, as well as traditional Italian and wholegrain breads. Mon–Wed 8.30am–7.30pm, Thurs–Sat 8.30am–1.30am, Sun 10am–4pm.

★**Caffè Sant'Eustachio** Piazza Sant'Eustachio 82 ☎ 06 6880 2048, ⓦ santeustachioilcaffe.it; map p.36. Just behind the Pantheon you'll find what many believe is Rome's best coffee, usually served very sweet. You can ask for it "*amaro*" if you'd prefer it without sugar. They also do a good line in coffee-based sweets and cakes. Daily 8.30am–1am, Fri till 1.30am, Sat till 2am.

Chiostro del Bramante Via Arco della Pace 5 ☎ 06 6880 90 35, ⓦ chiostrodelbramante.it; map p.36. This *caffetteria*-bistro is an atmospheric and rather stylish hideaway located on the first-floor loggia of a historic fifteenth-century palace (the Raphael fresco in the adjacent church dates to about 1515; see p.45). A great

venue for breakfast, lunch (salads, risottos), cakes and *aperitivi* at reasonable prices, and it's open even when there are no exhibitions on. The food is fine, but the location is exquisite. Mon–Fri 10am–8pm, Sat & Sun 10am–9pm; lunch served 11.30am–3pm.

La Caffetteria Piazza di Pietra 65 ☎ 06 679 8147, ⓦ lacaffettieraroma.it; map p.36. Bureaucrats flock to this Neapolitan café from the nearby Parliament: the pastries are imported from Naples daily, and the espresso is among Rome's best. Good for lunch, too, with pasta dishes, quiches and suchlike for around €12 and up. Tables outside offer a charming view of the Corinthian columns of an old Roman temple (see p.39). Mon–Sat 7.30am–9pm, Sun 9am–9pm.

La Cucina del Teatro Via di San Simone 70 ☎ 06 4547 4880; map p.36. On a charming cul-de-sac off the picturesque Via dei Coronari, this takeaway has *supplì* and pizza by the slice and quick and tasty pasta dishes and main courses, with organic wine and beer to go with it. There are a few tables outside at no extra charge (though there's no toilet). Standards have slipped since pizza maestro Gabriele Bonci left the partnership, but it's still better than average for the area, and the location is super. Daily 10am–10pm.

Lo Zozzone Via del Teatro Pace 32 ☎ 06 6880 8575; map p.36. This Roman legend, just around the corner from Piazza Navona and with seating both outside and in, serves *pizza bianca* filled with whatever you want, as well as lots of delicious *pizza al taglio* choices. Daily 10am–9pm, Sat & Sun till 11pm; closed Sun Oct–March.

Pascucci Via di Torre Argentina 20 ☎06 686 4816, ⓦpascuccifrullati.it; map p.36. This small, stand-up bar is *frullati* central: your choice of fresh fruit whipped up with ice and milk – the ultimate Roman refreshment on a hot

ICE CREAM

Italian **ice cream** (*gelato*) is justifiably famous. However, there is a big difference between the artisanal kind made in the traditional way with wholesome natural ingredients and the highly coloured, industrial pap that is increasingly available across the city centre, so be sure to choose carefully and when in doubt look for the words "*artigianale di produzione proprio*" or "*gelato artigianale*". You should reckon on paying around €2 for a cone (*un cono*) filled with one or two flavours (*gusti*), the price rising with each flavour you add. Most bars have a fairly mediocre selection, so for real choice go to a proper **gelateria**, where the range is a tribute to the Italian imagination and flair for display; our favourites are below.

★**Fatamorgana** Piazza degli Zingari 5, Monti ☎06 4890 6955, ⓦgelateriafatamorgana.com; map p.114. Undoubtedly one of the top *gelaterie* in Rome, *Fatamorgana* serves up scoops of creative and seasonal flavours; look out for the one-of-a-kind "Kentucky" – chocolate with tobacco. There are other branches in Piazza San Cosimato in Trastevere (☎06 580 3615), on Via Laurina near Piazza del Popolo (☎06 3625 2238) and on Via Leone IV near the Vatican Museums (☎06 3751 9093). Mon–Thurs & Sun noon–midnight, Fri & Sat noon–1am.

Fior di Luna Via della Lungaretta 96, Trastevere ☎06 6456 1314 ⓦfiordiluna.com; map p.160. Seasonality, invention and fair trade are the buzz words at this Trastevere establishment. If you're feeling adventurous try the donkey-milk *gelati*. Mon–Fri 11.30am–11pm, Sat & Sun 11.30am–midnight.

Gelateria dei Gracchi Via dei Gracchi 272, Prati ☎06 321 6668, ⓦgelateriadeigracchi.it; map p.188. This unassuming place is the most popular *gelateria* in Prati, with a small but choice range of flavours, such as hazelnut, pistachio and melon. Daily noon–12.30am.

★**Gelateria del Teatro** Via dei Coronari 65, Centro Storico ☎06 4547 4880; map p.36. The *laboratorio* is on view at this *gelateria*, so you can watch the ice cream being made while you decide what to have. Traditional flavours are executed with great panache, while equally tempting are the more exotic flavours such as rosemary, honey and lemon, and strawberry sorbet with champagne. Unusually for central Rome, there is seating both inside and out at no extra charge. A second branch can be found by the Tiber at Lungotevere dei Vallati, near Ponte Garibaldi (☎06 9436 6517). Daily 10.30am–midnight.

Giolitti Via degli Uffici del Vicario 40, Centro Storico ☎06 699 1243, ⓦgiolitti.it; map p.36. An Italian institution, always very busy, with a choice of seventy flavours. It once had a reputation – now lost – for the country's best ice cream, but is still decent. Daily 7am–1am.

★**Il Gelato di Claudio Torcè** Viale Aventino 59,

Aventine ☎06 574 6876, ⓦilgelatodiclaudiotorce .com; map p.140. One of eight outlets serving the outstanding ice cream of Claudio Torcè, founder of the city's natural *gelato* movement. Flavours range from classic hazelnut and chocolate to the more obscure habanero pepper and black sesame. The other centrally located shop is near the Vatican, at Piazza Risorgimento 51 (☎06 9788 2939). Daily 11am–10pm.

★**Palazzo del Freddo di Giovanni Fassi** Via Principe Eugenio 65/67a, Esquiline ☎06 446 4740, ⓦgelateriafassi.com; map p.114. "Fassi" is the place to see the Roman consume *gelato* in his natural habitat. This huge old-school ice-cream parlour is a piece of Roman cultural history and has been doing business since 1880. It's no longer the best in town, but is still a solid choice. Mon–Thurs noon–midnight, Fri & Sat noon–12.30am, Sun 10am–midnight.

★**Punto Gelato** Via dei Pettinari 43 ☎06 6839 5030; ⓦgunthergelatoitaliano.com; map p.36. Gunther Rohregger, from the Alto Adige, creates unique and organic ice creams. All the ingredients are carefully selected, from the Piedmont hazelnuts to the water that comes from the Italian Alps. The classics are great, but go for something adventurous such as buffalo milk and pink peppercorns, or alpine milk and pine-tree essence. There is a second outlet near the Pantheon in Piazza Sant' Eustachio (☎06 6880 8292). Mon–Sat 10am–2am, Sun 10am–midnight.

★**San Crispino** Via della Panetteria 42, Trevi ☎06 679 3924, ⓦilgelatodisancrispino.com; map p.91. Near the Trevi Fountain, this place was once considered to make the best ice cream in Rome. They've slipped in recent years, but still do interesting flavours such as ginger and cinnamon, and their meringue is stellar. There are other branches at Piazza Maddalena 3, right by the Pantheon (☎06 8781 1582), at Via Acaia 56 in San Giovanni (☎06 7045 0412), and in Terminal 1 at Fiumicino airport (☎06 6576 0626). Mon–Thurs & Sun 11am–12.30am, Fri & Sat 11am–1.30am.

15

day – although it does coffee and all the usual bar stuff, too. Daily 6am–midnight.

Tazza d'Oro Via degli Orfani 84 ☎06 678 9792, ⊛tazzadorocoffeeshop.com; map p.36. Just a few paces from the Pantheon, *Tazza d'Oro* ("Golden Cup") is well named, since it is by common consent the home of one of Rome's best cups of coffee, and also serves decent iced coffee and sinfully rich *granita di caffè*, with double dollops of whipped cream. Tasty pastries and sandwiches are available too. Mon–Sat 7am–8pm, Sun 10.30am–7.15pm.

Vitti Piazza San Lorenzo in Lucina 33 ☎06 687 6304, ⊛vitti.it; map p.36. A Roman institution, serving a wide selection of pastries and sandwiches, along with delicious coffee; there are a few tables inside and lots on the (very chic) square. A short lunch menu is served from 12.30pm – pasta dishes and suchlike – though it's not always the best value. Daily 6am–11pm.

RESTAURANTS

★**Armando al Pantheon** Salita de' Crescenzi 31 ☎06 6880 3034, ⊛armandoalpantheon.it; map p.36. You'll find surprisingly unpretentious surroundings and reasonably priced food in this long-standing staple close by the Pantheon (open since 1961). The menu features great Roman classic pasta dishes and main courses, from *cacio e pepe* to *saltimbocca*, *trippa alla Romana* (tripe, Roman-style, with lots of tomato sauce) and *abbacchio allo scottadito* (lamb chops). It's very popular; booking is a must. Mon–Fri 12.30–3pm & 7–11pm, Sat 12.30–3pm.

★**Casa Bleve** Via del Teatro Valle 48 ☎06 686 5970, ⊛casableve.com; map p.36. Not strictly a restaurant, more an *enoteca*, this atmospheric Renaissance hall, in the heart of the Centro Storico, is where Rome's beautiful folk come to enjoy great wine and the food to go with it. There's a huge wine list and a menu of assorted cured meats and cheeses, pastas, fish and meat courses. It's not cheap – most mains go for €18–22, and there are no wines under €25 – but the food is excellent and the service attentive and knowledgeable. There's also a wine shop out front. Tues–Sat 12.30–3pm & 7.30–11pm.

Da Alfredo e Ada Via dei Banchi Nuovi 14 ☎06 687 8842; map p.36. A tiny, long-established restaurant that used to be the domain of the formidable Ada and continues her tradition of serving good home-cooked food just like your Italian granny used to make. There's no menu, just three or four pasta dishes, which may include a *carbonara* or lasagne, followed by three or four hearty dishes such as veal stew with peas or chicken *cacciatore* with lots of tomatoes and herbs. The joy is, you won't know what you're going to get till you sit down. Reckon on spending around €25 for two courses including wine. Mon–Fri 12.30–3pm & 7–10.30pm; closed Aug.

Da Baffetto Via del Governo Vecchio 114 ☎06 686 1617, ⊛pizzeriabaffetto.it; map p.36. This cramped pizzeria has long been a Rome institution, though it now tends to be swamped by tourists. Nevertheless, it's still good value, with pizzas from €6. It has tables outside in summer, although you will always have to queue. Another branch – *Baffetto 2* (☎06 6821 0807) – is on Piazza del Teatro di Pompeo near Campo de' Fiori. Wed–Mon noon–3.30pm & 6pm–1am.

Da Francesco Piazza del Fico 29 ☎06 686 4009 ⊛dafrancesco.it; map p.36. You'll get not just delectable pizzas in this full-on pizzeria in the heart of the Centro Storico, but good antipasti, *primi* and *secondi*, too. The service can be slapdash, but the food is decent and the atmosphere second to none. A two-course dinner with wine costs around €25 a head. Daily noon–3.30pm & 7pm–12.30am.

★**Da Gino al Parlamento** Vicolo Rosini 4 ☎06 687 3434, ⊛ristoranteparlamento.roma.it; map p.36. Down a small alley right by the Parliament building, Gino presides over his constantly bustling restaurant with unhurried authority, serving a determinedly traditional Roman menu at keen prices – pasta dishes €8, mains €9–10. Try the house speciality – *tonnarelli ciociara*, with peas, mushrooms and ham – and top it off with the excellent *saltimbocca alla romana*. It's been very much discovered by tourists, but at heart it remains a locals' joint. No credit cards. Mon–Sat 1–3pm & 8–10.30pm.

★**Da Tonino** Via del Governo Vecchio 18/19 ☎333 587 0779; map p.36. Basic Roman food, always freshly cooked, and always delicious, is the order of the day at this unmarked Centro Storico favourite. It's a little more upmarket than it once was, but still serves the same simple Roman pasta dishes for around €6–8 and main courses for €8–10. The few tables fill up quickly, so come early or be prepared to queue. No credit cards. Mon–Sat noon–3pm & 7pm–midnight.

Enoteca al Parlamento Achilli Via dei Prefetti 15 ☎06 687 3446 ⊛enotecalparlamento.com; map p.360. Located in the very heart of the city, Massimo Viglietti's one-Michelin-star *Enoteca al Parlamento Achilli* is practically a household name among Romans. This isn't

15

TEN TRADITIONAL ROMAN RESTAURANTS

Armando al Pantheon See above
Checchino dal 1887 See p.260
Da Alfredo e Ada See p.248
Da Tonino See p.248
Flavio al Velavevodetto See p.260
Matricianella See opposite
Nonna Betta See p.251
Piperno See p.251
Pommidoro See p.258
Trattoria Lilli See opposite

your conventional fine-dining establishment; every thirty days the menu has a complete overhaul, which keeps dining at this historic, family-run restaurant fun, dynamic and full of surprises. The front part of the restaurant is a wine bar (over 6000 labels), and wine and other gourmet products are also for sale. Main courses from around €30. Daily noon–11.30pm.

Enoteca Corsi Via del Gesù 87/88 ☎06 679 0821, ⓦenotecacorsi.com; map p.36. Tucked away between Piazza Venezia and the Pantheon, this is an old-fashioned Roman trattoria and wine shop where you eat what they happen to have cooked that morning. The menu changes each day, and it gets very busy at lunchtimes; you may have to wait for a table. The food is solid and pretty cheap – €8 for a pasta dish, €10 or so for a main course. Mon–Sat noon–3pm, Thurs & Fri 7–10.30pm; closed Aug.

Il Bacaro Via degli Spagnoli 27 ☎06 687 2554, ⓦilbacaroroma.com; map p.36. This tiny restaurant tucked away down a small side street has a small, focused menu featuring an interesting selection of antipasti and pasta dishes (€14–18) and mostly meaty mains, particularly beef (€22–24). The feel of the place is quite romantic, though it's too cramped for a truly private tête-à-tête. Daily noon–midnight.

La Montecarlo Vicolo Savelli 13 ☎06 686 1877, ⓦlamontecarlo.it; map p.36. This busy pizzeria not far from Piazza Navona is run by the daughter of the owner of *Da Baffetto* (see opposite) and serves similar crisp, blistered pizza from €6, along with heaped dishes of pasta (from €8) and decent Roman *fritti*. It does good, simple food, and there are tables outside in summer; it will always be crowded, but is pretty big, so you don't usually have to wait for a table. Service is brisk – this is not the spot for a lingering romantic supper. Tues–Sun noon–1am.

La Terrazza Bramante Hotel Raphaël, Largo Febo 2 ☎06 682 831 ⓦraphaelhotel.com; map p.36. The picturesque, secluded piazza and ivy-covered facade of the hotel *Raphaël* (see p.230) is home to *La Terrazza Bramante*, with a flower-filled roof terrace that exudes romance. The menu emphasizes organic products, and, refreshingly for a high-end hotel restaurant, the focus is on vegetables and fish – saffron risotto, vegetable *carbonara* and a good aubergine *parmigiana*. *Primi* €16–18, *secondi* €18–24 – not bad for food and surroundings of this quality. Daily 12.30–2.30pm & 7–10pm.

Maccheroni Piazza delle Coppelle 44 ☎06 6830 7895, ⓦristorantemaccheroni.com; map p.36. This friendly restaurant enjoys a wonderful location right in the heart of the Centro Storico, a stone's throw from the Pantheon. Inside, it's plainly decorated yet comfortable, with marble-topped counters and the kitchen in view, while the outside tables make the most of the pretty square. The food is basic Roman fare – not outstanding but affordably priced and cheerfully served. Daily 12.30–3pm & 7–11.30pm.

La Matricianella Via del Leone 4 ☎06 683 2100, ⓦmatricianella.it; map p.36. Handily placed just off Via del Corso, this old favourite is perhaps the best place to try real Roman food in the city centre, with classic deep-fried dishes such as *filetti di baccalà* and various vegetable *fritti*, as well as traditional Roman pasta dishes such as *cacio e pepe*, and a great wine list. You can eat in the bustling main dining room or on the outside terrace. Pasta dishes around €11, main courses €16. Mon–Sat 12.30–3pm & 7.30–11pm.

Osteria dell'Ingegno Piazza di Pietra 45 ☎06 678 0662, ⓦosteriadelingegno.com; map p.36. A relaxed bistro on a happening square, with tables outside and plenty of room within. The inventive menu breaks free from the Roman specialities you'll find elsewhere, with dishes inspired by most of the country's regions. There are variations on traditional classics like pumpkin gnocchi and *cacio e pepe* with "square" pasta, and buffalo steaks and seafood with couscous – all to a background of cool jazz. There's a wide choice of wine, too. Main courses from around €14. Daily noon–11.30pm.

Osteria del Pegno Vicolo Montevecchio 8 ☎06 6880 7025; map p.36. Set on the ground floor of a fifteenth-century *palazzo*, tucked away and hard to find, this small restaurant (just eight to ten tables) serves Roman classics – *carbonara, abbacchio al forno* – alongside earthier food from the countryside such as fettuccini with porcini mushrooms and Ischian-style rabbit (stewed in wine, tomatoes and herbs), as well as a few fish dishes such as delectable *gnocchetti* with clams. They also serve pizzas cooked in a wood-burning oven. Expect good service and prices – *primi* €8–12, *secondi* €10–13 – and a lovely location. Daily except Wed noon–3pm & 7–10.30pm.

The Perfect Bun Largo del Teatro Valle 4 ☎06 4547 6337, ⓦtheperfectbun.it; map p.36. Sometimes you just have to have a burger, and this, by Rome standards, is burger heaven. Burgers, steaks, grilled chicken and other Tex-Mexish delights are served in a vast, vaulted room on the ground floor of a Renaissance palace; seating is at a long, high table down the middle, or at more discreet tables downstairs or around the upstairs mezzanine. Burgers come with every kind of accessory and cost from about €15, although this doesn't include the stupidly priced options – one comes topped with three fried eggs, six rashers of bacon, cheese and cheesy fries. It's also a good spot for a drink, or for the Sunday brunch buffet. Daily noon–2am.

★**Trattoria Lilli** Via di Tor di Nona 23 ☎06 686 1916, ⓦtrattorialilli.it; map p.36. One of the city centre's most authentic and un-touristy trattorias, tucked away below the riverbank, on the northern edge of the Centro Storico. It serves a good selection of classic Roman staples, including a broad range of earthy pasta specials, well prepared and served with gritty Roman directness – *primi* and *secondi* for

15

€10–12. There's outside seating, too. Tues–Sat 12.30–3pm & 7.30–11pm, Sun 12.30–3pm.

Vino e Camino Piazza dell'Oro 6 ☎ 06 6830 1332, ⓦ vinoecamino.it; map p.36. This friendly restaurant has its origins in northern Lazio, and the menu is mainly meat-based, with fine-quality steaks and other grilled meats, although there are plenty of vegetarian options, such as pasta with walnut pesto. Mon 7.30–10.30pm, Tues–Sat 12.30–3pm & 7.30–10.30pm.

CAMPO DE' FIORI AND THE GHETTO

CAFÉS AND BARS

★ **Antico Forno Roscioli** Via dei Chiavari 34 ☎ 06 686 4045, ⓦ anticofornoroscioli.it; map p.50. Part of the Roscioli empire, this traditional bakery is owned by the same branch of the family who run the excellent but pricey restaurant (see opposite) and deli (see p.299) round the corner. As you might imagine, it does great bread (which it provides to some of Rome's top restaurants), delicious pizza by the slice and other savoury and sweet delights to eat either perched at the counter or to take out. Mon–Sat 7am–8pm, Sun 8.30am–7pm.

Barnum Café Via del Pellegrino 87 ☎ 06 6476 0483, ⓦ barnumcafe.com; map p.50. This friendly, circus-themed café with free wi-fi is handy for breakfast, coffee and cake or a light lunch. After dark, it's a relaxing bar (see p.268) with great cocktails, and there's a popular nightly *aperitivo* buffet. Mon–Sat 9am–2am.

Caffè Farnese Via dei Baullari 106 ☎ 06 6880 2125; map p.50. Popular with business types and beautiful young things, but actually not expensive, this café, right on Piazza Farnese, is an enjoyable place to come for breakfast or lunch, as well as evening drinks. Excellent cappuccino, *cornetti*, pizza and sandwiches. There's free seating at the window bar, but you might want to pay to sit outside on a warm evening for the view of Palazzo Farnese. Sun–Thurs 8am–11.30pm, Fri & Sat 8am–12.30am.

Caffè Peru Via di Monserrato 46 ☎ 06 687 9548; map p.50. Run by a friendly young owner, this family bar serves great coffee (some say it's the best in Rome), as well as home-made, hot lunch specials. There's also an *aperitivo* hour in the evening, when you'll pay around €8 for a small hot dish and a glass from the good selection of wines. The clientele is mixed, from local families to priests and nuns and the odd diplomat, while late evening brings young revellers spilling onto the street. Mon–Sat 6.30am–2am, Sun 9am–9pm.

Caffè Camerino Largo Arenula 30 ☎ 06 689 2166; map p.50. Conveniently located near Largo Argentina, this café has excellent coffee and mouthwatering pastries and also serves inexpensive cafeteria-style lunches and sandwiches. Mon–Sat 6.45am–8pm, Sun 8.30am–8pm.

Il Forno di Campo de' Fiori Campo de' Fiori 22 ☎ 06 6880 6662, ⓦ fornocampodefiori.com; map p.50. A great Campo bakery that's always busy with devotees. The *pizza rossa* here (with a smear of tomato sauce) and *pizza bianca* (just drizzled with olive oil on top) are Roman legends, while porcini mushrooms or mozzarella with anchovies and courgette blossoms are especially good. No seating. Mon–Sat 7.30am–2.30pm & 4.45–8pm; closed Sat pm in summer.

RESTAURANTS

Al Pompiere Via Santa Maria dei Calderari 38 ☎ 06 686 8377, ⓦ alpompiereroma.com; map p.50. Housed in a frescoed old *palazzo*, in the heart of the Ghetto, this old-fashioned restaurant exudes tradition and serves up some of the best Roman-Jewish food you'll find (especially good *fiori di zucca*) and at decent prices, too, in its busy warren of high-ceilinged rooms. The owner's delightfully eclectic wine list features her favourites, many from small wineries. Mon–Sat 12.30–3pm & 7.30–11pm.

Ar Galletto Piazza Farnese 104 ☎ 06 686 1714, ⓦ ristoranteargallettoroma.com; map p.50. Situated on one of Rome's stateliest piazzas (and just off one of its trendiest), this place offers traditional Roman cookery with a homely touch (*coda alla vaccinara* and all the pasta classics), along with other more mainstream Italian dishes. In warmer months, you can sit outside and enjoy the magnificent Renaissance square. *Primi* €10–12, *secondi* €16–22. Daily 12.30–3pm & 7.30–11pm.

Ba' Ghetto Via Portico d'Ottavia 57 ☎ 06 6889 2868, ⓦ baghetto.com; map p.50. This moderately priced meat-kosher restaurant in the middle of the Ghetto serves Roman, North African – the owners are Libyan Jews – and Middle Eastern Jewish specialities. The *börek* (cheese pie) and *shacsuca* (eggs served in a piquant tomato sauce) are particularly good, and there is another branch serving dairy-kosher food, couscous and pizzas diagonally across the street at Via Portico d'Ottavia 2a. Mon–Thurs noon–11pm, Fri noon–3pm, Sat 6–11pm, Sun 11.30am–11pm.

Baires Corso Rinascimento 1 ☎ 06 686 1293, ⓦ baires. it; map p.50. The 2013 arrival of a new pope shone a spotlight on Argentina, and on this long-running Roman mini-chain of Argentinian steakhouses, which has been a convivial fixture on the city's dining scene for a decade and more. The steaks are excellent – mostly Argentine with some Tuscan Chianina beef too – and they serve some good Argentine wines that aren't so easy to find elsewhere. Other menu options reflect their Italian location, with mainly pasta *primi*. The lunch specials are generous and popular, attracting both local families and Senate staff to the flagship city-centre location. Tues–Sun noon–3.30pm & 6.30pm–midnight.

Ditirambo Piazza della Cancelleria 74 ☎ 06 687 1626, ⓦ ristoranteditirambo.it; map p.50. In a fantastic location around the corner from the Campo de' Fiori, this restaurant offers much more than your typical tourist haven. Food is an inventive take on traditional Italian dishes and ingredients, and there are lots of vegetarian options; if you don't want to sample their more complex offerings, you can always go for their *tonnarelli cacio e pepe* (€10), which is as tasty as anywhere in the city centre. There are a few tables outside plus lots of room within, and service is breezy and bright. Mon 7–11.30pm, Tues–Sun 12.45–3.15pm & 7–11.30pm.

★**Emma** Via Monte della Farina 28 ☎ 06 6476 0475, ⓦ emmapizzeria.com; map p.50. The Roscioli clan have a hand in this great pizzeria near Campo de' Fiori. As one might imagine, the pizza (€12) is excellent, the slightly higher-than-average prices reflecting the top-notch ingredients. There are also pasta dishes and *secondi* (excellent tartare), delicious *fritti* (try the *supplì* or *fiori di zucca*) and an unusually good wine and beer list. Some outdoor seating. Daily 12.30–3pm & 7.30–11pm.

Grappolo d'Oro Piazza della Cancelleria 80 ☎ 06 689 7080, ⓦ hosteriagrappolodoro.it; map p.50. Owned and run by the same team as nearby *Ditirambo* (see above), this place is a long-running Campo favourite but remains relatively unscathed by the tourist hordes. It serves Roman cuisine in a traditional trattoria atmosphere, and is excellent value, with pasta dishes costing €9–10 and mainly meat main courses at €15–17; try the pasta with bacon and artichokes followed by roast pork. Lots of *fritti* and *baccalà* too. Daily 12.30–3pm & 6.30–11pm, closed Wed lunch.

Il Sanlorenzo Via dei Chiavari 4/5 ☎ 06 686 5097, ⓦ ilsanlorenzo.it; map p.50. Between Largo Argentina and Campo de' Fiori, this fine fish restaurant serves the freshest and most creatively prepared catch in the city centre. The sleek dining rooms attract a rather pretentious clientele, but if you can tolerate the slightly snooty atmosphere and service you will be treated to quite exceptional food such as spaghetti with sea-urchin roe and tilapia with braised fennel and saffron. Pasta *primi* €20–22, *secondi* from around €30. Mon 7.30–11pm, Tues–Fri 12.45–2.45pm & 7.30–11pm, Sat 7.30–11pm.

Nonna Betta Via del Portico d'Ottavia 16 ☎ 06 6880 6263, ⓦ nonnabetta.it; map p.50. The best kosher restaurant in the Ghetto serves all the classics of the *cucina Romana: ebraica carciofi alla giudia* (deep-fried artichokes; €5), *aliciotti con indivia* (a sort of tart of anchovies with curly endive; €10) – as well as a selection of Middle Eastern dishes such as falafel (€5) and couscous (€10–15). Daily except Tues 11am–11pm.

★**Piperno** Via Monte de' Cenci 9 ☎ 06 6880 6629, ⓦ ristorantepiperno.it; map p.50. There's perhaps no more atmospheric place to sample Roman food than at *Piperno*, tucked away on a tiny piazza. It's not cheap, and the service can be a bit snooty, but it's a lovely space and the food is great, plus there's outside seating on the secluded hill square in the summer. You'll find all the traditional Roman starters – *carciofi alla giudia*, fried *baccalà, fiori di zucca* – for around €15, pasta dishes for about the same, and mains for €25. There's a good wine list, too, with lots of decent choices from €18 a bottle. Tues–Sat 12.45–2.30pm & 7.45–10.30pm, Sun 12.45–2.30pm.

★**Roscioli** Via dei Giubbonari 21 ☎ 06 687 5287, ⓦ salumeriaroscioli.com; map p.50. Is it a deli, a wine bar or fully fledged restaurant? Actually, it's all three, and you can either just have a glass of wine (good selection) and some cheese, or go for the full menu, which has great antipasti and pasta dishes. Nothing is cheap here, and the service can be a bit high-handed, but the food is excellent – standouts include the buffalo mozzarella, *burrata* (mozzarella with cream) and the *carbonara*, which is one of the best in Rome. Basic pasta dishes start at €12, main courses can be anything from €15 to €30. Deli Mon–Sat 8.30am–8.30pm; restaurant Mon–Sat 12.30pm–midnight.

Supplizio Via dei Banchi Vecchi 143 ☎ 06 8987 1920; map p.50. Not really a restaurant, but more than a café, this place is great for street-food fans. Named for the *supplì* (deep-fried rice balls with various additions; from €3) – how every Roman matron uses up leftover risotto – *Supplizio* is the offspring of Arcangelo Dadini, whose fancy restaurant *L'Arcangelo* is across the river in Prati. The vaulted Renaissance setting is elegant, though the street-food vibe means plates are paper and there is no table service. Other fried goodies and sandwiches are also available. Mon–Thurs noon–8pm, Fri & Sat noon–3.30pm & 6.30–10.30pm.

Taverna degli Amici Piazza Margana 37 ☎ 06 6992 0637, ⓦ latavernadegliamici.net; map p.50. The outside tables at this long-established restaurant, on a quiet, lovely square, offer a decent place for lunch after the rigours of

15

TEN REGIONAL RESTAURANTS

Baia Chia (Sardinia) See p.257
Cantina Cantarini (Le Marche) See p.254
Colline Emiliane (Emilia-Romagna) See p.256
Dal Bolognese (Emilia-Romagna) See p.253
Dal Toscano (Tuscany) See p.264
Palatium (Lazio) See p.254
Piccolo Abruzzo (Abruzzo) See p.256
Tajut (Friuli) See p.259
Tram Tram (Puglia) See p.258
Trattoria Monti (Le Marche) See p.258

15

SUMMER DINING AND ENTERTAINMENT BY THE TIBER

Summer brings all manner of **taverns** out along the **Tiber River**, pop-up places that set up on the embankment between early June and early September, and are generally good quality and value; look out for the pointy tent tops that line the riverbanks. On **Isola Tiberina** – a splendid location, cool and refreshing by the river rapids, even on a hot, sticky night – **L'Isola del Cinema** (ⓦisoladelcinema.com; see box, p.281) shows open-air movies (at least two nightly), and, sometimes, a region of Italy or an embassy will set up a booth for a night or two to promote travel and culture, or a free jazz concert will pop up.

---

the Forum or Ghetto, and are an atmospheric spot for dinner, too. The menu is relatively unadventurous, but there are lots of Roman classics, as well as less obvious options. Prices are moderate and the food decent – pasta dishes €12, mains €15–20 – but really, it's the location you pay for here. Tues–Sun 12.30–3pm & 7.30–11pm.

Vecchia Roma Piazza Campitelli 18 ☏06 686 4604, ⓦristorantevecchiaroma.com; map p.50. Located on a peaceful square on the fringe of the Ghetto, but a much slicker experience than the earthy Jewish restaurants of that neighbourhood, this traditional Roman restaurant has a lovely terrace and frescoed interior perfect for a special night out. It can be quite pricey, but the antipasto table is usually loaded and can be good value – just watch out for extras. Expect great fish and seafood, too, and top pasta dishes all-round. *Primi* €13–18, *secondi* €20–22. Daily except Wed 12.30–3pm & 8–11pm.

PIAZZA VENEZIA AND THE CAPITOLINE HILL

RESTAURANT

Terra e Domus – Enoteca della Provincia di Roma Largo di Foro di Traiano 82 ☏06 6994 0273; map p.61. The Provincia di Roma's wine bar reopened in late 2014 and is now run by folk from the very successful *Osteria Lotto* north of Rome. It's in a great location beside Trajan's Column and does a brisk lunch business serving government bureaucrats from the surrounding office buildings. The focus is on local ingredients, and the short menu features traditional and seasonal dishes. Unusually, it's open all day, from breakfast through to supper, so you won't need to curtail your visit to the ruins for fear of missing lunch. Daily 7.30am–12.30am.

THE TRIDENTE AND TREVI

CAFÉS AND BARS

Antico Caffè Greco Via Condotti 86 ☏06 679 1700, ⓦanticocaffegreco.eu; map p.91. Founded in 1760, and patronized by Casanova, Byron, Goethe and Stendhal, among others, this is nowadays a bit of a tourist joint, but Romans still use the stand-up area in the front. It is for curiosity value only, although the *granita di caffè* (iced coffee) is a hit on a hot summer's day. Daily 9am–9pm.

Babington's Tea Rooms Piazza di Spagna 23 ☏06 678 6027, ⓦbabingtons.com; map p.91. In business for over a hundred years, *Babington's* serves light lunches and English teatime delicacies such as scones with jam. It is extremely expensive – from €10 for a pot of tea for one, €22 for a burger, €29 for a full English breakfast – but very handy, has a great selection of teas and serves Sunday brunch, too. Daily 10am–9.30pm.

Buccone Via di Ripetta 19/20 ☏06 361 2154, ⓦwww .enotecabuccone.com; map p.91. One of the best places for lunch in the Tridente/Piazza del Popolo area, with lots of tables laid out amid its bottle-lined shelves (see p.296), a separate room out the back and a menu that changes daily. You can eat as much or little as you like – a salad or cold-cut platter (€8–10), a simple slice of *torta rustica* (savoury tart) or *aubergine parmigiana*, or one of the hot daily specials of pasta and meat courses (€7–10) – plus the wine list is very wide-ranging, with lots of choices by the glass. Mon–Sat 12.30–3pm & 7.30–11.30pm.

Museo-Atelier Canova-Tadolini Via del Babuino 150a ☏06 3211 0702, ⓦcanovatadolini.com; map p.91. It's a bit odd eating among the grand sculptures of this café-cum-museum (see p.96), and it's certainly not cheap, but it's very handy and provides one of the few places to sit down along this busy street, plus it serves decent sandwiches, salads and simple pasta dishes, as well as a few hot mains. There are a few outside tables, too, from which you can watch the designer bags bustle by. Bar daily 8am–midnight; food served noon–11pm.

RESTAURANTS

Alla Rampa Piazza Mignanelli 18 ☏06 678 2621, ⓦallarampa.com; map p.91. An unashamedly touristy joint, but it has a good-value antipasti buffet, decent service and pretty good food. The outside terrace, just off Piazza di Spagna, is large and undeniably appealing. Moderately priced; no credit cards. Daily noon–11pm.

Antica Birreria Peroni Via di San Marcello 19 ☏06 679 5310 ⓦanticabirreriaperoni.net; map p.91. A big, bustling *birreria* with an excellent and cheap

Italian-German fusion menu of simple food that's meant to soak up the beer. There are the usual starters and pasta dishes, plus a good selection of meat dishes, *scamorza* (grilled cheese) and various sausage dishes. Its walls are decorated with photos of old Rome and a frieze adorned by cherubs and slogans urging you to drink more beer – something that's very hard to resist in this lovely old wood-panelled space. Pasta dishes go for around €9, as do the *scamorza* and sausages; steaks and suchlike are around €15. Mon–Sat noon–midnight.

Babette Via Margutta 1/3 ☎06 321 1559, ⓦ babetteristorante.it; map p.91. Yes, the name is derived from the Danish foodie film, *Babette's Feast*, but the food here is Italian with a few twists, not Danish. The à la carte menu is thoughtful and regularly changing – you might find *paccheri* with tomatoes, aubergine and ricotta, followed by rabbit or beef fillet onion compote and gratin *dauphinoise* – plus there's an all-you-can-eat buffet lunch on weekends (€28 a head). There's a lovely courtyard to eat out in, too. Tues–Sun 1–3pm & 7–11.30pm.

Buca di Ripetta Via Ripetta 36 ☎06 321 9391, ⓦ labucadiripetta.com; map p.91. This smallish restaurant not far from Piazza del Popolo has friendly and attentive service, and though it primarily caters to tourists it does the Roman classics very well, with beautifully executed pasta dishes and classics such as *saltimbocca* and *coda alla vaccinara* as flavoursome as you'll get anywhere in the city. There are lots of straightforward grilled fish dishes, too, and regular daily specials. Starters €7–12, mains €12–20. Daily 12.30–3pm & 7–11pm.

Ciampini al Café du Jardin Piazza Trinità dei Monti 2 ☎06 678 5678, ⓦ caffeciampini.com; map p.91. Across the road from the French Academy, and part of a well-known local chain, *Ciampini* is handy for coffee and snacks in the morning and at lunchtime, but it is a restaurant above all, with a great setting in an enclosed garden overlooking the roofs and domes below. Prices are pretty good, considering the location, with a selection of pasta dishes and salads for €10–12, and fish, steaks and chicken from the grill for €16–20. It's a good place for kids, too, who can watch the turtles playing in the fountain between courses. Daily 8am–11pm.

Dal Bolognese Piazza del Popolo 1 ☎06 3222 799, ⓦ dalbolognese.it; map p.91. This elegant – and expensive – restaurant is the place to go to treat yourself to Emilian cuisine; their *tortellini in brodo* is a must, if you like chicken soup. Reservations are recommended, especially if you'd rather eat outside and watch the passers-by in the piazza, but be prepared for some unbelievably sniffy service. Food is great though, and prices moderate: excellent pasta, including lovely home-made ravioli, *bollito misto* (boiled beef) and veal and pork dishes. Tues–Sun 12.45–3pm & 8.15–11pm.

Fiaschetteria Beltramme Via della Croce 39 ☎06 6979 7200; map p.91. Originally, this place sold only wine, but it's been a full-blown restaurant for some time; just a few blocks from the Spanish Steps, it is thriving and nearly always packed. Service can be a bit slow, but if you want authentic Roman food, such as *spaghetti pomodoro e basilica* and *saltimbocca alla romana* in a good atmosphere at affordable prices, it's a good option in this area. Two courses with wine €40; no credit cards. Daily 12.15–3pm & 7.30–10.45pm.

Hamasei Via della Mercede 35/36 ☎06 679 2134, ⓦ roma-hamasei.com; map p.91. This elegant Japanese restaurant right in the centre of town has a tranquil, refined atmosphere and a full range of very authentic dishes, including a sushi bar. It's moderately priced for such fresh fish, too: main courses are around €15, while various sushi and sashimi mixes go for €13–40, and the lunch specials are super value at €15 a head. Tues–Sun noon–2.30pm & 7.15–10.45pm.

Il Chianti Via del Lavatore 81 ☎06 6792 470, ⓦ vineriailchianti.com; map p.91. Just metres from the Trevi Fountain, this Tuscan specialist, both in wine and food, is a find in a part of town not generally known for its value food and drink. There are spreads of cheese and cold meats (€15), a good selection of beef and other meat dishes, and all the usual pastas and decent pizzas at reasonable prices; however, if you don't fancy a full meal you can just stop by for a drink. Sit outside in summer if you can bear the travelling musicians who congregate to entertain the tourists. Daily 10am–1am.

Imàgo Hassler, Trinità dei Monti 6 ☎06 699 34726, ⓦ hotelhasslerroma.com; map p.91. The *Hassler* hotel

15

TEN ETHNIC RESTAURANTS

Chinese restaurants – most of them pretty average – abound in Rome, and there's a slowly growing list of other international options in and around the centre. Here is our pick of the best.

Akropolis (Greek) See p.261
Baires (Argentinian) See p.250
Charly's Sauciere (French) See p.259
Doozo (Japanese) See p.257
Hamasei (Japanese) See above

Hong Kong Food & Beverage (Chinese) See p.257
Maharajah (Indian) See p.258
Mesob (Ethiopian) See p.259
Take Sushi (Japanese) See p.263
The Perfect Bun (American) See p.249

15

(see p.232), at the top of the Spanish Steps, opens its formal restaurant *Imàgo* only at dinner, but its famous view is always matched by its flawless service and refined Italian cuisine, which includes such signature dishes as terrine of foie gras with morello cherries, saddle of deer with wild mushrooms and sake-glazed black cod; tasting menus are €110–140 a head. Daily 7–10.30pm.

Jardin de Russie Hotel de Russie, Via del Babuino 9 ☎ 06 3288 8870, ⓦ hotelderussie.it; map p.91. It's the magical enclosed terrace garden that makes the *Jardin de Russie* restaurant special, tucked away a stone's throw from the crowds of Via del Corso. As you would expect from a hotel of this calibre, service is faultless and quality high, and the prices reflect that, but the beautifully presented food has a heartiness not usually associated with fine dining, with dishes such as *cacio e pepe* ravioli, *paccheri* with fish sauce and a lovely frittata of calamari, prawns and veg. The weekday buffet lunch (€40 per head excluding drinks) attracts the Roman business elite, as well as hotel guests. Weekend brunch is a treat, too (served 12.30–3pm Sat & Sun; €58 per head excluding drinks). Daily 12.30–3pm & 7.30–11pm.

La Terrazza dell'Eden Hotel Eden, Via Ludovisi 49 ☎ 06 4781 2752, ⓦ laterrazzadelleden.com; map p.91. *La Dolce Vita* might not be much in evidence on Via Veneto anymore, but some of the hotels here still serve up great food in lovely surroundings, in particular the Michelin-starred *La Terrazza dell'Eden*, which consistently offers high-quality creative Roman cuisine (and fabulous views) in its lovely dove-grey-and-cream rooftop perch. The food is pretty wonderful, presented and served with all the ceremonial aplomb you would expect, but it's extremely expensive so it's worth knowing you can still enjoy the view with a drink in the bar. Wed–Mon 7–10.30pm.

Otello alla Concordia Via della Croce 81 ☎ 06 679 1178, ⓦ otelloallaconcordia.it; map p.91. Situated off a courtyard just off Via della Croce, this used to be one of the film director Fellini's favourites – he lived just a few blocks away on Via Margutta – and it remains a blessing in a neighbourhood not stacked with great choices. It's an unapologetically traditional place, with an emphasis on classic Roman dishes, all at very affordable prices considering the location (pasta around €12, mains around €15); try their *spaghetti Otello* – just fresh tomatoes and basil with garlic. Daily 12.15–3pm & 7–11pm, closed Sun eve.

Palatium Via Frattina 94 ☎ 06 6920 2132, ⓦ enoteca regionalepalatium.com; map p.91. Cool and sleek, this wine-bar-cum-restaurant celebrates the produce of the Lazio region and Rome, with a short, regularly changing menu of inventive takes on traditional dishes using local, seasonal ingredients and a long list of Lazio wines. You can settle for just a plate of salami and cheese, or opt for a classic such as *tonnarelli cacio e pepe*, Viterbese vegetable soup or mains such as sausages or rabbit from the hills to the north and south of the city. After a great start its reputation has begun to take a bit of a bashing, but its location, near Piazza di Spagna, is great, and it's good value, too (most *primi* and *secondi* cost between €12 and €16). Daily 11am–11pm.

Pizza Re Via di Ripetta 14 ☎ 06 321 1468, ⓦ pizzare.it; map p.91. A short walk from Piazza del Popolo, this place serves up authentic Neapolitan pizza (thicker than Roman) made in a wood-stoked oven (€9 including a drink), and the same people own the posher and more expensive *Recafé* (see below). Daily noon–midnight.

Recafé Piazza Augusto Imperatore 36 ☎ 06 6813 4730, ⓦ recafe.it; map p.91. The entrance on Via del Corso is a Neapolitan café, while, on the Piazza Augusto Imperatore side, you can enjoy proper Neapolitan pizzas (€10 with a drink), pasta and salad dishes and excellent grilled *secondi* for moderate prices: €11–14 or so for a *primo*, €13–22 for a *secondo*. There are Neapolitan desserts and *fritti*, too. The ambience is deliberately chic, and the large outside terrace always has a buzz about it. Daily noon–midnight.

THE QUIRINALE AND VIA VENETO

CAFÉS AND BARS

Lotti Via Sardegna 19 ☎ 06 482 1902; map p.104. A local institution with great coffee and good-value sandwiches, pastries and the like, just a stone's throw from uber-touristy Via Veneto. Ideal for breakfast, a coffee break or a quick lunch. There's seating both inside and out. Daily except Sat 6.30am–9pm.

Strabbioni Via Servio Tullio 2 ☎ 06 487 3965, map p.104. Tucked away in the neighbourhood near Piazza Sallustio, this bar dates back to 1888 and has a great atmosphere, plus Neapolitan pastries and sandwiches. For more substantial fare, their restaurant a few doors down serves Roman staples including *amatriciana* and *cacio e pepe*, as well as dishes with a Calabrian twist. Bar daily 7.30am–10pm; restaurant Mon–Fri 11am–4pm & 5pm–midnight, Sat & Sun 7pm–midnight.

RESTAURANTS

Al Forno della Soffitta Via Piave 62 ☎ 06 4201 1164, ⓦ alfornodellasoffitta.it; map p.104. Always busy, this popular restaurant and pizzeria does excellent *fritti* and thick-crusted Neapolitan-style pizzas, as well as pasta and grilled meat dishes, all very affordable. They also do really good Neapolitan cakes and desserts. Daily noon–3.30pm & 6pm–midnight.

Cantina Cantarini Piazza Sallustio 12 ☎ 06 485 528 ⓦ ristorantecantinacantarini.it; map p.104. This old-style trattoria just off Via XX Settembre serves a very simple

15

menu of food from the Marche region, including fish and seafood (at the end of the week) and rabbit. The place has a reassuringly unprepossessing interior, and good prices, too – pasta from €7, main courses €10–12. There are tables outside for much of the year. Mon–Sat 12.30–3pm & 7.30–10.30pm.

★**Colline Emiliane** Via degli Avignonesi 22 ☎ 06 481 7538 ⓦ collineemiliane.com; map p.104. Many Italians consider the cuisine of the Emilia Romagna region to be the country's best: here, you can try it for yourself, lovingly prepared at reasonable prices by a family, oddly enough, from the Marche region. Try the *bollito* (boiled) leg of pork or the veal, both cooked in milk. It's located just down from Piazza Barberini, on a quiet backstreet parallel to Via del Tritone. Tues–Sat 12.45–2.45pm & 7.30–10.45pm, Sun 12.45–2.45pm.

★**Giuda Ballerino!** Hotel Bernini Bristol, Piazza Barberini 23 ☎ 06 4201 0469, ⓦ giudaballerino.com; map p.104. Chef Andrea Fusco's fine-dining establishment, originally located down in the 'burbs, soared to the lofty heights of the eighth floor of the *Bernini Bristol* hotel in 2015. The swish new minimalist location, with great views across the city, features artwork referencing comic-book hero Dylan Dog (from which comes the eponymous exclamation). Food is modern Italian; tasting menus cost from €60, mains from €38. An outdoor branch opened recently on the Isola Tiberina serving a scaled-down selection in an informal setting (eves only). Mon–Sat 12.30–3pm & 7–11pm.

Mirabelle Splendide Royal, Via di Porta Pinciana 14 ☎ 06 4216 8838, ⓦ mirabelle.it; map p.104. The old-fashioned *Mirabelle* at the *Splendide Royal* continues to excel, and has stunning views over the umbrella pines of Villa Borghese. If you're looking for a special night out, you could do worse, especially as the food is both unusual and beautifully cooked and presented – expect the likes of goose-liver terrine and truffles, crispy rolls of corn with ricotta cheese, or suckling pig with pumpkin and liquorice. They do a decent children's menu, too. Reckon on spending at least €250 for a meal for two. Daily 12.30–3pm & 7.30–11pm.

Piccolo Abruzzo Via Sicilia 237 ☎ 06 4282 0176, ⓦ piccoloabruzzo.it; map p.104. A 5min stroll up unprepossessing Via Sicilia from Via Veneto, this place is a great alternative to the glitzy, mob-run places on the *Dolce Vita* street. There's no menu, just a seemingly endless parade of goodies plonked on your table at regular intervals. What you get depends on what they have that day, but there's a fair chance it will include mozzarella and/or ricotta, a vegetable course, a couple of pasta dishes, a meat course and a dessert – plus as much wine as you can manage from the barrel. All for around €35 a head. Daily 12.30–3pm & 6.30pm–12.30am.

★**Trattoria Cadorna** Via Raffaele Cadorna 12 ☎ 06 482 7061; map p.104. This old-school trattoria (think functional rather than romantic) has been in business since 1947. The abundant antipasto plate (€15) will easily do two people, and classic *primi* and *secondi* include pasta *alla gricia* and *carbonara*, *osso buco* and *saltimbocca*. Mon–Fri noon–3pm & 7–11pm, Sun 7.30–11pm.

MONTI, TERMINI AND THE ESQUILINE

CAFÉS AND BARS

Antico Caffè del Brasile Via dei Serpenti 23, Monti ☎ 06 488 2319; map p.114. A reliable old Monti café that has been selling great coffee, snacks and cakes for around a century; there are a handful of seats and tables at the back. Mon–Sat 6am–8.30pm, Sun 6am–3pm.

Caffè Fagi Piazza dei Cinquecento 39, Termini ☎ 06 488 3885; map p.114. In the piazza just to the left as you come out of Termini, this is the flagship café of the *Paranà* coffee group and serves excellent coffee made with their own blend of fair-trade organic beans, along with an assortment of sweet and savoury snacks – a blessing, in what is a relative wasteland for palatable food and drink. Daily 7am–10pm.

★**Dagnino** Galleria Esedra, Via E. Orlando 75, Termini ☎ 06 481 8660, ⓦ pasticceriadagnino.com; map p.114. A time machine to 1960s Rome, this long-established Sicilian bakery, *gelateria* and café-restaurant is a peaceful retreat in the Termini area, with tables outside in a small shopping arcade. It's good for a coffee and snack or a light lunch, with great pastries and sandwiches; there's a less commendable menu of pasta and other hot dishes, too. Daily 7am–11pm.

La Bottega del Caffè Piazza Madonna dei Monti 5, Monti ☎ 06 474 1578; map p.114. Bang in the heart of

CITTÀ DEL GUSTO

The hub of the **Gambero Rosso** food empire can be found in Monteverde, southeast of Trastevere. From humble beginnings as a food and wine supplement in the Communist newspaper *Il Manifesto*, it has become Italy's most successful gourmet publisher, with a bestselling magazine, TV programmes, cooking schools and a series of restaurant guides. At their headquarters at Via Ottavio Gasparri 13 (☎ 06 5511 2273, ⓦ gamberorosso.it; tram 8) they run **food and wine tastings**, and **cookery courses**. There is also a **shop** selling cookbooks and kitchen equipment (Mon–Fri 9.30am–3.30pm).

the best bit of Monti, just a short walk from the Colosseum, this is a good place for a lunchtime snack or an early-evening drink, with tables outside on the square. Expect excellent value and service, and, later on, when the square becomes crowded with drinkers, it's a great place to take in the action. Daily 8am–2am.

Mercato Centrale Roma Termini, Via Giovanni Giolitti 36, Termini ☎ 06 9293 9569 ⓦ mercatocentrale.it/roma; map p.114. Florence's popular central market and food-space concept hit Rome in 2016 and is conveniently located at Termini train station. On the ground floor there are around twenty vendors, selling cheese, meat and fish, pasta, ice cream, wine and craft beer, including some of the city's most famous foodie names, such as Trapizzino and Gabriele Bonci. Seating is at communal tables with waiter service. A gourmet bistrot (by Michelin-star chef Oliver Glowig) is located on the top floor. Daily 8am–midnight.

RESTAURANTS

Alle Carrette Via Madonna dei Monti 95, Monti ☎ 06 679 2770; map p.114. An inexpensive and large pizzeria just up Via Cavour from the Imperial Forums. It's always crowded in the evenings. Great homemade desserts. Daily noon–4pm & 7–11.30pm; closed Wed lunchtime.

Baia Chia Via Machiavelli 5, Esquiline Hill ☎ 06 7045 3452, ⓦ www.ristorantebaiachia.it; map p.114. This moderately priced Sardinian restaurant – pasta €9–12, mains €14–16 – has lots of good fish starters and tasty first courses, and the fish baked in salt is spectacular. For dessert, try the *sebadas* (hot pastries stuffed with cheese and topped with Sardinian honey). Mon–Sat 12.30–3.30pm & 7.30–11.30pm.

Da Danilo Via Petrarca 13, Esquiline Hill ☎ 06 7720 0111, ⓦ trattoriadadanilo.com; map p.114. This determinedly traditional restaurant sticks to what it knows best, and that's what makes it more of a locals' than a tourist joint. A short menu zeroes in on classics like *cacio e pepe* and simple rigatoni with tomato sauce, along with an *abbacchio allo scottadito* that is as good as it gets. It's homely trattoria food, though at perhaps slightly more than trattoria prices, owing to its long-standing fame – something evidenced by the photos of the proprietor with all manner of celebs that plaster the walls; pasta dishes go for around €10, mains €15. Mon 6.30–11pm, Tues–Sat 11am–3.30pm & 6.30–11pm.

★**Da Marcello** Via dei Campani 12, San Lorenzo ☎ 06 446 3311, ⓦ osteriadamarcello; map p.114. A super old-school trattoria frequented by university types, students and lecturers alike, with a surprisingly good wine list. Isidoro, Marcello's son, presides over the noisy dining room, while his mother rules the kitchen. Booking is always a good idea. Mon–Sat 7.30–11pm.

Doozo Via Palermo 51/53, Monti ☎ 06 481 5655, ⓦ doozo.it; map p.114. Arguably the best Japanese

restaurant in Monti, a zone known for its ethnic eateries. Part restaurant, part art gallery and bookshop, *Doozo* serves affordable lunch menus (€15–20), while dinner is a bit pricier (around €40). There are bento boxes at lunchtime, great sushi and sashimi, tempura and soba noodles, among other things. In the summertime the outdoor seating is in a leafy courtyard with an ancient wall. Tues–Sat 12.30–3pm & 7.30–11pm, Sun 7.30–11pm.

Enoteca Cavour 313 Via Cavour 313, Monti ☎ 06 678 5496, ⓦ cavour313.it; map p.114. This lovely, wood-panelled old wine bar has long stood out among the pizza joints at this end of Via Cavour, just a stone's throw from the Forum. You can enjoy mixed plates of salami and cheese on wooden benches for around €10 or a daily selection of different hot dishes, from couscous to lasagne, as well as a selection of veggie alternatives. There's excellent and enthusiastic service, too, and a great choice of wine. Mon–Sat 12.30–2.45pm & 6–11.30pm, Sun 7–11pm; closed Sun in July & Aug.

Formula 1 Via degli Equi 13, San Lorenzo ☎ 06 445 3866; map p.114. A cheap and justifiably popular San Lorenzo pizzeria, with tables outside in summer. Try their delicious *pizza all'ortolana* (with courgettes, aubergines and peppers), and courgette-flower fritters. Pizzas cost around €7. Mon–Sat 6.30pm–12.30am.

Hong Kong Food & Beverage Via Giolitti 105, Termini ☎ 06 4436 1626; map p.114. Rome's most authentic Chinese eatery is in an unprepossessing spot by the railway station – hardly what you came to Rome for, you might imagine, but expats and long-term travellers yearning for something un-Italian need look no further. The chilled cabinet at the back has ducks' tongues, chicken feet and other goodies which don't make it onto the Western part of the menu. Daily 11am–midnight.

Il Tempio di Mecenate Largo Leopardi 14/18, Esquiline Hill ☎ 06 487 2653; map p.114. A top location right by the Maecenas temple, with lots of outside seating. Unsurprisingly, it's popular with tourists of all stripes, but the service is friendly and there's an excellently executed array of Roman staples – a decent *carbonara*, *sauté di cozze e vongole* (mussels and clams), *saltimbocca* – okay pizzas and moderate prices: €8–10 for a *primo*, €12–14 for a *secondo*. Daily 12.30–3pm & 7pm–midnight.

★**L'Asino d'Oro** Via del Boschetto 73, Monti ☎ 06 4891 3832; map p.114. This is the Rome location of legendary Orvieto chef Lucio Sforza, who blends traditional Roman ingredients in both complex and simple combinations that you won't find anywhere else in the city. His bacon with sage and vinegar starter is delicious; follow it with lamb with artichokes or rabbit with vinegar and tomato. Desserts are great, too, using unexpected ingredients such as sage and rosemary, and it's excellent value for such high quality, especially considering the cool Monti vibe and bustling outside terrace – *primi* from €10, *secondi* from €13. It's a

15

15

good idea to book ahead. Mon–Sat 12.30–2.30pm & 7.30–11pm.

La Barrique Via del Boschetto 41b, Monti ☎ 06 4782 5953; map p.114. A regularly changing seasonal menu that always hits the spot – think simple, well-cooked pasta dishes, meat courses like rabbit confit and steaks – all of which you can enjoy inside or at the few tables out on the street, accompanied by an extensive wine list which reflects *La Barrique*'s past incarnation as a wine bar. Mon–Fri 1–3pm & 6.45pm–12.30am, Sat 6.45pm–12.30am.

La Carbonara Via Panisperna 214, Monti ☎ 06 482 5176, ⓦ lacarbonara.it; map p.114. Always crowded, this staple of the Monti eating scene maintains a refreshing distance from the more rarefied offerings of the neighbourhood, with a very seasonal menu in a bustling, wood-panelled dining room. You can expect to wait for a table, but it's no hardship to sit at the small bar and take in the activity before tucking into a selection of low to moderately priced Roman pasta staples (good *allagricia* and *carbonara*) and mainly meat-oriented *secondi* – *straccetti* (slices) or fillet of beef, *saltimbocca*, *coda alla vaccinara*, fish on Fri and tripe on Sat. There's a pretty decent wine list, too. Mon–Sat 12.30–2.30pm & 7–11pm.

Maharajah Via dei Serpenti 124, Monti ☎ 06 474 7144, ⓦ maharajah1.com; map p.114. This long-established neighbourhood favourite on Monti's main street serves Indian classics at reasonable prices. It's always busy, and one of the best bets for a decent curry in town. The popular lunch specials start at around €12. Daily 12.30–2.30pm & 7–11.30pm.

Monti DOC Via Giovanni Lanza 93, Monti ☎ 06 487 0942; map p.114. A comfortable Santa Maria Maggiore neighbourhood wine bar, with an excellent wine list and decent food – cold cuts and cheese, soups, quiches, salads and pastas (including some good veggie dishes) – all chalked on the blackboard daily. Most things go for €10–15. Tues–Sat 12.30–2.30pm & 7.30–10.30pm, Sun 12.30–2.30pm.

Pastificio San Lorenzo Via Tiburtina 196, San Lorenzo ☎ 06 9727 3519, ⓦ pastificiocerere.com; map p.114. The big interior space and windows give a contemporary feel to the old Cerere pasta factory, where the ground-floor restaurant, with its elegant long bar and generously spaced tables, is the perfect environment to enjoy the modern twists on classic Roman food that they specialize in here. Mains go for €15–19, pasta dishes €10–12, and might include a *carbonara* or *cacio e pepe*, a lamb dish or their house burger. The rest of the building houses an art foundation which hosts regular exhibitions. Mon–Fri 12.30–3pm & 8–11.30pm, Sat 8–11.30pm; bar 7pm–2am.

★**Pommidoro** Piazza dei Sanniti 46, San Lorenzo ☎ 06 445 2692; map p.114. A family-run Roman trattoria that's been around forever – it was once the favourite haunt of film-director Pasolini – and serves great Roman home-cooking. It's very seasonal, with an emphasis on grilled lamb and game cooked on a big open grill; all the pasta classics are here, too, with an excellent *carbonara* among other things, all at good prices. There's a breezy open veranda outside on the square in summer. Mon–Sat 1–3.30pm & 8–11.30pm.

Tram Tram Via dei Reti 44/46, San Lorenzo ☎ 06 490 416, ⓦ tramtram.it; map p.114. A grungy location but a cosy spot, this trendy, animated San Lorenzo restaurant serves Pugliese pasta dishes, fish and seafood and unusual salads, with mains at €15–18. Reservations are recommended. There's also a bar if you want to carry on drinking after dinner. Tues–Sun 12.30–3pm & 7.30–11pm

★**Trattoria Monti** Via di San Vito 13, Monti ☎ 06 446 6573; map p.114. This small, family-run and moderately priced restaurant specializes in the cuisine of the Marche region, which means hearty food from a short menu: great pasta and interesting cabbage-wrapped *torte* as *primi*, and mainly meaty *secondi*, with beef, lamb and rabbit predominating. Close enough to Termini to be convenient, but also homely and friendly – something places in this neighbourhood often aren't. Tues–Sat 1–2.45pm & 8–10.45pm, Sun 1–2.45pm.

Urbana 47 Via Urbana 47, Monti ☎ 06 4788 4006, ⓦ urbana47.it; map p.114. This Monti stalwart takes itself pretty seriously, with its "zero food kilometres" and post-industrial decor, not to mention a slight attitudinal approach to service. But, when it comes to the food, it's a thoroughly agreeable café/restaurant, and it's open right throughout the day, too. The menu offers a variety of intriguing takes on traditional Roman cuisine as well as more international dishes, including a good burger. Pasta dishes go for around €14 and mains for €16–18, and the menu changes every month – if you can't decide, just settle for a wine-bar-style plate of cheese and salami. Daily 7am–midnight.

Valentino Via del Boschetto 37, Monti ☎ 06 488 0643; map p.114. Easy to miss, with only a faded Peroni sign above the door, but well placed at the top of one of Monti's most atmospheric streets, this is both trattoria and *birreria*, and as cheap as that implies. Inside, it's always buzzing, with waiters zipping between the closely packed tables. You'll find lots of grilled meat options, and it also has a *scamorza* (grilled cheese) menu, making it a good bet for vegetarians. Mon–Sat 12.30–3pm & 8–11pm.

THE CELIAN HILL AND SAN GIOVANNI

CAFÉS AND BARS

Valentini Piazza Tuscolo 2, San Giovanni ☎ 06 7720 7427; map p.128. A lovely café, pastry shop and *tavola calda*, just 5min from San Giovanni. It's a great spot for lunch, and has the bonus of outside seating, too. Daily 6am–midnight.

FIVE PLACES FOR VEGGIES

It's relatively easy for **vegetarians** to survive and even eat extremely well all over Italy, even in Rome, whose core traditional cuisine consists of the unmentionable and rarely eaten parts of animals – though to be honest there are plenty of non-meat dishes besides. You certainly don't need to go to a specifically vegetarian restaurant, which is just as well, as there aren't many in Rome. Here are some of our favourite places to eat top-notch, meat-free meals across the capital.

Arancia Blu See p.263
Ditirambo See p.251
Mesob See below

Metamorfosi See p.264
Valentino See opposite

RESTAURANTS

Al Grottino Via Orvieto 6, San Giovanni ☎ 06 702 4440, ⓦ algrottino.com; map p.128. You can always tell a decent Roman pizzeria by the crowd of people hanging about outside waiting for takeaways, and this one – a 10min walk from San Giovanni metro station – fits the bill perfectly. There's a huge choice of pizzas, though as ever the classics are best not overloaded so you can appreciate the crispy charred bases – slightly less thin than the usual Roman style, and cooked to perfection. There's a good choice of antipasti too, with *fritti* and suchlike, plus an amazingly complete selection of Belgian beers. Expect to wait for a table, especially if you want to sit outside – it's always busy. Pizzas from €5. Daily 7.30pm–midnight.

Aroma Palazzo Manfredi, Via Labicana 125, Celian Hill ☎ 06 7759 1380, ⓦ palazzomanfredi.com; map p.128. A meal at *Aroma*, in the beautifully revamped *Palazzo Manfredi* hotel, is worth a splurge for the unsurpassed views of the Colosseum alone. But the food – Italian, somewhat Roman, but with a lot of twists – is so good that we'd recommend it if it were in a windowless basement. As you might expect, it's not cheap – *primi* around €30, *secondi* around €40, tasting menu €130 for seven courses (or €200 with wine pairings); service is excellent and understated. Daily 12.30–3pm & 7.30–11pm.

Caffè Propaganda Via Claudia 15, Celian Hill ☎ 06 9453 4255, ⓦ caffepropaganda.it; map p.128. Very handily placed for the Colosseum, this Celio bar-restaurant is unashamedly not of the traditional trattoria school: this is more the kind of place that offers bread in a paper bag and where the menu is a faux newspaper. It's a nice bright space though, and the food (*primi* €10–13, *secondi* €18–22) isn't at all bad: there's a simple if unadventurous menu of pasta dishes – *carbonara*, *amatriciana* – and a short list of main courses that includes a decent if overpriced burger and a few specials, and there are bar snacks to go with their fantastically mixed cocktails. Service is brisk and friendly. Daily noon–2am.

Charly's Saucière Via di San Giovanni in Laterano 270, Celian Hill ☎ 06 7049 5666, ⓦ charlyssauciere.com; map p.128. If the background *chansons* don't make you think you're in France – albeit a mythical one from the 1930s

– the menu certainly will, with lots of French classics, including *coq au vin*, onion soup and excellent steaks, plus fondues, too. Moderate prices – soups and starters €10–12, mains around €18 – and a handy location just a 5min walk from the Colosseum. Mon–Sat 12.30–3pm & 8–11.30pm.

Il Bocconcino Via Ostilia 23, Celian Hill ☎ 06 7707 9175, ⓦ ilbocconcino.com; map p.128. Not the greatest service, but a cut above most of the other places within sight of the Colosseum, with high-quality Roman food served in an old-fashioned environment. Their *tonnarelli cacio e pepe* is a great bargain for €7, while most main courses – meatballs, roast lamb, stewed rabbit – cost €9–11. Daily except Wed 12.30–3.30pm & 7.30–11.30pm.

Luzzi Via di San Giovanni in Laterano 88, Celian Hill ☎ 06 709 6332 ⓦ trattorialuzzi.it; map p.128. Midway between San Giovanni in Laterano and the Colosseum, this bustling joint is cheap and cheerful with no frills. The food is hearty and simple (if unspectacular), there's outside seating, and it's cheap – *secondi* go for around €6–9. There's pizza, too. Daily except Wed noon–midnight.

Mesob Via Prenestina 118, Pigneto ☎ 338 251 1621, ⓦ mesob.it; map p.128. Arguably the city's most interesting ethnic food – Ethiopian – reaches its zenith at *Mesob*, located in a renovated garage on the cusp of Pigneto. The vegetarian options, including rich lentil and vegetable stews, are the highlight, and the home-made *injera* (flatbread) is the best in town. Mains are very reasonable, starting at around €8. Tues–Sun 7pm–midnight.

Tajut Via San Giovanni in Laterano 244, Celian Hill ☎ 349 641 8088, ⓦ iltajut.it; map p.128. This cosy restaurant claims to be the only Friulian restaurant in Rome, which seems a crime, because the food here is excellent – sort of Italian with a Central European twist (good pasta and duck dishes) – and with its relaxed wine-bar vibe you can eat as much or as little of it as you like. It's not a million miles from the Colosseum, but is definitely more of a neighbourhood than a tourist restaurant. There's no outside seating – the pavement's not wide enough – but it's good for a leisurely evening dinner. Tues–Sun 7pm–1.30am.

15

★**Taverna dei Quaranta** Via Claudia 24, Celian Hill ☎ 06 700 0550, ⓦ tavernadeiquaranta.com; map p.128. This very relaxed locals' joint with chequered tablecloths offers good, very reasonably priced home-cooking. The dishes (*primi* €7–9, *secondi* €10–14) are Roman with a twist: classics such as roast lamb and courgette flowers, but polenta, too, and some interesting pasta dishes, on a menu that changes regularly. Only in Rome could this sort of place exist, 5min from the tourist scrum at the Colosseum. There are also a few tables outside. Daily noon–3.30pm & 7.30pm–midnight.

THE AVENTINE HILL AND SOUTH

CAFÉS AND BARS

Il Seme e la Foglia Via Galvani 18, Testaccio ☎ 06 574 3008; map p.140. This is a pleasantly low-key café popular with Testaccio trendies and students from the nearby music school. During the day it's good for sandwiches and big salad lunches, and in the evenings it's a mellow place to relax before visiting the area's more energetic offerings. Mon–Sat 8am–2am, Sun 6pm–2am.

★**Mordi e Vai** Mercato Testaccio (Box 15), Via B. Franklin, Testaccio ☎ 339 1343 344, ⓦ mordievai.it; map p.140. Head to Sergio Esposito's stand in what will forever be referred to as the "new" Testaccio Market (opened 2012) for one of the finest sandwiches you'll ever taste. Crusty rolls are filled on the spot with classics of the *cucina Romana* such as beef stew, tripe or veal kidneys. Take a number and wait your turn: you won't regret it. A second branch opened in 2016 at Re di Roma, Via Appia Nuova 221 (☎ 06 9441 4675; Mon–Sat 9am–10pm). Mon–Sat 8am–3pm.

Palombini Piazzale Adenauer 12, EUR ☎ 06 591 1700, ⓦ palombini.it; map p.155. This is a great EUR café where the outside terrace and large interior are a haven amid the brutal boulevards. Appropriately housed on the ground floor of EUR's official "restaurant building", it's a café, *tabacchi* and wine shop all rolled into one, and serves excellent cakes and sandwiches. Mon–Thurs 7am–10pm, Fri & Sat 7am–1am, Sun 8am–10pm.

Taverna Volpetti Via Alessandro Volta 8, Testaccio ☎ 06 574 4306, ⓦ volpetti.com; map p.140. Attached to the famous deli a few doors down (see p.299), this casual restaurant serves up all the roman classics from *cacio e pepe* to carbonara and cheese and charcuterie boards with local wine. Mon 11.30am–3.30pm, Tues–Sat 11.00am–11pm, Sun 11.30am–3.30pm.

★**Trapizzino** Via Giovanni Branca 88, Testaccio ☎ 06 4341 9624, ⓦ trapizzino.it; map p.140. A great spot for a taste of Roman street food. The patented *trapizzino* (a hybrid of *tramezzino* and *pizza*) is a pocket of pizza bread filled with a stew of your choice: Roman tripe, tongue, or meatballs if you're feeling less adventurous. There are also vegetarian options and a good selection of bottled beers, as well as stools on which to perch. Tues–Sat noon–1am.

RESTAURANTS

Agustarello Via G. Branca 98, Testaccio ☎ 06 574 6585; map p.140. *Agustarello* is a moderately priced Testaccio standard serving genuine Roman cuisine in a simple, old-fashioned atmosphere. It's resolutely traditional, serving a deliberately seasonal menu (no artichokes outside autumn/winter for example) that includes all the Roman offal classics – *coda alla vaccinara*, *pajata*, *coratelle* – as well as great steaks, pork chops and tripe. As with most Italian restaurants, even vegetarians can find good choices. *Primi* go for €10, mains €12–18. Mon–Sat 12.30–3pm & 7.30–11.30pm.

Checchino dal 1887 Via di Monte Testaccio 30, Testaccio ☎ 06 574 3816, ⓦ checchino-dal-1887.com; map p.140. Right in the heart of Monte Testaccio's bars and clubs, *Checchino dal 1887* is a historic (and expensive) symbol of Testaccio cookery, and one of the best places to sample the stalwarts of Rome's offal-based cuisine – appropriate, as it's right opposite the old slaughterhouse. It has an excellent wine cellar, too. Tues–Sat 12.30–3pm & 8–11.45pm.

Da Felice Via Mastro Giorgio 29, Testaccio ☎ 06 574 6800, ⓦ feliceatestaccio.it; map p.140. Always crowded, this joint isn't quite the rough-and-ready establishment it used to be when Felice used to choose his customers from a line outside, and there are those who feel it has lost some of its charm. But it still serves honest, seasonal Roman cooking – *bucatini cacio e pepe*, lamb, and in winter, artichokes: all the classics, well cooked and served. Listen for the daily specials, usually just half a dozen *primi* (€8–10) and *secondi* (€12–15). Daily 12.30–3pm & 7–11pm.

★**Da Remo** Piazza Santa Maria Liberatrice 44, Testaccio ☎ 06 574 6270; map p.140. *Da Remo* is the best kind of pizzeria: usually full of locals, very basic and serving the thinnest, crispiest Roman pizza you'll find. Try also the heavenly *bruschette* and other snacks such as *supplì* and *fiori di zucca*. Almost worth travelling out to Testaccio for – and very cheap. Mon–Sat 7pm–1am.

★**Flavio al Velavevodetto** Via di Monte Testaccio 97, Testaccio ☎ 06 574 4194, ⓦ ristorantevelavevodetto.it; map p.140. A very reasonable Testaccio restaurant carved out from Monte Testaccio, ancient Rome's pottery landfill site – a glass wall offers a view of all those amphorae. All the standard Roman classics are on offer, as well as some fish dishes, and its outdoor patios are a delightful venue for summer meals. Tues–Sun 12.30–3pm & 7.30–11.30pm.

Giulietta Piazza dell'Emporio 28, Testaccio ☎ 06 4522 9022, ⓦ giuliettapizzeria.it; map p.140. Alongside *Romeo Chef & Baker* (see opposite), and housed in the same

15

building, sits *Giulietta*, a pizzeria that boasts two pizza ovens – one producing Roman and one Neapolitan pizzas. Even the traditional fritti starters are regionally divided, with items such as *supplì* on the Roman menu and *frittata di pasta* (a pasta croquette of sorts) on the Neapolitan. Pizzas €8–10. Daily 12.30–3.30pm & 7.30–11pm.

La Maisonette Via Giacinto Pullino 103, Garbatella ☎ 06 8376 5543, ⓦ lamaisonnetteristrot.it; map p.140. Located in the hip working-class district of Garbatella, La Maisonette has a pretty French bistrot feel and a gorgeous garden setting for the warmer months. From ceviche to onion soup, the menu offers modern and of course, French-inspired cuisine and cocktails. But there are also some Roman classics on offer such as *pasta amatriciana* and a deconstructed *cacio e pepe* with figs. With an open-all-day

format, it's great for meals, afternoon tea or an after-dinner drink. Mains from €15, pasta from €12. Daily 11am–2am.

Romeo Chef & Baker Piazza dell'Emporio 28, Testaccio ☎ 06 3211 0120, ⓦ romeo.roma.it; map p.140. The brainchild of Michelin-star chef Cristina Bowerman, this huge restaurant occupies a former Testaccio warehouse. You can get a light lunch, while salumi, cheese and baked goods are available all day at the bar counter. On the dinner menu, instead of the traditional antipasti, *primi* and *secondi*, dishes are organized by produce – meat, fish and vegetables, for instance. Aperitivo time is a treat; sit at the huge bar and enjoy Bowerman's carefully constructed finger-food snacks, such as *gyoza* and vegetable tacos, as well as creative cocktails by expert mixologists. Mains cost around €20. Daily 10am–2am.

TRASTEVERE AND THE JANICULUM HILL

15

CAFÉS AND BARS

Caffè Di Marzio Piazza di Santa Maria in Trastevere 15 ☎ 06 581 6095; map p.160. This bar isn't much on the inside, but it's a friendly place, and the terrace right on Piazza Santa Maria makes it one of the best people-watching spots in Trastevere. There's not much in the way of food – just a toasted sandwich or panini. Daily 7am–1am.

Gianicolo Piazzale Aurelia 5 ☎ 06 580 6275; map p.160. This pleasant, wood-panelled café and bar has a long, shady terrace facing the Porta San Pancrazio, and is something of a hangout for Italian media stars, writers and academics from the nearby Spanish and American academies. Most customers come here for a drink, but they also serve tasty sandwiches and snacks. Tues–Sat 6am–1am, Sun 6am–11pm.

La Renella Via del Moro 15 ☎ 06 581 7265; map p.160. A long-standing bakery, right in the heart of Trastevere, with focaccia and *pizza al taglio*. Take a number and be prepared to wait at busy times. You can take away or eat on the premises at its long counter. Daily 7am–2am.

★**Sisini (La Casa del Supplì)** Via San Francesco a Ripa 137 ☎ 06 589 7110; map p.160. Just half a block from Viale di Trastevere, this hole-in-the-wall serves great *pizza al taglio*, as well as roast chicken and potatoes and excellent *supplì*. Mon–Sat 9.30am–10pm.

RESTAURANTS

Ai Marmi Viale di Trastevere 53/59 ☎ 06 580 0919; map p.160. Nicknamed "the mortuary" because of its stark interior with strip lighting and marble tables, this place – which confusingly also goes by the name *Panattoni* – serves unique *supplì al telefono* (so named because of the string of mozzarella it forms when you take a bite), fantastic fresh *baccalà* and good Roman pizza. It has dcent house red wine, too, and service is quick, despite the crowds, if not always especially friendly. A couple of pizzas and a carafe of house wine will set you back about €30.

Daily except Wed 6.30pm–2am.

Akropolis Via San Francesco a Ripa 103 ☎ 06 5833 2600, ⓦ akropolistavernagreca.com; map p.160. This small Greek restaurant and takeaway has delicious *souvlaki* and all the usual snacks and honeyed sweets. Good prices, too – bank on around €20 per head for more food than you can eat. Tues–Sun 7.30–11.30pm.

★**Antico Arco** Piazzale Aurelio 7 ☎ 06 581 5274, ⓦ anticoarco.it; map p.160. Located above Trastevere, next to the Janiculum Hill, this is one of Rome's finest restaurants, serving superb, exquisitely presented dishes, accompanied by an enormous fine-wine list. It's always good, and reservations are definitely required. Daily noon–midnight.

Bir and Fud Via Benedetta 23 ☎ 06 589 4016, ⓦ birandfud.it; map p.160. This fashionable little place, in one of Trastevere's busiest squares, does great wood-fired pizzas which can be washed down with what is an exemplary range of beers. It gets very busy, so come early or reserve. Mon 12.30pm–2am, Tues & Wed 6pm–2am, Thurs–Sun 12.30pm–2am.

Da Augusto Piazza de' Renzi 15 ☎ 06 580 3798; map p.160. This is a reliable diner-style joint serving Roman basics in an unpretentious, bustling atmosphere. Fine pasta and soup starters, and daily meat and fish specials – not haute cuisine, but decent, hearty Roman cooking. Daily 12.30–3pm & 8–11pm.

★**Da Enzo** Via dei Vascellari 29 ☎ 06 581 2260, ⓦ daenzoal29.com; map p.160. A tiny restaurant close to the river in Trastevere that does tasty basic Roman food at decent prices – a million miles away from some of the glitzy new places that have opened up over in the district's busier quarter. Mon–Sat 12.30–3pm & 7.30–11pm.

Da Ivo Via di San Francesco a Ripa 158 ☎ 06 581 7082, ⓦ ivoatrastevere.lt; map p.160. *The* Trastevere pizzeria, almost in danger of becoming a caricature, but still solid and with quite reasonably priced pizzas (€7–9), and cheap wine (from €8 a bottle). A tasty assortment of desserts as well – try the *monte bianco* for the ultimate chestnut cream and meringue confection. Arrive early to avoid a chaotic queue. Mon & Wed–Sat 6pm–12.30am, Sun noon–4pm & 6pm–12.30am.

Da Lucia Vicolo del Mattonato 2b ☎ 06 580 3601; map p.160. Outdoor Trastevere dining in summer is at its best at this wonderful old trattoria, which serves great Roman food at decent prices (€20–25 a head for two courses with wine). Spaghetti *cacio e pepe* is the speciality here – arrive early or book ahead to nab a table outside. Tues–Sun 12.30–3pm & 7.30–11pm.

Da Olindo Vicolo della Scala 8 ☎ 06 581 8835; map p.160. This is a great, family-run Trastevere trattoria that offers traditional Roman food in smart and cosy premises. There's a small menu of staples, and prices are very competitive: *primi* cost around €7, *secondi* around €9. Mon–Sat 12.30–3pm & 7.30–11pm.

★ **DOT** Via Natale del Grande 52 ☎ 06 581 7281; map p.160. Run by Simone Dordei, the son of the owners of nearby *La Gensola* (see below), *DOT* is Sicilian inspired, and its menu runs from "street food" offerings such as *panelle* (chickpea fritters) to fresh tuna "meat" balls *alla Favignese*. As at *La Gensola*, the fish is excellent, though non-fish-eaters are also catered for. *Primi* cost around €10–14, mains from €15 upwards, and there are tasting menus at €45 and €62. It also has a cocktail bar. Mon–Sat noon–3pm & 7pm–1am.

★ **La Gensola** Piazza della Gensola 15 ☎ 06 581 6312, ⓦ osterialagensola.it; map p.160. One of the best fish spots in town, in a little piazza on the quieter side of Viale di Trastevere. Specials vary daily, but you can expect to find the likes of *spaghetti con colatura* – a version of ancient Roman *garum* (fish sauce) from the Amalfi Coast – and Sicilian-influenced fish *secondi*. The catch is always fresh, as proven by the raw fish and shellfish specials. You can expect to spend about €50 per person without wine, which for such fresh fish isn't bad. Daily 12.30–3pm & 7.30–11.30pm.

Le Mani in Pasta Via dei Genovesi 37 ☎ 06 581 6017, ⓦ lemaniinpasta.net; map p.160. This small and cosy restaurant cooks up fantastic pasta and fish dishes (*primi* €10–12, *secondi* €16 or so) and has excellent service. It's often very crowded, and it's worth reserving to be sure of getting in. Tues–Sun 12.30–3pm & 7.30–11.30pm.

Osteria der Belli Piazza di Sant'Apollonia 11 ☎ 06 580 3782; map p.160. Sardinian-born Leo and his family have been running this restaurant for the past 35 years and have picked up a loyal clientele of both locals and foreigners. Situated next to the beautiful Piazza di Santa Maria in Trastevere and boasting a picturesque streetside terrace, this is just the spot for balmy summer nights. The emphasis is on fish and the daily catch is prepared with fresh ingredients and simple cooking to allow the quality to shine through. Don't miss the amazing antipasti table in the back room which groans under the weight of fabulous grilled vegetables and fish dishes such as sea bass carpaccio, marinated anchovies and smoked salmon. Mains start at €18 and pasta around €12. Tues–Sun noon–2.30pm & 7.30–11.30pm.

Paris Piazza San Calisto 7a ☎ 06 581 5378, ⓦ ristoranteparis.it; map p.160. This old-fashioned place serves Roman-Jewish food on one of Trastevere's most atmospheric piazzas, with tables outside in summer. It's fairly expensive – reckon on €50 a head, without wine – but offers good cooking in a firmly traditional and elegant environment. Tues–Sun 12.30–3pm & 7.30–11pm.

THE REVOLVING DOOR: CUTTING-EDGE CUISINE IN ROME'S HOTEL RESTAURANTS

In the past decade or so, some of the **best chefs** working in Italy (both Italian and foreign) have exited and entered the revolving doors of Rome's major **hotels**, and it's the cuisine of these establishments that is often at the cutting edge of Italy's food trends, with fresh local ingredients, some exotic touches and fantastic presentation. Not surprisingly, it's **expensive** to eat at any of these places, but bear in mind that the food and service are extra special and invariably accompanied by breathtaking views. You should also be aware that a lot of hotel restaurants offer a more economical, pared-down **lunch menu** (or even buffet) to attract business diners, but do check, because some chefs are active only at dinner, with lunch under a separate team that may produce an entirely different style of food. Here's our current top ten:

All'Oro Restaurant at the *H'All Tailor Suite Hotel* (see p.264)
Aroma at *Palazzo Manfredi* (see p.259)
Giuda Ballerino! at the *Bernini Bristol* (see p.256)
Imàgo at the *Hassler* (see p.253)
Jardin de Russie at *De Russie* (see p.254)

La Pergola at the *Cavalieri Hilton* (see p.264)
La Terrazza Bramante at the *Raphaël* (see p.249)
La Terrazza dell'Eden at *Hotel Eden* (see p.254)
Mirabelle at the *Splendide Royal* (see p.256)
Vivavoce at the *Gran Meliá Rome* (see opposite)

TEN PLACES FOR PIZZA

There's nothing like thin, crispy Roman pizza, baked in a wood-fired oven. Naturally there are loads of places to try it, but here are our ten favourites:

Ai Marmi See p.261
Al Grottino See p.259
Alle Carrette See p.257
Da Francesco See p.248
Da Remo See p.260

Emma See p.251
Formula 1 See p.257
Giggetto See below
Giulietta See p.260
Pizzarium See p.264

Sette Oche Via dei Salumi 36 ☎06 580 9753, ⓦsetteoche.com; map p.160. Based in a cellar, this restaurant, pizzeria and wine bar also has outside seating on a quiet street in the more tranquil part of Trastevere. The menu is short and not ambitious, but they do the basic Roman *primi* and *secondi* well, and prices are decent (*primi* €9, *secondi* €12), plus they also do a selection of focaccia and *bruschette*. Daily noon–midnight.

Take Sushi Viale di Trastevere 4 ☎06 581 0075, ⓦtakesushi.it; map p.160. Located on Trastevere's main avenue, this cosy place comes as a real – and affordable – surprise, serving delicious sushi and sashimi, as well as light, crispy tempura. The sashimi salad is very special, too. Start off with a flawless *miso* soup and finish with home-made green-tea ice cream. A sixteen-piece sushi set costs €26. Tues–Sun noon–3pm & 7pm–midnight.

Vivavoce Gran Meliá Rome, Via del Gianicolo 3 ☎06 925 901, ⓦristorantevivavoce.com; map p.160. Up on the Janiculum Hill, the *Vivavoce* in the *Gran Meliá Rome* is overseen by master chef Alfonso Iaccarino (of *Don Alfonso 1890* fame), who brings his famous take on fresh Mediterranean cuisine from Campania to Rome. They do a tasting menu for €95; *primi* are about €20, *secondi* €30. Mon–Sat 7.30–10.30pm.

VILLA BORGHESE AND NORTH

CAFÉS AND BARS

Caffè delle Arti Via Antonio Gramsci 73, Villa Borghese ☎06 3265 1236, ⓦcaffedelleartiroma.com; map p.173. Attached to the Galleria Nazionale (see p.176), this elegant café/restaurant is a great place for a refreshment. Its proximity to smart Parioli makes it a favourite haunt for ladies who lunch, and it's also popular with the archeologists and artists from the British School of Rome next door. Sandwiches, drinks and a limited lunchtime menu are all served with panache in the elegant interior dining room, or under the large umbrellas on the terrace. Mon 8am–5pm, Tues–Sat 8am–midnight.

Gianfornaio Largo Maresciallo Diaz 16, Flaminio ☎06 333 3472, ⓦilgianfornaio.com; map p.170. A great bakery serving pizza and other goodies, with lots of seating inside and out. There are a couple of other branches, too, in posh residential neighbourhoods around the city, notably on Largo Apollinaire in EUR and at Viale dei Parioli 95 in Parioli. Mon–Sat 7.30am–9pm, Sun 9am–3pm.

Sesto Piazza Buenos Aires 1/4, Trieste ☎06 855 9652; map p.170. *Sesto* is a modern *tavola calda*-style café and restaurant, where you can order at the counter from a range of salads, pasta dishes and hot meat and fish options, and then eat from your tray in the cool, functional interior. It's open all day for breakfast, lunch, dinner and everything in between (and after). There's a €10 *aperitivo* buffet from 6pm. Daily 5.30am–1.30am.

RESTAURANTS

Arancia Blu Via Cesare Beccaria 3, Flaminio ☎06 361 0801; map p.170. This long-standing vegetarian restaurant has moved all over town but is now settled in a Flaminio location. It still reckons itself a cut above the rest – and with some justification, although, in a city with very few vegetarians, it doesn't have to try too hard. *Arancia Blu* prides itself on serving good food using fresh ingredients in an imaginative fashion, and decent salads – red pesto spaghetti, asparagus and cheese risotto, courgette *parmigiana*. *Primi* and *secondi* are both around the €10–12 mark. Daily noon–4pm & 7pm–midnight.

Casina Valadier Piazza Bucarest, Villa Borghese ☎06 6992 2090, ⓦcasinavaladier.com; map p.173. The splendid setting is undoubtedly the great selling point of this restaurant, which is housed in an elegant, early nineteenth-century building designed by the eponymous Valadier, with spectacular views across the city from the Pincio. But the great service and food are also worthy of mention. *Primi* from €20, main courses from €30. Tues–Sat 12.30–3pm & 7.30–11pm.

Da Emilio Via Alessandria 189, Nomentano ☎06 855 8977; map p.170. A real regular's joint, that bills itself as specializing in "*cucina casareccia*" or rustic cuisine. It is indeed very simple, serving classic Roman dishes with the odd seasonal variation – asparagus in spring for example, plus the usual pasta specialities and *secondi* such as *vitello al forno*, meatballs with mash and *coda alla vaccinara* or oxtail stew. *Primi* and *secondi* €9–12. Mon–Fri 12.30–2.30pm & 7.30–10.30pm.

Giggetto Via Alessandria 43/49, Nomentano ☎06 841 2527; map p.170. Namesake of the more famous Jewish

15

15

Ghetto restaurant, this big and bustling pizzeria proclaims itself "king of pizza". It does great, crispy-thin Roman pizzas for just €6–8, lots of *fritti* and main dishes too. Daily 12.30–3pm & 7pm–1am.

La Pergola Rome Cavalieri, Via Alberto Cadiolo 101, Balduina ☎06 3509 2152, ⊛romecavalieri.com; map p.170. The undisputed pioneer of Rome's creative fine-restaurant dining is Heinz Beck, the chef at three-star *La Pergola*, situated atop the spectacular *Rome Cavalieri* hotel. It's frequently voted Italy's best restaurant, and is probably Rome's most expensive, too: the nine-course tasting menu costs €210, and à la carte prices start at €44 for antipasti, about the same for pasta dishes (*fagotelli carbonara* is Beck's signature dish) and €54 for mains such as John Dory with liquorice, or soya-poached beef fillet with garlic dandelion and wasabi. The dress code requires jackets for men. Tues–Sat 7.30–10.15pm.

★**Metamorfosi** Via Giovanni Antonelli 30, Flaminio ☎06 807 6839, ⊛metamorfosiroma.it; map p.170. Roy Caceres' Michelin-starred *Metamorfosi* in super-smart Parioli is an absolute delight, with spectacular food and wine served with grace, but not pomposity, in the elegantly restrained split-level dining room. Prices for à la carte are around €25–30 for a *primo*, €35–40 for a main course, while tasting menus are excellent value for such extraordinary quality (€80 with vegetarian option, €90

with "traditional" option). If you're going for the tasting menu, you'll find sommelier Paolo Abballe's wine pairings a dream. Mon–Fri 12.30–2.30pm, 8–10.30pm, Sat 8–10.30pm.

Osteria Flaminio Via Flaminia 297, Flaminio ☎06 323 6900, ⊛osteriaflaminio.com; map p.170. Convenient for MAXXI and the Auditorium, this airy and informal bistro-style restaurant has a focus on traditional dishes with a modern touch – both Roman and not – and high-quality ingredients. Pasta dishes are around €10, mains €15–18. Daily 12.30–2.30pm & 7.30–11.30pm.

Ristorante All'Oro Via Giuseppe Pisanelli 23/25 Popolo, ☎06 9799 6907, ⊛ristorantealloro.it; map p.170. *Ristorante All'Oro*, formerly at the *First Luxury Art Hotel*, has a stylish new home at the five-star boutique hotel opened by chef Riccardo di Giacinto and his partner Ramona Anello in 2017. This is not your average hotel-restaurant but a fun, fine-dining outfit done out with plush, colourful decor. The menu brings the same spunk to the restaurant's age-old signature dishes, with a few new ones on the list. Some of the standout dishes include the potato and salt-cod tiramisù and a deconstructed *carbonara* cream in an eggshell. *All'Oro* is a gastronomic journey that surprises and makes you smile at every turn. Mains cost around €30. Mon–Fri 7–11pm, Sat & Sun 12.45–2.45pm & 7–11pm.

THE VATICAN AND PRATI

CAFÉS AND BARS

Fa-Bìo Via Germanico 43 ☎06 6452 5810, ⊛fa-bio.com; map p.188. Favoured by local office workers and tour guides on a break from the Vatican Museums, this tiny café makes delicious made-to-order sandwiches, juices and salads from organic (*bìo*) ingredients. There are a few stools on which to perch, and often a queue out of the door. The friendly staff also speak perfect English. Mon–Fri 10.30am–5.30pm, Sat 10.30am–4pm.

Mondo Arancina Via Marcantonio Colonna 38 ☎06 9761 9213, ⊛mondoarancina.it; map p.188. There are great savoury Sicilian classics at this takeaway place, but the real treats are the *arancini*, of which there are any number of varieties – tomato and mozzarella, ham and cheese, bolognese – all delicious and just €2 a throw. There are several locations, including a second branch at Via Flaminia 42–44, just north of Piazza del Popolo (☎06 361 1069). Daily 10am–midnight.

★**Pizzarium** Via della Meloria 43 ☎06 3974 5416; map p.188. Undoubtedly Rome's best pizza-by-the-slice joint, where celebrity baker Gabriele Bonci uses top-notch ingredients to create creatively topped pizza: think rabbit and raisin or *trippa alla Romana*, though purists will also find classics such as *pizza rossa* and *margherita*. There is also an assortment of *fritti*: *supplì*, *filetti di baccalà* and *crocchette*. You can either take away or sit in. Mon–Sat

11am–10pm, Sun noon–4pm & 6–10pm.

Sciascia Caffè Via Fabio Massimo 80a ☎06 321 1580, ⊛sciasciacaffe1919.it; map p.188. One of Prati's best coffee bars, with not only excellent coffee but also pastries and places to sit inside. Free wi-fi, too, so not a bad place for a quick pick-me-up between Vatican sights. Mon–Sat 7am–8pm.

RESTAURANTS

Cantina Tirolese Via G. Vitelleschi 23 ☎06 6813 5297, ⊛cantinatiroleseroma.com; map p.188. This rustic Prati restaurant was reputedly the last pope's favourite lunch spot when he was still a cardinal, and no wonder – the cuisine here is hearty and wholesome Austrian and German cuisine. Choose from dumplings and goulash soup to start (for around €8), and then various meaty Central European meat specialities for your main course; fondue for around €26 for two is about the only vegetarian option you'll find. The lunchtime buffet (noon–3pm) is excellent value at €9.50 a head. Tues–Thurs 6.30pm–midnight, Fri–Sun noon–3.30pm & 6.30pm–midnight.

★**Dal Toscano** Via Germanico 58/60 ☎06 3972 5717, ⊛ristorantedaltoscano.it; map p.188. Don't come here for a salad. This restaurant specializes in *fiorentine* (the famous thick Tuscan T-bone steaks), perfectly grilled on charcoal, delicious *pici* (thick home-made spaghetti) and *ribollita* (veg and bread soup) – all at honest prices: *primi* around €10, mains for €12–15. Not far from the Vatican, it's tremendously popular with Roman families, so reservations are recommended for dinner. Tues–Sun 12.30–3pm & 8–11.15pm.

Del Frate Via degli Scipioni 118/122 ☎06 323 6437; map p.188. This large wine and spirits shop is a wine bar, too, and has a great selection of cheeses and cold meats (large mixed cheese and salami plates go for €16–18), as well as regular pasta dishes. There's a good choice of artisanal Italian beers, too, plus wines by the glass. Very handy for the Vatican, for lunch or at the end of the day. Mon–Sat noon–3pm & 6pm–midnight.

Il Sorpasso Via Properzio 31/33 ☎06 8902 4554, ⓦsorpasso.info; map p.188. A wine bar and restaurant with a great choice of wines by the glass, and a menu that runs from lovely prosciutto, cheese and cold cuts, to risotto and pasta dishes that change daily, steaks and other mains. Enjoy the full menu in the comfier back room, or just snack at the table outside or by the marble-topped bar. Mon–Fri 7.30am–1am, Sat 9am–1am.

L'Osteria di Birra del Borgo Via Silla 26a ☎06 8376 2316, ⓦosteria.birradelborgo.it; map p.188. Combining one of the best pizzas in town (that of pizzamaker Gabriele Bonci) and the top Roman beer brewers, Birra del Borgo, this is Rome's version of the gastropub – that is, inexpensive and quality food, stylish interiors and quality drinks. Aside from the excellent pizza, there's a full menu with gourmet dishes such as *orecchiette* with pork ragù and fennel, and fried meatballs in tomato sauce. And don't worry if beer is not your thing, there's an extensive cocktail list, too. Daily noon–2am.

Mamá Via Sforza Pallavicini 19 ☎06 6813 9095; map p.188. Open from breakfast right through to dinner, this contemporary yet homely little restaurant serves an inexpensive menu of hot breakfasts and sandwiches, pasta dishes (including Roman favourites and others which change daily; €9–12), salads, and fish and meat dishes (€12–18). They serve a good-value three-course lunch, too, for €15 including water and coffee, and a good range of artisanal Italian beers. Daily 10.30am–11.30pm.

★**Osteria dell'Angelo** Via G. Bettolo 24 ☎06 372 9470; map p.188. Above-average traditional Roman food at extremely reasonable prices, in a highly popular restaurant run by an ex-rugby player. There is an obligatory tasting menu priced at €25 a head, and booking is advisable, as it's often heaving with locals. Mon–Fri 12.30–2.30pm & 7.30–11pm, Sat 7.30–11pm.

Passaguai Via Pomponio Leto 1 ☎06 874 1358, ⓦpassaguai.it; map p.188. A basement wine bar with seating outside on the street that serves great platters of cheese, cold cuts, salads and various other snacks to go with its excellent choice of wine. A lot of the food is home-produced, and it's always busy, with a great vibe and an emphasis on freshness, quality and seasonality. Unusually, there's no cover or bread charge, and as an added bonus the bread is from Roscioli bakery (see p.250); wines start at €13 per bottle. Mon–Fri 10am–2am, Sat & Sun 6pm–2am.

Ragno d'Oro Via Silla 26 ☎06 321 2362, ⓦragnodoro. org; map p.188. As likely to be full of locals as tourists, this bustling place is a family-run restaurant, which, despite the picture menu, has decent Roman cooking at moderate prices and good (if brusque) service – plus it's also just a 5min walk from the Vatican. Mon–Sat 12.30–2.30pm & 7–11pm.

Settembrini Via Luigi Settembrini 21 ☎06 9761 0325, ⓦviasettembrini.it; map p.188. A bit out of the way, about a 15min walk from the Vatican, but the food at this restaurant is consistently good, whether you tuck into one of their wonderful seafood pasta dishes, a risotto, or just make do with a spectacular plate of cheeses and salami. *Primi* go for €14–16, *secondi* €16–22 – all good, simple food, from a short, regularly changing menu, served in a light contemporary space. There's also a café a few doors down at no. 21 for coffee and snacks. Daily 7am–1.30am.

15

MA CHE SIETE VENUTI A FÀ, TRASTEVERE

Drinking

Drinking is not something Romans do a lot of, at least almost never to drunken excess. While you'll find plenty of bars in Rome as with the rest of Italy, many are functional daytime haunts and not at all the kinds of places you'd want to spend an evening (see Chapter 15). However, partly because of the considerable presence of Brits and Americans in Rome, partly owing to a growing craft beer and mixology trend, there are plenty of bars and pubs conducive to an evening's drinking, from spit-and-sawdust wine bars to a growing number of sleek cocktail bars and speakeasy-style venues. There are also numerous good wine bars, most of which serve food, so it's worth scanning these listings for places to eat, too. Our listings are divided into neighbourhoods: Campo de' Fiori and the Centro Storico, Monti, Trastevere and Testaccio are the densest and most happening areas.

ESSENTIALS

Aperitivi One phenomenon is worth noting: a lot of bars lay out an early-evening buffet to tempt drinkers in for a pre-dinner *aperitivo*, with a choice of food free with the price of a drink, or for a set price, and it's become a popular way to kick off an evening. We've noted where places offer "free" buffets in the reviews, and there's a list of our favourites on p.268.

Bars There can be considerable crossover between Rome's bars, restaurants and clubs: for the most part, the places listed in this chapter are drinking spots, but you can eat, sometimes quite substantially, at many of them. Several could also be classed just as easily as clubs, with loud music and occasionally even an entrance charge; places that are more restaurant than bar are listed in Chapter 15; places that are more club than bar are listed in Chapter 17.

Opening hours Many bars are slick and expensive excuses for people to sit and pose, but most have the advantage of late hours, sometimes until 3 or 4am in summer, and almost always until 1am. Note that many places are closed at least during part of August; where possible this has been noted, but it's worth checking with individual places, as holidays are very variable.

WHAT TO DRINK

Beer *Birra* was once always a lager-type brew, but the trend in craft-beer production in Italy means you'll have more to choose from these days than just the industrial Moretti, Peroni and Nastro Azzuro, all of which usually come in one-third or two-third litre bottles, or on draught (*alla spina*). A small beer is a *piccola* (20cl or 25cl), a larger one (usually 40cl) a *media* (pronounced "maydia"). If you want lager, ask for *birra chiara*. You may also come across darker beers (*birra scura* or *birra ambrata*). Prices start at €4–5 for a *media*, but anywhere remotely fancy won't charge less than €6–7.

Wine Much of the wine served in Rome comes from the Castelli Romani, just south of the city. The best known is Frascati, a light, easy-drinking white made from a blend of Malvasia and Trebbiano grapes – like many Italian wines, it's much better than the exported varieties would have you believe. Elsewhere in Lazio, the big wine is called Est! Est! Est!, another drinkable white that hails from Montefiascone. The story goes that in the twelfth century a bishop's servant was sent to find the best wines of the region and to indicate the ones he liked by daubing the word "Est" on the door of the producer. He liked the wines of Montefiascone so much he daubed the word three times for emphasis.

Spirits All the usual spirits are on sale and known mostly by their generic names. There are also Italian brands of the main varieties: the best Italian brandies are Stock and Vecchia Romagna. A generous shot of these costs about €3, imported stuff much more. The home-grown Italian firewater is *grappa*, available just about everywhere. It's made from the leftovers from the winemaking process (skins, stalks and the like) and is something of an acquired taste; should you acquire it, it's probably the cheapest way of getting plastered. You'll also find fortified wines such as Campari; ask for a Campari-soda and you'll get a ready-mixed version from a bottle; a slice of lemon is a *spicchio di limone*; ice is *ghiaccio*. You might also try Cynar – an artichoke-based sherry, believe it or not, often drunk as an aperitif.

Liqueurs There's also a daunting selection of liqueurs. Amaro is a bitter after-dinner drink: it has a base of pure alcohol in which different herbs are steeped, according to various family traditions. It's highly regarded as a digestive aid to cap a substantial meal. Amaretto is much sweeter with a strong taste of almond; sambuca is a sticky-sweet aniseed concoction; while strega – yellow, herb-and-saffron-based stuff in tall, elongated bottles – is about as sweet as it looks but not unpleasant.

16

TEN WONDERFUL WINE BARS

One of Rome's more traditional types of drinking establishment is the **wine bar**, known as an *enoteca* or *vineria*. The old ones have gained new cachet in recent years, and newer ones, with wine lists the size of unabridged dictionaries, are weighing in too, often with gourmet menus to go with the superb wines they offer: we have reviewed those that feature great food as well as wine in Chapter 15. There's also been a recent proliferation of wine tastings (*degustazioni*), which offer a chance to sample some interesting vintages, often at no cost. Here are our ten favourite places.

Al Vino al Vino See p.269
Cavour 313 See p.270
Cul de Sac See p.268
Il Goccetto See p.268
Il Piccolo See p.268

La Barrique See p.270
L'Angolo Divino See p.268
Monti DOC See p.258
Passaguai See p.265
Vinaietto See p.269

CENTRO STORICO

Abbey Theatre Via del Governo Vecchio 51 ☎ 06 686 1341, ⓦ abbey-rome.com; map p.36. The most central and perhaps most convivial Irish pub in the city, with a good mix of Italians and expats, regular sport on TV and live music, as well as basic pub food. Daily noon–2am.

Bar del Fico Piazza del Fico 26 ☎ 06 6889 1373; map p.36. One of the nicest places for an outside drink in the Centro Storico, on its own peaceful square but right at the heart of Rome's urban buzz. Mon–Sat 9am–2am, Sun noon–2am.

Cul de Sac Piazza Pasquino 73 ☎ 06 6880 1094, ⓦ enotecaculdesacroma.it; map p.36. A busy, long-running wine bar with an excellent wine list, a great city-centre location with outside seating and decent wine-bar food – cold meats, cheeses, salads and soups. One of the best Centro Storico locations for a snack. Daily noon–4pm & 7pm–12.30am.

Enoteca Achilli Via dei Prefetti 15 ☎ 06 6877 3446, ⓦ enotecalparlamento.com; map p.36. A magnet for politicians and the well-heeled, this wine shop and bar has an expensive menu, but at the table the bottles are priced the same as in the shop. They specialize in champagne, great if you're in a celebratory mood, and there is also a decent selection of regular wines. Mon–Sat 9.30am–11.30pm.

Etabli Vicolo delle Vacche 9a ☎ 06 9761 6694, ⓦ etabli.it; map p.36. In the heart of the Centro Storico's drinking triangle, this is a lounge-style bar and restaurant with comfy sofas, free wi-fi and a pleasant, not-too-cool vibe. Daily 12.30–3pm & 6pm–2am.

Il Piccolo Via del Governo Vecchio 74/75 ☎ 06 6880 1746; map p.36. As its name suggests, the place is tiny, but the wine selection isn't bad. A friendly happy hour and a few outdoor tables make this a nice, cosy, casual choice near Piazza Navona. Mon–Sat 10.30am–2am, Sun 4pm–2am.

Le Coppelle 52 Piazza delle Coppelle 52 ☎ 349 740 4620; map p.36. This snazzy bar, decked out in glowing red decor, very much functions outdoors during the warm months, when there's a nice array of sofas and chairs on the usually heaving small piazza to hang out on. Daily 6pm–2am.

Salotto 42 Piazza di Pietra 42 ☎ 06 678 5804, ⓦ www.salotto42.it; map p.36. This chic bar facing the ruins of Hadrian's temple does an excellent early-evening buffet and cocktails for around €10 a pop. Tues–Sat 10am–2am, Sun 11am–midnight.

Trinity College Via del Collegio Romano 6 ☎ 06 678 6472, ⓦ trinity-rome.com; map p.36. A warm and inviting establishment offering international beers and food, though its two levels can get quite loud and crowded. Food includes a bit of everything – pasta, burgers, salads, Tex-Mex – and is served until 1am, plus there's a brunch menu at weekends for €15. Daily noon–3am.

CAMPO DE' FIORI AND THE GHETTO

Barnum Café Via del Pellegrino 87 ☎ 306 6476 0483, ⓦ barnumcafe.com; map p.50. A café by day (see p.250), great cocktail bar by night, this trendy spot lies just off the Campo de' Fiori, but its cocktails are a million miles from the watery mojitos normally found in the piazza. Daily 8.30am–2am.

★ **Il Goccetto** Via dei Banchi Vecchi 14 ☎ 06 686 4268, ⓦ ilgoccetto.com; map p.50. A short walk from Campo de' Fiori, this is one of the city centre's nicest wine bars, with lots of options by the glass and good plates of cheese and salami to go with it. Mon–Sat 12.30–3pm & 6.30pm–midnight.

Jerry Thomas Project Vicolo Cellini 30 ☎ 06 9684 5937, ⓦ thejerrythomasproject.it; map p.50. Named for the author of the first known cocktail manual, this late-night speakeasy-style bar is a testament to the cocktail boom in Rome in recent years. Call in advance to gain entry to the smoky room, and your cocktail dreams will be granted. You will need to supply the password at the door to enter (updated regularly and available on their website and social media). Tues–Sun 10pm–4am.

★ **L'Angolo Divino** Via dei Balestrari 12 ☎ 06 686 4413, ⓦ angolodivino.it; map p.50. A cosy, bottle-lined wine bar tucked between Campo de' Fiori and Palazzo Spada, with a small but well-chosen menu. The proprietor Massimo Crippa knows all there is to know about the mostly Italian wine selection and will offer advice upon request. Daily 10.30am–3pm & 5pm–1.30am; closed Sun & Mon lunch.

★ **Open Baladin** Via degli Specchi ☎ 06 683 8989, ⓦ baladin.it; map p.50. Central Rome's ultimate *birreria*, founded by the Baladin brewing company in 2009, and with a stark, modern interior and literally hundreds of mainly artisanal Italian beers to choose from, forty of them on tap. You can eat, too – salads, sandwiches and finger food, most of it pretty good (the burgers are decent) – but beer is the main thing here. Daily noon–2am.

Scholars' Lounge Via del Plebiscito 101b ☎ 06 6920 2208, ⓦ scholarsloungerome.com; map p.50. One of the better city-centre Irish pubs, with regular live music and giant screens showing Premier League football and other

---

FIVE APERITIVO SPOTS

Baccano See p.269
Freni e Frizioni See p.273
Il Goccetto See above
Romeo Chef & Baker See p.272
Sesto See p.263

sports. The quiz night on Mon can be fun, as can the karaoke nights on Sun and Tues. Daily 11am–3am.

Vinaietto Via del Monte della Farina 38 ☎ 06 6880 6989; map p.50. This hole-in-the-wall *enoteca* has just a handful of tables, so most of its regulars drink their wine outside on the cobbles. Though it's mainly a wine shop, the enthusiastic owners offer a range of wines to drink by the glass – and it's far less expensive than nearby Campo de'

Fiori. Mon–Sat 10.30am–3pm & 6.30–10pm.

Wine Bar Camponeschi Piazza Farnese 52 ☎ 06 687 4927, ⓦ ristorantecamponeschi.it; map p.50. The posh, somewhat overpriced *Camponeschi* restaurant doesn't always hit the mark, but its wine bar next door not only has a great selection of wines but also decently priced pasta dishes and seating on the square. Winemakers sometimes hold tastings here. Mon–Sat 8pm–2am.

PIAZZA VENEZIA AND THE CAPITOLINE HILL

0.75 Via dei Cerchi 65 ☎ 06 687 5706, ⓦ 075roma.com; see map p.61. Right by the Circo Massimo, around the corner from the church Santa Maria in Cosmedin, this convivial bar does food and has a reasonable *aperitivo* buffet every evening, as well as several screens showing

live sport. With two largeish rooms and plenty of space to spill out onto the pavement outside, it's a handy place for a drink and a quick bite in a neighbourhood that has few options. Daily 11.30am–2am.

THE TRIDENTE AND TREVI

★**Antica Enoteca** Via della Croce 76b ☎ 06 679 0896, ⓦ anticaenoteca.com; map p.91. This friendly wine bar is one of Rome's oldest, and has a lively, casual feel despite the high-rent district. It's always open, even on major Italian holidays, and serves lots of wines by the glass, as well as a selection of hot and cold dishes, including great platters of cheese and cold cuts, soups and salads, and attractive desserts. While the food is fine, a drink at the bar is the main reason to drop by. There are intriguing trompe-l'oeil decorations inside, majolica-topped tables outside. Daily 11am–1am.

Baccano Via della Muratte 23 ☎ 06 6994 1166, ⓦ baccanoroma.com; map p.91. They spent a fortune to turn this Trevi bar and restaurant into an Italian version of New York's trendy *Balthazar*, but Rome isn't New York. The food and service are variable, but it's undeniably a haven in what is a bit of a desert for good places to eat and drink. It's best treated as an early-evening drink-and-snack stop-off (they do a good *aperitivo*), rather than a full dining experience. Daily 10am–2am.

Canova Piazza del Popolo 16 ☎ 06 361 2231, ⓦ canovapiazzadelpopolo.it; map p.91. Once the haunt of the monied classes, *Canova* is not really the place it was. Still, it does all sorts of cocktails and reasonable food, and is a fine place to sit and take the air and watch the world go

by on Piazza del Popolo. Politically, *Canova*'s clientele was traditionally a right-wing one, while dyed-in-the-wool lefties patronized *Rosati* across the square (see below). Daily 8am–midnight.

Do Bar Via delle Carrozze 61 ☎ 06 6979 7096; map p.91. A café for breakfast, coffee or a quick snack by day, but the narrow modern interior and its adjacent patio also make a fine place for a drink before or after dinner. Daily 8am–midnight.

La Vi Via Tomacelli 23 ☎ 06 4542 7760, ⓦ la-vi.it; map p.91. Short for "Latteria Vineria", this trendy, self-consciously minimalist bar-restaurant lures in young Romans with its excellent rooftop terrace. Service and food can be a bit uneven, but it's unquestionably a nice place for a drink. It has long opening hours, too. Daily 7am–2am.

Lowenhaus Via della Fontanella 16b ☎ 06 323 0410; map p.91. Just off Piazza del Popolo, this Bavarian-style drinking establishment serves beer and snacks – and full meals, too. It's a handy place to get a beer in this location. Daily noon–2am.

Rosati Piazza del Popolo 5 ☎ 06 322 5859, ⓦ rosatibar .it; map p.91. This was the bar that hosted left-wingers, bohemians and writers in years gone by, though now it's cocktails and food (and winter sunshine) that draw the crowds to its outside terrace. Daily 8am–midnight.

16

MONTI, TERMINI AND THE ESQUILINE

★**Ai Tre Scalini** Via Panisperna 251, Monti ☎ 06 4890 7495, ⓦ aitrescalini.org; map p.114. A great, easy-to-miss little Monti bar, cosy and comfortable, with a good wine list, beer on tap and decent food – cheese and salami plates plus *porchetta, lasagne, parmigiana melanzane* and other simple staples. It gets very crowded later on. Mon–Fri noon–3pm & 6pm–midnight, Sat & Sun 6pm–midnight.

Al Vino al Vino Via dei Serpenti 19, Monti ☎ 06 485 803; map p.114. The Monti district's most happening

street offers this seriously good wine bar with a choice of over five hundred labels, many by the glass. Snacks are generally Sicilian specialities. Daily 11.30am–2.30pm & 5.30pm–12.30am.

Bar à Book Via dei Piceni 23, San Lorenzo ☎ 06 4544 5438; map p.114. A welcome addition to studenty San Lorenzo, this friendly bookshop and wine bar makes a very laidback place for a drink. They also organize events, from poetry readings to DJ sets. Tues–Sun 7pm–2am.

★**Cavour 313** Via Cavour 313, Monti ☎ 06 678 5496, ⓦ cavour313.it; map p.114. One of the oldest wine bars in Rome (opened in 1979), *Cavour 313* serves hundreds of labels, mainly Italian, in a wood-clad interior. The food menu includes daily specials with a Middle Eastern flair, as well as the standard cheese, cured meat, salad and carpaccio that one expects in a Roman wine bar. Daily 12.30–3pm & 7.30pm–12.30am; closed Sun in summer.

Club Machiavelli Via Machiavelli 49, Esquiline Hill ☎ 347 454 0179, ⓦ clubmachiavelli.it; map p.114. Located off up-and-coming Piazza Vittorio in a historic palace, this place serves wines and cocktails, plus home-made desserts and other treats. There are piano-bar-style evenings, too, with occasional live-jazz combos and other cultural events. Thurs–Sat 8pm–1am.

Druid's Den Via San Martino ai Monti 28, Monti ☎ 06 4890 4781, ⓦ druidspubrome.com; map p.114. A cheap and lively Irish pub with a genuine Celtic feel (and owners) and occasional impromptu Celtic music. It has a mixed expat/Italian clientele, and is not just for the homesick. Their sister pub, *Druid's Rock*, is located nearby at Piazza Esquilino 1 (open daily noon–2am). Daily 5pm–2am.

Fiddler's Elbow Via dell'Olmata 43, Monti ☎ 06 487 2110, ⓦ thefiddlerselbow.com; map p.114. One of the two original Irish bars in Rome, one block closer to Santa Maria Maggiore than its sister pub, the *Druid's Den*. It's a bit roomier, with a decidedly more Latin feel. Mon–Fri 5pm–2am, Sat & Sun 3pm–2am.

Finnegan's Via Leonina 66, Monti ☎ 06 474 7026, ⓦ finneganpub.com; map p.114. Another of the area's crop of pseudo-Irish pubs, with live football on TV, pool and a friendly expat crowd. There's seating outside, too, on this bustling Monti street. Mon–Fri 5pm–2am, Sat & Sun 3pm–2am.

Ice Club Via della Madonna dei Monti 18/19, Monti ☎ 06 9784 5581, ⓦ iceclubroma.it; map p.114. Constructed entirely of ice, this bar – where in summer patrons are given coats to wear inside the freezing atmosphere – has been open for some years now. Maybe it's the heat of a Roman summer that drives people here? Whatever, you can be sure that your drink will be well-chilled. Daily 6pm–2am.

★**La Barrique** Via del Boschetto 41b, Monti ☎ 06 4782 5953; map p.114. This lovely Monti wine bar has an ample and well-chosen selection of wines from Italy and abroad (including some natural wines), with several offered by the glass. Accompany your drink with something from the small but delicious menu, which includes both cheese and *salumi* selections and some hot dishes. Mon–Fri 12.30–3.30pm & 5.30pm–1am, Sat 6pm–1.30am, Sun 6pm–midnight.

Trimani Via Cernaia 37b, Termini ☎ 06 446 9630, ⓦ trimani.com; map p.114. This classy wine bar (with Rome's biggest selection of regional Italian vintages) is nice for a lunchtime or evening tipple and an indulgent snack. You'll spend around €15 to sample a range of good-quality cheeses and cured pork meat, or a soup and salad, including a glass of wine. It is an offshoot of Rome's oldest wine merchant around the corner (see p.299). Mon–Sat 11.30am–3pm & 5.30pm–midnight.

THE CELIAN HILL AND SAN GIOVANNI

Caffè Propaganda Via Claudia 15, Celian Hill ☎ 06 9453 4255, ⓦ caffepropaganda.it; map p.128. This studiedly informal Celio restaurant has a bar area in the front room with an impressive display of bottles presided over by Rome cocktail star Patrick Pistolesi, the barman-in-chief. Daily noon–2am.

Pentagrappolo Via Celimontana 21b, Celian Hill ☎ 06 709 6301, ⓦ ilpentagrappolo.com; map p.128. A Celio wine bar with lots of good wines by the glass, cheese plates and the usual cold cuts; food is served right up until 1am, and there's live piano music several nights a week. Tues–Fri noon–3pm & 6pm–1am, Sat & Sun 6pm–1am.

Tree Folks Via Capo d'Africa 33, Celian Hill ☎ 329 055 6412; map p.128. Expect lots of Belgian and German brews, as well as food – plates of cold cuts, burgers and chips, salads. Their other speciality is whisky, with a selection of single malts that must be one of the city's best. Daily 6pm–2am.

PIGNETO

Enolibreria Il Tiaso Via Ascoli Piceno 20 ☎ 333 284 5283, ⓦ iltiaso.com; map p.128. This relaxed wine bar with free wi-fi has book-lined shelves and lots of wines to try by the glass, accompanied by cheese and salami platters, as well as some more substantial meals. There are often live acoustic sets, too – a great place to kick off an evening out. Daily 6pm–2am.

Necci dal 1924 Via Fanfulla da Lodi 68 ☎ 06 9760 1552, ⓦ necci1924.com; map p.128. Pasolini shot some of his films in the Pigneto district, and this bar-restaurant was one of his favourite places, though it's been considerably upgraded since then. Five minutes' walk from the busy stretch of Via del Pigneto, it has a lovely shady garden where you can have a drink, sandwich or a full meal from its short menu, chalked afresh on the blackboard each day, cooked for you by London-born chef Ben Hirst. Daily 8am–1am.

16

THE AVENTINE HILL AND SOUTH

Ketumbar Via Galvani 24, Testaccio ☎06 5730 5338, ⓦketumbar.it; map p.140. Convenient for all the district's clubs, this ultra-hip Testaccio venue plays laidback world music and has very attitude-free service, despite its chic clientele. There's a restaurant here, too (closes 11.30pm). Daily 8am–2am; closed Aug.

Oasi della Birra Piazza Testaccio 41, Testaccio ☎06 574 6122; map p.140. Unassumingly situated beneath an *enoteca* on Piazza Testaccio, the cosy basement rooms here house an international selection of beers that rivals anywhere in the world – five hundred in all, and plenty of wine to choose

from, as well. On the menu are generous plates of cheese and salami and a great selection of *bruschette* and polenta dishes. It's not particularly Roman, but it's a very appealing place for a drink and some good food nonetheless. Mon–Sat 8am–2.30pm & 4.30pm–1am, Sun 7.30pm–1am.

Romeo Chef & Baker Piazza dell'Emporio 28, Testaccio ☎06 3211 0120, ⓦromeo.roma.it; map p.140. The newest bar on Rome's drinking scene is a cocktail hotspot with ultra-modern decor and a long bar bench to match. Award-winning mixologists create innovative drinks such as candle-wax-infused liqueurs. There is a bar-snack menu with vegetable

---

TOP HOTEL BARS

Many of Rome's best bars are in **hotels**, and not just the most expensive ones either: some have fantastic or historic spaces, courtyards or gardens, an unusual and alluring clientele or just great views over the city. Here are some of our favourites:

Aleph Via di San Basilio 15, Quirinale ☎06 422 901, ⓦhotelalephrome.com; map p.104. The *Aleph's* cosy *Angelo* bar is the perfect place to sink a cocktail or aperitif, before proceeding upstairs to its *Sin* restaurant. Daily noon–midnight.

De la Minerve Piazza della Minerva 69, Centro Storico ☎06 695 201, ⓦgrandhoteldelaminerve.com; map p.36. Right behind the Pantheon, the outdoor roof-garden bar here (open in the summer months) gives about the best view you can get over the rooftops and domes of the old centre – an ideal spot to wind up after you've been trudging around at street level all day. Daily noon–1am, summer only.

De Russie Via del Babuino 9, Tridente ☎06 328 881, ⓦhotelderussie.it; map p.91. A haven for chic drinkers, plus the odd celebrity, the *De Russie's Stravinskij* bar always has a buzz about it. It's a minimalist neutral space, with a generous selection of champagnes and wines by the glass, as well as cocktails, and opens out to the lovely courtyard and tiered "secret" garden. Daily 9am–1am.

D'Inghilterra Via Bocca di Leone 14, Tridente ☎06 699 811, ⓦniquesahotels.com; map p.91. The folk at *Gambero Rosso* (see box, p.256) reckon this to be one of the best bars in Italy, and its clubby interior is a perfect place to enjoy an excellent cocktail. Daily noon–midnight.

Eden Via Ludovisi 49, around Via Veneto ☎06 478 121, ⓦedenroma.com; map p.104. Expansive views of Rome across the Spanish Steps, the umbrella pines of Villa Borghese and more rooftops and domes than you could count, made this terrace perch a favourite spot for film director Federico Fellini. Daily noon–midnight.

The First Via del Vantaggio 14, Tridente ☎06 9799 6907, ⓦthefirsthotel.com; map p.91. For a chic upscale drinking experience that has Ruinart champagne as a partner, *The First's Aquaroof* is a lovely

find near Piazza del Popolo, where even the snacks are overseen by a Michelin-starred chef. Daily 7pm–midnight.

Forum Via Tor de' Conti 25–30, Monti ☎06 679 2446, ⓦhotelforumrome.com; map p.114. The American bar at this Monti four-star commands magical views over the Forum and Colosseum – great for a drink just as the sun is setting. Daily 5pm–midnight.

Gin Corner Hotel Adriano, Via di Pallacorda 2, Centro Storico ☎06 6880 2451, ⓦhoteladriano.com; map p.36. Dedicated to all things gin, the *Gin Corner* was opened in 2014 in the *Hotel Adriano* by Patrick Pistolesi and is now tended by Dario Araneo. Tell him what you like and he'll come up with something to hit the spot. Mon–Sat 7pm–midnight.

Indigo St George Via Giulia 62, around Campo de' Fiori ☎06 686 611, ⓦhotelindigorome.com; map p.50. The open-air rooftop bar here is only open during the summer, but its views are great, over the river and the domes and towers of the Centro Storico – you can eat dinner up here, too. Tues–Sat, summer only.

★Locarno Via della Penna 22, Tridente ☎06 361 0841, ⓦhotellocarno.com; map p.91. The slightly decadent atmosphere graced with hip, modern cocktail-sippers and a clubby back room with cosy fireplace make the *Locarno* Rome's most egalitarian hotel bar. It's frequented by literati, artists, princes, paupers, poseurs, fashionistas and just ordinary folk, and the warm weather adds a roof terrace to the mix. Tues–Sat noon–12.30am.

Raphaël Largo Febo 2, Centro Storico ☎06 682 831, ⓦraphaelhotel.com; map p.36. The terraces of the *Raphaël* offer a fabulous view across the rooftops and domes of the Centro Storico. Drinks are nothing special, but the view is breathtaking. Daily 7pm–midnight.

16

tacos and Japanese *gyoza* dumplings. Daily 5pm–2am.
Tram Depot Via Marmorata 13, Testaccio ☎06 575 4406; map p.140. Fashioned from an old tram and with

(only) outside tables, this kiosk is open all day for drinks and snacks, but really comes into its own from *aperitivo* time onwards. Daily 8am–2am.

TRASTEVERE

Baylon Via di San Francesco a Ripa 151 ☎06 581 4275; map p.160. Decked out in vintage style with colourful chairs, artwork and books lining the back walls, *Baylon* is a great all-day dining and drinking option in Trastevere; the late-night vibe is a good mix of young Romans and foreigners. Both indoor and outdoor dining is available. Daily 8am–1am.

Bar San Calisto Piazza San Calisto 3 ☎06 583 5869; map p.160. An old-guard Trastevere bar which attracts a huge crowd on late summer nights; the booze is cheap, and you can sit at outside tables, too. Things are slightly less demimonde-ish during the day, when it's simply a great spot to sip a cappuccino, read and enjoy the sun. Mon–Sat 6am–2am.

Enoteca Ferrara Via del Moro 1a ☎06 5833 3920, ⓦenotecaferrara.it; map p.160. Just off Piazza Trilussa, this wine bar has a more restrained atmosphere than some of the nearby alternatives, and has a good selection of wines by the glass. There's a pricey restaurant next door that's not at all bad and also a more casual section with lower-priced traditional fare. Daily 7.30pm–1am.

Freni e Frizioni Via del Politeama 4/6 ☎06 4549 7499, ⓦfreniefrizioni.com; map p.160. Just off Piazza Trilussa, this former auto workshop – the name means "brakes and clutches" – is now home to a bustling bar with good cocktails. There's a long table piled high with buffet fare between 7 and 10pm, after which everyone gathers on the terrace by the river and DJs take over. Daily 7pm–2am.

★**Ma Che Siete Venuti A Fà** Via Benedetta 25 ☎06 645 2046, ⓦfootball-pub.com; map p.160. There's an amazing choice of artisanal beers from all over the world in this tiny Trastevere bar. Some of them can't be found anywhere else in the city, or even Italy, and this is a busy place to work your way through them. Daily 3pm–2am.

★**Ombre Rosse** Piazza di Sant'Egidio 12/13 ☎06 588 4155, ⓦombrerossecaffe.it; map p.160. A pubby yet very Italian café with a shady outside terrace and clubby interior that hosts live jazz and blues, and serves decent wine-bar-style snacks and light meals. It's something of a Trastevere institution, and is perhaps the neighbourhood's nicest bar. Daily 8am–2am.

VILLA BORGHESE AND NORTH

ReRe Bar Via Flaminia Vecchia 475, Flaminio ☎06 334 0483; map p.170. Just off Piazzale Ponte Milvio, this bar is all dressed up in a kitsch bordello style that draws folk from far and wide. It also serves food and has resident DJs. Daily 6pm–2am.

Tree Bar Via Flaminia 226, Flaminio ☎06 3265 2754, ⓦtreebar.it; map p.170. This place feels more north

European than Roman, with its dark-wood tables set under greenery and trees. It has a great range of local and international wines, and the cocktails and bar snacks (including pizza) are delicious. On Mondays they host an aperitivo with modern jazz and electro-soul. Daily 6.30pm–3pm.

THE VATICAN AND PRATI

Fonclea Via Crescenzio 82a ☎06 689 6302, ⓦfonclea .it; map p.188. This historic basement joint is loaded with devoted regulars and those who have happily discovered that there is life in the Vatican's sometimes somnolent Borgo and Prati areas. Happy hour (till 8.30pm) and often high-quality live music add to the fun (see p.275). Daily 7pm–2am.

Four Green Fields Via C. Morin 38–42 ☎06 372 5091, ⓦfourgreenfields.it; map p.188. This large Irish pub, decked out in wood and terracotta, stretches over two floors. Draught Guinness and Kilkenny complement the scene, along with decent pub grub and sport on TV. Mon–Fri noon–2am, Sat 6pm–2am, Sun 6pm–1.30am.

Morrison's Via Ennio Quirino Visconti 88 ☎06 322 2265, ⓦmorrisons.it; map p.188. An Irish-themed pub – although not all is as it seems, for as well as the usual beers and (good) pub food they also make spectacularly good cocktails, and the knowledgeable staff will guide you through their top-notch whiskey and gin selection. Daily 4pm–2am.

Saxophone Via Germanico 26 ☎06 3972 3039, ⓦsaxophonelivepub.it; map p.188. A welcoming pub in the shadow of the Vatican walls that does a good line in international beers and has Italian football on TV, plus occasional live music. Mon 6pm–2am, Tues–Thurs & Sun 5.30pm–2am, Fri & Sat 5.30pm–3am.

Senza Fondo Via Germanico 168 ☎06 8936 4725; map p.188. A convivial Prati basement pub with a good choice of beers and decent food. There's sometimes live music, too. Mon–Thurs & Sun 8pm–2am, Fri & Sat 8pm–3am.

La Zanzara Via Crescenzio 84, Prati ☎06 6839 2227, ⓦlazanzararoma.com; map p.188. A short walk from St Peter's, this stylish venue, complete with French/New York bistrot decor and outdoor terrace, is the perfect spot for an after-dinner cocktail or an aperitivo (from 6pm), when waiters come round with a selection of Mediterranean and Asian-inspired canapé snacks. Daily 8am–2am.

16

Clubs and live music

As you would expect in a major European capital, there's plenty to do in Rome after dark. Club entrance prices tend to be high, and the scene retains some of the glamorous ethos satirized in Fellini's *La Dolce Vita*, with designer-dressing-up still the order of the day in some places, particular in the city centre, although the hippest venues are increasingly found in grungier neighbourhoods further out. If you're after live music, check out the regular summer festivals (see Chapter 19), with venues all over town, including free events in Circo Massimo and Piazza del Popolo, although the chances of catching big names are low, partly because promoters tend to favour other Italian cities. Capital city or not, Rome is still a little bit sleepy compared to northern hubs like Milan.

ESSENTIALS

Centri sociali To get around the licensing laws, some of Rome's night haunts are run as private clubs – usually known as *centri sociali* or *associazioni culturali*, a device that means you may be stung for a small membership fee, particularly where there's music, but entry will be free – although as a one-off visitor some places will let you in without formalities, and others charge no fee at all to be a member. In recent decades these sorts of places have sprung up all over the city, particularly in the suburbs, and are becoming the focus of political activity and the more avant-garde elements of the music and arts scene.

Where to go In the centre the best areas tend to be Ostiense and Testaccio (especially in summer), Trastevere, and the Centro Storico from the Jewish Ghetto to the Pantheon.

What's-on information For listings information, check *Wanted in Rome* magazine and their website (ⓦwantedinrome.com); the newspaper *Il Messaggero* lists major musical events, while *TrovaRoma* in the Thurs edition of *La Repubblica* is another handy guide to current offerings.

LIVE MUSIC

Rome's **rock and pop** scene is a relatively limp affair, especially compared to the cities of the north, focusing mainly on foreign bands and the big venues like the Stadio Olimpico. Summer sees local bands giving occasional free concerts in the piazzas – for example on Piazzale del Verano – while the "Rock in Roma" festival takes place at the Ippodromo Capannelle (see below). The city is much more in its element with **jazz**, with lots of venues and a healthy array of local talent.

BIG VENUES

For information about events at any of these venues – really the city's only options for big, internationally renowned visiting bands and solo acts – call the Orbis agency (see p.279).

Atlantico Live Viale dell'Oceano Atlantico 271d, EUR ☎06 591 5727, ⓦatlanticoroma.it; metro B EUR Fermi or bus #714 from Termini; map p.155. A giant tent-like structure 400m from Pala Lottomatica (see below), this is one of two arenas where major acts tend to end up. The venue holds about 1500 people and hosts everything from sporting events to club nights.

Ippodromo Capannelle Via Appia Nuova 1255, Capannelle ☎06 716 771, ⓦcapannelleippodromo.it; metro A to Cinecittà, then bus 6541; after-concert shuttle buses go back to Rome Termini. Horseracing circuit on the southern fringes of the city that hosts large-scale music events, including the annual "Rock in Roma" summer festival (see p.285).

Pala Lottomatica Piazzale dello Sport, EUR ☎06 540 901, ☎02 488 571, ⓦpalalottomatica.it; metro B EUR Palasport or bus #714 from Termini; map p.155. This circular hall has upgraded acoustics, and hosts major Italian and foreign acts, sporting events and entertainment spectaculars.

Stadio Olimpico Piazzale del Foro Italico, Flaminio ☎06 36851, ⓦstadiodi.it; bus #32 or tram #2 from metro A Flaminio; map p.170. When huge acts such as U2 and Madonna perform in Rome, they play in this massive, 82,000-spectator stadium in the northern part of the city between Monte Mario and the Tiber.

ROCK AND POP VENUES

★**Fonclea** Via Crescenzio 82a, Prati ☎06 689 6302, ⓦfonclea.it; map p.188. A busy basement bar in the Vatican area that hosts regular live music – usually jazz, soul and funk, but also the occasional cover band – from about 9.30pm. Fri & Sat €7; otherwise free. Happy hour 7–8pm. Daily 7pm–2am.

Forte Fanfulla Via Fanfulla di Lodi 5, Pigneto ☎06 8902 1632; map p.128. Just off the Via Prenestina, this cavernous multi-roomed space hosts live music and assorted cultural happenings, and also has a couple of bars and a bistro. Entry requires a membership card, which costs €10 on the door. Once you're inside drinks are cheap and all shows are free.

Forte Prenestino Via F. Delpino 100, Prenestino ☎06 2180 7855, ⓦforteprenestino.net; map p.114. Just south of Via Prenestina, this early twentieth-century fortress, and giant squat since 1986, is home to one of Rome's most active *centri sociali*, with regular live music, film screenings (sometimes in English) and other events held both inside and out in the castle courtyards. It also boasts a bookshop, various studios and a very inexpensive restaurant (Mon–Fri). Its May Day "non-lavoro" events, held to celebrate the anniversary of the occupation of the building, are popular. Opening hours vary according to the event. Live acts €15–18, otherwise €5.

Planet Roma Via del Commercio 36, Ostiense ☎06 574 7826, ⓦplanetroma.com; map p.140. Housed in an ex-factory off Via Ostiense, a little way beyond Testaccio, the old *Alpheus* club has space for three simultaneous events – usually a disco, concert and exhibition or piece of theatre. Sat night is GIAM XL – gay night. Daily 10pm–4am.

JAZZ, LATIN AND BLUES VENUES

Alexanderplatz Via Ostia 9, Prati ☎06 8377 5604 or ☎06 3974 2171, ⓦalexanderplatzjazzclub.com; map p.188. Rome's top live jazz club/restaurant with reasonable membership (€15 a month) and free entry, except when there's star billing. Reservations recommended. Doors

17

open at 8pm, concerts begin at 9.45pm Mon–Thurs & Sun, 10.30pm Fri & Sat.

Beba Do Samba Via dei Messapi 8, San Lorenzo ⓣ 393 2857 50390, ⓦ bebadosamba.it; map p.114. Brazil Central in Rome, each night they highlight a new group, with the focus on Latin sounds, while the chill-out room is replete with comfortable cushions and divans. Daily 9pm–2.30am.

★**Big Mama** Vicolo San Francesco a Ripa 18, Trastevere ⓣ 06 581 2551, ⓦ bigmama.it; map p.160. Trastevere jazz/blues club of long standing, hosting acts five nights a week. Membership is €14, and entry is free except for star attractions (when it's important to book ahead). Daily 9pm–1.30am; doors open at 9pm, concerts begin at 10.30pm.

Caruso Café de Oriente Via di Monte Testaccio 36, Testaccio ⓣ 06 574 5019, ⓦ carusocafe.com; map p.140. Three rooms – and a roof terrace in the warm months – host Latin music most of the week, with soul, r'n'b and occasional live cover groups. Daily except Mon 11.30pm–4.30am.

★**Casa del Jazz** Viale di Porta Ardeatina 55 ⓣ 06 704 731, ⓦ casajazz.it; map p.140. Sponsored by the city, and very much the project of Rome's former mayor, jazz-loving Walter Veltroni, this converted villa (once Mafia property, before being sequestered by the state) is the ultimate jazz-lovers' complex: the 150-seat auditorium hosts jazz names most nights of the week, plus there's also a book and CD shop, restaurant and recording studios. Admission is €10–15. Most acts start at either 7pm or 9pm, and there are Sunday lunchtime concerts at noon; the restaurant is open every night until midnight. Check website for hours.

Escopazzo Via d'Aracoeli 41, around Campo de' Fiori ⓣ 06 678 4371, ⓦ escopazzo.it; map p.50. Halfway between Piazza Venezia and Largo Argentina, this friendly bar attracts a crowd of thirty-somethings and offers food and wine along with live concerts or jam sessions most nights. Daily except Mon 10pm–5am.

Gregory's Via Gregoriana 54a, Tridente ⓣ 06 679 6386, ⓦ gregorysjazz.com; map p.91. Just up the Spanish Steps and to the right, this elegant nightspot pulls in the crowds with its live jazz, improvised by Roman and international musicians. Daily except Mon 8pm–3am.

CLUBS

Rome's **clubs** run the gamut. There are vast glitter palaces with stunning lights and sound systems, predictable dance music and an overdressed, over-made-up clientele – good if you can afford it and just want to dance (and observe a good proportion of Romans in their natural Saturday-night element). But there are also places that are not much more than ritzy bars with music, and other, more down-to-earth venues playing a more interesting selection of music to a younger, more cautious-spending crowd (we've listed some of these in Chapter 16 as well). There is also a small number of clubs catering specifically to the LGBT+ scene (see p.288). All clubs tend to open and close late, and **entrance fees** vary from €10 to €30, though they often include a drink and there is the occasional free admission for women. During the hot **summer** months, many clubs close down or move to outdoor locations like EUR's parks or the beaches of Ostia and Fregene.

CLUB VENUES

Akab Via di Monte Testaccio 69, Testaccio ⓣ 06 5725 0585, ⓦ akabclub.com; map p.140. One of the longest-running clubs on the Testaccio nightlife scene, *Akab* provides a big, impressive space for posing and dancing, to house and techno mainly but with the odd live act. Tues–Sat 10pm–4am.

Art Café Via del Galoppatoio 33, Villa Borghese ⓣ 340 620 7432, ⓦ art-cafe.it; map p.173. Housed in the underground car park at Villa Borghese, this is one of Rome's trendiest clubs. Expect to queue, and dress up – otherwise you might not get in. Tues–Sat 9pm–6am.

Black Out Via Casilina 713, San Giovanni ⓣ 06 9784 1880, ⓦ blackoutrockclub.com; map p.128. A murky industrial San Giovanni club that plays punk, heavy metal and Goth music, with occasional gigs by US and UK bands. Thurs–Sat 11pm–4am; closed in summer.

Boeme Via Velletri 13, Villa Borghese ⓣ 06 841 2212; map p.104. The two halls here feature Baroque splendour and modernistic monochrome. Music ranges from Latin to techno. Daily except Mon 11pm–4am.

Brancaleone Via Levanna 13 ⓣ 339 507 4012, ⓦ brancaleone.it; map p.170. Featuring minimalist spaces with the feel of a Berlin squat, this *centro sociale* off the Via Nomentana hosts live acts and DJ sets, including reggae (Thurs), techno (Fri) and drum 'n' bass (Sat). Tues–Sat 11pm–5am.

Gilda Via Mario de' Fiori 97, Tridente ⓣ 06 678 4838, ⓦ gildabar.it; map p.91. Just a few blocks from the Spanish Steps, this slick, stylish and expensive club is the focus for the city's minor celebs and wannabes. You'll need to dress smart to get in. Thurs–Sun 11pm–5am.

Goa Via Libetta 13, Ostiense ⓣ 06 574 8277, ⓦ goaclub.com; map p.140. This long-running Ostiense club near the Basilica di San Paolo is where all the biggest DJs who come to Rome spin. There's a superb sound system playing techno, house and jungle, and an ethnic feel – a shop sells handmade crafts and there's incense burning, plus sofas to help you recover after high-energy dancing. Tues–Sat 11pm–4am.

Jackie O' Via Boncompagni 11, around Via Veneto ⓣ 06 4288 5457, ⓦ jackieoroma.com; map p.104. Amazingly, this 1960s Via Veneto jet-set glitter palace is still going strong, even attracting its share of celebs from time to time. It can actually be fun if you enjoy its rather retro notion of a night out, including a preponderance of mainstream Italian pop. Daily 8pm–4.30am; closed Mon in winter.

Lanificio 159 Via di Pietralata 159, Pietralata ☎06 4178 0081, ⓦlanificio.com; map p.104. Set in the restored remains of an industrial textile complex, *Lanificio* is a big, garage-style club hosting DJs, concerts and art installations. Thurs–Sun 10pm–4am.

★**Micca Club** Trevi Club Via degli Avignonesi, Quirinale ☎393 3236 244, ⓦmiccaclub.com; map p.104. Burlesque is the theme at the *Micca Club*'s relatively new home off Piazza Barberini. Check website for dates.

Qube Via di Portonaccio 212, Tiburtina ☎06 438 5445, ⓦqubedisco.com; map p.128. This big Tiburtina club hosts a variety of different nights each week, including live music. Not the most original for music but its well-established gay and drag night on Fri – Muccassassina ("Killer Cow"; ⓦmuccassassina.com) – draws a big crowd. 11pm–4am, though check website for dates as opening can be irregular.

Rashomon Via degli Argonauti 16, Ostiense ☎349 555 9926 ⓦrashomonclub.com; map p.140. A live music,

performance space and electronic music venue which walks the line between underground club and trendy point of reference for Roman indie musicians, artists and DJs. Fri nights draw the biggest crowds. Wed & Thurs 10pm–2am, Fri & Sat 11pm–4am.

Vicious Via Achille Grandi 7, Termini ☎06 7061 4349, ⓦviciousclub.com; map p.114. A low-rent Termini club that's more about underground vibes than dressing up, playing everything from indie and grunge to house and electronica. They also host a monthly gay night, enticingly entitled "Butter". Tues–Sat 10pm–4am.

Vinile Via Giuseppe Libetta 19, Ostiense ☎06 5728 8666, ⓦvinileroma.it; map p.140. Well known to Romans as the former Ostiense hotspot *45 Giri*, *Vinile* is open from aperitivo-time till late, with DJ sets following live music or dance events from around 11pm. Daily except Mon 7pm–4am.

Zoobar Via Generale Roberto Bencivenga 1, Nomentano ☎339 272 7995, ⓦzoobar.roma.it; map p.104. Out near Nomentana station, this club plays a wide range of different music – oldies, ska, funk, r'n'b and much more. Thurs–Sat 11pm–3.30am.

THE AUDITORIUM

Culture and entertainment

Northern Italy is where creativity in music, dance and, of course, opera flourishes, and even locals would admit that Rome is a bit of a backwater for the performing arts. Relatively few international-class performers put in an appearance here. Nevertheless, the city does have a cultural life, and what the arts scene may lack in quantity or quality is made up for by the charm of the city's settings. Also, various foreign academies, especially Villa Medici, put on a stimulating array of cultural events, from retrospectives to cutting-edge openings. Rome's summer festivals ensure a good range of classical music, opera, theatre and cinema throughout the warmer months, often in picturesque locations, and the summer opera performances at the Baths of Caracalla are resounding occasions.

During the winter, you'll find a regular programme of **classical music** mounted by the city's principal orchestra, the **Accademia Nazionale di Santa Cecilia**, and other sporadic musical offerings of mixed quality, sometimes in beautiful churches or palatial halls, and on occasions free. **Opera** is well established in Rome and now and again approaches world-class levels. High-quality **dance** performances are a rarity in Rome, although international companies do show up from time to time, usually at the Teatro Olimpico, Teatro dell'Opera, Auditorium (see below) and the Teatro Argentina (see p.280). Unfortunately, cinema-lovers will find few **films** in the original language, as Italy clings as strongly as ever to its historic dubbing tradition, but we've listed a few places where you might be able to find films in their unadulterated forms.

18

ESSENTIALS

Information For current listings information see the monthly *Wanted in Rome* magazine, or their website (W wantedinrome.com) – or the *TrovaRoma* booklet in newspaper *La Repubblica*'s Thursday edition. The website W romeing.it is also a good source of what's-on information, as is W anamericaninrome.com, a blog written by American Natalie Aldern Kennedy, which publishes a monthly listing of events in English. It's worth looking out, too, for old-fashioned street posters and playbills posted around town.

Ticket agencies HelloTicket ☎ 800 907 080, W helloticket.it; Orbis, Piazza Esquilino 37 (Santa Maria Maggiore) ☎ 06 474 4776; TicketOne ☎ 892 101, W ticketone.it.

CLASSICAL MUSIC AND OPERA

Rome's own **orchestras** are approaching international standards, and although the city attracts far fewer prestigious artists than you might expect of a capital, it is becoming more and more a magnet for contemporary works – a sea-change inspired by Renzo Piano's **Auditorium Parco della Musica**, completed over a decade ago (see below). Listings magazines (see above) and posters around town advertise little-known concerts – a wide range of choral, chamber and organ recitals – in **churches** such as Sant'Agnese in Agone and Sant'Ignazio or other spectacular venues, including the private halls and courtyards of Renaissance or Baroque palaces. Otherwise, the many national academies and **cultural institutes** – Belgian, Austrian, Hungarian, British, American, French, German, et al – frequently host concerts. In the **summer**, concerts are staged in cloisters, in the Teatro di Marcello, just off Piazza Venezia, and in the ancient Roman theatre at Ostia Antica and at Villa Adriana. It may be that you'll just stumble across a concert-in-progress while out on an evening stroll, passing by some ancient church with all its lights on: Rome is a city where such magical musical moments can still happen. The city's **opera** scene has long been overshadowed by that of Milan, Venice, Parma and Naples, grand opera's acknowledged birthplace, but it is improving and attracts an increasing number of mainstream and international performing artists. In summer, opera moves outdoors, with performances held in the stunning setting of the ancient **Baths of Caracalla**, as well as at several churches and venues all around Rome, as part of the various festivals that take place over the summer (see p.284).

VENUES

Accademia d'Opera Italiana All Saints' Church, Via del Babuino 153, Tridente ☎ 06 3600 1881, W accademiadoperaitaliana.it. Performances generally include popular standards such as *La Traviata*, *Tosca* and *The Barber of Seville*, as well as Mozart's *Requiem* and *Carmina Burana*. Tickets €15–35.

Auditorium Parco della Musica Viale Pietro de Coubertin 30, Flaminio ☎ 06 8024 11, box office ☎ 892 982, W auditorium.com; metro Flaminio, then tram #2, or bus to Viale de Coubertin. This landmark musical complex is Rome's most prestigious venue. It is home to the city's premier orchestra, the Accademia Nazionale di Santa Cecilia, who are resident part of the year in its largest hall, while two smaller venues host smaller chamber, choral, recital and experimental works. The complex also hosts major rock and jazz names when they come to town, as well as Rome's Film Festival in October (see p.286). Some critics have said that beauty has been sacrificed for acoustics here; the three halls definitely deliver on sound quality, while the outdoor space can be used for anything from rock to opera, and even as a skating rink in the winter. You can also visit or take a tour of the building without attending a concert (see p.179).

Aula Magna dell'Università La Sapienza Piazzale Aldo Moro 5, Termini ☎ 06 361 0051, W concertiiuc.it. La Sapienza University's Istituzione Universitaria dei Concerti is deliberately experimental and eclectic, with musical offerings ranging from Bach to Miles Davis, and from Chopin to Kurt Weill. There are concerts year-round, and performances are usually held Tues and Sat evenings. Tickets €15–35; discounts for under-30s.

Oratorio del Gonfalone Via del Gonfalone 32a, around Campo de' Fiori ☎ 06 687 5952,

18

Ⓦ oratoriogonfalone.com. This lovely frescoed theatre stages performances of chamber music, with an emphasis on the Baroque, every Thurs at 9pm, with the season running from Nov to May. Tickets cost €22; telephone reservations are strongly recommended. You can also arrange a tour of the Oratorio (Mon–Fri 10am–4pm; tours €8; call to pre-book).

Sala Casella Via Flaminia 118, Flaminio Ⓣ 06 320 1752, Ⓦ filarmonicaromana.org. This 200-seat concert hall within the Palazzina Vagnuzzi, renovated by Valadier in 1810, hosts the Accademia Filarmonica Romana during their summer season. Tickets cost €10.

Teatro dell'Opera di Roma Piazza Beniamino Gigli 7, Termini Ⓣ 06 481 60255, Ⓦ operaroma.it. Nobody compares it to La Scala, but cheap tickets are a lot easier to come by at Rome's opera and ballet venue – they start at €17 for opera, €12 for ballet – and important artists do sometimes perform here. If you buy the very cheapest tickets, bring some high-powered binoculars, as you'll need them in order to see anything at all. Don't miss the summer opera season, set in the Baths of Caracalla (tickets from

€20). Box office Mon–Sat 9am–6pm, Sun 9am–1.30pm.

Teatro di Villa Torlonia Via Nomentana 70, Nomentano Ⓣ 06 440 4768, Ⓦ casadeiteatri.roma.it/ teatro-di-villa-torlonia. Restored in 2013 to its former glory (see p.184), this small theatre mainly hosts plays in Italian, but also puts on music concerts, often with free entrance.

Teatro Ghione Via delle Fornaci 37, Vatican Ⓣ 06 637 2294, Ⓦ teatroghione.it. This traditional little theatre offers chamber music and recitals, often by well-known musical lights. Tickets €23–30. Box office daily 10am–2pm & 4–7pm.

Teatro Olimpico Piazza Gentile da Fabriano 17, Flaminio Ⓣ 06 326 5991, Ⓦ teatroolimpico.it; metro Flaminio, then tram #2. Classical standards, chamber music and ballet are performed here by the Accademia Filarmonica Romana (Ⓦ filarmonicaromana.org), as well as other companies. The theatre also hosts the occasional contemporary work. Performances run from end Oct to mid-May. Tickets (generally €25–30) are relatively easy to come by. Box office daily 10am–1.30pm & 2.30–6pm.

THEATRE AND DANCE

There is a great deal of **theatre** in Rome, but it's virtually all in Italian, or even Roman dialect. Very occasional English-language musicals, usually put together by some travelling American company, come to town during the winter season. The venue for such rare events is almost always either the Teatro Olimpico (see above) or the Teatro Sistina (see opposite). Check the listings magazines (see p.279) for current programmes. As for **dance**, apart from the very occasional international company, it's generally home-grown troupes doing their thing on the city's stages. Though the origins of ballet can be traced back to eighteenth-century Italy, there are at present few Italian companies that rise above amateurish levels. The Teatro dell'Opera (see above) also puts on ballet performances.

THEATRES

Miracle Players Ⓣ 06 7039 3427, Ⓦ miracleplayers. org. One of Rome's two English-language theatre companies, performing light-hearted renderings of the classics and lots of material with an ancient Rome theme, often in authentic venues – for example the Roman Forum in summer. Tickets are usually free.

Salone Margherita Via dei Due Macelli 75, Tridente Ⓣ 06 679 1439, Ⓦ salonemargherita.com. Traditional Roman political satire and cabaret – worth it for the atmosphere, even if you don't understand the admittedly difficult verbal sallies. Tickets from €25.

Teatro Argentina Largo di Torre Argentina 52, around Campo de' Fiori Ⓣ 06 6840 00314, Ⓦ teatrodiroma.net. One of the city's most important theatres for dramatic works in Italian and for dance. Tickets €15–60. Box office Tues–Sun 10am–2pm & 3–7pm.

Teatro Eliseo Via Nazionale 183, Esquiline Ⓣ 06 8351 0216, Ⓦ teatroeliseo.com. One of Rome's main theatres, hosting plays by Italian playwrights, and adaptations into Italian of foreign works, though it was under threat of closure at the time of writing. Tickets start at €15. Box office Mon–Sat 9.30am–1.30pm & 2.30–7.30pm.

Teatro Greco Via R. Leoncavallo 10–16, Trieste Ⓣ 06 860 7513, Ⓦ teatrogreco.it; metro Libia or bus to Largo Somalia. Located well out of the centre, on the far side of Villa Ada, this theatre generally offers some of the best Italian dance and even has its own company, with tickets starting at €15. Box office Mon, Tues & Thurs–Sun 4–7pm.

Teatro India Lungotevere Vittorio Gassman 1, Trastevere Ⓣ 06 6840 00311, Ⓦ teatrodiroma.net; bus, tram or train to Stazione Trastevere. The sister theatre to the Teatro Argentina is housed in an ex-factory across the Tiber from Ostiense. Tickets €18.

Teatro L'Arciliuto Piazza Montevecchio 5, Centro Storico Ⓣ 06 687 9419, Ⓦ rometheatre.com. Rome's longest-established English-language theatre group, the English Theatre of Rome, performs a few plays each season between Nov and June in this tiny theatre off Piazza Navona. Tickets €15.

Teatro Romano di Ostia Antica Ostia Antica Ⓣ 06 5635 0215, Ⓦ www.ostiaantica.beniculturali.it; Lido train from metro B Piramide to Ostia Antica. In July and Aug, specially scheduled performances of all kinds are offered in the restored ancient Roman theatre – a spectacular, unforgettable setting, even if you don't speak Italian. Performances begin at 8pm, but go early for a chance to visit the ruins. It's a 30min train ride to Ostia Antica, then a short walk over the footbridge into the ruins. A great Roman summer experience. Box office Tues–Sun 4–7pm.

Teatro Sistina Via Sistina 129, Tridente ☎ 06 420 0711, ⓦ ilsistina.it. Every now and then an English-language (American, very off-Broadway) musical revue blows into town and it generally ends up here, just up from

Piazza di Spagna. Gershwin seems to be a perennial favourite, along with other jazzy-bluesy musical confections. Box office Mon–Sat 10am–8.30pm.

Teatro Vittoria Piazza Santa Maria Liberatrice 8–11, Testaccio ☎ 06 578 1960, ⓦ teatrovittoria.it. In Testaccio's main square, this large theatre sometimes books cabaret-like acts or dance-theatre companies that need no translation. Tickets from €19. Box office Mon 4–7pm, Tues–Sat 11am–8pm, Sun 11am–1.30pm & 4–6pm.

18

FILM

There tends to be limited **English-language cinema** in Rome, partly owing to lack of foreign demand, partly to the Italian penchant for dubbing. Look out for the words *versione originale* (abbreviated "VO" in listings) to be sure a film isn't dubbed. If your Italian is up to it, you'll naturally find current productions, as well as programmes for movie buffs, from silent films with live music to experimental cinema. **Listings** can be found in all newspapers and at ⓦ romereview.com or at ⓦ mymovies.lt; **tickets** cost €6–10, though some cinemas offer bargain early shows. Watch out for **film festivals** (see below & p.286) across the year (generally showing films in the original language) from one to five days, some of which show excellent films, especially from France, Spain and northern Europe, but plenty from further afield as well. Also, a week or so after the major festivals in Cannes, Locarno and Venice, a selection of those films presented comes to Rome.

CINEMAS

Barberini Piazza Barberini 24/26, Quirinale ☎ 06 4201 0392, ⓦ cinemabarberini.it. This central cinema offers first-run English-language films, some in VO.

Casa del Cinema Largo Marcello Mastroianni 1, Villa Borghese ☎ 06 423601, ⓦ casadelcinema.it. Right by the Porta Pinciana entrance to the Villa Borghese, this cinema hosts film premieres, festivals, reruns and retrospectives, often in the original language. In summer it moves outside (see box below).

Cinema dei Piccoli Largo Marcello Mastroianni 15, Villa Borghese ☎ 06 855 3485, ⓦ cinemadeipiccoli.it. Near the Casa del Cinema, this charming, tiny cinema in a little green house in the Villa Borghese hosts children's

films in the daytime, and in the evenings shows films for adults, sometimes in the original language.

Farnese Campo de' Fiori 56 ☎ 06 686 4395, ⓦ cinemafarnesepersol.com. This cinema has a good programme of independent films, many of which are shown in their original language.

Filmstudio Via degli Orti d'Alibert 1c, Trastevere ☎ 334 178 0632, ⓦ filmstudioroma.com. Arty films and themed retrospectives are shown in this renovated old cinema with tiny screens in Trastevere near the Tiber. Check first that the film is VO. Closed July–Sept.

Multisala Lux Via Massaciuccoli 31, Trieste ☎ 06 8639 1361; metro Sant'Agnese. It's a bit out of the way, but this multiplex with ten screens often shows blockbusters in

---

SUMMER FILM VENUES

Summer film offerings tend to be lightweight fare and "popolare", geared to a mainstream local audience, therefore the selection, even though it may lean heavily towards Hollywood fare, is mainly dubbed. Here are a few of the outdoor venues that offer alternatives, all in magical settings.

Casa del Cinema Largo Marcello Mastroianni 1, Villa Borghese ☎ 06 0608, ⓦ casadelcinema.it. The director here puts together interesting programmes with themes based on studios, actors, directors, and subjects that range from Shakespeare to futuristic Science Fiction, almost all in original language. Set among umbrella pines, with a handy café.

L'Isola del Cinema Isola Tiberina, around Campo de' Fiori ⓦ isoladelcinema.com. Although few films are shown in their original language, there are the occasional special events that bring in directors or actors for VO films. Either way, the setting by the river is

magical and there are plenty of good stalls offering everything from cocktails to creative gourmet food (see box, p.252).

Villa Medici Viale della Trinità dei Monti, Tridente ☎ 06 676 11, ⓦ villamedici.it (see p.96). In summer the French Academy's film programme moves outdoors into the glorious sculptural formal garden and always explores interesting themes; films are shown in the original language, the international selection often includes English and there's always something interesting to see.

their original language.

Nuovo Olimpia Via in Lucina 16, Tridente ☎06 8880 1283. Very central, just off Via del Corso, with two screens, and featuring foreign films in the original language most days. Reduced-price tickets weekday afternoons and Wed evenings.

Nuovo Sacher Largo Ascianghi 1, Trastevere ☎06 581 8116, ⓦsacherfilm.eu. Nanni Moretti's Trastevere film theatre, housed in the old Fascist youth HQ, occasionally shows current films in their original version on Mon, tending towards independent, left-leaning works.

Politecnico Fandango Via Tiepolo 13a, Flaminio ☎06 3608 6566, ⓦfandango.com; metro Flaminio then tram #2. This small cinema is carved out of what looks like an old garage. Run by a left-leaning film production and distribution company, it often shows feature films in the original language, usually with a social message. Its enchanting little courtyard also houses *Bistrot*, a cosy café and trattoria.

Quattro Fontane Via Quattro Fontane 23, Quirinale ☎06 8880 1283. Lots of mainstream films and the occasional art-house choice, with regular screenings in VO.

The Space Moderno Piazza della Repubblica 45, Termini ☎892 111, ⓦthespacecinema.it. This American-style multiplex shows dubbed Hollywood blockbusters.

Trevi Vicolo del Puttarello 25, Trevi ☎06 678 1206, ⓦfondazionecsc.it. This is a treasure-trove for buffs seeking films from the Cineteca Nazionale archives, some recently restored or featured in intriguing themes, although you have to check for VO, otherwise films are dubbed.

Villa Medici Académie de France à Rome Viale della Trinità dei Monti, Tridente ☎06 676111, ⓦvillamedici. it. Of all the foreign academies in Rome, the French is arguably the most international in its approach and most active in its cultural programmes, often showing English-language films and sometimes hosting a surprising line-up of guests. The small cinema is lovely, as is the garden, where films are shown in summer, plus there's a great bar.

Festivals

Rome puts on an array of festivals and events throughout the year, from ceremonious religious processions marking important saints' days to summertime cinema under the stars. Austerity cuts have put paid to some of the city's music festivals and cultural events in recent years, but there's still plenty on, especially over the summer. On public holidays (see p.31) many sights and shops are closed, as well as some bars and restaurants. When a public holiday falls midweek, Romans generally take it as an excuse to "fare il ponte" – "make a bridge" between the holiday and the weekend. Some of Rome's festivals run for months, especially over the summer, so check the preceding months' events in the list below too.

19

JANUARY

New Year's Day Jan 1. Thousands gather in St Peter's Square for the pope's New Year's Day blessing, and marching bands parade along Via della Conciliazione. The annual Tuffo nel Tevere ("Dive into the Tiber"), at noon, sees hardy souls jumping from the Ponte Cavour into the freezing waters below. Most museums are closed on this day.

Epiphany (La Befana) Jan 6. Epiphany sees the culmination of Piazza Navona's Christmas market, when La Befana herself touches down in the square (see box opposite).

FEBRUARY

Carnevale Mid-Feb. For ten days Roman kids dress up and are paraded around the city by their proud parents, and clubs put on themed nights. Look out for the carnival delicacies sold throughout the city: *frappe* (deep-fried pastry strips) and *castagnole* (bite-sized pastries). Piazza Navona hosts good Commedia dell'Arte performances and Piazza del Popolo puts on a horse show.

MARCH

Rome Marathon Mid-March ⓦ maratonadiroma.it. 17,000 runners take part in the city's annual marathon, one of the world's most scenic (see p.305).

Giornate FAI One weekend in spring ⓦ giornatefai.it. For one weekend in spring, buildings usually closed to the public open their doors to show off their spectacular interiors.

APRIL

Easter During Holy Week, Catholics from across the world descend on Rome to witness the pope's address. On the night of Good Friday, a solemn procession makes its way from the Colosseum to the Capitoline Hill, while on Easter Sunday the main events are the 10am Mass in St Peter's Square, followed by the pope's "Urbi et Orbi" blessing.

Pasquetta Easter Monday. Many Romans head out of town, traditionally for a picnic in the countryside.

Mostra delle Azalee Mid- to late April. The Spanish Steps are lined with pots of colourful azaleas.

Natale di Roma April 21. Rome's birthday is marked by a spectacular fireworks display set off from the Campidoglio and a weekend costume parade.

Liberation Day April 25. Commemorates the liberation of Italy by the Allies at the end of World War II. A solemn procession marches from the Colosseum to Piazza Porta San Paolo, and cycling events take place across the capital.

MAY

Primo Maggio May 1. "Primo Maggio" is celebrated with a free rock concert in Piazza San Giovanni. Most museums are closed.

Rome Masters First two weeks of May. Rome's international tennis tournament (see p.305) is a warm-up event for the French Open.

Mille Miglia Mid-May ⓦ 1000miglia.eu. Many antique cars roll through the city as part of a Brescia–Rome–Brescia tour.

Festival Piazza di Siena Late May ⓦ piazzadisiena. org. This swanky show-jumping event takes place in Villa Borghese.

JUNE

Festival delle Letterature Throughout June ☏ 06 0608, ⓦ festivaldelleletterature.it. June's international literature festival is set in the Casa delle Letterature (see p.46) and the Piazza del Campidoglio. Celebrated authors, some English-speaking, lecture or read their works, collaborating with actors and musicians.

Notti d'Estate a Castel Sant'Angelo June to early Sept ⓦ castelsantangeloestate.it. Classical, opera and jazz concerts on Wednesday, Friday, Saturday and Sunday nights, as well as special guided tours of Castel Sant'Angelo from Tuesday to Sunday.

Eutropia Festival June to mid-Sept ⓦ eutropiafestival. it. Taking place in the ex-Mattatoio in Testaccio, this summer-long music festival features mainly Italian rock bands, with the odd big international act.

Day of the Republic June 2. The day is marked with a military parade along Via dei Fori Imperiali at 10am (the Colosseum and Forum are usually closed on this day), and the gardens of the Quirinale Palace are open to the public for free in the afternoon (expect long queues).

Infiorata Two days in June. Genzano, a town in the Castelli Romani, holds its famous Infiorata every year on the Sunday and Monday following Corpus Christi. Locals completely cover one of the town's main streets with a carpet of flower petals in intricate patterns and pictures. Every year there's a different theme – the colours of Michelangelo, say. The finished result is a sight to behold – though it's trampled underfoot by a masked parade at the end of the festival.

Estate Romana Mid-June to Sept ☏ 06 0608, ⓦ estateromana.comune.roma.it. The main cultural focus of the summer is the Estate Romana, with events organized throughout the city, including musical and theatrical performances, film projections, art exhibits and events for children, staged in venues throughout the city, such as the cloister of San Pietro in Vincoli, the MACRO and the Isola Tiberina.

Rock in Roma Mid-June to early Sept ⓦrockinroma.com. The annual Rock in Roma festival has survived austerity, with sponsorship. It's basically a series of gigs throughout the summer staged at the Ippodromo Capannelle on the southern edge of the city (see p.275).

Isola del Cinema Mid-June to early Sept ⓦisoladelcinema.com. A summertime film festival (see p.281), with films shown nightly in the atmospheric setting of the Isola Tiberina (see p.58), with lots of food stalls, too.

Teatro dell'Opera Late June to mid-Aug ⓦoperaroma.it. The prestigious Teatro dell'Opera's summer season takes place in the spectacularly floodlit setting of the Baths of Caracalla.

Festa di Santi Pietro e Paolo June 29. Rome celebrates its two patron saints, St Peter and St Paul, with a Mass at St Peter's and a street fair on Via Ostiense, near the basilica of San Paolo fuori le Mura.

JULY

Roma Incontra il Mondo Throughout July ⓦvillaada.org. A series of outdoor pop, rock and indie concerts (with dining facilities) in Rome's largest park, Villa Ada. Tickets cost around €12.

Villa Celimontana July & Aug ⓦvillacelimontana jazzfestival.com. Open-air jazz festival in Villa Celimontana park.

Festa de' Noantri Mid-July. A procession in honour of the Madonna del Carmine begins a fortnight of street performances and events in Trastevere; a huge fireworks display marks the end of the festivities.

International Chamber Ensemble Mid-July to mid-Aug ⓦwww.interensemble.org. A series of evening chamber concerts in the splendid setting of the courtyard of Sant'Ivo alla Sapienza (see p.44). Tickets €21.

19

AUGUST

Festa delle Catene Aug 1. The chains of St Peter are displayed during a special Mass in the church of San Pietro in Vincoli.

Festa della Madonna della Neve Aug 5. The miracle of a summer snowfall (see box, p.116) is remembered in the Basilica of Santa Maria Maggiore with a shower of white petals in front of the main altar.

Ferragosto Aug 15. Original "holiday of Augustus", later the Feast of the Assumption; Rome empties as locals in search of cooling breezes head for the sea and mountains.

SEPTEMBER

Macchina di Santa Rosa 3 Sept ⓦmacchinasantarosa.it. The locals of Viterbo rebuild the Macchina di Santa Rosa, a thirty-metre-high tower in honour of their patron saint, every summer. On the evening of 3 September a hundred men lift the tower and carry it through the town's narrow streets. The procession draws thousands of spectators, and the night's festivities culminate in a spectacular fireworks display.

RomaEuropa Festival Late Sept to early Dec ☎06 4555 3050, ⓦromaeuropa.net. This international contemporary arts festival has gathered pace in recent years, and is now a pretty big deal, with dance, drama and highbrow music events at various theatres around town, and other venues such as MACRO. Some events are free, but most are priced at €15–35.

Taste of Roma 5 days in Sept ⓦtasteofroma.it. Rome's big food festival, held at the Auditorium Parco della Musica, is worth planning a trip around, with demonstrations from top Italian chefs and lots of food stalls.

LA BEFANA

There are many stories about **La Befana**, always depicted as an ugly old woman who flies along on a broom draped in black. The most recognized version is that she was outside sweeping when three kings walked by; she stopped them and asked where they were going. The kings responded that they were following a star in search of a newborn baby. They invited her to come along, but she declined, saying she had too much sweeping and cleaning to do. When she found out who it was the kings were off to find, her regret for not having joined them was so great that she has spent eternity rewarding good children with presents and sweets and bad children with pieces of coal on the day of Epiphany, **January 6**. Each year, from early December until this day, Piazza Navona sets up the **Befana toy fair**, where endless stalls tempt children with every sort of sticky sweet and even chunks of black sugar made to look like coal. There are also toy stands and manger scenes where children leave letters for La Befana, asking her for specific presents and toys.

OCTOBER

Sagra dell'Uva First Sun of Oct. Marino, in the Castelli Romani, has a great wine festival in early October, at which the town's fountains flow with wine and you can sample the local *vino novello* to your heart's content.

Rome Film Festival 8 days in mid-Oct ☎ 06 4040 1900, ⓦ romacinemafest.it. This international film festival is held at the Auditorium and a variety of other venues around town. Tickets generally cost under €20 and can be purchased from the Auditorium box office (see p.279) or from ⓦ listicket.it.

NOVEMBER

Ognissanti & Giornata dei Defunti Nov 1 & 2. On All Saints' Day (a public holiday), the pope usually celebrates Mass at Verano cemetery in San Lorenzo. The following day, All Souls' Day, Romans visit family graves.

Roma Jazz Festival Nov ⓦ romajazz.it. Two-week festival at the Auditorium that showcases the best of Italian jazz and experimental music, and attracts big names from around the world.

DECEMBER

Immacolata Concezione Dec 8. In honour of the Immaculate Conception of the Blessed Virgin Mary, a religious ceremony takes place in the Piazza di Spagna, often attended by the pope.

Christmas (Natale) Dec 25. In the build-up to Christmas, from mid-December, a Christmas fair sets up in Piazza Navona (see box above) and there's an outdoor ice rink near Castel Sant'Angelo. Elaborate Christmas cribs (*presepi*) appear in churches all over the city; those in Piazza di Spagna and St Peter's Square draw the biggest crowds. On Christmas Eve the pope celebrates Midnight Mass in St Peter's (tickets are in high demand; contact the Prefettura as far in advance if possible – see box, p.187). The pope also leads Mass on the day itself and a blessing at noon in St Peter's Square. All of the major sights are closed.

Santo Stefano (St Stephen) Dec 26.

New Year's Eve Dec 31. Known as Capodanno or the Festa di San Silvestro in Italy, New Year's Eve sees a free concert in the Circus Maximus, featuring Italian acts and a fireworks display. The Piazza del Popolo, Campo de' Fiori and Piazza Navona are all lively places to spend the evening. The city's metro stays open late (usually till 2.30am), though there are generally no nightbuses running.

19

LGBT+ Rome

Italy has never had any laws prohibiting same-sex couplings, but until recently remained quite conservative concerning rights and gay sex. In 2016, however, the Italian courts finally ruled to recognize and legalize same-sex civil unions. Rome has also made huge progress over the past decade; the former mayor, Ignazio Marino, was pro-gay rights and worked to make the capital a more gay-friendly place. The city has a number of LGBT+ clubs and bars, as well as all sorts of hetero clubs organizing gay nights to cater for the growing scene. There's also the tremendously successful Gay Village (ⓦgayvillage.it), which holds events throughout the summer at an open-air venue in EUR, and the ever-popular Gay Pride in June (ⓦromapride.it), twinned with that of San Francisco, no less.

The scene is well spread out: apart from a short stretch of **Via di San Giovanni in Laterano**, optimistically dubbed "Gay Street" for its nightlife scene (⟳gaystreetroma.com), there's no specifically gay area. You need a membership card to enter gay cruise bars, saunas and clubs in Italy, generally the **Anddos card** (see below), or sometimes you will have to become a member of the venue itself for a small fee. Photo ID is generally required to buy a card. Choices exclusively for **women** remain very few, although most places welcome both gay men and lesbians. Bear in mind that while great strides have been made, Rome remains a city where eyebrows may still be raised at men holding hands in the street and the city is certainly not quite ready for kissing in public. There are a couple of useful **websites** aimed at LGBT+ visitors: ⟳gayrome4u.com and ⟳patroc.com/rome.

CONTACTS AND SERVICES

Anddos Via Flavia 47 ☏06 6482 4220, ⟳anddos.org. The National Association against Sexual Orientation Discrimination sells the Anddos Card, which most cruise bars, saunas and clubs require for entry. You can generally buy it at the entrance for €17 (or €10 for just one bar, sauna or club); it's valid for a year.

Arcigay Via Zabaglia 14 ☏800 713 713, ⟳www.arcigayroma.it. The Rome branch of the Italian gay organization hosts gatherings for those new to the city on Wed (7–9pm). Annual membership costs €15 and will get you into Arcigay-organized events. The helpline is open Mon & Fri 4–9pm, Tues, Wed, Thurs & Sat 4–8pm.

Casa Internazionale delle Donne Via della Lungara 19 ☏06 6840 1720, ⟳casainternazionaledelledonne.org. Not a gay organization but rather a group of facilities for women only, including a bookshop, library, restaurant and café, housed, appropriately enough, in an old convent. It also has accommodation in its *Orsa Maggiore* hostel (☏06 689 3753, ⟳foresteriaorsa.altervista.org).

Circolo di Cultura Omosessuale Mario Mieli Via Efeso 2a ☏06 541 3985, ⟳mariomieli.org. Rome's most important gay activist organization offers a broad range of social and health services, including counselling and a helpline – ☏800 110 611. Weekly welcome group, political group and volunteer group meetings; call for details.

BARS AND CLUBS

In addition to the dedicated gay bars and clubs below, a few hetero clubs put on **gay nights**, including the long-established Muccassassina at *Qube* (see p.277) and Butter, which takes place on a Friday once a month at *Vicious* (see p.277). The city's most popular gay and lesbian club night is Saturday night's GIAM XL at *Planet Roma* (see p.275), with three dancefloors, a women-only room and an r'n'b and house soundtrack.

Beige Via del Politeama 13, Trastevere ☏347 389 1974, ⟳beigeroma.com; map p.160. This Trastevere lounge bar has occasional live music and DJ sets, and there's a good *aperitivo* buffet on Fri and Sat (drink with free buffet €10). Tues–Thurs 7pm–2am, Fri & Sat 6pm–3am.

Coming Out Via di San Giovanni in Laterano 8, Celian Hill ☏06 700 9871, ⟳comingout.it; map p.128. If any area has developed as Rome's gay zone, it is the stretch between the Colosseum and San Clemente. This little pub with its street terrace is the epicentre of the scene, frequented mostly by a younger clientele. Daily 7am–2am.

Garbo Vicolo di Santa Margherita 1a, Trastevere ☏06 581 2766, ⟳garbobar.it; map p.160. A friendly Trastevere bar, just behind Piazza di Santa Maria in Trastevere, with a relaxed atmosphere and a nice setting. Tues–Sun 10pm–5am.

L'Alibi Via Monte Testaccio 44, Testaccio ☏06 574 3448, ⟳lalibi.it; map p.140. This predominantly, but by no

GAY FESTIVALS AND EVENTS

A number of **gay festivals and events** take place over the summer, and can be worth planning a trip around. A favourite summer fixture, **Gay Village** (mid-June to mid-Sept Thurs–Sat; ⟳gayvillage.it), sees music, films, theatre and parties organized in the open-air location of the Parco del Ninfeo in EUR. A week of events leads up to **Roma Pride** in mid-June (☏06 541 3985, ⟳romapride.it), when a colourful parade snakes through the city centre. A more leftfield event, but increasingly popular, is the **Italian Gaymes** (⟳italiangaymes.it), an annual sports tournament that takes place over four days in mid-July, with a run around EUR, football, tennis and volleyball, among other activities.

20

means exclusively, male venue is one of Rome's oldest gay clubs, situated in the heart of the city's alternative night scene in Testaccio. It's no longer quite cutting-edge, but is a good all-round hangout, with a multi-room cellar disco, an upstairs open-air bar and a big terrace to enjoy in the warm months. Oct to mid-June Fri–Sun midnight–5am.

My Bar Via di San Giovanni in Laterano 12, Celian Hill ☏06 700 4425, ⓦmybar-roma.it; map p.128. Another popular spot on lively Via di San Giovanni in Laterano, *My Bar* has a good terrace, an extensive cocktail menu and a buzzy vibe later on. Daily 9am–2am.

Skyline Via Pontremoli 36, San Giovanni ☏06 700 9431, ⓦskylineclub.it; map p.128. Gay male strippers, dark zones and a decidedly macho decor make this San Giovanni club a magnet for various creatures of the night, possibly drawn by the heavy cruising on the balcony. Various regular theme nights, including "Naked Party" on Mon. Mon–Thurs & Sun 10.30pm–3am, Fri & Sat 10.30pm–4am.

SAUNAS

Europa Multiclub Via Aureliana 40, Quirinale ☏06 482 3650, ⓦeuropamulticlub.com. This sauna has pleasantly stylish, clean facilities and a snack bar. Mon–Thurs 1pm–midnight, Fri 1pm nonstop until Sun at midnight.

Mediterraneo Via Pasquale Villari 3, Celian Hill ☏06 7720 5934, ⓦsaunamediterraneo.it. This is a sauna on two levels, with all the usual choices, attracting mainly older men. Notably clean and has a snack bar. Daily 1–11pm.

ACCOMMODATION

Ares Rooms Via Domenichino 7, Termini ☏334 959 2057, ⓦaresrooms.com; map p.114. This gay-friendly bed-and-breakfast near Termini station has functional, spotless rooms, not all en suite. Staff are very welcoming and helpful and there's a small kitchen with microwave and fridge. **€70**

Relais Conte di Cavour Via Farini 16, Termini ☏347 182 9387, ⓦbed-and-breakfast-rome.com; map p.114. Very comfortable double rooms in a small, gay-friendly Via

Cavour *pensione*. Breakfast costs €5 extra. **€110**

Second Floor Via di San Giovanni in Laterano 10, Celian Hill ☏06 9604 9256, ⓦ2floor.it; map p.128. This bed-and-breakfast is situated on "Gay Street", directly above the popular *Coming Out* bar (see opposite) – bring earplugs. More than gay-friendly, it's actually aimed at gay couples, with bright, stylishly decorated rooms, some with a terrace and Colosseum views. **€120**

20

Shops and markets

At first glance, you may wonder where to start when it comes to shopping in a big, chaotic city like Rome. In fact, the city promises a more appealing shopping experience than you might think, abounding with pleasant, frequently car-free shopping streets and markets, many of them in the city centre. What's more, Rome hasn't yet been entirely overrun by the international chain stores that characterize most European city centres. One-stop shopping opportunities are rare, but you will find corners of the city that have been colonized by stores selling the same sort of merchandise – fashion, antiques, food – making it easy for you to check out the competition's products and prices. You will also still find true artisans in central Rome, some of whom sell their products directly to the public.

ESSENTIALS

Opening hours Quite a few shops in the centre of Rome stay open all day and are open on Sun too. However, many still observe the city's traditional opening hours: roughly Mon 3.30–7.30pm, Tues–Sat 9.30am–1.30pm & 3.30–7.30pm, and are closed on Sun. Food shops are also often closed on Thurs afternoon in winter and Sat afternoon during the summer. Markets tend to open early – around 7am – and close up by 2pm. Supermarkets are generally open all day from 8am until 8pm. Bear in mind that a lot of stores close down around mid-Aug for their annual holiday.

Tax-free shopping It's worth knowing that non-EU residents can save up to 14.5 percent of the purchase price, on a minimum purchase of €154.95. To do this you need to request a Tax Refund Cheque at the time of purchase. Then, before leaving Italy, go to the customs desk at the airport with your purchases, receipt, refund cheque and passport, and afterwards go to the designated Tax Free service desk for your credit, either on a card or as a cash refund. Allow plenty of time, as there's often a long queue.

Credit cards Most places accept all major credit cards, but a few stalwarts remain cash-only.

WHERE TO SHOP

Fashion Fashion straight from the catwalk is well represented on the stylish streets close to the Spanish Steps – Via dei Condotti, Via Borgognona, Via Frattina and Via del Babuino – where you'll find all the major A-list designers (see box, p.292) as well as lots of alluring, one-off boutiques. You can find more mainstream fashions and all the chains on Via Cola di Rienzo, near the Vatican, and also on Via Nazionale, near to which the streets of Monti are home to an increasing number of stylish independent stores. Bang in the centre of town, Via del Corso is the home of mainstream young fashion stores and various downscale chains (aside from Fendi and a mammoth Zara). Via dei Giubbonari, near Campo de' Fiori, is a good place to shop for affordably priced yet stylish clothes and shoes, and Via del Governo Vecchio is probably the city centre's best stretch of funky, stylish independent fashion boutiques and vintage stores. For more traditional and very stylish shops, especially for men, try the area between the Pantheon and Piazza San Lorenzo in Lucina.

Art and antiques Antique shops line Via dei Coronari and neighbouring Via dell'Orso and Via dei Soldati, just north of Piazza Navona. Via Giulia, southwest of Campo de Fiori, as well as Via del Babuino and Via Margutta, between Piazza del Popolo and the Spanish Steps, are also good sources of art and antiques; other worthwhile haunts are southwest of Campo de' Fiori, along Via Giulia, Monserrato and Banchi Vecchi.

Markets The city's many markets offer a change of pace from Rome's busy shopping streets. Many of these are bustling local food markets and, even in the centre, are still very much part of Roman life, especially in the mornings. The market in Campo de' Fiori is probably the most central, and certainly the best known, but we've listed others (see p.302). Otherwise, dedicated bargain-hunters still prowl Trastevere's Porta Portese flea market, selling heaps of antiques, clothing, books and indeed virtually anything else, every Sun morning (see p.166).

ANTIQUES

Antichità Archeologia Largo della Fontanella di Borghese 76, Centro Storico ☎ 06 686 4054; map p.36.

If you want to take home your own piece of ancient Rome, this is the place for you. Certified genuine Greek, Etruscan

MUSEUM SHOPS

Once almost entirely absent, **museum shops** have flourished in Rome in recent years. Most specialize in books, but those that feature modern exhibitions, like the Palazzo delle Esposizioni, often have designer items too, from jewellery and sculpture to desktop accessories. Hours will generally be the same as the museum's hours – you should never have to pay admission to gain entry.

Galleria Borghese Piazzale del Museo Borghese ☎ 06 841 3979. Great for titles on the major artistic periods, from the Renaissance to the Baroque.

MAXXI Via Guido Reni 4a ☎ 06 320 1954. Good art bookshop, as you would expect, with an emphasis on contemporary art, architecture and design.

Musei Capitolini Piazza del Campidoglio 1 ☎ 06 0608. Good book selection on ancient Rome as well as art through the Renaissance and Baroque periods.

Palazzo delle Esposizioni Via Nazionale 194 ☎ 06 3996 7500. Great all-round art and design shop situated in the basement of the building.

Scuderie del Quirinale Via XXIV Maggio 16 ☎ 06 3996 7500. Excellent art bookshop, covering all the major periods and artists.

Trajan's Markets Via IV Novembre 94 ☎ 06 0608. Particularly good for books about Rome, especially on ancient sites and archeology.

21

and Roman antiquities, such as terracotta oil lamps, figurines and incised jewels, start at about €100. Mon 3.30–7pm, Tues–Sat 10am–1pm & 3.30–7pm.

Oasi Antiquariato Via del Babuino 83, Tridente ☎06 320 7585; map p.91. One of several fine antiques stores in the area, with a large collection of stunning Italian furnishings from the 1700s. There is also an entrance on Via Margutta. Mon–Sat 9.30am–7.30pm.

Valerio Turchi Via Margutta 91a, Tridente ☎06 323 5047; map p.91. A bit different from the other antiques shops on Via Margutta, with exquisite pieces from Rome's past – various pieces of Roman statues and sarcophagi dating from as early as 300 AD. Mon–Fri 10am–7pm, Sat 10am–1pm.

BOOKS

★**The Almost Corner Bookshop** Via del Moro 45, Trastevere ☎06 583 6942; map p.160. Of all Rome's English bookshops, this stalwart Trastevere store is the best bet for having the very latest titles on your list of must-reads. Mon–Sat 10am–8pm, Sun 11am–8pm.

★**Anglo-American Bookshop** Via della Vite 102, Tridente ☎06 679 5222, ⓦaab.it; map p.91. An excellent city-centre English-language bookshop, with one of the best selections of new English books in Rome. It's especially good on history and academic books, but has lots of fiction, too. Sept–June Mon 3.30–7.30pm, Tues–Sat 10.30am–7.30pm; July to mid-Aug Mon–Fri 10.30am–7.30pm, Sat 10.30am–2.30pm; closed mid-to end Aug.

Feltrinelli International Via Vittorio Emanuele Orlando 84, Esquiline ☎06 482 7878; map p.114. Just off Piazza della Repubblica, this international branch of the nationwide chain has a great stock of books in English, as well as French, German, Spanish and Portuguese. The large store at Largo di Torre Argentina (☎06 6866 3001) also has an English-language selection and a coffee bar upstairs. Mon–Sat 9am–8pm, Sun 10.30am–1.30pm & 4–8pm.

Open Door Bookshop Via della Lungaretta 23, Trastevere ☎06 589 6478, ⓦbooks-in-italy.com; map p.160. Although they do have some new titles, especially on Rome and Roman history, used books dominate the shelves at this friendly Trastevere bookshop, where you never know what treasures you might turn up. They also have a selection of books in Italian, German, French and Spanish. Mon–Sat 10.30am–8pm; closed Sat in July & Aug.

Ottimomassimo Via Luciano Manara 16, Trastevere ☎06 9021 5070, ⓦottimomassimo.eu; map p.160. A local Trastevere institution for families and children, this bookshop not only boasts a wide range of educational items, books and games for kids of all ages, but hosts regular family-friendly events and readings. Daily 10am–7.30pm.

CLOTHES

Alberta Ferretti Philosophy 34a Via dei Condotti, Tridente ☎06 699 1160; map p.91. Almost every season this designer incorporates a few dresses that hark back to the fluid, soft lines of ancient Rome, as well as some very contemporary styles. Mon 4–7pm, Tues–Sat 10am–7pm.

Anteprima Roma Via delle Quattro Fontane 38–40, Quirinale ☎06 484 8445; map p.114. High-spirited elegant fashion with a dose of tongue-in-cheek style. Labels include Florence-based "Save the Queen". A definite cut above the nearby Via Nazionale shops. Mon–Sat

---

THE BIG DESIGNERS

Blumarine Via Borgognona 31 ☎06 679 0951
Bulgari Via dei Condotti 10 ☎06 679 3876
Dolce & Gabbana Via dei Condotti 51 (women) and Piazza di Spagna 93 (men) ☎06 6992 4999
Fendi Largo Goldoni ☎06 334 501
Ferre Piazza di Spagna 70 ☎06 678 6797
Giorgio Armani Via dei Condotti 77 ☎06 699 1460
Gucci Via dei Condotti 8 ☎06 679 0405
Krizia Piazza di Spagna 87 ☎06 679 3772
MaxMara Via dei Condotti 17/19; Via Nazionale 28 ☎06 6992 2104
Missoni Piazza di Spagna 78 ☎06 679 2555
Moschino Via Borgognona 32/A ☎06 678 1144
Prada Via dei Condotti 88/95 ☎06 679 0897
Roberto Cavalli Via Borgognona 25 ☎06 6992 5469
Salvatore Ferragamo Via dei Condotti 65 & 73/74 ☎06 678 1130/679 1565
Valentino Piazza di Spagna ☎06 679 0479
Versace Via Bocca di Leone 23 & 26/2 ☎06 678 0521

9.30am–8pm, Sun 11am–2pm & 3–8pm; closed Sun in Aug.

Antichi Kimono Via di Monserrato 43b–44, around Campo de' Fiori ☎ 06 6813 5876, ⓦ antichikimono.com; map p.50. Vintage kimonos paired with Italian separates. Also check out their reasonably priced jewellery and accessories. Mon 3.30–7.30pm, Tues–Sat 10am–7.30pm.

★ **Arsenale** Via del Pellegrino 172, around Campo de' Fiori ☎ 06 6880 2424, ⓦ patriziapieroni.com; map p.50. Just off Campo de' Fiori, this funky womenswear boutique has great dresses by the owner Patrizia Pieroni and lots of other stuff by small independent designers. Mon 3.30–7.30pm, Tues–Sat 10am–7.30pm.

Aspesi Via del Babuino 144, Tridente ☎ 06 323 0376, ⓦ aspesi.com; map p.91. In the heart of the Piazza di Spagna area, this is the very sleek flagship store of the contemporary Italian designer, with cool designs for both men and women, as well as textiles. Mon–Sat 10am–7pm.

Atipika Via di Monserrato 103, around Campo de' Fiori ☎ 331 944 9140; map p.50. The former Eckletika shop has enlarged its collection, adding some antique furniture, lamps and accessories to its sensual textiles of Venice, shown off to full effect in dresses of brocade, cashmere, silk and wool. Look for flirty capes, fashion jewellery from 1930s-inspired to modern, and smart Parisian bags; prices from €15 to €300. Mon 3.30–7.30pm, Tues–Sat 11am–7.30pm; closed 2 weeks mid-Aug.

Cinzia Via del Governo Vecchio 45, Centro Storico ☎ 06 683 2945; map p.36. The best of several used-clothing shops along this street, where you can find anything from an elegant raincoat to black leather biker jeans, and much more. Daily 10am–8pm.

Davide Cenci Via di Campo Marzio 1–7, Centro Storico ☎ 06 699 0681, ⓦ davidecenci.com; map p.36. The flagship store of this long-established purveyor of elegant and refined clothing, which always seems to be expanding down the block, offers conservative, high-quality fashion, decidedly more interesting for men than women, as well as threads for pampered children. Mon 4–8pm, Tues–Sat 10am–8pm.

Degli Effetti Piazza Capranica 75, 79 & 93, Centro Storico ☎ 06 679 0202; map p.36. Since 1987, these fashion forecasters have been choosing a stylish core collection featuring top Japanese houses Miyake, Comme des Garçons and Yohji Yamamoto. The shop prides itself on fashion quality, research, and its stylish feel for market niches. Mon–Fri 10am–2pm & 3.30–7.30pm, Sat 10am–7pm.

Diesel Piazza di Spagna 12, Tridente ☎ 06 678 6817, ⓦ diesel.com; map p.91. The flagship store of this Italian manufacturer of trendy styles for studiously disaffected youth. Mon–Sat 10.30am–7.30pm.

Emporio Armani Via del Babuino 140, Tridente ☎ 06 3221 5881, ⓦ armani.com; map p.91. The city-centre branch of the designer's chain of more affordable yet still very stylish stores. Daily 10am–7pm.

Ermanno Scervino Via del Babuino 97, Tridente ☎ 06 679 3173, ⓦ ermannoscervino.it; map p.91. The Florence-based designer's flagship Rome outlet is on super-cool Via del Babuino. Sporty, contemporary styles, mainly for women, and beautiful lingerie. Mon 4–7pm, Tues–Sat 10am–7pm.

Ermenegildo Zegna Via dei Condotti 58, Tridente ☎ 06 6994 0678, zegna.com; map p.91. This is a leading contender for the ultimate suit-maker for men. At least one Zegna suit hangs in every Italian CEO's wardrobe. Mon 4–7pm, Tues–Sat 10am–7pm.

FG Albertelli Via dei Prefetti 11, Tridente ☎ 06 6880 4960, ⓦ fgroma.com; map p.91. Shirts, bespoke and off-the-peg suits, coats, accessories and all that a chap could desire, as well as a very nice "casual" range. Though, of course, such effortless style doesn't come cheap. Mon 3.30–7.30pm, Tues–Sat 10am–7.30pm.

Kolby Via Nazionale 203–203a, Esquiline ☎ 06 482 4532, ⓦ kolby.it; map p.114. Casual styles for men at reasonable prices. There's also a branch on the more picturesque Via del Governo Vecchio 64 (☎ 06 6880 3732), near Piazza Navona. Mon–Sat 10am–7pm.

La Perla Via Bocca di Leone 28, Tridente ☎ 06 6994 1934; map p.91. The Bologna-based international chain stocks some of Rome's prettiest and most coveted lingerie. Tues–Sat 10am–8pm.

Le Gallinelle Via Panisperna 60, Monti ☎ 06 488 1017; map p.114. Choose your own fabric from among their own stylish designs, and have a garment made up on the spot at this cool Monti store. Mon 3.30–7.30pm, Tues–Sat 10am–1pm & 3.30–7.30pm, Sun noon–4pm.

Loro Piana Via dei Condotti 24, Tridente ☎ 06 6992 4906, ⓦ loropiana.com; map p.91. Luxurious cashmere is woven and knitted into fine, mostly classic styles by this Piemonte-based company. Mon–Sat 10.30am–7.30pm, Sun 11am–2pm & 3–7pm.

Luna & L'Altra Piazza Pasquino 76, Centro Storico ☎ 06 6880 4995; map p.36. Contemporary but not faddish store that stocks designs by Yohji Yamamoto, Issey Miyake, Martin Margiela, Dries Van Noten, Limi feu, + Noir, Rick Owens, Haat, Final Home and others. Mon 3.30–7.30pm, Tues–Sat 10am–2pm & 3.30–7.30pm.

Maga Morgana Via del Governo Vecchio 27, Centro Storico ☎ 06 687 9995; map p.36. Named for Morgan La Fey (literally the "witch Morgan"), this offbeat store makes and sells attractive and original women's tops, skirts and knitwear, and great dresses. Mon–Sat 10am–8pm.

Malo Via Belsiana 68, Tridente ☎ 06 679 1331, ⓦ malo.it; map p.91. A Florence-based designer who's famous for luxury cashmere, stocking everything from ultra-classic to

21

some very trendy lines. Mon 4.30–7.30pm, Tues–Sat 10.30am–7.30pm.

Max & Co Via Condotti 46, Tridente ☎ 06 678 7946, ⒲ maxandco.com; map p.91. The central Rome branch of MaxMara's more accessible and more youthful chain. Mon–Sat 10am–8pm, Sun 11am–7.30pm.

Miu Miu Via del Babuino 91, Tridente ☎ 06 3600 4884, ⒲ miumiu.com; map p.91. Miuccia Prada used her nickname to launch this spunky Prada spin-off, often sporting some of the more fun, if pricey, fashions. Mon–Sat 10am–7.30pm, Sun 10am–7pm.

Nadiamari Via Monserrato 104, Campo de' Fiori ☎ 06 6933 5463, ⒲ nadiamari.com; map p.50. This is Roman fashion designer Nadia Mari's second flagship store in the heart of Rome, a short walk from Campo de' Fiori. Her distinctive signature looks are for the urban yet elegant woman, and all pieces are made with Italian fabrics. Mon 3–7.30pm, Tues–Sat 10.30am–7:30pm.

104 Pandemonium Via dei Giubbonari 104, Campo de' Fiori ☎ 06 686 8061, ⒲ 104pandemonium.it; map

p.50. Conveniently located between Campo dé Fiori and Largo Argentina, this two-floor store stocks a fashionable collection of casual men's and women's clothing and accessories. They have some pretty cool backpacks, too. Daily 10am–7.30pm.

SBU Via di San Pantaleo 69, Centro Storico ☎ 06 6880 2547, ⒲ sbu.it; map p.36. Rome's coolest jeans store, the Strategic Business Unit (SBU), is housed in a former draper's shop (with original features and furniture) just around the corner from Piazza Navona. As well as SBU's Japanese denim jeans, there is a plethora of deceptively casual clothes, shoes and accessories. SBU caters mostly to men, but there is also a small women's section. Mon–Fri 10am–1pm & 3.30–7.30pm, Sat 10am–7.30pm.

Stella McCartney Via Borgognona 6, Tridente ☎ 06 6919 0779, ⒲ stellamccartney.com; map p.91. Eco-luxury flagship store from the Beatle daughter who uses no fur or leather and designs women's clothes which are sexy, sassy and modern. Also lingerie, dresses, sunglasses and children's wear. Mon–Sat 10am–7pm.

SHOES, BAGS AND ACCESSORIES

Antica Manifattura Cappelli Via degli Scipioni 46, Prati ☎ 06 3972 5679, ⒲ antica-cappelleria.it; map p.188. When Patrizia Fabri took over this historic hat shop, she kept its aura but added her own elegant and quirky styles for theatre, movies, special occasions, and just plain glamour. She designs and makes the hats right here and buys vintage pieces, too. Mon–Sat 9am–7pm.

★**Borsalino** Piazza del Popolo 20, Tridente ☎ 06 3265 0838, ⒲ borsalino.com; map p.91. Home of the classic fedora as sported by Jean-Paul Belmondo, Johnny Depp and others, as well as a whole host of other kinds of hats. There are also sister shops at Via Sistina 58 (☎ 06 678 821) and Via Campo Marzio 72a (☎ 06 678 3945). Mon 3–7.30pm, Tues–Sat 9.30am–1.30pm & 3–7.30pm.

Bottega Veneta Piazza San Lorenzo in Lucina 9–13, Tridente ☎ 06 6821 0024, ⒲ bottegaveneta.com; map p.91. Top-quality leather bags and purses, most featuring Bottega Veneta's trademark intricate braiding, in a prime spot on a super-chic square. Some of the supple leather is also transformed into jackets and dresses. Mon 4–8pm, Tues–Sat 9.30am–8pm.

Giorgio Sermoneta Piazza di Spagna 61, Tridente ☎ 06 6920 2066, ⒲ sermonetagloves.com; map p.91. This long-standing glove specialist has a large collection of Italian gloves in every price range, and has catered to celebrities, politicians and tourists for 35 years. Mon–Sat 9.30am–8pm, Sun 10.30am–7pm.

★**Ibiz** Via dei Chiavari 39, around Campo de' Fiori ☎ 06 6830 7297, ⒲ ibizroma.it; map p.50. Great leather bags, purses and rucksacks in exciting contemporary designs made on the premises. Mon–Sat 10am–7.30pm.

Il Gancio Via del Seminario 82–83, Centro Storico ☎ 06

679 6646; map p.36. High-quality leather bags, purses and shoes, all made in the workshop on site. Mon–Sat 10.30am–7.30pm.

La Cravatta su Misura Via di Santa Cecilia 12, Trastevere ☎ 06 8901 6941, ⒲ cravattasumisura.it; map p.160. This shop sells only one thing – ties. Choose from among the hundreds of ties on display, or from the hundreds of rolls of material and have your own made up. Mon–Fri 10am–2pm & 3.30–7.30pm, Sat 10am–2pm; closed Aug.

★**Loco** Via dei Baullari 22, around Campo de' Fiori ☎ 06 6880 8216; map p.50. A very cool shoe store just off Campo de' Fiori with plenty of styles for men and women. Mon 3.30–8pm, Tues–Sat 10.30am–8pm.

Mandarina Duck Via dei Due Macelli 59, Tridente ☎ 06 678 6414, ⒲ mandarinaduck.com; map p.91. The main branch of the trendy Bologna bag company is a tribute to how to be both practical and stylish. Mon 3.30–7.30pm, Tues–Sat 10am–7.30pm.

★**Marta Ray** Via del Moro 6, Trastevere ☎ 06 581 1108, ⒲ martaray.it; map p.160. Young local designer Marta Anna Ratajczak creates the prettiest ballet flats and more at this shoe, handbag and leather boutique in Trastevere, with two other locations in the city. Her signature style is elegant but functional, with rainbow colours and super-soft leather. Daily 10am–8pm.

Natural Shoes Via della Lungaretta 94, Trastevere ☎ 06 581 1190, ⒲ naturalshoes.it; map p.160. This Trastevere shop's comfortable shoes come to the rescue of those who can't navigate Rome's cobblestones in heels – or simply need a break from them. It also has styles for wider feet, a rarity in Italy. Mon–Thurs 10am–9pm, Fri & Sat 10am–10pm, Sun 11am–9pm.

21

Pineider Via dei Due Macelli 68, Tridente ☎06 679 5884, ⓦpineider.com; map p.91. This exclusive store has been crafting beautiful stationery items and handmade bags and wallets for Roman society since 1774. There's another branch at Via della Fontanella di Borghese 22 (☎06 687 8369). Daily 10am–7pm.

Sciú Sciá Calzature Via di Torre Argentina 8–9, Centro Storico ☎06 6880 6777, ⓦsciusciachic.com; map p.36. If you can't swing Bottega Veneta's prices (see opposite), try the working gal's alternative – lower-priced leather crochet bags (€165), made in Tuscany near Arezzo. Mon–Sat 9am–7.30pm.

JEWELLERY

Bozart Via Belsiana 49, Tridente ☎06 3105 2147, ⓦbozart.it; map p.91. These fakes are truly fabulous; this is just the spot to pick up crowns, diadems and body jewellery. Semiprecious stones, as well as Swarovski crystal pieces and resin and wooden elements are freely used to create dazzling costume jewellery, ranging in price from €25 to €300. Mon 4–8pm, Tues–Sat 9.30am–8pm.

Diana Molayem Via Belsiana 97, Tridente ☎06 679 6808; map p.91. The elegant Molayem jewellery boutique exudes crisp, cool calm. From cutting-edge modern designs to pieces modelled on ancient Roman jewellery, their collection is super-chic – and expensive. Mon–Fri 11am–1pm & 3–6pm.

Fabio Piccioni Via del Boschetto 148, Monti ☎06 472 837; map p.114. A vintage jewellery store with some original Art Nouveau and Art Deco pieces, though most are 1920s-to-1970s-inspired reproductions and one-of-a-kind adornments made in the workshop. Mon–Sat 10am–1pm & 3–8pm; closed Sat in summer.

Lefevre Via del Pellegrino 99, around Campo de' Fiori ☎06 6880 1881, ⓦadolfolefevre.it; map p.50. Exclusive designs here include seed-pearl ropes hung with cut crystals of ruby, emerald and sapphire matrix, for under €100. There are silver frames too, as well as fine porcelain. Mon 4–8pm, Tues–Sat 10am–1pm & 4–8pm.

Materie Via del Gesù 73, Centro Storico ☎06 679 3199, ⓦmaterieshop.com; map p.36. A small, independent jewellery and accessories shop featuring an eclectic range of hand-picked designers (both from Italy and not), just a stone's throw from the Pantheon. Mon–Sat 10.30am–7.30pm.

Migian Via dei Banchi Nuovi 13, Centro Storico ☎06 6880 5560; map p.36. Tucked away behind the Chiesa Nuova, these working goldsmiths sell jewellery at a wide range of prices. Mon 4–7pm, Tues–Sat 10am–7pm.

Novità Via Sora 17a, Centro Storico ☎06 686 8685; map p.36. Heaven for do-it-yourselfers, who flock here to find glass, plastic, wood, stone and crystal beads. They also have a wide stock of one-off pieces to repair vintage jewellery. Mon 3.30–6.30pm, Tues–Sat 10am–1pm & 3.30–7pm.

Percossi Papi Atelier Via di Sant'Eustachio 16, Centro Storico ☎06 6880 1466, ⓦpercossipapi.com; map p.36. Housed in an ivy-covered building near the Pantheon, this venerable goldsmith designs his work to flatter the skin tones of the wearer. His necklaces and other pieces have graced stars in major feature films, including Cate Blanchett as Queen Elizabeth I. Tues–Sat 10am–1pm & 4–7pm.

Petochi Via Margutta 1b, Tridente ☎06 321 5143; map p.91. A long-established jeweller's who have counted Audrey Hepburn and Ingrid Bergman among their customers over the years. Visitors today are often intrigued by their small mosaic pieces with Rome scenes, a classy Grand Tour souvenir. Mon 3–7pm, Tues–Fri 10am–7pm, Sat 10am–1pm.

Tempi Moderni Via del Governo Vecchio 108, Centro Storico ☎06 687 7007; map p.36. Inexpensive jewellery inspired by Art Deco and other retro styles, along with a few vintage pieces. Daily 10am–1pm & 3.30–7.30pm.

Zannetti Via Monte d'Oro 18–23, Centro Storico ☎06 6819 2566, ⓦzannetti.com; map p.36. The flagship store of the distinctive Italian handmade watch specialist and jeweller. Mon–Fri 9am–1pm & 4–7pm.

DEPARTMENT STORES AND MALLS

COIN Via Cola di Rienzo 173, Prati ☎06 3600 4298, ⓦcoin.it; map p.188. A nationwide chain that's good for high-street fashion and smarter kids' clothes, beauty products and so on. Also at Termini (☎06 4782 5909) and at Piazzale Appio 7, by San Giovanni metro station (☎06 708 0020). Mon–Sat 10am–8pm, Sun 10.30am–8pm.

TERMINI: A SHOPPING CENTRE WITH TRAIN STATION ATTACHED?

Time was when the postwar concrete masterpiece was looking past its best, but **Termini station** has been updated massively over the past decade or so and is now almost as much a place to shop as take a train, with the new Mercato Centrale, the city's best bookshops (Borri Books – English books are upstairs), a branch of the department store COIN and two supermarkets, plus the Sephora perfumery, new Victoria's Secret store, a wine shop and branches of several of the big Italian chains including Benetton. All very useful, though it's not a place for a relaxing shopping experience – watch out for pickpockets.

21

La Rinascente Galleria Alberto Sordi, Piazza Colonna, Tridente ☎ 06 6919 0769, ⊛ rinascente.it; map p.91. Rome's first department store, and Italy's oldest chain. Still a good place to browse cosmetics, handbags, accessories and mainstream fashion. The new Rinascente flagship store on Via del Tritone was on hold at the time of writing following archeological finds; the next-largest branch is at Piazza Fiume (☎ 06 884 1231). Daily 10am–9pm.

M.A.S. Piazza Vittorio Emanuele 138, Esquiline ☎ 06 446 8078; map p.114. It doesn't get any cheaper than this. Situated among the arcades of Piazza Vittorio, the "Magazzini allo Statuto" (Statutory Warehouses) is like one vast, multi-level rummage sale, but take your time and you

might find something you want. There's everything from clothing to housewares. Mon–Sat 9am–1pm & 4–7.45pm.

Oviesse Industry Via del Tritone 172, Tridente ☎ 06 678 3336, ⊛ ovs.it; map p.91. A nationwide chain that specializes in well-priced, sometimes stylish men's, women's and children's clothes and accessories. Mon 3.30–7.30pm, Tues–Sat 10am–7.30pm.

Zara Via del Corso 189, Tridente ☎ 06 6979 17210, ⊛ zara.com; map p.91. The Spanish retail giant's flagship Rome store, in Palazzo Bocconi, offers fashion savvy at budget prices, attracting Romans as well as tourists. Mon–Sun 10am–8pm.

FOOD AND WINE

Antica Caciara Trasteverina Via San Francesco a Ripa 140a/b, Trastevere ☎ 06 5811 2815, ⊛ anticacaciara.it; map p.160. Although the cheeses and wines they sell here come from various parts of Italy and also abroad, the chances are it's the aged pecorino cheeses that you can smell from down the street. This Trastevere institution dates from about 1900 and has a loyal following spanning generations. Mon–Sat 7am–2pm & 4–8pm.

Beppe e I Suoi Formaggi Via Santa Maria del Pianto 9a/11, Ghetto ☎ 06 6819 2210, ⊛ beppeeisuoiformaggi .it; map p.50. All you could possibly desire from a cheesemonger, plus cured meats, all of excellent quality. Their butter outclasses its counterparts from most of central and southern Italy, and you can taste the products on site with a glass of wine. A branch recently opened at Termini Station's Mercato Centrale (see p.302). Mon 4–7pm, Tues–Sat 10am–7pm.

BiblioTèq Via dei Banchi Vecchi 124, around Campo de' Fiori ☎ 06 4543 3114, ⊛ biblioteq.it; map p.50. A decent cup of tea is a rarity in Rome, so most likely you'll

want to make your own. Here you can find black, green and white teas, some coffee and chocolate, plus pots and accessories. Mon 3.30–7.30pm, Tues–Sat 10am–1.30pm & 3.30–7.30pm.

★ **Biscottificio Innocenti** Via della Luce 21, Trastevere ☎ 06 580 3926; map p.160. Trastevere's best *biscottificio*, a family operation for over a hundred years; keep an eye out for the glorious, massive (and still-functioning) old oven. Expect wonderful, chewy *croccantini* – half chocolate, half vanilla – plus *amaretti*, *brutti ma buoni* (hazelnut biscuits), *straccetti* (almond and hazelnut biscuits) and dozens more varieties. Mon–Sat 9am–1pm & 4–7.30pm, Sun 9am–1pm; closed mid-Aug to mid-Sept.

★ **Buccone** Via di Ripetta 19, Tridente ☎ 06 361 2154, ⊛ enotecabuccone.com; map p.91. Every alcoholic beverage you could dream of, with a large selection of wines from all over the world, plus spirits, and even ten-litre bottles of *grappa*. A good place to grab lunch, too (see p.252). Mon–Thurs 9am–8.30pm, Fri & Sat 9am–11.30pm.

CITY-CENTRE SUPERMARKETS

Rome's food stores and delis are so good that you shouldn't need to use a **supermarket** too often, but for pasta and other basics the supermarkets in the city centre can be useful, especially if you're self-catering or just want somewhere easy to pick up a picnic. Some of the more conveniently located ones are below.

Billa Via Cola di Rienzo 173, Prati.
Conad Viale Trastevere 62, Trastevere.
Carrefour Express/Dì per Dì Villa Borghese Parcheggio, Villa Borghese; Via del Gesù 58, around Campo de' Fiori; Via Vittoria 22, Tridente; Piazza Nicosia 35, Centro Storico; Corso Vittorio Emanuele 290, Centro Storico; Via Monterone 5, Centro Storico; Via Poli 47, Trevi; Via dei SS. Quattro Coronati 53, Celian Hill.

De Spar Corso V. Emanuele 42, Centro Storico; Corso Rinascimento 7, Centro Storico; Vicolo di Moretta 10 (off Via Giulia), around Campo de' Fiori; Via del Pozzetto 123, Tridente; Via San Bartolomeo de' Vaccinari 78, Ghetto; Via Nazionale 212–213, Esquiline; Via Alberico II 3, Prati; Termini station; Via Guicciardini 2, Esquiline.
Elite Via Cavour 230–234, Monti.
Sma Via della Frezza 8, Tridente; Piazza Santa Maria Maggiore, Esquiline.

21

Castroni Via Cola di Rienzo 196, Prati ☎ 06 687 4383, ⓦ castroni.it; map p.188. A huge, labyrinthine food store selling a large selection of Italian treats, including chocolates, pastas, sauces, olive oils, and hard-to-find international favourites such as plum pudding, Vegemite, peanut butter and Mexican specialities. As renowned for its good coffee blend (also served at the bar) as for its rude service. Their other branches at Via Ottaviano 55 (☎ 06 3972 3279), Via Frattina 79 (☎ 06 6992 1903) and Via Nazionale 71 (☎ 06 2036 9680) are a bit friendlier and also have coffee bars. Mon–Sat 7.30am–8pm.

Centro Macrobiotico Italiano Via della Vite 14, Tridente ☎ 06 679 2509; map p.91. The most central shop for natural foods, with wholegrain pastas and other such products from Italy's rich countryside. Mon–Fri noon–4pm & 7–11pm, Sat 7–11pm.

Colapicchioni Via Tacito 76–78, Prati ☎ 06 321 5405; map p.188. A long-running Prati bakery cum deli selling the family's excellent *pangiallo* and other foodie goodies. Mon–Sat 9am–8pm.

Comptoir de France Via Vitelleschi 20–24, Prati ☎ 06 6830 1516; map p.188. This Prati favourite is your one-stop shop for all sorts of French food and wine. There is an impressive selection of French cheeses and all the pastries and baked goods you'd expect from a French patisserie. Mon 4–8pm, Tues–Sat 9.30am–8pm.

Costantini Piazza Cavour 16, Prati ☎ 06 320 3575; map p.188. Prati claims one of the city's best wine stores; it has a fantastic selection in its basement *enoteca*, with *grappas*, spirits and liqueurs upstairs. Next door is their elegant and expensive restaurant. Mon 4.30–8pm, Tues–Sat 9am–1pm & 4.30–8pm.

Cristalli di Zucchero Via San Teodoro 88, around Piazza Venezia ☎ 06 6992 0945, ⓦ cristallidizucchero.it; map p.61. Down at the far end of Via San Teodoro, just off the Circus Maximus, this place has refined tarts, cakes and pastries – delicate works of art that melt in your mouth, and make the perfect accompaniment if you're queueing for the "Mouth of Truth" (see p.69) just around the corner. They do great coffee and more down-to-earth pastries, too, if all you want is a *cornetti*. There's another branch across the river in Monteverde at Via di Val Tellina 114 (☎ 06 5823 0323). Daily except Tues 7.30am–8.30pm.

De Bellis Pasticceria Piazza del Paradiso 56/57, around Campo de' Fiori ☎ 06 6861 480, ⓦ andreadebellis.it; map p.50. Cakes to swoon over. A French pastry chef comes in to make macaroons, and there are elegant tarts, biscuits, and a millefeuille bar where you can choose the creamy filling that you want. Late hours accommodate the Campo crowd and there's a small seating area. Daily 9am–8pm.

★ **Del Frate** Via degli Scipioni 118–122, Prati ☎ 06 323 6437, ⓦ enotecadelfrate.it; map p.188. This large wine and spirits shop is located on a quiet street near the Vatican, and has all the Barolos and Chiantis you could

want, alongside shelves full of *grappa* and some 2500 labels of liqueurs. It's also open for lunch, aperitifs and dinner (see p.265). Mon–Sat 9am–1pm & 4–8pm.

Eataly Piazzale XII Ottobre, Ostiense ☎ 06 9027 9201, ⓦ roma.eataly.it; map p.140. A prime example of the resurgence of the Ostiense district, housed in the former air terminal right by Ostiense station (to which it's linked by subway). It's a giant, high-quality artisanal supermarket, with four floors of food, wine, beer, books, kitchenware and more. The last word in just about every Italian foodstuff and edible product you could think of, and each section has its own eatery, so salivating non-residents can sate their appetites right away. A smaller branch opened in 2015 at Piazza della Repubblica 41, close to the Termini station, offering the same mix of intriguing groceries, kitchenware and eateries. Daily 10am–midnight.

Franchi Via Cola di Rienzo 200, Prati ☎ 06 687 4651; map p.188. One of the best old-school delis in Rome – a triumph of cheeses, sausages and an ample choice of cold or hot food to go, including delicious *torta rustica* and roast chicken. They'll make up customized lunches for you, and they also have the wines to go with it. Mon–Sat 8.30am–8.30pm.

Gay-Odin Via Stoppani 9, Villa Borghese ☎ 06 8069 3023, ⓦ gay-odin.it; map p.170. The best Italian chocolate shop in Rome gets its chocolates from its Naples base, changing the recipe slightly to suit the Roman sweet tooth. Mon–Sat 10am–1pm & 4–8pm.

★ **I Dolci di Nonna Vincenza** Via Arco del Monte 98a/b, Ghetto ☎ 06 9259 4322, ⓦ dolcinonnavincenza .it; map p.50. Excellent Sicilian pastries from Catania and ice cream, too. A superb way to begin the day is with a brioche smeared with pistacchio *granita*. There's another branch at Piazza Montecitorio 116 (☎ 06 6994 2185), but the baking is done here. It's run by friendly staff and there are a few tables as well. Daily 9am–9pm.

Il Boccione Via del Portico d'Ottavia 1, Ghetto ☎ 06 687 8637; map p.50. This marvellous tiny kosher Jewish bakery, unmarked but in the heart of the Ghetto, has unforgettable ricotta pies, *cornetti*, cinnamon biscotti and *pizza giudia* (a hard cake, crammed with dried and candied fruit) that draw quite a crowd. Famously indifferent service. Mon–Thurs & Sun 7.30am–7.30pm, Fri 7.30am–3.30pm.

Innocenzi Via Natale del Grande 31, Trastevere ☎ 06 581 2725; map p.160. Not to be confused with the famed Trastevere *Biscottificio Innocenti*, this is a great dry-goods grocer, with all the usual rice and pasta and Italian goodies, but also a large selection of stuff from around the world – tomato ketchup, teas, peanut butter, the works. A good option for homesick expats and foodies alike. Mon–Wed, Fri & Sat 7.30am–1.30pm & 4.30–8pm, Thurs 7.30am–1.30pm.

La Tradizione Via Cipro 8, ☎ 06 3972 0349; map p.188. People who live in the Prati/Cipro neighbourhood have been buying their cheeses and salumi at this historic delicatessan for decades. With hundreds of types of cold meat cuts and local and imported cheeses, gourmet food products including jams, honey and even oil, La Tradizione is a food lovers' wonderland. Mon 3–8pm, Tues–Sat 8am–2pm & 4.30–8pm.

Ladurée Via Borgognona 4, Tridente ☎ 06 6994 1625, ⓦ laduree.com; map p.91. This French chocolatier is a strong contender for the very best chocolate in the city – though it's maybe better known for its macaroons. Daily 10am–7.30pm.

Le Levain Via Luigi Sanini 22, Trastevere ☎ 06 6456 2880; map p.160. This French patisserie is perfect for a quick lunch or for anything baked, from baguettes and bread rolls to macaroons, elegantly decorated small and large cakes and baked savoury treats like quiches and the classic croque-monsieur. Packaged home-made sweet and savoury biscuits, plus a small selection of organic wine and local extra virgin olive oil, are also available. Mon–Sat 8am–8.30pm, Sun 9am–6.30pm.

Moriondo & Gariglio Via del Pie' di Marmo 21–22, Centro Storico ☎ 06 699 0856; map p.36. Just a short walk from the Pantheon, this shop is great for exquisitely wrapped gifts of handmade chocolate. Mon–Sat 9.30am–1pm & 3.30–7.30pm.

★**Panella** Via Merulana 54, Esquiline ☎ 06 487 2435, ⓦ panellaroma.com; map p.114. Probably the city's priciest bakery, with fantastic bread and pastries, delicious pizza and a small grocery section. They also do pasta (for example colourful, hat-shaped *sombrerini*, packaged to take home). Sample the goods at their café, which has tables indoors and out, and does a good *aperitivo* buffet. Mon–Fri 8am–midnight, Sun 8.30am–1.30pm.

Peperita Via della Reginella 30, Ghetto ☎ 347 367 6352; map p.50. Right near the turtle fountain in the Ghetto, this tiny shop specializes in hot chilli peppers – fresh, in sauces, powdered and in other forms. Daily 10.30am–8pm.

Punturi Via Flavia 48, Quirinale ☎ 06 481 8225; map p.104. One of Rome's many great delis, with a bakery, cheese and cold meat counter, and superb pizza by the slice. Mon–Fri 7.30am–8.15pm, Sat 8.30am–8.15pm.

Regoli Pasticceria Via dello Statuto 60, Esquiline ☎ 06 487 2812, ⓦ pasticceriaregoli.com; map p.114. Generations of Roman families have come to this pastry shop, which still turns out great sweets and pastries and usually is packed. Mon–Sat 9am–7pm.

Roscioli Via dei Giubbonari 21–23, around Campo de' Fiori ☎ 06 687 5287, ⓦ salumeriaroscioli.com; map p.50. First-rate and extremely pricey cheeses and salamis are joined by a surprisingly well-priced and good selection of wine at this deli, which doubles as a restaurant/wine bar (see p.251). The *Antico Forno Roscioli* bakery nearby at Via dei Chiavari 34 is also worth a visit (see p.250). Daily 9am–midnight.

Tea and Teapots Via dei Banchi Nuovi 37, Centro Storico ☎ 06 686 8824; map p.36. This shop hosts periodic tastings and sells over a hundred varieties of tea, including white, green, black and naturally perfumed. Also stocks teapots, cups and accessories from the Orient and Europe. Mon–Fri 11am–2pm & 4.30–7.30pm.

Totò Via Portico d'Ottavia 2, Ghetto ☎ 06 6880 6038; map p.50. A coffee bar in the Ghetto since 1890, this place sells a great coffee blend (Teichner). Ask for a can of ground coffee from the shelf behind the barman. Daily except Sat 7am–9pm.

Trimani Via Goito 20–22, Termini ☎ 06 446 9661, ⓦ trimani.com; map p.114. One of the city's largest, best and most historic (since 1821) wine shops, and handily close to Termini if you want to stock up before heading off to the airport. They have a wine bar around the corner, too. Mon–Sat 9am–8.30pm.

Un Punto Macrobiotico Via dei Volsci 119b–121, San Lorenzo ☎ 06 4938 2279; map p.114. This macrobiotic food shop near San Lorenzo also sells soaps and natural cotton T-shirts. Try the self-service café for an economical macrobiotic lunch or early dinner. There are other branches at Cinecittà (☎ 06 721 7741) and Valle Aurelia (☎ 06 3975 1039). Mon–Sat 10.30am–7.30pm.

Valzani Via del Moro 37, Trastevere ☎ 06 580 3792; map p.160. One of the oldest of the city's confectioners, still keeping up tradition with marvellous *mostaccioli* and *pangiallo* (both are traditional dried fruit and nut honey bars, the former chocolate-covered), *torrone*, *Sachertorte* and, at Easter, huge, gift-filled chocolate eggs which you can have your name etched on. Wed–Sun 10am–8.30pm; closed June to mid-Sept; extended hours at Christmas & Easter.

★**Volpetti** Via Marmorata 47, Testaccio ☎ 06 574 2352, ⓦ volpetti.com; map p.140. It's worth seeking out this Testaccio deli, which is one of Rome's very best. If you're lucky, one of the staff will give you samples of their truly incredible *mozzarella di bufala*. Volpetti also has its own restaurant round the corner (see p.260). Mon–Sat 8am–2pm & 5–8pm.

HOME AND DESIGN

Arcon Via della Scrofa 104, Centro Storico ☎ 06 683 3728, ⓦ arconroma.com; map p.260. This sleek, contemporary store is a visual feast for lovers of Italian contemporary furniture design, with lots of easy-to-carry accessories as well as larger pieces. Mon 3.30–7.30pm,

Tues–Sat 9am–1pm & 3.30–7.30pm; closed Sat pm in July & Aug.

C.U.C.I.N.A. Via Mario de' Fiori 65, Tridente ☎ 06 679 1275, ⓦ cucinastore.com; map p.91. A shop filled with modern kitchen appliances, including a large selection of

21

Italian cafetieres. There's also a branch near Piazza Navona on Via di Parione 21 (☎ 06 324 3723). Mon 3.30–7.30pm, Tues–Sat 10am–7.30pm.

De Sanctis Piazza di Pietra 24, Centro Storico ☎ 06 6880 6810, ⓦ desanctis1890.com; map p.36. This city-centre shop has been selling ceramics since 1890, and offers a slightly classier souvenir than you'll find anywhere else around here. Mon 10am–1.30pm & 3–7.30pm, Tues 3.30–7.30pm; occasionally open Sun in May, June, Sept & Oct.

Frette Piazza di Spagna 11, Tridente ☎ 06 679 0673, ⓦ frette.com; map p.91. This famous luxury linen shop is happy to fill custom orders and will ship their products anywhere. Mon 3–7pm, Tues–Sat 10am–7pm.

Il Giardino di Domenico Persiani Via Torino 92, Esquiline ☎ 06 488 3886; map p.114. An experience not to be missed – a quiet garden filled to the brim with all sorts of creations in ceramic: everything from glazed tiles to full-sized copies of famous statuary. Pieces made to order. Mon–Sat 9am–1pm & 3–6pm.

Lelli Via Margutta 5, Tridente ☎ 06 361 4000, ⓦ lelli1924.com; map p.91. A panoply of high-end homeware – fabrics, hand-printed wallpapers, floor coverings, ceramics, you name it – can be found in this shop, which has occupied this spot on the charmingly tranquil Via Margutta since the 1920s. Mon 2.30–7.30pm, Tues–Sat 10am–7.30pm.

Le Tele di Carlotta Via dei Coronari 228, Centro Storico ☎ 06 689 2585; map p.36. Simona hand-embroiders lace finishes on lingerie and linens in this small shop (the name of which translates as "Charlotte's Web"), which is situated among Rome's antique dealers. Mon–Fri 10.30am–1pm & 3.30–7pm.

Passamanerie Crocianelli Via dei Prefetti 40, Centro Storico ☎ 06 3735 3178, ⓦ passamaneriecrocianelli. com; map p.36. Rome's oldest haberdasher's has the most beautiful selections of ornaments for home furnishings. Don't forget to bring a fabric swatch from home to select the perfect colour cords, tassels, trims or pom-poms to embellish your chair, sofa or curtains. Mon 3.30–7.30pm, Tues–Sat 10am–1.30pm & 3.30–7.30pm.

Yaky Via Santa Maria del Pianto 55, Ghetto ☎ 06 6880 7724; map p.50. Quality contemporary and antique Asian crafts and furniture from Japan, Tibet, Mongolia and China. Mon–Fri & Sun 10am–2pm & 3.30–7.30pm, Sat 10am–7.30pm.

MUSIC AND DVDS

Feltrinelli Largo Torre Argentina 18, around Campo de' Fiori ☎ 06 689 3121, ⓦ lafeltrinelli.it; map p.50. One of central Rome's largest branches of the nationwide chain, and really more of a bookshop than a music shop, but still with a good selection of CDs and DVDs, and a café upstairs to browse your latest purchases. It has a good English book section, too. There's another branch in the Galleria Alberto Sordi. Mon–Fri 9am–9pm, Sat 9am–10pm, Sun 10am–9pm.

★ **Soul Food** Via di San Giovanni in Laterano 192–194, Celian Hill ☎ 06 7045 2025; map p.128. This vinyl junkie's paradise is the city centre's only dedicated CD-free music shop. Lots of stuff from the 1960s and 1970s, and the staff are genuinely enthusiastic. Tues–Sat 10.30am–1.30pm & 3.30–8pm.

PERFUMERIES

Campo Marzio 70 Via Vittoria 52, Tridente ☎ 06 979 7739, ⓦ campomarzio70.it; map p.36 and p.91. Some of the best "noses" from France and far-flung parts of the world come to Campo Marzio 70's flagship store, where they reckon they can tell the perfect scent for a man or woman as soon as they walk through the door. There's a private room upstairs for the high-rollers. The original perfume shop is at Via di Campo Marzio 70 (hence the name; ☎ 06 6920 2123). Mon 3–7.30pm, Tues–Sat 10.30am–7.30pm.

Essenza 2000 Piazza di San Cosimato 49, Trastevere ☎ 06 589 4579; map p.160. This place stocks all the big-name international brands from Armani to Chanel for cosmetics, make-up and toiletries. They also have a wide selection of perfumes and gift packs for all budgets and tastes. There is a small booth at the back for regular make-up and beauty-treatment promotions. Daily 8am–8pm; limited hours in the summer.

Profumum Via della Colonna Antonina 30, Centro Storico ☎ 06 6920 8008; map p.36. This perfumery, run by the Durante family, seeks to stray as far from the big-name brands as it can. A favourite scent with exotic overtones is "Volo AZ686", named for the Alitalia flight from Rome to Caracas. Mon–Sat 10am–8pm.

Roma-Store Via della Lungaretta 63, Trastevere ☎ 06 581 8789; map p.160. Not a football merchandise store but a shop selling classic perfumes – Acqua di Parma, Penhaligons and suchlike – scented soaps, lotions and candles. Only the very finest from Italy, France and England. Mon–Sat 10am–8pm, Sun 11am–8pm.

STATIONERY

Antica Cartotecnica Piazza dei Caprettari 61, Centro Storico ☎ 06 687 5671; map p.36. A long-running and beautiful pen store near the Pantheon, with lots of new as well as antique models. Mon–Sat 10am–1.30pm & 3–7.30pm.

Campo Marzio Via di Campo Marzio 41, Centro Storico

☎ 06 6880 7877, ⓦ campomarzio70.it; map p.36. Part of a chain that has now also spread to the UK, this store is dedicated to cool, brightly coloured pens and writing accessories, briefcases and pencil cases. Daily 10am–1pm & 2–7pm.

Cartoleria Internazionali Via Arenula 8, Centro Storico ☎ 06 6880 1050; map p.50. Your one-stop shop for stationery and paper goods. This shop stocks everything thing from pens to gift bags and printer cartridges, plus a selection of paper-based gifts. Mon–Sat 10am–7.30pm.

Ditta G. Poggi Via del Gesù 74–75, Centro Storico ☎ 06 679 3674, ⓦ poggi1825.it; map p.36. A fantastic, long-established art materials shop, selling a huge range of specialist paints and accessories, as well as pens, pencils and stationery. Mon–Sat 9am–2pm & 3–7.30pm.

Fabriano Via del Babuino 173, Tridente ☎ 06 3260 0361, ⓦ fabrianoboutique.com; map p.91. Fabriano

paper from the Marche has been around for hundreds of years and is of the highest quality; it's even used for the printing of euro notes. This central Rome branch sells bright and contemporary stationery, pens, wallets and briefcases. Daily except Thurs 10am–1pm & 3–7.30pm.

Il Papiro Via del Pantheon 50, Centro Storico ☎ 06 679 5597; map p.36. The timeless interior of the most central branch of this originally Tuscan chain stocks fine paper and notebooks, as well as the fancy pens to go with them. Daily 10am–8pm.

Stilo Fetti Via degli Orfani 82, Centro Storico ☎ 06 678 9662, ⓦ stilofetti.it; map p.36. A great city-centre pen shop that's been going since 1893, with lots to choose from and all the major brands – as well as elegant leather briefcases. Mon 3.30–7.30pm, Tues–Sat 9am–1pm & 3.30–7.30pm.

MISCELLANEOUS AND GIFTS

AS Roma Store Piazza Colonna 360, Tridente ☎ 06 6978 1232; map p.91. The best-stocked and most central location for AS Roma merchandise, with the usual shirts, leisurewear and baby-gros. Mon–Sat 10am–6pm.

Becker & Musicò Via San Vincenzo 29, Tridente ☎ 06 678 5435; map p.91. This long-established store sells beautiful pipes, inlaid wooden boxes and other lovely handcrafted objects. If you smoke a pipe, hours of fun can be had just lounging around chatting to the guys here about their favourite subject. Mon–Sat 10am–7pm.

Collalti Via del Pellegrino 82, around Campo de' Fiori ☎ 06 6880 1084, ⓦ collatibici.com; map p.50. Bicycle-sellers since the nineteenth century, Collalti sells new bikes and accessories, repairs bikes and rents them by the hour or day (see p.26). Mon–Sat 9am–1pm & 3.30–7.30pm.

Faraoni Via dei Banchi Vecchi 137, around Campo de' Fiori ☎ 06 683 2832; map p.50. The ancient Roman technique of micro-mosaic experienced a resurgence in the eighteenth and nineteenth centuries when Grand Tourists were looking for portable souvenirs. Luigi Faraoni and his workshop are among the few micro-mosaicists still working today. As well as producing ancient-Roman inspired cufflinks, brooches and watches, they are happy to work to commission on larger works. Mon 3–7.30pm, Tues–Sat 10am–2pm & 3–7.30pm.

Gammarelli Via di Santa Chiara 34, Centro Storico ☎ 06 6880 1314, ⓦ gammarelli.com; map p.36. In an area bursting with ecclesiastical outfitters, this is the official papal outfitter. Before being taken to the Sistine Chapel for conclave the papal robes are displayed in the window. Pick up some red cardinal socks as a souvenir of your trip to Rome. Mon–Fri 9am–1pm & 2–6pm, Sat 9am–1pm.

La Bottega del Marmoraro Via Margutta 53b, Tridente ☎ 06 320 7660; map p.91. Enrico and Sandro

Fiorentini, a father-and-son team, are skilled artisans, creating personalized marble plaques for every occasion, as well as statuary, both ancient and modern reproductions. They may sometimes take a break for lunch, but hang around and they'll reappear. Mon–Sat 8.30am–7.30pm.

Le Artigiane Via di Torre Argentina 72, Centro Storico ☎ 06 6830 9347, ⓦ leartigiane.it; map p.36. Italian artisans – who are often present themselves – sell everything from fashion accessories to home design in this shared space, between Largo Argentina and the Pantheon. Daily 10am–7pm.

★**Old Soccer** Via di Ripetta 30, Tridente ☎ 06 9684 6111; map p.91. This great shop revels in the past, selling old-fashioned Italian and international football shirts and other nostalgic soccer paraphernalia. Shirts (most of which, ironically enough, are made in England) cost from around €70. Daily 10am–8pm.

Polvere di Tempo Via del Moro 59, Trastevere ☎ 06 5880 0704; map p.160. For that astrolabe you've always dreamed of, as well as a huge array of ancient and medieval devices for telling the time, stop by this arcane little shop. They also have alchemists' rings that double as sundials and loads more oddities and curiosities. Mon 3.30–8pm, Tues–Sat 10am–1pm & 4–8pm.

Profondo Rosso Store Via dei Gracchi 260, Prati ☎ 06 321 1395, ⓦ profondorossostore.com; map p.188. Horror-film fans flock to director Dario Argento's store, which is dedicated to his own films as well as the genre, with costumes, masks, videos, books (some in English) and various paraphernalia including a stuffed raven. Argento himself makes an appearance every October 31. The basement – or is it dungeon? – has a small museum (€3 admission). Mon–Sat 11am–1pm & 4–7.30pm.

21

FOOD MARKETS

Rome's **food markets** are a perfect place to pick up a snack or picnic provisions. The one on Campo de' Fiori is the city's most famous and picturesque, and has been around for the last four hundred years. Other central options include: the market between the Termini rail tracks and Piazza Vittorio Emanuele, off Via Lamarmora; Piazza San Cosimato in Trastevere; Piazza dell'Unità in Prati; Piazza Alessandria, east of Villa Borghese; and Testaccio market. Most are **open** Monday to Saturday 7am–2pm, excepting public holidays. Also check out the **farmers' market** at the Circus Maximus end of Via San Teodoro (opposite the church of Sant'Anastasia), which is dedicated to food produced by local Lazio farmers (open Saturday and Sunday only) and the new Mercato Centrale at Termini Station.

MARKETS

Borghetto Flaminio Piazza della Marina 32, Flaminio; map p.170. A partly covered flea market with plenty of knick-knacks, designer clothing and antiques. Rummage alongside Rome's well-heeled shoppers and celebrities. Entrance €2. Sun 10am–8pm; closed Aug.

Fontanella Borghese Largo della Fontanella di Borghese, Centro Storico; map p.36. A small print and book market off Via del Corso, where you can find expensive antique prints and etchings along with inexpensive reproductions. Mon–Sat 9am–7pm.

La Soffitta Sotto I Portici Piazza Augusto Imperatore, Tridente ☎ 06 3600 5345; map p.91. Flea market selling a diverse mix of bric-a-brac, jewellery and old records. First & third Sun of the month 10am–7pm; closed Aug.

Mercato Centrale Roma Termini, Via Giovanni Giolitti 36, ☎ 06 9293 9569, ⓦ mercatocentrale.it/roma; map p.114. Florence's popular central market and food space concept hit Rome in 2016 and is conveniently located right at Termini train station. On the ground floor there are around twenty vendors, selling cheese, ice cream, meat, fish, pasta and more. Daily 8am–midnight.

Mercato Esquilino Between Via Lamarmora and Via Ricasoli, Esquiline; map p.114. The market that used to take place in Piazza Vittorio Emanuele is now over by the Termini railway tracks. One building houses cheap clothes and household goods, the other fresh fruit and veg and other food stalls. Mon–Sat 7am–2pm.

Mercato Monti Hotel Palatino, Via Leonina 46, Monti ⓦ mercatomonti.com; map p.114. With approximately thirty stands, this small but perfectly formed weekend market has been running in hip Monti since 2009. Vintage clothing, artisanal jewellery and vinyl vie for attention on the cobbled Via Leonina, a stone's throw from the Cavour metro station. Sat & Sun 10am–8pm; check website for openings, especially in July & Aug.

Porta Portese Trastevere; map p.160. Rome's most famous and largest market by far, stretching from Piazza di Porta Portese a mile or so down Via Portuense and into the streets around, with hundreds of stalls, legitimate and not, selling myriad goods, including antiques, Eastern imports, clothing, carpets, art, tools, appliances, underwear, linens and even puppies. Jewels can be found among the tat, especially at the southern end. Go early or not at all, and do watch out for your wallet. Sun 5am–2pm.

Via Sannio San Giovanni; map p.128. Near the San Giovanni metro station, and somewhat diminished by works on the new underground line, this market has its origins in the postwar period and sells mostly cheap clothing, bags and trashy jewellery, with a secondhand section at the back. Mon–Fri 9am–1.30pm, Sat 9am–6pm.

STADIO OLIMPICO DEL NUOTO

Sports and outdoor activities

Spectator sports are popular in Italy; the hallowed *calcio*, or football, is far and away the most avidly followed, and tends to overshadow everything else. Rome, with two clubs in the top division (Serie A), is no exception, and football is at the heart of so much of what goes on in the city – just look at the number of people reading sports papers. As for participation in sport, there isn't quite the same compulsion to hit the hell out of a squash ball or sweat your way through an aerobics class after work as there is, say, in Britain or the US. However, the notion of keeping fit is becoming as fashionable here as it is in most European countries, especially when it offers the opportunity to wear the latest designer gear.

SPECTATOR SPORTS

Italians are as mad about **sport** as most other European nations, and watching sport, especially **football**, is as valid a part of your holiday in Rome as seeing the sights, whether you catch Roma-Lazio at the Stadio Olimpico or just drop in to a bar to watch a game. And don't forget **rugby**, which galvanizes the city almost as much as the football when an international match is on.

FOOTBALL

Teams Rome's two big football teams are AS Roma (ⓦasroma.it) and SS Lazio (ⓦsslazio.it). Unsurprisingly, feelings run extremely high between the two teams, and derby games are big – and sometimes violent – occasions. Roma are traditionally the team of the inner-city urban working class, and historically the better of the two sides, while traditionally right-wing Lazio – the team of the outer suburbs – have trailed somewhat over the years. Lazio won the championship in 2000, only to have Roma bounce back in 2001 to take their third *scudetto*. Since then, neither team has been champions but Roma has finished runner-up on several occasions, and it's a breathless rivalry that can go either way when the two sides meet.

Matches Roma and Lazio currently play on alternate weekends between Sept and May at the Stadio Olimpico (ⓦstadiodi.it/olimpico-roma), northwest of the city centre, though Roma are due to move to a brand-new stadium in time for the 2017/18 season. Serie A is the top Italian division and the majority of matches take place on Sun afternoons, although games are nowadays staggered across the weekend, between Fri and Mon; Roma and Lazio take turns to play at the Stadio Olimpico so will never both be playing at home the same weekend. Midweek games are rare, although both clubs are often involved in European competitions, which are played on weekday evenings.

Ticket types The Stadio Olimpico is enormous, with a capacity of 70,000, and at most games, except perhaps Roma–Lazio clashes, you should be able to get a ticket for all but the cheapest seats. Lazio supporters, who wear blue and white with the eagle symbol, traditionally occupy the Curva Nord end of the ground, where you can sometimes get seats for €15–25 (but the atmosphere can be intimidating and not altogether pleasant); seats in the *distinti* (corners of the ground) or the *tribuna* (along the sides) are more expensive. *Distinti* tickets go for about

€25–35, and you should reckon on paying around €60–150 for a reasonable *tribuna* ticket. Fans of Roma, who wear red and yellow with the symbol of a wolf, occupy the Curva Sud, which is usually completely sold out to season-ticket holders, making a visit to a Roma game a slightly more expensive business, since the cheapest seat you'll find will be in the *distinti*.

Purchasing tickets Though there are a number of online ticket agencies such as ⓦlisticket.it, ⓦticketone.it or ⓦviagogo.co.uk, it's best (and cheapest) to get tickets from one of the dedicated outlets for Roma or Lazio. For AS Roma, the most central locations are Piazza Colonna 360 (on Via del Corso) and Via Arenula 82 (near Largo di Torre Argentina). There's a Lazio store near the Stadio Olimpico at Via Calderini 66. Note that you'll need ID to buy tickets.

Getting to the stadium Matches are currently played at the Stadio Olimpico, Piazzale del Foro Italico, though plans are afoot for Roma to move to a new stadium. On public transport, you can take tram #2 from Piazzale Flaminio (by metro A Flaminio) to Piazza Mancini or bus #910 from Termini and then walk across the river; alternatively, take bus #32 from Piazza Risorgimento or #628 from Via Plebiscito by Piazza Venezia. Make sure that you bring ID to the stadium as you'll need it to enter.

RUGBY

For information on Italian rugby current fixtures and tickets, go to ⓦfederugby.it.

International rugby Since Italy joined the Five Nations (since renamed the Six Nations) tournament over a decade ago, rugby union has grown in popularity, and the national team is followed enthusiastically by a small but committed group of supporters. International matches take place in the Stadio Olimpico, Piazzale del Foro Italico (ⓦstadiodi.it/olimpico-roma); the stadium is easy to reach from the centre by public transport (see above).

CALCIO IN INGLESE

If you want more information about the **Italian football season** in general, take a look at ⓦfootball-italia.net, which is one of the best and most up-to-date of several English-language websites, with **calcio** (football) fixtures, club details and lots of news, including a summary of the main stories in the Italian sports papers. Others include ⓦforzaitalianfootball.com and ⓦfootballitaliano.co.uk. If your Italian is good enough, get hold of one of the Italian sports newspapers, which are published daily and inevitably focus heavily on football. The Rome-based *Corriere dello Sport* (ⓦcorrieredellosport.it) will have details of any upcoming games, as will the other two papers: *Tuttosport* (ⓦtuttosport.com) and the pink *Gazzetta dello Sport*, which has an English version of the website (ⓦenglish.gazzetta.it).

National rugby Domestic rugby is mainly confined to the north and central regions of Italy, where teams compete in the National Championship of Excellence. Rome's teams are SS Lazio Rugby 1927 (a sister side to the Lazio football team) and Fiamme Oro.

TENNIS
Rome Masters The massive Foro Italico sports complex (see p.180) by the Stadio Olimpico hosts the Italian Open, or Rome Masters as it's now known, one of the city's biggest annual sporting events, held over two weeks in early May. Tickets for the final matches sell out several months before the event, but you can get seats for other matches nearer the time from ⓦ internazionalibnlditalia .com or the Foro Italico box office itself (☎ 800 622 662).

For more information contact the Federazione Italiana Tennis, Via Eustachio 9 (☎ 06 324 0422, ⓦ federtennis.it).

RUNNING
The Rome Marathon Rome has one of the most scenic marathon routes in the world. It starts by the Colosseum and heads south to the basilica of San Paolo before going back up the Tiber and skirting the city centre, passing through Prati as far north as Ponte Milvio. It then returns south, heading straight through the heart of the city to end where it began, at the Colosseum. The start/finish is probably the best place to view the race, which takes place in March, but there are loads of vantage points and none gets too off-puttingly crowded. You can, of course, also take part (see p.306).

22

PARTICIPATORY SPORTS AND ACTIVITIES

There are lots of opportunities to spend time on your favourite sport or hobby while you're in Rome, whether it's **tennis**, **golf** or just going to the **gym**, and of course there are few more scenic places to go for a jog. Time your visit around the Rome Marathon, and you can join a 40km city sightseeing tour of the city and keep fit at the same time.

GOLF
If you simply can't go a week or two without hitting a ball, it's worth knowing that golf is becoming a popular sport in

Italy, aided recently by the success of the country's most famous pro players, the Molinari brothers. Most clubs welcome non-members, but you must be able to produce a

---

SPLASHING OUT: ROME'S HOTEL POOLS

Hotel swimming pools are relatively rare in Rome, especially in the centre, and not surprisingly the hotels that have them are generally five star. However even if you're not splashing out on a fancy room, you can still cool off in one of the hotel pools listed below; outdoor pools are generally open from May or June to September. **Entrance fees** to non-guests are fairly hefty: reckon on paying €25–95 for a full day (weekends are generally at the upper end of this range; half-days are sometimes possible), and more if you opt for one of the spa treatments that are often available.

One of Rome's prettiest, most secluded pools is at the **Aldrovandi Palace** (see p.238) on the northern edge of Villa Borghese. Surrounded by lush foliage, it's large enough for a good swim. Nearby is the **Parco dei Principi**, Via Frescobaldi 5 (☎ 06 854 421, ⓦ parcodeiprincipi.com), whose 25m pool, set in a garden edged by umbrella pines, is close enough to the zoo that you can hear the lions roar at late-afternoon feeding time. More centrally, the **Radisson Blu Es** (see p.236) has a lovely rooftop pool that's open from 9am until 6pm, and the **Exedra** (see p.236) nearby stays true to the area's ancient function as the Baths of Diocletian, with an outdoor pool that's close to the bar and restaurant and has a view over the rooftops beyond the square, though it's really designed for a cooling soak rather than a vigorous swim; there's also a spa.

On Via Veneto, the **Westin Excelsior** (☎ 06 47081, ⓦ westinrome.com) has a small indoor pool, set among Neoclassical columns intended to suggest the baths of ancient Rome; spa treatments are available, as well as a jacuzzi, steam bath, sauna and gym. Across the Tiber, the **Rome Cavalieri** (see p.238) has lovely gardens and four swimming pools – three of them outdoor – which are about as good as they get in Rome. West of the Vatican, along Via Aurelia Antica, the **Crowne Plaza St Peter's** (☎ 06 66420, ⓦ crowneplaza.com) has a 25m outdoor pool and spa with a small indoor pool and gym, and is open until 9pm. The black-tiled pool at **Black Hotel** (☎ 06 6641 0148, ⓦ blackhotel.it) is deep enough for a good swim, though it's a bit of a trek from the centre. North towards Trastevere is the **Gran Meliá Rome** (see p.237), which has a secluded outdoor pool by a lovely garden, while further up the Janiculum Hill, the **Grand Hotel del Gianicolo** (see p.237) – the cheapest of the hotel pools – features a curvaceous mosaic-tiled outdoor swimming pool to keep visitors from plunging into the nearby seventeenth-century fountain.

22

membership card from your hometown club. For more information, get in touch with the Federazione Italiana Golf, Viale Tiziano 74 (☎06 323 1825, ⓦfedergolf.it).

Circolo del Golf di Roma Aquasanta Via Appia Nuova 716a ☎06 780 3407, ⓦgolfroma.it. This year-round, 18-hole golf course is just south of the centre of Rome, not far from the catacombs and Cinecittà. In addition to the par-71 course, there's also a bar, billiards room and an outdoor pool, so plenty to keep non-golfing friends occupied. Green fees range from €60 to €160. Tues–Sun.

Country Club Castel Gandolfo Via Santo Spirito 13, Castel Gandolfo ☎06 931 2301, ⓦcountryclub castelgandolfo.it. Situated in Castel Gandolfo, down in the Castelli Romani (see p.224), this is the pope's local course – open year-round, 18 holes, par 72 – and it has excellent facilities, including a restaurant, outdoor pool and bar. Green fees are €60–80. Open daily.

GYMS

Farnese Fitness Vicolo delle Grotte 35, near Campo de' Fiori ☎06 687 6931, ⓦfarnesefitness.com. This is a decent gym right in the centre of town, with good equipment and lots of regular fitness classes. Entry is €10 per day. Mon–Fri 7am–10pm, Sat 9am–7pm, Sun 9am–2pm.

Hard Candy Fitness Via Capo d'Africa 5, Celio ☎06 7049 0452, ⓦhardcandyfitnessroma.it. Madonna's fitness club franchise has opened a couple of locations in the centre of Rome; this one is very near the Colosseum, and there is another in the residential district of Parioli (Viale Romania 4; ☎06 807 5577). Check the website for a free one-off guest pass. Mon–Fri 7am–11pm, Sat 9am–7pm, Sun 10am–6pm.

HORSERIDING

Riding Ancient Rome ☎392 788 5168, ⓦridingancientrome.it. This company offers guided jaunts on horseback along the Appian Way, with tours of 1hr, 2hr or 3hr (€35 per person per hour, or €90 for the 3hr tour).

SWIMMING

If you feel like cooling off on a hot summer's day, a dip in a swimming pool may be the perfect cure. Unfortunately, most of Rome's pools are privately run and can be quite expensive, especially in hotels (see box, p.305), though there are a couple of affordable public pools, as well as a nearby waterpark, Aquafelix (see p.311), and you can also use the pools in some gyms (see above). If you fancy a spot of proper pampering it's worth booking a day at a hotel spa.

Centro Sportivo Jolly Via Concesio, Prima Porta ☎06 3361 3375, ⓦjollysportingclub.it. A sports club in the

north of the city that has both indoor and outdoor pools. Sessions cost €10–12 per person. Indoor pool Mon–Fri 8.30am–9.40pm, Sat & Sun 9am–6.30pm; outdoor pool June–Aug 9am–7pm.

Oasi di Pace Via degli Eugenii 2, Appia ☎06 718 4550, ⓦct-oasidipace.it. The "Oasis of Peace" sports club is just off the Via Appia and has an open-air pool that makes for a wonderfully atmospheric place to take a dip, as well as spa treatments. Cost is a flat fee of €12 per day. June–Sept daily 9.30am–6.30pm.

Piscina delle Rose Viale America 20, EUR ☎06 5422 0333, ⓦpiscinadellerose.it. Down in EUR, and easily reachable on metro line B, this is Rome's largest public pool, accessible for a rate of €14 per half-day, €16 per day. Mid-May to Sept Mon–Fri 10am–10pm, Sat & Sun 9am–7pm.

Stadio Olimpico del Nuoto Piazza Lauro de Bosis 3 ☎06 320 1498 or ☎06 3272 3315. The swimming complex at Mussolini's Foro Italico is used for high-profile international competitions, but anyone can swim here if they sign up for five swimming sessions (€52). The indoor pool has some fantastic Fascist-era sporty mosaics on the walls. Mon–Sat 9am–2pm.

TENNIS

Centro Sportivo Jolly Via Concesio, Prima Porta ☎06 3361 3375, ⓦjollysportingclub.it. A large sports and fitness centre in the north of the city, where you can hire outdoor tennis courts in spring and summer for €10–12 an hour.

Oasi di Pace Via degli Eugenii 2, Appia ☎06 718 4550, ⓦct-oasidipace.it. South of the centre of Rome, just off the Via Appia and near the Aquasanta golf course (see above), this big sports club has courts for €14 per hour. Mon–Fri 8am–9pm, Sat & Sun 8am–7pm.

RUNNING

Jogging Running on the roads in Rome when there is no official race on is impossible, and sometimes even dangerous, owing to the traffic and congestion, but luckily there are plenty of green spaces to escape the traffic. The most popular is Villa Borghese, where there are plenty of places to jog, including the Piazza di Siena, a grass horse-track in the centre of the park. Other good options include the Villa Ada, a lush and vast green space north of the city centre, which has a running track, and the Villa Doria Pamphilj above Trastevere, which offers nice paths with exercise stations along the way. For more central – and public – jogging, the Circus Maximus is the perfect size and shape, though it does sometimes feel like you're jogging around a vast traffic roundabout.

The Rome Marathon Held on the third Sun in March, the Rome Marathon (ⓦmaratonadiroma.it) circles around the city's most famous monuments, and is a nice opportunity to run through the city centre free of cars and crazy drivers. It starts and finishes on Via dei Fori Imperiali and the course follows the river, going as far north as the Ponte Milvio and as far south as the Basilica di San Paolo. If you're not up for a full marathon, or even anything like it, it's worth knowing that there's also a 5km fun run through the Centro Storico on the same day.

The Rome–Ostia Half Marathon Held every Feb/March, the Rome–Ostia Half Marathon (Ⓦromaostia.it) goes from EUR in the south of the city to the seafront in the heart of Ostia Lido.

The Roma–Appia 14k Taking you past all the sights of the Appian Way, the Roma–Appia 14k (Ⓦappiarun.it) takes place in mid- to end April.

22

Kids' Rome

Italians love children. Don't be surprised by how much attention people pay them here: peeking into strangers' buggies and cheek-pinching are quite normal, as is helping lug pushchairs up steps and giving up a seat for parents and their children on public transport. That said, though there have been significant improvements of late, Rome has a surprisingly limited number of activities specifically geared towards children. Luckily, just touring the sights of Rome might be enough – there are plenty of things that will appeal to kids of all ages, from sights specifically targeted at children, such as the Explora museum for children, to the perennially popular sites of ancient Rome.

This city is in many ways a natural one for kids: there are lots of open spaces, squares and pedestrian areas for just dashing about and playing, and some of the sights can really appeal to a younger audience. Hopping on and off an **open-top bus tour** (see box, p.24) can be a fun introduction to the highlights, and some of the sights in between have a special appeal – dramatic **Castel Sant'Angelo** (see p.209), the **Colosseum**, where you'll always find a gladiator or two (see p.72), throwing coins into the **Trevi Fountain** (see p.101) and of course sticking a hand in the **Bocca della Verità** and daring to tell a fib (see p.69). There are also a handful of attractions aimed at children, notably the **Explora museum for children** (see p.310); the **Time Elevator** (see p.311); and the city centre's largest park, **Villa Borghese** (see p.169), which has rowing boats and bikes for hire. On the park's northeastern side, there's also the Bioparco or **city zoo** (see p.310) – as well as plenty of open space for little ones to let off steam. There are always **shops** if you're desperate, but if it's hot and you're having a hellish time in the city itself, it might just be best to get away for a **day-trip**, perhaps to a beach (see box, p.225) or a quiet town, such as Bracciano (see p.220), Tivoli (see p.212), with its villa and Roman site, or one of the sites out of Rome listed in this chapter (see p.311). Finally, if you're here in December or early January, don't forget to check out the **Befana Toy Fair**, held in Piazza Navona (see box, p.285).

23

ESSENTIALS

Babysitting English-speaking babysitters are available through Angels (❶06 678 2877 or ❶338 667 9718, ⓦweb.tiscali.it/angelsstaff). If you're staying in a smart hotel, reception will generally be able to organize a babysitter for you.

Food Eating out with kids in Rome is easy – the numerous pasta and pizza options ensure that there's something for even the fussiest of eaters, while relaxed waiting staff go out of their way to charm and amuse the kids. If the menu fails to offer anything suitable, the kitchen is almost always willing to rustle you up a plate of plain spaghetti with butter or parmesan. And if you're on the go, you can always head to the nearest *gelateria*, or grab a slice of pizza.

Transport Rome is a reasonably kid-friendly city when it comes to getting around: children under 10 travel free on all public transport, and there are lots of streets and squares that enable you to plan a fairly traffic-free route across the city centre. If you've got very small children, a pushchair or buggy isn't much help and can be a positive hindrance, given the number of steps, cobbles, and – most irritatingly – scooter-jammed kerbs and pavements.

Information If you speak Italian, you may find the website ⓦromaperbambini.it a useful resource for kids' activities in the city. The blog ⓦlolamamma.wordpress. com also has useful information.

PARKS

Janiculum Hill High up on the Janiculum, this park is a good place to keep kids amused, with pony rides, carousels, balloon-sellers and puppet shows, while adults enjoy a great view of the city below. The puppet shows (see box, p.311) are top-notch and children can choose to take their favourite character home with them from the colourful selection on sale. You might want to time your visit to coincide with the daily firing of the cannon at noon (see p.167).

Orto Botanico Via Corsini, Trastevere ❶06 4991 7107, ⓦweb.uniroma1.it/ortobotanico. A peaceful oasis in the heart of Trastevere, the city's botanical gardens have palm-lined paths, fountains, a meandering rose garden, towering bamboo patches and lush greenhouses. Adults €8, 6–11yrs €4, under-6s free. Mon–Sat: April to end Oct 9am–6.30pm; end Oct to March 9am–5pm.

Villa Ada This is a large, beautiful park just north of the city with plenty to keep youngsters happy, including a roller-skating rink, bike paths, two playgrounds and ponds

(see p.181).

Villa Borghese This huge park offers plenty of entertainment for young ones. Enter at the northern side, via the Viale delle Belle Arti entrance, to find pony rides, a children's train, swings and paddleboats on the lake – which comes complete with a Greek temple. On the southern side of the park, the Pincio Gardens have a playground and carousels and places to rent bikes or a *risciò*, the latter particularly good fun for families (see p.169).

Villa Celimontana Celian Hill. These public gardens have nice views over the river and a playground (see p.129).

Villa Doria Pamphilj Main entrance on Via di San Pancrazio, Monteverde. A 10min walk east from the Janiculum Hill, Rome's largest park is a great place for kids to let off steam – more like real countryside in parts, it's the perfect walking, cycling or picnic spot and has a pretty lake filled with basking turtles and surrounded by woods (see p.167).

PIAZZAS, PLAYGROUNDS AND PUSSYCATS

Rome's abundant **piazzas**, with their cobbled expanses, fountains and cafés, are often just as much fun for kids to run around in as playgrounds – especially in the early evening when everyone's out for a stroll and the street sellers and buskers liven things up even more. **Piazza di Santa Maria in Trastevere** (see p.159) is always an energetic place, as are **Piazza di Spagna** (see p.94) and **Piazza Navona** (see p.42) – which has the added attraction of two toy shops. **Villa Borghese** (see p.169), **Villa Sciarra** (see below), **Villa Ada** (see p.181) and **Villa Celimontana** (see p.129) all have **playgrounds**; there are also very good play areas in **Piazza Vittorio Emanuele** (see p.120), **Piazza di Santa Maria Liberatrice** in Testaccio (see p.142) and **Piazza San Cosimato** in Trastevere.

The city's **cat colonies** are usually a big hit with kids – check out the one at **Largo di Torre Argentina** (see p.54) where cat-spotting among the ancient ruins is a popular pastime. At the cat sanctuary alongside, kids can get up close to some of the inhabitants that are up for adoption. The volunteers who look after the cats here are always happy to show you round, and they also take care of other colonies around the city, including **Pyramid of Caius Cestius** in Testaccio (see p.144).

23

Villa Sciarra Entrances on Via Calandrelli and Viale delle Mura Gianicolensi, Monteverde; tram #8 from Piazza Venezia to Viale Trastevere. A little way to the south of the Janiculum Hill, this small park is a bit out of the way but has a lovely little playground.

ATTRACTIONS AND MUSEUMS

IN THE CITY

Bioparco Via del Giardino Zoologico, Villa Borghese ☎ 06 360 8211, ⌨ bioparco.it. Rome's zoo, on the northern edge of Villa Borghese (see p.169), is a large, typical city-centre offering, focusing on conservation and education, yet still providing the usual animals kids are after, including tigers, apes, giraffes, elephants, hippos and a reptile house. The Museo di Zoologia next door (see below) is also worth a look. Adults €15, children over 1m tall €12, under 1m free. Daily: end March–end Oct 9.30am–6pm (till 7pm Sat & Sun); end Oct–end March 9.30am–5pm.

Castel Sant'Angelo Lungotevere Castello 50 ☎ 06 681 9111, ⌨ castelsantangelo.com. Along with the Colosseum, this is one of the most exciting of the city's ancient monuments for kids. Through the centuries, Hadrian's mausoleum has served as a papal escape route in times of trouble and the city's prison; it has all the grisly, dungeon-like spookiness you'd expect from such a history, and a wide, spiral ramp leading to the mausoleum itself adds to the atmosphere. There are also great views over the city from the top (see p.209). Adults €10, children free; free first Sun of the month. Tues–Sun 9am–7.30pm; last entry 1hr before closing.

Colosseum Piazza del Colosseo ☎ 06 3996 7700, ⌨ coopculture.it. Loaded with atmosphere given its setting as the stage for many a grisly end for both humans and beasts, Rome's most famous ancient monument can't fail to capture kids' imaginations (see p.72). Book tickets in advance to skip the queue. Adults €12 combined ticket with Forum (p.77) & Palatine Hill (p.84); under-18 EU citizens free, non-EU €7.50; free first Sun of the month. Daily: mid-Feb to mid-March 8.30am–5pm; mid- to end March 8.30am–5.30pm; April–Aug 8.30am–7.15pm; Sept 8.30am–7pm; Oct 8.30am–6.30pm; Nov to mid-Feb 8.30am–4.30pm; last entry 1hr before closing.

Explora – Museo dei Bambini di Roma Via Flaminia 82, Flaminio ☎ 06 361 3776, ⌨ mdbr.it. A short walk from Piazzale Flaminio, this learn-as-you-play centre, geared towards kids under 12, aims to teach children about themselves and the world they live in through hands-on activities. It's all laid out in the form of a small city and there's also plenty of purely fun stuff, such as a puppet theatre and a playground. Adults and children over 3 €8, 1–3yrs €5, 0–1yrs free. Timed entry for 1hr 45min slots: Tues–Sun at 10am (except In Aug), noon, 3pm & 5pm; advance booking recommended.

Museo della Civiltà Romana & Planetario Piazza Agnelli 10, EUR ☎ 06 0608, ⌨ museociviltaromana.it; metro line B to EUR Fermi. Closed for restoration at the time of writing, this museum has lots of stuff that will interest ancient Rome-addicted kids, among them replicas of the city's famous statues and buildings as well as more everyday artefacts. But the real favourite is the museum's scale model of Rome in the time of Constantine, which takes up a whole room. On the same site, there's also a planetarium and astronomy exhibition (also closed for restoration), but it's not as thrilling as you'd expect, and audio shows are only in Italian.

Museo di Zoologia Via Aldrovandi 18, Villa Borghese ☎ 06 6710 9270, ⌨ museodizoologia.it. Located next to the Bioparco (see above), this museum has a permanent exhibit – Animals and their Habitats – in one wing, while a variety of stuffed animals fill the older part of the museum. Adults and children over 6yrs €7, under-6s free. Tues–Sun 9am–7pm.

Time Elevator Via dei SS. Apostoli 20, Trevi ☎ 06 6992 1823, ⓦ time-elevator.it. Flight-simulator seats and headphones (English audio available) set the stage for a virtual tour of three thousand years of Roman history: an excellent way to prime the kids (not to mention their parents) for the sights they will be seeing. Adults €12, children 5–12yrs €9; not suitable for under-5s. Daily 10.30am–7.30pm; shows every hour, lasting 45min.

BEYOND ROME

Aquafelix Via Terme di Traiano, Civitavecchia, 80km northwest of Rome ☎ 0766 32221, ⓦ aquafelix.it. Situated on the edge of Civitavecchia, this is one of the most popular waterparks near the capital, and isn't too hard to reach on public transport – there are regular trains to Civitavecchia from Termini (40min–1hr), and a bus from the station to the park at 10.15am and 11.15am, returning at 6.30pm. Adults €20, children €17.50, afternoon ticket (from 2pm) €13. Mid-June to mid-Sept daily 10am–6.30pm.

Cinecittà World Via di Castel Romano 200, 25km from central Rome ☎ 06 4041 1541, ⓦ cinecittaworld.it. Cinecittà, Rome's historic film studios (see p.154) opened this cinema-inspired theme park in 2014. With twenty attractions and three film sets, there's plenty to keep kids

entertained, and it's been impressively put together: Oscar-winning composer Ennio Morricone created the soundtrack for the Western film set, and art director Dante Ferretti, another Oscar-winner, did the designs for the park. It's about a 20min drive from Fiumicino airport, or there's a shuttle bus from Via Marsala 58, by Termini, at 9.30am, returning at 6.15pm (€10). Prices vary depending on the month and day of entry, but adult tickets cost €24–32, afternoon tickets €18, children over 1m and up to 15yrs €15–19, children under 1m free; it's cheaper to buy tickets online. April Mon & Wed–Sun 10am–6pm; May Wed–Sun 10am–6pm; first half of June Mon–Fri 10am–6pm, Sat & Sun 10am–11pm; mid-June to mid-Sept daily 10am–11pm; mid-Sept to Oct Sat & Sun 10am–10pm; Dec & Jan check website for hours.

Ostia Antica Viale dei Romagnoli, Ostia Antica ☎ 06 5635 0215, ⓦ ostia-antica.org. Every bit as atmospheric and mesmerizing as Pompeii, the ruins of Rome's ancient port, Ostia, will give kids a great feel for what a Roman city was like. It's a must-see for any child who's read *The Thieves of Ostia*, the first in the *Roman Mysteries* series by Caroline Lawrence, in which a sea captain's daughter solves a mystery in 79 AD. To get there, take metro line B to Piramide and then a train (25min) from Porta San Paolo on the Lido di Ostia line (€10). Tues–Sun: Nov to mid-Feb 8.30am–4.30pm; mid-Feb to mid-March 8.30am–5pm; late March 8.30am–5.30pm; end March to Aug 8.30am–7.15pm; Sept 8.30am–7pm; Oct 8.30am–6.30pm; last entry 1hr before closing; Museo Ostiense 9.30am–1hr before the site closing time.

PUPPETRY AND FILMS

Puppetry has been delighting Italian children for hundreds of years, and Rome has a few venues for viewing puppeteers in action. Sometimes you can find a show in English, but the storyline is visually explanatory and kids don't seem to care whether they understand the words or not. Most **films** will be dubbed into Italian, but occasionally you can find one showing in the original language and there's also an excellent children's cinema in the Villa Borghese.

PUPPET SHOWS

Teatro di Pulcinella Piazzale Giuseppe Garibaldi, Trastevere ☎ 06 582 7767. This is said to be one of only two places left in Rome to view true puppeteers. Usually puts on Punch & Judy shows. Free, although a small donation is expected. Shows Sat & Sun.

Teatro San Carlino Viale dei Bambini, Pincio Villa Borghese ☎ 06 6992 2117, ⓦ sancarlino.it. Newer than the Teatro Verde (see below), this theatre puts on regular weekend shows for kids throughout the year. Adults €11, children under 14 €10.50, under-2s free.

Teatro Verde Circonvallazione Gianicolense 10, Trastevere ☎ 06 588 2034, ⓦ teatroverde.it; train to Trastevere from Termini or Ostiense, or tram to

Stazione Trastevere. Located just by Trastevere station, this children's theatre puts on weekend musicals and marionette shows as well as plays. Tickets €10. Shows Oct–May Sat & Sun at 5pm.

CINEMA

Cinema dei Piccoli Viale della Pineta 15, on the Via Veneto side of Villa Borghese ☎ 06 855 3485, ⓦ cinemadeipiccoli.it. Almost opposite the Casa del Cinema, this is not only the smallest public cinema in the world, with just 63 seats, but also one of the oldest, in business since 1934. Children's films are generally shown in Italian. Most showings Sat & Sun at 3.30pm, 5pm & 6.30pm.

23

Parco dei Mostri Località Giardino, Bomarzo, 93km north of Rome ☎ 0761 924 029, ⓦ bomarzo.net. "The Park of Monsters" is basically a garden but with crazy sculptures, weird buildings and surreal conceits that make it one of north Lazio's top tourist attractions. You can get to Bomarzo by COTRAL bus from Viterbo (6 daily; 40min), which in turn is easily reached by train from either Ostiense station or the Laziale platform at Termini. Adults €10, 4–13yrs €8, under-4s free. Daily 8am–sunset.

Zoomarine Via dei Romagnoli, 38km from central Rome ☎ 06 91534, ⓦ zoomarine.it. A marine park with all the usual dolphins, seals, penguins and the rest, along with a handful of waterpark attractions. A shuttle bus runs from Termini at 9.30am (April & May Sat & Sun; June–Sept all opening days; €10 return; 1hr). Adults €32, children €26, children under 1m free; discounts online. Mid-April to mid-June Thurs & Fri 10am–5pm, Sat & Sun 10am–6pm; mid- to end June Mon–Fri 10am–6pm, Sat & Sun 10am–7pm; July & Aug daily 10am–7pm; Sept, Oct & first half of April check website for hours.

SHOPS: CLOTHES, BOOKS AND TOYS

For **children's clothes**, your best bet is either Oviesse (see p.296) or COIN (see p.295), which both sell cheap and cheerful kids' clothes and shoes, though there's any number of tempting boutiques selling fancy childrenswear at eye-watering prices, especially in the Centro Storico.

Al Sogno Piazza Navona 53, Centro Storico ☎ 06 686 4198, ⓦ alsogno.com; map p.36. Perfectly located at the north end of Piazza Navona, with two floors of cuddly toys, handmade dolls, board games and replicas of Roman soldiers. Daily 10am–10pm; closes 8pm in winter.

Bertè Piazza Navona 108, Centro Storico ☎ 06 6574 4143, ⓦ bertegiocattoliroma.it; map p.36. One of Rome's oldest toy stores at the other end of the piazza from Al Sogno (see above), with toys for children of all ages. Daily 10am–7pm.

Città del Sole Via della Scrofa 65, Centro Storico ☎ 06 6880 3805, ⓦ cittadelsole.it; map p.36. This shop sells toys, games and books for kids in a great central location. There is a second store in Piazza San Cosimato, Trastevere. Mon–Sat 10am–7.30pm, Sun 11am–7.30pm.

Il Pesciolino Rosso Via Bocca di Leone 49, Tridente ☎ 06 6992 2059, ⓦ ilpesciolinorosso.eu; map p.91.

Located near the Spanish Steps, this lovely toy store sells a wonderful selection of toys – mainly of the tasteful wooden variety – plus plenty of pocket-money-priced items. Daily 10.30am–2.30pm & 3.30–7.30pm.

Little Big Town Via Cesare Battisti 120, Piazza Venezia ☎ 06 6992 4226, ⓦ littlebigtown.it; map p.61. Just off Piazza Venezia, this is billed as one of the largest toyshops in Italy, but in reality it's relatively modest. However, it's hard to imagine that your little ones won't find something they like. Mon 1–7.45pm, Tues–Fri 10.30am–7.45pm, Sat 10.30am–8.30pm, Sun 10.30am–7.30pm.

The Little Reader Via Conte Verde 66b, Esquiline ☎ 06 877 84678, ⓦ thelittlereader.it; map p.114. This is a fantastic specialist kids' bookshop, mainly Italian but with a small stock of books in English. It also has a great little café, and there are regular readings and events. Mon–Sat 10am–6.30pm.

STATUE OF BEARDED DIONYSUS, CENTRALE MONTEMARTINI

Contexts

History

The history of Rome is inextricably part of the history of the Western world. A hilltop settlement eventually grew into a city that would rule territories from Scotland to the Sahara, and from the Atlantic to Iraq. Its complex and various political and legal systems are at the root of all systems of Western government, those of despots and democracies, and everything in between. Some Roman history is crucial to an understanding of the city – its sights and monuments are often interconnected and a grasp of the continuum of events is helpful. We've tried to contextualize as much information in the Guide as possible, but we recommend you take a look at some of the historical texts we list in "Books" (see p.328) and "Films" (see p.332). Here follows a basic framework of the city's history.

Beginnings

Rome's history has its beginnings in the hazy realm of legend. Its founder Romulus and his twin brother Remus were the sons of Mars, god of war, and a local princess called Rhea Silvia. After their birth, Rhea Silvia's wicked uncle, fearing that the babies were the true claimants to his throne at Alba Longa, had them abandoned in a river in flood. They washed up in an inlet of the Tiber (the Velabrum) where they were found and suckled by a she-wolf. Brought up by a shepherd, they reached adolescence and began to argue. Remus founded his settlement on the Aventine Hill, Romulus on the Palatine. On 21 April 753 BC, Romulus, thrown into a fit of rage by his brother, killed him and became the first of the seven kings of Rome.

Legend tends to be rooted in actuality: the Velabrum where Romulus and Remus are said to have been suckled by the wolf was also once a point at which the Tiber was once fordable. The establishment of a settlement on the defensible Capitoline and Palatine hills overlooking this crossing is a very logical one. It was a key node on the trade routes between the valuable salt marshes at the mouth of the river at Ostia, and the neighbouring regions of Etruria and Campania.

The Etruscans

The **Etruscans** dominated the area of Italy to the north of the Tiber which extended in parts as far as the Po. According to the Greek historian Herodotus, they came to Italy from Lydia in modern-day Turkey. Another theory suggests they were an indigenous Italian tribe in close contact with the Greek world. The Etruscan language was of non-Indo-European origin, and written from right to left, though using Greek characters. The discovery of the Etruscan equivalent to the Rosetta Stone, the Pyrgi Tablets (at the excellent Etruscan Museum at Villa Giulia; see p.177), were only discovered in 1964.

8th century BC	753 BC	509 BC	509 BC–82 BC
First Iron Age settlement on Palatine Hill	Romulus assumes power in Rome	End of reign of Tarquinius Superbus – and of Rome as a kingdom	Period of the Roman Republic

The Etruscan architecture that survives is almost exclusively funerary: their houses were built of wood, but the tombs that emulated them were carved into the rock outside their cities. Long before other Italic tribes, they took important steps towards creating central urban nuclei, with twelve city-states. At the height of their civilization, in the sixth century BC, one of their greatest cities, Cerveteri (or Caere) had a population of over 25,000. Undoubtedly, the overriding official Roman line that Rome conquered Etruria is, at best, simplistic: the last three of the city's legendary seven kings were Etruscan, the first of whom was **Tarquinius Priscus** (616–579 BC). Under his rule, Rome began to develop an urban infrastructure: tradition attributes the creation of the Cloaca Maxima to him. This "great drain" reclaimed the valleys which then became the site of the Forum and the Circus Maximus. He also is credited with the building of the Temple of Jupiter Optimus Maximus on the Capitoline Hill, which would remain the most important temple of the Roman world for over a millennium.

The Roman Republic

The last of the kings of Rome emerge from the mists of myth into documented history. Around 509 BC, the people rose up against the last, tyrannical Etruscan monarch, **Tarquinius Superbus** (535–509 BC). Tarquinius's son raped a Roman noblewoman, Lucretia. She committed suicide shortly afterwards, and her husband, along with Lucius Junius Brutus, helped to lead an uprising that led to the establishment of a **Republic**. The Roman Republic would last nearly five hundred years, and was a (relatively) democratic form of government, based on the acknowledged fact that the fates of the Roman people and its patrician classes were inextricably bound up together. (The acronym SPQR, which you still see everywhere, stands for "Senatus Populusque Romanus" or "The Senate and the People of Rome".) The **Senate** represented the patrician families, and elected two consuls from their number to lead Rome, while the people were allowed to elect two tribunes to represent their interests.

The city prospered under the Republic, growing greatly in size and subduing the various tribes of the surrounding areas – the Volsci and Etruscans to the north, the Sabines to the east, the Samnites to the south. The Etruscans were finally beaten in 474 BC, at the battle of Cumae, and the Volsci and Sabines soon afterwards. Rome later drew up its first set of laws, in 451 BC, inscribing them on bronze tablets and displaying them prominently in the Forum, by now the city's most important central space.

The expanding Empire

Despite a heavy defeat by the **Gauls** in 390 BC, by the following century Rome had begun to extend its influence beyond the boundaries of what is now mainland Italy, pushing south into Sicily and across the ocean to Africa. In the meantime, Rome was also trying to subdue the **Samnites**, who occupied most of the land in the southern part of what is now Italy, waging sporadic wars between 343 and 290 BC that led eventually to the Roman occupation of most of the region that is now Campania.

Beyond mainland Italy, the next century was dominated by the **Punic Wars**, against **Carthage**, the other dominant force in the Mediterranean, and the only obstacle between Rome and total dominance of the region. The First Punic War, fought over

474 BC	264 BC	146 BC	87–82 BC	44 BC
Defeat of the Etruscans	First Punic war	Defeat of Carthage	Civil war in Rome	Assassination of Julius Caesar

Sicily, began in 264 BC and continued for around twenty years until Carthage surrendered all rights to the island; the Second Punic War famously began in 218 BC with Hannibal's march across the Alps with war elephants, and eventually ended with the Romans' defeat at Cannae in 202 BC. Rome's sacking of Carthage (Third Punic War, 146 BC) saw it become the dominant power in the Mediterranean, subsequently taking control of present-day Greece and the Middle East, and expanding north into what is now France, Germany and Britain.

Domestic turmoil

On home soil, the Romans built **roads** (the first paved example being the Via Appia, 312 BC) as military tools to move troops, and developed their civic structure, with new laws and far-sighted political reforms, one of which cannily brought all of the Republic's vanquished enemies into the fold as **Roman citizens**. However, the history of the Republic was also one of internal strife, marked by factional fighting among the patrician ruling classes, as everyone tried to grab a slice of the riches that were pouring into the city from its plundering expeditions abroad – and the plebeians, enjoying little more justice than they had under the Roman monarchs. In 87 BC, a power struggle between two consuls, Lucius Cornelius Sulla and Gaius Marius, led to a **civil war** in which Sulla, in 82 BC, eventually emerged as the sole leader of Rome. He initiated terrifying revenge against his opponents and introduced laws which greatly reduced the powers of the city's elected officials.

Gaius Marius's nephew, **Julius Caesar**, later emerged as a powerful military leader and over the course of eight long years conquered Gaul and Britain before returning to fight another civil war against his rival Pompey, which he won. Following this victory, he proclaimed himself "dictator of Rome", first for one year, then three years, then in perpetuity. It was the last straw for those eager to restore the Republican vision, and Caesar was assassinated at the Theatre of Pompey on March 15, 44 BC. Rather than returning Rome to the glorious days of the Republic, the murder of Caesar in fact threw it into even greater turmoil.

After his death, Julius Caesar's deputy, **Mark Antony**, briefly took control, joining forces with Lepidus and Caesar's adopted son, Octavian, in a **triumvirate**. Their armies fought against, and defeated, those controlled by Caesar's assassins, Brutus and Cassius, in a famous battle at Philippi, in modern-day Greece, in 42 BC. Their alliance was further cemented by Antony's marriage to Octavian's sister, Octavia, in 40 AD, but in spite of this, things did not go well for the triumvirate. Lepidus was imprisoned and Antony, unable to put his political ambitions before his emotional bond with the queen of Egypt, Cleopatra, was defeated by Octavian at the battle of Actium in 31 BC. Antony escaped to Alexandria, where he committed suicide with Cleopatra, leaving Octavian in command.

The Imperial Era

Julius Caesar's adoptive son and great-nephew, Octavian, was 19 when Caesar was assassinated. Seventeen years later, in 27 BC, he was given a new title by the Senate: Augustus. With its overtones of a divine mandate, the title referred to Augustus's own illustrious ancestry which included (he claimed) Romulus himself. The first ruler to

27 BC	**27 BC–337 AD**	**44 BC–68 AD**	**69–96 AD**
Accession of Octavian Caesar (Augustus)	Period of imperial Rome	Julio-Claudian dynasty	Flavian dynasty

have the absolute power of the army (the Imperium), he is considered the first Emperor. Indeed "Augustus" became the name by which all future Roman emperors were known. He began rebuilding the ramshackle Republican city with a new imperial grandeur. Soon before his death he claimed that he had found a city of brick and left one of marble.

Augustus was succeeded by his stepson, **Tiberius** (14–37 AD), who ruled from the island of Capri for the last years of his reign, and he in turn by **Caligula** (37–41 AD), a possibly insane ruler who was assassinated after just four years in power. **Claudius** (41–54 AD), his uncle, followed, at first reluctantly, and proved to be a wise ruler, only to be succeeded by his stepson, **Nero** (54–68 AD), whose reign became more notorious for its excess than its prudence, and led to a brief period of

---

THE RULERS OF ROME

ROMAN KINGS
Romulus (753–716 BC)
Numa Pompilius (715–674 BC)
Tullus Hostilius (673–642 BC)
Ancus Marcius (642–617 BC)
Lucius Tarquinius Priscus (616–579 BC)
Servius Tullius (578–535 BC)
Lucius Tarquinius Superbus (535–509 BC)

ROMAN REPUBLIC
c.509 BC–82 BC (death of Marius)

ROMAN DICTATORS AND TRIUMVIRS
Sulla (82–78 BC)
Triumvirate of Julius Caesar, Pompey and Crassus (60–53 BC)
Pompey (52–47 BC)
Julius Caesar (45–44 BC)
Triumvirate of Antony, Octavian Caesar (Augustus) and **Lepidus** (43–27 BC)

ROMAN EMPERORS
Augustus (27 BC–14 AD)
Tiberius (14–37)
Caligula (37–41)
Claudius (41–54)
Nero (54–68)
Galba (68–69)
Otho (69)
Vitellius (69)
Vespasian (69–79)
Titus (79–81)
Domitian (81–96)

Nerva (96–98)
Trajan (98–117)
Hadrian (117–138)
Antoninus Pius (138–161)
Lucius Verus (161–169) co-emperor with
Marcus Aurelius (161–180) co-emperor with **Commodus** (177–192)
Pertinax (192–193)
Didius Julianus (193)
Septimius Severus (193–211) co-emperor with **Geta** (209–211) co-emperor with **Caracalla** (211–217)
Macrinus (217–218)
Elagabalus (218–222)
Alexander Severus (222–235)
Maximinus Thrax (235–238)
Gordian III (238–244)
Marcus Philippus (244–249)
Decius (249–251)
Trebonianus Gallus (251–253)
Aemilianus (253)
Valerian (253–260) co-emperor with
Gallienus (253–268)
Claudius II (268–270)
Quintillus (270)
Aurelian (270–275)
Marcus Claudius Tacitus (275–276)
Florianus (276)
Probus (276–282)
Carus (282–283)
Carinus (283–285) in competition with
Diocletian (284–305)
Constantine (306–337)

193–235 AD	275 AD	590 AD	753 AD	800 AD
Severan dynasty	Building of the Aurelian Walls	Accession of Pope Gregory I	Lombard invasion	Charlemagne is proclaimed Holy Roman Emperor

warring and infighting after his murder in 68 AD, with Vitellius, Galba and Vespasian all vying for the position of emperor. **Vespasian** (69–79 AD) was eventually proclaimed emperor, thus starting a dynasty – the **Flavian** – which would restore some stability to Rome and its empire.

The Flavian and Severan dynasties

Vespasian began with the obliteration of all traces of Nero, not least by building an enormous amphitheatre – later known as the Colosseum – in what had been a vast lake at Nero's palace. Vespasian was succeeded by his elder son, **Titus** (79–81 AD), and then by Titus's younger brother **Domitian** (81–96 AD). Domitian reverted to imperial type, becoming an ever more paranoid and despotic ruler until his murder in 96 AD, when all his decrees were declared void. **Nerva** was declared emperor (96–98 AD), thus beginning the rule of the "five good emperors", known for their moderate policies and for giving Rome much-needed stability. He was succeeded by his nominated successor, **Trajan** (98–117 AD), who expanded the empire greatly, conquering lands to the east (Turkey and modern-day Romania). It was under his rule that the empire reached its maximum extent.

Trajan died in 117 AD, giving way to his cousin, **Hadrian** (117–138 AD), who continued the grand and expansionist agenda of his predecessor, and arguably provided the empire's greatest years. The city swelled to a population of a million or more, its people housed in cramped apartment blocks, or *insulae*; crime in the city was rife, and the traffic problem apparently on a par with today's, prompting one contemporary writer to complain that the din on the streets made it impossible to get a good night's sleep.

But it was a time of peace and prosperity, the Roman upper classes living a life of indolent luxury, in sumptuous residences with proper plumbing and central heating, the most extraordinary example being Hadrian's own villa at Tivoli. Hadrian's successors, **Antoninus Pius** (138–161 AD) and then **Marcus Aurelius** (161–180 AD), ruled over a largely peaceful and economically successful empire, until 180 AD, when Marcus Aurelius's son, **Commodus** (180–192 AD), assumed the throne but wasn't up to the task, and Rome entered a more fragile phase. Predictably, Commodus was murdered, and eventually replaced by **Septimius Severus** (193–211 AD), thus initiating the Severan dynasty – again a time of relative calm, although the political and military skills of Severus unfortunately weren't matched by those of his sons, Geta and Caracalla. **Caracalla** (211–217 AD) murdered his brother before assuming power for himself in 211 AD.

The decline of the city

The decline of Rome gathered speed in the third century. Towards the end of this "troubled century" the Emperor **Diocletian** (284–305 AD), an army officer from present-day Croatia, attempted to consolidate the rapidly fragmenting empire, by dividing it into four parts. Known also for his relentless persecution of Christians, Diocletian abdicated in 305 AD, retiring to the vast palace he had built for himself on the Dalmatian coast (Split). This led to a power struggle which culminated in the battle of the Milvian Bridge in Rome. Here **Constantine** (306–337 AD) defeated his co-ruler, Maxentius, and eventually reunited all four regions under his sole rule.

1305	1347	1376	1503	1527
Transfer of papal court to Avignon	Cola di Rienzo crowned "Tribune of Rome"	Return of papal court to Rome from Avignon	Accession of Julius II	Sack of Rome by Charles V

Legend says that before the battle Constantine saw a vision of a cross and converted to Christianity. Whether because of his conversion or as a political expedient (or both), Constantine legitimized the by now very popular religion, much to the chagrin of old-school patrician Romans. He would issue a further blow to the city, which was rapidly becoming marginalized: in 330 AD, he moved the capital of the Empire to Byzantium and renamed it Constantinople. Less than a century later, Rome was sacked by the Goths (410 AD), the first of a series of invasions which hastened its collapse. The imperial city was looted and abandoned, and by the sixth century was a devastated shadow of its former self: a city once populated by over a million people was reduced to just twenty thousand.

The rise of the papacy

It was the **papacy**, under Pope **Gregory I** ("the Great"; 590–604), that rescued Rome from its demise. Thomas Hobbes described the papacy as none other than "the Ghost of the deceased Roman Empire, sitting crowned upon the grave there of", and in an echo of empire, Gregory sent missions all over Europe to spread the word of the Church. The missions drew pilgrims, and their money, to the city, and in time the papacy emerged as the natural authority in Rome. Several of the city's great churches were built during this time, and those Roman buildings that were still standing were converted – the Castel Sant'Angelo was fortified to repel invaders; the Pantheon became a church. In 800AD, the crowning of Charlemagne as **Holy Roman Emperor**, with dominions spread Europe-wide but answerable to the pope, intensified the city's revival, though this would be short-lived.

Conflict: Pope versus Emperor

The apparent triumph of Charlemagne's coronation would sour, and subsequent centuries would see conflict raging between the pope and the Holy Roman Emperor. While the Holy Roman Emperor could claim absolute power over the secular world, the pope claimed not only spiritual power but also the right to crown and therefore validate the emperor. At times popes excommunicated emperors, at other times emperors imprisoned popes. The Ghibellines (supporters of the emperor) and the Guelphs (supporters of the pope) ravaged many Italian cities, and Rome was attacked on several occasions. Robert Guiscard, the Norman king, sacked the city in 1084; a century later, a dispute between the city and the papacy led to a series of popes relocating to Viterbo. Things became so unstable, that, in 1308, the French-born Pope **Clement V** (1305–14) transferred his court to Avignon. In the mid-fourteenth century, Cola di Rienzo, a self-styled "tribune" of Rome, seized power, setting himself up as the people's saviour from the decadent ways of the city's rulers and forming a new Roman republic. But the increasingly autocratic ways of the new ruler soon lost popularity; Cola di Rienzo was deposed, and in 1376, Pope **Gregory XI** (1370–78) returned to Rome. Shortly after Gregory's death a dispute over his successor's election led to the Great Schism, and the unnerving proposition of two popes – one in Rome and the other in Avignon. This was finally resolved in 1417, with the election of Martin V of the Colonna family, but the decades of papal absence had taken their toll on the fabric of Rome.

1585	1623	1798–1815	1849–70	1870
Accession of Sixtus V	Accession of Urban VIII	Napoleonic Republic	Italian Wars of Unification	Rome becomes capital of the Kingdom of Italy

PAPAL REIGNS

Celestine III (1191–1198)
Innocent III (1198–1216)
Honorius III (1216–1227)
Gregory IX (1227–1241)
Celestine IV (1241)
Innocent IV (1243–1254)
Alexander IV (1254–1261)
Urban IV (1261–1264)
Clement IV (1265–1268)
Gregory X (1271–1276)
Innocent V (1276)
Adrian V (1276)
John XXI (1276–1277)
Nicholas III (1277–1280)
Martin IV (1281–1285)
Honorlus IV (1285–1287)
Nicholas IV (1288–1292)
Celestine V (1294)
Boniface VIII (1294–1303)
Benedict XI (1303–1304)
Clement V (1305–1314)
John XXII (1316–1334)
Benedict XII (1334–1342)
Clement VI (1342–1352)
Innocent VI (1352–1362)
Urban V (1362–1370)
Gregory XI (1370–1378)
Urban VI (1378–1389)
Boniface IX (1389–1404)
Innocent VII (1404–1406)
Gregory XII (1406–1415)

Martin V (1417–1431)
Eugenius IV (1431–1447)
Nicholas V (1447–1455)
Callixtus III (1455–1458)
Pius II (1458–1464)
Paul II (1464–1467)
Sixtus IV (1471–1484)
Innocent VIII (1484–1492)
Alexander VI (1492–1503)
Pius III (1503)
Julius II (1503–1513)
Leo X (1513–1521)
Adrian VI (1522–1523)
Clement VII (1523–1534)
Paul III (1534–1549)
Julius III (1550–1555)
Marcellus II (1555)
Paul IV (1555–1559)
Pius IV (1559–1565)
Pius V (1566–1572)
Gregory XIII (1572–1585)
Sixtus V (1585–1590)
Urban VII (1590)
Gregory XIV (1590–1591)
Innocent IX (1591)
Clement VIII (1592–1605)
Leo XI (1605)
Paul V (1605–1621)
Gregory XV (1621–1623)
Urban VIII (1623–1644)
Innocent X (1644–1655)

Alexander VII (1655–1667)
Clement IX (1667–1669)
Clement X (1670–1676)
Innocent XI (1676–1689)
Alexander VIII (1689–1691)
Innocent XII (1691–1700)
Clement XI (I700–1721)
Innocent XIII (1721–1724)
Benedict XIII (1724–1730)
Clement XII (1730–1740)
Benedict XIV (1740–1758)
Clement XIII (1758–1769)
Clement XIV (1769–1774)
Pius VI (1775–1799)
Pius VII (1800–1823)
Leo XII (1823–1829)
Pius VIII (1829–1830)
Gregory XVI (1831–1846)
Pius IX (1846–1878)
Leo XIII (1878–1903)
Pius X (1903–1914)
Benedict XV (1914–1922)
Pius XI (1922–1939)
Pius XII (1939–1958)
John XXIII (1958–1963)
Paul VI (1963–1978)
John Paul I (1978)
John Paul II (1978–2005)
Benedict XVI (2005–2013)
Francis (2013–)

The Renaissance

After the definitive return of the papacy from Avignon, there was a conscious effort to rebuild the crumbling and neglected city. Aristocratic families (most of whom produced a pope at some point) were encouraged, indeed often sponsored, to beautify Rome. The names of the families are etched on the city's buildings and street names – Palazzo Borghese, Palazzo Barberini, Piazza Farnese. Churches were built, the city's pagan monuments rediscovered and preserved, and artists began to arrive in Rome to work on commissions for the latest pope, who would invariably try to outdo his predecessor's efforts with ever more glorious buildings and works of art (replete with personal coats of arms for posterity).

Bramante, Raphael and Michelangelo all worked in the city throughout their careers. The reigns of Pope **Julius II** (1503–13) and his successor, the Medici pope **Leo X** (1513–21), were something of a golden age: the city was at the centre of Italian cultural

1922	1929	1943	1944
Mussolini leads the March on Rome	Lateran Pact guarantees independence for the Vatican	Rome is declared an "open city" in World War II	Liberation of Rome

life, and was the setting for the creation of great works of art: Michelangelo's frescoes in the Sistine Chapel, the Raphael Rooms in the Vatican Palace, Villa Farnesina, Palazzo Farnese and Palazzo Spada, not to mention the commissioning of a new St Peter's, as well as any number of other churches. The city was once again worthy of the name, and its population had increased to a hundred thousand. In 1527, this golden age was brought abruptly to an end. The armies of the Habsburg monarch and Holy Roman Emperor, **Charles V**, swept into the city, determined to avenge his excommunication by Pope Clement VII (1523–34). The soldiers occupied the city and wreaked havoc for a year while the pope cowered in the Castel Sant'Angelo.

The Counter-Reformation

The ensuing years were ones of yet more restoration, in the service of the **Counter-Reformation**, the Roman reaction to the Protestant Reformation. The Roman Church sought to reel in the faithful and huge, sensational monuments were designed to confound the scepticism of the new Protestant thinking. The grandeur of pagan artefacts (such as obelisks), and the ready supply of building materials provided by the city's ruins, were employed in ever more extravagant displays of wealth. The Farnese pope **Paul III** (1534–49) would approve the Jesuit order, a crack squad aimed at crushing anti-Catholic feeling and converting the New World; later, Pope **Sixtus V** (1585–90) was perhaps the most determined to mould the city in his own image, ploughing roads through the centre and laying out bold new squares at their intersections. This period also saw the completion of St Peter's under **Paul V** (1605–21), and the ascendancy of Gian Lorenzo **Bernini** as the city's principal architect and sculptor under the Barberini pope **Urban VIII** (1623–44) – a patronage that was extended under the Pamphilj pope, **Innocent X** (1644–55).

The eighteenth and nineteenth centuries

The **eighteenth century** saw the decline of the papacy as a political force, a phenomenon marked by the occupation of the city in 1798 by Napoleon's forces; **Pius VI** (1775–99) was unceremoniously captured and taken to France as a prisoner (where he died), and **Napoleon** declared another Roman republic which lasted a year before papal rule was restored under **Pius VII** (1800–23). The years that followed were fairly quiet in Rome, if not in the rest of Italy, where the relatively despotic rules of the various city-states and fiefdoms that made up what we now know as Italy were at odds with the new ideas of centralization and modernization espoused by the **unification movement**, led by Giuseppe Mazzini. The revolutionary year of 1848, when popular revolts were sparked all over Europe, led to widespread unrest in Italy. In 1849, a pro-Unification caucus under **Mazzini** declared the city a republic and forced Pope Pius IX to leave Rome in disguise. However, Mazzini was chased out after a short four months by Emperor Napoleon III of France, who restored the papacy.

Garibaldi and reunification

There was further fighting all over Italy in 1859 and 1860 as forces for the **Risorgimento** or Unification of Italy gathered strength. Victor Emmanuel II, King of

1970s	1978	1992	1994
Civil disruption during the "Years of Lead"	Assassination of Aldo Moro	Mani Pulite corruption investigations	Silvio Berlusconi becomes prime minister of Italy for the first time

Piedmonte and his prime minister, Camillo Benso, Conte di Cavour, managed to bring the French on board against the Austrians who had control of the Lombardy–Venetia region. But, despite winning the second war of independence, they were betrayed by the French, who made a private settlement with the Austrians, whereby the Austrians would hold on to Venetia while giving up Lombardy. This came to nothing, but growing anger at this outrage galvanized the movement still further and forces under Giuseppe **Garibaldi**, who had defended Rome with Mazzini in 1849, waged an effective guerrilla campaign in Sicily and southern Italy, which ceded the territories to King Victor Emmanuel II. Eventually, Florence became the capital of the new kingdom in 1864.

Garibaldi made repeated attempts to capture Rome – occupied by Pope Pius IX and protected by the French – but he was arrested and sidelined by the new regime, embarrassed by his growing power and charisma. In 1870, French troops were withdrawn from Rome to fight the Franco-Prussian War, allowing Italian forces to storm the walls at Porta Pia and retake the city. Rome was declared the capital of the new Italy under Victor Emmanuel II (now the first King of Italy, though he maintained his Piedmontese regnal number). The King moved into the Palazzo del Quirinale, and the now powerless pontiff, **Pius IX** (1846–78), was confined within the Vatican until agreement was reached on a way to coexist. The initial **Law of Guarantees** drawn up by the new government defined the relationship between the state and the papacy, and acknowledged the pope as sovereign within the Vatican but no further; it was rejected by the pope, leaving the status of the Vatican in limbo for years to come. In the meantime, **Agostino Depretis** became the first prime minister of the new Italian state, and one of its greatest politicians, remaining in power until 1887, and seeing the new country through the difficult early years.

Modern times

As capital of a modern European country, Rome was ill-equipped, with its narrow streets and a river subject to flooding. The new kings set about building a city fit for government, cutting new streets through Rome's central core (Via Nazionale, Corso Vittorio Emanuele) and constructing grandiose buildings (the Vittoriano, Palace of Justice). The style was often more of the royal family's home town of Turin than of Rome.

In 1922, **Mussolini** became Prime Minister, and in 1929, signed the **Lateran Pact** with Pope **Pius XI** (1922–39), a compromise which finally forced the Vatican to accept the new Italian state and in return recognized the Vatican City as sovereign territory, together with the key basilicas and papal palaces in Rome, which remain independent of Italy to this day. The Church also received constitutional guarantees and a large sum of cash. Mussolini had typically bombastic visions for the city, and not only constructed new buildings and neighbourhoods such as Foro Italico, the University, EUR and Cinecittà, but also new thoroughfares and vistas within the historic centre itself. He created grand avenues, the better to march his troops along, including Via della Conciliazione, which connected St Peter's to the river. He also "liberated" the monuments of imperial Rome from the surrounding tangle of buildings – the Arch of Janus, the Temple of Vesta, the Theatre of Marcellus – bulldozing his way through ancient sites and medieval *borghi* which got in the way

1993–2001	2001–08	2011	2012
Francesco Rutelli is mayor of Rome	Walter Veltroni is mayor of Rome; he is replaced by Gianni Alemanno	Berlusconi stands down; Mario Monti becomes prime minister	Ignazio Marino becomes mayor of Rome

Rome was declared an "open city" during **World War II**, and as such emerged from the war relatively unscathed. However, after Mussolini's death, and the end of the conflict, the Italian king, Victor Emmanuel III, was forced to abdicate and Italy was declared a republic – still, however, with its capital in Rome. **After the war**, and the creation of a constitution which sought to render impossible a future dictatorship, Italy became known as a country that changes its government, if not its politicians, every few months. For the rest of Italy, Rome came to symbolize the inertia of their nation's government – at odds with both the slick, efficient north and the poor, corrupt south. Despite this, the city's growth was phenomenal in the postwar years, its population soaring to close to four million.

Rome was in the spotlight during the **1960s**, when it was the home of Fellini's Dolce Vita and Italy's bright young things. However, in the **1970s**, when the so-called **Anni Piombi**, or "years of lead", arrived, the city became a focus for the polarization and terrorism that was going on nationwide in Italian politics; there were troops on the streets and the country often seemed on the brink of civil disruption. The politically motivated murder of former prime minister **Aldo Moro** in 1978 (see box, p.55) sent shockwaves through society, and prompted calls for change. Since then, beginning with the **"Mani Pulite"**, or "clean hands", investigations of the **early 1990s**, the landscape of Italian politics has changed massively. Rome in particular saw a period of stable government under mayor **Francesco Rutelli**, and a clean-up of the city for the **Millennium**, when buildings and monuments that had been closed for decades were restored and reopened.

The twenty-first century

This process continued under the popular and urbane mayor, **Walter Veltroni**, who worked hard to improve cultural life and public services, launching Rome's first annual film festival, opening the Casa del Jazz and Casa del Cinema and building the new Auditorium Parco della Musica on the north side of the city centre, which opened to great fanfare in 2006. Veltroni's successor, however, **Gianni Alemanno**, a former neo-fascist and the city's first right-wing mayor for sixty years, reversed many of his predecessor's initiatives, criticizing Veltroni's focus on the arts and picking up on popular concerns about immigration and public services. He was replaced in 2012 by the centre-left **Ignazio Marino**, a former surgeon, who pledged to run Rome in a more inclusive way. His projects included opening the Via dei Fori Imperiali to pedestrian and bike traffic; reducing outdoor restaurant tables in Piazza Navona; and defying Italy's gay marriage ban by registering gay couples in the city who had got married abroad. Since Marino's replacement by the wildly inexperienced **Virginia Raggi** of the populist Five Star Movement, any developments in the city, both in culture and infrastructure, have all but ground to a halt.

The **abdication of Pope Benedict XVI**, successor to the popular Pope **John Paul II** (canonized, along with John XXIII, in April 2013), was unexpected. Benedict was the first pope to resign in over seven hundred years, and the subsequent election of the Argentinian Jorge Mario Bergoglio as the 266th pope in March 2013, took even insiders by surprise. They were further taken aback when he became the first pontiff to take the name of **Pope Francis.** In contrast to his predecessor, Benedict XVI, Francis has won plaudits for the friendly, informal approach he has adopted and his apparent

2013	2013	2014	2014
Monti stands down; Enrico Letta becomes prime minister	Benedict XVI becomes the first pope to abdicate in more than 700 years – he is succeeded by Francis I	Letta stands down; Matteo Renzi becomes prime minister	A huge corruption scandal, implicating top-level politicians and a mafia-like gang, rocks Rome

indifference to the material baubles of the Vatican. Whether he manages to sort out the web of vested interests and mini-empires that make up much of the Vatican's administration is another matter.

In 2014, Rome was rocked by a huge **corruption and embezzlement scandal** when it emerged that a network of high-profile politicians, allegedly headed by former mayor Gianni Alemanno, was in cahoots with a mafia-like criminal gang. It is thought that the public figures took kickbacks in exchange for awarding city contracts worth millions of euros to the gangsters – in construction, waste management and housing for immigrants, among other areas. Mayor Ignazio Marino, though not under investigation, was under pressure: as several members of his Democratic Party (PD) were implicated, there were calls to disband the city government, which were quashed by Prime Minister Matteo Renzi, also of the Democratic Party. Marino – who refused police protection for his habitual bike rides round Rome after receiving death threats – ordered an urgent review of city contracts and a rotation of top-level city administration jobs; the investigations into the so-called **"Mafia Capital"** continue.

In the meantime, Rome's faith in its leaders and public figures has been seriously shaken, and the corruption scandal and other pressing difficulties – an ongoing recession, rising youth unemployment and a crumbling infrastructure that there isn't the money to repair – have pushed the city to crisis point.

2016	**2016**	**2018**
Virginia Raggi elected as the first woman mayor of Rome, representing the populist Five Star Movement	Matteo Renzi resigns as Prime Minister, succeeded by former Foreign Minister Paolo Gentiloni	Metro C's long-awaited city-centre station is due to open at San Giovanni

Architecture

Rome is an open-air museum, with its architecture as the main exhibit. The city's growth spurts are plain to see, the Renaissance jostling the Imperial, with a glimpse of medieval peeking through here and there. Historical periods are built one on top of the other (great examples are the Theatre of Marcellus, p.56, and San Clemente, p.132). It's this sense of the city as a living organism, the notion that each period has made use of what has gone before and then left its own mark, that makes Rome so endlessly fascinating. This process does rather grind to a halt, however, in the early twentieth century. The last big building boom followed the declaration of Rome as the capital of the unified Italy in 1870, and eventually delivered the Victor Emmanuel monument, a pinnacle of bombast. The Fascist era produced Mussolini's EUR experiment and some building in the centre of town (such as Piazza Augusto Imperatore), though more often the dictatorship saw demolition rather than construction, the creation of Via dei Fori Imperiali being the most obvious example. The rebuilding of Termini Station was completed in 1950, after which there is very little more recent architecture in central Rome, with the notable exceptions of Richard Meier's Ara Pacis building and Zaha Hadid's MAXXI.

The classical era

As well as assimilating architectural forms from the Greek world, the ancient Romans were also innovative architects, exploiting local materials and the requirements of a city on an unprecedented scale to create new forms. Their legacy is everywhere you look: they invented concrete, brickwork, domes, arches and aqueducts.

Most of ancient Rome lies in ruins, but the **Forum** and **Palatine Hill** still manage to conjure up a sense of its grandeur, as do the **Baths of Caracalla** just to the south. Among more intact structures, the dome of the **Pantheon** is still the second largest in the city; the design of the **Colosseum** is as impressive today as it ever was; and the ruins of **Ostia Antica** give us a glimpse of ancient urban life. But perhaps the most enduring structure of ancient Rome is the imposing **Aurelian Wall**, built by the eponymous emperor in the late third century AD to keep the barbarians at bay.

TOP TEN FOUNTAINS

Rome has fifty monumental fountains and hundreds of small *fontanelle* – with over two thousand fountains in all, more than any other city in the world. A perfect blend of form and function, the fountains both decorate the city's many piazzas and traditionally provided water to the city's inhabitants.

Fontana dell'Acqua Paola p.166
Fontana delle Api p.104
Fontana del Babuino p.96
Fontana della Barcaccia p.94
Fontana del Mascherone p.52

Fontana delle Naiadi p.122
Fontana dei Quattro Fiumi p.43
Fontana delle Tartarughe p.57
Quattro Fontane p.108
Trevi Fountain p.101

The Middle Ages

In the centuries that followed the collapse of imperial power, the city was peopled by the four horsemen of the apocalypse: plague, pestilence, famine and war. Rome became a vastly underpopulated backwater. However, from the ashes of the city of the Emperors would gradually emerge the city of the Popes. Even when the population reached an all-time low of just two thousand, Rome still punched above its weight architecturally: as it was the seat of Christendom, the building of churches never ground to a halt. From the early sixth century, the evangelizing activities of Pope Gregory the Great began to attract pilgrims in their droves.

The earliest of the city's official churches, which had been built during the reign of Emperor Constantine, adopted the Roman basilica as their model and were often erected on the site of saints' martyrdoms (for example the first basilica of St Peter's in the Vatican). From Pope Gregory's reign onwards many more churches were built, often incorporating ancient buildings and reusing columns recycled from the imperial city. These early churches are among the most beautiful in the city. Examples are **Santa Sabina** on the Aventine Hill, **San Clemente** in the Celio district, **Santa Croce in Gerusalemme** and venerable Santa Maria Maggiore on the Esquiline, although this last is encased within a cocoon of later buildings. Gregory I also, accidentally, preserved Hadrian's tomb as the **Castel Sant'Angelo**: it provided a convenient, ready-made citadel to withstand invaders – something that was much needed in the centuries that followed. The majority of ancient buildings which survive today became either churches or fortresses, the medieval buildings of choice.

The Renaissance and the Baroque

During the Renaissance, military and economic success across Italy funded a boom in the arts and, as the seat of the Pope, Rome drew the best artists and architects from across the peninsula. They remodelled Rome; no more a crumbling besieged backwater, it was to be transformed into a worldly capital. Michelangelo was active in the city throughout his long and prolific career. Most famous for his work at the **Sistine Chapel**, he also laid out the **Piazza del Campidoglio**, finished the **Palazzo Farnese**, and at the age of 71 was appointed architect of **St Peter's**, a project he worked on until his death at 88. Michelangelo left the greatest mark on the structure of St Peter's, though its construction and decoration would continue well into the **Baroque period** – an era of flamboyance in art and architecture that grew out of the Catholic Church's bid to reassert itself following the Reformation. The Baroque has massively altered the city: the curvy and playful buildings, fountains and sculptures of the style's main protagonists, Bernini and Borromini, are everywhere. The interior of St Peter's and its grand piazza, both largely the work of Bernini, are prime examples of the vehemently and deliberately un-Protestant style. There are also many other examples of the Baroque period in the city: the enormous **Palazzo Barberini**, built by Bernini's main patron, Pope Urban VIII; Borromini's small and clever **San Carlo alle Quattro Fontane**; the grand ceiling and dome of **Sant'Ignazio** and its theatrical square; and of course the studied histrionics of Piazza Navona itself, to name just a few.

The nineteenth century

Rome became capital of Italy in 1870, and the Torinese Italian royals were determined to turn the city into a worthy showpiece. Great embankments were built to prevent the Tiber from flooding, thus divorcing the city from the river (its ancient *raison d'être*) for the first time in its history. Corso Vittorio Emanuele II was driven through Renaissance palaces, Via Nazionale and Via Cavour cut through the buildings and fields of the Esquiline. The city expanded outwards into the new suburbs of Prati, Nomentana and Salaria, with their stately apartment blocks and rigid grid plans. Often turgid

Neoclassical palaces were built to house the newly formed departments of state, although the Savoy's most memorable legacy to Rome's skyline is without doubt the bombastic, and still controversial, **Vittoriano** in Piazza Venezia.

The twentieth and twenty-first centuries

The twenty years of Fascism (1922–1943) saw massive building projects right across Italy. Mussolini's preferred architect was **Marcello Piacentini**, responsible for some of the most emblematic of the Fascist era's architecture in Rome – the Stadio dei Marmi, the housing complex of Garbatella and the southern suburb of **EUR**, planned as a futuristic city extension in the 1930s. Apparently untainted by his association with the regime, Piacentini would later work on EUR's Palazzo dello Sport with **Pier Luigi Nervi** in preparation for the 1960 Olympic Games.

The early twenty-first century has seen a spate of successful and prestigious architectural projects overseen by internationally renowned architects. **Auditorium Parco della Musica** on the northern edge of the city centre, by **Renzo Piano**, opened in 2002; **Richard Meier** built a new structure to house the ancient **Ara Pacis**, inaugurated in 2006; the late **Zaha Hadid's** celebrated **MAXXI** arts complex was inaugurated in 2010; and, after an agonisingly slow project besieged by problems, **Massimiliano Fuksas'** Conference Centre was finally opened in 2016.

Books

There have been an enormous number of books published about Rome over the years, and the list below is inevitably extremely selective, concentrating on entertaining travelogues, key texts on history and art, and on works of fiction that might be instructive – or fun – to read while you're in the city. Books marked with the ★ symbol are particularly recommended.

ANCIENT HISTORY

Juvenal *The Sixteen Satires*. Savage attacks on the follies and excesses of Rome at the end of the first century and start of the second.

Livy *The Early History of Rome*. Lively chronicle of the city's evolution from the days of Romulus and Remus.

Marcus Aurelius *Meditations*. The classic text of Stoic thought, written by one of the few Roman emperors it's easy to admire.

Petronius *Satyricon*. A fragmentary, spicy narrative written by one of Nero's inner circle; Fellini's film of the same name gives a pretty accurate idea of the tone.

Suetonius *The Twelve Caesars*. The inside story of Caligula, Nero, Domitian and others, elegantly written and very enjoyable, by the private secretary to Hadrian, who made the most of his unique access to the annals of recent imperial history.

Tacitus *Annals of Imperial Rome*. Covers much of the terrain dealt with by Suetonius, but from the stance of the diligent historian and serious moralist.

Virgil *The Aeneid*. The central work of Latin literature, this epic book depicts the adventures of Aeneas after the fall of Troy, and in doing so it celebrates Rome's heroic lineage.

HISTORY

Mary Beard *SPQR*. An enjoyable, well-written gallop through Rome's history, from Romulus to Caracalla.

Jonathan Boardman *Cities of the Imagination: Rome*. Like other books in the series, this is both a history of Rome and a celebration of the city and how it has featured in literature through the years.

Jerome Carcopino *Daily Life in Ancient Rome*. Originally published in 1941, and consistently in print since, Carcopino's book is a classic, bringing to life the beliefs, social life and customs of ordinary Romans at the height of the empire.

Christopher Duggan *A Concise History of Italy*. The best all-round history of the Italian nation that you can buy – this is concise and well written, covering everything from the fall of the Roman Empire to Unification and beyond.

ANCIENT ROME IN FICTION

Robert Graves *I Claudius; Claudius the God*. Having translated Suetonius's *Twelve Caesars*, Graves used the madness and corruption of the Imperial Age to create a gripping, if not necessarily historically accurate, tale. The classic book on the imperial Caesars.

Robert Harris *Imperium; Lustrum*. No one brings to life the Roman Republic quite as vividly as Harris, viewing the power struggles and intrigues of the main protagonists through the eyes of Cicero's faithful secretary, the freed slave Tiro. There are several novels to choose from, but this is perhaps the best dramatization of the period you can read.

Conn Iggulden *The Gates of Rome; The Death of Kings; The Field of Swords; The Gods of War*. Iggulden's engaging four-book series, *Emperor*, is a historical romp documenting the rise and fall of Julius Caesar, from the rites of passage of the young man during the turmoil of the last decades of the Republic to his eventual murder in Pompey's theatre.

Allan Massie *Augustus; Tiberius; Caesar; Caligula*. Massie's series of novels aspires to recreate the Roman Empire at its height through the imagined memoirs of its key figures, and does so with great success, in a series of novels that offers a well-researched but palatable way into the minutiae of the era.

Steven Saylor *Roma; Empire*. Saylor is better known for his Giordanius detective yarns set in the days of the Roman Republic, but this epic novelization of the city's history up to the growth of the empire – two volumes so far – is perhaps more appealing to the general reader.

Thornton Wilder *The Ides of March*. A suppositional reconstruction of the last year of the life of Julius Caesar through his letters, writings and reports.

Edward Gibbon *The History of the Decline and Fall of the Roman Empire*. This classic text was conceived amid the ruins of the Roman Forum in the latter part of the eighteenth century and covers the period from the second century AD to the fall of Constantinople in 1453.

Christopher Hibbert *Rome: The Biography of a City*. Simply put, the most entertaining and accessible introduction to the city that you can buy – no less than you would expect from this most prolific of popular historians.

Tom Holland *Rubicon*. This readable book pinpoints a specific but crucial period of Roman history, beginning with the Roman Republic at the height of its greatness and charting its decline up to the death of Augustus in AD 14. Good narrative history, documenting a fascinating era.

Robert Knapp *Invisible Romans*. Knapp's book concentrates on the "Romans that history forgot" – the prostitutes, slaves, freedmen, criminals and other members of the Roman underclass who made the empire, and city, tick. It's not just about Roman lowlife, however, and is especially compelling on the everyday existences of ordinary Roman men and women.

★ **Anthony Majanlahti** *The Families Who Made Rome*. Part history and part on-the-ground itinerary, this book brings the buildings to life with "strange but true" histories of families such as the Borghese, Chigi and Farnese, whose stamp is all over Rome.

Philip Matyszak *Ancient Rome on Five Denarii a Day*. A mock guide to the city for the imperial-era visitor, with lots of entertaining advice along the lines of "there's no need to pack a toga", but it in fact provides a very detailed – and digestible – insight into the life, monuments and customs of the time.

Leonard Sciascia *The Moro Affair*. Sciascia is one of Italy's – and in particular Sicily's – greatest postwar writers, and this is one of his least-known works, a nonfiction account of the events that led up to the murder of the Italian prime minister in 1978 (see box, p.55). Grippingly written, with good background on the political landscape of the time, including many of Moro's own letters.

Paul Vallely *Pope Francis: Untying the Knots*. All is not quite what it seems with the new, more inclusive and socially liberal Pope Francis I, argues Paul Vallely, who has spent time researching the pope's past in Argentina. He discovers that it's true that the new pope took the part of the Argentine poor, albeit from a socially conservative position, but this same man was also badly compromised in his dealings with the military junta that ran the country for so many years. Well-written and well-researched, this is the best book to read for background on the new pope.

ART AND ARCHITECTURE

Amanda Claridge *Oxford Archaeological Guides: Rome*. This is an excellently written, concise guide to the archeology of the ancient city – a good investment if this is your particular area of interest.

★ **Andrew Graham-Dixon** *Caravaggio: A Life Sacred and Profane*. A page-turner in the best sense, charting the painter's dangerous life at the heart of the Rome art scene in racy yet informed prose that brilliantly analyses his most famous paintings but also grippingly conjures up the man and the period. So much more than a book about painting.

Andrew Graham-Dixon *Michelangelo and the Sistine Chapel*. This is the story of the most brilliant creation of the Renaissance, beautifully retold as a warts-and-all tale of gritty endeavour, political wilfulness and pure genius.

Keith Hopkins and Mary Beard *The Colosseum*. An extremely readable history of the famous monument, full of architectural, literary and often very funny anecdotes. Not only does it give you the background to its construction, demise and resurrection but also advice on site visits.

Robert Hughes *Rome*. The Australian art historian's stab at writing a definitive, chronological guide to the city's art and architecture, and not a bad effort – a big book, but an engagingly written one, with lots of cultural and historical background, anecdote and opinion.

Keith Miller *St Peter's*. Part of Profile's excellent series focusing on great monuments, this is the last word on St Peter's, covering both its long development and construction and its far-reaching influence.

Giorgio Vasari *The Lives of the Artists*. There is no better background work on the artists of the Renaissance, written by a contemporary and correspondent of his subjects, who include Raphael, Michelangelo and others less relevant to Rome. Available in a very readable English translation.

Margaret Visser *The Geometry of Love*. Basically an extended tour of the church of Sant'Agnese fuori le Mura, and an absorbing study not just of the building and its history but also of the iconography and architecture of all Christian churches.

David Watkin *The Roman Forum*. Another in Profile's "Wonders of the World" series, Watkin's book brings to life the stones and rubble of the Forum better than anyone else has yet managed.

TRAVEL, IMPRESSIONS AND FOOD

Elizabeth Bowen *A Time in Rome*. Though written in the 1950s, Bowen's book endures because it is so engaging, and because it summarizes so well the longevity and continuity of Rome.

Anthony Doerr *Four Seasons in Rome*. The American novelist Anthony Doerr's memoir captures the modern city with clarity and imagination, describing both domestic issues such as bringing up two tiny babies in a foreign city and earth-shattering events such as the funeral of Pope John Paul II with the same degree of wit and perspicacity.

One of the more relevant and evocative recent travelogues you could read.

David Downie & Alison Harris *Food Wine Rome*. Part of the "Terroir Guides" series, this beautiful book tells you everything you need to know about the food and wine of Rome and its region, with some fascinating background on local produce and ingredients, beautiful photos and great recommendations for authentic local restaurants and shops.

Tobias Jones *The Dark Heart of Italy*. Not specifically about Rome, indeed it barely touches on the city at all, but Jones's book is a refreshingly contemporary take on Italy, and as such is a good book to take with you on any trip to the capital – assuming, that is, you want to read about the sleaze, corruption and dysfunctionality that make up the contemporary nation.

Carlo Levi *Fleeting Rome*. Posthumously published in 2002, this collection of 33 essays, written over a decade spent in Rome in the Sixties and Seventies by the great twentieth-century writer and politician, skilfully and evocatively encapsulate a city that no longer exists.

Diane Seed *Love Food Love Rome*. A comprehensive illustrated guide to the best of the city's cuisine, with listings of shops, restaurants, wine bars and markets – and recipes for all the Roman classics – by a long-time Roman expat and foodie.

H.V. Morton *A Traveller in Rome*. Like all Morton's books, this is a marvellously personal stroll around the sights, reflecting on history, architecture and culture.

William Murray *Italy: The Fatal Gift*. Out of print, but worth trying to get hold of for its perceptive essays on history and modern Italian life and culture, especially with regard to Rome, where Murray lived for many years, filing regular pieces for the *New Yorker*. Try also the in-print *City of the Soul*, Murray's slim volume of essays, walks and musings on the city.

David Winner *Al Dente: Madness, Beauty and the Food of Rome*. Winner is clearly fascinated by every aspect of Rome past and present, and hops from one subject to another like any passionate devotee. Much more than a book about food, this is great to read on any trip to Rome, full of the sort of profound and trivial detail that enhances any visit.

FICTION

Niccolò Ammaniti *Let the Games Begin*. Ammaniti is one of Italy's most popular and successful literary novelists writing today. His latest book, set in a dysfunctional vision of Rome, is both a dystopian fantasy and a critique of a corrupt society that has become obsessed by money, celebrity and public image.

Carlo Emilio Gadda *That Awful Mess on Via Merulana*. Superficially a detective story, this celebrated modernist novel is so dense a weave of physical reality and literary diversions that the reader is led away from a solution rather

---

ROMAN CRIME

Lindsey Davis *Venus in Copper; The Jupiter Myth;* and others. These crime novels set in the age of the Emperor Vespasian follow super-sleuth Marcus Didius Falco as he unpicks mysteries and dastardly doings.

Michael Dibdin *Cabal; Ratking;* and others. Not all of the late Michael Dibdin's novels are set in Rome, but the author was as interested in Italy as in his characters, with the result that his Aurelio Zen novels tell us plenty about the way Italian society operates – and they're well-plotted whodunits to boot, with Zen as the classically eccentric loner detective.

Conor Fitzgerald *The Dogs of Rome; The Fatal Touch;* and others. Fitzgerald's complex thrillers, set in the capital, are crammed full of intrigue and local colour, and keep you reading until the last page.

David Hewson *A Season for the Dead; The Villa of Mysteries; The Sacred Cut;* and others. Hewson's popular series of thrillers, starring detective Nic Costa, are mostly set in Rome, and are good yarns, well told, and full of local Roman colour and locations.

Tobias Jones *The Salati Case*. The latest lover of Italy to set tales of murder and intrigue in the country, Jones – author of *The Dark Heart of Italy*; see above – understands the country better than most, and as such is eminently suited to assume the mantle of the late Michael Dibdin. His detective, Castagnetti, is a classic gumshoe – he doesn't do things by the book and has a chaotic personal life. This book, and the subsequent Castagnetti novels, *White Death* and *Death of a Showgirl*, and the true-crime *Blood on the Altar*, are not all set in Rome but are great accompaniments to any trip to the city.

Iain Pears *The Raphael Affair; The Bernini Bust; The Titian Committee; Death and Restoration;* and others. Pears' successful series of thrillers with an art-historical theme are all set in Rome and make great holiday reading. There are plenty of local settings and descriptions, not to mention fast-paced art-world intrigue, with robbery, forgery and general skulduggery.

than towards it; it enjoys the sort of status in Italian fiction that *Ulysses* has in English.

Nathaniel Hawthorne *The Marble Faun*. A nineteenth-century take on the lives of Anglo-American expats in the Eternal City: sculptors, passionate lovers – the usual mad mix and excessive goings-on that you'll still find today.

Margaret Mazzantini *Don't Move*. Intense psychological novel of midlife crisis, sex and obsession in Rome that was a massive bestseller in Italy and made into a movie directed by the author's husband. The city and its outskirts form a bleak, rain-soaked backdrop.

Elsa Morante *History*. Capturing daily Roman life during the last war, this is probably the most vivid fictional picture of the conflict as seen from the city.

★**Alberto Moravia** *The Conformist*. A psychological novel about a man sucked into the abyss of Fascism by his desperation to conform. In *The Woman of Rome*, Moravia uses the Rome of the Mussolini era as a delicate backdrop for this detached yet compassionate tale of a Roman model and prostitute. Also worth a read is *Roman Tales*, a collection of short stories that has the lives of ordinary Romans as its thread.

★**Glyn Pursglove** (ed) *Rome* ("Poetry of Place" series). A wonderful little book, made up of a well-chosen selection of poems and extracts relating to all aspects and all eras of the city.

★**Tom Rachman** *The Imperfectionists*. A collection of interwoven stories about the various people who work on a long-running but declining English-language newspaper in Rome. Very much a novel of the city, with an, at times, forensic scrutiny of the often sad, random and occasionally hilarious lives of a well-realized and credible set of characters. Literate and intelligent, but also very readable.

Matt Rees *A Name in Blood*. Crime writer Rees gets to grips with the story of Caravaggio's time in Rome and his flight to Malta following the murder of a rival, with bold storytelling and well-crafted, page-turning prose that brings the era to life in what is a high-quality historical thriller.

Irving Stone *The Agony and the Ecstasy*. Stone's dramatized life of Michelangelo, popular "faction" that is entertaining even if it doesn't exactly get to the root of the artist's work and times.

William Weaver (ed) *Open City: Seven Writers in Postwar Rome*. An anthology of pieces by some of the best modern Italian novelists – Bassani, Silone, Moravia, Ginzburg, among others – selected and with an introduction by one of the most eminent postwar Italian translators.

Marguerite Yourcenar *Memoirs of Hadrian*. Yourcenar's reflective narrative details the main events of the Emperor Hadrian's rule, most of it in the form of letters to his nephew, Marcus Aurelius, documenting at once the Roman Empire at its height and the very human anxieties of perhaps its wisest and most accomplished leader. See also Yourcenar's conceptual Roman novel, now out of print, *A Coin in Nine Hands*.

Films

Rome has been a focus for moviemakers over the years, whether it's trying to recreate the drama of ancient times, portray the modern city's dark side or just revelling in its ready-made grand settings. We've included a rundown of our favourite Roman movies to watch before a trip to the city. Films marked with the ★ symbol are particularly recommended.

1940s AND 1950s

★ **Bicycle Thieves** (1948). A young boy is the witness to his father's humiliation in De Sica's classic movie, set in the poorer quarters of Rome, when he sees him steal a bicycle out of desperation (to get his job back) and immediately get caught. The child's illusions are dashed, and society is held to account, although the masses are also hostile and the only hope seems to lie in the family unit, which the hero falls thankfully back on at the end.

Quo Vadis (1951). Imperial Rome gets the full Hollywood treatment in this epic movie, featuring Robert Taylor and Deborah Kerr in an all-star cast that includes Peter Ustinov as Nero and Sophia Loren as an uncredited extra. The focus in on the decadence and corruption of the empire under Nero, and – in true Hollywood style – the emergence of Christianity as the only viable alternative. Grand and compelling, but not really a history lesson.

Roman Holiday (1953). Gregory Peck and Audrey Hepburn (in her first major role) are at their sparkling best in this popular and successful romantic comedy, which uses the city, in particular Piazza di Spagna and around, as a backdrop, with flair and invention. Indeed, it gave the city an enormous boost in tourism after its 1953 release. Prize for the least obvious location is the scene in the "embassy", which is actually Palazzo Barberini.

★ **Rome Open City** (1945). As the tanks were rolling out of Rome in 1945, Roberto Rossellini cobbled together the bare minimum of finances, crew and equipment and started shooting this movie, using real locations, documentary footage and low-grade film, and coming up with a grainy, idiosyncratic style that influenced not only his Italian contemporaries, but also the American film noir of the late 1940s.

Three Coins in the Fountain (1954). Having chucked their coins into the Trevi Fountain, three American girls search for romance in Rome, and of course succeed big-time, with a variety of handsome suitors.

1960s AND 1970s

Accattone (1961). Pasolini's eponymous petty thief and pimp is perhaps one of cinema's least likeable creations, but the movie, relentlessly bleak in black-and-white, is most memorable for its no-holds-barred depiction of the hopelessness and amorality of life in Rome's poorest neighbourhoods in the 1960s.

The Conformist (1970). Bertolucci's bold and disturbing film of Moravia's novel follows the career of Fascist functionary and assassin Marcello up to the fall of Mussolini. It features some of Rome's more cinematic corners – among them Ponte Sant'Angelo and the Colosseum – among its locations.

The Eclipse (1962). Antonioni used the impersonal environs of EUR as the background to this slow-moving tale of doomed love. Short on plot, but with a memorable visual subtlety.

★ **La Dolce Vita** (1960). Marcello Mastroianni is the now-iconic paparazzo in Fellini's stylish 1960s movie about celebrity, style – and ultimately emptiness. Lots of scenes shot on the Via Veneto, in the days when it was considered the city's most fashionable street.

★ **Mamma Roma** (1962). Sort of *Rome Open City* part two – or at least two decades later – with Anna Magnani playing a Roman prostitute who tries to give up life on the street but is forced into petty crime and ends up in prison. One of Pasolini's earliest movies, and one of his most accessible, although it's no barrel of laughs by any means, deliberately showing a stark contrast between Rome the eternal city and the lives of the lowest strata of its underclass.

Massacre in Rome (1973). Based on the book by Robert Katz, this gritty black-and-white drama depicts the true story of an attack on a German SS brigade in Via Rasella and the merciless Nazi backlash that follows, resulting in the Via Ardeatine massacre. Tightly directed, it has a great cast too, starring an excellent Richard Burton as the Gestapo chief who orders the reprisal and Marcello Mastroianni as a conscience-wrangling priest.

Roma (1972). Fellini's collection of disconnected Roman scenes is completely compelling, switching between wartime and the present day, and including some unforgettable sequences, from a hyper-realistic brothel scene to a grotesque clerical fashion parade.

Yesterday, Today and Tomorrow (1963). This Vittorio

di Sica comedy tells the stories of three Italian women: a cigarette-seller in Naples, a prostitute in Rome and the wife of an industrialist in Milan. Marcello Mastrioanni is superb, as is Sophia Loren.

1980s AND 1990s

Belly of an Architect (1987). One of the best movies set in Rome made in (relatively) recent times, Peter Greenaway's film follows the (mis)fortunes of Brian Dennehey's middle-aged architect who arrives in the city to supervise an exhibition of the work of a French rival. A film about creativity, sickness, curvaceous forms (including bellies), but most of all about Rome.

★**Dear Diary** (1993). Director, actor and screenwriter Nanni Moretti is seen by some as Rome's Woody Allen, chronicling the lives and neuroses of the city's inhabitants with a series of gentle, well-acted and sophisticated human comedies. Moretti achieved great acclaim with this film in three parts. A gently idiosyncratic and comic work, it covers a range of the director's personal obsessions – apartment blocks, children, telephones, Pasolini's unsolved murder, as well as his own fight against cancer. Very entertaining.

The Talented Mr Ripley (1999). Matt Damon plays the cool and charismatic Ripley in this slick thriller, which is mostly set in the Naples area but has a few choice scenes set in Rome, including Piazza Mattei and the Ghetto (where Ripley bases himself while in the city), Piazza Navona and *Caffè Latino* in Testaccio.

THE 21ST CENTURY

Angels and Demons (2009). Ok, it's not the greatest Rome-based film ever made, but it's better than the other Dan Brown Vatican thriller (*The Da Vinci Code*), and does include a lot of Rome colour and locations; indeed it could have been subsidized by the tourist board, with Tom Hanks and sidekick Ayelet Zurer dashing dramatically from one classic location to another.

Caesar Must Die (2013). Filmed entirely on location in Rome's Rebibbia prison, this is the Taviani brothers' (*Padre Padrone* is their most famous film) first film for six years, a version of Shakespeare's *Julius Caesar* performed by the hardest-of-the-hard prison inmates. Harshly realistic, and shot in grainy black and white for enhanced realism.

Eat Pray Love (2010). Naturally the "Eat" part of this film takes place in Italy, specifically Rome, where Julia Roberts "finds herself" by discovering the true meaning of food, buying meat from a real butcher's shop just south of Campo de' Fiori.

Good Morning Night (2003). This powerful film tells the story of the kidnapping and eventual murder of the Italian prime minister Aldo Moro, from the point of view of one of the participants, who becomes increasingly uncomfortable with events as they unfold.

★**The Great Beauty** (2013). Paolo Sorrentino's latest film has achieved the rare distinction of being feted by arthouse movie critics and notching up commercial success at the same time. It's a Fellini-ish look at the lives of the city's beautiful people – visually ravishing, with gorgeous scenes of Rome, and extremely gripping in its way.

Mid-August Lunch (2008). The directorial debut of Gianni di Gregorio is a gentle comedy about a hapless middle-aged man who cares for his mother in a rundown but respectable Trastevere flat. For once, a movie that celebrates being old.

My Mother (2015). An on-form Nanni Moretti directs this witty tale (with plenty of autobiographical touches) of a director in meltdown, having to manage both a family crisis – her mother's illness – and on-set demands.

A Perfect Day (2008). Daily life for a number of characters in Rome, but a series of events leads to a tragedy. A fast-moving story of the contemporary city, well told and well acted.

Quiet Chaos (2008). Nanni Moretti is pitch-perfect in this tale of a successful Roman executive dealing with the sudden death of his wife. There are only glimpses of any bits of Rome you might recognize, and for the most part its focus is on the well-heeled suburbs of the city and the nearby beaches. But it's brilliantly acted, with the odd flash of humour, and rather gripping, despite the fact that nothing much happens.

To Rome with Love (2012). Woody Allen's homage to the city is laden with romantic clichés and feels a bit thrown together, but as a visual portrait of the city, it's very watchable indeed. Recognizable spots include Cinema Farnese, *Sabatino* in Trastevere, the *Caffè della Pace*, and the *Vecchia Pineta* restaurant, overlooking the sea in Lido di Ostia.

Sacro GRA (2013). This survey of the lives of the people who inhabit the areas around Rome's ring-road, the Grande Raccordo Annulare, was the first documentary to win the Golden Lion award at the Venice film festival, and you can see why – its portraits of the various characters are penetrating, insightful and entertaining. A compelling view of contemporary life in Italy, in the capital's nether regions.

We Have a Pope (2011). Nanni Moretti's film follows a man elected against his will as the new pope, and how he deals with the panic that ensues. Sadly, filming isn't allowed inside the Vatican, so Villa Medici and Palazzo Farnese substituted for the real Vatican interiors.

Language

The ability to speak English confers prestige in Italy, and there's often no shortage of people willing to show off their knowledge, especially in Rome. But using at least some Italian, however tentatively, can mark you out from the masses in a city used to hordes of tourists, and having a little more can open up the city no end. The words and phrases below should help you master the basics. If you want a decent phrasebook, look no further than the Rough Guide Phrasebook: Italian, which packs a huge amount of phrases and vocabulary into a handy dictionary format. There are lots of good pocket dictionaries – the Collins range represents probably the best all-round choice, with their Gem or Pocket formats perfect for travelling purposes.

When speaking to strangers, the third person is the polite form (ie: *lei* instead of *tu* for "you"). It's also worth remembering that Italians don't use "please" and "thank you" half as much as we do: it's all implied in the tone, but if in doubt, err on the polite side.

PRONUNCIATION

Italian is one of the easiest European languages of which to learn the basics, especially if you already have a smattering of French or Spanish. Easiest of all is the pronunciation, since every word is spoken exactly as it's written, and usually enunciated with exaggerated, open-mouthed clarity. Generally, Italian words are stressed on the penultimate syllable unless an accent (´ or `) denotes otherwise. The only difficulties you're likely to encounter are the few consonants that are different from English:

c before e or i is pronounced as in church, while ch before the same vowels is hard, as in cat.

sci or sce are pronounced as in sheet and shelter respectively. The same goes with g – soft before e or i, as in geranium; hard before a, o, u and h, as in garlic.

gn has the ni sound of onion.

gl in Italian is softened to something like li in English, as in stallion.

h is not aspirated, as in honour.

WORDS AND PHRASES

BASICS

Good morning	Buongiorno	Do you speak English?	Parla inglese?
Good afternoon/evening	Buonasera	I don't understand	Non ho capito
Good night	Buonanotte	I don't know	Non lo so
Hello/goodbye	Ciao (informal; to	Excuse me	Mi scusi
	strangers use phrases	Excuse me (in a crowd)	Permesso
	above)	I'm sorry	Mi dispiace
Goodbye	Arrivederci	I'm here on holiday	Sono qui in vacanza
Yes	Sì	I'm English	Sono inglese
No	No	Scottish	scozzese
Please	Per favore	Welsh	gallese
Thank you (very much)	Grazie (mille)	Irish	irlandese
You're welcome	Prego	American (masculine/	americano/a
All right/that's OK	Va bene	feminine)	
How are you? (informal/	Come stai/sta?	Australian (masculine/	australiano/a
formal)		feminine)	
		a New Zealander	neozelandese
I'm fine	Bene	Today	Oggi

Tomorrow	Domani
Day after tomorrow	Dopodomani
Yesterday	Ieri
Now	Adesso
Later	Più tardi
Wait a minute!	Aspetta!
Let's go!	Andiamo!
In the morning	Di mattina
In the afternoon	Nel pomeriggio
In the evening	Di sera
Here/There	Qui/Là
Good/Bad	Buono/Cattivo
Big/Small	Grande/Piccolo
Cheap/Expensive	Economico/Caro
Early/Late	Presto/Tardi
Hot/Cold	Caldo/Freddo
Near/Far	Vicino/Lontano
Quickly/Slowly	Velocemente/ Lentamente
With/Without	Con/Senza
More/Less	Più/Meno
Enough, no more	Basta

SIGNS

Entrance/Exit	Entrata/Uscita
Free entrance	Ingresso libero
Gentlemen/Ladies	Signori/Signore
No smoking	Vietato fumare
WC/Bathroom	Gabinetto/Bagno
Open/Closed	Aperto/Chiuso
Closed for restoration	Chiuso per restauro
Closed for holidays	Chiuso per ferie
Pull/Push	Tirare/Spingere
Cash desk	Cassa
Go, walk	Avanti
Stop, halt	Alt

ACCOMMODATION

Hotel	Albergo
Is there a hotel nearby?	C'è un albergo qui vicino?
Do you have a room…	Ha una camera…
for one/two/three person/people	per una/due/tre persona/e
for one/two/three night/s	per una/due/tre notte/i
for one/two week/s	per una/due settimana/e
with a double bed	con un letto matrimoniale
with a shower/bath	con una doccia/un bagno
with a balcony	con balcone
Hot/cold water	Acqua calda/fredda
How much is it?	Quanto costa?
It's expensive	È caro

Is breakfast included?	È compresa la prima colazione?
Do you have anything cheaper?	Ha qualcosa che costa di meno?
Full/half board	Pensione completa/ mezza pensione
Can I see the room?	Posso vedere la camera?
I'll take it	La prendo
I'd like to book a room	Vorrei prenotare una camera
I have a booking	Ho una prenotazione

QUESTIONS AND DIRECTIONS

Where? (Where is/ where are…?)	Dove? (Dov'è/Dove sono…?)
When?	Quando?
What? (What is it?)	Cosa? (Cos'è?)
How much/many?	Quanto/Quanti?
Why?	Perché?
It is/there is	C'e…? (Is it/is there…?)
What time is it?	Che ore sono?
How do I get to…?	Per arrivare a…?
How far is it to…?	Quant'è lontano…?
Can you tell me when to get off?	Mi può dire dove scendere?
What time does it open/close?	A che ora apre/chiude?
How much does it/ do they cost?	Quanto costa/costano?
What's it called in Italian?	Come si chiama in italiano?

DAYS OF THE WEEK

Monday	lunedì
Tuesday	martedì
Wednesday	mercoledì
Thursday	giovedì
Friday	venerdì
Saturday	sabato
Sunday	domenica

MONTHS OF THE YEAR

January	gennaio
February	febbraio
March	marzo
April	aprile
May	maggio
June	giugno
July	luglio
August	agosto
September	settembre
October	ottobre
November	novembre
December	dicembre

NUMBERS

1	uno	20	venti
2	due	21	ventuno
3	tre	22	ventidue
4	quattro	30	trenta
5	cinque	40	quaranta
6	sei	50	cinquanta
7	sette	60	sessanta
8	otto	70	settanta
9	nove	80	ottanta
10	dieci	90	novanta
11	undici	100	cento
12	dodici	101	centuno
13	tredici	110	centodieci
14	quattordici	200	duecento
15	quindici	500	cinquecento
16	sedici	1000	mille
17	diciassette	5000	cinquemila
18	diciotto	10,000	diecimila
19	diciannove	50,000	cinquantamila

MENU READER

BASICS AND SNACKS

Aceto	Vinegar
Aglio	Garlic
Arancini	Stuffed rice-balls
Biscotti	Biscuits
Burro	Butter
Caramelle	Sweets
Cioccolato	Chocolate
Formaggio	Cheese
Frittata	Omelette
Marmellata	Jam
Olio	Oil
Olive	Olives
Pane	Bread
Pepe	Pepper
Pizza al taglio	Pizza by the slice
Riso	Rice
Sale	Salt
Supplì	Breaded ball of risotto rice mixed with tomato and egg
Uova	Eggs
Yogurt	Yoghurt
Zucchero	Sugar
Zuppa	Soup

Gnocchi	Small potato and dough dumplings
Maccheroni	Macaroni pasta
Minestrina	Clear broth with small pasta shapes
Minestrone	Thick vegetable soup
Paccheri	Big hollow pasta tubes
Pasta al forno	Pasta baked with minced meat, eggs, tomato and cheese
Pasta e fagioli	Pasta with beans
Pastina in brodo	Pasta pieces in clear broth
Penne	Smaller version of rigatoni
Rigatoni	Large, grooved tubular pasta
Stracciatella	Broth with egg
Tagliatelle	Pasta ribbons, another word for fettuccine
Tonnarelli	The same as bucatini (see above)
Tortellini	Rings of pasta, stuffed with meat or cheese
Vermicelli	Thin spaghetti ("little worms")

THE FIRST COURSE (IL PRIMO)

Brodo	Clear broth
Bucatini	Thick, hollow spaghetti – classically Roman
Farfalle	Butterfly-shaped pasta
Fettuccine	Narrow pasta ribbons

PASTA SAUCES (SALSA)

Aglio, olio e peperoncino	With olive oil, garlic and fresh chillies
All'amatriciana	Tomato sauce with diced guanciale or bacon (literally pig's cheek)

All'arrabbiata	Spicy tomato, with chillies ("angry")
Alla carbonara	Bacon, pecorino cheese and beaten egg
Alla gricia	Pecorino cheese and chunks of guanciale or bacon
Alla puttanesca	Tomato, anchovy, olive oil and oregano ("whorish")
Alle vongole	With clams
Al pomodoro	Tomato
Al ragù	With meat sauce
Cacio e pepe	Pecorino cheese and freshly ground pepper
Con la pajata	With calves' intestines

THE SECOND COURSE (IL SECONDO)

MEAT (CARNE)

Abbacchio	Young, roast lamb
Agnello	Lamb
Bistecca	Steak
Carpaccio	Slices of raw beef
Cervello	Brain, usually calves'
Cinghiale	Wild boar
Coda alla vaccinara	Stewed oxtail
Coniglio	Rabbit
Coratella	Sweetmeats
Costoletta	Cutlet, chop
Fegato	Liver
Lingua	Tongue
Maiale	Pork
Manzo	Beef
Milza	Spleen
Ossobuco	Shin of veal
Pancetta	Bacon
Pollo	Chicken
Polpette	Meatballs
Porchetta	Roast suckling pig
Rognoni	Kidneys
Salsiccia	Sausage
Saltimbocca	Veal with ham and sage
Spezzatino	Stew
Trippa	Tripe
Vitello	Veal

FISH (PESCE) AND SHELLFISH (CROSTACEI)

Acciughe	Anchovies
Anguilla	Eel
Aragosta	Lobster
Baccalà	Dried salted cod, usually served fried in batter
Calamari	Squid
Cefalo	Grey mullet
Cozze	Mussels
Dentice	Sea bream
Gamberetti	Shrimps
Gamberi	Prawns
Granchio	Crab
Merluzzo	Cod
Ostriche	Oysters
Pesce spada	Swordfish
Polpo	Octopus
Rospo	Monkfish
Sampiero	John Dory
Sarde	Sardines
Sogliola	Sole
Tonno	Tuna
Trota	Trout
Vongole	Clams

VEGETABLES (CONTORNI), HERBS (ERBE AROMATICHE) AND SALAD (INSALATA)

Asparagi	Asparagus
Carciofi	Artichokes
Carciofini	Artichoke hearts
Cavolfiore	Cauliflower
Cavolo	Cabbage
Cipolla	Onion
Fagioli	Beans
Fagiolini	Green beans
Fiori di zucca	Courgette flowers, sometimes stuffed with anchovies
Finocchio	Fennel
Funghi	Mushrooms
Insalata verde/mista	Green/mixed salad
Lenticchie	Lentils
Melanzane	Aubergine
Patate	Potatoes
Peperoni	Peppers
Piselli	Peas
Pomodori	Tomatoes
Puntarelle	A kind of chicory, very Roman
Radicchio	Red salad leaves
Spinaci	Spinach

USEFUL TERMS

Ai ferri	Grilled without oil
Al dente	Firm, not overcooked
Al forno	Baked
Al sangue	Rare
Alla brace	Barbecued
Alla griglia	Grilled

Alla milanese	Fried in egg and breadcrumbs	Limone	Lemon
		Macedonia	Fruit salad
Alla pizzaiola	Cooked in tomato sauce	Mandorle	Almonds
Allo spiedo	On the spit	Maritozzo	Sweet bread roll split in two and filled with fresh cream – typically Roman
Arrosto	Roast		
Ben cotto	Well done		
Bollito/lesso	Boiled	Mele	Apples
Cotto	Cooked (not raw)	Melone	Melon
Crudo	Raw	Mirtillo	Blueberry
Fritto	Fried	Pangiallo	A heavy cake of fruit and nuts
In umido	Stewed		
Ripieno	Stuffed	Pastiera	Cakes made with eggs and ricotta, typically eaten at Easter
Stracotto	Braised, stewed		

CHEESE (FORMAGGIO)

Dolcelatte	Creamy blue cheese	Pere	Pears
Fontina	Northern Italian cheese, often used in cooking	Pesche	Peaches
		Pinoli	Pine nuts
Gorgonzola	Soft, strong, blue-veined cheese, available in "dolce" (creamy) or "piccante" (strong) varieties	Pistacchio	Pistachio nut
		Sorbetto	Sorbet
		Torrone	Nougat
		Torta	Cake, tart
		Uva	Grapes
		Zabaglione	Dessert made with eggs, sugar and Marsala wine
Pecorino	Strong, hard sheep's cheese, used in Rome instead of parmesan		
		Zuppa Inglese	Trifle
Provola/Provolone	Smooth, round, mild cheese, made from buffalo or sheep's milk; sometimes smoked		

DRINKS

		Acqua minerale	Mineral water
		Aranciata	Orangeade
		Bicchiere	Glass
Ricotta	Soft, white sheep's cheese	Birra	Beer
Scamorza	Soft cow's milk cheese, similar to mozzarella, that's often smoked	Bottiglia	Bottle
		Caffè	Coffee
		Cioccolato caldo	Hot chocolate
		Ghiaccio	Ice

SWEETS (DOLCI), FRUIT (FRUTTA) AND NUTS (NOCI)

		Granita	Crushed ice with coffee or fruit
Amaretti	Macaroons	Latte	Milk
Ananas	Pineapple	Limonata	Lemonade
Anguria/Cocomero	Watermelon	Spremuta	Fresh fruit juice
Arance	Oranges	Spumante	Sparkling wine
Banane	Bananas	Succo	Concentrated fruit juice with sugar
Cacchi	Persimmons		
Cannoli	Crispy pastry shells with a creamy ricotta filling	Tè	Tea
		Tonica	Tonic water
Ciliegie	Cherries	Vino	Wine
Crostata	Pastry tart with a jam, chocolate or ricotta topping	rosso/bianco/rosato secco/dolce	red/white/rosé/dry/ sweet
		Litro	Litre
Fichi	Figs	Mezzo	Half
Fichi d'India	Prickly pears	Quarto	Quarter
Fragole	Strawberries	Caraffa	Carafe
Gelato	Ice cream	Salute!	Cheers!
Lampone	Raspberry		

Glossary of artistic and architectural terms

agora square or marketplace in an ancient Greek city

ambo a kind of simple pulpit, popular in Italian medieval churches

apse semicircular recess at the altar (usually eastern) end of a church

architrave the lowest part of the entablature

atrium inner courtyard

baldacchino a canopy on columns, usually placed over the altar in a church

basilica originally a Roman administrative building, adapted for early churches; distinguished by lack of transepts

belvedere a terrace or lookout point

caldarium the steam room of a Roman bath

campanile bell tower, sometimes detached, usually of a church

capital top of a column

Cardo the main north–south artery in a Roman town

Catalan-Gothic hybrid form of architecture, mixing elements of fifteenth-century Spanish and northern European styles

cella sanctuary of a temple

chancel part of a church containing the altar

chiaroscuro the balance of light and shade in a painting, and the skill of the artist in depicting the contrast between the two

ciborium another word for baldacchino (see above)

clerestory row of windows in the upper part of the wall of a church that separates the nave from the aisle

cornice the top section of a classical facade

cortile galleried courtyard or cloisters

cosmati work decorative mosaic-work on marble, usually highly coloured, found in early Christian Italian churches, especially in Rome; derives from the name Cosma, a common name among families of marble workers at the time

cryptoporticus underground passageway

cyclopean walls fortifications built of huge, rough stone blocks, common in the pre-Roman settlements of Lazio

Decumanus Maximus the main street, usaully east-west, of a Roman town – the second cross-street was known as the Decumanus Inferiore

domus single-storey ancient Roman house occupied by a well-to-do family

entablature the section above the capital on a classical building, below the cornice

ex voto artefact designed in thanksgiving to a saint

fresco wall-painting technique in which the artist applies paint to wet plaster for a more permanent finish

frigidarium the large cold pool of a Roman bath

loggia roofed gallery or balcony

metope a panel on the frieze of a Greek temple

Mithraism pre-Christian cult associated with Mithras, the Persian god of light, who slew a bull and fertilized the world with its blood

mithraeum temple dedicated to Mithras (see above)

narthex portico or porch at the western entrance of a church

nave central space in a church, usually flanked by aisles

nymphaeum grotto or shrine dedicated to a nymph or nymphs

Pantocrator usually refers to an image of Christ, portrayed with outstretched arms

peristyle columned porch or open colonnade in a building surrounding a courtyard, often containing a garden

piano nobile main floor of a *palazzo*, usually the first

polyptych painting on several joined wooden panels

portico covered entrance to a building, or porch

presepio/presepe Christmas crib

putti cherubs

reliquary receptacle for a saint's relics, usually bones; often highly decorated

sgraffito decorative technique whereby one layer of plaster is scratched to form a pattern

stereobate visible base of any building, usually a Greek temple

stucco plaster made from water, lime, sand and powdered marble, used for decorative work

tepidarium the warm room of a Roman bath

thermae baths, usually elaborate buildings in Roman villas

triptych painting on three joined wooden panels

trompe l'oeil work of art that deceives the viewer by means of tricks with perspective

Small print and index

Rough Guide credits

Editor: Ruth Reisenberger
Layout: Pradeep Thapliyal
Cartography: Deshpal Dabas
Picture editor: Mark Thomas
Proofreader: Stewart Wild
Managing editor: Monica Woods
Assistant editor: Payal Sharotri

Production: Luca Bazzoli
Cover photo research: Roger Mapp
Editorial assistant: Aimee White
Senior DTP coordinator: Dan May
Programme manager: Gareth Lowe
Publishing director: Georgina Dee

Publishing information

This eighth edition published March 2018 by
Rough Guides Ltd,
80 Strand, London WC2R 0RL
11, Community Centre, Panchsheel Park,
New Delhi 110017, India
Distributed by Penguin Random House
Penguin Books Ltd, 80 Strand, London WC2R 0RL
Penguin Group (USA), 345 Hudson Street, NY 10014, USA
Penguin Group (Australia), 250 Camberwell Road,
Camberwell, Victoria 3124, Australia
Penguin Group (NZ), 67 Apollo Drive, Mairangi Bay,
Auckland 1310, New Zealand
Penguin Group (South Africa), Block D, Rosebank Office
Park, 181 Jan Smuts Avenue, Parktown North, Gauteng,
South Africa 2193
Rough Guides is represented in Canada by DK Canada, 320
Front Street West, Suite 1400, Toronto, Ontario M5V 3B6
Printed in Singapore
© Rough Guides 2018
Maps © Rough Guides

All rights reserved. No part of this publication may be
reproduced, stored in or introduced into a retrieval system,
or transmitted in any form, or by any means (electronic,
mechanical, photocopying, recording or otherwise) without
the prior written permission of the copyright owner.
368pp includes index
A catalogue record for this book is available from the
British Library
ISBN: 978-0-24130-640-6
The publishers and authors have done their best to
ensure the accuracy and currency of all the information
in **The Rough Guide to Rome**, however, they can accept
no responsibility for any loss, injury, or inconvenience
sustained by any traveller as a result of information or
advice contained in the guide.
1 3 5 7 9 8 6 4 2

MIX
Paper from
responsible sources
FSC™ C018179
www.fsc.org

Help us update

We've gone to a lot of effort to ensure that the eighth
edition of **The Rough Guide to Rome** is accurate and up-
to-date. However, things change – places get "discovered",
opening hours are notoriously fickle, restaurants and
rooms raise prices or lower standards. If you feel we've got
it wrong or left something out, we'd like to know, and if
you can remember the address, the price, the hours, the
phone number, so much the better.

Please send your comments with the subject line
"Rough Guide Rome Update" to mail@uk.roughguides
.com. We'll credit all contributions and send a copy of the
next edition (or any other Rough Guide if you prefer) for
the very best emails.

ABOUT THE AUTHORS

Agnes Crawford, originally from London, graduated from Edinburgh University with a degree in Architectural History in 1999. In 2000, she came to Rome for six months and stayed. She is registered as a licensed guide by the Province of Rome and organizes personalized tours through ⓦunderstandingrome.com

Maria Pasquale Born to Italian parents, though raised in Melbourne, Maria always knew Rome was her destiny. She contributes regularly to *USA Today*, *CNN* and *The Telegraph* and writes an award-winning food, travel and lifestyle blog, HeartRome. In Rome, you'll find her walking the streets of Trastevere, checking out the latest bar for an *aperitivo* or dining with friends. Maria's first book *I Heart Rome* – recipes and stories from the eternal city – came out in November 2017.

Readers' updates

Thanks to all the readers who have taken the time to write in with comments and suggestions (and apologies if we've inadvertently omitted or misspelt anyone's name):

Tone Matthews and Adam Tamas

Photo credits

All photos © Rough Guides, except the following:
(Key: t-top; c-centre; b-bottom; l-left; r-right)

Index

Maps are marked in grey

H

I

J

K

T

Map index

Listings key

■ Accommodation
● Eating
■ Drinking/nightlife
● Shopping

City plan

The **city plan** on the pages that follow is divided as shown:

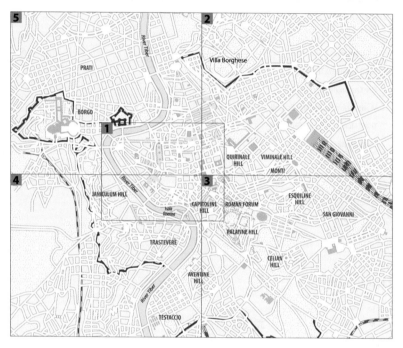

Map symbols

– – –	Chapter division boundary	♦	Place of interest	∴	Ruins	
	Road	⊠	Post office	☆	Viewpoint	
	Pedestrian road	⊞	Hospital	⋂	Arch	
⊓⊓⊓	Steps	ⓘ	Tourist information	⊙	Statue	
– – – –	Footpath	✡	Synagogue	⇨	Church	
▬▬	Wall	🅿	Parking		Building	
▬▬	Railway	🆃	Toilet	◯	Stadium	
⌣	Bridge	⊠	Gate	▭	Park/gardens	
✈	Airport	⊤	Fountain	⊞	Christian cemetery	
Ⓜ	Metro					

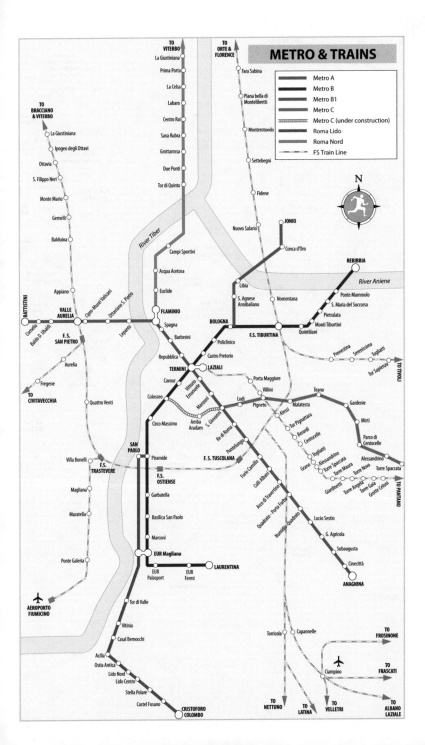

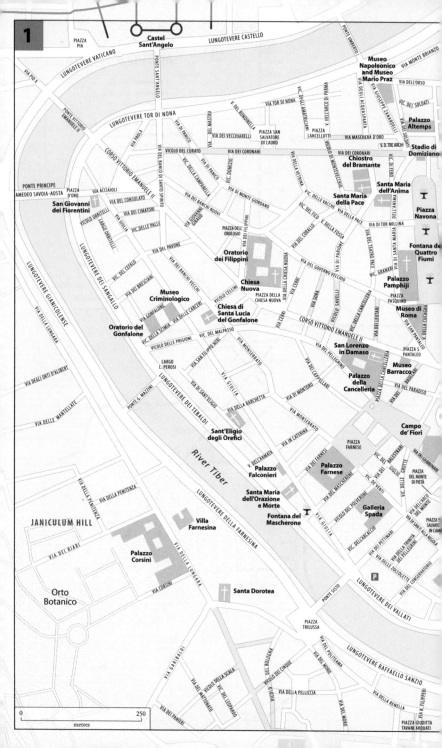

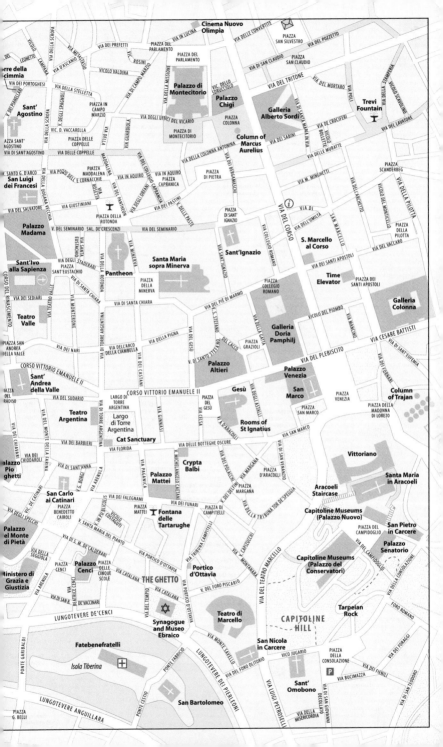

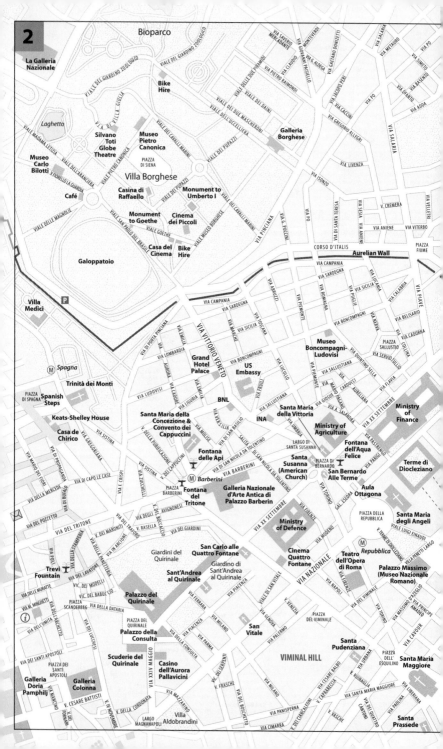

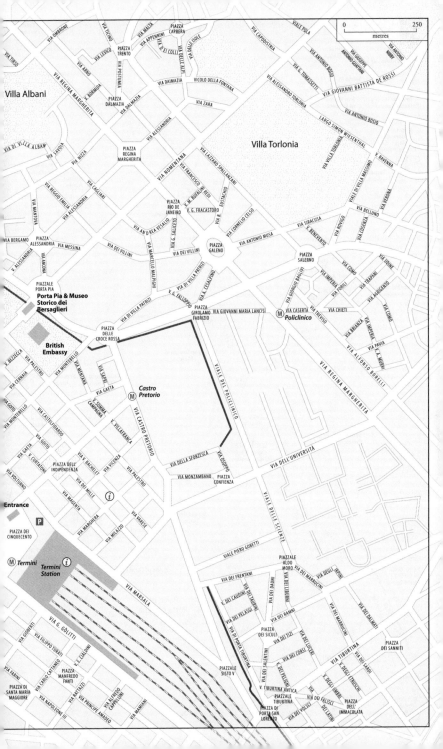

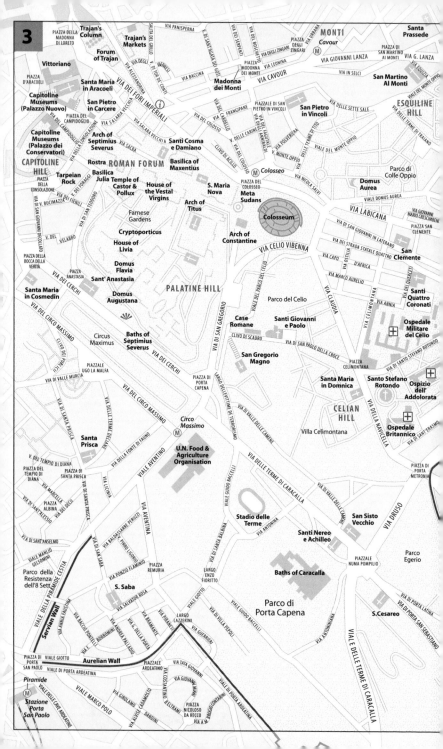

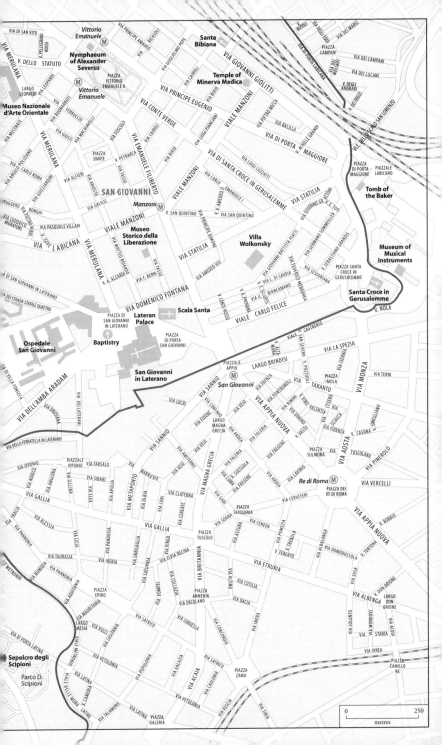

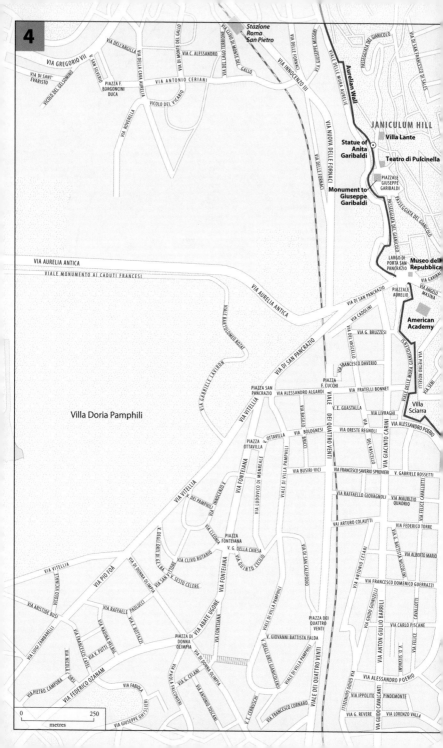

4

VIA GREGORIO VII

VIA DELL'ARGILLA

VIA DI MONTE DEL GALLO

VIA A. ALESSANDRO

VIA CLIVO DI MONTE DEL GALLO

Stazione Roma San Pietro

VIA DELLE FORNACI

VIA INNOCENZO III

VIA DI SANT'EVARISTO

VICOLO DEL GELSOMINO

VIA SAN SEVERO

VIA DELLA CAVA AURELIA

PIAZZA F. BORGONCINI DUCA

VIA ANTONIO CERIANI

VICOLO DEL V. VICARIO

VIA ROVERELLA

VIA NUOVA DELLE FORNACI

VIA DELLE FORNACI

PASSEGGIATA DEL GIANICOLO

VIALE DELLE MURA AURELIE

Aurelian Wall

VIA DI SAN FRANCESCO DI SALES

JANICULUM HILL

Villa Lante

Statue of Anita Garibaldi

Teatro di Pulcinella

PIAZZALE GIUSEPPE GARIBALDI

Monument to Giuseppe Garibaldi

PASSEGGIATA DEL GIANICOLO

PASSEGGIATA DEL GIANICOLO

VIA AURELIA ANTICA

VIALE MONUMENTO AI CADUTI FRANCESI

VIA AURELIA ANTICA

VIALE BARTOLOMEO ROZAI

VIA GABRIELE LAVIRON

VIA DI SAN PANCRAZIO

LARGO DI PORTA SAN PANCRAZIO

Museo della Repubblica

VIA GARIBALDI

VIA ANGELO MASINA

PIAZZALE AURELIO

VIA DI SAN PANCRAZIO

VIA CADOLINI

American Academy

VIA G. BRUZZESI

VIA DEL VASCELLO

VIA PIETRO ROSELLI

VIA SAN...

VIA CARLO ALBERTO RACCHIA

Villa Sciarra

FRANCESCO DAVERIO

PIAZZA F. CUCCHI

VIA FRATELLI BONNET

Villa Doria Pamphili

PIAZZA SAN PANCRAZIO

VIA ALESSANDRO ALGARDI

V.E. GUASTALLA

VIA LIVRAGHI

VIA ALESSANDRO POERIO

VIA VITELLIA

VIA BASCELLO

VIA BASCELLO

VIA ORESTE REGNOLI

VIA GIACINTO CARINI

OTTAVILLA

VIA BOLOGNESI

BRICCI

DEL VASCELLO

PIAZZA OTTAVILLA

OTTAVILLA

VIA BUSIRI-VICI

VIA FRANCESCO SAVERIO SPROVIERI

V. GABRIELE ROSSETTI

VIA FONTEIANA

VIA INNOCENZO X

VIA LUDOVICO DI MONREALE

VIALE DI VILLA PAMPHILI

VIA RAFFAELLO GIOVAGNOLI

VIA MAURIZIO QUADRIO

VIA FELICE CAVALLOTTI

VIA VITELLIA

V. DEI PAMPHILI

VAI ARTURO COLAUTTI

VIA FEDERICO TORRE

V.BEGLI ORTI DI GE'BA

VIA CELIMONTANA

PIAZZA FONTEIANA

VIA BATTISTA NICCOLINI

VIA ALBERTO MARIO

VIA CLEMENTE

VIA S.V. SESTO CELERE

V.G. DELLA CHIESA

VIA DI SAN CALEPODIO

VIA ANTONIO CESARI

VIA FRANCESCO DOMENICO GUERRAZZI

VIA VITELLIA

VICOLO VICINALE

VIA PIO FOA

VIA DI DONNA OLIMPIA

VIA SAN V. ETTORE

VIA CLIVO RUTARIO

VIA QUINTO CECILIO

VIA GUIDO GUINIZELLI

VIA CARLO PISCANE

VIA ARISTIDE BUSI

VIA RAFFAELE PAOLUCCI

VIA E. ROTELLI

PIAZZA DEI QUATTRO VENTI

VIA FELICE

VIA LUIGI ZAMBARELLI

VIA FRANCESCO CARINI

VIA MORINA DEL BIG.

VIA ABATE UGONE

VIA FONTEIANA

VIALE DI VILLA PAMPHILI

V. GIOVANNI BATTISTA FALDA

VIA ANTON GIULIO BARRILI

IPPOLITO TA X.

VIA V. PUTTI

PIAZZA DI DONNA OLIMPIA

VIA DI DONNA OLIMPIA

VIA BEGLI ORTI GIANICOLENSI

VIA ALESSANDRO POERIO

VIA NICOLA FABRI

VIA FABIOLA

VIA G. CELANI

VIALE DI QUATTRO VENTI

VIA IPPOLITO TA X.

PINDEMONTE

VIA PIETRO CAMPORA

VIA FEDERICO OZANAM

VIA PAOLA FALCONIERI

VIA ANTONIO TOSCANI

VIA GUIDO CAVALCANTI

VIA GUIDO CAVALCANTI

VIA GIUSEPPE GH. (SETTI)

K.E. CERBUSCHI

VIA FRANCESCO CORNARO

VIALE DI QUATTRO VENTI

VIA G. REVERE

VIA LORENZO VALLA

0 ————— 250

metres

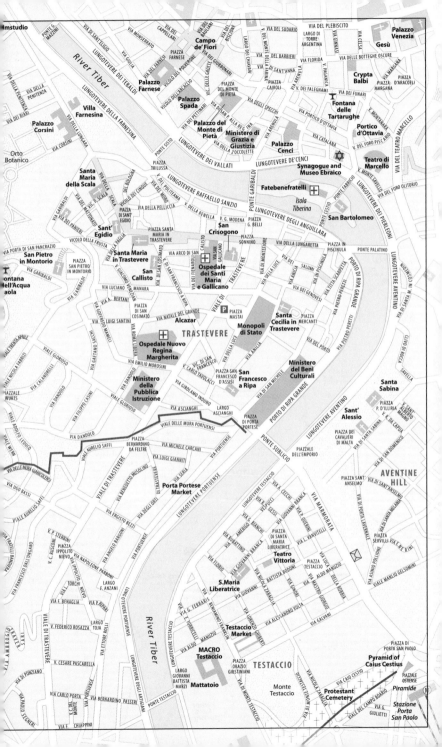

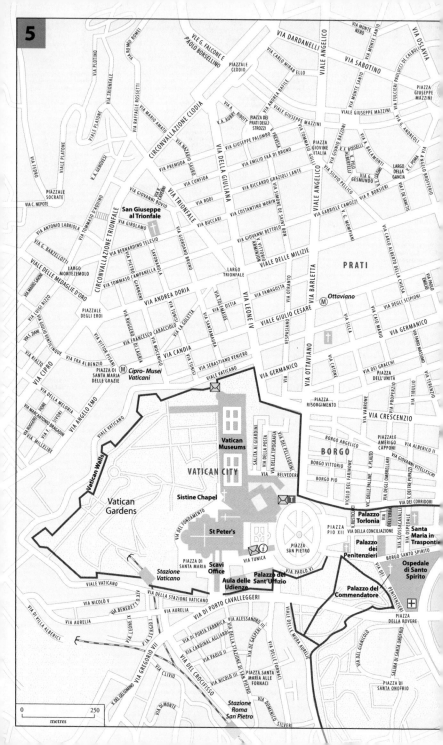

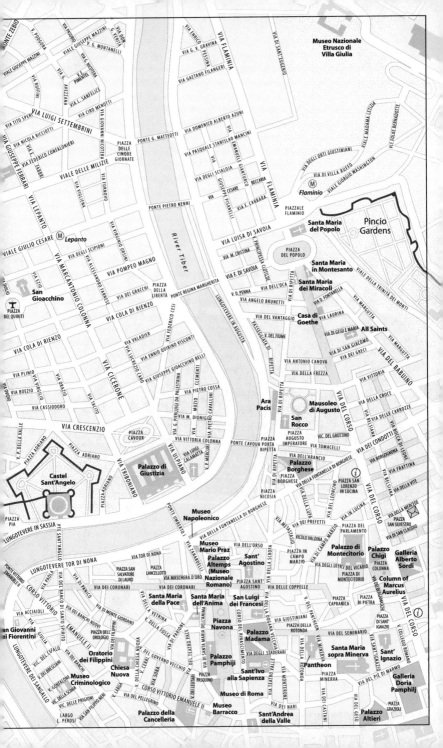

ESCAPE
THE EVERYDAY

ADVENTURE BECKONS
YOU JUST NEED TO KNOW WHERE TO LOOK

roughguides.com

1. **Denim, the pencil, the stethoscope and the hot-air balloon were all invented in which country?**
   a. Italy
   b. France
   c. Germany
   d. Switzerland

2. **What is the currency of Vietnam?**
   a. Dong
   b. Yuan
   c. Baht
   d. Kip

3. **In which city would you find the Majorelle Garden?**
   a. Marseille
   b. Marrakesh
   c. Tunis
   d. Malaga

4. **What is the busiest airport in the world?**
   a. London Heathrow
   b. Tokyo International
   c. Chicago O'Hare
   d. Hartsfield-Jackson
      Atlanta International

5. **Which of these countries does not have the equator running through it?**
   a. Brazil
   b. Tanzania
   c. Indonesia
   d. Colombia

6. **Which country has the most UNESCO World Heritage Sites?**
   a. Mexico
   b. France
   c. Italy
   d. India

7. **What is the principal religion of Japan?**
   a. Confucianism
   b. Buddhism
   c. Jainism
   d. Shinto

8. **Every July in Sonkajärvi, central Finland, contestants gather for the World Championships of which sport?**
   a. Zorbing
   b. Wife-carrying
   c. Chess-boxing
   d. Extreme ironing

9. **What colour are post boxes in Germany?**
   a. Red
   b. Green
   c. Blue
   d. Yellow

10. **For three days each April during Songkran festival in Thailand, people take to the streets to throw what at each other?**
    a. Water
    b. Oranges
    c. Tomatoes
    d. Underwear